NOT SEEING RED

American Librarianship and the
Soviet Union, 1917-1960

Stephen Karetzky

University Press of America,® Inc.
Lanham · New York · Oxford

Copyright © 2002 by
University Press of America,® Inc.
4720 Boston Way
Lanham, Maryland 20706
UPA Acquisitions Department (301) 459-3366

12 Hid's Copse Rd.
Cumnor Hill, Oxford OX2 9JJ

Library of Congress Cataloging-in-Publication Data

Karetzky, Stephen.
Not seeing red : American librarianship and the Soviet Union,
1917-1960 / Stephen Karetzky.
p. cm
Includes bibliographical references and index.
1. Library science—Soviet Union—History. 2. Libraries and
communism—Soviet Union—History. 3. Librarians—United
States—Attitudes. 4. Soviet Union—Foreign public opinion,
American. 5. United States—Public opinion. 6. International
librarianship. I. Title.

Z665.2.S65 K37 2001   020'.947—dc21   2001054031 CIP

ISBN 0-7618-2162-7 (cloth: alk. paper)
ISBN 0-7618-2163-5 (pbk. : alk. paper)

⊝™ The paper used in this publication meets the minimum
requirements of American National Standard for Information
Sciences—Permanence of Paper for Printed Library Materials,
ANSI Z39.48—1984

To Professor Charles J. Rooney,
distinguished scholar and friend to all

and

In memory of Anthony J. Ballestrasse and Harry Karetzky,
who embodied the ideals of generosity and tolerance

CONTENTS

ACKNOWLEDGMENTS

Numerous people have provided assistance in the production of this book.

Several prominent scholars took time from their own busy schedules to read the manuscript and offer suggestions and encouragement. These included Paul Hollander, Professor Emeritus at the University of Massachusetts at Amherst, and M. Stanton Evans, President of the National Journalism Center in Washington, D.C. Moreover, I believe that the influence of their well-known books is manifest throughout this volume. I refer here particularly to Hollander's *Political Pilgrims*, *Anti-Americanism*, and *Soviet and American Society: A Comparison*; and to Evans' *Politics of Surrender* and *The Theme is Freedom: Religion, Politics, and the American Tradition*. Two of the foremost scholars of the history of librarianship read my work. Professor George Bobinski, of the State University of New York at Buffalo, is not only an expert on American library history, but he has been personally involved with librarianship in Central and Eastern Europe for three decades. Dr. Lee Shiflett, Chair of the Department of Library Studies at the University of North Carolina at Greensboro, scrutinized all but the last chapter. He did so with the acuity and the commitment to objective research for which he is so widely known and admired.

The acknowledged dean of the historiography of American Communism and anti-Communism, Dr. John Earl Haynes of the Library of Congress, generously provided both valuable information and inspiriting countenance. Moreover, I was greatly instructed by his numerous books and articles.

Many of my co-workers at the Felician College Library—Mary

Zieleniewski, Helen Jamgochian, Genevieve Como, Vito Savino, and Rosalind Bochynski—aided in several ways, particularly in obtaining numerous items on interlibrary loan. Our reference librarian, Elisabeth Gatlin, expertly ferreted out even the most obscured facts.

Others at Felician who provided help were Dr. Sherida Yoder, with her invaluable input on stylistic matters, and Professor Alexandra Kirilovna Sinkowsky, who assisted in translating some difficult Russian texts. Aid was also received from Dr. Robert Ingoglia and Frederick Sochacki. Dr. Gerard O'Sullivan, our resident polymath and Dean of the Division of Arts and Sciences, served as an abiding source of information, knowledge, and wisdom. The College's Vice-Presidents for Academic Affairs—first Dr. Beate Schiwek and then Sr. Patricia Morris, O.P., Ph.D.—have been supportive of my efforts.

Many hard-to-find source materials were supplied by the knowledgeable and generous Lewe H. Sessions.

Information about the extraordinary Howard Aylwin Gregory and his visit to the Soviet Union was provided by his widow, Agnes Gregory. An accomplished librarian in her own right, she has proven to be a gracious and interesting correspondent.

The insight that even politically conservative librarians have tended to be liberal in their professional philosophies was first articulated by the doyenne of library historians, Phyllis Dain, Professor Emeritus at Columbia University. In parts of this book I have tried to expand on this thesis.

Auralie Phillips Logan crafted the thorough index with her usual diligence.

As with many previous projects, my greatest source of advice, help, and encouragement was Joanne Karetzky.

I must acknowledge the great advantage I had in growing up in New York City: it afforded me the opportunity to begin meeting Communists and anti-Communists when I was just a boy. This first-hand experience has provided some understanding apparently lacking among many who write about them and related historical subjects. (Indeed, a portion of these investigators even seem to doubt the very existence of Communists.) In a similar manner, my later encounters with Soviet librarians initiated my interest in their worldview and led to some comprehension of it. Many of the lessons first learned as a youth were again brought home, e.g., that one's personal friends and one's political allies are not necessarily the same.

I would like to thank those organizations and individuals noted below for permission to quote from works within their dominion. Sylva Simsova deserves special recognition because of her pioneering scholarship in this field.

Sylva Simsova for excerpts from *Lenin, Krupskaia, and Libraries*, ed. by Simsova, trans. by G. Peacock and Lucy Prescott (London: Clive Bingley; Hamden, CT: Archon Books, 1968), pp. 48-49, 53-54.

H. W. Wilson Company for excerpts from "America, Russia, and Adult Education," by Margaret P. Coleman, *Wilson Library Bulletin* 10 (Dec. 1935): 235-39.

Columbia University Press for excerpts from *Living with Books: The Art of Book Selection*, 2nd ed., by Helen E. Haines (New York: Columbia University Press, 1950), pp. 108-9, 187-88.

American Library Association for excerpts from:

ALA. "Overseas Library Statement." *ALA Bulletin* 47 (Nov 1953): 487.

ALA. "Statement on Labeling" [July 13, 1951]. As reprinted in ALA. *Intellectual Freedom Manual*. 5th ed. Chicago: ALA, 1996. Pp. 114-15.

Downs, Robert B. "The ALA Today—A 1953 Report." *ALA Bulletin* 47 (Oct. 1953): 397-99.

Waples, Douglas. "Guiding Readers in Soviet Russia." *Bulletin of the American Library Association* 26 (Oct. 1932): 762-67.

Stephen Karetzky

INTRODUCTION

For over seven decades, the leaders of the American library profession failed to understand, or oppose, the Soviet Union and its Communist form of librarianship. This lack of comprehension and dedication to democratic ideals was remarkable. Prominent, well-educated librarians visited the USSR to inspect this new type of society: many of its basic elements were there for the seeing. These professionals also had easy access to accurate written critiques of the revolutionary regime. Their task was made easier by the fact that the USSR—including its libraries—were essentially the same throughout this period, having been effectively initiated by Lenin. In addition, some elements of that society should not have been entirely unfamiliar: educated individuals could have seen some parallels in the Jacobins and their Reign of Terror. Nevertheless, these librarians generally thought very highly of Soviet librarianship, often considering it superior to that in the United States, and did their best to assist it. Moreover, after the onset of the Cold War, they vigorously fought American anti-Communism. Thus, in thought and deed, they betrayed the fundamental values, goals, and interests of their profession and their country.

The purpose of this work is to examine the reaction of American librarians to Soviet librarianship and to the Soviet Union as a whole. The focus is on the years 1917 through 1960, although there is an overview of the subsequent period ending with Gorbachev's rise to power in 1985. This latter era saw the American view of the USSR's libraries eclipsed by an Anglo-American philosophy of international librarianship which viewed the Soviet Union as merely another foreign country which should be treated like any other. In the years following the ascension of Gorbachev, librarianship in the USSR began to change in fundamental ways. This is not dealt with here: it is a different story that can best be treated in a separate study.[1]

While many studies have been made of the reactions of intellectuals, politicians, laborers, and others to the rise and development of this Communist state, the response of professionals—who constitute a significant element in highly developed democratic societies—has received scant attention: no major studies have focused on librarians.[2] Of prime significance is the fact that, from its very beginnings, the totalitarian approach to librarianship established in the USSR was clearly antithetical to that in the United States. Nevertheless, as this work shows, the American librarians—many of them highly esteemed members of the profession—who visited there and/or wrote about it in the first three decades after the 1917 Bolshevik coup d'état admired and helped Soviet librarianship and the Soviet Union. This repudiation of democratic American ideals was repeated by leaders of librarianship in later decades, albeit in different ways. The possible political, psychological, social, intellectual, and moral explanations for this behavior are offered: they can provide insight into some of the pathologies democracies continually face in maintaining their liberties. It is hoped that these revelations will help make librarians and others more steadfast in their commitment to free institutions. However, it is sobering to know that excellent scholarship dealing with analogous behavior among intellectuals has fared poorly in the book review pages of most academic journals.[3]

The possibility that most contemporary historians of librarianship are incapable of writing objectively about the history of Soviet-American library relations may be indicated by a recent contribution to the scant literature on this subject.[4] It asserts that the "establishments" in both countries prevented the exchange of valuable knowledge. This proposition of the moral equivalence of the adversaries—a thesis vigorously advanced by New Left historians and their intellectual followers—is accompanied by a legion of false assertions and factual errors. It is analyzed near the end of the book as part of an evaluation of the decayed state of library historiography.

The title of this book, *Not Seeing Red*, is in part a response to the several published works styled *Seeing Red*. This clichéd expression encapsulates the banal theme they have put forth: the Western democracies, particularly the United States, overreacted to the threat of

Communism in the twentieth century and saw agents of this movement where they did not truly exist.[5] The best recent scholarship shows more clearly than ever that American government officials and academics usually underestimated the threat of the USSR and Communism, undervalued the extent and significance of pro-Soviet activity within the United States directed from Moscow, and frequently failed to regard Communists as such.[6] The same can be said about the leaders of the library profession. It is relevant that for the past thirty years, the public has been bombarded by fanciful books, films, and televised documentaries that are positive about Communists and negative about anti-Communists.[7]

Lenin and his wife Krupskaya were directly responsible for the ideological and institutional formation of the new totalitarian library system. This is described in some detail because their creation remained largely unchanged, in its essentials, for seventy years. For most of the American professionals, it was the USSR's library world which constituted their primary arena for first-hand interaction with Soviet society. The world of books, readers, and libraries in Czarist Russia is outlined to further demonstrate the disastrous consequences of the Bolshevik putsch.

Little research has been done on the history of Soviet librarianship aside from that conducted by Russians during the years of Communist ascendancy. However, library historians in Russia have begun to write more accurate accounts of library developments both before and after 1917. In general, they have been extremely critical of the Communists.[8] The work by Americans and others in the democracies has not only been fragmentary but has generally failed to describe—or even note—the calamitous consequences of the Bolshevik seizure of power. This significant error of omission is compounded by errors of commission. For example, many of these limited investigations blame Stalin for the despotic policies actually begun by Lenin.[9] Fortunately, there have been a few researchers who have analyzed Soviet libraries more objectively.[10]

It was only with the beginning of the Cold War that a portion of the librarians in the United States finally began to show a greater understanding of the Soviet Union and its libraries. Many of these librarians had academic backgrounds in Soviet studies or were refugees who had faced the reality of living under Communist regimes. Unfortunately, their work—much of it quite scholarly—had little effect on the leaders of the profession, who worked effectively to prevent the mobilization of librarians into active opponents of Communist totalitarianism.

Some recent scholarship has at long last begun to present a more accurate history of American anti-Communism, showing it to be largely a rational, measured, and eventually successful reaction to a very real evil.[11] However, the great bulk of those writing about anti-Communism as it relates to librarianship's past do not do so as objective scholars but as amanuenses, echoing the canards of the anti-anti-Communist librarians of the Cold War era who claimed to be protecting the ideals of intellectual freedom against assaults by the ignorant, neofascist masses in the United States. What we have here is a failure to illuminate. This book demonstrates the flawed thought and actions of those in the professional pantheon of these writers on library history,[12] who diligently emulate the work of academia's left-wing historians. As Michael Kazin, Professor of History at American University and a self-described member of the Left, declared in 1992: American historians are "overwhelmingly cosmopolitan in their cultural tastes and liberal or radical in their politics."[13] It should also be pointed out that no one in the field of international and comparative librarianship has ever put forth a theory for a *nationalist* or anti-Communist approach to this area of scholarship and practice.

Many in the history profession and the liberal "mainstream" media have tried to downplay—or even deny—the revelations emerging over the past decade from the archives of the United States and the former Soviet Union. Some even want the study of the struggle between democracy and Communism—the greatest political conflict of the twentieth century—to be dropped, fearing the consequences of further analysis.[14] While the Cold War with the USSR was won, a neo-Marxian adversarial culture has grown strong in the United States, making the triumph less than complete. We are faced with the unusual problem that most of the victorious nation's academics and scribes are either loath to write this particular war's history or are averse to doing so objectively. This is highly significant because there still remain dangerous countries abroad—Communist and otherwise. Moreover, as already indicated, the perverse, contrarian ethos that has flourished possesses the capacity to transmogrify our free society.

The new archival research has made it it clearer than ever that, from 1917 on, the conservative American (and British) appraisal of

Communism at home and abroad was generally the most accurate one—as was its view of how to deal with it.[15] The absence of a vital conservative philosophy of librarianship was one element that impaired the profession's ability and desire to understand and counter this prototype of totalitarianism. The story that follows will help to confirm this.

A few remarks on wording, form, and documentation may prove useful to the reader.

Those who are unacquainted with the literature of those actively opposed to Communism may start at the ungraceful term *anti-anti-Communist*. Over the past several decades, many, like Sidney Hook and Norman Podhoretz, have used it with frequency. It is utilized in this work because of its precision as well as its honorable heritage.

The capitalization of the initial letter in the word *Communism* and its derivatives is found throughout this work. To some extent, the tendency over the past three decades to *not* capitalize the *C* is merely a matter of style, reflecting the contemporary minimalist inclination to dispense with the majuscule whenever possible. In addition, some now assert that the *C* should be capitalized only when one is writing of the Communist Party, its official pronouncements, and so forth. Since this work deals with the librarianship, the state, and the international movement controlled by the Communist Party and its precursor, the Bolshevik Party, a capital *C* is not only justifiable but preferable.[16]

Capitalization of the term *intellectual freedom* depends on whether the phrase is being used to denote free thought and expression themselves or to identify what I have chosen to call librarianship's *Intellectual Freedom movement*.[17] This crusade by librarians advanced the cause of anti-anti-Communism, thereby undermining their professed ideal world-wide.

For the sake of convenience and clarity, *full* citations for books and articles are occasionally given in the end-of-chapter notes even when they have appeared earlier in the book. In the bibliography, whenever several contributions in a collective work (like conference proceedings) have been utilized, the complete citation for the aggregate volume is given under the name of its editor or title.

There are a large number of quotations in this work, some of them quite lengthy. These are presented so readers can see for themselves what some people have stated instead of taking my word for it. This is particularly important when the ideas of those being discussed seem incredible.

Works published after December 2000 are not analyzed in this book.

NOTES

1. It is significant that librarians in the USSR were relatively slow to respond to *glasnost* and *perestroika*. For information on this period, see: Dennis Kimmage, ed., *Russian Libraries in Transition: An Anthology of* Glasnost *Literature* (Jefferson, NC, and London: McFarland, 1992); and E. Varvarina, comp., *Russian Librarianship During the Time of* Perestroika *(1987-1991): Digest*, trans. by E. Azarova and O. Azarova (Moscow: Rudomino All-Russia State Library for Foreign Literature, 1993). A few first-hand glimpses of the attempts to create a library profession devoted to democracy in post-Communist Russia can be found in James H. Billington's *Russia Transformed: Breakthrough to Hope* (New York: The Free Press, 1992).

2. No such studies are indicated in Donald G. Davis, Jr., and John Mark Tucker, eds., *American Library History: A Comprehensive Guide to the Literature* (Santa Barbara, CA, and Oxford, England: ABC-CLIO, 1989), particularly pp. 259-60, 263-65. A thorough perusal of the literature, as well as bibliographies of, and indexes to it (for example, *Library Literature* [New York: H. W. Wilson, 1921-]), reveals the same lack.

3. The most prominent example was the "hostile and dismissive" reaction to Paul Hollander's *Political Pilgrims*. (See Hollander, "An End to Political Pilgrimage? [Preface to the University Press of America Edition]," *Political Pilgrims: Travels of Western Intellectuals to the Soviet Union, China, and Cuba* [Lanham, MD, and London: University Press of America, 1990, p. 8; originally published: New York and Oxford: Oxford University Press, 1981.] Recently reissued as *Political Pilgrims: Western Intellectuals in Search of the Good Society*, 4th ed., with new intro. [New Brunswick, NJ, and London: Transaction, 1998].) His related title, *Anti-Americanism*, was not even reviewed by the two major scholarly periodicals in his field. Hollander's reaction was, "I take this to be simply a matter of not wasting space on a politically incorrect volume." (Hollander, "Introduction to the Transaction Edition," *Anti-Americanism:*

Irrational and Rational [New Brunswick, NJ: Transaction Publishers, 1995; originally published as *Anti-Americanism: Critiques at Home and Abroad, 1965-1990* (New York and Oxford: Oxford University Press, 1992)], p. xv.) Elsewhere, these books were lauded by C. Vann Woodward, Adam B. Ulam, Robert Nisbet, Jeane Kirkpatrick, Peter L. Berger, Irving Louis Horowitz, and Saul Bellow. Hollander is Professor of Sociology at the University of Massachusetts at Amherst and a Fellow of the Russian Research Center at Harvard University.

4. Pamela Spence Richards, "Soviet-American Library Relations in the 1920s and 1930s: A Study in Mutual Fascination and Distrust," *Library Quarterly* 68 (Oct. 1998): 390-405.

5. The first of these appears to have been Walter Nelles' "Seeing Red: Civil Liberty and Law in the Period following the War," (New York: American Civil Liberties Union, Aug. 1920, 12 pp.) Nelles, the ACLU's Consel, attributed the phrase to federal judge George W. Anderson. (See Nelles, p. 2.) Anderson was active in organizations focusing on labor and world peace, and he was also an office holder in the ACLU. He is probably best remembered for his 1920 ruling that the Communist Party in the United States was of no danger at all to the country and that it was not truly committed to either violence or the takeover of the government. *Despite its self-proclaimed goals and methods*, he declared, in reality it was similar to "a fraternal society constituted on the lodge system." (Ruling in Colyer et al. v. Skeffington, 265 F. 17, reprinted in Dan Whitehead, *The FBI Story*, foreword by J. Edgar Hoover [New York: Random House, 1956], p. 51. See also p. 52.) For the classic antithetical ruling by federal judge John C. Knox issued that very same year, see Whitehead, p. 52. Three decades later, Knox appointed Judge Irving Kaufman—whose ideas were similar to his—to preside in the Rosenberg trial. Dan Whitehead, Washington Bureau Chief of the *New York Herald-Tribune*, had been awarded Pulitzer Prizes for journalism in 1951 and 1953.

On the use of the term "Seeing Red," see also Theodore Kornweibel, Jr., *"Seeing Red": Federal Campaigns against Black Militancy, 1919-1925* (Bloomington and Indianapolis: Indiana University Press, 1998). Kornweibel contrasts his use of the term with that of Attorney General A. Mitchell Palmer in 1919. (See Kornweibel, pp. xiv-xv.) Another recent contribution to this genre is Charles H. McCormick, *Seeing Reds: Federal Surveillance of Radicals in the Pittsburgh Mill District, 1917-1921* (Pittsburgh: University of Pittsburgh Press, 1997). While their research deals only with the post-World War I era, McCormick and Kornweibel insist that the thoughts and actions of the general American public and their government during these few years—which they characterize as paranoid, oppressive, and racist—remained fixed as the core of anti-Communism for the next fifty years. (See McCormick, pp. 1-6, 201-4; and Kornweibel, pp. xi-xv, 1-2, 19-21, 35, 174-82.)

Still Seeing Red: How the Cold War Shapes the New American Politics (Boulder, CO: Westview Press, 1997) focuses primarily on the myriad evils that historian John Kenneth White claims existed in Cold War America. He barely addresses—let alone proves—his thesis that post-Cold War politics have been molded by anti-Communism. Even a sympathetic British scholar declares that "Where the book falls down . . . is in its central claim that Americans are still seeing 'red.' If they were, then why for goodness sake did they elect Clinton not just once, but twice?" (Michael Cox, untitled review of *Still Seeing Red*, by White, *Political Studies* 46 [Sept. 1998]: 841.)

   Similarly phantastic works have been issued in other Western-style democracies. See: The Evatt Foundation, *Seeing Red: The Communist Party Dissolution Act and Referendum, 1951: Lessons for Constitutional Reform* (Sydney, Australia: The Evatt Foundation, 1992); and George Fraser, *Seeing Red: Undercover in 1950's New Zealand* (Palmerston North, NZ: The Dunsmore Press, 1995).

   6. For example, see: Robert Louis Benson and Michael Warner, eds., *Venona: Soviet Espionage and the American Response, 1939-1957* (Washington, DC: National Security Agency and the Central Intelligence Agency, 1996); Allen Weinstein and Alexander Vassiliev, *The Haunted Wood: Soviet Espionage in America—the Stalin Era* (New York: Random House, 1999); and Richard Gid Powers' treatment of the years 1960-1979 in his *Not Without Honor: The History of American Anticommunism* (New York: The Free Press, 1995). See also the groundbreaking research by John Earl Haynes and Harvey Klehr in notes 11 and 16 below. John Lewis Gaddis has slowly and reluctantly come to acknowledge the Soviet Union's history of aggressiveness and its responsibility for the Cold War. (See his *We Now Know: Rethinking Cold War History* [Oxford and New York: Oxford University Press, 1997].)

   7. These included Warren Beatty's *Reds* (1981) and several about the blacklisting of Communist writers: *The Front* (1976), Woody Allen starring and directing; Walter Bernstein's *House on Carroll Street* (1988); and Irvin Winkler's *Guilty by Suspicion* (1991), starring Robert de Niro. Among the fraudulent documentaries was PBS's $5.6 million, thirteen-part *Vietnam: A Television History* (1983), which complemented *The Deer Hunter* (1978), *Apocalypse Now* (1979), Stanley Kubrick's *Full Metal Jacket* (1987), and a host of others. *Senator Joseph McCarthy: An American Inquisitor* (A&E, 1995), supposedly a documentary, was as inaccurate as NBC's 1977 docudrama *Tail Gunner Joe*. HBO's spurious *Citizen Cohn* (1992), starring James Woods, was equally damning. Oliver Stone's fanciful critiques of America's attempts to fight Communism (*Salvador* [1986], *Platoon* [1986], and *Born on the Fourth of July* [1989]) were applauded, but he was almost universally castigated as irresponsible when he dealt with a subject dear to liberals in *JFK* (1991).

   Some convincing critiques of the aforementioned have been made. Ronald

Radosh evaluated both print and film Blacklist revisionism in "The Blacklist as History," *The New Criterion* 16 (Dec. 1997): 12-17. Accuracy in Media responded to the multimillion dollar PBS series with the relatively few financial resources it could muster for its *Television's Vietnam* (1984, 1985). (The Public Broadcasting System's inaccurate treatment of the war did not prevent videotapes of its *Vietnam: A Television History* from being used as the basis of college courses throughout the country.) Roy Cohn provided "The Answer to 'Tail Gunner Joe' " in an addition (pp. vii-xviii) to his book, *McCarthy* (New York: Manor Books, 1977; originally published by New American Library, 1968). Ted Turner's version of the Cold War misled its CNN viewers for much of its nineteen hours. This 1998 documentary has been accurately evaluated in Gabriel Schoenfeld, "Twenty-Four Lies about the Cold War," *Commentary* 107 (March 1999): 28-35; and Thomas M. Nichols, "Mules, Missiles, and McCarthy: CNN's *Cold War*," *International Journal* 54 (Summer 1999): 418-25.

Librarianship's contribution to this subject has been a predictably snide, anti-anti-Communist web site at the University of Washington's Library titled "The Red Scare: A Filmography," <http://www.lib.washington.edu/exhibits/AllPowers/film.html>. It was compiled by Glenda Pearson, head of the Microforms and Newspapers Collection, and dated March 5, 1998.

8. An initial bibliographic work of studies from the Soviet era is Robert A. Karlowich's "Libraries, Bibliographies, and Books in Russia in 1917-1935: A Preliminary Bibliography of Books and Serials on the Period Published in the Soviet Union, 1946-1985," in *Books, Libraries and Information in Slavic and East European Studies: Proceedings of the Second International Conference of Slavic Librarians and Information Specialists*, ed. by Marianna Tax Choldin (New York: Russica, 1986), pp. 129-43. A brief overview of the historiography of Russian librarianship in pre-Communist, Communist, and post-Communist Russia can be found in Mary Stuart, "The Evolution of Librarianship in Russia: The Librarians of the Imperial Public Library, 1808-1868," *Library Quarterly* 64 (January 1994): 2-5.

9. For example, Harold M. Leich writes: "Beginning in the late 1920's the Communist party [*sic*] imposed the philosophy that librarianship's chief goal was to serve the propagation of party ideology. The work of many prerevolutionary Russian librarians was denounced, and emphasis turned to developing a new Communist librarianship." ("The Society for Librarianship and Russian Librarianship in the Early Twentieth Century," *Journal of Library History* 22, no. 1 [1987]: 55.)

10. See, for example, the work of Eugene Slon, a Slavic librarian at Cornell University in the 1970's. (Slon, *Open Access to Soviet Book Collections*, ed. by Donald C. Robbins [New York, Ukrainian Library Association of America; and Toronto: New Review Books, 1978].) Unfortunately, the impact of his research was limited by his inability to master

English after immigrating to the United States and his failure to obtain an experienced publisher for his work. A member of the profession raised in America who has demonstrated the negative consequences of Communist rule on library development is Marianna Tax Choldin, head of the Slavic and East European Library and Research Director at the Russian and East European Center, University of Illinois at Urbana. (See chapter one, note 29.)

Valuable contributions have been made by a Soviet emigré, Boris Korsch, at the Hebrew University of Jerusalem: *The Permanent Purge of Soviet Libraries* (Jerusalem: Soviet and East European Research Centre, Hebrew University of Jerusalem, 1983; "The Role of Readers' Cards in Soviet Libraries," *Journal of Library History* 13 (Summer 1978): 282-97, originally published in Hebrew in *Yad Lakoré* 15 (April 1976): 135-45; and *The Brezhnev Personality Cult—Continuity: The Librarian's Point of View* (Jerusalem: Marjorie Mayrock Center for Soviet and East European Research, Hebrew University of Jerusalem, 1987). Like Slon, Korsch underscores the continuity of the essentials in Soviet librarianship. The Israeli interest in librarianship in Eastern Europe—as well as the rest of the world—has been ably promoted by Shmuel and Irene Sever, two scholar-librarians at Haifa University. For example, see: Valeria D. Stelmakh, ed., *The Image of the Library: Studies and Views from Several Countries* (Haifa: University of Haifa Library, 1994).

A politically astute contribution to Russian and Soviet library history was made in an American journal in the 1990's by a Finnish professor of library and information studies. It is additional evidence that the terrible realities of the USSR have generally been best apprehended by those most affected by them. This researcher shows that libraries for prisoners were better under the Czars than the Communists. He also points out that, despite their differences, the approaches of the Stalinists and Krupskaya (Lenin's wife, who is admired by many in the United States) were basically the same. (See Ilkka Mäkinen, "Libraries in Hell: Cultural Activities in Soviet Prisons and Labor Camps from the 1930s to the 1950s," *Libraries and Culture* 28 [Spring 1993]: 117-42.)

11. The best of these works is by a historian at the Library of Congress: John Earl Haynes, *Red Scare or Red Menace? American Communism and Anticommunism in the Cold War Era* (Chicago: Ivan R. Dee, 1996). The author of several books on this subject, Haynes has done extensive research in recently opened archives in Russia and the United States. Another valuable work is by Richard Gid Powers, Professor of History at the College of Staten Island and the Graduate Center of the City University of New York: *Not Without Honor: The History of American Anticommunism.* Its title alludes to the lack of respect anti-Communists have received in the United States: "A prophet is not without honor, save in his own country and his own house." — Matt. 13:57. Powers' research for the book changed his mind entirely about his subject: "I began with the idea that anticommunism displayed America at its worst, but I came to see

in anticommunism America at its best." (Powers, p. 503)

12. For example, see Louise S. Robbins, *Censorship and the American Library: The American Library Association's Response to Threats to Intellectual Freedom, 1939-1969* (Westport, CT, and London: Greenwood Press, 1996).

13. Michael Kazin, "The Grass-Roots Right: New Histories of U.S. Conservatism in the Twentieth Century," *The American Historical Review* 97 (Feb. 1992): 136. See Edward Shapiro's critique of Kazin's review article in his "Liberalism and the College History Textbook: A Case Study," *Continuity: A Journal of History*, no.16 (Fall 1992): 27. Kazin's political views are presented fully in his *Populist Persuasion: An American History* (New York: Basic Books, 1995). In it, he declares: "I cherish the traditional convictions of the non-Communist Left. . . ." (p. 6)

14. See: John Earl Haynes, "The Cold War Debate Continues: A Traditionalist View of Historical Writing on Domestic Communism and Anti-Communism," *Journal of Cold War Studies* 2 (Winter 2000): 76-115; Hilton Kramer, "The 'Red Baiters' were Right—But *N. Y. Times* Ignores Spy Story," *Human Events* 52 (March 22, 1996): 5; Hilton Kramer, "Protecting the Rosenberg Myth: *N. Y. Times* Trying to Minimize Rosenbergs' Role as Soviet Spies," *Human Events* 53 (May 16, 1997): 14; John Corry, "Hissteria: Why Do They Insist on Distorting History?" *American Spectator* 29 (May 1996): 46-47. Kramer is editor of *The New Criterion*. Corry was, for many years, a media critic for the *New York Times*. He tired of being one of this newspaper's token conservative journalists and resigned.

15. The literature of the field is large, and some of it will be described on the pages that follow. A few of the works published over the years that illustrate the point are: Henry Arthur Jones, *My Dear Wells* (London: Eveleigh Nash & Grayson; New York, E. P. Dutton, 1921); Sir Winston Churchill's speeches: "Socialism," Jan. 21, 1926, "Disarmament and Europe," June 29, 1931, "The Iron Curtain Begins to Fall," Aug. 16, 1945, and "The Sinews of Peace," [the *famous* "Iron Curtain" speech] March 5, 1946, in *Churchill Speaks, 1897-1963: Collected Speeches in Peace and War*, ed. by Robert Rhodes James (New York: Barnes & Noble, 1998; originally published: Chelsea House, 1980), pp. 477-79, 540-43, 873-76, 876-84; James Burnham, *Suicide of the West: An Essay on the Meaning and Destiny of Liberalism* (Chicago: Regnery, 1985; originally published: New York: John Day, 1964); M. Stanton Evans, *The Politics of Surrender* (New York: Devin-Adair, 1966); Richard V. Allen, *Peace or Peaceful Coexistence?*, foreword by Bertram D. Wolfe (Chicago: American Bar Association, 1966); Richard Pipes, *Survival is Not Enough: Soviet Realities and America's Future* (New York: Simon and Schuster, 1984). See also Andrew E. Busch, "Ronald Reagan and the Defeat of the Soviet Empire," *Presidential Studies Quarterly* 27 (Summer 1997): 451-66.

16. See *The Chicago Manual of Style*, 14th ed. (Chicago: University of Chicago Press, 1993), pp. 235-36, 256-57; and the entries under *Communism* in: *Webster's Third New International Dictionary of the English Language*, ed. by Philip Babcock Gove and others (Springfield, MA: G. & C. Merriam Company, 1981) and *Webster's New Universal Unabridged Dictionary . . . Based on the Second Edition of the Random House Dictionary of the English Language* [*Unabridged Edition*, 1993] (New York: Barnes & Noble, 1996.) The Bolshevik Party officially changed its name to the Communist Party in March 1918.

Newly opened archives in Russia and the United States should leave no doubt that the Communist Party of the United States was controlled from Moscow. See: John Earl Haynes and Harvey Klehr, *Venona: Decoding Soviet Espionage in America* (New Haven, CT, and London: Yale University Press, 1999); Harvey Klehr, John Earl Haynes, and Fridrikh Igorevich Firsov, *The Secret World of American Communism* (New Haven, CT, and London: Yale University Press, 1995); and Harvey Klehr, John Earl Haynes, and Kyril M. Anderson, *The Soviet World of American Communism* (New Haven, CT, and London: Yale University Press, 1998).

17. On the non-capitalization of the initial *m* in *movement*, see *The Chicago Manual of Style*, 14th ed., pp. 256-57.

1

THE COMING OF COMMUNIST LIBRARIANSHIP

Librarianship in Pre-Revolutionary Russia

Librarianship in pre-Revolutionary Russia was highly developed and well on its way to creating institutions similar to those found in the democratic nations of the world.[1] From the mid-nineteenth century through the early 1900's, there were extraordinary advances in Russian librarianship paralleling those in Russian education, economic development, and political reform.[2] For example, there was an enormous growth in the number and size of libraries: by 1914, there were fourteen thousand public libraries in Czarist Russia holding a total of nine million books. There were also several major research libraries. The Imperial Public Library (renamed the Saltykov-Shchedrin Library after the Revolution) contained 2.3 million volumes; the Rumiantsev Museum in Moscow (designated the Lenin Library by the Soviets), 1.3 million books; and the Academy of Science Library, six hundred thousand.[3] Writing of those days in a 1924 *Library Journal* article, one American declared that "Every one knew, of course, that Russian libraries ranked high among the great book collections," and that the country "had several of the world's greatest reference and research collections."[4] Significantly, the Imperial Public Library—the third largest library in the world—was more accessible to the public than any other major library in Britain and Europe.[5]

In the production of books, Czarist Russia was one of the world leaders by the end of the eighteenth century. In 1913, Russia ranked a close second to Germany in the number of titles produced and equalled the figures for Great Britain, France, and the United States

combined. In terms of total output, the number of volumes printed in
1848 was only 766,000; but in 1913, it was 89 million. Thus, the
rapidly growing reading public was served by a great quantity of books
as well as much variety.[6]

The major research libraries were adequately staffed by highly
educated and skilled librarians. These librarians, particularly those in
Moscow and St. Petersburg, were the leaders in the development of the
Russian profession. There was an interest in the intellectual, social,
and behavioral aspects of librarianship in addition to the technical. The
Bibliographical Society, founded in Moscow in 1889, began to issue a
journal, *Knigovedenie* ("Book Science"), at the turn of the century
which dealt with the study of the production, distribution, and
utilization of books. Librarianship was initially regarded as a part of
this field rather than as a separate entity. In 1908, the library section
of the Society transformed itself into the independent Society of
Librarianship, and two years later the first Russian periodical devoted
specifically to library work made its appearance. There was an annual
guide to new books and periodicals (*The Bibliographic Yearbook*) as
well as yearly statistical summaries of publication trends. In 1911 the
first conference for librarians was held. A program in education for
librarianship was begun at Sheniavskii University in Moscow under
the direction of L. B. Khavkina (aka L. Haffkin Hamburger), and
bibliography became a university discipline when it was taught by
Professor N. M. Lissovski in St. Petersburg.[7]

The emerging profession of librarianship was politically liberal in
its orientation. In 1905 the Bibliographical Society petitioned the
government to decrease its censorship and its other controls over public
libraries, and there *was* a liberalization during this period. There was
also a strong tradition among the pre-Revolutionary librarians—like
Khavkina—of political nonpartisanship in book selection and other
library activities. The first All-Russian Library Congress in 1911
formally endorsed the principle that there should be no political,
national, or religious biases in library work.[8]

During the nineteenth and the early twentieth centuries, the basis
of what later became Soviet Communist librarianship was also established—outside of the professional mainstream. By the 1830's, the
Russian intellectual dissidents, influenced by German idealists such as
Hegel and Schiller, established their essential approach to social
transformation: correct ideas must be propagated because they are a

precondition to successful revolution. Understanding the potential significance of reading, it is not surprising that the radicals were early on involved in library work. Some of the *Decembrists*—so-called because of their abortive revolution in December 1825—were exiled to Siberia to serve various terms. There they formed libraries from the personal collections they brought and used them to continue their revolutionary education. (The relatively lenient treatment they clearly received should be noted.) Alexander Herzen, the "father" of Russian revolutionaries, considered libraries important. He served as an assistant public librarian in the 1830's during his exile in northern Russia. N. G. Chernyshevskii, author of the touchstone work *What Is To Be Done?*, was also interested in libraries.[9]

It appears that the liberal reforms under the Czars, in conjunction with the relatively mild consequences for those working to overthrow the government, paved the way for revolution. By 1860, a great number of non-aristocratic students were being admitted to universities; many became radicalized there. Quite a few dedicated revolutionaries were created by the growing freedom within institutions of higher education, the isolation of the college students from the realities of the general society, and the development of a radical political subculture that idealized the masses.[10]

There were student strikes and attempts to organize the peasants; such activities were assisted by Russian libraries. The research collections of the great national and university libraries played a large role as a source of information and ideas for several generations of left-wing intellectuals. Sometimes, as at Moscow University, a library served as both a means of disseminating radical material and as a cover for the formation of clandestine radical groups. Marxists like Lenin and Krupskaya made use of both legal and illegal libraries and books in their teaching activities. When Krupskaya was an instructor for workers in St. Petersburg, her major source of books was the library provided for the public by the wealthy, reform-minded Rubakin family. (Lenin and the other Communists later pilloried its librarian, Nicholas Rubakin, for his liberal ideas.) The revolutionaries saw the great potential of the book and paid much attention to its role in mobilizing the working class. Sometimes the Bolsheviks cleverly managed to take control of legal government libraries or libraries supported by liberal aristocrats; they then purged them of books they did not like. Contemporaries reported that the radicals feared a free exchange of opinions and worked to impose orthodox thoughts on each other as well as on their students.[11]

The First Decades of Communist Librarianship

There was chaos in the libraries for years following the Bolshevik coup, in part because of one significant act: their nationalization. In addition, funds for their support were scarce because the Communized economy had quickly collapsed. In October 1921, there were still 13,700 public libraries in the European part of the Soviet Union; one year later there were only 6,000. Many of the libraries had been plundered by the government or destroyed by its riotous supporters. Statistics reveal that at the end of the 1920's, the number of public libraries per person was still less than it had been before the Revolution. In the twenties and early thirties, most libraries had poor collections, were badly managed, and failed to cooperate with one another. Although some quality libraries had been established by the Bolsheviks in factories, these soon became the exclusive preserves of the new Communist administrators. In general, progress in most of the material aspects of librarianship was not made until 1932 and afterward with what is sometimes termed *Stalinization*.[12]

The primary "accomplishment" in the fifteen years after the so-called October Revolution was the destruction of the budding Western-style libraries and librarianship and the laying of the foundations for a monolithic library system which allowed no competition, contained highly tendentious collections, emphasized political propaganda in reader services, and was staffed by well-indoctrinated librarians dedicated to fulfilling the wishes of the Communist Party. Lenin and Krupskaya were largely responsible for this although the Party's Central Committee was also directly involved in numerous important decisions. One sign of the significance of libraries in the minds of the new rulers is the fact that Leon Trotsky was the keynote speaker at the 1924 All-Russian Library Congress.[13] Moreover, his lengthy speech was also printed in the official Communist Party newspaper, *Pravda* ("Truth").

One area in which the new Soviet librarianship was very successful in accomplishing its goal was in propaganda work with the Red Army. Many new, young recruits to librarianship worked with, and within, the armed forces. During the Civil War, their propaganda work was considered to be of the very highest importance, and thus the transport of books to the front-lines received the same priority as guns and ammunition.[14]

In addition to libraries for soldiers and industrial workers, collections were set up to serve other special groups. For example, in the early twenties, libraries were established for the purpose of distributing Communist works on pedagogy to teachers to help foster the new Communist education[15]—the "once respectable"[16] school system had been largely destroyed. Most teachers opposed the Communists, especially in Moscow and Petrograd. (St. Petersburg had been renamed Petrograd in 1914. This was changed to Leningrad in 1924. The original name returned in 1991.) In 1917, these educators began a three-month strike which was apparently supported by almost all members of the profession. In Petrograd, the teacher's association expelled three Bolsheviks 'for carrying out the orders of a self-proclaimed power,' viz., Russia's Communist leadership. In 1918 the Russian teacher's union was disbanded by the self-appointed "workers government."[17]

Krupskaya had direct conflicts with the teachers. There was a telling incident in 1919 in which Krupskaya was unsympathetic to some teachers who had appealed to her for help. As she reported it, they had 'shed crocodile tears about the Cheka [secret police], arrests, . . . and babbled on about freedom of the press.'[18]

Like the other Bolsheviks, Krupskaya engaged in systematic censorship and purges in her effort to create the new society. It was under her direct guidance that collection development in Soviet libraries became thoroughly politicized. This was not an easy task since, as already noted, there was a strong, widespread tradition and belief among pre-Revolutionary librarians that they should carry out educational work without political, national, or religious partisanship. At first, Krupskaya had the support of only a few librarians: a handful of her Bolshevik comrades. Her opponents—called the "objectivists"—included prominent members of the profession, such as L. B. Khavkina, A. A. Pokrovskii, and E. Medinskii.[19] Khavkina wrote in 1918 that she was an adherent of 'the American view-point [in which] the goal of libraries is to improve the life of the people, raise well-being and happiness.'[20] She and her allies put up a strong struggle against the Bolsheviks but, like the school teachers, they lost.

Krupskaya not only succeeded in eradicating the "non-alignment" policy of the library profession but the "objectivist" mainstream ideology of related groups, like the publishers.[21]

Krupskaya wrote that in the years following the Revolution, "Libraries had to be purged of narrow-minded and religious books and in the process the shelves of old, established libraries were almost denuded."[22] In 1923 Krupskaya ordered the following works removed from libraries: all "anti-artistic literature"; "counter-revolutionary" books; anti-Communist works; 'the agitational literature of 1917 for the constitution, the democratic republic, civil liberties, the Constituent Assembly, universal voting rights, . . . etc.'; and 'obsolete Soviet agitational literature from 1918, 1919 and 1920, on questions which have since been decided in a different manner by the Soviet state.'[23] Her stated purpose for these ukases was 'the simple protection of the interests of the masses.'[24] There were repeated "cleansings" of this type in the 1920's, often as part of propaganda campaigns. Many librarians were averse to implementing the new Communist regulations, so Krupskaya had her directives concerning library censorship mandate the active participation of the feared secret police.[25]

One Soviet study of rural libraries showed that the most common form of propaganda work was that carried out against religion.[26] Robert McNeal, the preeminent Western biographer of Lenin's wife, states: "It is not surprising to find Krupskaya taking a hard line on religion. Anti-religious education was one of her specialities."[27]

The 1923 mandate concerning censorship had a list of proscribed books attached. It drew some opposition in the USSR and received a great deal of attention and criticism in the West. (Krupskaya's defense of Communist censorship, originally issued in *Pravda*, the Party's official newspaper, was reprinted in the highly regarded American cultural magazine, *Living Age*.) The list, officialy issued by an agency headed by Krupskaya called the Commission for Book Revision, included works by Plato, Kant, Schopenhauer, and Tolstoy. Responding to the criticism, Krupskaya stated that this particular enumeration was merely a "mistake." The question of whether Plato and Kant should be proscribed was actually "irrelevant," she declared, since they were not read by the masses. Moreover, she asserted, there was no danger in the religiousness of Tolstoy or the anarchism of Kropotkin because the masses had already been sufficiently "saturated" with secular and Communist thought. Krupskaya added that if anything about the regulations truly deserved criticism, it was the fact that they had not been zealous enough in their attacks on religion.[28]

In its essentials, the Soviet system of censorship established in these early years remained for over seven decades. Compared to the censorship under the Czars, it was far more thoroughgoing, proactive, efficient, and effective. It has been suggested by some scholars that the term *censorship* is inadequate to describe the all-pervasive, totalitarian system of control the Communists established.[29]

In the second half of the 1920's, there was an increased emphasis on what could be termed "narrow" Party propaganda. It may be significant that it accompanied an increased Soviet effort to industrialize rapidly. After 1929, there were many administrative, technical, and financial improvements in the Soviet library system. At the same time, there was another major purge of book collections and library workers as well as another drive for rapid industrialization and collectivization.[30]

This purge within librarianship—like others—was part of a ruthless, society-wide bloodletting, accompanied by a national hysteria and a preoccupation with so-called "anti-revolutionaries" and "spies." Books and journal articles about newly discredited people and ideas were once again removed from libraries in great quantities. There were numerous generic attacks against unspecified enemies within librarianship, as well as vivid denunciations of many particular librarians—including prominent ones. The named and the unnamed, the seen and the unseen, were charged with being "purveyors of an alien bourgeois ideology of librarianship," or with being "counter-revolutionary" for not totally subjecting library work to the proletariat and the class struggle. Supporters of library centralization and cooperation were criticized for being "left-wing deviationists," the same label applied to Joseph Stalin's rival, Trotsky. (Stalin had ascended to power after Lenin's death in 1924.) Later, "right-wing deviation" was focused on. Even admitting guilt to such charges was frequently not enough to preserve one's freedom or save one's life. For example, V. Nevskii, a long-time Bolshevik who had participated in the November 1917 coup and later became director of the Lenin Library, was arrested in 1935 despite several public "confessions." Similarly, M. Smushkova, Krupskaya's Bolshevik co-worker and editor of the major Soviet library journal, admitted her "guilt," to no avail. In the early thirties, Khavkina, Pokrovskii, and most of the current and former leaders of Soviet librarianship were purged, except for

Krupskaya. (Apparently, the elder stateswoman of Communist librarianship worked to save her friends' lives.) They, like Krupskaya,
had offered a measure of resistance to some of the censorship orders
issued by the Central Committee of the Communist Party, which now
acquiesced to Stalin's wishes as it had once done to Lenin's. These
orders proscribed many works by, or about, former high-ranking
Communists who had become Stalin's political adversaries—real and
imagined—such as Trotsky, Zinoviev, Bukharin, and Kamenev. Like
those conducted under Lenin's rule, the chaotic library purges resulted
in the devastation of many library collections, the pulping of millions
of volumes, the disappearance of tens of thousands of book titles from
library shelves, and the growth of special collections of banned works
accessible to only a few.[31]

The careers of many librarians benefitted from successful attacks
on their professional colleagues.[32]   However, most of those who
gained power in these purges were in turn eliminated between 1937 and
1940, and their names were likewise anathema until Khrushchev came
to power in the fifties.[33]   As before, no one could do much to ensure
his or her safety.   V. Kirov, editor of the periodical *Krasnyi
Bibliotekar*, wrote in 1936 that '. . . librarians speak of their limitless
love and devotion to the Leninist-Stalinist Central Committee of our
party and to the dearest, beloved leader, father, teacher, and director
Iosif Vassavianovich Stalin.'[34]   He was purged the following year.

Despite the disorder and confusion created by the liquidations and
government reorganizations, there were many improvements in
librarianship in the 1930's in bibliography, children's work, library
education, and other areas.   There was a major growth of industrial
libraries which paralleled the growth of industry.   Bibliographic and
cataloging practices were improved, although the revised decimal
classification placed more stress on Marxism.   A great deal of money
was allocated for children's librarianship.   The shortage of competent
librarians was finally addressed: many new training schools were
established, and the curriculum was upgraded.   A Ph.D. program in
librarianship was begun in 1930.

Before her death in 1939, Krupskaya complained that, in the past
decade, Soviet adult education had come to resemble that under the
Czars in its mindless obsession with rote learning.   At the same time,
she said in disgust, some libraries were apparently being misused as
places for playing checkers and for other diversions.   One thing that

had not changed during this period was the low pay librarians received in the "workers state."[35]

There were no forceful public attacks made directly against Krupskaya by Stalin and his followers, but she was slowly stripped of power. Despite her misgivings about his policies, she usually endorsed them. Other longtime Communists generally failed to oppose Stalin in any meaningful way.[36]

In addition to the propaganda, pressure, and purges, changes were brought about within the library profession in the two decades following the 1917 Revolution by the recruitment of new members. The kind of work a librarian did in the new Communist state was often different from that in pre-Revolutionary times, so different types of people were drawn into the field. Moreover, the new regime made major efforts to create a library workforce sympathetic to its goals.

After the Bolshevik coup, it was active Communist Party members who were appointed to directorships of libraries[37] although there were relatively few such persons to choose from. Ten thousand loyal Party members were ordered to work in libraries and small rural "reading huts," and instructions were issued to recruit more librarians from among college-educated workers and peasants.[38] It is significant that those who worked as librarians in the Red Army in the first years after the Revolution were mainly young. They were not well educated in librarianship: most of what they knew about their new vocation came from special army training courses. The new government was quite successful in placing Communist library workers in the countryside. A 1926 study showed that 74% of the rural librarians in the USSR were of peasant origin, 84% were only 18-30 years of age, and fully 19% were members of the Communist Party.[39]

A study carried out fifteen years after the 1917 Revolution revealed some of the results of the drive to create the "New Soviet Man" and demonstrated that much of its success was with the young. This research on 2500 Leningrad-area metal workers showed that 46% knew about the great Russian classics but only 7% were acquainted with the new Communist literature. However, of the younger workers, 38% were acquainted with the classics and 20% with the post-Revolutionary authors.[40]

Lenin and Krupskaya: The Touchstones of Communist Librarianship

Lenin

Leninism was the bedrock of the Communist philosophy and practice of librarianship. Of course, the term derives from the name Vladimir Ilyich Lenin. He was born Vladimir Ulyanov in 1870, adopting the alias Lenin in 1901. His father was a school inspector, but his older brother was a revolutionary who was hanged in 1887 for plotting to blow up the Czar with a bomb he had made.[41]

Lenin was a frequent user and observer of libraries in Russia and elsewhere in the years preceding his seizure of power. His views on both the philosophy and the techniques of librarianship were expressed in numerous published articles, unpublished memoranda, letters, and official directives.[42] These were effectively implemented by Krupskaya, Stalin, and the subsequent leaders of Soviet librarianship and the Soviet state.

The primacy of his philosophy is evidenced by the fact that, for seven decades after his coming to power, Communist librarians frequently began their speeches, books, and journal articles with a quotation from him. At an International Federation of Library Associations (IFLA) conference held in Moscow forty years after his death, an exhibition on Soviet libraries began with a section on Lenin in recognition of the fact that his views on librarianship were still considered the theoretical foundations of the Soviet library system.[43] The Soviets traditionally claimed that the most popular book in the USSR on librarianship was the 1929 collection of his works edited by Krupskaya, *What Lenin Wrote and Said about Libraries*.[44] In 1972, the prominent library administrator and theoretician, O. S. Chubaryan, wrote that Lenin was the originator of modern Soviet librarianship and that the foundations of its principles were set out in his 270 articles and governmental communications relating to libraries.[45] Chubaryan also referred to Lenin's declarations as "prophetic words."[46] Two years later, N. M. Sikorsky, Director of the Lenin State Library, similarly asserted that contemporary librarianship in the Soviet Union was based on the principles developed by Lenin.[47] Vasilii Vasilevich Serov stated in 1969 that "V. I. Lenin played an enormous role in the development of the theory and practice of Soviet librarianship."[48]   When I. P. Osipova dealt with a significant professional question *before* the demise of Communism, she often turned to Lenin. In the 1970's she said: "'How great is book circulation among the people?' Lenin's question is the principal yardstick to measure the effectiveness of library activity and the entire book propaganda and work in the Soviet Union."[49] Lenin also held an exalted position in the other Communist countries. Thus, Horst Kunze of East Berlin stated that the teachings of Marx and Lenin on culture and cultural revolution constituted the essence of Communist library policy.[50]   The canonization of Lenin continued into the 1980's.[51]

Of the many political radicals who made great use of the libraries in Czarist Russia, none did so more than Lenin.   He also made intensive use of collections in England, Switzerland, France, Denmark, and other countries during his years of exile.   Krupskaya stated that when Lenin headed the USSR he spent much of his time devoted to library development because he considered them so significant.[52] Indeed, one student of this subject has gone as far as to say that his primary contribution to Communist librarianship may well have been that he legitimized libraries' activities by his frequent pronouncements that they were important.[53]   Lenin, writes McNeal, had "a lifelong respect for libraries."[54]   He and Krupskaya had large private libraries: Lenin's collection in the Kremlin had close to ten thousand books while Krupskaya's contained twenty thousand.   Moreover, they had a personal librarian to assist them.[55]   An interesting sidelight in the story of Lenin and libraries is the fact that when he was living abroad, he instructed the Communist groups throughout Russia to send two copies of their revolutionary publications—which were illegal of course—to the manuscript division of the library of the Academy of Sciences, the government's foremost learned organization: the Academy had begun a collection of such publications.[56]

In February 1918, Nicholas Rubakin, the anti-Czarist Russian librarian who knew both Lenin and Krupskaya, wrote a perceptive analysis of the new government leader for a newspaper in Switzerland, where he was living:

> He is above all a man of willpower and emotions. This iron will drives him not only to fight, but to do so without respite; everything standing in his way is crushed underfoot. . . . Any opinion contrary

to his own provokes his anger; his feeling of hatred for the bourgeois social system springs from a deep conviction. . . .

In the long run it is inevitable that a man with this keen mind, highly charged emotions and energy, and with such a monumental impatience about the opinions of others, should wind up as a political egocentric. His ideas, his efforts, his intentions, his party, his programme, his tactics, are for him the beginning and the end. The ultimate result, as the saying goes, is *"ultima ratio—potestas!"* From there to despotism—despotism for the sake of an idea—is only a short step.[57]

Lenin's premier biographers, as well as scholars of the Soviet regime, have fully documented Lenin's intolerance, obsession with power, drive for control, and penchant for mandating murder and terror.[58] He created the Soviet concentration camps (*gulags*) and ordered mass executions without hesitation. While ruling the Soviet Union, he penned numerous instructions like these to his apparatchiks:

'The preparation of terror in secret is necessary and urgent.'

'The dictatorship [of the proletariat] means . . . unrestrained power based on force and not on law.'[59]

"The greater the number of representatives of the reactionary clergy and reactionary bourgeoisie we succeed in executing . . . , the better."[60]

Rubakin asserted that Lenin was unconcerned with traditional Western ethics, with good and evil. The revolutionary's statements and actions, he reported, showed that he considered anything which helped him politically to be "good," anything which hurt him to be "bad."[61] Lenin openly proclaimed that his Communist government did not believe in bourgeois morality which, he declared, was based on either the alleged commandments of a God that did not exist or on ideals which led to very similar prescriptions. True morality, he asserted, stems only from the necessities of the proletariat's struggle.[62]

According to Solzhenitsyn,[63] the Communist movement had been fairly consistent since its inception, but Lenin made it more intolerant and inhuman:

It is Lenin who deceived the peasants about the land, and the workers about self-management. He is the one who turned the trade unions into organs of suppression. He is the one who created Cheka, the secret police, and the concentration camps. It is he who sent troops out to the border areas to crush any national movements for liberation and set up an empire.[64]

Bertram Wolfe, an American who lived in the Soviet Union and became a comrade of the Revolution's leaders, wrote that Lenin's followers did not love him but they admired him, obeyed him, and often adhered to his pronouncements blindly. Moreover, ". . . after his death, they glorified, sanctified, worshipped him, made his every utterance into a sacred text, . . . [and] raised his mummified corpse to the level of an ikon. . . ."[65]

The English librarian George Chandler noted that a November 1917 memorandum of Lenin concerning public libraries contained the essentials of his master plan for libraries: (1) the use of books for political ends, and (2) the promotion of approved books through centralization, systematic services, and easy access for patrons.[66] In 1919 Lenin declared that there must be a single "well planned and unified organization" of all libraries in the country; if this were not forthcoming, "then this revolution will remain a bourgeois revolution, because the basic characteristics of a proletarian revolution which is on the road to communism is this."[67] Back in 1905 Lenin had publicly stated that libraries, like everything else, should be run by the Bolshevik (later Communist) Party: "Newspapers must become the organs of the various party organizations, and their writers must by all means become members of these organizations. Publishing and distribution centres, bookshops and reading-rooms, libraries and similar establishments—must all be under party control."[68] He was true to his word concerning Party domination. For example, in 1918 and 1920 he ordered bookstores nationalized[69] and gave the Russian people a clear warning: "Owners of books and co-operative organisations [i.e., all individuals and groups] guilty of concealing stocks of books and other printed matter will be prosecuted."[70]

A wide variety of directives concerning books and libraries were issued by Lenin, frequently accompanied by threats of imprisonment for all uncooperative library personnel.[71] In 1920 he ordered the creation of special, locked book collections in large libraries that would

be open only to individuals granted special permission.[72] The following
year he ordered the pulping of all confiscated "pornography and books
on religious subjects."[73]

Lenin's views on literature were quite different from those found
in the West or in Czarist Russia, and they remained consistent
throughout his adult life. In 1905 he had written:

> Down with non-partisan writers! Down with literary supermen!
> Literature must become *part* of the common cause of the proletariat,
> "a cog and a screw" of one single great Social-Democratic
> [Bolshevik] mechanism set in motion by the entire politically-
> conscious vanguard of the entire working class. Literature must
> become a component of organized, planned and integrated Social-
> Democratic [Bolshevik] Party work. . . . I daresay there will ever
> be hysterical intellectuals to raise a howl about such a comparison,
> which degrades, deadens, "bureaucratises" the free battle of ideas,
> freedom of criticism, freedom of literary creation, etc., etc. Such
> outcries, in point of fact, would be nothing more than an expression
> of bourgeois-intellectual individualism.[74]

He would also not tolerate any related offenses that reflected what he
termed "bourgeois-anarchist individualism."[75]

Lenin knew that his propaganda system would not be effective
unless illiteracy was eliminated. Thus, in 1922 he stated:

> "The purpose of 'liquidate illiteracy' is only that every peasant
> should be able to read by himself, without help, our decrees, orders,
> and proclamations. The aim is completely practical. Nothing
> more."[76]

Lenin perceived the value of adapting some of the library policies
and procedures of the Western democracies which he saw or read
about. He publicly praised Western libraries for their efforts to
circulate their books to large numbers of people, and reported details
about such work by the New York Public Library which he had
obtained from his close reading of its 1911 annual report. Once in
power, he continued to point to the numerous services provided by
libraries in the West, particularly in the United States and Switzerland.[77]

Krupskaya

Nadezhda Konstantinovna Krupskaya Ulianova [78] was the person most directly responsible for redirecting Russian librarianship along Leninist lines. It would be difficult to exaggerate her importance in the shaping of Soviet librarianship, even though she could—and would—be overruled by Lenin and Stalin. [79]   Born in 1869, she was greatly influenced by her father, an active progressive. She became a teacher and propagandist among the workers in St. Petersburg. [80] Recollecting the adoption of her radical political philosophy, she wrote:

> "Marxism gave me the greatest happiness that a person could possibly hope for: the knowledge of where to go, the quiet conviction in the ultimate outcome of the work which I had tied my life to. The path was not always going to be easy, but there was never any doubt [in my mind] that it was the right one." [81]

After the Revolution, she became the country's director of adult education and propaganda and Deputy Commisar of Education, making her one of the very few women to ever attain a high rank in the Soviet educational system [82]—or, in fact, in any part of the Soviet power structure. She directed the course of librarianship on a daily basis until her death. [83]   After Lenin's demise in 1924, she became the living symbol of his ideas and an object of near-worship among the Communist Party's rank-and-file and the general public; they viewed her as a motherly protector. Her gathering of Lenin's writings on librarianship for publication in 1929 bolstered her political position, which had declined under Stalin. [84]

In Robert McNeal's biography, [85] she is characterized as "tough," stern, and honest. In 1972 he observed that in the Soviet Union she still remained "the symbol of the liberated woman as well as the devoted spouse." [86]   His judgement is that she became authoritarian only after coming to power and that the most prominent manifestation of this transition was in the field of librarianship.

Late in her life, Krupskaya complained about the constraints placed on her by the system she herself had helped set up. [87]   It can also be stated that "The balance of all available evidence seems to suggest that Krupskaya's attitude towards Stalinism, like that of a great many other old Bolsheviks, was not one of consistent and principled opposition." [88]

Solzhenitsyn writes with anger, scorn, and some bewilderment in the *Gulag Archipelago* that Krupskaya—like the other Bolsheviks—did not fight Stalin:

> "Why didn't Lenin's faithful companion, Krupskaya, fight back? Why didn't she speak out even once with a public expose like the old worker in the Roston Flax Works? Was she really so afraid of losing her old woman's life?"[89]

An American researcher supportive of Krupskaya stated in 1979 that her ideas about librarianship "shaped the basic guidelines which even today determine Soviet thinking and practice."[90]   Eugene Slon, a scholar in the field of Soviet library history who fled Eastern Europe for the United States, wrote that during Stalin's rule "Krupskaia inspired librarians in their work; she gave them advice and directions and helped them become active aids to the Communist Party in the struggle toward industrialization of the nation and the collectivization of the rural economy."[91]

Unfortunately, her chief "accomplishment" was making Russian librarianship subservient to the Communist Party of the USSR, in accordance with Leninist principles.   It was she who created the centrally-controlled library network staffed by disciplined workers to carry out the policies of the Party leaders. Her influence later followed the Soviet troops into Eastern Europe and reached both Communist and non-Communist developing countries throughout the world.[92]

The essential elements of her philosophy were formed in the 1890's, although her major written work on education, a short book titled *Education and Democracy*, was published in 1917. She usually claimed that all her theories were derived from Lenin, but many came from Marx and a few others.[93]

Krupskaya, like Lenin, had an unquestioning, dogmatic belief in the power of Marxism to rapidly transform a society, and a faith in the unlimited power of political indoctrination. She accepted Lenin's thesis that the "New Communist Man" could be created in a short time and that a total transubstantiation of the masses could be effected. The Communist Party, Krupskaya felt, was morally obligated to direct the masses through the necessary metamorphosis.

As already indicated, essential to Krupskaya's philosophy and approach to life and librarianship was her blind faith in Marxism. It was only this science of society, she held, that could reveal the truth, and only the leaders of the Communist Party (particularly Lenin) who could fully comprehend it. The decisions of these political scientists were infallible, inevitable, and beneficial for the proletariat. To Krupskaya, a refusal to accept Marxism-Leninism—or even a passive indifference to it—was a sign of either reactionary, class-based hostility or of political ignorance. McNeal states that she was devoted to abstractions and that one could accurately say she was married to the Revolution. Accordingly, his biography of her is titled *Bride of the Revolution*.[94]

Krupskaya was firm in her belief of the necessity for an all-powerful role in library affairs for the Party's ruling elite. All library work had to be consonant with the political and economic goals set by the Party, and she maintained that it was this organization's responsibility to determine both the general functions of librarians and their specific tasks. She firmly believed in the total politicization of librarianship.[95]

Marxism-Leninism dominated all aspects of the philosophy and practice of librarianship that Krupskaya worked to institute throughout the USSR. She believed that knowledge of the theory and practice of Marxism was essential for librarians in all elements of their work. For example, on the subject of writing an evaluation of a book for inclusion in a bibliography or a card catalog, she stated: "It is no simple matter to evaluate a book, but a large question and one must be a good Marxist to tackle it."[96] Similarly, bibliographic annotations had to be done with a 'Marxist evaluation of the book, rather than in an objectivist [i.e., objective] spirit.'[97] She averred that 'The book . . . is like a rifle in battle. This of course, is true not of every book, but only of a good book, one which is needed for the raising of political consciousness, and for the practical work of a socialist reshaping of life. . . .'[98]

Not surprisingly, Krupskaya maintained that the most important quality in a librarian is not technical expertise, but the capacity to be a good propagandist for Marxism.[99] She described contemporary Soviet librarians thusly: ". . . with every step do librarians feel how much they need to study Marxism-Leninism and everywhere in the country passionately to offer their readers works of Marx and Engels."[100] One suspects that she was moved by wishful thinking here. On the question of book collections, Krupskaya had already

decided before the turn of the century that public libraries throughout
Russia should only have books conforming with Party policy.[101] She
asserted that '. . . a librarian must necessarily learn to be a
propagandist'[102] and held that the primary didactic method of the
librarian was the recommendation of books that would lead readers to
hold Communist views. This necessitated learning about people, as
well as books.[103]

The cataloging and classification of materials were radicalized by
this revolutionary. She wrote: "It is important to arrange books in the
best way from the Marxist point of view, both in catalogs and on the
shelves."[104] According to one Soviet librarian, she made 'a categorical
demand that there be an organic connection between the construction
and content of a catalog and the general ideological tasks of the Soviet
library.'[105]

Krupskaya was very interested in library services to young people,
and her pedagogical ideas shaped children's libraries.[106] She asserted
that, in general, strong supervision of children was necessary to ensure
that they 'actually form the kind of public opinion that is required.'[107]
And she stated explicitly what the primary aim of children's library
service was: to make them loyal to the Communist Party. This was to
be accomplished through structuring a youngster's perceptual categories
so that he or she viewed the world in the same way as the Party.[108]

Krupskaya was forthright about the quality of early Soviet
literature: "In our children's books there are no living people, nothing
happens; . . . there are tractors, combines, but no living people—all are
alike."[109] Consequently, she conceded that some traditional classics
still had to be utilized because of their capacity to widen the intellectual
and emotional horizons of children. However, they did have to be
rewritten to purge them of non-Communist ideas.[110]

She feared and hated what she called "foreign ideologies." In
reality, the term signified ideologies foreign to Communism and to the
new state. To her, such beliefs reflected the values of the Church,
Czarism, and the Russian bourgeoisie. Children's books were altered
or replaced, so whereas under the Czars children read biographies of
the saints, under the Bolsheviks they read about Lenin and the leaders
of the Communist Party. The content of books had to be materialist,
with no elements of mysticism, religion, or belief in God.[111] Libraries
for children, she asserted, were supposed to propagate Marxism-
Leninism, teach about the Communist Party and the government,

develop Soviet patriotism, prepare children to work, and indoctrinate them on the subject of science and atheism. Krupskaya stressed that children's library books not only had to be properly selected, but that they needed appropriate introductions and supplements to ensure correct interpretation. Since she believed that books could do either good *or* evil, she opposed any uncontrolled access to them by the young.[112] By the early 1930's, she was somewhat pleased with the progress made in developing textbooks and school libraries, but she still felt there was a dearth of exciting, high-quality children's books "imbued with the spirit of Communism."[113]

Krupskaya studied the culture and the educational agencies of Western Europe and the United States.[114] Her estimation of the values these reflected and reinforced was essentially negative. For instance, she condemned American and European films for poisoning people's minds with bourgeois values.[115] However, Krupskaya did express admiration for some aspects of Western life—like the American appreciation of the significant influence of children's reading—and she acknowledged the Soviet need to progress in these areas. In some of her work in librarianship, she believed she was following American models.[116]

Despite Krupskaya's central role in the development of librarianship, after her death her name was rarely mentioned by Soviet librarians until the death of Stalin in 1953. Even then, little was said of her until Khrushchev denounced "The Man of Steel" three years later.[117] By the end of the 1970's, there was a good deal of material written in the USSR about Krupskaya's contributions to librarianship—all of it laudatory.[118] Her work is being reappraised in post-Communist Russia.

NOTES

1. The facts do not support the picture traditionally put forth by Soviet librarians. These decried or ignored developments in Russia before the Bolshevik coup in November 1917 while extolling those which followed. (The

putsch is frequently referred to as the *October Revolution* because this was the month according to the old style Russian calendar.) Typical were those of Vasillii Vasilievich Serov, Head of the Soviet Ministry of Culture's Library Directorate, as expressed in his "Union of Soviet Socialist Republics," *ALA World Encyclopedia of Library and Information Services* (Chicago: American Library Association, 1980), pp. 567-71. To some extent, the politically acceptable version changed over time, contorted to satisfy contemporary political exigencies. For example, in 1968 Lev Vladimirov, the Soviet director of the UN Library, stated that library development in the Czarist era had been extremely bad; under Lenin, very good; under Stalin, bad; under Khrushchev, not too bad; and under "The New Leadership" (Brezhnev and Kosygin), very good. (Speech at Columbia University School of Library Service, New York, March 16, 1968.)

2. For earlier progress in librarianship, see Mary Stuart, *Aristocrat-Librarian in Service to the Tsar: Aleksei Nikolaevich Olenin and the Imperial Public Library* (Boulder, CO: East European Monographs, 1986; distributed by Columbia University Press, New York). For information on Russia's impressive economic development before the Revolution, see: W. W. Rostow, *The Stages of Economic Growth: A Non-Communist Manifesto* (Cambridge, England: Cambridge University Press, 1961), pp. 93-100; Zbigniew Brzezinski, *Between Two Ages: America's Role in the Technetronic Era* (Harmondsworth, England: Penguin, 1976 [paperback]; originally published by Viking Press, New York, 1970), p. 189; and John A. Armstrong, *Ideology, Politics, and Government in the Soviet Union*, 3rd ed. (New York: Praeger, 1974), p. 15.

3. Boris Raymond, *Krupskaia and Soviet Russian Librarianship, 1917-1939* (Metuchen, NJ, and London: Scarecrow Press, 1979), pp. 22-23. These libraries served the growing number of people able to read. The figures on the rapid development of literacy during this period are impressive. (See Carlo M. Cipolla, *Literacy and Development in the West* [Baltimore, MD: Penguin, 1969], pp. 90, 116, 118, 11.) For a description of what was read, see Jeffrey Brooks, *When Russia Learned to Read: Literacy and Popular Literature, 1861-1917* (Princeton, NJ: Princeton University Press, 1985).

4. "Russian Libraries Today," *Library Journal* 49 (Sept. 1, 1924): 727, 728.

5. The two largest were the British Museum and the Bibliothèque Nationale. It was noted by a contemporary student of this subject that the Library of Congress would probably overtake the Imperial Public Library within a few years. (See Theodore W. Koch, "The Imperial Public Library, St. Petersburg, Second Paper: The Story of a Hundred Years," *Library Journal* 40 [Feb. 1915]: 108.) Earlier American assessments of its size were reported in B. Fernow's "The Imperial Public Library of St. Petersburg," *Library Journal* 30 (Nov. 1905): 860.

Concerning its accessibility, see Mary Stuart, " 'A Potent Lever for Social Progress': The Imperial Public Library in the Era of the Great Reforms," *Library Quarterly* 59 (July 1989): 208. Eugene Slon describes the openness of Russian public and private libraries, and even a few university libraries, in his *Open Access to Book Collections*, ed. by Donald C. Robbins (New York: Ukrainian Library Association of America; and Toronto: New Review Books, 1978), pp. 5-12. All public libraries had reading rooms, loaned books, and were open every day, including Sunday. (L. Haffkin Hamburger [L. B. Khavkina], "Russian Libraries," *Library Journal* 40 [March 1915]: 169.)

6. In contrast, a careful analysis of the books published in the Soviet Union decades later indicated that except for professional books and translations of Russian works into other languages, the selection of books available in the USSR was actually smaller than it had been before the Revolution and that there was little political or artistic diversity. (See Maurice Friedberg, *Russian Classics in Soviet Jackets* [New York and London: Columbia University Press, 1962], pp. x-xi.) The Russian librarian, L. Haffkin Hamburger (L. B. Khavkina), stated before the Revolution that over thirty thousand different titles were published annually in Russia. (See her "Russian Libraries," p. 169.)

Under the Czars, an independent, critical press arose relatively unhindered by government censorship. (See Charles A. Ruud, "The Printing Press as an Agent of Political Change in Early Twentieth-Century Russia," *The Russian Review* 40 [Oct. 1981]: 378-95.)

7. Marianna Tax Choldin, "The Russian Bibliographical Society, 1889-1930," *Library Quarterly* 46 (Jan. 1976): 1-19; Leich; Raymond, p. 23; "Russian Libraries Today"; Stuart, "The Evolution of Librarianship in Russia"; and Pal Molnar, "The Conception and Interrelation of Bibliology and Library Science Formulated in Recent Debates in Socialist Countries," *Libri* 18, no. 1 (1968): 9-10. The Soviet study of bibliology decades later resembled Lissovski's work, which greatly influenced it.

8. See Stuart, "The Imperial Public Library," pp. 216-18, on the triumph of the progressives in the Imperial Public Library in the 1860's. See also Raymond, p. 63; and Leich.

9. Raymond, pp. 19, 24-26.

10. See W. W. Rostow, with Alfred Levin, *The Dynamics of Soviet Society*; and Raymond, pp. 26-27. Aleksandr Solzhenitsyn has argued convincingly that there was far more freedom under the Czars than under the Communists: people could leave the country freely, there were few prisons, and there was general cultural freedom. (See Solzhenitsyn, *The Mortal Danger: How Misconceptions about Russia Imperil America*, 2nd ed., trans. by Michael Nicholson and Alexis Klimoff [New York: Harper & Row, 1981], pp. 14-19.)

11. Raymond, pp. 15; 18; 27-40; 13n12; Stuart, "The Imperial Public Library," pp. 212-15; and "Library of Kazan Students," in *Great Soviet Encyclopedia: A Translation of the Third Edition*, vol. 3, Moscow: Sovetskaia Entsiklopedia Publishing House, 1970 (New York: Macmillan, 1973), p. 716.

12. Nadezhda K. Krupskaya, "Foreword," *What Lenin Wrote and Said About Libraries* [*Chto Pisal I Govoril o Bibliotekakh*], 1st ed. (Moscow: 1929), trans. and reprinted, in part, in *Lenin, Krupskaia, and Libraries*, ed. by S[ylva] Simsova, trans. by G. Peacock and Lucy Prescott (London: Clive Bingley, 1968), p. 10. While Krupskaya mentioned that the Whites burned some libraries and used others as hospitals during the Civil War, she described in some detail the destructive acts of the Reds. See also Raymond, pp. 81, 108-13, 118-19, 122.

13. Raymond, pp. 100-101, 88. The conference was initiated by Glavpolitprosvet, the Chief Committee for Political Education, which was headed by Krupskaya. She presided over the conference. In his speech, Trotsky declared that in the Soviet Union, ". . . a librarian—and everyone who has read the remarks of Vladimir Ilyich on this subject knows this—here a librarian is not an official dealing with books, but rather he is, must be, must become a cultural warrior, a Red Army soldier fighting for socialist culture." (See Trotsky's "Leninism and Library Work," trans. by Tom Scott, in *Problems of Everyday Life and Other Writings on Culture and Science*, by Trotsky [New York: Monad Press, 1973; distributed by Pathfinder Press; first published in *Pravda*, July 10, 1924], p. 143.)

14. Stephen J. Main, "The Creation and Development of the Library System in the Red Army during the Russian Civil War (1918-1920): A Historical Introduction," *Library Quarterly* 65 (July 1995): 319-32; and Raymond, pp. 56-57.

15. *Soviet Education* 25 (Nov. 1982): 17.

16. McNeal, p. 204. He writes: "The disaster that swept over Russia's once-respectable system of public education in 1918-20 was not simply the result of half-baked reforms. The country was racked by civil war and economic collapse. . . ." Richard Pipes presents a devastating portrait of the educational system created by the Communists in his *Russia under the Bolshevik Regime* (New York: Knopf, 1993), pp. 314-21.

17. *Soviet Education* 25 (Nov. 1982): 11-12.

18. McNeal, p. 200. Most of the Russian intelligentsia, dedicated to free inquiry, reform, and speaking on behalf of the nation's welfare, opposed the Bolsheviks. Lenin and his comrades in power wanted them shot, jailed, or exiled. (See Jane Burbank, *Intelligentsia and Revolution: Russian Views of Bolshevism, 1917-1922* [New York and Oxford: Oxford University Press, 1986].) Krupskaya was also involved in the destruction of the autonomy and intellectual freedom widely supported among academics and students at the

universities. Most of the latter did not back the Bolsheviks. (See Peter Konecny, "Conflict and Community in Soviet Institutes of Higher Education, 1921-1928," in *History of Higher Education Annual, 1992* [University Park, PA: Pennsylvania State University, 1992], particularly pp. 70-73.)

19. Raymond, pp. 199, 159, 63-64, 93-94, 160. The Bolshevik librarians included M. Smushkova, V. Nevskii, A. Kravchenko, and F. Dobler.

20. Khavkina, quoted in Raymond, p. 64. For additional information on Khavkina, see Edward Kasinec, "L. B. Khavkina (1871-1949): American Library Ideas in Russia and the Development of Soviet Librarianship," *Libri* 37 (March 1987): 59-71.

21. Krupskaya, "We Shall Fulfill Lenin's Instructions on Library Work," [1936] in *Lenin, Krupskaia, and Libraries*, ed. by Simsova, p. 48; Raymond, pp. 63-64, 93-94, 160, 197.

22. Krupskaya, "Foreword," in *Lenin, Krupskaia, and Libraries*, ed. by Simsova, p. 10.

23. *Glavpolitprosvet*, "Instructions," as quoted and attributed in Raymond, p. 91.

24. Quoted in McNeal, p. 210.

25. McNeal, pp. 201-2.

26. Raymond, pp. 125, 85.

27. McNeal, p. 210.

28. N. K. Krupskaya ["Nadezhda Krupskaia"], "A Bolshevist *Index Expurgatorius*," *Living Age* 322 (July 5, 1924): 26-28, reprinted from *Pravda* (April 9, 1924); McNeal, pp. 201-2; Bertram D. Wolfe, "Krupskaya Purges the People's Libraries," *Survey*, no. 72 (Summer 1969): 141-55; Raymond, pp. 91-93, 103n53, 103n47. See Inge Antonie Rader, "Krupskaya: Pioneer Soviet Educator of the Masses," (Ph.D. dissertation, Southern Illinois University, 1974), pp. 100-101. The foremost name on the government directive was Krupskaya's. The document was reprinted in "The 'Index' of the Soviet Inquisition," *The Slavonic Review* 4 (March 1926): 725-32, where it was erroneously dated 1926, not 1923.

29. See the following works by Marianna Tax Choldin: "*CA [Current Anthropology]* and Soviet Censorship: An Interrupted Conversation with My Father," *Current Anthropology Supplement* 37 (Feb. 1996): S129; "Censorship in the Slavic World: An Exhibition in the New York Public Library, June 1-October 15, 1984," (New York: New York Public Library, 1984), pp. 7, 9-11; "The New Censorship: Censorship by Translation in the Soviet Union," *Journal of Library History* 21 (Spring 1986): 336; "Censorship Via Translation: Soviet Treatment of Western Political Writing," in *The Red Pencil: Artists, Scholars, and Censors in the USSR*, ed. by Choldin and Maurice Friedberg, with translations by Friedberg and Barbara Dash (Boston and London: Unwin Hyman, 1989), pp. 30, 34-40, 48. Her major study of censorship in Czarist

Russia began as a doctoral dissertation at the Graduate Library School of the University of Chicago: *A Fence Around the Empire: Russian Censorship of Western Ideas under the Tsars* (Durham, NC: Duke University Press, 1985).

30. Raymond, p. 79.

31. Ibid., pp. 113-14, 125-30, 149-50, 160-61; Szekely, "Introduction," *Soviet Education* 25 (Dec. 1982): 4; and Boris Korsch, *The Permanent Purge of Soviet Libraries* (Jerusalem: Soviet and Eastern European Research Centre, Hebrew University of Jerusalem, 1983), pp. 5-8, 11-13, 16, 24-27, 36. Despite her misgivings about Stalin's library purges, Krupskaya publicly supported them and the call for creating a new kind of librarian. (Korsch, *The Permanent Purge*, pp. 24-25.)

32. Raymond, pp. 129-30, 161, 124. For the sad stories of scholarly librarians who had to suppress or contort their work to survive under Communism, see: Edward Kasinec, " 'Old Cadres' in Practical Service of the 'Book and Revolution': The Case of A. Iu. Malein (1869-1938)," *Libri* 35, no. 3 (1985): 250-52; and Kasinec's "Iurii O. Ivaniv-Mezhenko (1892-1969) as a Bibliographer during His Years in Kiev, 1919-1933," *Journal of Library History* 14 (Winter 1979): 1-20.

33. Szekeley, "Introduction," p. 4.

34. Quoted in Raymond, p. 162. See also p. 124.

35. Ibid., pp. 113, 117-18, 144, 151-59, 163, 190. Krupskaya and Lenin both advocated *study* which led one to the correct, Communist view as opposed to the mere rote learning of a few slogans. The former, they believed, would be more efficacious. See, for example, Krupskaya, "Organization of Self-Education," [1922] in *On Education: Selected Articles and Speeches*, by Krupskaya, trans. by G. P. Ivanov-Mumjiev (Moscow: Foreign Languages Publishing House, 1957), pp. 213-42; and Lenin, "The Tasks of the Youth Leagues," [1920] in *V. I. Lenin: Selected Works*, vol. 3 (Moscow: Progress Publishers, 1971; reprinted from Lenin's *Collected Works*), pp. 470-83. In the latter, Lenin stated: ". . . we must replace the old system of instruction, the old cramming and the old drill, with an ability to acquire the sum total of human knowledge, and to acquire it in such a way that Communism shall not be something to be learned by rote, but something that you yourselves have thought over, something that will embody conclusions inevitable from the standpoint of present-day education." (p. 474)

36. Robert V. Daniels, *Russia: The Roots of Confrontation* (Cambridge, MA, and London: Harvard University Press, 1985), pp. 165-68; Raymond, pp. 128-31, 163, 10-11; and Dmitri Volkogonov, *Stalin: Triumph and Tragedy*, ed. and trans. by Harold Shukman (New York: Grove Wiedenfeld, 1991), particularly pp. 92-116. Volkogonov was the first scholar to have full access to Soviet archives after *perestroika*.

37. Slon, *Open Access to Soviet Book Collections*, p. 25.

38. Korsch, *The Permanent Purge*, pp. 22-23.

39. Raymond, pp. 56, 10.

40. Ibid., p. 110.

41. On Lenin's pseudonyms, see Folke Dovring, *Leninism: Political Economy as Pseudoscience* (Westport, CT, and London: Praeger, 1996), pp. 19-20; and Dmitri Volkogonov, *Lenin: A New Biography*, trans. and ed. by Harold Shukman [New York: The Free Press, 1994], pp. 1-2. On Lenin, see also Paul Johnson, *Modern Times: The World from the Twenties to the Eighties* (New York: Harper & Row, 1983), p. 50.

42. Many of these can be found in *Lenin and Library Organization*, comp. by K. I. Abramov (Moscow: Progress Publishers, 1983); *Lenin and Books*, comp. by A. Z. Okorokov (Moscow: Progress Publishers, 1971); and *Lenin, Krupskaia and Libraries*, ed. by Simsova, pp. 9-44.

43. George Chandler, *Libraries, Documentation and Bibliography in the USSR, 1917-1971: Survey and Critical Analysis of Soviet Studies, 1967-1971* (London and New York: Seminar Press, 1972), p. 14.

44. Ibid., p. 165.

45. O. S. Chubaryan, "Librarianship in the System of the Sciences," *Libri* 21, no. 4 (1971): 338; Chandler, pp. 143-44.

46. O. S. Chubaryan, "Reading in Modern Society: Reading and the Motivating Forces of Modern Society," *Reading in a Changing World: Papers Presented at the 38th Session of the IFLA General Council, Budapest, 1972*, ed. by Foster E. Morhardt (Munich: Verlag Dokumentation, 1976), p. 55.

47. N. M. Sikorsky, "Library Planning in the Soviet Union," *National and International Library Planning: Key Papers Presented at the 40th Session of the IFLA General Council, Washington, D.C., 1974*, ed. by Robert Vosper and Leone I. Newkirk (Munich: Verlag Dokumentation, 1976), pp. 35-36.

48. V. V. Serov, "Library Science and Some Problems of Library Education in the USSR," *Libri* 19, no. 3 (1969): 117.

49. I. P. Osipova, "Popularity of Reading in the USSR," *Reading in a Changing World*, ed. by Morhardt, p. 93.

50. See Pal Molnar, pp. 20-23.

51. See, for example, N. S. Kartashov, "The Unified Library System in the USSR," *International Librarianship Today and Tomorrow*, comp. by Joseph W. Price and Mary S. Price (New York and Munich: K. G. Saur, 1985), pp. 82-83.

52. McNeal, p. 89; Raymond, pp. 15, 18; and Krupskaya, "Foreword," in *Lenin, Krupskaia, and Libraries*, ed. by Simsova, p. 9. For more details, see Lenin's own writings in the compilations *Lenin and Books* and *Lenin and Library Organization*.

53. Raymond, p. 46.

54. McNeal, p. 124.

55. Ibid., pp. 189-90; Rader, p. 102n.

56. McNeal, p. 124.

57. Rubakin, 'Lenin-Ul'ianov—The Man and the Revolutionary," from *Die Internationali Rundschau* 3, 1918: 97-105, in *Lenin, Krupskaia, and Libraries*, ed. by Simsova, pp. 53-54. The Latin saying Rubakin employed can be translated as "The ultimate consideration—power!"

58. See: Volkogonov, *Lenin*, pp. 27, 82-83, 233-46; Pipes, *Russia under the Bolshevik Regime*, pp. 265-66, 270; Harold Shukman, *Lenin and the Russian Revolution* (New York: G. P. Putnam's Sons, 1967), pp. 48-49; Robert Payne, *The Life and Death of Lenin* (New York: Simon and Schuster, 1964), pp. 480-84, 516-18; Louis Fischer, *The Life of Lenin* (New York: Harper & Row, 1964), pp. 350-53; and Bertram D. Wolfe, *An Ideology in Power: Reflections on the Russian Revolution*, intro. by Leonard Schapiro (New York: Stein and Day, in conjunction with the Hoover Institution, Stanford University, 1969), pp. 166-80. Rubakin's accurate portrait was only confirmed by the much lengthier one of Stefan T. Possony over four decades later. Possony's psychological analysis stresses Lenin's impulse for destruction. (See Possony's *Lenin: The Compulsive Revolutionary* [Chicago: Henry Regnery, 1964], particularly pp. 376-99.) One highly relevant chapter in Dovring's 1996 evaluation of Lenin is entitled "Pathological Personality" (*Leninism*, pp. 119-28). Most of this succinct book is revealing. (See, for example, pp. 141-43.) Materials made accessible in the 1990's from previously closed Russian archives confirmed the most negative analyses and interpretations of Lenin's behavior that had heretofore been made. (See Richard Pipes, ed., *The Unknown Lenin: From the Secret Archive* [New Haven, CT, and London: Yale University Press, 1996.])

59. As quoted in Volkogonov, *Lenin*, pp. 82, 236. Such statements were numerous. Shortly before the coup in November, he publicly asserted that his forthcoming seizure of power would be successful and that the country's 150,000,000 people could easily be governed by the 240,000 in his Bolshevik Party. (See "Can the Bolsheviks Retain State Power?" pamphlet, 1917, reprinted in *Lenin: Selected Works*, vol. 2, p. 413.)

60. Letter to Molotov for Politburo Members (March 19, 1922), in *The Unknown Lenin*, ed. by Pipes, p. 154.

61. Rubakin, 'Lenin-Ul'ianov,' in *Lenin, Krupskaia, and Libraries*, ed. by Simsova, pp. 53-54.

62. Lenin's concept of morality is so foreign to most of those from Western countries that it would be useful to read his precise words:

> In what sense do we reject ethics, reject morality? In the sense given to it by the bourgeoisie, who based ethics on God's commandments. On this point we, of course, say that we do not believe in God, and that we know perfectly well that the clergy, the

landowners and the bourgeoisie invoked the name of God so as to further their own interests as exploiters. Or, instead of basing ethics on the commandments of morality, on the commandments of God, they based it on idealist or semi-idealist phrases, which always amounted to something very similar to God's commandments.

We reject any morality based on extra-human and extra-class concepts. We say that this is deception, dupery, stultification of the workers and peasants in the interests of the landowners and capitalists.

We say that our morality is entirely subordinated to the interests of the proletariat's class struggle. Our morality stems from the interests of the class struggle of the proletariat.

(From "The Task of the Youth Leagues," speech, Oct. 2, 1920, printed in *Pravda*, Oct. 5-6, 1920, as translated in *Lenin: Selected Works*, vol. 3, pp. 476-77.)

63. Solzhenitsyn, *The Mortal Danger*, pp. 61-62.

64. Ibid., pp. 62-63. This is also dealt with in Robert Conquest's *The Harvest of Sorrow: Soviet Collectivization and the Terror-Famine* (New York: Oxford University Press, 1986).

65. Bertram D. Wolfe, *A Life in Two Centuries: An Autobiography* (New York: Stein and Day, 1981), p. 469.

66. Chandler, pp. 15, 17-18.

67. Lenin, "Two Speeds in the First All-Russian Conference on Adult Education," pamphlet (Moscow: 1919), in *Lenin, Krupskaia, and Libraries*, ed. by Simsova, p. 24.

68. "Party Organization and Party Literature," *Novaia Zhizn* 12 (Nov. 13, 1905) reprinted in *Lenin and Books*, p. 16.

69. See Lenin's decrees made as Chairman of the Council of People's Commissars, "Requisitioning Libraries, Book Depots and Books in General" and "Nationalisation of Stocks of Books," in *Lenin and Library Organization*, pp. 135-36, 144-45. Both were originally published in *Izvestia*.

70. Ibid., p. 145.

71. See, for example, his letter to Y. A. Litkens of May 17, 1921, in *Lenin and Library Organization*, p. 74.

72. Korsch, *The Permanent Purge*, pp. 7-8.

73. Lenin, "Draft Decision . . . , " Sept. 13, 1921, in *Lenin and Library Organization*, p. 87.

74. "Party Organization and Party Literature," *Novaia Zhizn* 12 (Nov. 13, 1905) in *Lenin and Books*, p. 15. The Social-Democratic Party referred to was not like those which later became prominent in several European countries. Rather, it was the Russian Marxist party which in 1903 had split into two

groups: the Mensheviks and the more militant Bolsheviks led by Lenin.
75. Ibid., p. 16.
76. Lenin, quoted in Tom Bethell's "But Can Juanito Really Read?" *National Review* 35 (Sept. 30, 1983): 1199.
77. See: Lenin, "What Can Be Done for Public Education," in *Rabochaia Pravda* 5 (July 18, 1913); and "The Tasks of the Public Library in Petrograd," written Nov. 1917, published in 1933 in *Lenin Miscellany* 21; reprinted in *Lenin and Library Organization*, pp. 29-30 and 38.
78. On the changes in her name over time, see Bertram D. Wolfe, *Three Who Made a Revolution: A Biographical History* (New York: Stein and Day, 1984; first ed.: Dial Press, 1948), p. 99n; and Rader, p. 78. After 1924, her primary appellation was *Krupskaya*.
79. Georgij Fonotov, "Nadezhda Krupskaya," *ALA World Encyclopedia of Library and Information Services*, 2nd ed. (Chicago: American Library Association, 1986), pp. 424-25; Szekeley, "Introduction," *Soviet Education* 25 (Dec. 1982): 5; McNeal, p. 206; and Raymond.
80. Wolfe, *Three Who Made a Revolution*, pp. 100-103; Rader, pp. 8, 10-11. It is interesting—and significant—that many of the books which she (like others) used for her radical activity in St. Petersburg were borrowed from the public library of the politically liberal Rubakin family. Nicholas Rubakin, who came to head the library, was later criticized vigorously by Lenin and the Communist librarians. (See Raymond, p. 13n12; and Stephen Karetzky, *Reading Research and Librarianship: A History and Analysis* [Westport, CT, and London: Greenwood Press, 1982], pp. 307-19.)
81. Krupskaya, *O bibliotechnom dele* (Moscow: n.p., 1957), p. 9, as translated in Raymond, p. 6. See also Krupskaya, "My Life," in *On Education: Selected Articles and Speeches*, by Krupskaya, pp. 5-20.
82. Szekeley, "Introduction," p. 5.
83. Serov, "Library Science," p. 177; Raymond, p. 12. See Fonotov's "Nadezhda Krupskaya" for an overview of the scope and magnitude of her involvement.
84. Raymond, pp. 8-9, 196-97. Similarly, Soviet librarians in later years reinforced their claims of social importance by identifying themselves with the work of both Krupskaya and Lenin.
85. The admiring researcher, Rader, has lauded Krupskaya for her alleged "simplicity, kindness, and self-effacing manner." (Rader, p. 42. See also p. 26.) Bertram Wolfe, who knew her, called her "modest." (Wolfe, *A Life in Two Centuries*, p. 412.) Volkogonov describes her as "exceptionally intelligent and hard-working" as well as "obliging, even-tempered and balanced." (*Lenin: A New Biography*, p. 33.) He believes she was totally dominated by Lenin and his ideas.
86. McNeal, p. 296.

87.　Ibid., p. 202.
88.　Raymond, p. 11.
89.　Aleksandr I. Solzhenitsyn, *The Gulag Archipelago, 1918-56: An Experiment in Literary Investigation*, Parts III-IV (Vol. 2), trans. by Thomas P. Whitney (New York: Harper and Row, 1975), p. 333. Solzhenitsyn also attacks her in *Cancer Ward* (London: Bodley Head, 1962), p. 280. An account of her relationship with Stalin is given by Lazar Moiseevich Kaganovich, Stalin's right-hand man, in Stuart Kahan, *The Wolf of the Kremlin* (New York: Morrow, 1987), pp. 142-45.
90.　In keeping with the rest of her adulatory study of Krupskaya, Rader defends Krupskaya's behavior. (See Rader, pp. 159-62.)
91.　Slon, *Open Access to Soviet Book Collections*, p. 32. See also p. 36 concerning her great influence over library legislation during Stalin's reign.
92.　See Raymond, p. 191.
93.　Ibid., pp. 174-75, 168. Raymond notes the influence of Tolstoy, and Rader describes this influence in some detail. (See Rader, pp. 27-42.) Wolfe calls Krupskaya "Lenin's loyal wife and unquestioning follower." (Wolfe, *Three Who Made a Revolution*, p. 612) He believes it was Lenin who perverted her philosophically, politically, religiously, and emotionally. (See his "Krupskaya Purges the People's Libraries," p. 147, and compare the person he condemns in that article with the younger woman in *Three Who Made a Revolution*, pp. 100-103.)
94.　Raymond, pp. 200-201, 174-75, 39, 169; McNeal.
Jane Barnes Casey, the author of a novel about Krupskaya's personal life, says that she got the idea for the book while reading Krupskaya's memoirs: "It was inconceivable to me that anyone could be as literal and serious, as dully civic minded as she seemed to be in her reminiscences." ("Author's Note," *I, Krupskaya: My Life with Lenin—A Novel* [Boston: Houghton Mifflin, 1974], p. v.) Casey may well be wrong. Krupskaya resolutely denied herself many pleasures, e.g., alcohol and the theater. (Rader, p. 23; and Wolfe, *Three Who Made a Revolution*, p. 101.)
Krupskaya's faith in the absolute and all-embracing truth of Communist doctrine has been characteristic of both the founders and the adherents of the movement from its very beginnings. Thus, in 1844 Marx wrote with assurance, "Communism is the riddle of history solved, and it knows itself to be this solution." (Noted in *Karl Marx Dictionary*, ed. by Morris Stockhammer [New York: Philosophical Library, 1965], p. 43.) On the philosophical, psychological, and political dynamics and consequences of this faith in the inevitability of the revolutionary cause, see Arthur P. Mendel, "The Formation and Appeal of 'Scientific Socialism,' " in *Essential Works of Marxism*, ed. by Mendel (New York: Bantam, 1965), pp. 1-10. Highly relevant are Hannah Arendt's *The Origins of Totalitarianism*, new ed. (New York: Harcourt Brace, 1975), pp. 468-

74; and Thomas Molnar, *Utopia: The Perennial Heresy* (Lanham, MD: University Press of America [with the Intercollegiate Studies Institute], 1990), pp. 225-40. Insights can also be found in Eric Hoffer's breezy *True Believer: Thoughts on the Nature of Mass Movements*, intro. by Sidney Hook (New York: Time, 1963).

95. Raymond, pp. 180-81.

96. Krupskaya, "We Shall Fulfill Lenin's Instructions on Library Work," speech, Dec. 1936, in *Lenin, Krupskaia, and Libraries*, ed. by Simsova, p. 48.

97. Krupskaya, *O Bibliotechnom Dele* (Moscow: n.p., 1957), p. 95, as quoted in Raymond, p. 150.

98. Krupskaya, *Pedagogicheskie Sochinenia* (Moscow: 1857-1963), vol. 8, p. 406, as quoted in Raymond, p. 172. See also Rader, pp. 99-100.

99. Rader, p. 101; Raymond, p. 100.

100. Krupskaya, "Lenin's Instructions," in *Lenin, Krupskaia, and Libraries*, ed. by Simsova, pp. 48-49.

101. Raymond, p. 63.

102. Krupskaya made this statement to library school students. Noted by K. Abramov, and cited in Raymond, p. 156. See also p. 155 and p. 166n61.

103. Raymond, p. 178.

104. Krupskaya, "Lenin's Instructions," in *Lenin, Krupskaia, and Libraries*, ed. by Simsova, p. 51.

105. Z. Ambartsumian. See Raymond, pp. 182; and 192n45.

106. Slon, *Open Access to Soviet Book Collections*, pp. 142-43.

107. Krupskaya, quoted in Ravkin, "The Development," p. 20.

108. Raymond, p. 185.

109. Krupskaya, *Pedagogicheskie Sochinenia*, vol. 3, p. 631, as quoted in Raymond, p. 189.

110. Raymond, p. 189.

111. Ibid., pp. 186-87; 190; McNeal, p. 210.

112. Raymond, pp. 154, 185. However, see her remarks concerning children's freedom to choose their own reading in "All-Round Development of Children," [1937] in *On Education*, by Krupskaya, pp. 127-131.

113. Krupskaya, "Our Children Need Books that Would Bring Them Up as Genuine Internationalists," in *On Education*, by Krupskaya, p. 124.

114. See Fonotov, p. 424, for an overview.

115. Krupskaya, *Pedagogicheskie Sochinenia*, vol. 7, p. 349, as quoted in Raymond, p. 173.

116. Raymond, p. 188; Rader, pp. 98, 99n.

117. McNeal, pp. 294-95.

118. Rader, pp. 75, 177; Raymond, p. 1.

2

ACCURATE CRITIQUES OF THE SOVIET UNION, 1917-1939

From the very beginning of the Bolshevik seizure of power, there were accurate analyses of the ideology and actions of the new regime that were freely available throughout America, Britain, and the other democracies. Some of those who understood the significance of the so-called October Revolution wrote newspaper stories, magazine articles, and books. Some gave speeches. As with almost all political affairs, there were conflicting accounts of the events in Russia after the coup.[1] However, educated individuals were trained to evaluate sources and statements, and thus there was no justifiable reason for them to either grossly misconstrue events there or, as many did, declare that the developments were *impossible* to fathom. Of all the major political phenomena of the twentieth century, no other had as many highly schooled individuals claiming—year after year—that it was a grand mystery and that judgment of this alleged "Great Experiment" should be put off to some unspecified time in the future (when its longed-for benefits would supposedly materialize).

What follows clearly shows that the facts were apprehended quite early by those willing to see them. As the years passed, additional damning evidence accumulated: the material below is merely a small, representative sample of the many insightful, objective works written about the Communist regime. They provide a standard against which the inaccurate accounts discussed later in this book can be evaluated. It is particularly significant that many negative accounts of the new state did not come from reactionary emigrés, as its supporters (like John Dewey) usually maintained, but rather from liberals, socialists, and radicals, as well as conservatives.

Winston Churchill's Insights

Winston Churchill, then a member of the Liberal Party, understood the nature of the new Communist regime from its very birth—as well as the wisdom of crushing it. Unfortunately, this is much less widely known today than his similar comprehension of National Socialism in the 1930's and the proper method of dealing with it. Within *weeks* after the Bolshevik coup, he began making declarations to political and military figures, as well as the general public, about the utter barbarity of this new form of government, its dependence on brute force for its existence, its expansionist desires, and its international, conspiratorial nature. He himself did all that he could to snuff it out.[2] In early 1919, he declared in a speech:

> Of all the tyrannies in history the Bolshevik tyranny is the worst, the most destructive, the most degrading. . . . The political, economic, social, and moral life of the people of Russia has been utterly smashed. Famine and terror are the order of the day. . . . Resist by every means at your disposal the advances of Bolshevist tyranny in every country in the world.[3]

It is important to point out that Churchill understood the Soviet Union without having any knowledge of the Russian language. Similarly, his failed attempt as a youth to learn German proved no impediment to his understanding the Nazis.

E. H. Wilcox, Journalist

E. H. Wilcox, an authority on European political and military affairs and the Petrograd correspondent for the British *Daily Telegraph*, had his detailed, factual descriptions and analyses of the Russian revolution published in the United States by Charles Scribner's in 1919[4] after they had been serialized in England. Annoyed with those who misunderstood the Communists' behavior and put forth exotic theories to explain it, he declared that

> those whose business it is to instruct and guide the public should have known better. Seventy years had passed since the publication of the

Communist Manifesto by Marx and Engels, and the whole Bolshevik policy was summed up in the culminating passage of that document: "The proletarians have nothing to lose but their chains: they have a world to win. Proletarians of all lands, unite!" The Internationale was not a secret society, and its theories and objects were accessible to all. The purpose of the Zimmerwald and Kiental conferences was perfectly well known. Lenin had for years before the War preached in the Press the doctrines which he promulgated on his return to Russia, and he has done nothing grossly inconsistent with his previous thirty years' political work.[5]

He proceeded to declare that Lenin was a fanatic, and that "No man is so dangerous as the fanatic of a false idea, and the only way to disarm him is to treat him as what he is."[6] Of Lenin and his fellow Communists, Wilcox declared that "It would not be difficult to convict them, under common law, of every kind of murder, atrocity, robbery, fraud and forgery. In duplicity and mendacity they have probably surpassed all political parties in history."[7] A strong critic of the Czar's regime, Wilcox nevertheless maintained that the new form of government was far worse:

To the skeptics—those who do not believe in the promises of Bolshevism—it can only appear as one of the greatest scourges that has ever afflicted humanity. To everything that was bad in the Tsardom, it has paid the tribute of imitation; and the wrongs of the new tyranny have been infinitely worse than those of the old. No Tsar of modern times ruled so autocratically as Lenin, and none was more ruthless. The tsars restricted freedom of speech—Lenin has absolutely abolished it. The Tsars suppressed this or that newspaper—Lenin allows none which opposes his views. The Tsars put people to death for offences which existed only in Russia—Lenin has massacred thousands against whom no charge at all was brought.[8]

Isaac Don Levine Describes Totalitarianism

Born in Russia in 1892, Isaac Don Levine immigrated to the United States in 1911. He returned to his birthplace as a newspaper correspondent to cover events in the revolutionary country. Levine saw the evils of the new Soviet system and its leaders, and he made them manifest in his 1924 book, *The Man Lenin*, published in New York by Thomas Seltzer.[9]

In this volume, he described how the Soviet power structure was roughly pyramidal in shape, with dicta flowing downward. Its architect, Lenin, was amoral, had contempt for the mass of humanity, and scorned democracy and liberty.[10] Essentially, wrote Levine, "Bolshevism is a step backward to the primitive civilization of brutal force."[11] Nothing good could ever come of it.[12] It was also clear to this newsman that Marxism was a flawed prism through which the world could not be viewed accurately.[13]

Levine, like Churchill, understood what most at that time did not. He pointed to Lenin—and his student, Mussolini—to emphasize that in the twentieth century, democracy could be undermined by a ruthless and skilled minority waving the flag of an ideology. While the isms might differ, the psychology and soul of such tyrannies were the same.[14] Levine, a consistent supporter of democracy, was an early critic of Mussolini as well as Lenin. He not only tried to explain the essence of *Il Duce* to the general American public, but also to his friends and colleagues like Lincoln Steffens and Ernest Hemingway, both early admirers of the Italian dictator.[15]

A Perceptive Youth: William Adams Brown, Jr.

Along with many other Americans, William Adams Brown, Jr. went to Russia in September 1917 to work in the humanitarian aid program of the YMCA. This recent graduate of Yale University soon joined the American Committee on Public Information to disseminate pro-American and pro-Allied news and analysis. He returned to the United States in March 1919 when the work of the Committee ceased.

In his book, *The Groping Giant: Revolutionary Russia as Seen by an American Democrat*,[16] published by Yale University Press in 1920, he gave a discerning description and analysis of the situation in the new USSR. He was strongly opposed to the dictatorial Bolshevik regime:

> The first feeling of almost everyone leaving revolutionary Russia after a protracted stay in that unhappy country is an exhilarating sense of liberation and release. It is as if one breathed the outside air once more after passing through the gates of a prison to be free of the

restraint and the tension from which no one in Russia can escape.[17]

Ethel Snowden inside the "Iron Curtain"

Ethel Snowden, the prominent English suffragette and labor leader, was one of those sent to the USSR by the Labour Party and the Trades Union Congress in early 1920 to discern the truth about this new country. It was believed by the organized workers that the criticisms expressed in the English newspapers could not be assumed valid.[18] Despite great efforts by the Soviets to hide the truth from this delegation,[19] Snowden's major conclusion, after piercing what she termed the 'iron curtain'[20] at the country's borders, was that

> I am not hostile to the Russian Revolution which the tyrannous regime of the Czars made necessary and inevitable; but I am utterly opposed to the *coup d'état* of the Bolsheviki, as I should be to the seizing of power by any small minority of the people; for out of this action has sprung a large part of the misery the unhappy people of Russia endure.[21]

Snowden met with Lenin and was struck by his "fanaticism" and "his firm belief in the necessity of violence for the establishment throughout the world of his ideals."[22] She was surprised by his inaccurate belief that a revolution was imminent in Britain[23] and thought that he was proof that world affairs should not be entrusted to academics: ". . . Lenin is above all things the keen-brained dogmatic professor in politics."[24] Snowden went on to report that Lenin's "army of spies and police agents, largely the same men as served the Czar's régime, arrest for the most trivial offences and on the slightest suspicion."[25] As a result,

> I know that everybody I met in Russia outside the Communist party [*sic*] goes in terror of his liberty or his life. The pervading fear worked terribly on the subconscious selves of some of us, and we lived hourly in a spirit of hot hate of the cruelties and tyrannies which met us at every turn.[26] . . .
> The people are afraid of the police and spies, the spies are afraid of one another. All dwell in an atmosphere of suspicion, and the Red Terror is a terrible reality.[27]

Emma Goldman's Paradise Lost

One of the most widely read of the early criticisms of the Communist regime was *My Disillusionment in Russia* by the well-known anarchist, Emma Goldman. The full text of her account was published in both England and the United States by 1925. Goldman, who had been deported to the USSR from America in 1920 because of her political activities, documented the evolution of her attitude from exultation upon arriving in "the promised land"[28] to hatred when she left it one year later. The Soviet Union, she declared to the world, was devoid of freedom and humanity, and well along the path of ruthless brutality.[29] Goldman also wrote one of the first critiques of the political pilgrims who traveled to the USSR and blithely failed to perceive the realities there.[30]

Stan Harding, Imprisoned Journalist

While the Soviet state was extremely cordial to foreign journalists who toed the line, it was ruthless with those it considered uncooperative or guilty of spying. It often refused admission to those it believed might be critical. Stan Harding (aka Mrs. Stan Harding), a British reporter hired to be the New York *World*'s correspondent in the USSR, was arrested soon after her arrival in 1920. She was sentenced to death three days later without a trial. Finally released after five months in prison—much of it spent in solitary confinement—she wrote a revealing account of the Communists' rule through terror.

Harding admitted that before her incarceration her political views had been "pretty far to the Left."[31] (This was a major reason she had received this job, she said, because *The World*'s two previous choices had been refused entry by Soviet authorities.) Distrusting the published accounts of atrocities in the USSR, she had thought she would love the country. She admitted learning through her experiences and the people she met that the country was far more barbarous than it had been under the Czars: the entire "population may be divided into three categories—those who have been, are, or will be in prison."[32]

Harding had been "exposed" as a spy for the United States by an American journalist who had spent ten months in a Soviet jail facing charges of espionage. She correctly believed that making this accusation against Harding would gain her own release. Tellingly, the greatest anger expressed by Harding and her supporters in England—Bertrand Russell, the Institute of Journalists, and the National Union of Journalists—was not directed at the Communist state that had incarcerated her but rather at the American government!

The ACLU's Letters from Russian Prisons

In 1924, the International Committee for Political Prisoners, established by the American Civil Liberties Union, began an investigation of the Soviet incarceration of those whose only crime was the peaceful expression of views contrary to that of the Communist govenment. The Committee was headed by Roger N. Baldwin of the ACLU and included Jane Addams, Clarence Darrow, W.E.B. Dubois, Elizabeth Gurley Flynn, Felix Frankfurter, and Eugene V. Debs. The study, edited by the anarchist Alexander Berkman, was published as *Letters from Russian Prisons*.[33] It included numerous photographs of prison letters and the sympathetic reactions of well-known cultural figures, such as Harold Laski, Albert Einstein, Bertrand Russell, and Rebecca West.[34]

In his introduction, Baldwin declared:

> The essential fact stands out clear and unchallenged,—that the Soviet Government exiles and imprisons political opponents for their political activities and expressions in speech and print. Socialists, Syndicatists and Anarchists are the principal targets for attacks, but Zionists and Tolstoians have also suffered.[35]

Baldwin maintained that such persecution was unnecessary since the Soviet government appeared to be more secure than any other in Europe. He also claimed that while there had been many accusations in the past of political imprisonment in the USSR, they had always come from opponents of Bolshevism. He made it quite clear that most on his Committee were sympathetic to the revolutionary cause.[36] In his influential book published three years later, *Liberty under the Soviets*,[37] Baldwin showed that his devotion to the Communist cause overrode the evidence presented in this earlier work. This will be discussed later.

Will Durant, World Famous Author

Will Durant reported on his first-hand view of the Soviet Union in 1933 with *The Lesson of Russia*.[38] Earlier, he had spent years teaching in anarchist, socialist, and labor schools in New York City, earned a Ph.D. in philosophy at Columbia University, and become widely known and respected through his book, *The Story of Philosophy*. It had sold over one million copies, making it the best-selling non-fiction work of 1927.[39] Durant confessed that he had gone to the USSR "loving her not wisely but too well."[40] His views, he believed, had been those of perhaps "a hundred thousand intellectuals and liberals"[41] believing that he would see a country engaged in a heroic struggle against injustice and ignorance. And while he did see an impressive amount of industrialization, growth in literacy, and increased rights for women vis-à-vis men, he saw far more which appalled him:

> . . . never had I known such despotism, such herding and hounding of men, such industrial serfdom and conscription of labour; never had I seen a people so unhappy, so suspicious of one another, so obviously living in endless terror of universal secret police; never had I observed so ruthless an exploitation of the country by the town, or so complete a militarization of the schools, or so thorough a deception of the people by a government-owned radio and Press, or so rigid a censorship of every drama and every book, or so brutal an application of exile or death as deterrents to criticism and dissent.[42]

Durant was also shocked by the fact that so many in Europe and America, plagued by economic depression and deluded by propaganda, looked upon the Soviet Union as a model for their own societies. He declared himself willing to put up with their expected attacks: "I know how unpopular such a position must be with critics and students whose natural liberalism and sympathetic interest in social experiments will be offended by this apparent betrayal of the liberal cause."[43] However, he asked his anticipated opponents to remember that fidelity to freedom is central to liberalism, and that freedom is both the lifeblood of Western Civilization and the most precious inheritance of modern man.

Emigré Accounts

Reports on the Communist regime appeared in the West that were written by emigrant Russians who had lived and suffered under it. Unfortunately, these accounts were usually dismissed by American and European intellectuals and academics as the work of aristocratic, monarchist reactionaries. Ignored was the reality that in Russia many of these eyewitnesses had actually been progressive political figures, scholars, active socialists of humble means, and so forth. Discounted was the fact that many of them still had reliable sources of information inside the USSR that were unavailable to others. The term *emigré* was frequently used by anti-anti-Communists as a code word to indicate a mendacious, malevolent, and deluded conspirator.

The former foreign minister in the Kerensky government, Paul Miliukov, was a leader of the left-of-center refugees and a widely respected, and productive, historian. In one of his many books, he described Communist intrigues throughout the world including contemporary America. Published in 1920 by Allen & Unwin of London, it bore the descriptive title, *Bolshevism: An International Danger: Its Doctrine and Its Practice through War and Revolution.*[44]

Another prominent emigré author was Sergey Melgounov. The son of a well-known historian, he was educated in this discipline at the University of Moscow, wrote several scholarly books, and founded a publishing house which served academics as well as literate workers and peasants. A leader of a democratic, socialist party, he was arrested by the Communists and deported late in 1922 after serving a year in prison in solitary confinement. He spent the rest of his life in Paris. In 1925, the first of his books on the Revolution was translated into English and published by J. M. Dent in London as *The Red Terror in Russia.*[45] The book contained two hundred and seventy-one pages detailing brutalities by the Communists. Also included were fifteen photographs, many of them quite gruesome: a row of executed ecclesiastics, the skin ripped from prisoners' bodies in Bolshevik torture chambers, and so forth.

Conclusion

Accurate reports and analyses of the treachery, ruthlessness, and despotic nature of the Soviet Communists were made public by world-famous statesmen, labor leaders, socialists, journalists, and writers. A handful of these accounts have been described here, but there were many others, such as John Spargo's widely read books published on the heels of the revolution.[46] (André Gide's later critique of 1936 was different from others, because, in part, it openly criticized the harsh measures taken against those who were not heterosexual.[47]) However, as we shall see, such newspaper stories, speeches, and books seem to have had little impact on those leaders of the American library profession who took an interest in the Soviet Union. Like many educators and intellectuals, they elected to view this revolutionary country in highly positive terms.

NOTES

1. Accurate descriptions of many of the various perspectives and those who held and disseminated them can be found in a memoir by one who knew many of the individuals involved firsthand: Isaac Don Levine, *Eyewitness to History: Memoirs and Reflections of a Foreign Correspondent for Half a Century* (New York: Hawthorn Books, 1973).

2. See Sir Martin Gilbert, *Winston S. Churchill*, vol. 4: *The Stricken World: 1916-1922* (Boston: Houghton Mifflin, 1975), pp. 219-442 for a full account of his thoughts and actions regarding the Bolsheviks after their coup.

3. Winston S. Churchill, "An Aggressive and Predatory Form," speech, London, April 11, 1919, reprinted in *Blood, Toil, Tears and Sweat: The Speeches of Winston Churchill*, ed. and intro. by David Cannadine (Boston: Houghton Mifflin, 1989), pp. 86, 91, 92.

4. E. H. Wilcox, *Russia's Ruin* (New York: Charles Scribner's Sons, 1919).

5. Ibid., p. 246. At the Zimmerwald and Kiental conferences in Switzerland in 1915 and 1916, Lenin and his Bolshevik allies reiterated their belief that worldwide, violent revolution should be the goal of all true socialists.

6. Ibid., p. 249.

7. Ibid.

8. Ibid., p. 290.

9. Seltzer issued works by distinguished authors such as Marcel Proust and Ford Maddox Ford.

10. See Isaac Don Levine, *The Man Lenin* (New York: Thomas Seltzer, 1924), pp. 34-39, 57, and 128-30. It appears that he obtained much of his information about Lenin's personality from Raphael Abramovich, the leader of the socialist Jewish Bund. Abramovich actively opposed the Bolshevik coup and later went into exile, warning the socialists of Europe of the Communist movement.

11. Ibid., p. 196.

12. Ibid., p. 207.

13. Ibid., pp. 201, 206.

14. Ibid., p. 202. Hitler acknowledged that he was a student of Mussolini.

15. See Levine, *Eyewitness to History*, pp. 165-69. Levine collaborated with Hemingway on translating Russian poetry. He worked alongside both Steffens and Hemingway as a correspondent.

16. William Adams Brown, Jr., *The Groping Giant: Revolutionary Russia as Seen by an American Democrat* (New Haven: Yale University Press, 1920; London: Humphrey Milford and Oxford University Press.).

17. Ibid., p. 186. While he declared his love of American democracy, he did state that his exposure to Communism made him more sensitive to the needs of the working class in America. (See Brown, Jr., *Groping Giant*, pp. 186-99.) Brown eventually received a doctorate in economics from Columbia University and became an academic and government adviser specializing in international monetary policy. He was the son of William Adams Brown, a clergyman and professor at the Union Theological Seminary, who was not only a prolific writer but a social activist.

18. Mrs. Philip [Ethel] Snowden, *Through Bolshevik Russia* (London and New York: Cassell, 1920), p. 7. Her husband was one of the leading Labour parliamentarians for many years.

19. See Emma Goldman's description in *My Disillusionment in Russia*, [includes *My Further Disillusionment in Russia*], intro. by Rebecca West, biographical sketch by Frank Harris, (as reprinted from an apparent 1925 edition: Gloucester, MA: Peter Smith, 1983), pp. 58-59. The first American edition in 1923 accidentally omitted the material soon afterwards published as *My Further Disillusionment in Russia* (Garden City, NY: Doubleday, Page, 1924).

20. Snowden, *Through Bolshevik Russia*, p. 32.

21. Snowden, p. 11.

22. Ibid., p. 117.

23. Ibid., pp. 117-18.

24. Ibid., p. 119. In 1920 Bertrand Russell wrote about his meeting with
Lenin: "He resembles a professor in his desire to have the [materialist] theory
understood and in his fury with those who misunderstand or disagree, as also
in his love of expounding." (Bertrand Russell, *The Theory and Practice of
Bolshevism*, 2nd ed. [New York: Simon and Schuster, 1964; originally
published: London: Allen & Unwin, 1920], p. 32.)
25. Snowden, pp. 154-55.
26. Ibid., p. 156.
27. Ibid., p. 161.
28. Goldman, *My Disillusionment in Russia*, p. 241.
29. Ibid., pp. 58-59, 212-20.
30. For a description of her early attempts (and those of others) to
disseminate information about the bloodthirsty, oppressive Communist regime,
see Emma Goldman, *Living My Life* (New York: Knopf, 1931), pp. 962-84.
31. Stan Harding, *The Underworld of State*, intro. by Bertrand Russell
(London: George Allen & Unwin, 1925), p. 40.
32. Ibid., p. 150.
33. Alexander Berkman, ed. *Letters from Russian Prisons* (New York:
Albert and Charles Boni, 1925).
34. H. G. Wells and Romain Rolland expressed their opposition to the
project, and Upton Sinclair declared that the treatment of political prisoners in
the USSR was apparently as bad as that in the United States. (See ibid., pp. 5-
16.) The correspondence with these influential figures was done by Isaac Don
Levine. (See Levine, *Eyewitness to History*, p. 169, where he appears to claim
editorship of the book. The footnote on page five of *Letters from Russian
Prisons* acknowledges only his aid in collecting the damning primary sources
and his correspondence with the noted intellectuals.)
35. Roger N. Baldwin, "Introduction," in *Letters from Russian Prisons*,
ed. by Berkman, p. xiv. Israel Zangwill's response to the horrific evidence
ended with this remark: "Incidentally I note that a number of the prisoners are
Jews, which serves at least to show how untrue is the identification of the race
with Bolshevism." (Israel Zangwill, letter to Isaac Don Levine, Jan. 31, 1925,
as reprinted in *Letters from Russian Prisons*, ed. by Berkman, p. 16.)
36. Baldwin, "Introduction," in *Letters from Russian Prisons*, pp. xiii-xix.
37. Roger N. Baldwin, *Liberty under the Soviets* (New York: Vanguard
Press, 1927).
38. Will Durant, *The Lesson of Russia* (London: G. P. Putnam's Sons,
1933).
39. Will Durant, *The Story of Philosophy* (New York: Simon and Schuster, 1926). Several of its chapters had been published earlier for 5¢ each by E.
Haldeman-Julius in its Little Blue Books series. Some of these had sold
150,000 copies. (See Frank Luther Mott, *Golden Multitudes: The Story of Best*

Sellers in the Unites States [New York: MacMillan, 1947].) Over the years, the book's sales in the United States and overseas have amounted to several million copies.

40. Durant, *The Lesson of Russia*, p. ix.

41. Ibid.

42. Ibid., pp. ix-x.

43. Ibid., p. x.

44. The work was reprinted: Westport, CT: Hyperion Press, 1981.

45. Sergey Petrovich Melgounov, *The Red Terror in Russia* (London and Toronto: J. M. Dent, 1925; trans. from Russian version: Berlin: Vataga, 1924).

46. For example, see John Spargo, *The Psychology of Bolshevism* (New York and London: Harper & Bros., 1919); and *"The Greatest Failure in All History": A Critical Examination of the Actual Workings in Russia* (New York and London: Harper & Bros., 1919).

47. See André Gide, *Return from the USSR*, trans. by Dorothy Bussy (New York: Alfred A. Knopf, 1937), pp. 38-39; originally published as *Retour de l'URSS* (Paris: Librairie Gallimard, 1936).

3

EARLY WESTERN ASSISTANCE TO
SOVIET LIBRARIANSHIP

From the beginning of Communist rule, American librarians nurtured Soviet librarianship and the USSR as a whole. Their assistance took many forms, such as giving useful professional information to the new country, furnishing the fledgling state with technical advisers, and publicly portraying the brutal government to the West in positive terms. These efforts were sometimes interrelated.

Professional Expertise and Technical Information

The development of libraries in the USSR was directly aided by American professionals and those who had found sanctuary in the United States. One of the first was Henrietta Derman, a revolutionary born in 1882 in Russian Latvia who fled Europe for the United States in 1914. Three years later, she graduated from the Simmons Library School in Boston and eventually went to work in the Slavic and Yudin collections of the Library of Congress. Her political notions were able to find expression in the library press when she was working in Washington as a Classifier and Cataloger in the Russian Collection. In 1921 she wrote an obituary of the Russian bibliographer, S. A. Vengerov, for the widely read, influential *Library Journal*. In it she blamed the famine which had brought about his lethal typhus on World War I, the Russian Civil War, and the West's economic policies towards the USSR. Apparently, the Bolsheviks bore no responsibility for the disastrous social and economic conditions in their country.

Moreover, she asserted that the Czar's government—unlike the Soviet regime—had been unwilling to support Vengerov's important work during wartime. In addition, she sneered that during the Czarist era the country had had to import most of its paper, type, and printer's ink.

Later that year, Derman returned to her newly independent homeland, but found the democratically elected, anti-Communist government of Latvia unpalatable. The sentiment was mutual and she soon found herself in the USSR. Being one of the few people in the country who possessed both a knowledge of librarianship and a proven zeal for Communism, it was not long before she began getting appointed to high-ranking posts. Among her prestigious positions in the following years were: director of the library of the country's premier ideological institute (The Communist Academy), head of the Lenin Library, and director of the USSR's foremost library school. She assisted the American consultant, Harriet G. Eddy, write a pro-Soviet article that appeared in *Library Journal* in 1932. An upbeat American visitor reported upon returning to the United States in 1936 that Derman had reorganized her half-million book library of the Communist Academy according to American principles.

Derman was purged before the decade ended.[1]

In 1925 and 1926, the Soviet Commissariat for Education studied the administration of libraries in other countries. The ministry concluded that the well-developed county library system in California could serve as a partial model for their own polity.[2] Harriet G. Eddy, an Assistant Professor of Agricultural Extension in Los Angeles and the former organizer of the county library system for the State Library, was invited to visit the Soviet Union as a consultant. She was granted a five-month sabbatical in 1927 and traveled throughout the USSR inspecting the organization and the services of fifty libraries. At the invitation of the Chief Committee for Political Education (headed by Krupskaya), which directed all public libraries, movies, and museums, Eddy returned to the Communist state in December 1930 for another five-month period.[3]

At the suggestion of Eddy, the Commissariat of Education had sent Krupskaya's long-time Bolshevik comrade, Anna Kravchenko, to the United States for several months in 1928 to observe county-wide library planning, particularly in California. She reorganized part of the Soviet system when she returned home. Kravchenko was made director of the Institute of Library Science at the Lenin Library; its responsibility was the development of theory and research on the role and practice of librarianship in the USSR. With Henrietta Derman, she assisted Eddy in writing her enthusiastic *Library Journal* article about Soviet librarianship.[4]

In the Soviet Union's first two decades, most of its technical advances were made by purchasing or stealing them from Western countries. (US military intelligence understood the significance of this, but the State Department did not.)[5] Even the modernization of Soviet library equipment was accomplished by aping American products.[6] It is not surprising, therefore, that the acquisition of scientific and technical information from non-Communist countries was an essential function of Soviet science libraries. In 1918 the State Scientific-Technical and Economic Library was founded and in 1920 the Foreign Literature Reading Room was created. Seven years later, these were combined into the State Scientific Library—the pinnacle of the Soviet science library network. A new building was erected to house it and in 1932 it was put under the direct control of the Commissariat for Heavy Industry.[7] The following description of the local branches of the State Scientific Library indicates the importance of foreign information in Soviet development:

> The tasks of these branches were to help the factory-level special libraries by informing them of the newest material relevant to their particular factory's work, carry out large-scale bibliographical surveys for the factory libraries, *provide them with all available material on imported machinery, gather and translate relevant foreign technical literature, coordinate subscriptions to foreign technical periodicals, and provide them with over-all methodological guidance.*[8] (Italics mine)

In 1931 the Soviet Union was one of the two largest foreign purchasers of Library of Congress catalog cards.[9] This indicates both the scope of their acquisition of Western printed material and the willingness of American librarians to facilitate its use. Soviet libraries were expert at obtaining foreign publications through exchange. Thus, by the late 1930's the Lenin Library had trade agreements with libraries in fifty foreign countries which brought in close to 187,000 volumes from 1936 to 1941. This library also purchased almost 3,000 titles from abroad each year. The Society for Cultural Relations with

Foreign Countries ("VOKS") exchanged books with fifty-nine countries and thereby acquired as many as 32,000 volumes annually.[10]

Contemporary Coverage of Developments in The Soviet Union

A significant form of assistance to the Soviet Union was the overwhelmingly positive coverage of developments there in the library profession's periodicals. In a few instances, these were reprinted in the mainstream media. Librarians who visited the USSR and wrote their impressions for their colleagues produced pieces that praised the Communist library system. Unfavorable facts that were widely reported and condemned in general Western newspapers and magazines, like the strict censorship in Soviet libraries,[11] were glossed over in the reports by librarians, many of whom were leaders of the profession. This favorable coverage frequently included calls to assist the USSR. One can reasonably hypothesize that this slanted treatment affected librarians' selection of books and periodicals about the Soviet Union for their collections.

R. R. Bowker and Library Journal

In the first decade after the Bolshevik putsch, the premier American periodical in the profession, *Library Journal*, provided its readers with numerous editorials, news items, and articles on library developments in the USSR. The overwhelming thrust of these was that much progress was being made in the Soviet Union, that a great social and political experiment was proceeding nicely, and that American librarians should assist their beleaguered, idealistic colleagues there with food as well as with materials for their professional education and advancement. The Soviet librarians, one was told, were soldiering on despite all adversity. There was no indication that the Communist regime was in any way responsible for the disastrous economic and social conditions that beset these librarians. Similarly, there was no mention of the fact that a totalitarian regime was destroying a progressive library profession and perverting the institutions in which it had been based.

The person most responsible for this misleading campaign was the journal's editor and publisher, Richard R. Bowker. A politically active liberal in the 1890's, by the early twentieth century he could best be described as a member of the Progressive movement.[12] Although a professed opponent of socialism, he supported the socialist candidate for mayor of New York when it became clear that the reform aspirant could not beat the Tammany choice. Known for his liberal political views and opposition to discrimination against Jews and African-Americans,[13] in his writings criticizing socialism he did not hesitate to malign Catholicism, which he found analogous to it:

> Socialism is the offer of a social Catholic and infallible church to give peace of mind to the perplexed Protestant willing to surrender his liberty of action to a state Pope called the People. It transfers tyranny from monarchy to democracy.[14]

This anti-Catholicism presaged that of later so-called progressives in librarianship, particularly among those in the Intellectual Freedom movement in the 1950's and 1960's.

Bowker had been involved with Russian affairs as vice-president of the Society of Friends of Russian Freedom, an organization begun before the turn of the century to support change in that country.[15] (He had also long been interested in international library cooperation.) Not surprisingly, he was delighted by the overthrow of the Czar's government. At the American Library Association conference following the February Revolution, he reported on his 1914 visit to Russia with his wife, and urged—successfully—that a message of support be sent to the new government.[16] In this speech and in an essay he edited for *Library Journal* the following year, Bowker expressed his admiration for Russia's cultural achievements and his belief in the Russian people's "democratic nature, their love of freedom, and their great yearning for education."[17] At the conference he had noted that "There are still murky clouds on the horizon, but we may hope that the horrors of the French commune, which were the prelude to the French Republic, may be spared to Russia."[18] Nevertheless, when the Bolsheviks—who openly admired and emulated the Commune—soon seized power,[19] Bowker was unable or unwilling to see them for what they were.

Bowker used his editorial pages to support the Communist regime. Thus, in November 1923 he declared, "It must be admitted that Soviet

Russia has shown remarkable developments in the literary and library field. . . ."[20] Four months later he proclaimed:

> Every bit of added information regarding the library situation in Russia . . . makes more clear the achievements of the Soviet in intellectual relations. It was not supposed that the intellectuals, who are a recognized class throughout the Russian federation, have much part in the government, but the results seem to show that Soviet officialdom is either constituted in a great part of this class or has its full co-operation in what it is working out. Everyone who knows Russia at all recognizes its enormous potentiality in all sorts of directions, likely to be in the future when its form of government is finally developed, a strong rival in wholesome competition with our own great country.   Despite all criticism, what has been accomplished in some respects under the Soviet government must command admiration.[21]

Later in 1924 he asserted:

> Whatever the criticism on [*sic*] Soviet Russia, it must be conceded that in this experiment of government, many advances have been made. Nationalization has accomplished, at least for the present time, some remarkable results in the library field. . . .[22]

Unfortunately, Bowker never described the criticisms of the Soviet Union he alluded to in these two pieces. They were followed in late 1925 by an editorial in which he declared that most Americans would be surprised to learn of the advances made in Soviet adult education and its great efforts to reduce illiteracy.[23]

Library Journal editorials were invariably optimistic about the future of Soviet libraries. Bowker held that when the economic problems of the USSR (and Germany) would begin to be solved, great library development would follow. He wrote that "Czar despotism," which had stymied public library development, was no longer there to hold back progress. Bowker did mention that the Soviet Union was *temporarily* "netted in a new despotism," but he did not elaborate on this; he seemed to consider it unimportant.[24]

Library Journal editorials contributed by others generally agreed with the views of the editor/publisher. One discussed an article on censorship that had appeared in the Soviet periodical *Red Librarian* entitled "Concerning the Purification of Libraries."[25]   The American contributor wrote that ". . . one is pleasantly surprised to find very sensible remarks on the subject" and quoted approvingly the words of a high-ranking Communist official:

> "The sense of removing certain books . . . does not consist in concealing from the readers those thoughts with which we do not agree. It must be remembered that by means of removal and prohibition of books, we do not struggle against other peoples' thought, but merely against the attempts to falsify thought thru an appeal to passions and to wicked emotions, or to deceive the readers by a mendacious representation of the facts."[26]

The acceptance of such transparent claims served to help excuse one of the most thoroughgoing censorship campaigns of the century, a program that was attacked in other circles in America and Europe. As reported earlier, many people in the West opposed the 1923 censorship orders promulgated by Krupskaya.

Not all the opinions about the Soviet Union expressed in *Library Journal* were positive. A brief item contributed by the author of the aforementioned editorial contrasted sharply with the usual fare.   It charged that "An article on the past and future of library work in the first number of the *Red Librarian*, published in Moscow, contains some figures telling a sad story of the theoretical beginnings and the pitiful ending of Bolshevist 'reforms.'"[27]   While not going into great detail, it was correctly asserted that any claimed increases in library holdings since the October Revolution had resulted from the confiscation of privately-owned book collections.[28]

The pages of *Library Journal* contained upbeat news items and stories on alleged advances in Soviet library administration, library services, library education, and library literature.[29] Perhaps the most significant ones were those written by L. B. Khavkina (L. Haffkin Hamburger).   Editorials about her also reinforced important myths. All items by, or about, Khavkina either stated or implied that she was the leader of Soviet librarianship, which was making great strides and developing along American lines.   None of this was true, although it doubtlessly reflected the fervent wishes of both Khavkina and Bowker. In a 1923 article, she characterized the Czarist regime as "reactionary," and in a contribution two years later she called Lenin a "great man."

Given her political views, it is probable that the latter statement, at least, was made to insure her own survival, professional and otherwise.[30] Unfortunately, American librarianship depended too much on her as a source of information. Her very strong ties to American librarians and librarianship, which had been created, in part, by visiting the United States, were unequalled by any of her colleagues and predated the November 1917 coup. To many in America, she continued to personify her country's profession even after the Bolsheviks seized power, although (as described earlier) she and the other "objectivists" were marginalized and then suppressed by the Communists, who opposed their dedication to intellectual freedom and democratic ideals. Thus, regular *Library Journal* readers might not have been shocked when the highly respected Arthur E. Bostwick, head of the St. Louis Public Library, erroneously declared in its pages in 1924 that "The indications are that the Soviet Government is now turning its attention intensively upon the popularization of libraries as a regular policy and that it is attempting to carry this out on decidedly American lines."[31] Khavkina's articles also appeared elsewhere, like the American Library Association's *Bulletin*.[32] This particular contribution in the ALA's premier magazine was then reprinted in other library related periodicals in the United States and Britain, and uncritically excerpted in the widely read cultural magazine *Literary Digest*.[33]

However, damning evidence of the Communists' policy of seizing complete control of libraries and all other agencies of communication managed to slip into the pages of Bowker's periodical.[34] In March 1919, *Library Journal* reprinted some edicts that had been issued a year earlier by the People's Commissioner of Education of the Western Provinces and then published in the left-wing American journal, *The Nation*. The nationalization of all libraries and all but small personal book collections in the area under the Commissioner's control was part of this official's self-proclaimed move "to regulate the library business and its reorganization on new principles." There was not even a hint of criticism of these measures by R. R. Bowker. In fact, *Library Journal*'s scholium downplayed their importance with the incorrect statement that "The private libraries mentioned in [Order] No. 2 apparently include only private *circulating* libraries." (Italics mine) The significance of the "reorganization on new principles" was further mitigated by the bland, misleading title *Library Journal* gave to this item: "The Soviets Take Stock of Russia's Schools, Libraries and Movie Houses." The word *Control* would have been more accurate than *Stock*.

A speech made to Midwest librarians before the Communist putsch was printed in *Library Journal* in March 1918 as "The Library and the Book in Russia's Revolutionary Movement."[35] Its author had been what he called a "socialist-revolutionist" and underground librarian in Czarist Russia until his flight to America. While he briefly mentioned the Bolsheviks in his work, his recommended reading for understanding his subject was comprised largely of Russian moderates or anti-Bolsheviks, such as Paul Vinogradoff, Peter Kropotkin, and Paul Milyukoff. Bowker appended a note to this recommending the works of Lenin and Trotsky.

There were numerous pleas for donations of library literature and food to nourish the minds and bodies of Soviet librarians. Bowker wrote: "Under the difficult circumstances of transition and experiment, those in Russia who are leading in library progress should have hearty cooperation in America. . . ."[36] These calls elicited responses from individuals, institutions, and library-related companies.[37] It was apparent that the humanitarian contribution of food—part of a popular American effort which saved millions of lives in the USSR—provided the necessary sustenance for some librarians. It should have been just as obvious that the professional assistance could have no beneficent results in a state where the Communists held power. Fortunately, the impulse to provide such technical assistance was not nearly as widespread among most Americans, who, in the main, wisely limited their largesse to the provision of foodstuffs.

In 1924 an unidentified "representative" from *Library Journal* interviewed Harry M. Lydenberg, head of the Reference Department—and later Director—of the New York Public Library, and Dr. Avrahm Yarmolinsky, Chief of the Library's Slavonic Division, after they returned from their three-month book-buying trip to the Soviet Union.[38] (Yarmolinsky stayed there a few additional months to carry out his literary and social investigations.) What was afterwards printed in the pages of the periodical was a combination interview/article/editorial highly favorable to the new Communist system. It is difficult to know precisely whose views this journalistic hodgepodge represents. The main reaction of these travellers was reportedly sympathy because of the warfare, civil strife, and famine suffered there for the past several years. (This piece mentioned "The appeals for food sent to American librarians during the famine years,"[39] and declared that "None of us has had to live thru conditions . . . such as those that faced our fellow *workers* in eastern Europe."[40]   (Italics mine. The use of the term *workers* rather than *human beings* or *librarians* was, in this context and era, a political statement.) Their second major impression was said to be the great desire of Soviet librarians to learn about library developments in the United States,[41] particularly "anything about the library as an instrument of social betterment."[42]

Ignoring the widespread destruction of libraries and their collections, the confiscation of private collections open to the public, and the massive purging of library shelves, the unidentified voice of *Library Journal* erroneously proclaimed that "The world of learning will be glad to know that the public libraries throughout Russia have not suffered during these years, suffered physically, that is to say. Their collections are intact."[43] One is given to believe that the visitors were impressed by the developments under the Communists, such as the great interest in libraries by those in power, the support for bibliographic activities, the large number of books circulated, the attention paid to the "untutored," the publication of what *Library Journal* considered to be "the only book in any language on library statistics,"[44] and the administrative reorganization that had been effected. That perfidious act—the nationalization of private and public book collections—was commended: "Russian public libraries will, of course, benefit largely as the gatherings from the nets of 'nationalization' are digested."[45]

One finds the statement, "In some ways they are ahead of us,"[46] and various public services were mentioned. It was also noted that "It was not easy to explain [to the Communist librarians] that American libraries used any [classification] system they chose."[47] Unfortunately, there was no elaboration of this important point.

The interview/article/editorial ended with a reference to Krup-skaya, identified as "Mme. Lenin, the widow of the great Russian,"[48] as well as this exhortation followed by the names and addresses of nine Soviet libraries:

What the Russian librarians need greatly today is information about current movements and developments on our side of the water. Every one of us can help if we will send our reports and any other printed matter to some if not all of the following libraries:[49]

The actual thoughts of Lydenberg and Yarmolinsky about the Soviet Union were far more negative than one would gather from reading this work in *Library Journal*. Lydenberg's personal letters reveal that he considered the censorship in the Soviet Union as stringent as it had been under the Czars. He was affronted by the fact that the acquisitions for the New York Public Library were subjected to scrutiny and censorship before shipment home. He also thought that the government's so-called "nationalization" of books and other property should more accurately be called "confiscation." However, he did admire the librarians for working in difficult physical conditions as well as for their techniques of instruction and propaganda. Robert Karlowich has pointed out that Lydenberg was apparently not fully aware of the political and social goals of the Bolsheviks nor of the faithful attention given the two librarians by watchful Communist apparatchiks.[50] If he had been, his views of the USSR would certainly have been even more negative. For some reason, this very productive author[51] and internationally esteemed librarian never wrote an article or gave a speech presenting his impressions of Soviet libraries and society. Lydenberg did not oppose such evaluations by foreign librarians—at least when they were done by Europeans visiting the United States. He welcomed studies of this type for the perspective they could offer.[52] In the following decades, Lydenberg continued his involvement in international librarianship. In 1943, he became the first director of the American Library Association's International Relations Office.

Yarmolinsky had been born in the Ukraine in 1890 but came to the United States in 1913 after studying in Switzerland. In 1921 he earned his doctorate from Columbia University and wrote or translated a dozen books and scores of articles—primarily on Russian literature—before, during, and after his long tenure as head of the New York Public Library's Slavonic Division from 1918 until 1955.[53] His writings reflect a love of Russian belles lettres as well as a belief that the Czarist regime was wicked.[54] He maintained that this government's censorship was oppressive, and, after it was overthrown in March 1917, he thought that an era of freedom had begun.[55] However, less than half a year after the Bolsheviks seized power he wrote an extremely negative analysis of their regime for the reputable periodical, *Current History*. In it, he condemned the "disastrous" effect of the government's seizure of the land and means of production, its analogous takeover of the press, and the destruction of the traditional financial and legal systems. The north of Russia, he wrote, had never been nearer starvation than under the Bolsheviks.[56] Two months later, this was followed by another highly critical article.[57] He was still on the attack in 1925: "The Soviet Union is run by a small, opinionated, energetic group of people who conduct a dictatorship in the name of the workers and peasants."[58] Their treatment of the individual is cavalier, their goal is regimentation, and their posture includes an "implacable hostility to all forms of religion."[59]

Despite his professional dedication and his prolific, sharply pointed pen, in the ensuing decades Yarmolinsky wrote only a single article greater than one page in length that focused on Soviet librarianship: a pedestrian piece in 1944 on wartime conditions in the USSR's libraries.[60]

Harriet G. Eddy

At the request of *Library Journal*,[61] Harriet G. Eddy wrote an article, in collaboration with Henrietta Derman and Anna Kravchenko, titled "Beginnings of United Library Service in the USSR." It was published in its January 15, 1932 issue. Eddy's service as a library consultant in the Soviet Union now totalled over ten months and her article was an enthusiastic celebration of that country.

She trumpeted that the developments in librarianship were part of "the new life spreading out like a net all over the USSR,"[62] and that ". . . all educational activity in Russia is a part of life, not a preparation."[63] She was impressed by the way that "those characteristics—organization, cooperation, teamwork—are developing in all phases of Russia's new life."[64] Librarianship was being shaped by "a tremendous building program going on all over this country 'covering one-sixth of the earth's surface.' "[65]

With much emotion, Eddy contrasted this with a bleak portrait of conditions in Russia before the Revolution. She claimed that it had been a country in which many nationalities had been subjugated and where the government had been a strong opponent of education. Her implication here was that the Communists oppressed no nationalities and supported true education. Eddy alleged that, in Czarist times, libraries had played a negligible social role because of widespread illiteracy, high fees for borrowing books, and an emphasis in library collections on religious books and political histories.[66]

Ignoring the facts and alluding to the preternatural, Eddy enthused: "From 1917 to 1922 library service in Russia grew with magic swiftness. . . ."[67] Disregarding the intentions and efforts of the Communists, she averred that the developments in library services in this period were due to the public's "thirst for knowledge."[68] The result, she claimed, was a plethora of libraries with little central organization: "Is there any other country in the world where distribution of books has become so thoroughly decentralized?"[69] Eddy thus ignored the negative impact of the Communist takeover of all libraries and the heavy-handed regulations emanating from Moscow. The books included in libraries were certainly receiving much greater scrutiny by central authorities than ever before.

Our Californian easily alternated between utopian, anarchist fantasy and support for some of the most ruthless aspects of centralized Communism. Her article concentrated on the developments in a new "unified" library system which was serving as a model for the rest of the Soviet Union. (What was to come of the alleged decentralization she so loved?) She stated in a blasé manner that in rural areas the unified libraries were "a most natural outgrowth of the land collectivizations."[70] Eddy also noted that "The numbers of peasants' holdings that have been collectivized in each rayon [county] average 20,000 families."[71] She displayed neither an awareness of, nor a concern for, the bloody ruthlessness with which the expropriation of these people's lands took place.[72] Eddy blithely went on to compare the library funding in Russian "counties" with that in Fresno County, California.

Margaret P. Coleman

Another earnest—yet confused and superficial—report of a visit to the Soviet Union was made by Margaret P. Coleman of the Omaha Public Library in the widely read periodical issued by the H. W.

Wilson Company, *Wilson Bulletin for Librarians*.[73] There were many
elements in her 1935 contribution that were common in contemporary
analyses of the USSR. For example, there was the failure to deal with
the lack of freedom in the Soviet Union as evidenced by the inability
to clearly distinguish between propaganda and true education, between
tyranny and liberty. Coleman wrote:

> It is not necessary for me to remind librarians that Russia is doing
> a tremendous job in adult education; propagandistic education, yes,
> but none the less tremendous for that reason.[74]
>
> . . . .
>
> I can hear protests at this point to the effect that these ideas embody
> true education, that they are propaganda. Granting that, I cannot
> help thinking of one of our [American] university lecturers this
> summer who said: "Look at our advertising; look at our movies;
> look at the teaching in our public schools and tell me if we haven't
> been training our children to be good little capitalists just as surely
> as Russia trains hers to be good little communists."[75]

She confessed that she did not know if education for democracy
was fundamentally different from education for Communism or
fascism.[76] She also seems to have been more tolerant of incessant
Communist political propaganda than of advertising by America's
capitalist entrepreneurs:

> They use radio, not occasionally and with the grudging consent of
> the makers of toothpaste and face powder, but constantly and all the
> time with the enthusiastic support of the powers that be. There must
> be times when the Moscow worker, pursued by the blare of
> loudspeakers from his factory to his apartment and even to his Park
> of Culture, prays for silence. But at least his education is going
> on.[77]

The only reason she proffered for opposing the Communists'
suppression of ideas—which she incorrectly compared to that of the
much more lenient Czarist government—was superficial, amoral, and
inhumane. Such suppression was bad, she said, solely because it might
provoke a counterrevolution.[78]

Coleman asserted that American libraries were—*in theory*—bound
up with democracy, but she was not certain to what extent they had

actually supported it.[79]   She asked:

> . . . are our libraries, our government, really as democratic as they
> pretend to be? Are we not, in organization, an oligarchy; in book
> selection policy unconscious propagandists for the status quo, for
> capitalism? If in doubt, see the Roving Eye in the September 1935
> *Wilson Bulletin* discussing "So-called Radical Literatures."[80]

This librarian reported that she had taken a summer class for adult
educators at a teachers' college in which she was told by the faculty
that the American education system was undemocratic and "highly
aristocratic."[81]   Apparently, she lacked both the intelligence and the
knowledge required to critique such extreme charges.

Coleman was unexcited about Western librarianship. In contrast,
she was impressed by, and envious of, the dynamism she perceived in
the Soviet Union and the feeling of centrality the Soviet librarians had.
She envied their certainty concerning their role in society: "The thing
to get excited about in these libraries, it seems to me, is not that
Moscow is reclassifying its collections according to Marx but that the
Soviet librarians are actively conscious of their place in the social
scene, of their importance to the new education."[82]   She believed that
many librarians in the United States, unlike those in the USSR, were
indifferent to their societal role. Coleman wanted American librarians
in the vanguard of social change rather than at what she perceived to
be the tail end. She expressed some doubt as to whether these
allegedly apathetic librarians in the United States even favored progress.[83]

The librarian from Omaha was skeptical about the robustness of
Western civilization and had no faith that it would survive much longer.
She comforted herself with the idea that if it did indeed fall, libraries
would nevertheless survive and fulfill the requirements of any
subsequent society.[84]

Like many of the other vocal professionals in that minority who
were dissatisfied with the federal government's laissez-faire policy
towards most libraries, she envied the Soviet government's involvement
in libraries and other agencies of communication. In a demonstration
of her support for increasing the federal government's involvement in
library affairs, she made an inaccurate claim about the new Communist
system in an attempt to reassure her readers: "Here is a system

sponsored and supported by the State (Federal aid, if you will) yet without loss of individual adaption to locales."[85]

Coleman's article was not the only one in the *Wilson Bulletin for Librarians* in this decade to provide a rosy picture of the Red state and a bleak portrait of the US. This will be treated later in the discussion of its editor, Stanley J. Kunitz, and his self-proclaimed "Roving Eye."

Douglas Waples

Following a brief visit to the Soviet Union,[86] Douglas Waples, the professor at the University of Chicago Graduate Library School who led the movement to base librarianship upon scientifically derived data,[87] made a speech to the readers' advisers at the 1932 American Library Association annual conference that was later printed in the Association's primary periodical, *ALA Bulletin*. Waples' first sentence set the tone for his presentation: "Moscow is the happy hunting-grounds for readers' advisers."[88] He was impressed with what he perceived to be the youthful energy, scope, social importance, and thoroughness of Soviet librarianship, and he held that when compared with librarians in the West, the Communists fared very well.

He seems to have been captivated by the "extraordinary zeal"[89] behind library-related enterprises, and he intoned: "The Soviets take libraries seriously."[90] Waples offered this naive, idyllic description:

> In Moscow, at least, nearly everyone reads for information and nearly every reader seeks and receives advice from some quarter. *The official regulations which virtually oblige everyone to read are not distasteful.* They find a ready response in the somewhat adolescent hunger for ideas that urges young Russia to its books.[91] (Italics mine)

Here, as elsewhere in his talk, Waples was strangely accepting of the coercion in the Soviet system. In contrast, this social scientist's work in America was intertwined with his commitment to fostering freedom.[92] Having received his Ph.D. in education and having been a professor of education before entering librarianship, it is also surprising that this usually careful thinker and precise writer used the term *educational* to characterize the Soviet propaganda system. For example, he declared that "There are no private publishers in the USSR, hence the publishing industry is largely devoted to the *educational* needs of the state."[93] (Italics mine) Similarly, when Waples described the system of selecting which books were to be published, he acknowledged the possibilities for censorship here but insisted that this was merely a part of "guiding readers." In fact, the title of his ingenuous presentation was "Guiding Readers in Soviet Russia."

To some extent, he equated many workers in the Soviet book world with American librarianship's readers' advisers.[94] This was fallacious since these American librarians were preoccupied with the question of how to guide readers *without* coercing them: they stressed the significance and the dignity of the individual and his or her desires.[95] Waples then uncritically reported about the USSR: ". . . every citizen belongs to at least one institution. . . . In each institution is a library. In the library is a librarian who advises not merely on the selection but also on the interpretation of the books read."[96] This is a country of learners and teachers, with "an army of volunteer workers to assist."[97]

Waples attributed much of the thorough attention the Soviets paid to readers to *concern*, to their great humanity. He said of the librarians who assisted users of the special libraries in Moscow: "As compared with the intelligent and frigid desk attendants in the British Museum for example, they are far less intelligent but infinitely more helpful to the novice. In short, they have a heart."[98]

He believed that the *essential* difference between Soviet and American librarianship was that the latter was geared to the person who 'just wants to read' or who does not know a particular author's name or book title. Soviet library work was more significant. He claimed that the thorough methods of the Communist librarians were necessitated by their goals as well as by their interest in the *ideas* contained in books rather than their mere titles and authors. The strong implication was that Western librarians were preoccupied with superficialities. Waples was pleased that Soviet cultural programs were "ruthlessly pedagogical" and were carried out with "an extraordinary zeal" which, he said, John Dewey had correctly characterized as "religious."[99] (This demonstrated that both Dewey and Waples misunderstood some of the most significant aspects of religion.) Surprisingly, Waples failed to even mention the primary goal of the

librarians he observed in that foreign country: the creation of a
Communist society.

This University of Chicago professor indicated that there was a
lack of interest in books among American adults, and he believed that

> There is probably a much larger quantity of simple reading matter
> about adult problems in Russia than in any other country. It is the
> lack of such material and the necessity of using reading matter
> intended for children instead that accounts for our own lack of
> success in teaching adults to find satisfaction in useful books.[100]
> . . . .
> The only thing harder to enter than a Moscow bookstore is a
> Moscow trolley car. Moscow buys books. There are more than a
> hundred bookstores in the city.[101]

Waples made a snide comparison of literacy education in America
and the Soviet Union in which—incredibly—it was the United States
that was caricatured as the nation that mingled literacy education with
jingoism:

> This Soviet system is greatly superior to the American practice
> in at least one particular, namely, the after treatment of adults who
> have managed to pass our so-called literacy tests. In Russia the
> business of teaching adults to read does not stop with the ability to
> decipher such sentences as: "THE UNITED STATES OF
> AMERICA IS THE GREATEST COUNTRY IN THE WORLD
> WHERE EVERYBODY IS RICH AND HAPPY."[102]

The Soviet government agents who distributed the books to libraries received high marks from Waples because he naively believed
that their motivation could only have been one of service since they
received no immediate, direct, financial profit. Such a Soviet official
"has nothing to gain by recommending books on any other basis than
their value to the community. Would that all book agents [in the West]
had motives as pure!"[103]   Similarly, ". . . the interesting fact about the
Moscow bookstores is that the salesmen (being indifferent to sales,
since their incomes are not affected) give advice to readers of a purely
disinterested sort."[104]

Why did Waples not perceive—or even conceive—that ideological
impulses, a need to meet a quota, fear of those in power, a desire for

a job promotion, a wish to rid one's self of unwanted stock, sloth, or other such factors could also have influenced the Soviet book distributors? One also wonders why he believed that those who successfully fulfilled the goals of the Communist Party did not receive better housing, food, or other perquisites than those who did not.

Waples was impressed by the magnitude of the Soviet book world. He presented a table that indicated the quantity of book titles published in the USSR in one year, broken down by subject area in order "to give some notion of the number and variety of Soviet publications."[105] The amount of magazines and newspapers, he wrote, was similarly "impressive."[106]

In the 1930's, Waples was the scholarly leader of the American movement in librarianship to study the sociological aspects of reading with scientific rigor. It is surprising, therefore, to see his totally uncritical, unscientific appraisal of reading interests and behavior in the USSR. He presented an annotated list of the nine 'Most Read Novels' with the remark: "Note that each of them has to do with the background, aims, and work of the revolution."[107] (For example, one was about the Young Communists' League, while another concerned the New Economic Policy.) He declared that they were "chosen at random from those mostly sold at the time of my visit, early in December, 1931."[108] However, in a footnote he indicated that these were the most widely read novels "As chosen by [the] head of [the] largest fiction bookstore in Moscow."[109] It is not totally clear whether Waples meant that the list, or all of the bookstore's stock, was chosen by the director, but it appears that at least the former was true. Why did this usually skeptical social scientist take the store manager's word for what was popular? Why did Waples have so much faith in this highly informal "study" when he ordinarily insisted on scientific sampling? Where was his frequent criticism of research in America and Western Europe that inferred reading *interests* from *actual* reading? The latter, he insisted, is primarily determined by what is, or is not, available.[110]

In his own country, Waples displayed an extraordinary concern for democracy and true education. He made great efforts to be a scrupulous scientific researcher. However, these traits were not in evidence when he painted his idyllic portrait of the Soviet Union. For some reason, he showed little interest in the pernicious goals of the Communist librarians and the noxious messages they were working so hard to propagate.

William E. Haygood

William Haygood, a doctoral student at the Graduate Library School of the University of Chicago, traveled to the Soviet Union and in 1936 wrote an article for *Library Journal* about what he saw.[111] While not uncritical of the Communist library system, he was awed by it and supported its program enthusiastically. Haygood chided the Soviets for disapproving of everything pre-Revolutionary.[112] He also reproved their propagandists for exaggerating the smoothness with which the Communist library system ran. However, his article began with one-sided, contemptuous attacks on librarianship under the Czars, and the remainder included a positive description of the new institutions being established.

Haygood began his rebuke by focusing on the great collections of "Old Russia": "These great institutions were ornaments to the Czarist regime, and access to their vast resources was an envied prerogative of the privileged classes."[113] He continued: "A photograph taken in the reading room of the Imperial Public [Library] about the time of the outbreak of the World War speaks more eloquently than a complete file of the Red Librarian."[114] In this photo, "tropical palms nod in buckets in the far corners; the room is half filled with well-dressed, well-nourished readers. . . . The atmosphere is expensive, exclusive, refined."[115] One wonders whether Haygood ever saw the photo of the "Leningrad Library" accompanying Margaret P. Coleman's December 1935 *Wilson Bulletin for Librarians* article.[116] This showed a huge palm tree in the middle of the reading room of this Communist institution.

Haygood went on to quote the complaint of a Russian at a 1915 American Library Association conference that librarians in his country lacked assistants. Haygood was not struck by the fact that this Russian had traveled overseas freely and was willing and unafraid to publicly point out the defects he saw in his nation's libraries. These were things that Haygood's contemporaries in the USSR could not do. Haygood's inaccurate treatment of this professional and of pre-Revolutionary Russia continued: ". . . the life of such a library functionary was hazardous as well as harried. Censorship was rigid."[117] Each public library, he claimed, was "regarded by the government as dangerous to the civil population, and was the continual object of hostile and suppressive measures."[118]   Haygood wrote that there had been more than five thousand public libraries in Czarist Russia—there had actually been three times that number—yet he made the patently lugubrious statement that at one point there had been "such stringent supervision that libraries were closed at the rate of *four* a year."[119]   (Italics mine) This meant, according to his figures, that only 1 out of every 1250 were closed down in an average year by a disapproving government. This was nothing compared to the wholesale confiscations and book "cleansings" conducted later by the totalitarian Communists.

Vitriolic in his attack on the unseen, long-gone Czarist society, Haygood gave his readers no taste whatsoever of the savagery of the Communist country he visited.   He was writing in the mid-1930's amidst mass purges, including those of librarians and their family members.   He did state that the books in Soviet libraries served "political" functions,[120] but he never gave his readers any idea of what the essence of these so-called "political" functions was: the formation of a Communist society by any means necessary.[121]   Haygood's readers were certainly not well served when he told them that ". . . the Soviet librarian is as much social worker as librarian. . . ."[122]

Haygood did not even heed his own mild warnings concerning the new Communist state.   He cautioned that the Soviet government defined a *book* as any publication of two or more pages: "This fact tends to bring some of the Gargantuan statistics quoted in this article down to the mundane and less frenetic plane that obtains in countries where progress is slower and less perfervid than in the USSR."[123]   All the same, he declared that the State Library of the USSR in Leningrad (the former Imperial Public Library) "contains a collection of between four and five million volumes and is the largest library in the world."[124]

Perhaps Haygood did not question these Communist claims because he believed that they doubtlessly *would* be true some day, as would all the aims of the new librarianship. He stated: "That this plan for the future library system will be fully and intelligently developed, or that some more successful variant will take its place, there can be small doubt."[125]   The library system was already "as massive and extraordinary as the land it serves."[126]

Haygood did provide an accurate description of the relationship between the thorough bibliographic work and the tight control over the production and distribution of books. However, he was naive when he enthusiastically described the centrally produced, annotated catalog cards: "As these annotations are the work of experts in every field, the library is liable to receive more help from the source than if he read the book himself."[127]   He said nothing of the propaganda purposes of the annotations, a use stressed by Krupskaya and the Communist librarians.

Haygood compared the motives for building the Soviet library system to the desire of some American librarians for more financial support and involvement by their federal government. He referred to ". . . the library system which it [the Communist government] fosters with a zeal and liberality a trifle terrifying *to even the most visionary American librarian. . . .*"[128]   (Italics mine) The words "liberality" and "visionary" generally have positive connotations: Haygood was well disposed to the system the Communists had set up as well as to the goals of these particular American librarians.

Much of Haygood's 1936 *Library Journal* article—the subjects covered, the wording, even a joke—is very similar to Waples' contribution in the *ALA Bulletin* four years earlier. It appears that Haygood depended heavily on this work by his teacher, or perhaps on a lengthier, unpublished version. It is also conceivable, albeit unlikely, that Haygood and Waples both drew heavily from some unnamed source. The footnoting in both men's articles is inadequate and provides no hints.

John Richmond Russell

Librarian John Richmond Russell ardently defended Soviet librarianship after a mere six-day tour of Moscow's libraries in 1935 organized by that city's Institute of Library Science.   In the major periodical issued by the American Association for Adult Education, he asserted that adult education was the primary concern of the librarians he met.[129] While admitting that "Adult education, like other education in the USSR, is marked by a single point of view and a unified purpose,"[130] he contended that most of what librarians there helped people learn—mathematics, ancient literature, and so forth—were not subjects amenable to propaganda.   Russell's enthusiasm even extended to their work on collective farms where, he told his readers, ". . . librarians took books into the fields, told stories during the lunch periods, and organized newspaper clubs."[131] Remarkably, he related these particular activities and their educational import as if he had personally witnessed them during his brief stay in Moscow. If he had been taken on a day-trip to a Potempkin collective farm, he did not report it.

Russell had had little professional experience in library public services at this time, having spent most of his early career in cataloguing and classification at the New York Public Library. He left in 1935 to become Chief of the Division of Cataloguing at the National Archives, a post he held until beginning his long-term tenure as Director of Libraries at the University of Rochester five years later. In 1942 he became a member of the Executive Board of the American Library Association; in 1945, President of the New York Library Association.[132]

Articles by Soviet Librarians

Several articles were written by Soviet librarians specifically for publication in the West during this period. Most of these described the alleged advances made in the field since the Communists came to power. Eager to receive assistance from the United States, Britain, and other countries, most of the Soviet librarians spoke openly of their eagerness to adopt Western techniques and said only positive things about Western librarianship. Unlike many works published abroad in the decades after World War II, these did not criticize any aspects of the democratic library ideology in America and England.

As reported earlier, the most prolific of these writers was L. B. Khavkina, who actually did admire the ideals, as well as the techniques, of Anglo-American librarianship. However, after 1927 her presence in Western journals as the writer of articles and long letters abruptly ceased, reflecting her professional decline in the USSR caused by her discredited bourgeois ideology. Librarians who were committed to Communism took her place as spokespeople, but they too would pass from the scene, victims of wave after wave of purges. This unusual phenomenon of disappearing librarians was never a subject of speculation or discussion in the Western library press.

In 1928 Eugenia Khmelnitsky, Chief Bibliographer of the Institute

of Labor Research in Kharkov, Ukraine, presented an extremely
enthusiastic overview of changes since the October Revolution at an
American library conference. It was later published in the primary
journal of the Special Library Association. After complimenting the
"expert librarians in the country which is famous for splendid methods
and technique [*sic*] of library organization,"[133] she gave her phantastic
view of Russian and Soviet library history:

> "In the field of library work in these ten years after the revolution
> more has been accomplished than perhaps in a hundred years
> before."

> "I cannot remember even one conference of libraries before the
> revolution."

> "*All* books taken away from the churches, monasteries, and
> institutions were put in the public libraries, where they became
> available for every one."[134] (Italics mine)

In addition to charging that few people in Czarist Russia had been
allowed to use the libraries, she implied that censorship was done away
with when the Communists came to power.

In keeping with the general aims of the USSR, Khmelnitsky ended
with a plea that Western librarians increase their communication with
those in the Soviet Union so that the latter could acquire more Western
professional expertise as well as reference books in all subject fields.
She ended on a grandiloquent note that would have appealed to
librarians of internationalist sentiment: "Like science itself, to which
the library opens the door, library and bibliographical work is and
should be international."[135]

Approximately one year later, an article by the Soviet librarian and
historian Dmitri N. Egorov appeared in the Scottish journal *Library
Review*. It purported to describe the progress in Soviet libraries since
1917. Egorov began with elegant horticultural metaphors. Thus, when
noting the innumerable books that "fell into the possession of the
state," he wrote of "the harvest of books that fell to the libraries of the
state."[136] He bragged that "Soviet book publishing is carried out
according to a definite plan: there is nothing casual in it. Only books

thought to be helpful and necessary are issued."[137] Other evidence of supposed progress spurred on by "enthusiasm and a consciousness of duty"[138] were duly described. Egorov went out of his way to note the emulation of Western library *techniques*:

". . . the most up-to-date Western European methods are being adopted and promoted with striking success."

"Many of the most active workers in the library have had training in libraries in the United States and the brilliant example of the American achievement is ever before them."

"Western European and American construction [of libraries] has been studied."[139]

An American library periodical issued by the Library Bureau in Chicago summarized the *Library Review* article by Egorov, whom it described as a "distinguished Russian author."[140] However, by the time this compliment appeared Egorov had already been arrested, and he soon afterwards met the Grim Reaper.[141]

Britain Views Soviet Librarianship

The primary British report on Soviet librarianship in the 1930's was part of a 659 page qualitative and quantitative evaluation of libraries in Britain, the United States, Canada, and seventeen European countries. Published in 1938, the project, like many others in Britain, was underwritten largely by the Rockefeller Foundation. It was overseen by Lionel R. McColvin, the leading public librarian in England and the long-term holder of a position of central importance: Honorary Secretary of the Library Association. In a statement that reflected a major declared goal of the Rockefeller Foundation and also expressed a core belief of the growing number of internationalist librarians, McColvin wrote that the purpose of the study went beyond that of merely ascertaining the status of libraries with an eye towards their improvement—it would increase "international understanding":

We believed, too, that more knowledge of library conditions in other

countries and personal contact with our foreign colleagues would
help to promote that better international understanding that all desire
so heartily—would even help us, in the course of our own work, to
further that understanding in a wider sphere than that of librarianship
itself.[142]

Thirty-six pages of this volume were devoted to the Soviet Union,
which was surveyed by H. M. Cashmore, City Librarian of Birming-
ham. In general, his report was quite positive. He declared that he
had never before been in a country where as much reading was done
and that nowhere were libraries as well supported as in the USSR.
Like other visitors, he declared that (1) there had been a tremendous
increase in library services since the Revolution, (2) librarians were not
well paid but were enthusiastic, and (3) the emphasis in librarianship
was on education. While he stressed that the use of all libraries was
free of charge, he reported that open access to library shelves was rare
and that only those with special authorization had access to anti-Soviet
materials—most of which, he said, were foreign in origin. He noted
more than once the detailed records kept on people's reading but failed
to discuss the political implications of this practice.[143] Cashmore also
presented his findings in a speech at a Library Association conference.
As printed in the Association's primary periodical,[144] it was even more
enthusiastic than his lengthier treatment.

Writing at the end of the 1930's, James Wellard, the English
librarian who had studied under Douglas Waples, was critical of
librarianship in both Germany and the Soviet Union. However, he was
far more negative about the former than the latter.[145] In this, he was
like many librarians in the United States, as will be shown below.

The Antipodal Position of H. A. Gregory

Were there no librarians from democratic countries who were
outraged by the censorship in the Soviet Union and who openly
declared so? Were there no speakers at conferences who understood
the essential propagandistic nature of the extensive library apparatus in
the USSR and the dominant role of Communist ideology in the
librarians' activities? Unfortunately, for public enunciations of this
kind we must go to the end of the earth.

H. A. Gregory was the Acting City Librarian of Prahran, located in greater Melbourne, Australia. After a trip to the Soviet Union shortly before the outbreak of World War II, he reported his observations at a conference of the Australian Institute of Librarians. It was a balanced presentation. He provided interesting qualitative and quantitative information and recognized that in the USSR—more so than Australia—the potential impact of the librarian was understood by government authorities.[146] However, he was emphatic in expressing his disgust at having his newspapers and magazines confiscated when he entered the country, even those that were purely literary. Similarly, he was not afraid to note the "lack of freedom of thought and speech"[147] there and to "deplore the political shackles which fetter and cramp the usefulness of the Soviet libraries."[148] The Bolshevik leaders, Gregory declared, were smart enough to understand the propaganda value of directed reading, and he went on to describe how this and "the rigid state censorship"[149] were embodied in library practices.

While acknowledging the courteous assistance given him by Soviet librarians,[150] he was able to see the dark side of their worldview:

> As an instance of the fanatical devotion of the Orthodox Communist to this single set of ideas [Communism], and of the amazing extent to which they have permeated the intellectual life of the country, I may quote the reply given to me at the Odessa State Scientific Library when inquiring as to the system of cataloguing adopted there. I was gravely informed that while the decimal system at present in use worked very efficiently from a technical point of view, the authorities were determined shortly to supplant it with another system based on the Marx-Lenin methodology simply as a proof of their political loyalty.[151]

Finally, Gregory was the only librarian who traveled to the USSR in this period who called it precisely what it was—"a totalitarian state."[152] Even in future decades, librarians would avoid this most apt of terms.

Who was Howard Aylwin Gregory? Is there any accounting for the unique perspicacity displayed in his speech and article on the USSR? Some attention to this man is warranted.

Gregory, born in 1900, had a lifelong interest in history, geography, and international relations. Adept at languages and a skilled writer, he earned a master's degree in Language and Literature from the University of Melbourne. He taught school until he earned enough money to spend the year 1929 in Western Europe, which included taking short courses at Cambridge University, the Sorbonne, and the University of Heidelberg. Upon his return to Australia, he became a librarian at the Prahran Municipal Library. He worked his way up to Deputy City Librarian and, in 1941, to City Librarian. Except for his years of army service in World War II, he remained in that position until 1952.

In 1938 Gregory took a year's leave to travel throughout Europe. On this trip, he became the first Australian librarian to visit the Soviet Union. As before, he paid his own way. Unlike many of the American visitors who had preceded him, he received no library funds, university stipends, or Rockefeller grants.

In the three years after his return, he wrote fifty articles for *The Age Literary Supplement* of Melbourne about the history and current affairs of Europe. In addition to his significant activities within the Australian library profession, he was a member of the Australian Institute of International Affairs. He maintained his interest in global developments until he passed away in 1975.[153]

H. A. Gregory understood the essential differences between the democracies and the tyrannical countries. He also recognized the dangers posed by the latter if the former did not act with sagacity and a willingness to use effective military force.[154] While certainly no guarantors of wisdom, in Gregory's case his strong background in world history and languages and his extensive, purposeful travels through Europe helped enable him to comprehend what he saw in the Soviet Union. His work also reflected his initiative, courage, good judgment, acute knowledge of right and wrong, and keen sense of duty.

Fascism and Communism: The Double Standard in American Librarianship

In the 1930's, librarians in the United States displayed a measure of concern about fascism in Europe—and even in America—but almost none about Communism on either continent. Moreover, American anti-Communists and overt patriots were criticized vehemently, while professed anti-fascists of any political persuasion were reflexively identified as being pro-American.

Overview of the Library Press

The library press expressed some disapproval of totalitarian librarianship in Europe—but only in Germany, not the Soviet Union. In the 1930's, there were no major articles in either *Library Journal* or the *Wilson Bulletin for Librarians* to offset those they published praising the USSR.

A 1934 piece by Arthur Berthold in the *Wilson Bulletin* did refer to Soviet censorship, but he stated that this was already well-known and that he would confine himself to a description of Nazi librarianship, contrasting it with the ideals of the American profession. Interestingly, he declared that one reason for exploring fascism was that some "writers," as he termed them, had been claiming that the United States was drifting in that direction.[155] In 1947, Berthold became one of the first American librarians to write a strong indictment of Communist librarianship.[156]

The same month in 1934 that Berthold's work appeared, *Library Journal* ran a description of censorship in German libraries written by Leon Carnovsky, who had just returned from a short visit there.[157] (It appears that the librarians he met displayed no enthusiasm for the new system.[158]) He contrasted the American approach to freedom of inquiry with that of the Nazis. Carnovsky made no similar studies of the Soviet Union.

Actions in the USSR that were praised by Americans were not applauded when they occurred in the other powerful totalitarian country. Thus, no one in the American library community lauded the National Socialists for increasing government support for, and coordination of, public libraries.[159]

Stanley J. Kunitz's Astigmatic "Roving Eye"

From 1928 through 1943, Stanley J. Kunitz was editor of the *Wilson Bulletin for Librarians*, renamed *Wilson Library Bulletin* in September 1939. He made this widely read professional journal second only to *Library Journal* in its willingness to deal with contemporary political and social issues. He regularly used his editorial column, "The Roving Eye," to decry any form of overt patriotism. Kunitz also utilized his platform to loudly criticize any unwillingness of public libraries to distribute pro-Communist or radical literature: to him, this constituted censorship. In contrast, he did not consistently and unambiguously champion the distribution of fascist materials.[160] There was no uproar from Kunitz, others in the library press, or the leaders of the profession when the University of Miami removed literature from its library that it considered pro-fascist or pro-Nazi.[161]

Kunitz criticized other efforts that might have inhibited Communist activities, like the institution of loyalty oaths. Increasingly used for state employees, teachers, and college professors in the 1930's, in general these merely had them affirm that they would obey the law and not abet any efforts to violently overthrow the government. Kunitz considered such a requirement oppressive. As with questions of censorship, he viewed loyalty oaths primarily as they related to Communism, ignoring the fact that federal, state, and local governments were concerned about activities inspired by Berlin as well as those directed from Moscow.[162]

Kunitz published several articles in the thirties praising Soviet libraries, none criticizing them. Margaret P. Coleman's pro-Communist, anti-American contribution[163] in 1935 has already been described. Another example of such wonder accounts by visitors to the USSR was written by Jessica M. Fredricks for the December 1937 issue.[164] It implied that all Soviet citizens had full and free access to reading materials from all over the world. This music librarian from the San Francisco Public Library trilled, "Russia would appear to be the Special Librarians paradise on earth. . . . Every institution of learning has a library and no association of librarians has to persuade uninterested executives to believe in the value of a library."[165] In case anyone missed the point of where library heaven was, directly following her propaganda piece was another one written by a Soviet librarian.[166]

One article selected by Kunitz for the *Wilson Bulletin* tried to graft Communist visions, aims, and means on to those of traditional American librarianship. Gretchen Garrison of the Bennington College Library expressed great concern about the alleged dangers of nationalism in her 1934 "Public Libraries and the World-Mind." She asserted that ". . . the new interdependent world demands a new kind of citizen—a world citizen."[167]   It was therefore incumbent upon America's public librarians that they be part of a *"planned* effort"[168] to create this new type of person.   (All italics in this section are Garrison's.) Adapting the specious socialist slogan "Production for use, not [financial] profits," she declared that "Production for *use* is nowhere better applied than in the book world."[169] The results of properly guided reading would be manifested in new attitudes and social behavior:

> This was forcibly brought to my attention a short time ago, during the course of a study group on Russia, when an older woman, who had been notably anti-Russian at the beginning of the reading and discussion, said emphatically, "Why I had no idea about these things. I have been reading the *wrong things* about Russia!"[170]

Garrison closed with additional radical cant.   She appealed to librarians to help avert "disaster" and to "promote economic security, productive leisure and true social democracy."   Proclaiming that "A new day, demanding new loyalties and social techniques has dawned," she said that the question was whether librarians would be "among those proving that it is not a false dawn."[171]

Stanley Kunitz gained fame as a poet soon after graduating from Harvard University in 1926. (His verse earned him a Pulitzer prize in the 1950's.) He was also widely known as an editor of literary reference books and a translator of Russian poetry. Long-lived, in 2000 he was appointed Poet Laureate of the United States by the Librarian of Congress.

However, when it came to Kunitz's editorial work at the *Wilson Bulletin for Librarians*, his self-proclaimed "Roving Eye" was actually quite fixed when it came to the USSR and anti-Communism. Moreover, the eye was astigmatic, had major blind spots, and could not perceive objects in depth. In terms of his role in librarianship, Kunitz is frequently considered one of the early leaders of the Intellectual Freedom movement. Indeed, he did maintain the double-standards and the anti-anti-Communism of many of its primary exponents.

Archibald MacLeish's Class Warfare

American librarianship has suffered from yet another Pulitzer Prize winning poet: Archibald MacLeish. In late 1939, this recently appointed Librarian of Congress began to endear himself to the profession. In an October speech entitled "Libraries in the Contemporary Crisis,"[172] which became an honored classic in the literature of the profession, he declared that the most critical problem facing the United States was a growing domestic fascism and that the only way to combat it was through education, particularly through the public library. He alleged that the primary standard-bearers of American fascism were the same as in Germany: those in the lower-middle class. Supposedly, this segment of the population lacked the knowledge, or any of the other positive qualities, of the working class—which MacLeish romanticized. Moreover, they were ignorant of the culture of the upper class (into which he, one should keep in mind, had been born):

> Deprived on the one hand of the realism, the hard-headedness, the piety, the traditional human wisdom, the salt sense, the kindness of those who labor the earth and the earth's metals with their bodies, they were equally deprived on the other of that different wisdom of those whose life is in the mind. . . . The reason why fascism is so brutal, so vulgar, so envious, so superstitious, so childish, so shrewd, is that these are the characteristics of a social class excluded from the moral and emotional and intellectual traditions of its society.[173]

Ironically, this biased, paranoid snob charged that America's overt patriots were prejudiced and that anti-Communists were distrustful of their fellow citizens. Entirely secure economically, socially, and professionally, he found it easy to complain about those who feared radical ideas.[174]

Interestingly, most librarians at the time would probably have been classified by sociologists as members of MacLeish's dreaded and despised lower-middle class. As for our poet, he had been raised on his family's estate and educated at private schools before attending Yale and Harvard. His appointment as Librarian of Congress by his friend, Franklin Roosevelt (who called him "Archie"), was opposed by most librarians. The American Library Association formally criticized the President's assertion that a professional librarian was not needed for the position, but rather "a gentleman and a scholar."[175] Within librarianship, only the leftists and Communists who comprised the recently formed Progressive Librarians' Council enthusiastically approved of his preferment.[176] MacLeish was a frequent participant in Popular Front activities right up to the time he was appointed.[177] It was noted in Princeton University Press' landmark scholarly work, *Socialism and American Life*, that "The penetration of leftist thought into the work of non-Marxian poets is perhaps best illustrated in the work of Archibald MacLeish during the middle thirties. . . ."[178]

In 1944, MacLeish began his short-term service as the US Assistant Secretary of State for Cultural Affairs. As described later, Macleish was to become instrumental in the formation of the United Nations and of Unesco. It is not surprising that he became an early critic of Senator Joseph McCarthy.

MacLeish won Pulitzer Prizes for Literature in 1932, 1953, and 1959. Unfortunately, his political and social views foreshadowed the elitist, internationalist, anti-anti-Communism that became predominant among librarianship's leaders after World War II.

NOTES

1. See: Henriette M. Derman, "Semen Afanasevich Vengerov, 1855-1920," *Library Journal* 46 (April 15, 1921): 349-50; Harriet G. Eddy, "Beginnings of United Library Service in the USSR," *Library Journal* 57 (Jan. 15, 1932): 61, 66-67; Raymond, pp. 151, 165n47. The optimistic visitor was William Haygood. (See William Converse Haygood, "Libraries in the Union of Socialist Soviet [*sic*] Republics," *Library Journal* 61 [June 1, 1936]: 437, 439.)

2. Haygood, pp. 436-37.

3. Eddy, p. 61; Raymond, p. 114.

4. Eddy, pp. 61, 67; Raymond, pp. 114, 63; Haygood, p. 437.

5. See Antony C. Sutton, *Western Technology and Soviet Economic Development*, 3 vols. (Stanford, CA: Hoover Institution on War, Revolution, and Peace, Stanford University, 1968-1973.) Sutton was a professor of economics at the California State University at Los Angeles. He became a research fellow at the Hoover Institution.

6. Haygood, p. 438.

7. "Russian Libraries," p. 727; Raymond, pp. 146-47.

8. Raymond, p. 147.

9. Noted in *Library Journal* 57 (Jan. 15, 1932): 74.

10. Arthur B. Berthold, "Survey of Recent Russian Library Literature," *Library Quarterly* 17 (April 1947): 146.

11. McNeal, p. 302ff.; Raymond, p. 103n53.

12. On Bowker's domestic and international political and social views described here, see E. McClung Fleming, *R. R. Bowker: Militant Liberal* (Norman, OK: University of Oklahoma Press, 1952), pp. 257-79, 358.

13. Ibid., pp. 284, 358, 188.

14. Bowker, *The Arts of Life* (1903), p. 209, as quoted ibid., p. 276.

15. Fleming erroneously states that the Society arose in response to the 1905 Revolution. Founded by George Kennan and Samuel Clemens, among others, it came to include other prominent individuals such as Robert M. La Follette, Julius Rosenwald, Ida Tarbell, Cyrus L. Sulzberger, and Stephen S. Wise.

16. R. R. Bowker, "For Russia," *Library Journal* 42 (Aug. 1917): 599-605; American Library Association, "Message to Russia," *Bulletin of the American Library Association* 11 (June 1917): 328-29.

17. Bowker, in his and Zinovi Rechkoff's "Literature and Science in Russia," *Library Journal* 43 (March 1918): 164.

18. Bowker, "For Russia," p. 605.

19. See Lenin, "Destruction of the Parasite State," in *Lenin Reader*, ed. by Stefan Possony, pp. 199-200. In his adoration of the Commune, Lenin was in full accord with Marx, who wrote, "Workingmen's Paris, with its Commune, will be forever celebrated as the glorious harbinger of a new society." ("The Civil War in France," [1871] reprinted from the Foreign Languages Publishing House [Moscow] edition, in *Basic Writings on Politics and Philosophy: Karl Marx and Friedrich Engels*, ed. by Lewis Feuer [Garden City, NY: Doubleday, 1959], p. 390.) The versions in Feuer's book are very close to those published in the Soviet Union but are slightly less stilted. Compare, for example, the English language texts in Karl Marx and Frederick Engels, *Selected Works* (Moscow: Progress Publishers, 1975).

20. Bowker, untitled editorial, *Library Journal* 48 (Nov. 15, 1923): 967.

21. Bowker, untitled editorial, *Library Journal* 49 (March 15, 1924): 287.

22. Bowker, untitled editorial, *Library Journal* 49 (Sept. 1, 1924): 741.

23. Bowker, untitled editorial, *Library Journal* 50 (Dec. 1, 1925): 1006. He noted that he was basing, this, in part, on information received from L. Haffkin Hamburger (L. B. Khavkina).

24. Untitled editorial, *Library Journal* 47 (April 15, 1922): 363.

25. *Red Librarian* (Oct. 1923).

26. N. L., untitled editorial, *Library Journal* 49 (April 1, 1924): 342.

27. N. L., "Russia," *Library Journal* 49 (April 1, 1924): 336.

28. Ibid., p. 338.

29. See Avraham [Avrahm] Yarmolinsky, "The Russian Public Library," *Library Journal* 47 (April 15, 1922): 352-53; "Library Activities in Russia," *Library Journal* 49 (March 15, 1924): 292; "Libraries in Soviet Russia," *Library Journal* 44 (Nov. 1919): 724. See also Bowker, untitled editorial, *Library Journal* 47 (April 15, 1922): 363.

30. See: R. R. Bowker, untitled editorials, *Library Journal* 48 (Feb. 15, 1923): 179, and *Library Journal* 50 (Dec. 1, 1925): 1006; L. Haffkin Hamburger, "State Institute for Library Science in Russia," *Library Journal* 48 (Feb. 15, 1923): 171-72, and Hamburger, "The Institute for Library Science at Moscow," *Library Journal* 50 (Dec. 1, 1925): 991-93.

31. A. E. Bostwick, "Russia," *Library Journal* 49 (June 1, 1924): 540. Bostwick, a leading figure in the American library profession for decades, was interested in a broad array of subjects, including international and comparative librarianship. For example, he edited the book, *Popular Libraries of the World* (Chicago, American Library Association, 1933).

32. L. Haffkin Hamburger, "Libraries in the Soviet Union," *ALA Bulletin* 20 (Oct. 1926): 260-64; reprinted in *Libraries* [Chicago] 31 (Dec. 1926): 502-6; and *The Librarian and Book World* [London] 16 (Dec. 1926): 134-39. *Libraries* was published by the Library Bureau; the English journal by R. Atkinson, Ltd. Both periodicals had played an important role in the profession for many years.

33. "Libraries in Soviet Russia," *Literary Digest* 93 (April 9, 1927): 28.

34. "The Soviets Take Stock of Russia's Schools, Libraries and Movie Houses," *Library Journal* 44 (March 1919): 184-85.

35. Victor Yarros, "The Library and the Book in Russia's Revolutionary Movement," *Library Journal* 43 (March 1918): 147-51.

36. Bowker, untitled editorial, *Library Journal* 49 (Sept. 1, 1924): 741.

37. Money for food was channeled through the American Relief Association in New York, with the American Library Association sometimes serving as an intermediary. Library literature was sent directly to the libraries and to Haffkin Hamburger's library school. The donors included the Library of Congress, New York Public Library, New York State Library School, Los Angeles Library School, American Library Association, New York Special Libraries Association, the Bowker Co., H.W. Wilson Co., Gaylord Brothers, The Library Bureau, T. W. Koch, and William Warner Bishop. (See: L. Haffkin Hamburger, letter ["Russian Librarians Send Thanks"], *Library Journal* 48 [Feb. 1, 1923]: 128; Carl H. Milam, "Help for Russian Librarians," *Library Journal* 47 [Oct. 15, 1922]: 870; Bowker, "Relief for Russian Librarians," *Library Journal* 47 [June 1, 1922]: 495; Bowker, "Who Will Help Russian

Librarians?" *Library Journal* 47 [April 1, 1922]: 310; and Bowker, "Who Will Help Russian Librarians?" *Library Journal* 47 [April 15, 1922]: 358.)

38. See "Russian Libraries." For an account of what they acquired, see Avrahm Yarmolinsky, "The Slavonic Division—Recent Growth," *Bulletin of the New York Public Library* 30 (Feb. 1926): 71-79.

39. "Russian Libraries," p. 727.

40. Ibid.

41. Ibid.

42. Ibid., p. 728.

43. Ibid. Compare the contrary observations made by Krupskaya and others that are noted in chapter one.

44. "Russian Libraries," p. 729. The volume referred to was written by V. A. Stein of the library school at the Rumiantsev Museum.

45. Ibid., p. 728.

46. Ibid.

47. Ibid. In 1921 the Soviet government had *mandated* that the Universal Decimal Classification be adopted in all libraries whenever it was possible to do so.

48. Ibid., p. 729.

49. Ibid.

50. See Robert A. Karlowich, "Stranger in a Far Land: Report of a Bookbuying Trip by Harry Miller Lydenberg in Eastern Europe and Russia in 1923-24," *Bulletin of Research in the Humanities* 87, nos. 2-3 (1986-87): 199n, 210-11, 203, 203n43, 215n47, 205-6, and 199. Much of this information also appears in Karlowich's "Harry Miller Lydenberg and Soviet Libraries in 1923," *Newsletter of the Slavic and East European Section, Association of College and Research Libraries* 3 (1987): 35-44. See Phyllis Dain's interesting "Comments" which follow this article: *Newsletter . . .* 3 (1987): 44-49.

51. See George L. McKay, "A Bibliography of the Published Writings of Harry Miller Lydenberg [1909-1942]," in *Bookmen's Holiday: Notes and Studies Written and Gathered in Tribute to Harry Miller Lydenberg*, ed. by Deoch Fulton (New York: New York Public Library, 1943), pp. 5-26; and David H. Stam, "A Bibliography of the Published Writings of Harry Miller Lydenberg, 1942-1960," *Bulletin of the New York Public Library* 64 (June 1960): 298-302.

52. Harry Miller Lydenberg, "What Some Friends in Europe Say about Us," *Library Journal* 53 (May 15, 1928): 437. Lydenberg was instrumental in several international projects in the 1920's. For example, he was Chair of an American Library Association committee that oversaw the distribution of money to over a dozen financially strapped European countries—including the USSR—to help them purchase books and periodicals. Germany was by far

the largest recipient. (See Harry Miller Lydenberg, "Books for Europe," *Bulletin of the American Library Association* 18 [Aug. 1924]: 222; and his "Books for Foreign Countries," *Bulletin of the American Library Association* 20 [Oct. 1926]: 368-69.)

53. Many of his works are listed in "Avrahm Yarmolinsky—The List [of his Writings, 1909-1955]," *Bulletin of the New York Public Library* 59 (March 1955): 110-32. He continued to publish for many years after his retirement.

54. See, for example, Abraham [Avrahm] Yarmolinsky, "The Kennan Collection" (New York: New York Public Library, 1921), p. 13; reprinted from the *Bulletin of the New York Public Library* (Feb. 1921).

55. See Avrahm Yarmolinsky, "Censorship in Russia," *The Russian Review* 3 (July 1917): 98-103.

56. Abraham [Avrahm] Yarmolinsky, "The Internal Policy of the Bolsheviki," *Current History* 8 (April 1918): 68-72. He was also considered sufficiently knowledgeable to review recent books on Russia and the Soviet Union for *The Bookman* (For example, see Abraham [Avrahm] Yarmolinsky, "Exploring Russia," *The Bookman* 46 [Dec. 1917]: 481-86) and the *New York Herald Books* section. In 1924 the *Herald* and the *New York Tribune* merged to form the *New York Herald-Tribune.*

57. Abraham [Avrahm] Yarmolinsky, "More Bolshevist Legislation," *Current History* 8 (June 1918): 455-58.

58. Avrahm Yarmolinsky, "New Ideas and Ideals in Soviet Russia," *Current History* 22 (June 1925): 402.

59. Ibid., pp. 404-5.

60. Avrahm Yarmolinsky, "Soviet Libraries," *College and Research Libraries* 5 (Sept. 1944): 351-56. A major book in the following decade described the oppressive and anti-Western literature mandated in the USSR after 1945: Avrahm Yarmolinsky, *Literature under Communism: The Literary Policy of the Communist Party of the Soviet Union from the End of World War II to the Death of Stalin* (Bloomington, IN: Russian and East European Institute, Indiana University, 1960). He noted (p. 160) that the policy remained unchanged at the time he completed this book in 1957, four years after Stalin's death.

61. See the editor's paragraph inserted in Eddy's article, p. 61.

62. Eddy, p. 61.

63. Ibid., p. 66.

64. Ibid., p. 61.

65. Ibid., p. 65.

66. Ibid., pp. 62-63.

67. Ibid., p. 63.

68. Ibid.

69. Ibid.

70. Ibid., p. 65.

71. Ibid.

72. For a full account of the murder of millions of peasants and kulaks in the years following the Communist takeover, climaxing in the murder of several more million in the collectivization Eddy was so enamored of, see Robert Conquest's *Harvest of Sorrow*.

73. Margaret P. Coleman, "America, Russia, and Adult Education," *Wilson Bulletin for Librarians* 10 (Dec. 1935): 235-39.

74. Ibid., pp. 235-36.

75. Ibid., p. 237.

76. Ibid., pp. 238-239.

77. Ibid., p. 236.

78. Ibid., p. 237.

79. Ibid., pp. 236-38.

80. Ibid., p. 238. "The Roving Eye" was the column of the journal's editor, Stanley J. Kunitz.

81. Ibid.

82. Ibid., p. 236.

83. Ibid., pp. 239, 236-38.

84. Ibid., pp. 238-39.

85. Ibid., p. 236.

86. Waples stated that he visited "early in December 1931." See his "Guiding Readers in Soviet Russia," *Bulletin of the American Library Association* 26 (Oct. 1932): 765.

87. See Stephen Karetzky, *Reading Research and Librarianship*, particularly pp. 93-148.

88. Waples, p. 762.

89. Ibid.

90. Ibid., p. 766.

91. Ibid., p. 762.

92. Again, see Stephen Karetzky's analysis of Waples in *Reading Research and Librarianship*.

93. Waples, p. 762.

94. Ibid.

95. For example, see Jennie M. Flexner and Sigrid A. Edge, *A Reader's Advisory Service* (New York: American Association for Adult Education, 1934), pp. 7, 36, 54-57. These two leaders of the Readers' Advisory movement worked at the New York Public Library.

96. Waples, p. 766.

97. Ibid., p. 763.

98. Ibid., p. 767.

99. Ibid.

100. Ibid., p. 763.

101. Ibid., p. 766.

102. Ibid., p. 763.

103. Ibid., p. 765.

104. Furthermore, Waples asserted, "Unlike the book clerks in most other countries, . . . the clerks do occasionally read some of the books they sell." (Waples, p. 766)

105. Waples, p. 764. There were 14,230 titles.

106. Ibid., p. 764.

107. Ibid., p. 765.

108. Ibid.

109. Ibid., p. 765n.

110. Waples did note in his article that there was censorship in the Soviet Union.

111. Haygood, "Libraries in the Union of Socialist Soviet [*sic*] Republics."

112. Ibid., p. 436. For example, he noted that M. A. Ziboulenko fully adopted Lenin's belief that pre-Revolutionary literature had been—and still was—evil because it obscured the truth. He cited Ziboulenko's *Le Travail des Bibliothèques dans la Russe Prerevolutionnaire et en URSS.*

113. Haygood, p. 435. He neglected to explain their extensive use by the revolutionaries, many of whom were not particularly well-to-do, albeit not penurious.

114. Haygood, p. 435. He was referring to the Soviet periodical, *The Red Librarian.*

115. Ibid.

116. Coleman, p. 237.

117. Haygood, p. 435.

118. Ibid.

119. Ibid., p. 436.

120. Ibid., p. 438.

121. An American reader might well have been misled by Haygood's use of the term *political* solely for the reason that its definition in the United States has always connoted a power which is rather limited in scope and which has generally been formed by a democratically arrived at consensus. The so-called political function in the USSR was actually the antithesis of this: coercion by an elite reaching into almost all aspects of human life.

122. Haygood, p. 439.

123. Ibid., p. 438.

124. Ibid., p. 437.

125. Ibid., p. 439.

126. Ibid. Haygood opined that the Communist system had not yet reached its fulfillment "hampered as it is by undeveloped natural and human resources, and having only partially mastered the tools of technology."

127. Ibid., p. 438. Waples made the same claim, but only in reference to technical books. See Waples, p. 765.

128. Haygood, p. 438.

129. John Richmond Russell, "Library Service in the USSR," *Journal of Adult Education* 8 (April 1936): 165. Russell mentioned in his article that the Institute of Library Science had recently issued a collection of articles on "American library methods" as an instructional aid for Soviet librarians.

130. Russell, p. 169.

131. Ibid.

132. See *Who's Who in American Education, 1957-58*, 18th ed., ed. by Robert C. Cook (Nashville: Who's Who in American Education, 1957).

133. Eugenia Khmelnitsky, "Research in the Bureau of Labor, Kharkov, Ukraine," *Special Libraries* 19 (July-August 1928): 183.

134. Ibid, pp. 183, 184.

135. Ibid, p. 185.

136. Dmitri N. Egorov, "Russian Libraries since the Revolution," *Library Review* 2 (1929-30): 329.

137. Ibid, p. 330.

138. Ibid, p. 332.

139. Ibid, pp. 330, 331, 332.

140. "Library Progress in Russia," *Libraries* 35 (Dec. 1930): 454.

141. See Konstantin F. Shteppa, *Russian Historians and the Soviet State* (New Brunswick, NJ: Rutgers University Press, 1962), pp. 17, 25, 38, 43.

142. Lionel R. McColvin, "Introduction," in *A Survey of Libraries: Reports on a Survey Made by the Library Association during 1936-1937*, gen. ed. by McColvin (London: The Library Association, 1938), pp. 2-3. McColvin reported that a major goal of the Rockefeller Foundation was "the promotion of international intellectual co-operation and understanding" (p. 3) and that this was influential in the shaping of the study. The same Foundation grant also helped to build the Library Association's library.

143. H. M. Cashmore, "Russia," in *A Survey of Libraries*, ed. by McColvin, pp. 308-44.

144. H. M. Cashmore, "Libraries in Russia," *Library Association Record* 39 (June 1937): 298-300. Cashmore made a pithy remark on a subject ignored by American librarians visiting the USSR: "Discipline everywhere is satisfactory and, in spite of what critics of Russia say, there is neither equality of standing among library staffs nor dragooning of subordinates." (p. 299) This was dealt with at greater length in his full report. (See Cashmore's "Russia," in *A Survey of Libraries*, ed. by McColvin, pp. 341-42.)

145. See Karetzky, *Reading Research and Librarianship*, pp. 196-98, 204-5.

146. H. A. Gregory, "Libraries in Soviet Russia," in *Australian Institute of Librarians Meeting and Conference Proceedings*, vol. 2 (Melbourne: Brown, Prior, and Anderson; Dec. 1940), p. 119.

147. Ibid., p. 118.

148. Ibid., p. 119.

149. Ibid., p. 118.

150. Ibid., p. 124.

151. Ibid., p. 119. At the time, the word *totalitarian* was still fairly new, having been coined in the mid-1920's. (See: Abbott Gleason, *Totalitarianism: The Inner History of the Cold War* [New York and Oxford: Oxford University Press, 1995], pp. 9-10; and Michael Curtis, *Totalitarianism* [New Brunswick, NJ, and London: Transaction Books, 1979], p. 6.)

152. Gregory, "Libraries in Soviet Russia," p. 119.

153. Agnes Gregory, letters to the author (May 8, 1997; May 13, 1997). Howard and Agnes Gregory were wed in 1947. She too was a librarian.

154. See H. A. Gregory, "Why I Enlisted: Some Talks with the Man in the Street in Central Europe," Talk over Radio Station 3XY (Melbourne, Feb. 8, 1939). Gregory's attempt to enlist in the army was unsuccessful because of his age and the malaria he had contracted in Eastern Europe in 1938. However, the need for manpower increased during the war, and he wound up serving in the armed forces for several years, primarily in educational and library services. (Agnes Gregory, letters.)

155. Arthur Berthold, "Dispensing Library Ammunition," *Wilson Bulletin for Librarians* 9 (Nov. 1934): 130-32, 135. Berthold also criticized the Soviet government's use of libraries to control people's reading in "The Young Librarian," *Wilson Bulletin for Librarians* 8 (Jan. 1934): 296-97. As this latter article makes clear, he was very wary of *all* national governments' involvements with their public libraries, and he did not share the enthusiasm of some of his young colleagues, like Jesse Shera, for a greatly enhanced role by the US federal government.

156. Arthur B. Berthold, "Survey of Recent Russian Library Literature," *Library Quarterly* 17 (April 1947): 138-47.

157. Leon Carnovsky, "Libraries in Nazi Germany," *Library Journal* 59 (Nov. 1934): 893-94.

158. The only librarian he named, Dr. Walter Hoffmann, was later put in a concentration camp because of his socialist views. (On Hoffmann, see Karetzky, *Reading Research and Librarianship*, pp. 277-78, 295-98.)

159. On developments under the Nazis, see Margaret F. Stieg, *Public Libraries in Nazi Germany* (Tuscaloosa and London: University of Alabama Press, 1992).

160. For the rare occasion when he even brought up the subject of fascist materials, see Stanley J. Kunitz, "The Roving Eye," *Wilson Bulletin for Librarians* 9 (Nov. 1934): 137-38.

161. See John Earl Haynes, *Red Scare or Red Menace? Communism and Anticommunism in the Cold War Era* (Chicago: Ivan R. Dee, 1996), pp. 25-27. The move on the part of the university was applauded by the American Council Against Nazi Propaganda, nominally headed by the liberal historian and US ambassador to Germany from 1933 to 1938, William Dodd. Despite its reputable sponsors, much of the group's financial support secretly came from Communists, and many of its staff members were covert members of the Party. (John Earl Haynes, letter to the author [Oct. 30, 1998].) The Miami affair is dealt with in the Council's publication, *The Hour*, no. 104 (July 5, 1941).

162. For example, see Stanley J. Kunitz, "The Roving Eye," *Wilson Bulletin for Librarians* 10 (Nov. 1935): 194-95; and 10 (March 1936): 469-70.

163. Coleman, "America, Russia, and Adult Education."

164. Jessica M. Fredricks, "A Glance at Russian Libraries," *Wilson Bulletin for Librarians* 12 (Dec. 1937): 233-37.

165. Ibid., p. 236.

166. V. Semenev, " A Russian View of the Lenin Library," *Wilson Bulletin for Librarians* 10 (Dec. 1937): 237-38.

167. Gretchen Garrison, "Public Libraries and the World-Mind," *Wilson Bulletin for Librarians* 9 (Sept. 1934): 19.

168. Ibid.

169. Ibid., p. 20.

170. Ibid., pp. 20, 31.

171. Ibid., p. 31.

172. Archibald MacLeish, "Libraries in the Contemporary Crisis," *Library Journal* 64 (Nov. 15, 1939): 879-82.

173. Ibid., p. 881.

174. Ibid., pp. 880-82.

175. See John Y. Cole, "Archibald MacLeish," in *World Encyclopedia of Library and Information Services*, 3rd ed., p. 529. The ALA countered that the holder of this post should be an experienced library administrator as well as "a gentleman and a scholar."

The 1939 correspondence between Roosevelt and Supreme Court Justice Felix Frankfurter about the possible appointment of their mutual acquaintance, "Archie," is revealing. Frankfurter, who mentioned that when he was a boy his uncle was director of the library at the University of Vienna, supported MacLeish vigorously. He favored a scholar or literary figure for the position rather than a "technical librarian." Moreover, he though that "promotions from within the staff" in libraries had elevated librarians to positions they could not do well. MacLeish's left-wing views were never mentioned in their letters.

(See Franklin Delano Roosevelt, memo to Felix Frankfurter, May 3, 1939; and Frankfurter's reply, May 11, 1939; published in "Judging Librarianship: Are Library Leaders Trained—Or Born?" intro. by David Streeter, *American Libraries* 26 [May 1995]: 408, 411.)

176. See "Archibald MacLeish," *P.L.C. Bulletin* 1 (Sept. 1939): 3. As with other Popular Front organizations controlled by Communists, the PLC lobbied against any direct, or indirect, American involvement in World War II while the Soviet Union and Germany maintained their cooperation pact. After the Soviet Union was attacked, the PLC reversed its stance and became a vigorous supporter of an immediate "Second Front" in Europe to take pressure off the USSR. Pro-Communists, like Rockwell Kent and Vito Marcantonio, participated in its conferences and wrote for its magazine. A short, generally favorable overview of its history has been written: Joe W. Kraus, "The Progressive Librarians' Council," *Library Journal* 97 (July 1972): 2351-54. It is analyzed later in this book.

Some members of the American Library Association's Junior Members Round Table, like Edwin Castagna, tried to have that group support the PLC's efforts to lobby President Roosevelt on the war issue. (See letters, *ALA Bulletin* 34 [Sept. 1940]: 478-80.)

177. Willard Thorp, "American Writers on the Left," in *Socialism and American Life*, vol., 1, ed. by Donald Drew Egbert and Stow Persons (Princeton: Princeton University Press, 1952), pp. 606-7, 617; and Daniel Bell's contribution in the same volume, "The Background and Development of Marxian Socialism in the United States," p. 361. Thorp was Chairman of the American Studies Program at Princeton University and coeditor of the scholarly, three-volume work, *The Literary History of the United States*, along with Robert E. Spiller, Thomas H. Johnson, and Henry Seidel Canby (New York: Macmillan, 1948).

178. *Socialism and American Life*, vol. 2; ed. by Donald Drew Egbert and Stow Persons; bibliographer: T. D. Seymour Bassett (Princeton: Princeton University Press, 1952), p. 492. With parts of the book a cooperative effort, this sentence may have been written by Egbert, Persons, Bassett, David Bowers, or Willard Thorp. (See vol. 1, pp. viii, 600; and vol. 2, p. viii.)

4

AUTHORS, INTELLECTUALS, AND EDUCATORS APPLAUD THE USSR

The attitude of librarians towards the Soviet Union from 1917 through the 1930's can be better understood when compared with those of leading intellectual and cultural figures of the time, including prominent members of librarianship's sister profession, education. It is significant that many of the foremost educationists, writers, and intellects in the United States were even more positive than librarians about the Communist country. Some of the major figures in this anti-American, philo-Soviet movement, like John Dewey and George S. Counts, became disillusioned with the USSR by the end of the thirties. In contrast, the overwhelming majority of the American people never thought well of either Communism or the Soviet Union.

Overview of Americans' Attitudes towards the USSR, 1917-1939

A brief sketch of Americans' attitudes towards Communism and the Soviet Union during this period will help put those of librarians and others into perspective. The general views of liberals, intellectuals, religious leaders, typical Americans and their representatives, and those I term *Conservative Anti-Communists* are described below in turn. Naturally, there are many nuances and exceptions that would be cited in a lengthier treatment.[1]

American liberalism had a history of frequent support for the

Soviet Union that went back to the very founding of the Communist State. It stemmed from several sources, including the liberals' dismay resulting from World War I, disillusionment with the Versailles Treaty, dislike for America's conservative opponents of Communism, hope that innovation in the revolutionary country would promote change in the United States, belief that the Soviet Union was treated poorly by the Western countries, faith that the USSR would become more democratic, and general disaffection from America. They maintained that the problems in Soviet-American relations were caused by the United States.

Liberals were preoccupied with the Soviet Union from its very inception. As with many American intellectuals, their fascination and dependence merely increased in the twenties because in the US the general public's satisfaction, the healthy economy, and the absence of major social upheaval in this era of "Normalcy" both betokened, and created, the lack of widespread interest in the large-scale political, social, cultural, and ideological transformation the liberals greatly desired. Feeling alienated from, and betrayed by, their own people, they turned to those of the USSR to sustain their hopes and visions. Throughout the twenties, they yearned for what they considered a truly "human," idealistic culture and a society opposite to theirs, which they perceived as materialistic and decadent.

In the course of the 1920's, the early assertions by liberal spokespeople that the Soviet Union would become more democratic became less tenable, so they were replaced, to some extent, by claims that the USSR should not be judged by democratic values. When liberals did criticize the Communist state, excuses for its failings were invariably made.

The onset of the Depression deepened the liberals' attraction to the Soviet Union, resulting in an increased affinity for its economic system and a relish for the state's emphasis on planning most aspects of life. The illusory "full employment" there proved beguiling; in reality, it was massive forced labor. Given the growing despair in America—particularly among themselves—the dedication and purpose they believed they saw in the USSR attracted them more than ever. While not universal among liberals, the failure to perceive the oppression in the Soviet Union was the rule, not the exception. When it *was* discerned, it was usually condoned.

In the 1920's, most American intellectuals, particularly writers, were not pro-Soviet, merely anti-American. To some extent, the causes of this were similar to those that moved the liberals. These intellectuals tended to be rebels, not revolutionaries, and were attracted to a vague liberalism or cynical aestheticism. However, with the coming of the Depression in 1929, most intellectuals, writers, and artists very quickly became as radical in their collectivism as they had been in their individualism: Dada was replaced by Big Brother. Their new positive views of the USSR were symptomatic of this.

Most Americans were religious, but while the bulk of these believing citizens were firmly opposed to the Soviet regime—particularly during its frequent anti-religious campaigns—spiritual leaders varied in their opposition. The clergy most staunchly opposed to Communism throughout the decades was that of the Catholic Church. It included intellectuals and scholars like Father Edmund A. Walsh, head of the School of Foreign Service at Georgetown University and a widely respected expert on the Soviet Union. Rabbis were initially divided over whether the conditions for Jews were better, or worse, under the Communists than under the Czars, but even then very few thought well of the new rulers. Many prominent Protestant clergymen and theologians, like Harry F. Ward and Reinhold Niebuhr, frequently excused the Communist suppression of religion. In this, they were unlike their less famous coreligionists.

Not surprisingly, the early reaction of the American business community to the new Communist state was negative given the Soviet view of free enterprise and private property. Like their fellow citizens, they supported democracy and religion, and shared the widespread feeling of betrayal when the Soviet Union withdrew from the Great War. There were major business organizations, like the Chamber of Commerce, that remained steadfast in their opposition decade after decade. (For example, it opposed any trade with the USSR throughout the 1920's.) However, some businessmen were encouraged by Lenin's partial reintroduction of capitalism in his New Economic Policy, and believed that the industrialization of the Soviet Union and opening it to trade could only work to liberalize the government. Of course, many of them also saw more involvement with the USSR as a way to enrich themselves. (Henry Ford was the most prominent of the business leaders seeking increased ties with the Communist country.) With the onset of the Depression, an increasing number of businessmen wanted trade with the Soviet Union because they were desperate and thought it would benefit them financially.

The overthrow of the Czar was widely celebrated by the American people. This was reflected in the action of their government, which was the first in the world to formally recognize the legitimacy of the democratically oriented government that succeeded that of Nicholas II. However, unlike many liberals and intellectuals, over the next several years the general public continued to support the views of the sitting presidents—Wilson, Coolidge, and Hoover—as well as the great majority of the members of Congress. The belief of the government and the people was that the Bolshevik coup had brought to power a regime which was evil at its core and violated the essential decencies of Western civilization by opposing God, freedom, morality, and the generally accepted ideals of honorable behavior. The Soviet Union's attempts to provoke revolution throughout the world were considered both a threat and a gross violation of the basic elements of peaceful, civilized, international relations. (Despite their resolute opposition to the Soviet regime, the American populace—along with their government and most other elements of society—fully supported the massive provision of food begun in 1921 to try to stave off famine in the Communist country.) Most Americans disliked the USSR so much that they even seemed opposed to any commercial intercourse with the renegade country throughout the twenties, although trade was restored. In the thirties, the general public still maintained its negative view of the Soviet government's denial of its subjects' basic political, social, and religious rights. Unlike the situation in liberal, intellectual, and literary circles, no excuses for this lack of freedom were common among the mass of the population.

Like the people they spoke for, almost all of the most prominent union leaders were among the strongest and most consistent anti-Communists from the very rise of the Bolsheviks. In part, this was a result of the Communist efforts—which began soon after the October Revolution—to take over these instruments of the American workers. This provided the democratic labor activists with excellent lessons in Soviet aims and techniques. It is telling that most would-be labor leaders who *were* Communists attempted to hide it from the rank and file.

One can identify a core of people that remained unalterably, vocally, and actively opposed to the USSR throughout the interwar period, and even during World War II: the Conservative Anti-

Communists. To some extent, they were also members of other groups mentioned here, but these particular elected representatives, government officials, Catholic clergy and laypeople, and members of patriotic and anti-Communist organizations maintained a resolve that merits special acknowledgment. Unfortunately, the variegated Conservative Anti-Communist circles maintained only loose networks of communication with each other.

Within a few years of its establishment, the Soviet government had set up an extensive, sophisticated public relations program to help increase its power and undermine that of its chosen foes—the capitalist countries.[2] The belief was that, sooner or later, Communists would overthrow the weakened states. Intermediate goals included the bolstering of its image in the West and a concomitant undermining of the self-images of the democratic societies. (This was facilitated by the faltering self-confidence of some in the democracies because of the Great Depression.) Other Soviet aims included the acquisition of technical information and expertise in all areas; diplomatic recognition by foreign governments, which could be followed by loans and credit; and the acquisition of foreign currency expended by visitors.

The USSR did everything possible to accomplish these goals. To gain widespread foreign approval, it presented itself to those abroad and to visitors by being all things to all people. To intellectuals, it portrayed itself as the embodiment of ideals to which they could dedicate their lives. To educators, it was refashioned as a society devoted primarily to schooling in all of its forms. Businessmen were told of the great market potential for their goods as well as the cheap labor for the factories they could build. Moderate union leaders were shown things that would hopefully lead them to believe that only in the USSR could workers get fair wages and decent living conditions. It was solely with the small number of radicals and potential extremists that the subject of a worldwide proletarian revolution was discussed. In other words, whatever the itch of the foreigner or visitor—intellectual, moral, emotional, or financial—the Communists were prepared to scratch it.

American Cultural Figures

It is generally accepted that many American cultural leaders, particularly those involved in literary pursuits, worked to support the Soviet Union and Communist causes after 1917, especially during the thirties. Among those one can name are Sherwood Anderson, Waldo Frank, Theodore Dreiser, Dashiell Hammett, John Dos Passos, James T. Farrell, Philip Rahv, Langston Hughes, Erskine Caldwell, John Chamberlain, Clifton Fadiman, Richard Wright, Edmund Wilson, Granville Hicks, Max Lerner, and Kenneth Fearing. Their ideology dominated the influential literary pages of the *New York Times*, *The Herald-Tribune*, and the *New Yorker*, as well as the more high-brow publications.[3]

The title of Eugene Lyons' incisive book on pro-Communist intellectuals of the thirties— *The Red Decade*—created a label for this cultural period that has not been successfully challenged since its appearance in 1941.[4] It should be pointed out that, unlike Lyons' book, many later accounts of the intellectuals' support for the brutal, totalitarian country that opposed the Western democracies shamelessly excuse, or even praise, their behavior. Most claim that no harm came of it, and some brazenly declare that there was actually a redeeming value to their apostasy. Many of those writing on this subject appear to defend the actions of these Communists or fellow travellers because of their own overwhelming animosity towards Cold War anti-Communism.[5] Their tendentious accounts agree with the self-appraisals of the recreants themselves: few have ever admitted to more than minor offenses.[6]

Frank Warren's significant study of "left-wing liberals" (his term) who made common cause with the Communists in the thirties accurately criticized their gullibility when it was published by Indiana University Press in 1966. It should be added, however, that when it was reprinted in 1993 by Columbia University Press, his new preface expressed regret that his volume may have fed "conservative or Cold War liberal anti-Communism." Like many of his fellow academics who moved to the Left in these years, he now thought more highly of the Communists than before.[7]

Roger N. Baldwin's Seminal Study

Roger N. Baldwin, founder of the American Civil Liberties Union, visited the USSR in 1927 and issued his findings as *Liberty under the*

Soviets.[8] It was published by Vanguard Press, which had been established by the American Fund for Public Service and continued to be funded by it. The Fund's board of directors was comprised mainly of prominent members of the Communist Party, like William Z. Foster and Benjamin Gitlow, as well as some socialists. Baldwin's work was part of the "Vanguard Studies of Soviet Russia" series, edited by Yale University's Jerome M. Davis, a leading member of numerous Communist-front organizations throughout his life.[9] The distinguishing feature of the books in this series was that while they were always positive about the Soviet Union in their general thrust, they usually assumed the guise of impartiality and avoided blatant propaganda.[10]

Frank Warren maintains that Baldwin's book and John Dewey's 1929 volume on the USSR (analyzed below) were, among intellectuals, the most influential works of the period about that country.[11] *Liberty under the Soviets* certainly did serve as a model of obfuscation and exculpation. It described and criticized many of the negative aspects of Soviet life, like the strict censorship, but it consistently went to great pains to rationalize them by discussing the political theories or psychological factors supposedly underlying these evils. Some parts of the work—like the benign treatment of the hellish Communist prison system—were ludicrous.

Baldwin, who was active in several Russian-American projects, declared that he titled his book *Liberty under the Soviets* "because I see as far more significant [than political or civil liberty] the basic economic freedom of workers and peasants and the abolition of classes based on wealth."[12] Economic liberty, he insisted, underlies all others.[13] These views must make one question the name and the aim of the ACLU, which he created and headed for thirty years. Such *apparent* political and philosophical inconsistencies were a hallmark of Baldwin's life. For example, while he claimed to be a pacifist during World War I, he was, at the same time, a member of the violent International Workers of the World. Pronouncing himself an anarchist, he also supported their Communist opponents—who were intent on murdering them. Underlying such apparent contradictions was his very consistent attempt to undermine the political and social structure of the United States.

Despite Baldwin's previous association with the revealing book *Letters from Russian Prisons*, in his *Liberty under the Soviets* he dismissed all evidence of widespread brutality in the USSR. Moreover, he declared throughout the work that any negative aspects of Communist rule were probably just the manifestations of its adolescent stage; hopefully, things would work themselves out in time. In addition, he repeatedly stated that the Communists would become more tolerant if they felt less threatened by the capitalist world. Baldwin therewith placed the onus for their barbarity on the Western democracies and advocated a policy of appeasement towards a state dedicated to the destruction of the free nations.[14] These ideas were staples of books of this genre.

Educators

Major studies of the USSR's education system began in the late 1920's. By this time, a self-styled field of *international comparative education* was already developing in the United States, more than two decades before the term *comparative librarianship* was first used. This is understandable, given the different sizes of the professions. The number of (1) school teachers and administrators, (2) schools of education, and (3) faculty members in these professional schools dwarfed the analogous figures in librarianship.[15]

Lucy L. W. Wilson

The first major book about Soviet pedagogy by an American educator was Lucy L. W. Wilson's *The New Schools of New Russia*. Issued in 1928, it was, like Roger Baldwin's *Liberty under the Soviets*, published by Vanguard Press as part of its series "Vanguard Studies of Soviet Russia." Wilson, a high school principal in Philadelphia, held a Ph.D. in biology, had written several books on education, and had visited numerous countries throughout the world in addition to the USSR.

She maintained that no educator should ignore Soviet education. While it was not perfect,

> For the first time in history, a new school has risen out of the ethos
> of the people. For the first time in history, a people has a new
> cultural ideal on which to build. For the first time in history, the

education of a people is blossoming forth out of the natural life and experiences of a generation.[16]

Wilson claimed that an understanding of the USSR's *successful* efforts was vital for Westerners, while a comprehension of its failures was of value primarily to Soviet citizens.[17] This is not logical, but it did provide her with a rationale for consistently emphasizing the supposedly positive aspects of the Soviet Union while ignoring, or glossing over, the negative. Thus, she mentioned—almost in passing—that in education ". . . the important things are decided by the Communist Party. . . ."[18] No indication of the ruthless, totalitarian nature of the Soviet system was given in this book. As with other prominent American educators who visited the Soviet Union, she met with its foremost educationists, including Krupskaya, whom she described in the most flattering terms.[19]

John Dewey

What impression did the USSR make on the most influential American philosopher of education in the twentieth century and one of the nation's most prominent intellectuals? John Dewey was a professor of philosophy at Columbia University who held a joint appointment at the University's Teachers College. He visited the Soviet Union for sixteen days in 1928 and published his reactions in a series in *The New Republic*, a liberal periodical. These were issued as a book in 1929 along with some of his earlier writings on other countries undergoing major transformations: *Impressions of Soviet Russia and the Revolutionary World—Mexico, China, Turkey.*[20] The great impact in America made by his report on the USSR has been noted by scholars who have studied this period.[21]

Dewey was not a Marxist,[22] but that did not prevent him from writing a paean to the Soviet Union and its educational system. He was a rabid anti-anti-Communist at this time. This analysis of his book will quote liberally from it to give a sense of its flavor and to present Dewey's preposterous views as precisely as possible.

Dewey's methodological approach in his investigative tour was admittedly highly subjective: ". . . I am dealing only with impressions received at first hand and not with information proceeding from systematic inquiries. . . ."[23] He defended the validity of his technique: ". . . I am dealing with impressions rather than with matters capable of any objective proof."[24] He noted that this was the same procedure used by the novelist Anatole France when he had visited Russia, as if this validated the methodology. (France, incidentally, had been pro-Communist.)[25] Dewey averred that his "impressions" enabled him to see how wrong the typical foreign view of the Soviet Union was.[26] Strangely, this insistence on the validity of subjective notions formed during a short tour coexisted with his hearty approval of the Communists' declared aim of evaluating and planning their educational system—indeed their entire society—scientifically. He reported with admiration that it was the first country in the world to do so.[27]

Neither the brevity of his stay nor the small, skewed sample of people he met and relied on for information—mainly Soviet educational leaders—made Dewey question whether he had learned the central truths about the Communist country. He assured his readers that what he had heard from these educators led him to a more accurate understanding of the USSR than would have been possible if he had spoken with powerful political or economic figures. The major undertaking in the Soviet Union, he explained, was the development of a new mentality among its people. In this endeavor, it was those high up in the educational hierarchy who were most influential in creating the New Soviet Union and the New Soviet Man. (This displayed Dewey's gross ignorance of the power structure in the USSR.) He dismissed Western analysts who understood the Russian language, had wide contacts in the Soviet Union, and wrote political and economic analyses of the new state. Their works, he declared, missed the truly essential elements of the country.[28] One must point out that while Dewey claimed to have discerned the key elements of Soviet education and society, he saw little of the most significant instructional institutions there: the schools were closed for summer break when he arrived in July!

Dewey was entranced by the USSR. To him, it was a country of "movement, vitality, energy,"[29] an "outburst of vitality, courage, confidence in life."[30] This, he believed, was the essence of Revolution itself; it had less to do with the supposed principles of that upheaval, namely, Communism.[31] Dewey was certain that what he was seeing was the "liberation of a people to consciousness of themselves as a determining power in the shaping of their ultimate fate."[32]

He was awed by the stated goal of Soviet education, and a prime aim of all institutions in the USSR: the aforementioned creation of "a new mentality in the Russian people."[33] He insisted that this educational effort to create "a new collective mentality; a new collective morality I should call it, . . . is . . . succeeding to a considerable degree."[34] He was thrilled that people were being taught to act "coöperatively and collectively as readily now as in capitalistic countries they act 'individualistically.'"[35] The entire country was "an enormous psychological experiment in transforming the motives that inspire human conduct."[36]

Dewey greatly admired what he accepted as the connection of education to "social life" and to "socially useful work" in the Soviet Union.[37] This, he claimed, was "the idea that underlies all attempts at thorough-going [educational] reform"[38] wherever it occurs. It is prevented in capitalist countries by the "personal competition and desire for private profit in our economic life."[39] In fact, these unsavory characteristics make it necessary for education in the Western countries to be *protected* from the society at large.

Dewey complained that educational improvements in the United States could only be made piecemeal. The Soviet Union shows that "only in a society based upon the coöperative principle can the ideals of educational reformers be adequately carried into operation."[40] The Soviet view of cooperative, socially useful work and proper education is the opposite of that advocated by capitalist leaders in the United States.[41]

Dewey claimed to dislike the consistent, systematic, and centrally controlled propaganda that he saw pervading all aspects of life in the Soviet Union. He remarked that it outstripped any other effort of its kind elsewhere. However, he not only managed to reconcile himself to this brainwashing but to defend it.[42] Thus, he maintained that in some ways it was no different from attempts in all other countries to use schools to fulfill societal goals:

> There are many elements of propaganda connected with this policy, and many of them obnoxious to me personally. But the broad effort to employ the education of the young as a means of realizing certain social purposes cannot be dismissed as propaganda without relegating to that category all endeavor at deliberate social control.[43]

Dewey's incapacity here to distinguish between limited guidance and wholesale regimentation is striking.

He went on to assert that propaganda in this Communist country is not propaganda as Westerners usually conceive it: furtive communication which serves the interests of one particular social group. Instead, it is overt and carried out on behalf of a "public faith."[44] Its purpose, the Soviet leaders believe, is not for "private or even a class gain, but is [for] the universal gain of universal humanity."[45] (Dewey declared that even if one disagrees with the Communists, one could not question their sincerity. In other words, he believed that the supposed candidness of the Communists went a long way towards excusing any possible deficiencies in their ideology, morality, intelligence, and so forth.) Dewey concluded this treatment of the subject with a declaration that reflected his easy acceptance of Communist propaganda and his failure to insist on differentiating it from true education. In the USSR, he stated, ". . . propaganda is education and education is propaganda. They are more than confounded; they are identified."[46]

Dewey believed it was inevitable that the brainwashing and agitprop would die out as the Soviets began to feel more secure, knowing that they would be left alone by other countries to work out their own destiny.[47] The implication here was that their propaganda was merely a reaction to the hostile posture of others: the Americans, the English, and the Poles were actually to blame, not the Communists. He also believed that the propaganda would be overcome by the intellectual freedom and cooperative mentality he saw developing in the USSR:

> There is, of course, an immense amount of indoctrination and propaganda in the schools. But if the existing tendency develops, it seems fairly safe to predict that in the end this indoctrination will be subordinate to the awakening of initiative and power of independent judgment, while coöperative mentality will be evolved. It seems impossible that an education intellectually free will not militate against a servile acceptance of dogma as dogma. One hears all the time about the dialectic movement by means of which a movement contradicts itself in the end. I think the schools are a "dialectic" factor in the evolution of Russian communism.[48]

Once again, Dewey's illusions obscured the truth. He saw what he hoped to see and was entirely ignorant of who the real power holders in the Soviet Union were.

Dewey maintained a double-standard for Communist and non-Communist countries. In his support for the Soviet regime's attempts to destroy the traditional social fabric and all other countervailing forces, he applauded its attempts to eradicate the family structure. In contrast, he complained bitterly that industrialization was rending the family in the West.[49]

Dewey vigorously defended the Communist state against attacks by those who said they preferred democracy. He maintained that the major goal of the Soviet enterprise was the cultural development of all levels of society. (The spirit and force driving this work were intrinsically religious, he maintained, and resembled early Christianity.[50] This revealed Dewey's lack of understanding of religion in general, as well as this particular one. For one thing, unlike the Communists, the early Christians did not throw their opponents to the lions.) This educational effort was "nobly heroic, evincing a faith in human nature which is democratic beyond the ambitions of the democracies of the past."[51] He considered the USSR an experiment to see if democratic ideals—liberty, equality, and brotherhood—could best be realized in a cooperative, socialist regime. He asserted that there was more democracy in Soviet schools than in America's, and that students there were being better prepared for active participation in democratic communities and industry.[52] He also declared that critics should stop contrasting the governance of the USSR to "an imaginary democratic system."[53] Rather, it should be compared to that under the Czars. This would show that "like the old system, it has many repressive traits. But . . . ."[54]

As already indicated, Dewey saw that teaching and teachers played a central role in Soviet society. Not surprisingly, it pleased the leader of America's educationists to believe that the prominent role of the Soviet-style "educators" was to "liberate" the people of that revolutionary country.[55] He specifically noted "the added dignity"[56] that teachers have in the USSR because of their part in directing the social course of their society. This, he remarked, was something "an educator from a bourgeois country may well envy."[57] (The apparent centrality and social power of their counterparts did appeal to visiting American librarians.) Dewey also happily announced that intellectuals were an integral part of all endeavors. In other countries, he believed, sincere intellectuals *had* to be primarily critical of their societies.[58] He did not elaborate here, but one can assume that it was because he deemed the capitalist countries to be essentially flawed.

Dewey was aware of some of the brutalities of the Communist system but consistently downplayed their scope and significance:

> In spite of secret police, inquistions, arrests and deportations of *Nepmen* and *Kulaks*, exiling of party [*sic*] opponents—including divergent elements in the [Communist] party [*sic*]—life for the masses goes on with regularity, safety, and decorum.[59]

The mass of people were happy, he reported, and it was this that made the country stable, not "espionage and police restriction, however excessive the latter may be."[60] He did not elaborate.

The one thing about the Soviet Union that did seem to truly disturb Dewey, although he did not spend much time discussing it, was the Communists' assertion that violent class warfare and world revolution were a necessity. However, he was confident that their zeal for inciting civil wars abroad would disappear if there were free intercourse with the rest of the world: this would convince them that other countries were not their enemies. Thus, Dewey again deftly shifted the onus for the USSR's belligerent philosophy and behavior onto its targets, particularly the United States and Britain.[61]

Apparently alluding to the lack of diplomatic relations between the United States and the Soviet Union, and to negative reports in the West about the Communist country, Dewey declared that he deeply regretted

> those artificial barriers and that barricade of false reports that now isolates American teachers from that educational system in which our professed progressive democratic ideas are most completely embodied, and from which accordingly we might, if we would, learn much more than from the system of any other country.[62]

Visitors from the United States, he said, could only feel "humiliated"[63] on seeing how progressive educational ideas and practices first developed in America have been incorporated more thoroughly into the Soviet educational system than into their own. As for the alleged "artificial barriers," Dewey seemed to take for granted the fact that the US government did not impede the travel of Americans to the USSR, or commerce between the nations, despite its refusal to formally recognize the Communist regime committed to international revolution.

As already indicated, Dewey's benightedness when it came to the Soviet Union was manifest throughout this work. He wrote of a "free and democratically conducted coöperative movement"[64] while, in reality, collectivization was imposed through widespread bloodshed. Similarly, he claimed that there was religious freedom and a "scrupulous regard for cultural independence"[65] when, in truth, there were stringent anti-religious measures and determined efforts by the Russians to dominate, and eventually Russify, the national groups within their empire. Dewey went so far as to say that Soviet institutions, unlike those of Western countries, were free of racial prejudice.[66]

Given the popularity of Dewey's pedagogical writings among Soviet educators, it is not startling that he, along with some others, met with Krupskaya. He said that because of her high-ranking position, he was surprised that the views she expressed on education were "distinctly maternal, almost housewifely."[67] This seemed to please him.

Strangely, Dewey's book was not reviewed by any American journals of education. However, it was evaluated in the nation's major newspapers and intellectual periodicals. The most accurate of these critiques appeared in the *New York Herald-Tribune Books* section:

> It is a curious fact that the philosopher of pragmatism has a boyish enthusiasm for revolutions. He liked the schoolboy revolutionists of China, the Moslem revolutionists of Turkey, the Indian revolutionists of Mexico, and in Russia he hailed the psychological revolution. . . . Perhaps the book is more significant as a revelation of John Dewey than as a picture of Russia.[68]

In 1964 the volume was reprinted by Teachers College as the first volume in its "Comparative Education Studies" series. This project was dedicated to reissuing classics as well as to publishing new works. The series editor noted in his preface to Dewey's book that it was "little remembered."[69]

The reprint included a lengthy introduction by William W. Brickman, a professor of education at the University of Pennsylvania and a leading scholar in both international comparative education and the history of education. Brickman pointed out that Dewey's books had been well-known to the early Soviet educators, including Krupskaya, and that his ideas had influenced Soviet education a great deal. He also reported that the "progressive education" in the USSR that had excited Dewey so much was abruptly discarded in 1931.[70] While Brickman was critical of many elements of the book, he tended to downplay the extent and significance of Dewey's misapprehensions and greatly exaggerate his perspicacity. He came to this astonishing conclusion: "One senses that Dewey understood the essential nature of Soviet education. . . ."[71]

Five years after the publication of *Impressions of Soviet Russia*, Dewey wrote a strongly worded article, "Why I Am Not a Communist."[72] Gone were many of the fantasies about the USSR evident in the 1929 volume. He attacked "the implicit or explicit domination of the Communist party [*sic*] in every field of culture, the ruthless extermination of minority opinion in its own ranks, the verbal glorification of the mass and the actual cult of the infallibility of leadership."[73] He assailed the Party's suppression of civil liberties and its obstinate attempt to create a unified and uniform social entity comprised of members of the so-called "proletariat." He maintained that the official Communist theory of historical development could be avowed only by those who were either ignorant or disingenuous. Dewey now affirmed Americans' enduring belief in the importance of individuality, declaring that the Communist refusal to accept this fact verged on "political insanity."[74] Instead of extolling their supposed sincerity, he now found repugnant their lack of elementary honesty and commitment to fair play. He also condemned as devious their behavior in so-called "united front" campaigns with liberals in the West, and he characterized as odious their belief that their ends always justify their means. The rejection of his "progressive education" techniques within the USSR in 1931, and any relationship it may have borne to his reevaluation of Communism, were not mentioned in his proclamation.

As indicated, Dewey was now not only attacking the Soviet Communists, but those who followed their creed elsewhere in the world. He believed that the revolutions they desired in modern societies, like the United States, would only result in massive destruction. Moreover, their doctrine of inciting revolution in the West had elicited fears that successful upheavals would lead to dictatorial governments run from Moscow. This, he declared, had encouraged the rise of fascism in Italy and Germany and could do so in other countries. He concluded, "As an unalterable opponent of Fascism *in every form*, I cannot be a Communist."[75] (Italics mine)

In contrast to his complete rejection of fascism, Dewey emphasized that the Communism he opposed was solely that which was modeled on that of the Soviet Union.[76] He had still not abandoned all of his earlier visions: "I cannot blind myself . . . to the perceptible difference between communism with a small *c*, and Communism, official Communism, spelt with a capital letter."[77] In sum, Dewey was unable to discard his fantasies[78] of reshaping human beings to fit into collectivist societies, but he had given up his beliefs that they might well be achieved in the USSR and that the Soviet Union could serve as a model for other countries. American solutions would have to be found for American problems:

> Our problems flow from the oppressive exercise of power by financial over-lords and from the failure to introduce new forms of *democratic* control in industry and government consonant with the shift from individual to corporate economy.[79]

George S. Counts

George S. Counts was one of the most prominent educationists in twentieth-century America. Through his numerous publications, his professional position at the International Institute at Teachers College, Columbia University, and his leadership of the American Federation of Teachers, he strove to radically transform education so that it would, in turn, radically transform the United States. He has been called "The Father of Comparative Education."[80] Counts studied Russian and gained some proficiency in both reading and speaking the language. He visited the USSR for a total of ten months in 1927 and 1929. Throughout the twenties and thirties, he was a frequent writer and lecturer on the Soviet Union, Soviet education, and American civilization, and was widely considered an expert on these subjects.

In 1931, Houghton Mifflin published his translation of a Soviet propaganda book for young people on the virtues of Communism, specifically the economic and social planning entailed in the Five Year Plan begun in 1928.[81] Counts wrote an enthusiastic introduction to the work in which he expressed the hope that readers of all ages in the United States would adopt the vision expressed in the volume.[82] With the coming of the Great Depression, interest in centralized planning had increased greatly among Americans, so this book outsold all other non-fiction books but nine the year it was issued. *New Russia's Primer: The Story of the Five Year Plan* was, according to Alice Payne Hackett, "the first best seller to illustrate public interest in the Soviet régime."[83]

Counts' vision for American education was presented in a speech to the Progressive Education Association in February 1932, and it so rocked the conference that it actually altered its agenda.[84] In "Dare Progressive Education Be Progressive?" he charged that this education movement primarily reflected the interests of the upper-middle class, the background of most of the children in progressive schools. He declared that its educational theories and practices should be socially transformative, not child-centered, individualistic, or anarchistic.[85] In creating a new American social and political order, progressive education must become "less frightened than it is today at the bogeys of *imposition* and *indoctrination*."[86] There is little chance of the latter causing any harm, he asserted: "We may all rest assured that the younger generation in any society will be thoroughly imposed upon by its elders and by the culture into which it is born."[87]

The same month as this speech, Counts elaborated on these themes in addresses before the Department of Superintendence and the National Council of Education in Washington, D.C. The three presentations were then published together under the title, *Dare the School Build a New Social Order?*[88]

Counts' first book comparing the Soviet and American social and educational systems appeared in 1931 as *The Soviet Challenge to America*.[89] In it he declared that the essential differences between the USSR and the United States—and the factors that presented the *real* challenges to America—were the USSR's centralized planning and its educational system. He asserted that the gauntlet was *not* being thrown down by the Communist International, the Soviet secret police, or the Red Army, "as most of our citizens naively and timorously believe."[90] Americans, said Counts, were being distracted by those who em-phasized these peripheral agencies: "Only mischief can come from reports of Soviet Russia that keep attention centered on the most melodramatic and in all probability the more ephemeral aspects of the [Soviet] experiment. . . ."[91]

Counts believed that science and technology had created extraordinary new opportunities: "The dreams of mankind through the ages are at last capable of realization. . . ."[92] However, the leaders of America's educational, political, and economic affairs had failed to avail themselves of these new tools, had failed to coordinate their efforts, and had failed to engage in social planning. As a result, our civilization faced collapse.[93]

Counts applauded the Soviets for what he considered to be their obvious competence, honesty, dedication, passion, courage, and heroism.[94] Less certain, he said, was whether their view of human nature and history were accurate. However, the answer to this crucial question was apparently of no great significance to Counts because he believed that Soviet achievements were already great and that the Communists had the capacity to learn from their experiences.[95] He was enthusiastic about the attempt in the USSR to create a collective society: "Such an ideal state has been the dream of poets and prophets through the centuries. . . ."[96] What would come of this effort, "only time can answer."[97]

America compared poorly with the Soviet Union in Counts' eyes. He was unimpressed with the political freedoms in the United States, questioning the value of political elections in a capitalist country where some people were rich while others were poor. In contrast, he was captivated by the social and economic equality the Communists appeared to stress.[98] He went so far as to claim that in the Soviet Union, unlike the United States, there was racial and ethnic equality.[99] Counts even preferred Soviet patriotism: it was part of everyday life while in America it was militaristic.[100] Tellingly, he almost completely ignored the officially authorized brutalities and terror in the USSR, which vitiated any pretenses of a just or moral society.[101]

Counts' disgust with America and the other highly developed Western countries was almost total, and his admiration for the Soviet Union equally unrestrained. While he challenged the leaders of America to boldly refashion and humanize their civilization (guided by what appears to be a simplistic rationalism),[102] he offered few specific suggestions. One does not get the impression that he thought such an undertaking would ever be initiated:

In the societies of the West in general, and in the United States of
America in particular the evolution of institutions proceeds for the
most part without plan or design, as a sort of by-product of the
selfish competition of individual groups, and enterprises, for
individual gain. In Russia, on the other hand, since the days of
1917, the Soviet government has sought to promote the rational and
orderly development of the entire social economy.[103]

He considered modern industrial society a "monster," with its
members either isolated from each other or at war. Such societies were
in moral chaos, having ethics that were antiquarian and irrelevant and
religions that avoided the realities of life. Their art existed only in
museums. He pronounced his final judgment: if industrial capitalism
could not meet people's spiritual needs, it should cease to exist.[104]

Counts again and again contrasted the capitalist democracies with
the Soviet Union, presenting a caricature of the former and an
idealization of the latter:

The revolutionary movement embraces much that is rich and
challenging in the best sense of the word. The idea of building a
new society along the lines developed by the Communists should
provide a genuine stimulus to the mind and liberate the energies of
millions. It is certainly no worse than the drive towards individual
success which permeates not only the schools but every department
of culture in the United States. If one were to compare the
disciplined effort of the Soviets to industrialize the country, to
socialize agriculture, to abolish poverty, to banish disease, to
liquidate unemployment, to disseminate knowledge, and generally to
raise the material and spiritual level of the masses, with the selfish
scramble for wealth and privilege, the cruel disregard of the less
sensational forms of human suffering, the relative absence of a sense
of social responsibility, the reluctance to come honestly to grips with
the major problems of the time, and the apparent decay of the
political, ethical, and religious life in America, one would find small
grounds for complacency.[105]

Counts believed in the efficacy of revolution in all conceivable
areas: philosophy, social organization, education, and so forth. Thus,
he maintained that in the USSR, "new principles of right and wrong are
being forged."[106] He urged that *no* educational theory, such as those
advocating freedom, be held true everywhere or for all time.[107]

Moreover, he believed that "The *new man* is already appearing on the broad steppes of ancient Russia."[108]

Counts not only consistently defended Soviet censorship and propaganda activities but considered them virtuous activities that proved Communist society superior to that of the degenerate West. True, he admitted, some leaders had been arrested for not adhering closely to the Party line, but he claimed that the majority of the population is comprised of young Communists who have almost complete freedom of speech.[109] While Soviet movies are full of propaganda, at least they have meaning, unlike those produced in Hollywood.[110] He also declared the massive Soviet programs of indoctrination to be entirely understandable and acceptable because the Communists believe strongly in their causes. In contrast, people in the West are skeptical and disillusioned and hold their faiths—like democracy and Christianity—lightly. Moreover, he maintained that Western objections to Soviet propaganda and educational manipulation do not stem from any authentic ideals but arise solely because the ideas being promoted are Communist ones.[111]

Counts continued: The Soviet devotion to social justice and the common good for all people throughout the world does often lead to the censorship of quality art and the promotion of crude cultural products. However, the latter are "authentic and vital."[112] (Moreover, underlying even "the excesses and the imbecilities"[113] of Communist programs there is a great ideal which may in time harmonize art, science, and philosophy. The world should pay close attention.) It is inevitable and acceptable that Communist idealism should lead to censorship and repression:

> Whatever may be said on the other side concerning the regimentation of opinion and the restriction of individual freedom, there exist in Soviet Russia today an idealism and a driving passion for human betterment which contrast strangely with the widespread cynicism of the United States. It is only natural that this idealism and this passion should sweep through the schools as well as through the rest of the social order.[114]

Counts preferred the Communist concept of freedom in education to that in American "progressive education." He concurred with the Soviets, who said that the latter consisted largely of egotistical liberty for the privileged.[115]

Not surprisingly, Counts pronounced the progress made in Soviet education "stupendous."[116]   As with other admiring visitors to the USSR, he was pleased by the central role played by educators in the society.[117]

Counts paid little attention to the libraries in the Soviet Union except to state that a large number had been created since the Revolution and great increases were expected to ensue from Stalin's Five Year Plan.[118] He noted that his investigations for his book were "greatly aided by Mrs. N. K. Krupskaia, Head of the Department of Political Education in Moscow."[119]

Counts' views of the United States and the Soviet Union were remarkable in their inaccuracy. The so-called "Father of Comparative Education" credulously believed that the despotism he was so willing to accept throughout the world was creating a "new man."   He gratuitously discounted the significance of the Communist International, the secret police, and all other instruments of Soviet global intrigue and domestic suppression while wantonly deriding the American public as ignorant and cowardly for fearing these agencies. Counts considered American civilization bankrupt—morally, spiritually, and ideationally—when in fact it was he himself who had lost his reason and moral compass.

In the late 1930's Counts became anti-Soviet. The reason for this turnaround is not clear, but it could well have been due to his position as president of the politically-oriented union, the American Federation of Teachers. As head of the second largest teacher's organization in the United States, he found that he had to fight off a major effort by Soviet-directed American Communists to seize control of it. He now declared that the USSR had been, from its very inception, a totalitarian country. He believed, however, that this was due to a Russian perversion of its Communist ideology, rather than to something inherent in this philosophy. The vision of Communism, he asserted, was still of value; in this regard it was distinct from fascism. He feared greatly that democracy—particularly American democracy— would not survive these two threats to its existence.[120]

After World War II and throughout the 1950's, Counts was very liberal on domestic issues. However, most of his numerous writings during these years dealt with the serious challenge posed by the Soviet

Union and Soviet education. He now focused on the fact that they were totalitarian, anti-Western, and extremely dangerous.[121]

Thomas Woody

The most comprehensive American study of Soviet education in this period was Thomas Woody's *New Minds: New Men? The Emergence of the Soviet Citizen*. This five hundred page book was published in New York by Macmillan in 1932. Woody, a professor of education at the University of Pennsylvania, had already written several scholarly volumes on the history of education in the United States and Europe. He had taken an early interest in the Soviet Union, providing humanitarian assistance there for five months in 1918 under the auspices of the YMCA. He returned for three months in 1928. *New Minds: New Men?* was informed by firsthand contact with Soviet educators and a great deal of background reading on the USSR, including works in Russian.

In this book, Woody appears to have striven for a middle-ground between the supporters and the critics of the USSR. However, he failed to describe the negative aspects of Communist rule with the same verve that he reported what he considered positive. It is particularly significant that he did not even mention the widespread terror and murder that were an integral part of Communist governance.

A few years earlier, Woody had written articles in education periodicals about the USSR and Soviet education, based largely on his enthusiastic journal entries made during his 1918 and 1928 visits. These publications were paeans to that country. He stressed what he believed to be the high quality of Soviet life, while dismissing as fabrications the negative reports reaching the West. Moreover, he frequently compared the USSR with the USA: the former was *always* judged to be superior. Woody did briefly mention the propaganda in the Soviet Union, the illegality of anti-Communist activities, and the apparent omnipresence of the secret police, but—incredibly—these did not seem significant to him.[122]

Woody maintained that the indoctrination carried out by Soviet schools and libraries was no different from that implemented in all countries of the West, except that in the latter the practice was frequently not acknowledged. He went to some lengths to impress upon his readers that it was not the Communists who invented such practices but rather Western societies; he even traced the idea back to ancient Greek philosophy. The Soviets, he asserted, were mere imitators in this area. Significantly, his article on this subject was titled, "Political Education in Russia," not "Political Propaganda [or Indoctrination] in Russia." [123]

Woody made clear his central views concerning the primary goal of education in the United States and other Western countries in a 1932 radio broadcast made under the auspices of the Women's International League for Peace and Freedom. (At the time, WILPF was an internationalist, pacifist organization that often cooperated with Communist Party enterprises.) His presentation was later published in *Educational Outlook*, a periodical issued by his School of Education. In it, he asserted that social change *can* be controlled: to succeed, it need only be well-planned and in accord with new, visionary ideas.[124] As proof of this thesis, he declared that "Soviet Russia has succeeded, to a marked degree, in forming a new mind during the past fifteen years."[125] The specific vision he advocated for Western countries stressed internationalism and a "world society." The instruments for accomplishing this—which, as in the USSR, necessitated the creation of a "new mind"—would be the educational institutions. The goals were obvious, he said, because commerce and communication had already become international.[126] More importantly, declared Woody, nationalism, which currently held sway, was nothing more than savage, infantile, provincial, and dangerous.[127]

I. L. Kandel

I. L. Kandel is far more worthy than Counts of the honorific, "Father of Comparative Education." A colleague of Dewey and Counts at Teachers College, he was an Associate at its International Institute and edited the Institute's *Educational Yearbook* from its inception in 1924. His landmark book, *Comparative Education*, was published nine years later. This nine hundred page work attempted to define the scope and method of the field and compare the educational systems of England, France, Germany, Italy, the USSR, and the United States.[128] It was one of a half-dozen volumes he wrote on international and comparative education by 1945.

Like the other educationists discussed above—Dewey, Counts, and Woody—Kandel yearned for some overarching, integrating social purpose with which to link the American educational system, but he was far more willing to accept the United States and its schools as they were. Moreover, he had far fewer illusions about the Soviet Union and its educational institutions. In addition, he was able to view Italian-style fascism as being quite distinct from Soviet Communism and much less ruthless and destructive in its goals and methods.[129] In his studies, Kandel tended to keep a constant eye on the facts, unlike the other professors of education considered here, who frequently indulged themselves by basing their sweeping theories and conclusions on untested and untempered hypotheses, perceptions, and enthusiasms.

Carleton Washburne

Carleton Washburne was an influential professor of education and educational administrator who spent much of his career as the superintendent of schools in Winnetka, Illinois. His educational experiments, surveys, and books were well known. An active member of the Progressive Education Association who believed that American education, capitalism, and government needed change, he opposed George S. Counts' early ideas as utopian and his tactics as counterproductive.[130]

Washburne went to the USSR to study its educational system in 1927 and returned in 1931 as part of a Rosenwald Fund-sponsored tour of eleven countries in Europe, the Middle East, and Asia.[131] He compared what he saw to the situation in the United States, and his investigation was published in 1932 by John Day as *Remakers of Mankind*. Like many of his contemporaries in his profession, he believed that education has the potential to reshape human beings and the course of history,[132] which accounts for the title of the book.

Washburne understood that the Communist Party dominated the Soviet state. Nevertheless, he remarked:

> The impression often given by Russia's critics that a handful of communists are forcing their way against the will of a vast, stifled majority is, I believe, false. I think most impartial observers will agree that the party [*sic*] has the whole-hearted support of most of

the workers and either the support or the passive acceptance of a majority of peasants.[133]

Like so many other political tourists, he believed that the USSR considered itself "in active warfare against all capitalistic forces"[134] and that this excused many of its apparent excesses.   After all, said Washburne, Americans were similarly irrational in their hatreds during World War I. This was a false analogy. It was the Soviets who had declared and maintained their imperialist war. Americans had been reluctantly forced by aggressive nations into the Great War in an effort to protect its citizens and national honor—and, hopefully, "make the world safe for democracy" and "end all wars."[135]   At one level, Washburne understood this.[136]

Washburne saw the limitations on free speech in Soviet schools but, while he did not like them, he strove mightily to "understand" and excuse them.   They were analogous, he claimed, to limitations in American schools on discussing certain subjects, e.g., whether the United States should again become a British colony.[137] And while he thought that Communist education contained too much indoctrination, social engineering, and faith in positivistic materialism, he marveled at its certainty of aims and thoroughgoing efforts.   In the end, Washburne's awe of the "remakers of mankind" won him over: he concluded that ". . . as an example of what can be done in recreating human society through organized, well thought-out education toward a definitely envisaged goal, Russia is an inspiring example to the rest of the world."[138]

Journalists

Despite the efforts of the Communists to control the news coming out of their new state, some journalistic accounts of the first years of the regime were accurate, particularly those of Isaac Don Levine and others who wrote for the *New York Tribune*.[139] The energetic *Chicago Tribune* reporters there also contributed to the sound knowledge available in the West.[140] This newspaper was devoted to democratic principles and was thus also among the earliest and most accurate critics of the fascist regimes that later came to power in Italy and Germany.   (The work of other high-quality journalists has been described in chapter two.)

New York Times news stories of Lenin's October putsch and its aftermath were generally highly critical of the Bolsheviks but were filled with factual errors. Regrettably, an analytical exposé of the latter by Walter Lippmann and Charles Merz in the *New Republic*[141] was used for many years by supporters of the USSR, like Jerome Davis of Yale University, to indicate that all negative reports about that country were not based on solid evidence. Over the next two decades, the *Times'* coverage remained full of significant factual errors but was now generally supportive of the Soviet government, of Lenin, and of Stalin. This pro-Communist propaganda came primarily from the pen of its longtime correspondent, Walter Duranty. Unfortunately, Lippmann and Merz were never moved to analyze *his* reports, but many people knew of his unprofessional dissimulation. Apparently, this did not include those at Columbia University and its School of Journalism who awarded Duranty a Pulitzer Prize in 1932 for his coverage of the Soviet Union. This was the very time that this correspondent was covering up the fact that millions were being murdered in Stalin's forced collectivization of farms. In contrast, Malcolm Muggeridge reported the facts accurately back to his paper, the *Manchester Guardian*. The *Times* finally faced the facts about Duranty and quietly dismissed him in 1940.[142] It has never publicly repudiated his work.

Many of the pro-Soviet correspondents from the time of the Revolution through the 1930's also wrote many widely read books and magazine articles about the USSR. This was true of Duranty (who, in addition, co-authored the entries about the Soviet Union in the *Encyclopaedia Britannica* and the *Encyclopedia Americana* in the 1930's), Louis Fischer of the *Nation*, Albert Rhys Williams of the *New York Evening Post*, Maurice Hindus of *Century Magazine* and other periodicals, and Bessie Beatty of the *San Francisco Bulletin*. Highly influential for decades was the pro-Bolshevik book *Ten Days that Shook the World*, by John Reed, journalist and organizer of the Communist Labor Party, the forerunner of the Communist Party of the United States. First published in America in 1919, subsequent editions contained introductions by Lenin and Krupskaya attesting to its veracity. However, Krupskaya, presumably under pressure from Stalin, publicly criticized the work in December 1924 for containing some 'legends and inaccuracies.'[143]

The Evolution of British, European, and American Intellectuals' Attitudes towards Communism

The Soviet Union and Communism were attractive to many leading British intellectuals, particularly in the 1930's. Among the most prominent spokesmen for the cause were Sidney and Beatrice Webb, John Strachey, Harold J. Laski, J. B. S. Haldane, J. D. Bernal, Julian Huxley, V. Gordon Childe, W. H. Auden, Eric Hobsbawm, Christopher Isherwood, A. L. Morton, and Louis McNiece. Some enthusiasts rejected Communism by the beginning of World War II.[144]

One should not be surprised that twentieth century France, a fertile breeding ground for collaborators, produced a great number of prominent intellectuals and cultural figures whose highest devotion was to the Soviet Union and Communism. Louis Aragon, Henri Barbusse, Romain Rolland, and Jean-Richard Bloch remained engagé to their deaths. Some who were devoted Communists at the beginning of the period under consideration here renounced it by the late 1930's; André Gide and André Malraux were the most prominent of this latter group.[145] Albert Camus did not turn away from Communism until the 1940's, and, like the others mentioned here, he was known and read internationally. As Harry Karetzky once quipped, "Camus was famous. Camus was too."[146]

Throughout most of the thirties and forties, the small number of anti-Communist liberal intellectuals in America and Europe were barely heard from because the intellectual agencies of communication were, in the words of Peter Coleman, controlled by "the Communists and their fellow-travellers."[147] He has described the situation thusly:

> There was only one established magazine, *Partisan Review* in New York, that reflected their experience. Some of the writers among them found it hard to be published at all. When they managed to be published, contemptuous reviews of their books often minimized their sales. This was the period when Max Eastman's *Artists in Uniform* sold a total of five hundred copies; when George Orwell's publisher, Victor Gollancz, refused to look at the anti-Communist *Homage to Catalonia* (and when Fredric Warburg published it, it sold a mere seven hundred copies); when Orwell's *Animal Farm* was turned down by several London publishers; when Malcolm

Muggeridge, quarantined for writing *Winter in Moscow*, could barely earn a living in England and had to find work in India; when Boris Souvarine had difficulty finding a publisher for his now classic biography *Stalin*; when the French translator of Koestler's *Darkness at Noon* found it prudent to withdraw his first name and then his pseudonym from the translation; and when Hannah Arendt could not find a French publisher for her *Origins of Totalitarianism*. "An anti-Communist is a rat," said Jean-Paul Sartre, reflecting a general view. Anti-Communism, said Thomas Mann, is "the basic stupidity" (*die Grundthorheit*) of the twentieth century.[148]

At the end of the 1940's, more liberals, primarily in America, became vocal in their opposition to the USSR. The most notable of these was Arthur Schlesinger, Jr.[149] Unlike Conservative Anti-Communists, many proudly admitted to being anti-capitalist and anti-religious, particularly anti-Catholic.[150] The hostility towards religion was most blatant among those like Dwight Macdonald. It is significant that *The God that Failed*, the classic 1949 compilation of works by intellectuals who had forsaken Communism, contained an introduction by its British editor, Richard Crossman, that included traditional anti-Catholic canards.[151] While anti-Communism increased somewhat in the postwar years, anti-Americanism remained *de rigueur* among most intellectuals in England, France, Latin America, and elsewhere in the world.[152] This hurt the anti-Communist cause.

Conclusion

American librarians and their colleagues in other Western democracies were working within societies where many of the cultural and intellectual leaders thought positively about the USSR and Communism. There was also a failure of many liberals to declare their opposition to Soviet totalitarianism. These factors certainly influenced librarians' views about the Soviet Union and must be considered one reason that almost all of these American professionals who took an interest in Communist libraries thought well of them. Other likely explanations are noted later in this work.

As more information comes to the fore—partly as a result of greater research efforts, the opening of archives in Russia, and the release of formerly classified material in the United States—there is even more evidence than before of the widespread Soviet manipulation of Western cultural figures. The information and insights that strongly committed anti-Communists had been providing since the Bolshevik coup have again been reaffirmed and proven correct beyond any rational doubt. Whether it was organizing propagandistic tours of the Soviet Union, undermining Americans' faith in their own institutions, or whipping up worldwide support for Sacco and Vanzetti, Moscow's agents were very frequently directing the efforts. Willi Münzenberg, the mastermind behind many of these activites, referred to those he finessed as "innocents."[153] Lenin thought Western intellectuals were stupid and highly gullible. And he was dedicated to making use of these "deaf mutes,"[154] as he called them.

NOTES

1. This overview owes much to Peter G. Filene, *Americans and the Soviet Experiment, 1917-1933* (Cambridge: Harvard University Press, 1967).

2. The strategy and its implementation are described well in Sylvia R. Margulies, *The Pilgrimage to Russia: The Soviet Union and the Treatment of Foreigners, 1924-1937* (Madison: University of Wisconsin Press, 1968).

3. Eugene Lyons, *The Red Decade*, with new preface (New Rochelle, NY: Arlington House, 1970; originally published: Bobbs-Merrill, 1941), particularly pp. 128-33.

4. Lyons, *The Red Decade*. In his preface to the 1970 reprint of his book, Lyons declared that his volume may well have *understated* the influence of Communism on intellectuals and cultural leaders. Lyons had been an admirer of the Soviet Union and Communism for years and served in the USSR as a correspondent for United Press from 1928 to 1934. His experiences there changed his political views.

5. See, for example, the standard work by Daniel Aaron, *Writers on the Left: Episodes in American Literary Communism* (New York: Harcourt, Brace & World, 1961; reprinted: New York: Octagon Books, 1979); particularly his absurd conclusion, pp. 395-96. This study was sponsored by the Fund for the Republic, which consistently worked to downplay the dangers of Communism, past and present. Similar is the well known treatment by David Caute, *The*

Fellow-Travellers: A Postscript to the Enlightenment (New York: Macmillan, 1973).

6. See Lyons, *The Red Decade*, pp. 355-64.

7. Frank A. Warren, "Preface to the Morningside Edition," *Liberals and Communism: The "Red Decade" Revisited* (New York: Columbia University Press, 1993), pp. xi-xxiii; originally published by Indiana University Press, 1966.

8. Roger N. Baldwin, *Liberty under the Soviets* (New York: Vanguard Press, 1927).

9. On Davis' political proclivities, see Evan Stark, "Sociology," in *Encyclopedia of the American Left*, ed. by Buhle, Buhle, and Georgakas (Urbana and Chicago: University of Illinois Press, 1992; originally published: New York: Garland, 1990), p. 732. For a list and description of the scores of Front organizations he belonged to, see: US House of Representatives Special Committee on Un-American Activities, *Investigation of Un-American Propaganda Activities in the United States: Appendix, Part IX: Communist Front Organizations*, 3 vols. (Washington, DC: GPO, 1944).

10. One work in the series was Avrahm Yarmolinsky's *The Jews and National Minorities in Russia.* He was cautiously hopeful about the fate of Jews in the USSR, a theme that does not quite jibe with those of his other writings about the Soviet Union.

The logo of Vanguard Press depicted a worker with his hammer at rest while reading a book. The inside covers of its books bore the motto, "The vanguard of thought for the vanguard of humanity."

11. Frank A. Warren, *Liberals and Communism*, pp. 63-64.

12. Roger N. Baldwin, *Liberty under the Soviets*, p. 2.

13. Ibid., p. 3.

14. It was clear even in these early years that the rulers of the Soviet Union would always feel "threatened" unless the entire world were under their direct or indirect control. They avidly cultivated a siege mentality among the general populace to make it more pliable and willing to fight non-Communist nations.

15. For brief overviews of the history of comparative education up to this period, see: I. L. Kandell, "Comparative Education," in *Educating for Democracy*, ed. by John I. Cohn and Robert M. W. Travers (London: Macmillan, 1939; reprinted: Freeport, NY: Books for Libraries, 1970), pp. 422-42; and I. L. Kandel, *Comparative Education* (Boston: Houghton Mifflin, 1933), pp. xv-xxvi, 868-72.

16. Lucy L. W. Wilson, *The New Schools of New Russia* (New York: Vanguard Press, 1928), p. xiv.

17. Ibid., p. 1.

18. Ibid., p. 40.

19. Ibid., pp. 21-23.

20. John Dewey, *Impressions of Soviet Russia and the Revolutionary World—Mexico, China, Turkey* (New York: New Republic, 1929).

21. See Frank A. Warren, *Liberals and Communism*, pp. 63-64; and Lewis S. Feuer, "American Travelers to the Soviet Union, 1917-1932: The Formation of a Component of New Deal Ideology," *American Quarterly* 14 (Summer 1962): 122.

22. Dewey, *Impressions of Soviet Russia*, pp. 7-9.

23. Ibid., p. 30.

24. Ibid., p. 58.

25. Ibid., p. 5. On Anatole France's politics, see David Caute, *Communism and the French Intellectuals, 1914-1960* (New York: Macmillan, 1964), pp. 40, 42n, 26, 36, 75-77, 82.

26. Dewey, *Impressions of Soviet Russia*, p. 31.

27. Ibid., p. 125.

28. Ibid., pp. 47-51. It should be noted that a full-page ad for another New Republic book which appeared at the end of Dewey's work (p. [273]) contained a very positive blurb by him for Albert Rhys Williams' *The Russian Land* (New York: New Republic, 1927). Williams had gone to Europe as a journalist but ended up working for the new Soviet government for several years and was instrumental in Soviet military and foreign affairs. He "was one of the best-known sympathizers of Lenin's Bolshevik ideology." (David Shavit, "Albert Rhys Williams," *United States Relations with Russia and the Soviet Union: A Historical Dictionary* [Westport, CT, and London: Greenwood Press, 1993], p. 197.) Philip Grierson, who was not the slightest bit anti-Soviet, described *The Russian Land* as "Sketches of life since the Revolution, by an American Left-Wing sympathizer." (Grierson, *Books on Soviet Russia, 1917-1942: A Bibliography and a Guide to Reading* [London: Methuen, 1943; reprint: Twickenham: Anthony C. Hall, 1969], p. 81.) *The Russian Land* was one of several such books by Williams, who was a frequent lecturer in the United States.

29. Dewey, *Impressions of Soviet Russia*, p. 4.

30. Ibid., p. 14. Similarly, on page six he had underscored his perception of "courage, energy, and confidence."

31. Ibid., pp. 6-9, 14.

32. Ibid., p. 8.

33. Ibid., p. 39.

34. Ibid., p. 57.

35. Ibid., p. 61.

36. Ibid., p. 113.

37. Ibid., pp. 84, 88.

38. Ibid., p. 84.

39. Ibid., p. 86.

40. Ibid.

41. Ibid., pp. 85-88.

42. Ibid., p. 53.

43. Ibid., pp. 81-82.

44. Ibid., p. 54.

45. Ibid.

46. Ibid.

47. Ibid., p. 32.

48. Ibid., pp. 128-29. It is relevant to the subject of propaganda that the front cover and several pages of Dewey's volume had drawings taken from Soviet school books. (See "Publishers' Note," Dewey, *Impressions of Soviet Russia*, p. [iii].) Those on the cover depicted people parading with banners while most of those inside were extremely cheerful, showing children skiing, jumping rope, and planting. These were misleading. It would have been more accurate to reproduce the numerous idealized depictions in children's books of Lenin, Stalin, and factories, as well as the ever-present charts showing the goals of Stalin's Five Year Plan (1928-1933).

49. Dewey, *Impressions of Soviet Russia*, p. 78.

50. Ibid., pp. 117, 119-20.

51. Ibid., p. 32.

52. Ibid., pp. 114-16, 105-6.

53. Ibid., p. 67.

54. Ibid.

55. Ibid., p. 127.

56. Ibid., p. 100.

57. Ibid.

58. Ibid., p. 121.

59. Ibid., p. 24. *Nepmen* were those who had engaged in business under the recently discarded New Economic Plan (NEP) for development which had lasted from 1921 until 1928. *Kulaks* were peasants who owned their own land and were better off than the average agricultural toiler.

60. Ibid., p. 68.

61. Ibid., pp. 130-32. The United States did not recognize the Soviet government until Franklin Roosevelt became president in 1933, but there was a good deal of business between the two countries nevertheless. Recognition from Great Britain had come in 1924, but relations were not always good and were punctuated by British trade embargoes imposed in retaliation for Soviet attempts to foment revolution in that country.

62. Ibid., pp. 107-8.

63. Ibid., p. 107.

64. Ibid., p. 21.

65. Ibid., p. 96.

66. Ibid., p. 97.

67. Ibid., p. 112. See also p. 111.

68. "Young Dewey," *New York Herald-Tribune Books* (March 31, 1929): 10.

69. George Z. F. Bereday, "Series Preface," *John Dewey's Impressions of Soviet Russia and the Revolutionary World—Mexico, China, Turkey*, intro. by William W. Brickman (New York: Teachers College, Columbia University, 1964; includes reprint of *Impressions of Soviet Russia* by Dewey [1929],) p. [ix]. Parts of the original book had been reprinted in 1929 in John Dewey, *Characters and Events*, vol. 1 (New York: Holt), pp. 378-431.

70. William W. Brickman, "Introduction," *John Dewey's Impressions of Soviet Russia*, by Dewey, pp. 17-19.

71. Ibid., p. 31.

72. John Dewey, "Why I Am Not a Communist," *The Modern Monthly* 8 (April 1934): 135-37. John Tebbel and Mary Ellen Zuckerman have characterized *Modern Monthly* as "an unorthodox radical magazine . . . which opposed the [Communist] party [sic]." It provided serious competition for the *New Masses*, which generally did support the Party, particularly in its early years. (Tebbel and Zuckerman, *The Magazine in America, 1741-1990* [New York and Oxford: Oxford University Press, 1991], p. 211.)

73. Dewey, "Why I Am Not a Communist," p. 135.

74. Ibid., p. 136.

75. Ibid., p. 137.

76. Ibid., p. 135.

77. Ibid., p. 137.

78. The disagreements between Dewey and another liberal philosopher, Morris R. Cohen, illuminate the sources of some of Dewey's basic philosophical and political errors and illusions. (See Leonora Cohen Rosenfield, *Portrait of a Philosopher: Morris R. Cohen in Life and Letters* [New York: Harcourt, Brace, & World, 1962], pp. 169-85.)

79. Dewey, "Why I Am Not a Communist," p. 136.

80. On this honorific, see Lawrence J. Dennis and William Edward Eaton, eds., *George S. Counts: Educator for a New Age* (Carbondale and Edwardsville, IL: Southern Illinois University Press, 1980; London and Amsterdam: Feffer & Simons), p. 16. Dennis and Eaton provide a general overview and evaluation of his career on pp. 1-18.

81. M. Illin, *New Russia's Primer: The Story of the Five Year Plan*, trans. by George S. Counts and Nucia P. Lodge (Boston and New York: Houghton Mifflin, 1931).

82. See Counts, "Word to the American Reader," ibid., pp. v-x.

83. Alice Payne Hackett, *Seventy Years of Best Sellers, 1895-1965* (New York and London: Bowker, 1967), p. 144.

84. Lawrence A. Cremin, *The Transformation of the School: Progressivism in American Education, 1876-1957* (New York: Knopf, 1969), pp. 259-61. See pp. 261-66 for an estimation of its longer-term effect on the profession, as well as Robert L. Church and Michael W. Sedlak, *Education in the United States: An Interpretive History* (New York: The Free Press, 1976; London: Collier Macmillan), pp. 376-78.

85. George S. Counts, "Dare Progressive Education Be Progressive?" *Progressive Education* 9 (April 1932): 257-63.

86. Ibid., p. 259.

87. Ibid., p. 263.

88. George S. Counts, *Dare the School Build a New Social Order?* (New York: John Day, 1932). The titles of the other two speeches were "Education through Indoctrination" and "Freedom, Culture, Social Planning, and Leadership." The work was fifty-six pages long, twice the length of the typical "John Day Pamphlet." Some of the other authors in this important series were Rebecca West, Joseph Stalin, Walter Lippmann, Charles A. Beard, and Hendrik Van Loon.

89. George S. Counts, *The Soviet Challenge to America* (New York: John Day, 1931). This book was 372 pages in length.

90. Ibid., p. x.

91. Ibid. He also declared that the Soviet "anti-religious campaign . . . [was] generally misrepresented in the American press." (p. 293)

92. Ibid., p. ix.

93. Ibid., pp. ix, 11-13.

94. Ibid., p. 5, 11-13.

95. Ibid., p. 5.

96. Ibid., p. 25.

97. Ibid.

98. Ibid.

99. Ibid., pp. 27-28. He also believed that the Soviets were promoting the equality of women. (pp. 29-30)

100. Ibid., p. 314.

101. Counts did briefly mention "the severity and ruthlessness with which . . . conspiracies have been put down. . . ." (Ibid., p. 292)

102. Ibid., pp. 339, 11-13, 332.

103. Ibid., p. 7.

104. Ibid., p. 335.

105. Ibid., p. 329.

106. Ibid., p. 324.

107. Ibid.

108. Ibid., pp. 336-37.

109. Ibid., pp. 11-13, 73-75, 320, 314.

110. Ibid., pp. 73-74.

111. Ibid., pp. 323-28.

112. Ibid., p. 338.

113. Ibid., p. 338. See also p. 339.

114. Ibid., pp. 329-30.

115. Ibid., p. 336.

116. Ibid.

117. Ibid., p. 323.

118. Ibid., pp. 173, 281, 130-31.

119. Ibid., pp. xi-xii.

120. George S. Counts, *The Prospects of American Democracy* (New York: John Day, 1938), pp. 2-4, 143-49.

121. For example, see George S. Counts and Nucia Lodge, *The Country of the Blind: The Soviet System of Mind Control* (Boston: Houghton Mifflin, 1947) and Counts, assisted by Lodge, *The Challenge of Soviet Education* (New York: McGraw-Hill, 1957).

122. See these articles by Thomas Woody: "Ten Years Passed," [Parts I and II,] *Educational Outlook* 3 (Jan. 1929): 86-106; and "Ten Years Passed," [Part III,] *Educational Outlook* 3 (March 1929): 161-78.

123. Thomas Woody, "Political Education in Russia," *School and Society* 28 (Dec. 1, 1928): 665-73.

124. Thomas Woody, "International Versus Nationalistic Education," *Educational Outlook* 6 (March 1932): 149-50.

125. Ibid., p. 149.

126. Ibid., p. 152.

127. Ibid., pp. 151-52.

128. I. L. Kandel, *Comparative Education* (Boston: Houghton Mifflin, 1933). Born to English parents and having lived in Britain before immigrating to the United States and earning his doctorate at Columbia University, Isaac Leon Kandel tended to use the initials of his name, as was—and still is—common practice among academics in Britain.

129. For example, see I. L. Kandel, *Comparative Education*, pp. 64-76, 81.

130. See Carleton Washburne, *Remakers of Mankind* (New York: John Day, 1932), pp. 287-89; and Cremin, *The Transformation of the School*, pp. 262, 295-99, 382-83. Washburne's method stressed that each student should learn at his or her own pace.

131. Washburne studied the schools in Japan, China, India, Iraq, Syria, Egypt, Turkey, the USSR, Poland, France, and England.

132. Washburne, *Remakers of Mankind*, p. 2.

133. Ibid., p. 161.
134. Ibid., p. 160. See also p. 168.
135. Ibid., p. 160. On Americans' attitudes towards the Great War, see Joanne L. Karetzky, *The Mustering of Support for World War I by* The Ladies' Home Journal (Lewiston, NY, and Lampeter, Wales, UK: Edwin Mellen Press, 1997).
136. Washburne, *Remakers of Mankind,* p. 155.
137. Ibid., p. 169-70.
138. Ibid., p. 185.
139. See Levine's *Eyewitness to History,* pp. 32-38, 42-44. *The New York Tribune* was also a leader in cultural matters.
140. The owner of the *Chicago Tribune* understood that the events in that country were of monumental significance. See Lloyd Wendt, *Chicago Tribune: The Rise of a Great American Newspaper* (New York: Rand McNally, 1979), pp. 439-41, 472, 563-64, and 576. The *Tribune's* reports on widespread famine in the USSR encouraged the enormous relief efforts of Americans, led by Herbert Hoover, that saved millions from starvation.
141. Walter Lippmann and Charles Merz, "A Test of the News," *New Republic Supplement* (Aug. 4, 1920): 1-42; and Lippmann and Merz, "More News from the *Times,*" *New Republic* 23 (Aug. 11, 1920): 299-301. The authors of the study also criticized the newsmen's interpretations of the facts as being anti-Communist. Lippmann was then an editor of the *New Republic.* Interestingly, Merz was hired by the *New York Times* in 1931 and was befriended by Arthur Hays Sulzberger, who soon took over as publisher. Merz then became the paper's chief editorial writer. According to one historian of the newspaper, "Almost immediately, Merz and Sulzberger, who were about the same age, were liberal politically, and had much in common, became good friends." (Gay Talese, *The Kingdom and the Power* [New York and Cleveland: New American Library, 1969], p. 185.)
142. On Duranty, see: S. J. Taylor, *Stalin's Apologist: Walter Duranty, The New York Times's Man in Moscow* (New York and Oxford: Oxford University Press, 1990); Malcolm Muggeridge, *Chronicles of Wasted Time: An Autobiography* (Washington, DC: Regnery, n.d., pp. 254-58, 263, 271, 275; New York: William Morrow, 1973-74; originally published in two volumes: Chronicle I: *The Green Stick,* and Chronicle II: *The Infernal Grove*); and Gay Talese, *The Kingdom and the Power,* p. 438.
143. John Reed, *Ten Days that Shook the World,* foreword by V. I. Lenin, preface by N. K. Krupskaya, and new intro. by John Howard Lawson (New York: International Publishers, 1967). A 1960 edition with an illuminating introduction by Bertram D. Wolfe was issued by Vintage of New York. It lacks Krupskaya's introduction. On Krupskaya's shift, see Wolfe's note on page xlvi.

144. An excellent study of this subject is Neal Wood, *Communism and British Intellectuals* (New York: Columbia University Press, 1959). Malcolm Muggeridge's insights into this phenomenon are found throughout his memoirs, *Chronicles of Wasted Time.*

145. Gide's public repudiation of the Soviet Union created a furor when it was issued. See his *Return from the USSR*, trans. by Dorothy Bussy (New York: Alfred A. Knopf, 1937; originally published: *Retour de L'URSS* (Paris: Librairie Gallimard, 1936).

As with the studies of intellectuals in other countries during this period, many excuse, or defend, the allegiance to Communism. One of the most influential of these works has been David Caute, *Communism and the French Intellectuals, 1914-1960* (New York: Macmillan, 1964). An engaging account of the political involvements of French intellectuals is Herbert Lottman, *The Left Bank: Writers, Artists and Politics from the Popular Front to the Cold War* (Boston: Houghton Mifflin, 1982).

146. A widely published short story writer from the mid-thirties through the mid-fifties, Karetzky later worked in New York City's Office of the Mayor under John Lindsay, Abraham Beame, and Ed Koch.

147. Peter Coleman, *The Liberal Conspiracy: The Congress for Cultural Freedom and the Struggle for the Mind of Postwar Europe* (New York: The Free Press, 1989; London: Collier Macmillan), p. 7.

148. Ibid., pp. 7-8. The rejection of Communism by the *Partisan Review* editors and contributors is described in Terry A. Cooney, *The Rise of the New York Intellectuals: Partisan Review and its Circle, 1934-1945* (Madison, WI: University of Wisconsin Press, 1986).

149. Schlesinger's book, *The Vital Center*, provided a rallying point. See Arthur M. Schlesinger, Jr., *The Vital Center: The Politics of Freedom*, with a new intro. by Schlesinger (Boston: Houghton Mifflin, 1962; originally published 1949).

150. Peter Coleman, *The Liberal Conspiracy*, pp. 11-12.

151. Richard Crossman, "Introduction," in *The God that Failed* (New York: Bantam, 1965; first published 1949), pp. 2, 6-7. He declared in his introduction that a literary bent is "abnormal" in a Catholic and that Catholics are more willing than others to subject themselves to spiritual and political authoritarianism. He apparently believed that the British Protestant is the most individualistic of all people.

152. See Peter Coleman, *The Liberal Conspiracy*, pp. 72, 85, 142.

153. See Stephen Koch, *Double Lives: Spies and Writers in the Secret Soviet War of Ideas Against the West* (New York: Free Press, 1994). Willi Münzenberg directly or indirectly manipulated the activities of Lillian Hellman, Dorothy Parker, John Dos Passos, André Gide, and scores of others, as well as the course of numerous "protest movements."

154. Lenin had written:

From my own observations during my years as an emigre, I must say that the so-called educated strata in Western Europe and America are incapable of comprehending the present state of affairs, the real balance of power. Those elements should be regarded as deaf mutes and treated accordingly. . . . First, to soothe the fears of the deaf mutes, we must proclaim a separation . . . of our government . . . from the Party and Politburo and especially from the Comintern. We must declare that the latter entities are independent political organizations merely tolerated on Soviet soil. Mark my word, the deaf mutes will swallow it.

(As quoted in *Chekisty: A History of the KGB*, by John D. Dziak, foreword by Robert Conquest [Lexington, MA: Lexington Books/D. C. Heath, 1988], p. 45. See "Useful Idiots of the West," in *Safire's New Political Dictionary*, by William Safire [New York: Random House, 1993], pp. 837-38.)

5

AMERICAN LIBRARIANSHIP AND THE SOVIET UNION, 1940-1949

The World War II Years

During World War II, it was clear from the pronouncements of the library profession's leaders that they wanted the international cultural, book, and library programs begun before the war, and greatly augmented during it, to be increased after the end of hostilities. Flora Ludington, Harry Miller Lydenberg, Carl H. Milam, Archibald MacLeish, Luther Evans, and others made manifest their belief that such efforts should stress "international understanding" and American assistance, and not serve as instruments of propaganda or of the government's foreign diplomacy. It was equally clear that many in the State Department and most members of Congress expected such cultural activities to buttress America's foreign policy aims and security interests in addition to promoting intercultural communication.[1] These differences became more obvious after the end of the war.

American interest in, and aid to, Soviet librarianship continued during World War II. The Communist nation worked hard to maintain this, encourage the sympathy and goodwill of its wartime ally, and keep up the flow of donated and exchange books. American librarians, like the high-ranking officials of the US government, seemed to want to think well of their partner in arms. Ignored were the sage warnings of those who understood the Soviet Union best, like Max Eastman and Alexander Barmine, whose writings were readily available in *Reader's Digest*.[2]

M. I. Rudomino, Director of the State Central Library of Foreign Literature in Moscow, sent librarians overseas a bibliography on

English and American literature that her institition had prepared as a guide for Soviet readers. It was accompanied by a plea for much-wanted gifts in this area. She noted that a popular exhibit on US writers had been created in 1941 "during the most trying days for Moscow when the Hitlerites were almost at the very gates of our capital."[3] A librarian at the University of California forwarded her appeal to *Library Journal* along with his instructions on where to ship donated volumes. His communication[4] and Rudomino's were published under the rubric, "Russia Wants to Know Us." It should be pointed out that Rudomino's letter named five of the modern writers in America and Britain that she and her comrades had been working to bring to the attention of Soviet citizens: Jack London, Upton Sinclair, Theodore Dreiser, H. G. Wells, and George Bernard Shaw. American librarians in the 1940's were generally conversant with letters, so they should have known that these were all vehement critics of capitalist society and that all except London—who had died a year before the Revolution—had sometimes celebrated the USSR in their works. If Russia wanted to know us, as *Library Journal* claimed, it could not have done so through its libraries.

Photographs and news of an exhibit about US history at Moscow's Lenin Library in 1942 reached the pages of *Library Journal* via the Chief of the Division of Documents at the Library of Congress. He was impressed that such work took place "when the enemy was on the very threshold of Moscow."[5] The same issue of the periodical reprinted an article from the *Information Bulletin* distributed by the Soviet Embassy in Washington. Not surprisingly, it declared that the Lenin State Library and the Moscow Historical Library continued to function despite assaults by enemy ground and air forces.[6] (The reality was less dramatic: the German army had been stopped twenty to twenty-five miles from Moscow and the city suffered "virtually no war damage."[7]) Of course, the reader was reminded that the exchange of books with libraries of other countries was still being carried out. The author began the piece with the oleaginous statement that the Library of Congress was the only institution in the world with more holdings than the Lenin State Library, thereby flattering both countries. It is significant that Soviet declarations about the relative size of these two libraries changed after the Germans were defeated.

American Communists and Communist sympathizers also spread pro-Soviet propaganda through the library press. A laudatory article on "Soviet Libraries in the War" appeared in the May 1st (May Day) issue of *Library Journal*.[8] It was written by Ethel M. Takce, an Editorial Assistant at *Soviet Russia Today*, the official publication of the Friends of the Soviet Union and its successor, The National Council of American-Soviet Friendship. (The Friends had been headed by leading members of the Communist Party—such as William Z. Foster, Earl Browder, and Michael Gold—as well as those willing to ally themselves with them. Its name and nominal leadership were changed during the war to make it appear less threatening.)[9] The author described the pillage of numerous Soviet libraries by the Nazis and how the USSR's libraries continued to serve that nation. It declared that

> Since its inception, the aim of the Soviet government has been to achieve a great and expanding culture. Education for all, with everyone participating as creators and enjoyers, had been practically achieved. . . . More than anything else, the development of the libraries testifies that his [Lenin's] program has been realized.[10]

The reader was then subjected to the usual wonder stories of the Soviet Union's immense and active libraries.

The publication of this panegyric on Soviet libraries coincided with "Russia Book Week" in the United States, which began on May Day, 1944. Joseph E. Davies, U.S ambassador to the Soviet Union from 1936 to 1938 and a special emissary to that country during the war, declared that the future of the world depended on the nature of Soviet-American relations and that this essentially rested on what the people of these countries thought of each other. He declared, 'It is vital therefore that the truth should be known. There is no better source for truth than the public libraries of our country.'[11] He asserted that 'through their efforts in projecting this information program, libraries are contributing definitely to the cause for which our soldiers are fighting.'[12]

Toby Cole, Librarian of the American Russian Institute, described the New York library of this nationwide Communist organization in the pages of *Library Journal*.[13] Before coming to the Institute in 1942, Cole had worked for the Newark Board of Education Library helping to establish elementary school libraries. Like Ethel Takce, author of "Soviet Libraries in the War," she had studied in the accelerated Soviet Civilization program at Cornell University.

Cole declared fallacious the allegedly widespread American beliefs that it was difficult to find out the truth about the Soviet Union because of that country's secretiveness and that this very covertness should make Americans distrustful of it. Any lack of knowledge, she insisted, was due to the failure of America's educational institutions—including libraries—to gather and disseminate the necessary information. Her library, she declared, was the sole agency in the United States devoted entirely to the acquisition and distribution of the latest factual material on the USSR.

British Librarianship and the USSR

In the early 1940's, the primary contribution of British librarianship to the study of the Soviet Union was the bibliographic work of Philip Grierson. His 350 page volume, *Books on Soviet Russia, 1917-1942: A Bibliography and a Guide to Reading*,[14] was the first full-length English-language bibliography of its kind. Its potential usefulness was enhanced by its annotations, even though these tended to be supportive of the Communists. The work was updated by Grierson's articles in *The Slavonic and East European Review* until 1951. The original book was reprinted in 1969, which attests to its continued utility despite the existence of more evenhanded bibliographies by this time.

Grierson served as the library director at Gonville and Caius College, Cambridge, from 1944 until 1969, and president of the College, 1966-1976. He was a prominent scholar of numismatic history: most of the dozen or so volumes he wrote were about medieval or ancient coins. The bibliography was his sole book about the USSR.

The Postwar 1940's

Communist Propaganda

In November 1945, the American Russian Institute sponsored a one-day conference for librarians who dealt with Russian materials. A distorted account of the meeting appeared as an article by Toby Cole in *Library Journal.*[15]   Representatives from fifty establishments attended, ranging from the Hoover Institution to Communist-front organizations like the American-Soviet Science Society. Many associations like this "Science" Society had been established during the war and were affiliated with the National Council of American-Soviet Friendship. As already noted, the latter had replaced the more openly pro-Communist Friends of the Soviet Union. The National Council had stressed American-Soviet unity and friendship during the war, ostensibly to promote better understanding and friendly relations between the two countries in order to win the war and establish democracy and peace throughout the world. Like the American-Russian Institute, it was accurately described by a California State Senate Committee as being a "direct agent of the Soviet Union, engaged in traitorous activities under the orders of Stalin's consular service in the United States."[16]

In her article, Cole stressed the importance of international understanding based on the free exchange of information. The choice, she said, was between 'one world or none.'[17]   Two conference participants responded to her rendition in letters to *Library Journal.* Verner Clapp of the Library of Congress declared false the allegations made at the conference—and repeated in the article—that the US government was hindering the distribution of Soviet books to American libraries.[18]   Ralph R. Shaw, Librarian of the Department of Agriculture, was more vigorous in his protest, charging that both his own presentation, and the words and actions of other participants, had been misrepresented in Cole's work. He asserted that the major point they had made there was that while the USSR had unrestricted access to the same publications as American scholars, it had severe restrictions on the export of its scholarly, scientific, and technical literature.[19]

Objective Scholarship about Soviet Librarianship

The postwar era saw the beginnings of scholarly research on Soviet librarianship that produced a picture quite unlike the deluded ones of previous decades. In the second half of the 1940's, Nathalie Poliakoff Delougaz contributed three studies on Soviet librarianship to *Library Quarterly* that were among the most objective and revealing investigations done by a librarian to date. The first, published in 1945, gave an overview of Soviet librarianship from 1924 through 1940 based on an analysis of Soviet library periodicals. She was aware of the malignant political role of those who worked in libraries in Communist countries, but she nevertheless closed her work with the hope that Western countries could help rebuild Soviet librarianship materially while finding some inspiration in the enthusiastic zeal of the Russian librarian.[20] The second study analyzed the politically inspired changes made by Soviet librarians in the Universal Decimal classification, which had been based largely on Melvil Dewey's scheme.[21] The third, taken from her master's thesis at the University of Chicago's Graduate Library School, analyzed the trends in Soviet book publishing and compared them—not always favorably—with the situation in Czarist times.[22] Delougaz had been born in Leningrad but left Russia for France in 1922. Educated at the University of Paris, she came to the United States in 1942. She studied at the Graduate Library School while working as a cataloguer at the University of Chicago Library.

In a 1947 *Library Quarterly* article,[23] Arthur B. Berthold provided an insightful survey of Soviet library literature that emphasized the years since 1930. His shrewd reading of Soviet works resulted in a portrait of a field that had proven itself expert in gathering materials from abroad but which, in many other ways, was not highly developed. Moreover, he showed that it served a citizenry less interested in supposedly "educational" subjects than the Soviets liked to boast of.

Berthold had been born in Latvia in 1905 but educated in the United States. In 1939 he served as a delegate to the International Federation for Documentation Institute Conference in Zurich. He knew several European languages, including Russian, and used these, in conjunction with his bibliographical and research expertise, in his work for the OSS during World War II. He returned to government duty in 1948 at the State Department's library.

Unfortunately, this important scholarship had no impact on the leaders of American international librarianship.

Postwar International Librarianship: Its Philosophy and Organizations

The basic vision for American international librarianship put forth during World War II continued to develop along the same lines after the surrender of Germany and Japan.[24]

Ralph R. Shaw, a highly influential member of the profession, made it clear that he believed that international library relations were inextricably bound up with the increased involvement of the United States overseas.[25]   In 1946 he set the tone for American librarianship's enthusiastic and ambitious postwar approach to international librarianship with his hortatory article in the *American Library Association Bulletin*, "Wars Begin in the Minds of Men."[26]   Its title was taken from the preamble to the constitution of the United Nations Educational, Scientific, and Cultural Organization: "Since wars begin in the minds of men, it is in the minds of men that defences of peace must be constructed." Shaw proceeded to invoke the names and ideas of preeminent figures of American history and librarianship in an attempt to convince his readers to support Unesco. He asserted that leaders throughout history, like Thomas Jefferson, had understood that "international understanding is the surest road to peace"[27] and that this was the purpose of this UN agency. He reported that both Archibald MacLeish, former Librarian of Congress, and Luther Evans, his successor, had participated in its founding, as had numerous librarians from other countries.   The implications of Unesco's program for libraries were many, said Shaw, and could include the establishment of world bibliographic centers, the promotion of the international exchange and loan of print materials, the development of public libraries, and the lessening of copyright, currency, and political restrictions on the free circulation of knowledge. He agreed with the vision of MacLeish and Unesco that this organization (and thus libraries) should promote knowledge and understanding among all the people of the world, not just scholars and professionals.[28]

After the war, the International Relations Board of the American Library Association made manifest its intention to continue with its work and insure that it would be on firmer ground administratively within the ALA. It asserted that, "It is indeed in the minds of men that lasting peace is to be assured.   It is with [the] minds of men that librarians work."[29]   The Board further affirmed that "The international exchange of materials and information is essential if libraries are to be effective agencies in promoting international understanding."[30] A study by Shaw of the Board's activities from 1942 to 1947 also indicated its possible direction in the future.[31]

The anti-anti-Communist outlook of those involved with the IRB was also made quite clear soon after the war. Thus, the profession's commitment to the free international flow of print and other materials was the alleged focus of a 1946 conference sponsored by the American Library Association's Board on Resources of American Libraries and the ALA's International Relations Board. It was attended by approximately thirty leaders of the profession,[32] who provided concrete proposals for the attainment of their goals. Not surprisingly, the uninhibited restrictions on the free international flow of information by the Soviet Union and its occupied countries were downplayed, while those in the West—like those related to copyright—were distorted and magnified.[33] The conferees also recommended that the State Department's overseas libraries be "competently and thoroughly studied and evaluated by American librarians"[34] in an obvious attempt to put them under the profession's purview.

Other librarians created the complementary Round Table for Library Service Abroad within the American Library Association. At its organizing meeting could be heard these utopian catchwords and clichés: "world cooperation," "internationalism," and "world citizen." An alert participant from the State Department asserted to those in attendance that useful service required that one not lose one's identity as an American.[35]

The Library of Congress

A lifelong supporter of internationalism and world government, Luther Evans, MacLeish's protégé, spent a good deal of time promoting international library activities, Unesco, and other global projects after his appointment as Librarian of Congress in 1945. In the early fifties, these excessive involvements were one reason he came under fire from Congress, which was fulfilling its legal responsibility to maintain oversight of the Library. He consequently resigned his post in 1953 to become Director General of Unesco.[36] After five years in Paris, Evans returned to the United States and worked in a variety of positions at the Brookings Institution, the National Education Association, and Columbia University. He later served as president of World Federalists, USA, one of the many organizations working for world government that he had supported for decades.

At the same time, the Library of Congress had begun to produce informative, scholarly materials critical of the USSR and Communism, usually made at the behest of a member, or a committee, of Congress. One of the first of many that would be issued over the next several years was done for Congressman Everett Dirksen. *Communism in Action,*[37] a 141 page work, was conceived by Dirksen in reaction to what he perceived as a growing acceptance of Communism within the United States. He believed that an objective picture of the Soviet Union would convince Americans of the evil of its totalitarian system: "The real antidote to communism lay in a diffusion of knowledge and information on how it operates."[38]   Like many of the Library of Congress studies on Communism that followed, it was conducted by its Legislative Reference Service, which received assistance from other departments of the Library and other federal agencies.

Propaganda about Soviet Libraries

After World War II, Soviet officials increased their bombastic propaganda about libraries, both to their own people and to those in other countries. For example, in 1947 the Chair of the Committee in Charge of Institutions for Cultural Enlightenment declared that the Lenin Library had more books than any other library in the world, followed by the Saltykov-Shchedrin Public Library. In 1953 she became the Minister of Culture.[39]

Lev Rakov, Director of the Saltykov-Shchedrin State Library in Leningrad, described his library for the readers of England's *Library World* in 1949. He stressed that ". . . it is now one of the largest and best stocked libraries in the world,"[40] having "trebled its stocks in the years since Soviet power was established."[41] He reported:

> The Soviet government has awarded the Saltykov-Shchedrin Library the Order of the Red Banner of Labour. This award expresses the Soviet people's love for this great library, which disseminates amongst the working people knowledge acquired by mankind throughout the ages.[42]

That same year, an article in Scotland's *Library Review* by O. Moshensky emphasized the large number of libraries in the USSR—250,000—and the fact that they held 500,000,000 volumes.[43]

The public libraries, union libraries, college libraries, factory libraries and others "cater for the broad masses of the working people."[44] He enthusiastically described a new addition to this panoply of libraries serving the multitude:

> . . . a great many collective farms are setting up their own libraries and maintaining them at their own expense. The outlook and cultural interests of the Soviet peasantry has grown immeasurably. To have books, magazines and newspapers to read is one of the collective farmer's first needs.[45]

Some of the more phantastic declarations the Soviets made during this, and other periods, are described elsewhere. In general, they claimed to have the world's largest libraries, the greatest number of libraries, and the most (and best) readers. This was facilitated by defining all publications exceeding a few pages as a *book*, and designating any collection of fifty or more such books as a *library*.[46]

The American Dedication to "Balanced" Collections

While Soviet librarians were still dedicating themselves to propaganda work at home and abroad, American librarians were *in theory* more committed than ever to insuring that the nation's libraries provided (1) differing points of view and (2) balanced collections on controversial subjects, including the nature and policies of the USSR. Throughout the 1940's, librarians like Flora B. Ludington, Harry Miller Lydenberg, and other prominent members of the library profession fought to have "balanced" collections in American libraries at home and abroad. As will be shown later in this book, to the leaders of the profession the concept of "balance" increasingly seemed to mean the exclusion of conservative and anti-Communist materials.

The relatively new fixation of these leaders on what was termed *intellectual freedom* was exemplified by a 1949 study[47] to determine whether public libraries nationwide were providing "politically balanced" collections about the Soviet Union. Conducted by Howard Winger, then a Teaching Assistant at the University of Chicago's Graduate Library School, the subject was of potentially great professional interest and its approach was the statistical type then admired at the GLS. Winger asserted that (1) the nature of a democracy, (2) the earliest stated objectives of the American public library as an agency for adult education, and (3) the Library Bill of Rights all indicated that public library holdings on controversial issues should be "balanced." He sent a checklist of fifty book titles published between 1944 and the first six months of 1948—half "friendly" to the USSR and half "hostile"—to 161 public libraries. His statistical analysis convinced him that the American public library was indeed doing its job: approximately half their holdings were pro-Soviet, half antagonistic.

While technically proficient, the study was flawed in its concepts, assumptions, and analyses. The very title, "Public Library Holdings of *Biased* Books about Russia," (italics mine) was misleading. He was studying books that had a definable point of view; such works were not necessarily "biased." However, careful readers could have overcome Winger's misuse of this word. More problematic was his dismissal of the fact that many of the pro-Soviet books had been acquired while the USSR was still a comrade in arms. He maintained that the great significance here was that these works were not removed when the relationship changed "from that of a wartime ally to that of a diplomatic and commercial antagonist."[48] (His characterization of the contemporary relationship as diplomatic antagonism was an understatement, while his belief that the USSR was a commercial antagonist was entirely fanciful.) Moreover, Winger apparently believed that a 50-50 split on issues inherently indicated "balance," yet the revised 1948 Library Bill of Rights (first issued in 1939) that he quoted and used as a touchstone supported placing works of 'sound factual authority'[49] in libraries without partisanship. It said nothing of such things as specious wartime propaganda. (The phrase stipulating books "of sound factual authority" was removed from the profession's credo in 1967.) And while this investigator realized that his study left many significant questions unanswered and he recommended several valuable "subjects for further research" concerning the provision of library material on controversial issues, he missed the potential significance of some of his data, e.g., that showing that more books favorable to the Soviet Union than unfavorable had been published during these years.[50] The movement was clearly towards more unfriendly books after 1946.

Winger indicated that only during wartime should the principle of a "balanced collection" be discarded. He seemed oblivious to the fact that the United States was in the Cold War when he wrote this, with the possibility of a hot war quite real. Moreoever, democratically-oriented countries, whose libraries may well have held the "balanced collections" he claimed to hold so dear, had recently been subverted and/or subjugated by Moscow, and more were being threatened.

Finally, his assertion that the very history of the American public library argued almost solely for the intellectual freedom and balanced collection approach reflected a skewed interpretation of that history that overemphasized a relatively new ideology. Historically, the great preponderance of public librarians and supporters of public libraries had looked upon other responsibilities as being of equal or greater significance. Winger cited as his evidence a recently published history by Sidney Ditzion. The particular page that Winger referenced does not deal with the subject, and the book as a whole refutes Winger's claim.[51]

NOTES

1. This difference in opinion is clear if one reads closely Charles A. Thomson's "The Emerging Program of Cultural Relations," *ALA Bulletin* 75 (Feb. 1944): 75-78, and compares it with the following "Discussion" by four librarians: Flora B. Ludington, Charles H. Brown, Mary Gould Davis, and Ralph Munn, pp. 78-81. Thomson, who headed the State Department's Division of Cultural Relations, described the contemporary efforts as "a valuable factor in the war effort" that "contributes to the security of the United States by building a bulwark of friendship and understanding for this country in foreign lands." (p. 75)

The librarian's view was also articulated forcefully by Carl H. Milam in his "Libraries, Scholars, and the War," *Annals of the American Academy of Political and Social Science* 235 (Sept. 1944): 100-106, particularly 102. Milam maintained that reading the books of another country increases one's understanding and respect for it, thereby building a foundation for permanent peace. He not only warned against using cultural activities to support US foreign policy but of even giving the *appearance* of utilizing them for such a purpose.

In 1944 Harry Miller Lydenberg, director of the American Library Association's International Relations Office, wrote that "We are part and parcel of 'one world' physically, nervously, emotionally, intellectually, even more in the realm of thought and ideas than in that of commerce and travel." (Lydenberg, "An International Board? Why? What for? What Does It Do?" *ALA Bulletin* 38 [Nov. 1944]: 457.) He declared that internationalism had always been a strong element in the American Library Association, and that this entailed both responsibilities and opportunities. Lydenberg described America's assistance to other countries during the war, and he looked forward to its continuation after the cessation of hostilities. (Lydenberg, "An International Board?" pp. 457-64.)

The ideas of Archibald MacLeish and Luther Evans are discussed later in this chapter.

2. Many of these realists can be found in George Sirgiovanni, *An Undercurrent of Suspicion: Anti-Communism in America during World War II* (New Brunswick, NJ, and London: Transaction Publishers, 1990). As for the magazine articles referred to, see: Max Eastman, "We Must Face the Facts about Russia," *Reader's Digest* 43 (July 1943): 1-14; and Alexander Barmine, "The New Communist Conspiracy," *Reader's Digest* 45 (Oct. 1944): 27-33. This periodical also issued articles about the USSR which were far more favorable to it.

3. Margarita Ivanova Rudomino, untitled letter, Dec. 10, 1942, trans. by Gerda Beherns, reprinted in *Library Journal* 68 (Oct. 1, 1943): 777.

4. Jens Nyholm, "Russia Wants to Know Us," (Letter,) *Library Journal* 68 (Oct. 1, 1943): 777.

5. James B. Childs, "Russian Library Exhibit," (Letter,) *Library Journal* 68 (July 1943): 565.

6. N. Karintsev, "Moscow Libraries," *Information Bulletin* (Washington, DC: Embassy of the USSR, June 8, 1941), as reprinted in *Library Journal* 68 (July 1943): 565-66.

7. "Moscow," *The Columbia Encyclopedia*, 5th ed. (New York: Columbia University Press, 1993), p. 1837.

8. Ethel M. Takce, "Soviet Libraries in the War," *Library Journal* 69 (May 1, 1944): 384-88.

9. For information on *Soviet Russia Today*, the Friends of the Soviet Union, and the National Council of American-Soviet Friendship, see State of California, Senate Fact-Finding Committee on Un-American Activities, *Fourth Report: 1948: Communist Front Organizations* (Sacramento: The Senate, March 25, 1948), pp. 366, 244-47, and 321-27.

10. Takce, p. 385.

11. Joseph E. Davies, as quoted in Toby Cole, "A Library on the Soviet Union," *Library Journal* 70 (May 15, 1945): 476.

12. Davies, ibid., p. 479. Well-known for his book *Mission to Moscow*, Davies is less remembered for his postwar role as a strong advocate of confronting Soviet aggression with military force.

13. Cole, "A Library on the Soviet Union," pp. 476-79. The Germans surrendered on May 7th. Clearly, this article had been written before then.

For information on the American-Russian Institute, see "American Russian Institute," in California, *Communist Front Organizations*, pp. 169-78.

14. Philip Grierson, *Books on Soviet Russia* (London: Methuen, 1943; reprint: Twickenham: Anthony C. Hall, 1969.)

15. Toby Cole, "A Special Libraries Conference on Russian Materials," *Library Journal* 71 (May 15, 1946):730-33.

16. California, *Communist Front Organizations*, p. 327. See also pp. 321-26 for a description of these organizations.

17. Cole, "Special Libraries Conference," p. 733.

18. Verner W. Clapp, "About Russian Publications," (Letter,) *Library Journal* 71 (Aug. 1946): 1029.

19. Ralph R. Shaw, "About Russian Publications," (Letter,) *Library Journal* 71 (Aug. 1946): 1029.

20. Nathalie Delougaz, "Some Problems of Soviet Librarianship as Reflected in Russian Library Periodicals," *Library Quarterly* 15 (July 1945): 213-23.

21. Nathalie Delougaz, "Adaptions of the Decimal Classification for Soviet Libraries," *Library Quarterly* 17 (April 1947): 148-61.

22. Nathalie Delougaz, "Some Significant Trends in Soviet Book Production," *Library Quarterly* 19 (Oct. 1949): 250-62.

23. Arthur B. Berthold, "Survey of Recent Russian Library Literature," *Library Quarterly* 17 (April 1947): 138-47.

24. See the first paragraph of this chapter and note one above.

25. Shaw, "International Activities of the American Library Association," *American Library Association Bulletin* 41 (June 1947): 229. Norman D. Stevens, "Ralph Robert Shaw," in *Dictionary of American Library Biography*, pp. 476-81; and I. Bruce Turner, "Ralph Shaw," in *Leaders in American Academic Librarianship, 1925-1975*, ed. by Wayne Wiegand (Pittsburgh: Beta Phi Mu, 1983; distributed by the American Library Association), pp. 288-319, particularly pp. 291-92.

26. Ralph R. Shaw, "Wars Begin in the Minds of Men," *American Library Association Bulletin* 40 (Nov. 1946): 419-20.

27. Ibid., p. 419.

28. Shaw, "Wars Begin in the Minds of Men," p. 420.

29. Flora B. Ludington (Chairman), and others, in *American Library Association Bulletin* 41 (June 1947): 198.

30. Ibid.

31. Shaw, "International Activities of the American Library Association." Most of the Board's activities in the 1940's were paid for by the State Department and the Rockefeller Foundation.

32. American Library Association Board on Resources of American Libraries and [the] International Relations Board, *Conference on International, Cultural, and Scientific Exchanges*, Princeton University, Nov. 25-26, 1946 (Chicago: American Library Association, 1947). The conference was partly funded by the Carnegie Corporation.

33. See ibid., p. 122, for a gentle allusion to Soviet restrictions.

34. Recommendation #21, ibid., pp. xix-xx.

35. Anne V. Marinelli, "Librarianship from an International Point of View," *College and Research Libraries* 10 (Oct. 1949): 319-20. Marinelli, the reporter here, was a bibliographer at the University of Illinois Library and Chair of membership and recruiting for the new Round Table.

36. See John Y. Cole, "Luther Evans," in *Supplement to the Dictionary of American Library Biography*, ed. by Wiegand, pp. 22-26; and Betty L. Milum, "Luther Evans," in *World Encyclopedia of Library and Information Services*, 3rd ed., pp. 289-90. Evans' 1927 political science doctoral dissertation at Stanford University was on the League of Nations. He served as Chief Assistant Librarian under MacLeish and Acting Head during MacLeish's wartime absences and after his resignation in 1944.

37. *Communism in Action: A Documented Study and Analysis of Communism in Operation in the Soviet Union Prepared at the Instance and under the Direction of Representative Everett M. Dirksen by the Legislative Reference Service of the Library of Congress, under the Direction of Ernest S. Griffith* (Washington, DC: GPO, 1946). Soviet libraries received only three sentences in this study.

38. Everett M. Dirksen, "Foreword," ibid., p. iii.

39. See Arturs Baumanis, and Robert A. Martin, *Soviet Book Statistics: A Guide to Their Use and Interpretation* (Urbana, IL: University of Illinois Library School, Occasional Paper number 44, Dec. 1955), p. 3.

40. Lev Rakov, "The Leningrad Public Library," *The Library World* 51 (May 1949): 221.

41. Ibid., p. 222.

42. Ibid.

43. O. Moshensky, "Soviet Libraries," *Library Review* 91 (Aug. 1949): 157. This amounted to almost one library for every two thousand people in the Soviet Union, he pointed out.

44. Ibid.

45. Ibid.

46. On Soviet definitions, see: Baumanis and Martin, *Soviet Book Statistics*; and Maurice Friedberg, *Russian Classics in Soviet Jackets*.

47. Howard Winger, "Public Library Holdings of Biased Books about Russia," Occasional Paper number 1 (Urbana, IL: University of Illinois Library School, July 1949, 12 pp.)

48. Ibid., p. 9.

49. Ibid., p. 1.

50. Ibid., p. 3.

51. Winger's first paragraph cited page thirty of Sidney Ditzion, *Arsenals of a Democratic Culture: A Social History of the American Public Library Movement in New England and the Middle States from 1850 to 1900*, foreword by Merle Curti (Chicago: American Library Association, 1947). A more detailed portrayal of the history of the priorities of public librarians, particularly those related to intellectual freedom and censorship, is Evelyn Geller's *Forbidden Books in American Public Libraries, 1876-1939* (Westport, CT, and London: Greenwood Press, 1984). Geller is open in her support of those librarians who did advocate so-called intellectual freedom positions.

6

AMERICAN LIBRARIANSHIP AND THE SOVIET UNION, 1950-1959

The 1950's saw a dramatic change in the literature of American librarianship in its treatment of the Soviet Union and its library system. The new widespread understanding in the West of the dangers posed by Communist totalitarianism and imperialism had shaken some librarians loose from their naive fantasies. Objective reporting and scholarly research on the USSR's libraries increased, as did affirmations of the differences between democratic and Communist societies and their respective library systems. The insights of librarians who had fled from Communist countries began to be made better known.

Among some in the West, there still remained a degree of envy for the zeal evinced by librarians in the USSR. But unlike the past, when visiting Americans and others had been impressed primarily by their public services, the most positive views were usually accorded to their bibliographic enterprises. The former were now apprehended by many to be the tools of a tyrannous government. There was also a growing comprehension of the Soviet need for Western technological information. And finally, some of those interested in international and comparative librarianship were beginning to express a commitment to supporting democracy instead of declaiming the old pieties about "international understanding." *True* international understanding was finally growing among a segment of librarians in the West.

Unfortunately, the American librarians who best recognized the nature of the Soviet Union had little influence on the leaders of the profession, who were the spokespeople for the field on domestic and international matters. Position in the professional hierarchy, rather than scholarly or empirical knowledge of the USSR and Communism, proved to be the most significant factor. Those members of the small group that dominated the American Library Association year after year—or librarians who had close ties to these leaders—retained the power to speak on behalf of the tens of thousands of librarians in the United States and to dominate the conversation within the field. Apparently, the correct political orientation was requisite for admittance to this elite group.

Scholarly Research and Other Writings

The objective research on Soviet librarianship begun in the second half of the 1940's continued to be carried out, and it increasingly made manifest the shortcomings and evils of the libraries in the USSR. Two staff members of the Detroit Public Library, Arturs Baumanis and Robert A. Martin, wrote a revealing study based on a careful scrutiny of Soviet figures and Soviet publications. (Baumanis, a foreign-language specialist for the Library, was the primary force behind this and other studies of Soviet librarianship. He had immigrated from Latvia.) Their *Soviet Book Statistics: A Guide to Their Use and Interpretation* was published in 1955 as part of the University of Illinois Library School's series of Occasional Papers. It concluded with these words:

> Previous deductions on the nature of Soviet library holdings and the publishing industry should be revised in light of the above facts and observations. This, on its part, would contribute to a more realistic understanding of the manner in which the contemporary Russian library affects the library patron, particularly the so-called general reader.[1]

Baumanis and Martin pointed out the very generous Soviet definition of a *book*: it included any item of eight pages or more in length. The criteria used in most other countries was far greater; in the US it was sixty-five pages of text. This extremely low Soviet standard resulted in highly inflated figures for the size of their library holdings and belied their boasts of having the largest libraries in the world. The number of books produced in the Soviet Union was also shown to be far less prodigious than had been previously reported.[2] (A Unesco conference in 1964 declared that the international definition of a *book* should include the requirement that it be at least forty-nine pages in length.[3])

The authors also described the inefficiencies of the centralized selection of books for libraries. It frequently resulted in a dearth of many publicly desired works in libraries while these institutions sometimes received hundreds of copies of one unwanted title. The numerous destructive book purges dating from the beginnings of Communist rule were described as well.[4]

Baumanis and A. Robert Rogers produced a scholarly evaluation of Soviet classification and cataloging for *Library Quarterly* in 1958.[5] Based on a close reading of Soviet library literature dating primarily from the postwar era, the authors described the decades-old attempt to create a classification system that reflected Communist ideas. Supposedly, it would contrast with the 'unscientific,' 'pernicious,' 'warmongering' systems of the capitalist countries.   The two researchers detailed the propagandistic role of the card catalogs made available freely to the public and the restricted access to others used for banned books.   The continuity of the basic Soviet approach since the days of Krupskaya was underscored.

Another article in *Library Quarterly* that year analyzed Russian retrospective book bibliographies. The author, Karol Maichel, found that ". . . while some periods are covered fully and well, others are very poorly covered."[6] He did not note any efforts by the Soviets to remedy the inadequate bibliographic control of this pre-Revolutionary material. Maichel, originally from Czechoslovakia, was an expert in East European bibliography. Through most of the 1950's, he was a Russian and Slavic collections librarian at Columbia University.

Paul L. Horecky

Paul Horecky was perhaps the most outstanding of the scholars from Europe who found a professional home in American librarianship by specializing in Soviet and Slavic materials. Born in Czechoslovakia in 1913, he received a law degree from the University of Prague in 1936 and an M.A. in Soviet Area Studies from Harvard in 1951. He then began a twenty-six year career at the Library of Congress in the Slavic and East (later Central) European Division, becoming its Chief in 1972. In addition to his significant publications during this period, he was actively involved in the Slavic and East European section of the American Library Association (1966-1967) and the Library and Documentation Committee of the American Association for the Advancement of Slavic Studies (1970-1973).

The aim of his first major book, *Libraries and Bibliographic Centers in the Soviet Union*,[7] was to present an accurate, up-to-date portrait of these institutions, describing their everyday functioning and their distinct Communist aspects. In this he succeeded, writing the most comprehensive survey and analysis of Soviet librarianship done up to that time. Claiming to have begun his research with no theories to either promote or derogate, the work was mainly descriptive. However, he affirmed the necessity of making some analyses and viewing libraries in their proper cultural and political perspective: the failure to do so "might lead to the naive opinion that Soviet libraries are simply a regional variety of libraries as we know them."[8] Conversely, he believed, it would be equally false to view them merely as agencies of indoctrination, ignoring their educational and scientific roles.

The book was largely the result of Horecky's close study of Soviet journal articles, books, and government pronouncements. He stated that in recent years a great deal of these materials had become available, and that, when evaluated wisely, they provided valuable information. Horecky also gained facts and insights from scholars who had visited Soviet libraries, and he included in the book extensive firsthand observations from Thomas J. Whitby, his colleague at the Library of Congress.[9] (Whitby's work is dealt with below.)

The study was funded by the Council on Library Resources. Founded in 1956 with a $5 million gift from the Ford Foundation, it supported a wide variety of studies and projects, particularly those dealing with major research institutions. Its broad charter included the charge "to improve relations between American and foreign libraries and archives."[10]

Horecky's first chapter was titled "The Soviet Concept of Librarianship." He began it by describing Lenin's major views and pronouncements on libraries which, he reported, were frequently touted by Soviet librarians as representing the epitome of wisdom in the field. He reduced them to three major dicta:

1. Libraries must circulate books to the masses.
2. Libraries must serve as agencies of Communist indoctrination as well as education.
3. Libraries must be entirely state-owned and state-run; there can be no competing systems.[11]

He went on to describe Soviet legal deposit, bibliography, cataloguing, library architecture, professional education, and the major libraries. A ninety page appendix contained enlightening translations of library laws, regulations, classification systems, and so forth. The carefully researched, well-written text was informed, on occasion, by the scholarship on Communism by J. L. Talmon, Alex Inkeles, Gerhart Niemayer, and Robert N. Carew Hunt. Throughout the work,[12] Horecky reiterated that superficial similarities should not obscure the essential differences between Communist and democratic library systems: the former is an integral part of a totalitarian system and focuses on ideological and technical training to develop the USSR's economic and military strength. Nevertheless, the book was balanced throughout, pointing out both the positive and negative aspects of Soviet libraries. Thus, as part of his summary, he wrote:

> The total picture presented by this system is a rather strange blend of strength and weakness, assets and liabilities. Operational efficiency and dynamic activity are combined with bureaucratic regimentation. Great book repositories are maintained, but within their walls the reader is impeded in the sovereign inquiry of the human mind and subjected to an untiring indoctrination process. Priceless treasures of cultural history are preserved with great care, but the general public is barred from certain reading rooms which are restricted to a privileged and state-sanctioned elite. Bibliographic centers sponsor publications of impressive scope and quality, but at the same time they compile lists of *libelli non grati* earmarked for expulsion from library collections.
>
> Despite these divergent elements and despite the monotonous intellectual fare often served up, Western visitors to the USSR have taken note of the generally wide-spread enthusiasm for reading.[13]

Horecky maintained that the genuine accomplishments of Soviet librarianship could have been made under a democratic system without the undermining of truth and genuine learning.[14]

Popular Anti-Soviet Writings

Popular articles presenting a negative picture of libraries in the
Soviet Union and other Communized countries also began to appear in
American library journals in the 1950's. These were neither the result
of immediate scholarly research nor of brief visits overseas. A work
titled "Bookshelves behind the Iron Curtain," by Bela Talbot Kardos,
also of the Slavic and East European Division of the Library of
Congress, was reprinted from the *Christian Science Monitor* in a 1953
issue of the *Idaho Librarian*, published by the Idaho Library Association.[15] A native of Hungary, where he had earned a doctorate
in political science in 1929, Kardos described how Soviet librarians
had supervised the successful drive to change the fundamentals of
librarianship in the USSR's recently conquered countries. In colorful
terms, he described the Communist view that all aspects of library
work had to serve the cause of Marxist revolution and how classic
works of culture were butchered in Communist editions to destroy their
original themes. Works of discredited Leftists, he reported, were also
subject to removal, as "the Marxist revolution eats its own children."[16]

In 1959, Idahoans again spudded up Communist techniques in a
half-page article in the University of Idaho Library's *Bookmark*. Titled "Statistics on Stilts," it began:

> For many years the Library of Congress has been accepted
> throughout the world as the largest of its kind. In the past few
> years, however, Russia has put in its claim to having the largest
> collection of books gathered together in one institution. But don't
> you believe it! This claim to fame belongs in the same classification
> as many of their statements about having invented the first airplane,
> the first subway, etc. And this is how they get around the library
> boast.[17]

It proceeded to report the findings in Baumanis and Martin's 1955
research study.

Librarians in other Western countries produced a few popular
articles describing the evils of Soviet librarianship. For example, a
British librarian working in Canada wrote in the *Ontario Library
Review* about the essentially political nature of Soviet librarianship.[18]

Using only a handful of published articles as sources, she nevertheless accurately described the adherence of Soviet librarians to the goals of the Communist Party, their oppression of the Soviet people, and their agitation against Western society. She noted that the librarian's role had not essentially changed in the USSR from what it had been in the 1930's.

Writings on Soviet Bibliographic Control and Science/Technology Librarianship

In the 1950's, there was still a great interest in, and much admiration for, the bibliographic control of books and other printed materials in the Soviet Union. Descriptions of the mandatory submission of *all* printed matter (books, magazines, pamphlets, maps, broadsides, and so forth) to dozens of depository libraries, as well as their cataloging and classification, appeared in *Library Quarterly, College and Research Libraries*,[19] and other journals. Several were written by Thomas J. Whitby.

In 1959, the American Documentation Institute, the forerunner of the American Society for Information Science, published a revealing description of "Libraries and Information Services behind the Iron Curtain" in its primary journal, *American Documentation*. The author, Judith Szebenyi-Sigmond, who lived in the Netherlands, had been a science librarian in Hungary before fleeing that country in 1956. While much of her article described the organization of technical librarianship in her homeland, she stated that the principles were analogous to those in the USSR. The picture she drew was of a well-organized effort. In fact, she declared that while the equipment and facilities of Western technologic libraries were better, she believed that Communist technical librarianship was superior because of its greater vitality, sophistication, and attention to foreign publications. (She noted the vigor with which Western scientific articles were processed and translated.) The article, which included numerous jabs at Communist oppression, ended with a poignant remark about her former work and co-workers:

> We had many difficulties and were nearly always overburdened, but our work gave us some satisfaction too, because in some way it was through our activity that thousands of engineers could get a glimpse

of the free world from which they are cut off in such a cruel and insensible manner.[20]

The appreciation of Soviet bibliographic efforts and science librarianship was not confined to the United States. The journal of the British Association of Special Libraries published an evaluation of a mammoth Russian abstracting service. Begun in 1953, its goal was to keep Soviet scientists apprised of developments throughout the world.[21] While précis were made of articles written in thirty-four languages, more had been in English than any other language; a large percentage of these works had been published in the United States. Photocopies of the original articles were provided to Soviet scientists on request.

The author was impressed by the speed with which new titles from overseas were processed, as well as with the magnitude of the effort. She agreed with the director of the Soviet Institute of Scientific Information, which was responsible for this undertaking, that nothing like his organization could exist in a capitalist society. She concurred that such a marvel could only develop in a system where there was "centralization" rather than "competition."

Reports Stemming from Visits to the Soviet Union

Many of the visits by American scholars and librarians to the Soviet Union focused on the acquisition of Soviet books and journals. In part, this interest was the result of the increasing study of the USSR by scholars in the humanities and social sciences, a direct outgrowth of the heightened involvement of both the United States and the Soviet Union in international affairs. Reports by these visitors were published in the library press, as were the impressions of Soviet libraries by prominent figures in American higher education and political affairs.

In 1955 Martin E. Malia, assistant professor of history at Harvard University, spent five months in the USSR on behalf of the purchase and exchange programs of the Library of Congress and several university libraries.[22] He wrote an account of his findings in the *Library of Congress Information Bulletin* in which he reported that the exchange of books had become much easier in 1955 because of greater cooperation on the part of the Soviet government and its expansion of direct exchange privileges to more than the traditional three Soviet institutions. While a visiting Assistant Professor at Berkeley after his return, some of his thoughts—particularly those regarding the difficulties in acquiring Soviet materials—were reported in the University of California Library's *CU News* and thereafter reprinted in *Library Journal*.[23] In these works, Malia noted that many aspects of Soviet society were responsible for impeding the free international exchange of books, such as: the censorial aims of its totalitarian government, the ignorance of international exchange on the part of its librarians heretofore forbidden to partake directly of foreign fruit, and the encumbrances created by its recalcitrant bureaucrats.

A Slavic historian at the University of California at Davis presented his views on Soviet research libraries and the recent easing of Soviet restrictions on visitors in his *College and Research Libraries* account of his one-month tour in 1956. C. Bickford O'Brien believed that such visits played a vital role in scholarly research, international understanding, and international relations:

> International tensions of the last year, as everyone knows, have given little hope of improved relations between the world powers. Yet in spite of the misunderstandings and problems, there is reason to believe that some progress is being made toward a clearer understanding of differing points of view. One evidence of this is the fact that for the first time in about twenty years hundreds of Americans have been permitted to enter the Soviet Union. . . . There is hope, at least, that it will remove even further some of the misconceptions that persist on both sides of the iron curtain.[24]

Unfortunately, O'Brien never described what he thought these so-called mutual "misunderstandings" and "misconceptions" were.

As for the Soviet research libraries of interest to academics working in Slavic studies, O'Brien was impressed by the vastness of their collections and the assistance their scholarly librarians rendered him. He also noted the immense holdings of research libraries in general, although he did discern major gaps in some subject areas. The visitor reported that his hosts were aware of these lacunae.[25]

An article in *College and Research Libraries*[26] by Oswald P. Backus III, a University of Kansas librarian, gave practical tips on how to acquire Russian materials. He had gained this knowledge during his visits there in 1957 and 1958. Backus described the well-known Soviet desire to exchange, rather than purchase material, due to their lack of hard currency.[27] He remarked that the Soviets were interested in "obtaining primarily new works in physics, chemistry, engineering and related fields to be purchased on the open market by American institutions in exchange for [their] old books."[28]

On the subject of "exchange," Backus made an observation that—apparently unbeknownst to him—was fraught with meaning: the Soviet interest in visiting libraries that would also give them "an opportunity of observing life in various parts of the United States."[29] All Soviet citizens in the United States were obligated to inspect and analyze American society and report their findings back to their government. In effect, all of them were foreign intelligence agents. Solzhenitsyn later wrote eloquently about this phenomenon.[30]

The Alabama Librarian carried an enthusiastic and optimistic account of the two-week visit to the USSR in 1959 of Charlotte Forgey Chesnut, the director of a technical documents library focusing on ballistic missiles.[31] Chesnut was one of twenty-five librarians from all parts of the United States who, she asserted, went there together as "tourists" to sightsee and meet librarians. She stressed that they had *not* gone to study the Soviet political system nor the librarians' political role. Moreover, they had not been sponsored by the US government.

Chesnut described the large state libraries they visited and the All Union Institute for Scientific and Technical Information (VINITI). She was very impressed with the size of the collections and appreciated both the friendliness of the librarians and their eagerness to speak with them. She concluded:

> From our limited inspection of Russian libraries it was impossible to learn a great deal about their library philosophy, processes, and methods, but we could observe the enthusiasm and interest of the librarians in their work. It was an inspiration to talk to the Russian librarians and to exchange ideas which we hope will foster a better library understanding between the USA and Russia.[32]

American journals went far afield to obtain informed information on Soviet librarianship. *College and Research Libraries* printed an English-language version of an article that had originally appeared in the Swedish journal *Biblioteksbladet* in 1957.[33] It had been translated by Thomas R. Buckman, Head of the Acquisitions Department of the University of Kansas Libraries at Lawrence, who had studied in Scandinavia and received a master's degree in Scandinavian studies from the University of Minnesota. Valter Ahlstedt, a librarian at the Stockholm Public Library, based his article on the information he had gathered during a class tour by his library's school of librarianship as well as on a few articles by Swedish and German librarians. This informative report criticized the central role Communist propaganda played in Soviet librarianship, but, like so many others before it, expressed admiration for the government's support of libraries and for the enthusiasm of newly graduated librarians. Many of the novices, Ahlstedt claimed, had requested assignment to library jobs in remote geographic areas to fulfill their pioneering desires.

In 1959, *Ontario Library Review* published an article on "Book Selection in the USSR" by Charles Deane Kent, Assistant Director of the London (Ontario) Public Library and Museum. It was the product of a recent trip to the USSR (whose duration and itinerary were unspecified), a bit of reading, a good deal of speculation, and much pontificating. Early on, Kent showed his ignorance and lack of critical ability by declaring that ". . . something like 60,000 [book] titles (1,100 million copies) were published in the Soviet Union in 1958, according to a recent issue of *Soviet News* and I see no reason for disputing this figure."[34] The fraudulence of such numbers had by this time been fairly well reported in America's professional literature.

Kent charged that Soviet librarians were, to some extent, mere functionaries carrying out the will of their government when it came to selecting books. He asserted that librarians, not political officials, should choose library books. However, he added that in addition to the "existential" aspects of selecting books, a librarian must be "a servant of the community."[35] Soviet librarians—in actions analagous to those of their Western counterparts—were merely fulfilling the latter role when it came to works like the Nobel Prize winner, *Dr. Zhivago*, which was outlawed in the USSR:[36]

> Perhaps *Dr. Zhivago* is not available because the triumvirate of State-Librarians-people together just do not approve of this book and this type of literature. A little far-fetched? Possibly, but then it is easily noticeable in Russia that Russians have a quick readiness to

stand together, particularly when Russia is criticized or attacked. It is conceivable, I would say, that many of the sentiments and ideas in *Dr. Zhivago* are scandalous and shocking to the majority of Russian readers, and that if the book was available it would not be read too widely anyway except by the few who would, if they were in our country, read curiosa erotica and the like and nothing else. Possibly because these items are forbidden. [*sic*] The editors in Russia who rejected this work may have done so on firm grounds. It is not easy to judge the paradox of Russia with our standards. You will recall that Churchill said, "Russia is an enigma wrapped in a mystery." When enough Russians can read *Dr. Zhivago* without flinching, then perhaps it will be available.

Very often we in the West are inclined to overemphasize the division between the "people" and the "rulers" in Russia. Undoubtedly there are discordant elements but not in nearly the same hoped-for quantity or quality. Most people are behind the Russian government and this includes librarians. Thus Russian librarians seem to be providing the users of public libraries with "wanted" material according to all the statistical evidence that we have. Which is—within limits—standard professional practice anywhere. [*sic*][37]

Thus, Kent defended the Soviets with a mélange of speculation, illusory data, mystic cultural relativism, spurious comparison, and inappropriate quotation.

He went on to claim that there were many people in the West who supported censorship in libraries or, worse still, opposed the provision of libraries. (Kent maintained that a failure to provide library service to *all* was a particular sore point for him as a Canadian.) At least, he declared, in the USSR libraries and book selection are taken seriously, unlike most Western countries. Moreover, he insisted, "there is evidence" that most of what the libraries there do *is* educational and cultural, not propagandistic. He did not describe this evidence or indicate where one could find it.[38]

Kent ended by expressing dissatisfaction with "materialistic culture such as ours where taxes and money seem to govern everything."[39] He advanced a variety of different scenarios for the USSR, including the possibility that "Kruschev's" [*sic*] promise of more consumer goods would make the Russian people "exactly like ourselves: soft and senile."[40]

Thus were the librarians of Ontario enlightened by the primary journal of their Toronto-based Provincial Library Service.

Kent's other articles on this subject were not as bad. *Canadian Library Journal*, issued by the Canadian Library Association, published his relatively commonplace, mildly enthusiastic description of the Saltykov-Shchedrin Library. He also contributed articles about his trip to *Library Journal* and Scotland's *Library Review*. In the former, he warned that democratic countries had to increase their financial support for libraries and other such institutions or there would *be* no democracies. The latter work was a brief, straightforward description of the Hermitage Art Museum Library in Leningrad.[41]

One prominent visitor to Soviet libraries and other educational institutions was William Benton: he spent the month of October 1955 in the USSR. After a brief but lucrative career in advertising with Chester Bowles,[42] Benton had become a vice president of the University of Chicago where he served as an assistant to his Yale classmate, President Robert Hutchins. While at Chicago, he purchased the *Encyclopaedia Britannica* as a gift for the University and became chairman of the reference work's board of directors, a position he held until his death in 1973. He served in the federal government as Assistant Secretary of State from 1945 to 1947 overseeing international information programs. As the head of the US delegation to a Unesco conference, he proclaimed:

> "We are at the beginning of a long process of breaking down the walls of national sovereignty. In this UNESCO can be, and indeed must be, the pioneer."[43]

In 1949 Benton was appointed by Bowles, who was then Governor of Connecticut, to fill a vacant US Senate seat. He then ran for, and won, the unexpired two years of this position.

After returning from his trip to the Soviet Union, he traveled throughout America presenting his conclusions. His views appeared in *American Libraries* and *Library Journal* and were often cited by others.[44] A concerned Benton saw a library system in the USSR that was eager to serve a populace zealous for learning. He was quite aware that there was no intellectual freedom there, yet he nevertheless maintained that the primary threat from the Soviet Union was intellectual, not military, and that it was the USSR's dynamic educational agencies that posed the real danger to the United States. He did not explain why.

Benton believed that because the Soviet leaders understood the power of book publishing, schools, and libraries, they supported them with high levels of funding and well-trained personnel. In contrast, he asserted, until recently Americans had been coasting in these areas. He hoped that the desire for education among his fellow citizens would increase and that more funds would be made available to libraries.

Benton had an unduly high regard for the Soviet world of books and libraries. For example, he seemed to believe that any reader in the USSR received any book in the country he or she desired within forty-eight hours via airmail. Similarly, he accepted Soviet claims that they published almost fifty-five thousand book titles per year, compared to less than thirteen thousand in the United States. The latter number was factual; the former was factitious.

In his articles comparing the Soviet and American systems, he reserved his strongest condemnation for Senator Joseph McCarthy's staff members, Roy Cohn and David Schine, who had criticized the inclusion of pro-Communist books in the American overseas libraries that Benton had earlier overseen:

> At times in history when intellectual inquiry has fallen into disrepute, libraries have been bastions against barbaric attack and suspicion. It is no coincidence that the flamboyant sabotage of Messrs. Cohn and Schine found their worst excesses on this nation's overseas libraries.[45]

There were additional reasons for Benton's unfounded remarks about McCarthy's associates. In the US Senate, Benton had been an outspoken critic of McCarthy and had taken the unusual action of trying to have this duly elected politician expelled from that body in 1951. McCarthy accused Benton of protecting seven spies, fellow travellers, and dangerous innocents—all of whom he named—who had worked with Benton in the State Department. For example, he pointed out that Benton had refused to follow the 1946 recommendation of the State Department's own Loyalty Board that William T. Stone—who reported directly to Benton—be fired due to his close association with known Communists and spies. The Wisconsin senator added that Nathan

Silvermaster, the self-confessed head of a major Soviet spy ring in Washington, had more recently admitted that Stone had given him secret information.[46] In 1952 Benton sought election to a full six-year Senate term, but he was defeated by his Republican adversary, who had McCarthy's active support in the campaign.

A 1958 summer tour of eighteen Soviet institutions of higher education led the Chancellor of the University of Pittsburgh, Edward H. Litchfield, to declare that American university libraries were much smaller than those in the USSR and that this reflected the stronger commitment to higher learning in that Communist country. While he stated that comparative appraisals should be made by library specialists, he clearly thought that their basic conclusions would be the same as his, namely, that Soviet libraries dwarfed those in even the leading American institutions and that the use of their materials was very great. The implications, he asserted, were clear: American universities, including his own, must begin the task of catching up with their Soviet counterparts.[47] In other words, Litchfield, like Benton, mistakenly believed that there was a perilous library gap.

Thomas J. Whitby

One of the major writers on Soviet librarianship in the 1950's was Thomas J. Whitby. After graduating from the University of Chicago's Graduate Library School, where his thesis was "An Analysis of the Bibliographic Activities of the Book Chamber in Soviet Russia," Whitby served the Library of Congress as a Slavic cataloguer and acquisitions specialist from 1952 until 1961. His first publication in the field, "National Bibliography in the USSR," appeared in *Library Quarterly* in 1953. In this work, Whitby described their bibliographic system as unique and "remarkable" because of its completeness and masterful organization.[48] It was followed by articles on Soviet legal deposit and classification.[49] The latter demonstrated the frequent attempts to bring Soviet book classification into conformity with Marxist theory and the resulting dislocations and inefficiencies.

In 1957 Whitby spent thirty-six days in the USSR visiting thirty-four libraries and bibliographic centers. The trip was supported financially by a grant from Rutgers University. Whitby fulfilled part

of his agreement with Rutgers by writing a 103 page description of
what he saw.[50]   Unfortunately, it went unpublished, and generally
unheralded, within the library community. A few copies found their
way into large research libraries.[51]

He was captivated by the numerous large card catalogs in the
Lenin Library,[52] which he described as "possibly the largest library in
the world."[53] Unfortunately, Whitby did not make it clear whether he
meant this in terms of its book collection, building size, or some other
variable—an unpardonable lapse given the significance and sensitivity
of this subject. He was also impressed by the great amount of reading
and library use throughout the country. However, he did not fail to
describe some of the restrictions placed on the material available in
libraries and bookstores, and he observed that ". . . the average Soviet
citizen is starved for news."[54]   His report also noted how quickly
librarians throughout the country responded to instructions from above
in instituting propaganda programs.[55]

Whitby was the sole writer on Soviet libraries to point out the
seemingly obvious fact that the American authors who were promoted
in the USSR were mainly critics of US society.[56] This visitor was also
one of the very few to question his hosts about the closed collections
(*spetsfond*) in research libraries; he even asked why there were no
works by Trotsky listed in the public catalogs![57] (The straight-faced
response to the latter inquiry was that there was no longer any interest
among library users in Trotsky.) Unique among those who visited or
wrote about Soviet libraries in this period, he was interested in the
unrelenting anti-religious campaign that was waged.[58] Whitby's details
on his numerous meetings with librarians could have enabled a careful
reader to see how readily his or her cordial counterparts in the USSR
would dissemble when confronted with sensitive subjects like their
censorship and propaganda work.

While he was an admirer of Soviet bibliography and cataloging,
Whitby nevertheless pointed out shortcomings in these too.   For
example, he reported that while all libraries for the general public
utilized the same decimal classification system, research libraries used
"a veritable jungle of classification schemes."[59] And while ready-made
catalog cards were available for purchase, many librarians continued to
labor making their own. "Library handwriting," he pointed out, was
still taught in library schools.[60]

Whitby's valuable study did have flaws. His detailed descriptions of technical matters and library buildings seem purposeless at times; they are frequently mind-numbing. Despite his role at the Library of Congress in processing Slavic scientific materials, he did not visit some of the most significant, innovative, and energetic bibliographic centers and libraries handling this type of publication. Finally, he dismissed as worthless the literature already existing on Soviet librarianship—both Western and Soviet in origin—believing that only eyewitness accounts could be valuable.[61] His apparent lack of acquaintance with much that was available in both English and Russian would account for his failure to know who Anna Kravchenko was when he met this pioneering organizer of libraries in the USSR.[62]   Moreover, while Whitby understood the essential fact that Soviet libraries existed to carry out the dictates of the Communist Party,[63] his observations and analyses would have been more sophisticated if he had known more about Soviet politics and society.

Whitby wrote two popular accounts of his trip for publication. The first, in *D.C. Libraries*,[64] indicated that he had come back from the visit with his respect for Soviet bibliographic work largely intact. However, he reported that he had developed a negative view of Soviet library education and had gained only an incomplete understanding of the closed book collections. Moreover, he declared that he did not comprehend the reasons for the differences between libraries in the United States and the Soviet Union, submitting that they might be due to political, cultural, or geographic factors. This article could have given an informed contemporary the impression that Whitby was extremely naive and largely baffled by his experiences in the USSR.

Whitby created a different picture in his second report, which was published in the American Library Association's *ALA Bulletin*. It provided an excellent, albeit brief, overview of the Soviet library system based primarily on his visit. The essentially political nature of these institutions was made clear throughout. Unfortunately, Whitby's inadequate knowledge of the best Western literature in the field again made itself all too clear: in his very first paragraph he erroneously stated that fifty thousand book titles were being published in the Soviet Union each year, many times the actual number.[65]

Whitby's best overall work was his contribution to the 1958 "Iron Curtains and Scholarship" conference at the University of Chicago's Graduate Library School.

The *"Iron Curtains and Scholarship"* Conference

Perhaps the most visible scholarly effort of this decade to deal with
Soviet-American library relations was the 1958 annual conference at the
University of Chicago's Graduate Library School, "Iron Curtains and
Scholarship: The Exchange of Knowledge in a Divided World." As
usual, the papers were published as an issue of *Library Quarterly* as
well as a book.[66] The director of the conference, and the editor of the
printed proceedings, was Howard W. Winger, then an Assistant
Professor at the GLS. He had earned his master's and doctoral degrees
in librarianship at the University of Illinois in 1948 and 1953,
respectively, and served on the faculty of the Graduate Library School
from 1953 until 1981, for five of those years as Dean (1972-1977).
Winger was the editor of *Library Quarterly* from 1981 through 1985.
His flawed research on whether American public library collections
were "balanced" when it came to the Soviet Union has already been
described.

According to Winger, the raison d'être of the conference was
scholarship, not politics. He stated that while in the 1930's the
Graduate Library School had done pioneering work in mass communications, advances in that area had enabled a shift in interest to
scholarly communication. The conference, he declared, was a reflection of this: communication between scholars of East and West was
one of the most pressing problems in this newer field of inquiry.

In a major departure from the general consensus of the period,
Winger maintained that the term *iron curtain* in reference to East-West
communication was misleading. There were, he claimed, many
curtains (as he hinted in the name of his conference), and some had
been put up by the West. He neglected to provide any evidence for
these novel assertions, but the facts were apparently of little importance
to him here. Perhaps this was due to his avowed "desire to avoid
placing blame on either the East or the West."[67]

Winger, failing to face the essentially *political* nature of the East-
West antagonism, asserted that knowledge was socially based and that
the apparent political division was merely a reflection of cultural
differences. He then happily reduced the issue of the exchange of
knowledge in a divided world to "a problem of cross-cultural communication,"[68] that is, to a manageable problem capable of solution by

scholars wielding pens. In introducing the conference, its director pronounced one of its important premises: "that the world of knowledge *should* be one world."[69]

Winger's own conference paper reiterated what he had said in his opening remarks, but he declined to enlighten the attendees (or his later readers) by describing the divisions between East and West:

> To point out the obvious differences which provoke the conflict would be painfully commonplace. To attempt a deeper analysis would be too great a task for an introductory paper and would encroach upon the topics of other speakers.[70]

This reticence was unfortunate, since an elaboration of either his "multi-curtain" theory or his proposition of the primacy of culture might at least have proven interesting. Instead, he attempted to show the importance of cross-cultural communication by rehashing the stories of some of the great inventions of the past three thousand years.[71] He ended by asserting the importance of (1) promoting the interchange of ideas by librarians and scholars, (2) using areas where agreement exists to "punch holes in our iron curtains," and (3) exchanging ideas on particulars where broader agreement cannot be reached.[72]

Thus, Winger looked upon the adversarial relationship of the East and West not as a conflict between freedom and totalitarianism, nor as an antagonism which could devastate the globe, but primarily as an impediment to advances in science, the social sciences, and the humanities. Moreover, he overvalued the potential impact of exchanges in academic and cultural areas. Fortunately, the approach of the other conferees was less abstracted.

The next speaker at these proceedings was Douglas W. Bryant, Associate Director of Harvard University Library. Bryant had received his master's degree in librarianship in 1938 from the University of Michigan and subsequently held positions at several research libraries. He served as director of the United States Information Service Library in London from 1949 to 1952, gaining top administrative posts at Harvard University Library after his return from abroad. He was Chairman of the International Relations Committee of the American Library Association, 1952-1955. At the time of the "Iron Curtains" conference, he was Vice President of both the International Federation of Library Associations and the International Federation of Documentation.[73]

Some of the essentials of Winger's general approach and major theses were contradicted by Bryant's contribution, "The American Scholar and Barriers to Knowledge."[74] Unlike the Chicago professor's theories of manifold, bipolar curtains and cultural determination, Bryant placed the major onus for the contemporary situation on one politically motivated barrier erected by the Soviet Union: "The politically inspired creation of the Iron Curtain raised a new and fundamental barrier to East-West contact, from which derives the host of specific problems that plague scholarship today."[75] Knowledgeable about the specifics of Soviet-American communication, he showed that the United States government—unlike that of the USSR—was not hindering the flow of information to, or from, the Soviet Union. (Nevertheless, he was greatly displeased that the US government did have the *potential* to do so!)[76]

Bryant did not entirely dismiss all of Winger's points. He too kept central the idea that increased cultural interchange between East and West was important for scholarship. However, he did not mean scholarship in all fields, as Winger did, but rather that related directly to the "quest for knowledge and understanding of the peoples and the countries of eastern Europe."[77] Moreover, it was applied scholarship as opposed to basic scholarship that Bryant had in mind, i.e., that "which promotes that discrimination so basic to action."[78]

Despite Bryant's note of the significance of the political factors involved, almost half of his presentation described the *cultural* differences between the United States and the USSR. For example, he discussed the American concept of access to libraries as a right as opposed to the Soviet view of libraries as instruments of an "authoritarian" government. The Soviet approach, Bryant erroneously declared, was merely a continuation of the traditional one in Russia. He illustrated the Soviet conception with a quotation from a Czechoslovakian Communist librarian about libraries in his country.[79] This was a mistake on Bryant's part because it actually argued against his emphasis on the cultural in favor of the political—unless there was a previously unknown tradition of Czechoslovakian "authoritarianism" that was intimately linked with that of Russia's and was a more significant force than that of the Soviet army. The quotation Bryant used had been reprinted in an article by a Czechoslovakian refugee, an insightful work that contrasted traditional Czechoslovakian libraries with those imposed by what he termed "totalitarian" Communist forces. (As usual, those with a knowledge of the Soviet Union and political science referred to the USSR as *totalitarian*, not *authoritarian*.) This work that Bryant misused and apparently did not fully comprehend was written by one of his own colleagues, the head of public services at Harvard University's Law Library.[80] Thus, his misconceptions could have been prevented by better communication with this member of his staff.

Bryant went on to discuss some of the essential elements of the Russian psychology and worldview:

1. Alternating feelings of inferiority and superiority.
2. A belief in the Russian nation's essential purity and messianic destiny in the world.
3. A conviction that the West persecutes Russia whenever possible, but that eventually Russia would dominate the Continent.[81]

Bryant considered the Soviet Union nothing more than a continuation of the traditional Russian "authoritarian" regime. In terms of libraries, this ignored the negative changes instituted by the Bolsheviks after their seizure of power. Despite his lip-service to the role of the *political*, he never discussed Communism as a vital factor in and of itself. Lenin and Krupskaya were also absent from his analysis. The term *totalitarian*, far more apt than his word *authoritarian* for describing the USSR, was similarly missing in his appraisal. Even the two classic books Bryant relied on most to support his essential view, Nicolas Berdyaev's *The Origin of Russian Communism* and Hans Kohn's *Basic History of Modern Russia*, had acknowledged the significant transformation that Communism had wrought in Russia. Both scholars had perceived that in addition to reflecting traditional Russian approaches, Communism had introduced new elements and transmogrified the old.[82]

A valuable overview of the history, present state, and potential for "Eastern European Publications in American Libraries"[83] was presented by Melville J. Ruggles. He had received his library school degree from Columbia University and worked at the New York Public Library and the Council on Foreign Relations. During World War II, he served in the USSR Division of the Research and Analysis Branch of the Office of Strategic Services (OSS). Afterwards, he worked at the American Embassy in Moscow and later at the State Department. In 1956 he became Vice President of the Council on Library Resources, where he surveyed American library holdings of East European materials for the Association of Research Libraries' Committee on Slavic and East European Studies. Ruggles maintained that librarians had a responsibility to be engaged with both the Soviet Union and the books it produced. Paraphrasing Henry Roberts, director of Columbia University's Russian Institute, he stated that ". . . given a military stalemate and a diplomatic impasse, intellectual and cultural competition might play a more important role than usual in the power struggle between Communist and non-Communist worlds."[84] This view was not articulated by any other speaker at this conference.

Thomas J. Whitby contributed his best work of the 1950's on Soviet bibliographic work at this meeting.[85] It was as comprehensive as a seventeen page publication on the subject could be, and managed to include some information on the European countries under Soviet domination. Unlike many of his other publications of the period, it reflected a knowledge of the Soviet literature on this subject although it still ignored almost everything written in the West.

More than any other presentation at the conference, as well as any of his other works, Whitby put his contribution within a political framework. Its very title, "Libraries and Bibliographic Projects in the Communist Bloc," used the "C" word avoided by so many others at the conference and those involved in international librarianship. Similarly, using the term *bloc* rather than *Eastern Europe* showed his willingness to use a term quite popular at the time—outside of the library profession—that indicated a large political and military combine of a nature dissimilar from, and opposed to, that in the West. To his credit, Whitby made manifest the serious adversarial nature of that aggressive empire and its relationship to librarianship:

> My second general observation is that we are witnessing today the struggle between two titans, one of whom has flung challenge after challenge. While the Soviet military challenge is perhaps the

most obvious—and possibly the most dangerous—it is necessary to keep in mind that the Soviets are challenging the West in practically every sphere of human endeavor and knowledge. How the West responds to those challenges may determine the course of civilization for centuries.

As librarians, you and I realize how vital a role libraries and bibliographic services play in the accumulation and furtherance of knowledge. I venture to say, therefore, that one of the sources of Soviet strength today is the structure of its libraries and bibliographic facilities.[86]

The conference included papers evaluating the quality of the natural sciences, social sciences and humanities in the Soviet Union, each by a scholar in the field. They reported that the achievements in these areas were few, except in the hard sciences.[87] This confuted Winger's thesis of the importance of international communication for the development of scholarship: the West had little to learn from the Communists outside of the natural sciences.

There were other speeches. A presentation by a Sovietologist gave his subjective impressions of the three extant generations of scholars in the USSR.[88] The president of the Institute of International Education placed all blame for the problems in international communication on the Soviet Union.[89] The contribution by a Russian career diplomat on the accomplishments of Soviet book publishing and distribution rounded things out by presenting the usual myths.[90]

The Library of Congress

The Library of Congress played an active role in Soviet-American library relations. As already shown, it worked to obtain Soviet books for American research libraries after World War II. It also took over the work begun during the war by the American Library Association's International Relations Board in selecting works deemed valuable for libraries throughout the world.[91] Thus in the early 1950's, it prepared *The United States Quarterly Book Review*, published by Rutgers University Press. This contained information on 'currently published [American] books believed to make a contribution to the sum of knowledge.'[92] As it had in the second half of the 1940's, the Library of Congress continued to conduct excellent research on the Soviet Union at the behest of members and committees of the US Senate and House.[93]   Finally, as we have seen, many of the most important analysts of Soviet librarianship were staff members of this library.

The View from Britain

In 1959, Edward Dudley, then a lecturer in the Library School at London's Ealing Technical College, compiled an annotated bibliography of works on Soviet librarianship published within the previous fifteen years. Most of the two dozen or so items described were from the United States, but a few were from Britain, France, Germany, and the USSR itself. He remarked that "By contrast [to the situation in the UK], it would appear that interest and research in Soviet librarianship by librarians and others in the United States is both wide and detailed."[94]

Dudley speculated on the reasons for the small number of publications produced in the UK. It was a particularly interesting question because, as he pointed out, British librarians were not insular and were very involved with libraries throughout the world. He believed the situation could be attributed to three major factors. First, Russian was not a foreign language frequently selected for study in the United Kingdom, so few librarians were able to read Soviet publications. Moreover, not many Soviet books and journals about librarianship were available in Britain. This situation was exacerbated by the second factor: only a small number of librarians in the UK—probably less than ten—had ever been to the USSR. Dudley believed that such visits would both lead to, and result from, a relevant body of literature in Britain. The third reason, he thought, was the dislike librarians in his country had for the Soviet state.[95]

Dudley himself was not fully satisfied with these explanations. For example, he noted that

> . . . both lack of sympathy and, indeed, antagonism are more widespread in the USA than in this country and have proved to be less of a barrier to the determined acquisition of knowledge about many aspects of life in the USSR, including the provision and maintenance of library services. (One may be forgiven, perhaps, for

saying that the lack of sympathy and antagonism have positively *inspired* much research of this kind.)[96]

Dudley held that the achievements of Soviet librarians had been great and that studying them could prove useful for the British. (He pointed out that the converse was also true and that the USSR had always acquired useful Western techniques for its own use.) A knowledge of Soviet librarianship would facilitate the international exchange and loan of publications and improve the cataloguing and bibliographic control of the increasing number of Russian-language acquisitions.[97]

Even as Dudley wrote, the British involvement with Soviet librarianship was beginning to increase dramatically. Highly intelligent, capable, and gracious, he went on to become one of the leaders of the British library profession and to write the introduction to Sylva Simsova's excellent collection of writings on librarianship by Lenin and Krupskaya.[98]

As it had done in earlier decades, the *Library Review* of Scotland published works about Soviet libraries. In 1959 it carried two articles by recent visitors to the USSR. One was a quantitative and qualitative description by someone impressed by the size and scope of the Soviet library enterprise.[99] The other was an account of the author's attempts to obtain books written by novelists and political figures in the USSR who had fallen out of favor in the 1920's.[100] In doing so, it delineated the tortuous world of Soviet card catalogs, book collections, and regulations.

Propaganda by Soviet Librarians

Throughout the 1950's, Soviet librarians continued their coordinated, worldwide propaganda efforts to further the aims of the Communist party. One element of this was the rallying of their domestic colleagues to the supposed defense of world freedom against the threat posed by the capitalist countries, particularly the United States. Thus, a 1952 article in a periodical issued by the Library of the USSR Academy of Sciences put forth these claims:

"It must be said that the governments of certain capitalistic countries, and particularly that of the United States of America, trying to conceal the truth about the Soviet Union from their peoples, are placing obstacles of every kind with Soviet scientific institutions. . . . Pressure on the part of the imperialistic bosses of the U.S.A. hinders American scholars from maintaining normal relations in a book exchange with Soviet scholars. Several other capitalistic countries are also operating in accordance with orders from Washington, having sold their independence and freedom to American imperialism. . . .

Despite all this, Soviet scientific literature is well known in capitalistic countries. The works of Soviet scientists are highly valued beyond the frontiers of our country, because they reflect the accomplishments of the most advanced and progressive scholarship. . . .

In a situation in which the imperialists, and especially the imperialists of the United States of America, are making desperate efforts to separate and isolate peoples and to sow mistrust and hatred among them in order to plunge them into war against each other, the strengthening and extension of international cultural relations is a powerful means for achieving mutual understanding among peoples of various countries and for rallying fighters for world peace."[101]

In the 1950's, the Soviets used *The Unesco Bulletin for Libraries* as a public relations organ to reach librarians throughout the world. Their articles in it were written by leading Soviet librarians. They stressed the enormous size and cultural richness of library collections in the USSR and the extent of their services. They also wrote of their eagerness to engage in international book exchange and loan programs, as well as the strengthening of international cultural relations. These sophisticated propaganda articles were subdued in tone and almost free of overt Communist library theory.[102]

NOTES

1. Arturs Baumanis and Robert A. Martin, *Soviet Book Statistics: A Guide to Their Use and Interpretation* (Urbana, IL: University of Illinois Library School Occasional Paper number 44, December 1955), p. 8.

2. Ibid., pp. 1-3, 7-8. Moreover, Soviet officials counted any collection of fifty or more books as a *library*, thereby inflating the figures for this type of institution. (See Maurice Friedberg, *Russian Classics in Soviet Jackets* [New York and London: Columbia University Press, 1962], pp. x, 94n7, and 18n.)

3. "Book," in *Harrod's Librarians' Glossary*, 6th ed., comp. by Ray Prytherch (Aldershot, England: Gower, 1987), p. 92.

4. Baumanis and Martin, pp. 4-7.

5. Arturs Baumanis and A. Robert Rogers, "Soviet Classification and Cataloging," *Library Quarterly* 28 (July 1958): 172-86. In the 1970's, Rogers wrote two short pieces on Soviet librarianship: "Censorship and Libraries in the Soviet Union," *Journal of Library History, Philosophy, and Comparative Librarianship* 8 (Jan. 1973): 22-29; and "Some Impressions of Three Russian Libraries," *Ohio Library Association Bulletin* 4 (July 1973): 4-10. His interest in Communist librarianship is discussed in Eric G. Linderman, "A. Robert Rogers: The Influence of His Canadianism on His Work as a Library Educator," *Libraries and Culture* 35 (Fall 2000): 499-513.

6. Karol Maichel, "Russian Retrospective Bibliographies," *Library Quarterly* 28 (April 1958): 122. Maichel also wrote a scholarly article describing the vagaries of current national bibliographic efforts in Russia from 1772 to 1917. For much of this period, the listing of new books was attached to the state censorship apparatus. (Maichel, "Russian Current Bibliographies, 1772-1917," *Library Quarterly* 28 [Jan. 1958]: 38-44.) See also his "Czechoslovak National Bibliography: A Historical Sketch," *College and Research Libraries* 18 (July 1957): 269-74.

7. Paul L. Horecky, *Libraries and Bibliographic Centers in the Soviet Union* (Bloomington, IN: Indiana University, 1959). The book was part of the university's prestigious Slavic and East European Series.

8. Horecky, *Libraries and Bibliographic Centers*, p. v.

9. Ibid., pp. v-vi.

10. The Council was headed by Verner W. Clapp from its founding in 1956 until 1967. Prior to that time, he had worked for more than thirty years at the Library of Congress. The quotation from the Council's charter is from Foster E. Mohrhardt, "Verner Warren Clapp," *Dictionary of American Library Biography*, p. 79. Mohrhardt began this biographical sketch with the statement that "Verner W. Clapp was an internationalist . . . ," (p. 77) but the only major international projects Mohrhardt described were (1) a postwar cooperative acquisitions program to enable American research libraries to secure foreign publications, (2) a plan for a Japanese national library which grew out of Clapp's chairmanship of the US Library Mission to Japan, 1947-1948, and (3) his assistance to the United Nations Library. One major project of the CLR entailed the donation of $6.2 million to build the UN Library that was completed in 1961.

11. Horecky, pp. 1-2.

12. For example, see ibid., pp. 154-55.

13. Ibid., p. 150.

14. Ibid., pp. 160-61.

15. Bela Talbot Kardos, "Bookshelves behind the Iron Curtain," *Idaho Librarian* 5 (Oct. 1953): 25-27.

16. Ibid., p. 27. Early comparisons of revolutions to Saturn were made by Pierre Vergniaud (1753-1793), a French Girondist executed with his colleagues; and George Büchner (1813-1837), a German protoexpressionist playwright. See: *The Oxford Dictionary of Quotations*, 4th ed., ed. by Angela Partington (New York: Oxford University Press, 1992); and *Familiar Quotations*, 15th ed., ed. by John Bartlett and others (Boston: Little, Brown, 1980).

17. "Statistics on Stilts," *Bookmark* 12 (Dec. 1959): 48. Ironically, the University of Idaho was located in the town of Moscow, Idaho. According to George R. Stewart, the fifteen states in America that include Moscow as a place-name generally do so for no reason other than the nineteenth century fashion of naming new settlements after large foreign cities. (See his reliable *American Place-Names: A Concise and Selective Dictionary for the Continental United States of America* [New York: Oxford University Press, 1970.])

18. Elizabeth Bowen, "Libraries in the USSR," *Ontario Library Review* 42 (May 1958): 114-16.

19. Rudolph Smits, "Bibliographic Control in the Soviet Union," *College and Research Libraries* 17 (July 1956): 350-52. Smits worked at the Library of Congress.

20. Judith Szebenyi-Sigmond, "Libraries and Information Services behind the Iron Curtain," *American Documentation* 10 (April 1959): 115.

21. Elisabeth Beyerly, "A Russian Abstracting Service in the Field of Sciences: *Referativnyi zhurnal,*" *Aslib Proceedings* 8 (May 1956): 135-40.

22. The universities were the University of California, Columbia, Harvard, Indiana, and the University of Washington at Seattle. See Martin E. Malia, "Report on the Principal Results of Martin E. Malia's Acquisitions Trip to the USSR," Appendix to the *Library of Congress Information Bulletin* 15 (July 16, 1956): 389-92.

23. "Soviet Research Libraries," *CU News* (May 29, 1957), as reprinted in *Library Journal*, 82 (Nov. 15, 1957): 2892.

24. C. Bickford O'Brien, "Russian Libraries—The Door Swings Open," *College and Research Libraries* 18 (May 1957): 217.

25. O'Brien noted that *The World of Learning* (London: Europa Publications, 1955) estimated the size of the Saltykov-Shchedrin library at over ten million volumes and that the *Report of the Librarian of Congress* for 1955 confirmed this figure. (O'Brien, "Russian Libraries," p. 218, 218 notes.)

26. Oswald P. Backus III, "Recent Experiences with Soviet Libraries and Archives: Uncommon Resources and Potential for Exchange," *College and Research Libraries* 20 (Nov. 1959): 469-73, 499.

27. Ibid., p. 499.

28. Ibid., p. 470. See also p. 499.

29. Ibid., p. 473.

30. One Soviet director of the UN library reported that part of his job while in the United States was to analyze the organization of public libraries. However, unable to understand the concept of local control of educational institutions, he concluded that American public librarians were nothing short of "anarchists." (Lev Vladimirov, speech.) While Solzhenitsyn was correct in his pronouncements that the Soviets studied everything about the United States that they could, they were clearly wrong in some of their conclusions!

31. Charlotte Forgey Chesnut, "Russian Libraries," *The Alabama Librarian* 2 (July 1960): 68-69.

32. Ibid., p. 69.

33. Valter Alstedt, "Library Education in the Soviet Union," *College and Research Libraries* 19 (Nov. 1958): 467-70; reprinted from *Biblioteksbladet* 9 (1957), and translated by Thomas R. Buckman. Buckman later became Director of Libraries at Nothwestern University and then President of the Foundation Center in New York. He wrote about libraries in Japan, among other subjects.

34. Charles Deane Kent, "Book Selection in the USSR," *Ontario Library Review* 43 (Nov. 1959): 284.

35. Ibid., p. 285.

36. Boris Pasternak's novel about Russian history was denied publication in the USSR but was issued in Italy and afterwards in other countries. Awarded the Nobel Prize for Literature in 1958, Pasternak was forced by his government to refuse the award.

37. Kent, pp. 285-86. It is difficult to discern whether Kent's sentence fragments were flourishes or mere grammatical lapses.

38. Ibid.

39. Ibid., p. 286.

40. Ibid. The accepted transliteration of the Soviet leader's name has always been *Khrushchev*.

41. See Charles Deane Kent's articles: "The Leningrad State Library," *Canadian Library Journal* 16 (Sept. 1959): 67-70; "Leningrad State Library Institute," *Library Journal* 84 (Nov. 15, 1959): 3528-30; and "The Library of the Hermitage in Leningrad," *Library Review* 17 (Spring 1960): 320-21.

42. Bowles was later active in the founding of Unesco as well as the early development of other elements of the UN. He was prominent in liberal Democratic Party circles for three decades and served as a Congressman from Connecticut as well as an ambassador.

43. Quoted in "William Benton," *Biographical Dictionary of the Left*, consolidated vol. 1, p. 235.

44. The information that follows is taken from: William Benton, "Too Busy to Think?" *ALA Bulletin* 52 (June 1958): 441-43, and Benton, "William Benton Reports on Russian Libraries," *Library Journal* 81 (Nov. 15, 1956): 2650-51. Paul L. Horecky was one of many who took at least some of Benton's observations seriously. (See Horecky, *Libraries and Bibliographic Centers in the Soviet Union*, p. 151.)

45. William Benton, "Too Busy to Think?" p. 443.

46. See Joseph McCarthy, "Explanation of Why Names Were Made Public: Statement on Suspended State Department Officials under Investigation Being Allowed Access to Secret Files," Aug. 9, 1951, in *Major Speeches and Debates of Senator Joe McCarthy Delivered in the United States Senate, 1950-1951*, p. 317. On William T. Stone, see Buckley and Bozell, *McCarthy and His Enemies*, pp. 195-97.

47. "Report on Russian Libraries," *Library Journal* 84 (Jan. 15, 1959): 161. Litchfield was accompanied by seven other educators. He issued an account of the trip that was published by the University of Pittsburgh Press.

48. Thomas J. Whitby, "National Bibliography in the USSR," *Library Quarterly* 23 (Jan. 1953): 22.

49. Thomas J. Whitby, "Development of the System of Legal Deposit in the USSR," *College and Research Libraries* 15 (Oct. 1954): 398-406; and "Evolution and Evaluation of a Soviet Classification," *Library Quarterly* 26 (April 1956): 118-27.

50. Thomas Joseph Whitby, "Account of a Library Visit to the USSR, May-June 1957; A Report Submitted to the Graduate School of Library Service, Rutgers University," (Washington, DC: n.p., Oct. 1957, 103 pp., mimeographed).

51. In 1997 an OCLC search revealed one hard copy at the University of Kentucky and one "microfilm (negative) of original in Library of Congress" at the University of California at Berkeley.

52. Ibid., p. 22.

53. Ibid., p. 19.

54. Ibid., p. 37.

55. Ibid., pp. 62-63.

56. Surprisingly, one of the Soviet librarians he met asserted in front of his own colleagues that the American literature in Soviet libraries was dated. He declared that the best of the modern writers, like Willa Cather and Pearl Buck, were absent, while less capable authors, like Mitchell Wilson and Howard Fast, were well represented. (See Whitby, "Account," pp. 75-76.) Wilson wrote about the morality of nuclear scientists. Fast was a member of the Communist Party until 1956.

57. Whitby, "Account," pp. 22-23, 74-75, 95-96, 101.

58. For example, see ibid., pp. 39-41, 63.

59. Ibid., p. 100.

60. Ibid., p. 101. Whitby remarked that the quality of the cataloguing was lower than that done by either the Library of Congress or the H. W. Wilson Company. Both produced catalog cards for sale to libraries.

61. Ibid., p. 98.

62. Ibid., pp. 90-91.

63. Ibid., pp. 99-100.

64. Thomas J. Whitby, "Impressions from a Library Tour of the Soviet Union," *D.C. Libraries* 29 (Oct. 1958): 65-69.

65. Thomas J. Whitby, "Soviet Libraries Today," *ALA Bulletin* 53 (June 1959): 485-89.

66. Howard W. Winger, ed., *Iron Curtains and Scholarship: The Exchange of Knowledge in a Divided World: Papers Presented before the Twenty-Third Annual Conference of the Graduate Library School of the University of Chicago, July 7-9, 1958* (Chicago: Graduate Library School, University of Chicago, 1958); also published (with different pagination) as *Library Quarterly* 28 (Oct. 1958).

67. Howard Winger, "Introduction," in *Iron Curtains and Scholarship*, ed. by Winger, p. 1. See also p. 2. The term *Iron Curtain* was commonly used for decades in descriptions of the Soviet-inspired divide between East and West after it was emphasized in a speech by Winston Churchill on March 5, 1946. Churchill had used the term earlier to describe the boundaries of Soviet power, as had Viscountess Ethel Snowden (1920), Joseph Goebbels (1945), and Senator Arthur Vandenberg (1945). (See "Iron Curtain" in: William Safire, *Safire's New Political Dictionary* [New York: Random House, 1993]; Nicholas Comfort, *Brewer's Politics: A Phrase and Fable Dictionary* [London: Cassell, 1993]; Thomas Parrish, *The Cold War Encyclopedia* [New York: Henry Holt, 1996]; and Sir Martin Gilbert, *Winston S. Churchill* [Vol. 8]: *'Never Despair': 1945-1965* [Boston: Houghton Mifflin, 1988,] *passim*.)

68. Winger, "Introduction," pp. 1-2.

69. Ibid., p. 1.

70. Howard Winger, "The Exchange of Ideas in the Advancement of Knowledge," in *Iron Curtains and Scholarship*, ed. by Winger, p. 3.

71. Ibid., pp. 5-12.

72. Ibid., p. 12.

73. Bryant went on to become the Director of Libraries at Harvard.

74. Douglas W. Bryant, "The American Scholar and Barriers to Knowledge," in *Iron Curtains and Scholarship*, ed. by Winger, pp. 13-27.

75. Ibid., p. 13.

76. Ibid., pp. 23-25.

77. Ibid., p. 13.

78. Ibid.

79. Ibid., p. 15.

80. Vaclav Mostecky, "The Library under Communism: Czechoslovak Libraries from 1948 to 1954," *Library Quarterly* 26 (April 1956): 105-17. Compounding his other errors, Bryant footnoted the Communist quotation incorrectly, indicating that it was a statement by Mostecky rather than someone Mostecky was quoting and criticizing. Mostecky's article drew a vivid, well-documented portrait of a Communist effort to use libraries to help destroy a culture and replace it with a Soviet-style one.

81. Ibid., pp. 15-20.

82. See: Nicholas Berdyaev, *The Origin of Russian Communism*, trans. by R. M. French (London: Geoffrey Bles, 1937, 1948; as reprinted: Ann Arbor: University of Michigan Press, 1960), pp. 155, 183, 187, and elsewhere; and Hans Kohn, *Basic History of Modern Russia* (Princeton, NJ: Van Nostrand, 1957): pp. 107-18. All of Kohn's numerous books focus on nationalism as the prime determinant in modern history. Born and educated in Prague, he came to the United States in 1931 and thereafter taught in American colleges and universities. Berdyaev, the Russian philosopher, theologian, and historian, was exiled by the Communists in 1922 because of his criticism of their regime. He lived the rest of his life in Paris.

83. Melville J. Ruggles, "Eastern European Publications in American Libraries," in *Iron Curtains and Scholarship*, ed. by Winger, pp. 111-23.

84. Ibid., p. 120.

85. Thomas J. Whitby, "Libraries and Bibliographic Projects in the Communist Bloc," in *Iron Curtains and Scholarship*, ed. by Winger, pp. 51-68.

86. Ibid., pp. 51-52.

87. Everett C. Olson, "Russian Literature in the Natural Sciences"; Alexander Dallin, "The Soviet Social Sciences after Stalin"; and Edward J. Brown, "Literature of the Humanities"; all in *Iron Curtains and Scholarship*, ed. by Winger, pp. 69-81, 82-95, and 96-110, respectively.

88. Leopold H. Haimson, "Three Generations of the Soviet Intelligentsia," in *Iron Curtains and Scholarship*, ed. by Winger, pp. 28-42.

89. Kenneth Holland, "Prospects for a Freer Exchange of Knowledge," in *Iron Curtains and Scholarship*, ed. by Winger, pp. 124-29.

90. Yuri Gvosdev, "Publishing and Book Distribution in the USSR," in *Iron Curtains and Scholarship*, ed. by Winger, pp. 43-50.

91. Flora B. Ludington, "Strengthening the Forces for Peace," *MLA* [Massachusetts Library Association] *Bulletin* 41 (July 1951): 37-38.

92. As quoted ibid., p. 38n.

93. For example, see "Khrushchev on the Shifting Balance of World Forces: A Selection of Statements and an Interpretive Analysis: A Special Study Presented by Sen. Hubert H. Humphrey [and] Prepared by the Legislative Service of the Library of Congress" (Washington, DC: GPO, Sept. 1959).

94. Edward Dudley, "Libraries in the USSR," *Library Association Record* 61 (May 1959): 111.

95. Ibid., pp. 111-13.

96. Ibid., p. 113.

97. Ibid.

98. Edward Dudley, "Introduction," *Lenin, Krupskaia, and Libraries,* ed. by S. Simsova, pp. 7-8. In this 1968 work, Dudley noted the increased study of Soviet librarianship in both the UK and the USA in recent years. He believed that historical and comparative studies were necessary for the true development of a profession. He hoped that Simsova's work would, among other things, make possible "an understanding of many of the aims and practices of the contemporary Soviet library system; and, perhaps, a little more understanding and sympathy for Lenin the man and library-user." (p. 8)

99. W. W. Gottlieb, "Some Facts about Libraries in the USSR: Impressions from a Recent Visit," *Library Review* 130 (Summer 1959): 98-101.

100. Michael Futrell, "Banned Books in the Lenin Library," *Library Review* 130 (Autumn 1959): 184-86.

101. P. N. Vymenets, "International Book Exchange of the Library of the USSR Academy of Sciences," *Vestnik* (March 1952), as translated in Boris I. Gorokhoff, "Soviet Views on International Book Exchange," *Library of Congress Information Bulletin* 11 (Sept. 8, 1952): 11.

102. For example, see: G. A. Cebotarev, "The Library of the USSR Academy of Sciences," *Unesco Bulletin for Libraries* 10 (Oct. 1956): 225-26; Margarita Rudomino, "The All-Union Library of Foreign Literature," *Unesco Bulletin for Libraries* 10 (Oct. 1956): 226-28; and V. Barasenkov, "The Saltykov-Scedrin State Public Library, Leningrad," *Unesco Bulletin for Libraries* 11 (Feb.-March 1957): 32-35. Each author was the director of the library described. A major agency of library education was featured in N. Skrypnev, "The 'Krupskaja' State Library Institute, Leningrad," *Unesco Bulletin for Libraries* 13 (April 1959): 84-86.

7

THE PROFESSION OPPOSES
ANTI-COMMUNISM

The General Philosophy of International Librarianship

American Library Association Presidents:
Ludington, Downs, and Morsch

Writings and pronouncements on the philosophy of international librarianship were still not numerous or well developed in the United States in the 1950's, but some statements were made. Expressing the views acceptable to the leaders, and possibly the members, of the American Library Association was Flora Belle Ludington. This Chairman of the American Library Association's Board of International Relations from 1942 to 1944[1] and 1950 to 1952 described the goals of America's international endeavors as "Strengthening the Forces for Peace," the title of her 1951 article in the journal of the Massachusetts Library Association.[2] Ludington, the Librarian of Mount Holyoke College, declared that librarians could be effective agencies in this "battle for peace"[3] by mobilizing ideas, materials, and people. She considered it "inconceivable"[4] that members of the American profession would not be engaged on the international level. Every librarian, she believed, could make some contribution. She agreed with the thoughts expressed in a recent speech at an American Library Association conference by the political scientist and former Deputy Director General of Unesco, Walter H. C. Laves. Ludington quoted him in her attempt to stress the importance of "international understanding":

"Through exchange of ideas, through personal contact, the culture
of each people must be made known to others. The community of
librarians in the world, each pressing for the development of
libraries as centers of democratic action should and *can* be a potent
influence in the educational job to be done."[5]

(Laves had also asserted in his presentation that the current world
crisis did not consist simply of the antagonism between the United
States and the Soviet Union nor the opposition of capitalism and
Communism: it was essentially the battle between internationalism and
nationalism. The United States, he averred, had to continue its world
leadership by encouraging other countries to pledge themselves to the
United Nations, an institution whose charter expressed the essence of
American aspirations and institutions: human rights, democracy, and
peace. All nations must align their policies according to those desired
by the majority of countries in the United Nations. The duty of
American librarians was to adhere to the US National Commission for
Unesco and to educate the American people for what he termed "the
United Nations world."[6])

Ludington affirmed that librarians must make their patrons informed on issues of international affairs and cognizant of the views
held in foreign countries.[7] She maintained that the profession should
help identify those books "which adequately interpret the United
States,"[8] and assist programs that place them overseas. She spoke
positively of the Information Centers operated abroad by the Department of State. (In the late 1940's, Ludington had joined with
other leaders of the American Library Association in directly urging
the State Department to keep America's overseas libraries non-
propagandistic and inclusive of works critical of the United States.[9]
This is dealt with below.)

Her other major statement on international library relations was
presented at the 1953 *International Aspects of Librarianship* conference
at the University of Chicago's Graduate Library School. In it she
asserted the "basic internationalism of our profession"[10] and the belief
that "As keepers of the intellectual book, librarians can play an
important role in furthering world scholarship and world understanding."[11] She did not support these assertions with any facts, but
merely enumerated the ways American librarianship had bolstered
professional developments abroad. Again invoking the nostrum of

international communication, Ludington hinted that some American librarians in the early 1920's may have *predicted* World War II when they declared that the "intellectual isolation" of Germany, Austria, Hungary, Czechoslovakia, Poland, Russia, and the Baltic States was the greatest threat to global peace.[12] She insisted that the contemporary world was in a similar situation and mentioned the "free world."[13]

One finishes reading this confused work wondering what she is talking about. Amazingly, the contemporary Soviet Union was never mentioned, nor was the "C" word. Apparently, these were not necessary for "international understanding."

Like similar articles of this genre, most of the international activities Ludington described and approved of consisted of Americans assisting other countries with free books or professional expertise. Despite her earlier quotation of Laves on the role of "democratic" libraries, she neglected to note their failure to develop in the countries of America's political adversaries, and she offered no ideas for dealing with that reality. In truth, she seemed unable to face the grim fact that the United States was being challenged by a hostile, aggressive foreign power that was imbued with an antithetical ethos. Her incapacity or unwillingness to even name that country and its political philosophy was significant.

Ludington's views buoyed her position in American librarianship. In addition to serving as head of the committee overseeing the international activities of the American Library Association, she directed the United States Information Library in Bombay from 1944 to 1946. Over the next dozen years, she was sponsored by the ALA, the Ford Foundation, and the Rockefeller Foundation to serve as a library consultant in Japan, Turkey, and areas of Africa. In the domestic arena, she was a leader of the Intellectual Freedom movement, whose ideology and players were much the same as those seeking "democratic" American libraries overseas.[14] Ludington served as President of the American Library Association from 1953 to 1954.[15]

"One Library World" was the title of Robert B. Downs' inaugural address as President of the American Library Association in July 1952. The then director of the library school at the University of Illinois declared that the international events of the previous thirty years had made it clear that all peoples belonged to one world. He asserted that it was just as true that there was now just one library world. This was his evidence:

1. "Increasingly, librarianship as it is practiced in the United States has become accepted as a standard which the rest of the globe is striving to attain."[16] He noted the large number of foreign students at American library schools, American library educators who were teaching abroad, and the model libraries provided by the US Information Centers abroad.

2. The increasing efforts of the United States to acquire foreign books, and the international exchange of catalog cards.[17]

While this was certainly proof that America's libraries and librarians had become more involved in international enterprises, it was hardly sufficient to claim that there was now "One Library World." Downs also exaggerated the extent to which foreign countries were imitating the United States. Moreover, he seems to have entirely forgotten about the Soviet Union and its satellite countries, as well as the People's Republic of China. Clearly, the librarians there were not attempting to emulate those in the United States. Like Ludington, Downs was a leader of the Intellectual Freedom movement as well as the fight to model the US government's overseas libraries on domestic public libraries.

A uniquely patriotic, anti-Communist library theme was sounded in the presidential speech of Lucile Morsch at the 1957 annual American Library Association conference.[18] Morsch, whose lifelong professional interest was cataloging, utilized as its title the phrase added to the Association's charter in 1942 proclaiming its newfound mission of "promoting library interests throughout the world." Morsch berated American librarians for not being more involved in international activities. Significantly, she did not *decry* American foreign policy, like most leaders of the profession, but instead enumerated the ways librarians could help carry it out. She quoted from a statement by President Eisenhower declaring that there were not enough government diplomats and information officers to accomplish what needed to be done:

"Indeed, if our American ideology is eventually to win out . . . it must have the active support of thousands of independent private groups and institutions and of millions of Americans, acting through person-to-person communication."[19]

Morsch contrasted the ideals of American librarianship—which she said were sometimes taken for granted—with those in some other countries. In such nations, she declared, libraries are tools of the state and serve as agencies of indoctrination. (She left no doubt which countries she was referring to.) This is "an approach to librarianship that is repulsive to us and spurs us on to international activity on behalf of the system we champion."[20] American librarians should promote worldwide what she called "the American library gospel."[21]

The "International Aspects of Librarianship" Conference

As described above, Ludington spoke at the 1953 annual conference of the Graduate Library School of the University of Chicago. The very choice of the meeting's topic, "International Aspects of Librarianship," demonstrated the growing interest in this subject. It was organized by Leon Carnovsky, a Professor at the GLS who had joined the faculty after receiving his doctorate there in 1932. The conference dealt with a very wide range of subjects and lacked focus. However, there was some stress on the improvement of the international flow of information[22] and, in the words of Carnovsky, "international library improvement and understanding."[23] The failure of the conference to confront reality was betokened by the fact that most of the speakers avoided discussing, or even mentioning, the Soviet Union or Communism.

One presenter, a physiologist at the University of Minnesota, deplored both the limitations allegedly imposed by the United States government on the free international flow of scientific information and the supposed shortcomings of the American public. "These points need stress because the layman does not in general perceive the great importance of free exchange of basic information to scientific progress even in military affairs."[24] However, the ignorance, fears, and negative political motives of many Americans were not the only domestic causes for concern, he warned:

There are psychopathic personalities in every race and every
nation. In some, unfortunately, the psychopaths have great power.
We in the United States have a great problem on our hands to make
sure that psychopathic personalities do not exploit our national
troubles by unreasonable and unwise restrictions on the intra- and
international exchange of knowledge. This must be prevented in
order to protect our own future progress and safety and also to
improve the attitudes, which are rapidly deteriorating, of foreigners
toward our country.[25]

Carnovsky's own paper, "Patterns of Library Government and
Coverage in European Nations,"[26] devoted as much space to countries
like Belgium, Switzerland, and Denmark as to the USSR. He stated
that "enormous strides have been taken in the creation and development
of libraries for all"[27] in the Soviet Union; his elaboration of this point
constituted the bulk of his treatment of Soviet librarianship. He
devoted one paragraph to the use of Soviet libraries for propaganda,
declaring that "The role of the Soviet library in indoctrination or
thought control is too well known to require elaboration."[28] The only
speech at the conference that attempted to deal directly with the East-
West conflict was Dan Lacy's "Overseas Book Program of the United
States Government." It is discussed later.

One unintended consequence of this 1953 conference was the
impetus it apparently provided for Chase Dane, an American Library
Association staff member, to write an article entitled "Comparative
Librarianship."[29] Published in a British library periodical, it did much
to popularize this new term and the goals of the infant field it
described:
1. a comparison and evaluation of differing philosophies and
   practices of librarianship.
2. a broadened tolerance and understanding that would lead
   to international library cooperation.
3. shared techniques and practices on a global level.
4. improved library services throughout the world.
5. greater international understanding and cooperation through the
   profession itself, as well as indirectly to other areas of society
   through the products of international librarianship, particularly
   universal bibliographic control.

6. improved international relations through the knowledge and understanding gained with comparative librarianship.

The utopian, internationalist philosophy of the field of international comparative librarianship was to prove detrimental to the development of an objective, realistic discipline that would serve the interests of American librarianship and of the American people.

The Overseas Libraries Dispute

Soviet-American relations had a large impact on the numerous overseas libraries maintained by the US State Department. The precursors of these institutions had begun in the late 1930's and increased dramatically during World War II to improve political, and to a lesser extent cultural, relations with America's allies and with non-belligerents. They had been funded by the State Department, the Office of War Information, and the Rockefeller Foundation. As already noted, leaders of the library profession had fought to prevent these from becoming instruments of American propaganda or foreign policy.[30]

After World War II, there were curtailments in the financial support and staffing for US government libraries in other countries. However, visiting members of Congress and other observers in Europe soon reported on the successful Communist grabs for power there and on the poor state of America's libraries. In 1947, for example:

> In France, aided by a strong local Communist movement and a system of 1,500 binational associations known as "France-USSR," the Soviets were waging an effective propaganda campaign at the expense of the Americans who were concerned simply with averting starvation [in France]. The State Department estimated at the time that the British spent $440,000 annually in France for information and cultural relations, the Russians nearly ten times as much and the Americans only $125,000.[31]

A renewed involvement was forthcoming. With the advent of the Cold War, many in the government wanted these libraries to become more active in supporting America's foreign policy goals and in thwarting those of the USSR. (Nevertheless, throughout the 1950's these efforts remained dwarfed by those of the Soviet Union. The USSR flooded the libraries and bookstores of much of the world with inexpensive or free books.[32]) Many leaders of the profession continued to oppose making the US overseas libraries pro-American and anti-Soviet, maintaining that they should be modeled after the American public library and thereby serve as archetypal democratic institutions. Waving the banners of "democracy" and "intellectual freedom," their reaction was an unsophisticated reflex. They did not have the ability to distinguish between a locally run, domestic, educational institution and a federally controlled agency operating abroad in a world threatened by an aggressive foe. As Roy Cohn remarked about the overseas libraries he had inspected as part of Senator Joseph Mc-Carthy's investigation of them: "This wasn't the New York Public Library we were talking about, where free circulation of ideas is the reigning virtue."[33]

Throughout the 1940's, leaders of the American library profession, like Carl Milam, Harry Miller Lydenberg, and Flora Ludington, advocated what Gary Kraske has accurately labeled "liberal internationalism."[34] He notes that Milam, who served as the chief executive officer of the American Library Association from 1920 to 1948 and then Director of the UN Library for two years, readily admitted that he had little knowledge of foreign policy but rather held those ideas Kraske believes were "shared by most educational and cultural leaders of the day."[35] Milam maintained that an international cultural program should be a manifestation of domestic policy untainted by foreign policy considerations. It should simply attempt to spread knowledge around the globe. In so doing, it would create the kind of world and international relations he believed Americans would like. Soberly, Kraske has concluded: ". . . the efficacy of a cultural program with such indistinct aims and built upon some timeless American desire for free expression seemed debatable in a world full of malice."[36]

By the 1950's, there were better informed critics of the overseas libraries, such as Dan Lacy and Henry James, Jr., who—at least in their writings—presented careful analyses of many of the relevant policy considerations. James, who had worked as a script writer for the Voice of America from 1948 to 1951 and then earned a master's degree in library service from Columbia University, was even more critical of the US government's approach than Lacy.[37] Both men based some of their recommendations concerning the foreign libraries on the conclusion of the recent Public Library Inquiry that the natural audience for the American public library was the educated elite. Lacy and James considered this the proper function of the libraries abroad as well. Here, as elsewhere, the elitist propensities of those in the Intellectual Freedom movement were evident.

As already stated, the question of book selection for overseas and domestic libraries tended to be conflated in the 1950's, as they had been in the previous decade. Lacy declared in a 1993 interview that he believed that if Joseph McCarthy's policies on overseas libraries had been effected, the Senator would probably have turned his attention to libraries at home.[38] There is no evidence to support such a charge.

At the emotional American Library Association annual conference in 1953, the hysterical presidential speech of Robert B. Downs set the tone:

> Perhaps at the top of the list for discussion, because of its wide implications for librarians and the general public alike, is the current wave of anti-intellectualism, manifesting itself in attacks on books, on free speech, freedom of inquiry, freedom to teach, and all the rights which we have long held to be guaranteed by the First Amendment to the United States Constitution. A virulent disease, presently diagnosed as "McCarthyism," but antedating the distinguished Senator for whom it is named by centuries, is infecting nearly every segment of our governmental structure from national down to local levels.
>
> Look, for example, at the excellent system of 194 information libraries now operated by the Department of State in some 61 foreign countries. Stringent censorship directives, issued in the atmosphere of fear, hysteria, and repression now prevailing in Washington, threaten to place the entire information library program in jeopardy.[39]

After further distorting the situation, he again sounded the tocsin, warning of the

> spreading pressures on books, being manifested in attacks on libraries, textbook controversies, attempts to limit circulation and publication, repressive legislation by state and local governments, extra-legal measures by police officials, and the activities of such

private groups as the so-called National Organization of Decent
Literature.[40]

Librarians, he said, were the subject of "assaults by the forces of
darkness and reaction,"[41] but he assured his audience that the American Library Association was fighting back.

Shortly after this conference, the alleged "fear, hysteria, and
repression now prevailing in Washington" somehow did not prevent
Downs from being appointed to the United States Information Agency's
Committee on Books Abroad. He believed that he owed this position
to a recommendation by Lacy. Downs served in this capacity for eight
years during which, he reported, he "participated in many lively
discussions on policies."[42] Similarly, the supposed "fear, hysteria, and
repression" had not prevented the Librarian of Congress, Luther Evans,
from openly challenging Joseph McCarthy's allegations of subversives
in government, going so far as to hire someone who had been fired by
the State Department after being named by McCarthy as a security
risk.[43]

In the febrile atmosphere of the 1953 ALA conference, its
governing Council adopted a resolution, written primarily by Lacy,[44]
titled the "Overseas Library Statement."[45] It was a poorly organized,
redundant, and illogical pronouncement that was full of contradictions.
It began with an insistence that the American Library Association and
its members had been closely involved with the federal government's
overseas library program from its beginnings in the late 1930's, that
these institutions had always done an effective job, and that they had
been devoted entirely to "the interests of the United States." Today,
"With many impartial observers, we believe that they are among the
most effective weapons possessed by the United States in the battle to
preserve free men and free minds from the enslavement of Communist
political and intellectual tyranny."

It went on to criticize the "confused and fearful response of the
State Department to recent attacks upon this program." Naively and
illogically conflating the purposes of overseas and domestic libraries,
the Statement noted "the indispensable value of free libraries as the
enemy of enslaved minds abroad as at home." It indicated that the
overseas libraries should be modeled on the domestic public library:
"The [overseas] libraries must express in themselves and their services
the ideas of freedom for which they speak." It was not spelled out in

this particular Intellectual Freedom statement, but these were code words meaning, among other things, that book collections should be "balanced."

Twice in the Statement it was explicitly affirmed that the effectiveness of libraries was dependent on the certainty of their users that they were sources of "truth." It did not explain how libraries could dispense "the truth" *and* opposing sides of issues. In addition to these commitments to both "the truth" and intellectual freedom, the authors of the Statement supported yet a third responsibility, declaring that "no one could justify or would seek to justify the use of the overseas libraries to disseminate material harmful to the United States." Obviously, this charge was not necessarily compatible with the other two and seems to have been tossed in as a patriotic fig leaf. No rank order of goals was given, so the ALA did not declare which of these conflicting aims would be considered most important if, for example, there were a conflict between the truth and the well-being of the United States.

A firm stand was made in the Overseas Library Statement against the consideration of authors' political orientations when selecting books. There should be no "elaborate, irrelevant, and offensive schemes of 'clearance' of authors," nor should "irrelevant reasons of the past associations of authors" be part of any decision. It was not explained why considerations of an author's background or current political views were particularly "irrelevant" and "offensive" since library book selection had traditionally evaluated the aims and qualifications of authors. A member of the Communist Party would be, by the Party's own guidelines, pro-Soviet and committed to anti-American work. And as has been noted before, the financial remuneration and prestige accorded a Communist author by placing his or her works in US government libraries abroad would be incompatible with the legal aims of those libraries. It is relevant that members of the Party were expected to donate money, as well as time and energy, to it.[46] The "Overseas Library Statement" also attempted to undermine the scrutiny of authors when it proclaimed that only "the simple criterion of whether a book is useful to the purpose of the libraries" should be utilized. (This assertion reflected either innocence or feigned innocence.) The same sentiment was stated another way by declaring that a book should be included when it was "useful to the provision of . . . service." It was significant that the Statement annointed the professional librarians running the overseas libraries as the sole rightful arbiters in choosing the books.   Such a pronouncement would be popular in a field yearning for greater power and prestige.

The Statement ended with the simplistic idea that the overseas libraries did not truly belong to any agency of the government but "to the whole American people, who were entitled to have them express their finest ideals of responsible freedom." (Apparently, these ideals would somehow be apprehended by the overseas librarians and then acted upon.)   One can see how naive—or crafty—these high-flown words were if one compares them to the administration of all other government services: the latter have a legally sanctioned chain-of-command.

The American Library Association slyly tied its Overseas Library Statement to a few extemporaneous remarks made by President Eisenhower at Dartmouth College[47] earlier in the month.   The Statement read, "We are . . . enormously heartened by the President's recent vigorous attack on book-burning.   We support this position fully."[48]   However, Eisenhower declared explicitly in a lengthy, well-publicized press conference three days after his brief observations on June 14, 1953, that he had clearly been referring to the censorship of America's domestic libraries, not those in other countries.   He asserted to the badgering news reporters that Communist and pro-Communist works have no place in US libraries abroad: assisting an enemy that is bent on one's destruction would be "about the limit of silliness."[49]   Thus, the American Library Association misrepresented the President's position, as well as its own, in its shoddy Statement.

Gaining center stage at the conference was the two thousand word declaration titled the "Freedom to Read" written a few weeks earlier at a meeting of two dozen leading publishers and librarians presided over by Luther Evans.   It received quick support from President Eisenhower, numerous professional organizations, and many newspapers and magazines nationwide.   A *New York Times* editorial suggested that it and the declaration on overseas libraries 'ought to be prominently displayed and readily available in every public library at home or abroad.'[50]   It began:

> The freedom to read is essential to our democracy.   It is under attack.   Private groups and public authorities in various parts of the country are working to remove books from sale, to censor

textbooks, to label "controversial" books, to distribute lists of "objectionable" books or authors, and to purge libraries.[51]

Such actions, the "Freedom to Read" maintained, should be fought. While it addressed the situation only within the United States, it arose, in part, due to the debates about the overseas libraries.[52] Unfortunately, as I have said, many contemporaries, as well as later library historians, have erroneously viewed the controversies over the domestic and the overseas libraries as one.[53]

One library historian has writen that "The enhanced prestige and authority that came with ALA's firm articulation of *The Freedom to Read* and the Overseas Libraries Statement contributed to a sense of assertiveness, at least among those who attended the Los Angeles conference."[54] She indicates that "the exhilarating episode"[55] of the conference in defending intellectual freedom was intimately linked with the librarians' growing professionalism. Downs later claimed that the librarians' actions may well have been responsible "for turning the tide in the national hysteria over book purging and book burning which seized the country."[56] Thus, it appears that battling against censorship and alleged censorship had quickly become a hearty manifestation of many librarians' enduring and rueful yearning for greater prestige and professional status. Some apparently also wanted more power. Such longings were impelled largely by self-induced feelings of low self-esteem.

Two years before these events, the American Library Association had adopted its "Statement on Labeling." It was partly written in response to suggestions from the Montclair, New Jersey, chapter of the Sons of the American Revolution that Communist works and other subversive materials be labeled as such and given out only to those willing to sign a request for them. Much of the 250 word ALA document discussed Communism and other non-democratic systems; it affirmed that these were a threat to the free world that American librarians should resist. However, it opposed the mild proposition that Communist materials be labeled:

1. Although totalitarian states find it easy and even proper, according to their ethics, to establish criteria for judging publications as "subversive," injustice and ignorance rather than justice and enlightenment result from such practices, and

the American Library Association has a responsibility to take a stand against the establishment of such criteria in a democratic state.

2. Libraries do not advocate the ideas found in their collections. The presence of a magazine or book in a library does not indicate an endorsement of its contents by the library.

3. No one person should take the responsibility of labeling publications. No sizeable group of persons would be likely to agree whether on the types of materials which should be labeled or the sources of information which should be regarded with suspicion. As a practical consideration, a librarian who labeled a book or magazine pro-communist might be sued for libel.

4. Labeling is an attempt to prejudice the reader, and as such, it is a censor's tool.

5. Labeling violates the spirit of the Library Bill of Rights.

6. Although we are all agreed that Communism is a threat to the free world, if materials are labeled to pacify one group, there is no excuse for refusing to label any item in the library's collection. Because communism, fascism, or other authoritarianisms tend to suppress ideas and attempt to coerce individuals to conform to a specific ideology, American librarians must be opposed to such "isms." We are, then, anticommunist, but we are also opposed to any other group which aims at closing any path to knowledge.[57]

In 1971 the Statement on Labeling was substantially modified, and all references to Communism and subversive materials were taken out.[58] By this time, lip service to such concerns was no longer deemed necessary.

Throughout the 1950's and later decades, those who opposed the provision of Communist books in America's overseas libraries, or merely advocated the provision of anti-Communist books in domestic libraries, were routinely vilified as "book burners." The allusion, of course, was largely to the Nazis and their infamous public firings of books. This frequent defamation was thus particularly irresponsible and indecent when aimed at men and women who had served in the armed forces in World War II.

(It is telling that when the public burning of library books in Germany by the National Socialists was noted by those in the

Intellectual Freedom movement, it was not mentioned that these acts were carried out and led by university students and their professors.[59] This would not have conformed to their preconceptions about educated and cultured people of social standing: it was those in the supposedly ignorant lower classes that Movement librarians feared and despised. It is relevant that many generals in the SS held Ph.D.'s, and that Joseph Goebbels earned a doctorate in literature at the University of Heidelberg before embarking on his political career.)

Many in librarianship who used the slur "book burner" so freely, like Robert B. Downs, were not merely doing so metaphorically. They charged that books in overseas libraries actually were being burned, despite the lack of solid evidence to support this. The American press eagerly jumped on what seemed to be an exciting story with the potential for scandal if played correctly: a means of disposal could be transmogrified into something sinister. However, at a June 1953 press conference, Secretary of State John Foster Dulles, who had begun to investigate the rumors of incineration, declared that it *appeared* that out of the two million books in the overseas libraries a mere eleven works had been burned in one or two places "due to a rather fanatical interpretation of rules."[60] He called for "more common sense"[61] on the part of those carrying out their duties. Unfortunately, Dulles did not make public his belief—expressed at a Cabinet meeting—that if librarians overseas had indeed burned books they may have done so in an attempt to discredit McCarthy.[62] In the ensuing months, these alleged book burnings were ascribed by those eager to find them to a succession of different US libraries throughout the globe: Europe, Australia, and elsewhere. In each case, zealous journalists were informed by the local American officials that nothing of the sort had taken place, and a new venue for the supposed deed would then be contrived and investigated.

With a few exceptions, the epithet *bookburner* was used almost exclusively by the militant anti-anti-Communists. Already mentioned was its fraudulent use by the American Library Association to buttress its Overseas Library Statement with President Eisenhower's impromptu remarks at the Dartmouth College commencement.[63] The proximate cause for his brief—but frequently quoted—statement may have been the fact that before the ceremony the other recipients of honorary degrees had been "discussing with horror the [supposed] book burnings and [Eisenhower] joined in the conversation."[64] With McCarthy attacking both the executive branch of the government Eisenhower headed, as well as his personal associates, the President may have been striking back publicly at his political foe with a term that was being used by some to discredit the Wisconsin senator. On the conservative side, the term was used as a riposte by Freda Utley[65] and William T. Couch[66] when describing the widespread, successful efforts to prevent the publication and distribution of anti-Communist works.

Dan Lacy and the Overseas Libraries Debate

Dan Lacy, an historian and archivist, had overseen the US State Department's overseas information centers for close to two years. In 1953 he left government work to become managing director of the American Book Publishers Council. As already reported, he was the primary author of the American Library Association's Overseas Library Statement. Nevertheless, unlike most of the others involved in the ALA's campaign against anti-Communism, he had an informed fear and hatred of the USSR that was displayed in many of his articles and public statements.

In July 1953, Lacy debated the function of America's overseas libraries with Congressman Charles Kersten on the popular and prestigious, nation-wide ABC radio show, *Town Meeting of the Air*. Kersten, a Milwaukee lawyer, was a friend and supporter of Senator McCarthy. Lacy claimed more than once in this public exchange that there was little difference between his views and those of his opponent. The positions he articulated in this particular discussion were relatively moderate. He declared that the purpose of the overseas libraries was different from domestic ones, and stated that while books written by Communists should not automatically be excluded from the US libraries abroad, it was not likely that they would be appropriate. However, he expressed a vaguely worded and pregnant concern that users of the overseas libraries should not be allowed to think that they might not be given the truth about some subject. Kersten was adamantly opposed to including works by Communists in overseas libraries, declaring such individuals to be ipso facto anti-American. He also stressed the political and legal factors that mandated that such libraries be different from those within the US. He agreed that books which pointed out shortcomings of the United States were acceptable in American libraries abroad, but maintained that the focus of these agencies should be on defeating Communism.[67]

At the 1953 Graduate Library School conference on the theme, "International Aspects of Librarianship," there was a note of urgency in Lacy's presentation that was absent from the other contributions. In his "Overseas Book Program of the United States Government," he maintained that there was an imminent Communist threat to Western Europe and Asia. Several times in the course of his speech he mentioned this antagonistic "tyranny,"[68] this "Communist totalitarianism,"[69] this "Soviet menace so capable of overwhelming and indeed obliterating western European civilization."[70] Security could only be effected by building a countervailing force: a voluntary world order of independent countries which must, of necessity, be under American leadership.[71] Unafraid to use the terms "the free world" and "the free nations,"[72] Lacy asserted that "The only alternative to a free [order] is a totalitarian order, and the basis of a free order is a community of knowledge and purpose."[73] Unfortunately, he did not provide any specifics concerning this proposed "free order" and "community of knowledge and purpose," optimistically believing that these would emerge from (1) some sort of international dialogue (which would include the use of books) and (2) an American program that would hold up before the world those ideas and principles to which all free people would agree.[74]

Lacy charged that the US government's overseas programs involving books and libraries were insufficient, misguided, and ineffective. The major problem was that they were too small, particularly when compared with those involving radio and newspaper communication; this reflected the government's preference for making mass appeals. Moreover, the funds for books were ill-spent. He declared that the World War II orientation of the State Department and the Office of War Information still prevailed, with the stress being on short-term propaganda victories.[75] One result of this was that books were being promoted that were too stridently pro-American and anti-Russian.[76] In addition, Lacy maintained, overseas libraries should stress service to local intellectual elites rather than the broad masses. These leaders, he believed, would then influence their compatriots. In contrast to many of those involved in international librarianship who wanted the US libraries in other countries to serve as model public libraries, Lacy held that overseas libraries imitated domestic public

libraries too much in their attempt to be all things to all people.[77] The
similarity here between his views and those expressed in the Public
Library Inquiry are obvious.

While only a few days separated this speech from his presentation
on *Town Meeting of the Air*, in at least one important area the opinions
expresssed were contradictory.   In an oblique slap at those who
questioned the placing of books by American Communists in US
libraries abroad, he declared that ". . . uninformed and irresponsible
criticism has always plagued our overseas information effort."[78]
Sounding like the author of the Overseas Library Statement that he
was, he maintained that international book programs must be concerned
solely with success in attaining their goals.   He insisted that "The
intrusion of irrelevant political considerations—e.g., the screening of
books to be presented to an Indian medical school to aid, let us say, its
work in epidemiology, with a view to eliminating any by authors with
a prior record of 'listed' organizational affiliations—would be fatal to
the ultimate political objectives of the program."[79]

The Anti-Communist Critique of the Overseas Libraries and the International Information Programs

Lacy's politically-suspect epidemiologists were straw men, of
course, designed to make critics of the libraries abroad look foolish.
The US Senators and their assistants, as well as private citizens, who
had investigated the holdings of the libraries abroad were primarily
concerned because they contained (1) relatively few anti-Communist
books; (2) numerous copies of volumes by Communist Party leaders,
like Earl Browder; and (3) works that were essentially positive about
Communism, the USSR, and the People's Republic of China by
American and European authors such as Anna Louise Strong, Walter
Duranty, Maurice Hindus, Edgar Snow, Howard Fast, William Jaffe,
Louis Aragon, Ilya Ehrenberg, Egon Erwin Kisch, and Hewlett
Johnson (the self-proclaimed "Red Dean" of Canturbury). This meant
that the libraries were not carrying out their legally authorized
functions.   The investigators were also disturbed by the inability, or
unwillingness, of any government employees to determine who selected
the pro-Communist books for acquisition.   While some critics advocated a policy of eliminating from these libraries *all* works written

by those favorable to Communism, this was not their central goal. In fact, Roy Cohn, Chief Counsel for the Senate Investigating Committee evaluating the overseas libraries, later declared that this particular proposal had been a mistake.[80] However, one can make a good case that such book purchases financially benefited writers (and through them the Communist Party) who supported an organization then legally considered a dangerous foreign agency and provided these authors with a legitimacy they ill deserved.

The man running the investigation of the libraries was Joseph McCarthy. He and his staff revealed a good deal of useful information, partly through the numerous, workmanlike hearings held by the Senator. Unfortunately, historians—particularly historians of librarianship—discuss these inquiries without reading their transcripts! The probes are discussed elsewhere in this work, as at the end of the final chapter in the evaluation of both McCarthy himself and the wrongheaded, disparaging term, *McCarthyism.*

McCarthy and his colleagues had ample reason for concern. It was clear that the federal government's international information programs, which included the libraries under discussion, were not always run by individuals who thought more highly of the United States than of the Soviet Union. William T. Stone was appointed director of the State Department's Office of International Information and Cultural Affairs in late 1945. A few months later, the Department's Bannerman Security Screening Board declared that because of Stone's Communist affiliations he should be dismissed if he did not avail himself of the opportunity to resign. (This approach was the common one at the State Department. Not only was it considered "gentlemanly," but it helped the Department avoid public attention and public embarrassment.) However, his superior, Assistant Secretary of State William Benton, did nothing. In 1951 Stone was publicly attacked for the first time—by Joseph McCarthy. As reported earlier, the Senator also criticized Benton for his lack of action. In 1952 the federal Civil Service Loyalty Review Board expressed its displeasure over the State Department's handling of the case and declared that it would take the matter into its own hands. Stone resigned immediately.

The negative information about Stone was copious and much of it was easily available to anyone. From 1937 to 1941, he had been on the editorial board of *Amerasia*, a magazine issued by the Institute of Pacific Relations. During this period, the IPR, funded mainly by the

Rockefeller Foundation and the Carnegie Corporation, came under the control of open members of the Communist Party and its covert supporters, largely due to the efforts of the wealthy public figure, Frederick Vanderbilt Field.   Years later, Field admitted in his autobiography that he had considered himself a member of the Party and had bound himself to its dictates.   It is significant that Stone's background did not prevent his appointment as Assistant Administrator of the Board of Economic Warfare.   While there, he attempted to secure a position for Field in military intelligence and get his other colleagues at *Amerasia* jobs in the State Department.   Moreover, he leaked a confidential, adverse security report produced by Naval Intelligence to the very person it focussed on, Nathan Silvermaster. Silvermaster worked under Stone at the Board and soon became well-known as a central figure in one of the Soviet Union's spy rings within the federal government.[81]

In 1945, *Amerasia* became a household word when newspapers nationwide carried the story that its editor and five other staff members were arrested for violation of the Espionage Act.   The OSS had found seventeen hundred top secret government documents in the magazine's offices—many of them original reports, not copies—on subjects such as the making of the atomic bomb and the planned invasion of Japan.[82]

Conservatives, Anti-Communism, and the Helen Haines Debate

Librarians' Censorship of Anti-Communist and Conservative Materials

Newspapers and journals committed to conservatism and anti-Communism frequently attacked American libraries for carrying few books and magazines committed to these causes.   For example, the *Boston Post* pointed out that Joseph McCarthy's 1952 book, *Mc-Carthyism and the Fight for America*,[83] which was serialized in its pages, could not be found in the Boston Public Library while *Pravda*, *Izvestia*, and *New World Review* could.[84]   In general, the criticisms concerning library collections were generally not aimed at the mass of librarians who actually did the selecting of materials but at the major reviewing media librarians tended to depend on.   It would have been more accurate to blame both. Some of the book reviews, like those in *Library Journal*, were written primarily by librarians. More significant was the fact that librarians had the professional responsibility to read reviews critically and to seek information from sources other than those merely easily available. Several analyses showed that almost all of the major book review media espoused the same views: anti-conservative, opposed to vigorous anti-Communism, and often positive about Communism in the USSR, China, and elsewhere.[85]

The charge that conservative anti-Communist journals were rarely carried in libraries was accurate. Only one, *The American Mercury*, was indexed by the widely used *Readers' Guide to Periodical Literature*, an honor freely bestowed on internationalist, liberal, and anti-anti-Communist publications of dubious value, like *UN World* and *International Conciliation*. Ignored by *Readers' Guide* were *The Freeman*, *The National Republic*, *Plain Talk*, *Human Events*, and the widely circulated *American Legion Magazine*, which had 2,800,000 subscribers. *Readers' Guide* was published by the H. W. Wilson Company,[86] a business that usually worked hard to insure that its indexes reflected the desires of practicing librarians. Clearly, librarianship was burying conservative and vigorous anti-Communist thought.

Most conservative and anti-Communist groups merely wanted librarians to live up to what they considered basic "Americanism": providing truly balanced collections, like so many librarians—including the Intellectual Freedom zealots—claimed they wanted. This goal was almost always central, even among the most ardent of the anti-Communists of the 1950's. For example, broadcast journalist Fulton Lewis III (called "Fascist Fulton" by some of his critics) was upset when he saw works in school libraries authored by those he considered Communists, but he believed they should remain there: "Our greatest weapon is truth. But in order to find the truth, we must read, discuss, and determine. . . ."[87] Similarly, the Chairman of the House Un-American Activities Committee, Harold H. Velde, publicly declared, "I have always had the feeling that Communist books—that is, books or any literature written by members of the Communist Party—should be read by American students and American citizens. . . ."[88]

A 1954 article in *American Legion Magazine* urged readers to examine the shelves of their tax-supported school and public libraries:

". . . if there are books by and about the left on the library shelves, there can also be placed there the counteraction of books by and about the right, *in the fullest American tradition.*"[89] (Italics mine) At the top of the article was the statement, "A spot check of a public library will soon disclose if there is a desire on the part of officials to present *both sides. . . .*"[90] (Italics mine) The author also wrote of the need to "counterbalance" books on library shelves written by and about Communists; there was no call to expunge them.[91] She went out of her way to urge her readers to maintain their good manners and their respect for librarians when they evaluate these collections:

> . . . when you start checking into the situation in your town, do so as sensible citizens, not as crusading zealots looking for trouble. While you have every right to inquire and to study what is happening in your community, in the libraries, and in the schools, you do *not* have the right to make yourself obnoxious while doing so. . . .
>
> This is important too: don't start out with the assumption that the librarian is your enemy. The great majority of librarians are good, conscientious people, as patriotic as you.[92]

Throughout the 1950's and afterwards, the American Legion publicly censured the occasional individual members and errant local posts that attempted to limit freedom of speech in any of its forms. Both conservative and liberal historians have described how this association of several million war veterans maintained its dedication to intellectual freedom while vigorously opposing Communism abroad and at home.[93] Nevertheless, the primary book on the history of intellectual freedom and librarianship for the period 1939 to 1969 paints an entirely negative portrait of this organization, referring to "Self-appointed censors—mainly in the form of right-wing, super-patriotic groups, such as the American Legion. . . ."[94]

On occasion, a few overzealous individuals, organizations, and agencies of communication declared that they wanted Communist material banned entirely from public libraries. At one point, the *Boston Post* targeted its city's public libraries. As frequently occurred elsewhere in the country when such things happened, other conservatives and anti-Communists came to the fore to help insure that a range of materials would continue to be provided, including those which were openly Communist. The efforts of Monsignor Robert H. Lord, the Catholic diocesesan newspaper, and former FBI agent and counterspy Herbert A. Philbrick (the author of *I Led 3 Lives*) proved decisive in fending off the campaign begun by the young financier who had purchased the *Boston Post* four months earlier. The Archbishop of Boston soon returned to his traditional seat on the Library's five-member Board of Trustees, thereby insuring the permanence of this outcome.[95]

The resolution of the conflict in Boston did not calm the leaders of the Intellectual Freedom movement and the library profession, as one might have expected, but merely fuelled their hysteria. Resonating with the words and sentiments of *It Can't Happen Here*, Sinclair Lewis' best-selling 1935 novel about a takeover of the United States by domestic fascists, the library press was filled with scare articles. *Before* the events noted above, a lead article in the Massachusetts Library Association *Bulletin* was ominously titled, "Can It Happen in Massachusetts?"[96] *After* the campaign by the *Boston Post*'s publisher was defeated, an article in the same journal proclaimed, "It *Has* Happened in Massachusetts."[97] Reading this last-mentioned piece, one finds that the "It" referred to was not the coming of fascism but merely "a vicious attack on the Boston Public Library."[98] Fascism or a failed attempt at censorship—what was the difference? To many in the library profession, apparently none. Other unsuccessful attempts to have books removed from libraries, or labelled in some way as Communist or obscene, were similarly presented in the library press: "It Happened in Pasadena,"[99] "It Happened in Burbank,"[100] etc. The fact that these attempts were rarely successful and that "It" did not happen failed to compose or quiet the alarmists. There is little evidence that they had any desire to be mollified. It is difficult to know whether they were impelled by genuine paranoia or a calculated intent to create the illusion of a menacing fascist movement. Different individuals were probably moved by different forces. Whatever its origins, the movement to stifle anti-Communism in libraries thrived.

Parallel hyperthymia developed in other areas of American life at this time. *This Happened in Pasadena*, a book about an alleged attempt in 1950 by dangerous right-wingers to take over a school system, was favorably reviewed on page one of the book review sections of both the *New York Times* and the *New York Herald-Tribune* and became a best-seller. In actuality, the events in Pasadena were not at all like the work described them, and of course they did not presage a nationwide attempt to appropriate the country's schools, as implied by its author, David Hulburd.[101] Not surprisingly, Hulburd considered anti-Communism to be more dangerous than the Soviet Union and its agents.[102]

The Helen Haines Controversy

A significant indication of how some prominent American librarians in the 1950's and later decades viewed their own country and the USSR is revealed in the long-term controversy over the 1950 edition of Helen Haines' widely-used library school textbook, *Living with Books: The Art of Book Selection*.[103] The volume by this leader of the Intellectual Freedom movement and nationally-known book reviewer for the *Herald-Tribune* and the *Saturday Review of Literature* presented views of the works about the United States and the Soviet Union that were shamefully inaccurate. Haines lashed out at what she considered to be a "long continuing flow of books intensifying American fear, suspicion, and antagonism towards the Soviet state, and by anti-Soviet propaganda carried on in many newspapers and periodicals, by most radio commentators and numerous public leaders."[104] This was not entirely new, she declared, since the Soviets had been subjected to decades of such criticism following the West's armed intervention after World War I. Haines asserted that most works in library collections about the Soviet Union lacked the "sympathetic imagination"[105] so necessary to understanding another culture. Instead, one usually found volumes of "unqualified attack, reprobation, and denunciation."[106] She made no similar criticism of the Soviet literature about the United States, but she did allow that there had arisen a "*mutual* ignorance, bitterness, and hostility"[107] (italics mine) that was undermining the efforts to create the hoped-for 'one world.'[108]

In *Living with Books* she warmly commended Sartre's political writings—which had consistently defended Stalinism[109]—and books by the transparently pro-Communist Corliss Lamont, which she thought reflected a "warmly human philosophy"[110] based on "Marxian realism."[111] Haines insisted that most Americans were wrong in their thinking that ". . . communism stands for a fantastic devil realm of cruelty and oppression."[112] In her comparisons of the United States and the Soviet Union, she frequently declared that the two countries were merely *different*, with neither being superior to the other. However, the USSR Haines presented seemed to have no serious flaws. Moreover, it was "dedicated to the equality of rights of all people 'irrespective of their nationality or race.' "[113] In contrast, the second greatest totalitarian movement of the century, National Socialism, was reviled as despotic and aggressive.[114] Thus, she decried the Nazi takeover of Czechoslovakia in the 1930's but did not even mention the Communists' seizure of power there a decade later.

Haines lavished criticism on the United States. She issued what was becoming a commonplace charge among self-proclaimed "progressives": the post-World War I "anti-Bolshevik 'red scare' traced a coercive pattern of repression prophetic of the deeper menace to intellectual freedom that was to confront the nation in another quarter century."[115] Whenever possible, she intruded additional allegations of America's supposed political, economic, and social-psychological ills, such as "commercialism," the exploitation of workers, and "the mirage of everlasting prosperity."[116] American racism was frequently mentioned. Haines assured her readers that despite all these social, cultural, and political pathologies, not everything in the United States had degenerated in the twentieth century: the inspiration of both Communism and Marxism had improved American literature by enhancing its democratic elements.[117]

Haines recommended as authoritative and scholarly numerous shoddy works which were groundless, left-wing critiques of the USA or paeans to the Soviet Union, like E. H. Carr's *The Soviet Impact on the Western World* and Harold Laski's *The American Democracy*. The necessity of providing various sides of the Soviet-American conflict, she asserted, obligated libraries to purchase works like Sidney and Beatrice Webb's *Soviet Communism: A New Civilization?*[118] However, it is important to note that Haines' version of intellectual freedom did not extend to all books. For example, she declared that while librarians should be tolerant and responsive to public demand, this did not include books that "strengthen ignorance and foster char- latanism."[119] Within this category she placed what she considered pseudosciences, like astrology.[120] Apparently, only political pseudo- sciences, like Marxism and Communism, were acceptable to her.

The tendentious political views expressed in *Living with Books* were actually somewhat less extreme than those Haines had expressed elsewhere. In February 1948, *Library Journal* carried her article bearing the magisterial title, "Balancing the Books: Reason Enthroned."[121] Posing as a reassertion of the intellectual freedom principle of providing "balanced" collections, this diatribe against alleged "mass hysteria," "narrow, primitive nationalism," and an anti-radical "witch-hunt"[122] asserted that there was a campaign being waged by America's leaders to start a war with the irenic USSR. This effort was being

> incited and strengthened by the continuous flow of books intensifying American fear, suspicion, and hostility toward the Soviet Union, and by the violent anti-Soviet propaganda that is carried on by most of our newspapers and periodicals, by almost all radio commentators still broadcasting, and by nearly all our public leaders.[123]

Librarians should "balance" these assaults with the insightful, objective works by Edgar Snow, F. L. Schuman, E. H. Carr, and William Mandel.[124] Her favorite book was *Soviet Russia since the War*, by "the Dean of Canterbury, 'the Red Dean,' ardent Christian socialist, friend and champion of the Soviet Union."[125] Considering it "a contribution to peace and international understanding,"[126] she encouraged all librarians to read it and hoped it would be widely disseminated through bookstores and libraries.

Haines taught in library schools and wrote the text widely used in library school book selection courses in the three decades following its appearance in 1935. She was also an active leader of the field's Intellectual Freedom movement. However, she never became a librarian and there is no indication that the library profession's great affection and respect for her were ever reciprocated: she merely found librarians *useful*. Haines was enamored of fiction. Moreover, she maintained that it provided the ultimate medium for understanding the world. She believed that public libraries offered the greatest potential to distribute "good" fiction, which was of particular importance to her in the nuclear age because human survival was at stake.[127] Haines frequently expressed her contempt for librarians. For example, in a 1946 speech to librarians later printed in *Library Journal*, she claimed that "Librarians Don't Like People" and that "books, like people, waken little enthusiasm among librarians."[128] She added some peculiar assertions about the differences between men and women, including male and female librarians. For example, she declared that men "can disagree violently, exchange vilifications and mutual contumely, without permanent ill feelings, while women in much less violent encounter cherish unappeasable antagonism."[129] Many of her views have been downplayed in the adulatory writings about her. She is particularly revered today by those in the Intellectual Freedom movement.

The standard works about Haines, such as those in two mainstays of the profession, the *Dictionary of American Library Biography* and *The World Encyclopedia of Library and Information Services*,[130] are more hagiographical than biographical. Both of these treatments claim that criticism of the 1950 edition of her *Living with Books* was unwarranted but "inevitable" given the temper of the times:

> Robert D. Harlan: ". . . It was probably inevitable in the early 1950s that her representation of divergent points of view, particularly political ones, should provoke some harsh criticism."[131]

> Ruth Warncke: "By 1950 . . . the climate had changed. Haines, then 78 years old, again exhibited an open, liberal attitude toward the books of the period, including those on politics, religion, and science. It was inevitable that she should be accused of a pro-Soviet bias. . . ."[132]

As described below, both write-ups erroneously claimed that an excellent critique of *Living with Books* by the conservative Oliver Carlson was refuted. Moreover, both charged—without providing any evidence—that the bulk of librarians were not enthusiastic about this second edition of the book because of their timidity and failure to fully embrace the ideals of intellectual freedom.[133] Harlan was Professor and Associate Dean of the School of Library and Information Studies at the University of California at Berkeley. His academic expertise was the history of books and printing. Warncke, a longtime public librarian, directed the American Library Association's American Heritage Project in the 1950's. (Its anti-anti-Communist program is described later in this book.) Afterwards, she became the Deputy Executive Director of ALA.

The most influential anti-Communist treatment of library book selection in the fifties was an article by the educator and writer, Oliver Carlson, in *The Freeman* in 1952.[134]   According to a concerned supporter of Helen Haines, ". . . some of our library patrons are receiving and distributing reprints of the article. . . ."[135]   Carlson centered his attack on the new edition of Haines' *Living with Books*[136] because of the work's longtime influence in the library profession. He included numerous long quotations from the volume that demonstrated Haines' belief that a prejudiced, anti-Soviet 'bloc' of reviewers in the postwar world had resulted in many library collections that were not balanced.[137] According to Haines, the 'postwar reaction'[138] was part of a 'nation-wide hysteria,' an 'essentially nationalistic' reaction against liberal and left-wing ideas.[139]   Carlson described how Haines *consistently* recommended pro-Soviet works over anti-Soviet books in a wide variety of fields. He concluded, "She is the perfect 'innocent.' Like so many muddled European and American intellectuals, she has mistaken the fine and noble phrases of Communistic propaganda for Communist reality."[140]

This was not the last time Haines' ignorance of social and political processes would be pointed out.[141]   However, it is difficult to say whether she herself was definitely and enthusiastically pro-Soviet or pro-Communist.   Nevertheless, she clearly had an affinity for those who *were*, as well as an antipathy for conservatives and active anti-Communists.   In this, she was similar to many other leaders of the Intellectual Freedom movement.

Elinor S. Earle, director of the Reference Division of the Akron Public Library, wrote the sole rebuttal of Carlson's analysis in the 1950's.[142]   In 1961, Everett T. Moore wrote that it was not possible to know why the attack on Haines had gone unanswered in the library press aside for Earle's piece, but he opined that it might have been due to the belief that "*The Freeman* was not widely enough read to deserve serious reply."[143]   In fact, *The Freeman* had a circulation of twenty thousand and was possibly the most important American libertar-ian/conservative periodical of the period.   It was edited by the well-known journalists John Chamberlain, Henry Hazlitt, and Suzanne LaFollette. Its contributors included Isaac Don Levine, Eugene Lyons, William F. Buckley, Frank Chodorov, Ludwig von Mises, and the future Nobel Prize recipient in economics, Friedrich A. Hayek.[144] The failure of the library profession to respond to Carlson's critique may have been caused by its unfamiliarity with conservative and libertarian journals, arrogance, inability to respond to the charges, or even a recognition that Carlson's criticisms were accurate. Robert Harlan and Ruth Warncke believed that it was a lack of commitment to intellectual freedom among contemporary librarians that accounted for the lack of a broad-scale response to Carlson in the library press.[145]

In any case, Earle did try to refute Carlson's charges but a close study of the texts involved clearly shows that she failed. Her major accusation was that his article was primarily a contrivance consisting of quotations taken out of context.[146] In truth, his quotations were not misleading snippets but lengthy segments from Haines' book up to ninety words in length. Earle presented these quotations with Haines' sentences, or even paragraphs, which came before or after them— sometimes both before and after—and declared that she had thereby exposed Carlson's distortions. In fact, his quotations stood well on their own: Earle's lavish provision of additional text did not alter their meaning or undermine his arguments.

Let us examine her first example of alleged misrepresentation. Carlson quoted the following passage of Haines and countered with the assertion that the political slant of influential book reviewers was actually the opposite of what she stated. He followed the quotation with "Italics mine" in brackets.

> In the literature of the war and postwar years the clash of nationalisms, the conflict of ideologies, kindled impassioned warfare; and the great reviewing combat arena of the period is that devoted to books about Russia. *Balanced judgment and fair understanding were obscured and the scales of American public opinion were weighted by prejudice and hostility of a strong anti-Soviet "bloc" of well-known reviewers, so that the impartial, adequate book selection in this field deteriorated in many library collections.*[147]

Earle indicted Carlson for not including Haines' sentences that immediately preceded the above quote:

> There are no rigid rules binding critical judgment to a given formula. In book reviewing, as in every human activity, there are

'many men of many minds.' For literary criticism is essentially an
attempt to define the qualities of a certain piece of writing and to
decide whether or not it has been well done. The decision will be
influenced by the standards of judgment that the individual critic
accepts and applies—whether traditional and erudite, as in the
critical writings of Paul Elmer More, or vigorously factual and
ironic, as in the reviewing of Bernard De Voto, or intellectualized
and psychoanalytical, as in much of the work of Edmund Wilson.
Beyond certain boundary lines, however, critical judgment does not
function, and we enter a region of bad taste and fatuous opinion,
where adult infantilism seeks and finds books of its own caliber.
Within the canons that establish literature as an art, though all critics
agree on fundamentals, not many think alike. In all his years of
critical writing Howells was a champion of realism and disliked
romantic literature. Stevenson loved romance and continually pleads
for it in his charming critical essays.   Paul Elmer More was
indifferent to the most vital and significant modern literature. Stuart
Sherman in his earlier critical work sharply attacked writers whose
powers he later recognized. The intense anti-Puritanism of Ludwig
Lewisohn leaves its tinge on his critical judgments. Individual
convictions of political or social faith, personal intensities of
partisanship, find violent expression in contemporary reviewing.[148]

Clearly, these do not change the meaning of the material Carlson
quoted.
    Earle compounded her distortion by continuing her critique:

By quoting only the concluding lines and by preceding them with his
own statement that "The tremendous power wielded by book
reviewers who were apologists and defenders of the Soviet
government and communism has been reported in detail by several
writers during the past year," Carlson gives the impression that
Haines is an ardent Soviet partisan.[149]

Carlson's full passage reads as follows:

The tremendous power wielded by book reviewers who were
apologists and defenders of the Soviet government and communism
has been reported in detail by several writers during the past year.
Miss Haines, however, insists that the opposite is true.[150]

He then went on to his next point.

In truth, it was not Carlson but Haines herself who gave the impression in her book that she was a supporter of the Soviet Union. (The writers Carlson was referring to, those who had exposed the leftists' control of the book review media, will be discussed later. It should also be pointed out that with the growing use of the term *Communist bloc* in the late 1940's to describe the menacing empire in the East, Haines' use of the term *bloc* to describe an alleged cabal of sinister, anti-Communist writers was particularly mischievous and unsavory.)

Earle's second example of alleged distortion-through-quotation actually showed the opposite of what she had intended! If Carlson had quoted the entire paragraph from which he had taken a long, ninety-word quotation—as Earle implied he should have—his case against Haines' political positions would have been even stronger. The relevant material is reproduced in a note below.[151]

The rest of Earle's incompetent article continued in this mode, although she added other kinds of alleged distortion to the charges against Carlson. A favorite of hers was to accuse him of purposely presenting a false picture of Haines' work by discussing some of the books she had evaluated under rubrics that were different from those employed in Haines' text—or which Earle herself decided were more apt. Thus, Carlson was berated for describing serious, analytical works by John Fischer, V. A. Kravchenco, Albert Rhys Williams, Edgar Snow, Hewlett Johnson, and Walter Duranty as books on 'international relations, sociology and political science'[152] because Haines had included them in her discussion of travel books. Carlson's classification was certainly as accurate, but it was of little significance either way. Incidentally, Haines had described the books of Williams, Snow, Johnson, and Duranty as 'equally authentic' as the anti-Communist works of Fischer and Kravchenko.[153] This was an astonishing statement since the members of this pro-Communist quaternity had spent most of their careers as propagandists and were still unrepentant.

Not all of Earle's criticisms were unfounded. As she charged, Carlson had made an inference from a hasty comparision of the indices of the first and second editions of *Living with Books*.[154] He had incorrectly, but understandably, assumed that the first edition of this textbook for librarians published by prestigious Columbia University

Press had been adequately indexed.

Elinor Earle ended her distorted analysis of Carlson's article by saying that his approach to libraries resembled those of Nazis and Communists because they too wanted to purge libraries. She asserted that Haines' book was merely an attempt to reinforce the principles of intellectual freedom which mandated that all opinions be included in libraries.[155] However, Carlson had convincingly pointed out that there was no balance in Haines' volume when it came to Communism, and that this pillar of the profession appeared intent on "stacking"[156] library collections in favor of that totalitarian ideology.

For the past four decades, Intellectual Freedom movement activists, library historians, and biographers of Haines have written about Carlson's critique as if it had been refuted by Earle. In 1961, Everett T. Moore reported that Earle's "able" response provided "a point-by-point answer." In his opinion, she had revealed Carlson's technique of quoting Haines out of context and otherwise misusing quotations—to say nothing of his miscategorizing of books.[157] In 1978, Robert D. Harlan wrote that Earle had provided "an effective rebuttal, noting in particular Carlson's quoting and interpreting of passages."[158] Ruth Warncke's 1980 profile of Haines apparently accepted Earle's "point-by-point answer"[159] at face value, as does Louise Robbins' recent history of the Intellectual Freedom movement: "Carlson's article was rebutted point by point by Elinor S. Earle. . . ."[160] This gross misjudgment, failure to objectively scrutinize original texts, and parroting of stock phrases are indicative of the superficial nature of the anti-anti-Communist Intellectual Freedom movement and its unquestioning champions and historians.

The Intellectual Freedom Movement, Robert B. Downs, and Everett T. Moore

A closer look at two leaders in the fight against alleged censorship in the overseas libraries, both prominent in the Intellectual Freedom movement in the 1950's and afterwards, can clarify some of the aforementioned events. It should provide insight into how and why members of this campaign worked to undermine the attempt to provide libraries in foreign countries that could effectively oppose the expansion of Soviet power. Moreover, as with the treatment of Haines above, it will give some indication of the ideology and tactics that helped prevent American librarianship as a whole from becoming a committed and effective foe of an increasingly powerful Communist force.

The credo termed *intellectual freedom* was far more attractive to librarians than anti-Communism. While the early formal statements advocating the former were sometimes consistent with anti-Communism, or even espoused it in parts, the so-called "intellectual freedom" elements in these declarations were always preeminent. (As already indicated, the explicit anti-Communist pronouncements were all removed in later years.) In some cases, the fallacious and tendentious interpretation of these statements prevented any possible use they might serve as weapons in the fight against the greatest global threat of the century to free thought and speech. Moreover, when American anti-Communists were unjustifiably and repeatedly castigated by these professionals for being against intellectual freedom, their patriotic and anti-Soviet activities were undercut. This could not have been missed by those librarians who wanted to strongly oppose the USSR. Their professional status, to say nothing of their jobs, would have been jeopardized by countering the ethos of the intolerant, zealous crusaders leading their profession who had appropriated the term *intellectual freedom* and were using it for their own political purposes. Thus, in numerous ways the Intellectual Freedom movement not only helped prevent American librarianship from becoming strongly anti-Communist in the 1940's, 1950's, and afterwards, but it put pressure on all librarians to become "anti-anti-Communist."

Robert B. Downs after 1953

Robert B. Downs served as both the director of the library and of the library school at the University of Illinois from 1943 until 1970, when his active retirement years began. His interest in international librarianship was reflected in his involvement in establishing library schools overseas. After his American Library Association presidency in 1953, he continued to be one of the chief spokesmen for the Intellectual Freedom movement for the next thirty years. He proved to be an intolerant extremist and an elitist who was partial to world government. (This desire for a global government was necessarily accompanied by a willingness to forgo some of America's sovereignty.)

Like so many others in his movement, he made no distinction between restrictions on the holdings of libraries within the United States and of the US government libraries overseas.[161] If fact, he asserted that all censorship in all places and at all times is the same, and is never acceptable. One can find no room for nuance here. While Downs did note the influence of social forces, he maintained that the primary reason an individual would want to limit anyone's access to anything is because he or she has some kind of psychological disorder.[162]

Nevertheless, Downs himself may not have been above censoring the work of others; he was so accused in the mid-1950's by William T. Couch, former head of the University of Chicago Press. According to Couch, he had been asked to write an article for *Library Trends* on the topic of scholars' publishing problems and he did so, identifying the major one as censorship by influential pro-Communists in the trade. Downs, reported Couch, claimed that this charge was irrelevant to the subject and refused to publish his submission in this journal issued by the library school that Downs headed.[163]

In a revealing 1961 debate in *Library Journal* with author and journalist James J. Kilpatrick—whom our fervent opponent of book "labelling" did not hesitate to label "right-wing"[164]—Downs criticized Kilpatrick for "over-objectivity"[165] in a careful, considered volume Kilpatrick had written about censorship. One had to be entirely on one side or the other, Downs railed. Kilpatrick defended himself against what amounted to "guilt by association, exaggeration, misstatement of fact, and the use, ad nauseum, of ad hominem attacks."[166]

Some years later, Downs declared in a commencement address that he favored the outlook and ideas of intellectuals above all others. He seemed to believe that if their ideas had had more influence in the past, we would be living in a better world, one with some sort of 'limited Federal World Government.'[167]

Downs maintained his anti-anti-Communist zealotry to the end of his long life. In *Journalists of the United States*, published the year he died, 1991, he wrote an inappropriate introduction for this biographical dictionary. Unlike the book itself, it dealt mainly with censorship. Indeed, he even bestowed the rubric *Censorship* to this preliminary material. In it, he restated the emotional, misleading charges that in the early 1950's "McCarthyism" had "led to the burning of books accused of being communist propaganda and the closing of a number of US information libraries abroad."[168] In the body of the book, the biographies of the journalists and the descriptions of the newspapers and magazines were generally moderate in tone, but some did reflect Downs' prejudices: William F. Buckley's *National Review* was unjustifiably described as "ultraconservative"[169] while the pro-Communist newspaper *PM* (1940-1948) was rendered "idealist."[170] A major anti-Communist of the forties and fifties, columnist and author George E. Sokolsky, was characterized thusly: "He was noted for his highly conservative views. According to one critic, he was 'a one-man intellectual front for conservative capital.' "[171] The profundity of Sokolsky's reporting and of his scholarship was not mentioned.[172] The most shameful entry of this volume demonstrated Downs' ignorance of journalism, Communism, and the Soviet Union. His laudatory description of Walter Duranty,[173] *The New York Times'* correspondent in the USSR throughout the 1920's and 1930's, was almost the antithesis of reality. Duranty's purposeful coverup of the brutalities of Stalin's regime had been widely acknowledged for decades and was written about as early as 1934.[174] Many had suggested that his Pulitzer Prize be rescinded. None of this was mentioned by Downs.

Everett T. Moore

Everett T. Moore spent most of his career at the library of the University of California at Los Angeles. He served as president of the California Library Association and was a leader in a variety of professional activities, particularly those related to intellectual freedom. He was editor of the *Newsletter on Intellectual Freedom*, issued by the American Library Association's Intellectual Freedom Committee; wrote a column on censorship for the Association's primary journal, *ALA Bulletin*; and served as vice-president and lead plaintiff for the Freedom to Read Foundation, ALA's legal pit bull in disputes over alleged instances of censorship.

His obituary in the newsletter he had edited declared: .

> Through his writings, Everett T. Moore chronicled a significant chapter in the history of American freedom. He generated light rather than heat in the intellectual controversies of three decades of American librarianship. . . . His writings were scholarly, judicious, and of continuing interest in the world of books and ideas, . . . and

[he] served as the author of the most complete account of the purging of American overseas libraries of controversial books. . . .[175]

In truth, Moore was one of the chief propagandists who helped
create and sustain the myths concerning the overseas libraries,
censorship, and the profession's proper role. In a 1971 *festschrift* in
honor of Robert B. Downs, the first contribution after the obligatory
biographical sketch was by Moore writing on the subject "Intellectual
Freedom." It dealt entirely with the events surrounding the overseas
library controversy and Senator McCarthy. Concerning the events of
summer 1953, he trumpeted: "The challenge to American librarianship
was accepted, and the events . . . are among the most notable in our
[professional] history."[176]

In this fable, Moore idealized the libraries overseen by the Office
of War Information, as well as those that succeeded them.[177] Despite
his assertions, neither the OWI nor Congress intended for these
libraries to include works critical of the Allied war effort or, after
Germany and Japan were defeated, of works with "dangerous
thoughts"[178] that might negatively impact America's international
position or foreign policy. In Moore's imagination, these near-idyllic
libraries had been greatly damaged by Senator McCarthy and the
lingering fear he had instilled in government officials.

Nevertheless, according to Moore, these overseas institutions later
recovered much of their old mission. He did report a recent setback,
however: ". . . USIA Director Frank Shakespeare's instruction to the
libraries, sent out in early 1970, to order certain 'conservative' books
if their existing collections were 'preponderantly liberal,' betrays a sad
misapprehension as to the art of developing a balanced and
representative collection of books. . . ."[179] Given the plentiful public
pronouncements of the Intellectual Freedom advocates in support of
evenhanded collections, one must wonder about Moore's opposition to
Shakespeare's action aimed at insuring this very balance, which
apparently did not exist in some of the overseas libraries. It seems that
the moralistic intonations of Moore were fraudulent, like those of many
other self-proclaimed Intellectual Freedom advocates. Evidently,
anything that increased the presence of conservative or anti-Communist
books was anathema to him. If one wants to be charitable, one can
hypothesize that he, and others in the Movement, mistakenly believed
that anything liberal or left-of-center was inherently balanced—or even

non-political—being merely an objective account of things as they truly are.

Moore's muddled historical account of developments in the early 1950's is reminiscent of the confusion among many in those earlier years as to what was a domestic library and what was an overseas library. While insisting that librarians did indeed understand that there was "an essential distinction"[180] between the libraries within the United States and those abroad involved in the Cold War (it seems that Moore believed domestic libraries should not be involved in this conflict), he went on—in the very same sentence—to declare that the attempts to place restrictions on overseas libraries constituted a "threat to our principles of free selection and free access to ideas [and] was recognized as striking at home as well as abroad."[181] While many Intellectual Freedom supporters asserted that the events concerning the overseas libraries had *created* a similar situation domestically, Moore held the opposite view: "The attacks on the American libraries abroad was an extension of a movement which had already gained momentum at home."[182]

As reported earlier, except for a few notable exceptions, like Dan Lacy, the danger of Communism was not high on the list of concerns of the Intellectual Freedom movement's leaders. They rarely spoke or wrote about it except when it related to their cause—and then primarily to oppose those who were attempting to combat the totalitarian movement. In addition to ignoring the reality of Communism abroad, they were unable to see it at home. Here too, our case study of Everett T. Moore is revealing. From the vantage point of 1971, when even more information about Communist subversives was publicly available than in the early fifties, Moore still claimed that in Joseph McCarthy's overseas library investigation the Senator's definition of a Communist had been too broad because he had wrongly used that designation for highly-regarded people like Rockwell Kent and Corliss Lamont.[183] The fact is that Kent had been identified as a Communist in the late 1940's by Benjamin Gitlow, a former leader in the US Communist movement, as well as by Louis Budenz, the former editor of the Communist Party's *Daily Worker*. Max Eastman had castigated Kent publicly in 1950: "I learn from a Tass dispatch that your career as a pro-Communist artist and writer has brought you to Moscow, and to the extreme statement, in a speech to the Kremlin: 'The American government is not my government.' "[184] Kent donated much of his artwork to the USSR, was an honorary member of the Soviet Academy of Arts, and won the Lenin Peace Prize in 1967, donating his $10,000 prize to North Vietnam. Moore's admired Corliss Lamont, the author of numerous pro-Soviet books, had been singled out in 1944 by the House Committee on Un-American Activities as the most sedulous propagandist for the Soviet Union in the United States. In 1956, a US Senate Internal Subcommittee had included his name on its list of the most active sponsors of Communist-front organizations. Peter Viereck, a literary figure and political analyst known for his willingness to criticize both the Left and the Right, called Lamont 'America's leading intellectual enthusiast for Communist Russia.'[185]

In short, Moore did not seem able or willing to call any American a Communist, despite the evidence. It is difficult to know whether this failure was caused by intellectual, psychological, or political factors. In any case, it is clear that the views of Moore (and like-minded librarians) are not tenable.

A corollary of the inability or unwillingness of Moore and many other librarians after World War II to recognize the existence of Communists was their frequent use of the term *witch-hunt* to describe some of the activities of the anti-Communists.[186] More than a half-century later, library historians are still utilizing this accusatory label when describing those years.[187] However, the term is misleading because while there is no such thing as a witch, Communists did exist and were dangerous. One reason it has been a favorite term of many is because it hearkens back to the infamous New England witch-hunts of the 1690's. It can thus be used by those who dislike mainstream America to give the false impression that such nefarious activities—which were actually short-lived, very restricted in scope, and negligible when compared with similar undertakings in Europe[188] and elsewhere in the world—are a deeply ingrained part of American history and civilization. The relatively small scope of American witch-hunting has been known for centuries by any educated person wishing to know the truth.[189] The same can certainly be said for "witch-hunting" in its metaphorical sense.

In January 1962, the American Library Association's principal journal published Everett Moore's article "Why Do the Rightists Rage?"[190] An arrogant and manipulative piece, it used propagandistic scare tactics (e.g., deceptive name calling, distortion, and the use of inflammatory words) to sound the alarm about a purported uprising of ferocious, ignorant Americans trying to destroy the country's freedoms and its libraries. Unfortunately, it typified the more extreme literature of the anti-anti-Communist movement of the 1950's and later decades.

The article began, "The wrath of the extreme rightists which has been aimed for some time at the public schools is now being directed vengefully toward our public libraries as well."[191] Moore maintained that his goal was to insure that library collections remained balanced.[192] However, we have already seen that his concept of "balance" was quite skewed; this article merely reinforces this fact. In actuality, the individuals, organizations, periodicals, and newspapers he belittled and vilified, such as Rosalie Gordon, the Cardinal Mindszenty Foundation, the Christian Anti-Communism Crusade, *National Review*, and *Human Events*, were not part of any "battle being fought by the extreme rightists to compel libraries to change their principles of book selection."[193] Rather, it was a movement by mainstream conservative anti-Communists who, by and large, wanted librarians to live up to widely accepted views of fairness and to the profession's principles by providing some measure of balance in their collections. It was first and foremost the exclusion of anti-Communist and conservative materials from public libraries that rankled these critics, not the inclusion of left-wing, or even Communist, books. They usually placed the blame for this situation on the reviewing media relied on by librarians when making their selections, not the librarians themselves. (As stated elsewhere, they were being far too indulgent here. They *should* have criticized the political prejudices, sloth, and intellectual and professional flaccidity of many of the librarians, who not only ignored anti-Communist review sources but wrote many of the biased evaluations in the highly influential *Library Journal*.) These beliefs and aims of the conservative anti-Communists appeared again and again in their periodicals and organizational literature, yet Moore ignored the contents of the very articles he cited.

He invoked a caricature[194] of the conservative authors and their compatriots as paranoids who were more worried about Communist conspiracies within the United States than about the threat of Communism from without. His charge was untrue, although these anti-Communists did understand that the internal and external threats were intertwined. Moore also falsely claimed that the conservatives openly declared that their true enemies were not really the Communists at all, but rather "the liberals, who are the actual architects of the conspiracy."[195] Moreover, as a side-bar in his article proclaimed, they were allegedly " 'Anti' Everything But War."[196] Part of the plot that Moore thought he saw were the conservatives' supposed efforts to "undermine the public's confidence in the judgment of librarians."[197] Echoing the arguments by the Intellectual Freedom advocates in the debates about the overseas libraries, he appeared to support the hubristic view that librarians were always to be the sole arbiters of what was to be included in the collections they worked with. Either Moore's imagination and/or paranoia were running wild, or he was dissembling.

As we shall see later, careful analyses of the influential book reviews in the *New York Times*, *New York Herald-Tribune*, *Saturday Review*, and *Library Journal* that Moore defended—with no evidence—showed that they did not present many favorable critiques of conservative or strongly anti-Communist books but frequently praised works that were positive about the USSR and the Chinese Communists.[198]   However, Moore, ever an elitist, found the articles criticizing these review media to be "crude and unlettered."[199] He supported this claim, in part, by citing the opinion expressed by Ralph Ellsworth and Sarah Harris in their bigoted study, *The American Right Wing*. (It too will be analyzed later.) This duo claimed that 'many of the rightists lack any real acquaintance with the great books of the world or the specialized disciplines of learning that have developed in the universities.'[200] Moore declared that:

> our [librarians'] communication with the extremists breaks down, for our ways of thought are, admittedly, closely akin to and influenced by many of the intellectual lights that are anathema to the rightists.
> These are the university people, writers, and people in public life who make their ideas widely known through books, articles, and lectures, and in public service.[201]

Moore then proceeded to list names such as Arthur Schlesinger, John Galbraith, Adlai Stevenson, and William O. Douglas. For Moore and the librarians who shared his views and placed him in positions of leadership within the profession, this was a war between the supposedly enlightened, liberal, educated elite and the yahoos.

The Fund for the Republic, Fiske's Censorship Study, and Danton's Library School

A politically inspired study of book selection and censorship in California was conducted by Marjorie Fiske, a social scientist who found a temporary home at the University of California's School of Librarianship in Berkeley. The School agreed to officially sponsor the enterprise after it was endorsed by the California Library Association. As the School had expected, the Fund for the Republic gave it $36,000 to help defray the cost of the large-scale investigation. Most work on the project was done from 1956 through 1958.

Fiske and her staff depended on the director of the School of Librarianship and his faculty for information concerning the profession since none of them were librarians. Thus, she acknowledged that "In the planning and analysis phases, Dean J. Periam Danton and Professors Frederic J. Mosher and LeRoy C. Merritt were invaluable in orienting the study staff to the profession of librarianship and the problems of censorship in California."[202] The University of California Press published the study as part of its energetic program in this period to issue books that would help undermine America's anti-Communist efforts: an ad for two of these works filled the back of the dust jacket.[203] The jacket flap, also the responsibility of the publisher, claimed that Fiske's book investigated an area of public life "too often . . . preempted by cranks and bigots."

It is clear from the interviewers' questionnaire that those responsible for this survey were eagerly looking for evidence of politically conservative public pressure to censor library materials.[204] However, the librarians queried declared that there had been no increase in such initiatives in recent years and that they were rare occurrences. Moreover, they stated, the great majority of complaints from the public did not concern political matters, but profanity and sexuality in school library books.[205] The volume most frequently objected to was *Peyton Place*.[206]

Not finding what she and the others behind the survey had wanted, Fiske still managed to fill the report with unsubstantiated, politically motivated assertions and hypotheses. Her baroque thought processes produced so-called "conclusions" which even she admitted several times were "largely impressionistic."[207] However, Fiske abandoned all restraint in the last paragraph of her work and blamed any existing censorship on the librarians' "internalization of indirect public pressures, one of the major findings of this study."[208]

Fiske contradicted her own data and findings by referring several times to "the restrictive pressures of the post-war period"[209] in which there was little "respect for ideas, knowledge, and intellectual freedom."[210]   She mentioned book banning campaigns by the late Senator McCarthy despite the fact that his investigations had dealt with government libraries overseas, not locally sponsored school and public library collections in the United States.[211]   Fiske also alluded to "extremist groups whose programs include campaigns to decimate the library,"[212] but offered no evidence of this.   In fact, she declared that while there were generally no proven links between censorship efforts and supposed "extremist" groups, their "mere presence" was *somehow* conducive to it.[213]   She also implied that such organizations were conspiring nationwide.[214]

Fiske's capacity for speculation was limitless when she wrote about conservatives. She even detailed their *possible* thought processes that, she asserted, *could* lead them to want to (1) look over the shoulders of librarians, (2) prevent change of any type, and so forth.[215] Legitimate, traditional American concerns that international organizations like the United Nations could compromise US sovereignty were dismissed as evidence of a psychological disorder ("displacement") that served to mask the actual motivation for such ideas, particularly racism.[216] This far-fetched notion about those who were leery of any move in the direction of ceding America's sovereign powers became a fixture among those in the Intellectual Freedom movement for years to come, as did the gratuitous charge that such ideas were based on racism.[217]

In her study, Fiske alludes to attempts to "censor" works written by Paul Blanshard, who specialized in popular books about the alleged threat that Catholics posed to American democracy. The *New York Times Book Review* section, rarely positive in its treatment of traditional religion, said of his 1949 *American Freedom and Catholic Power*:

> Unfortunately, this reviewer can find little in these pages that is not on a very prejudiced plane. . . . Mr. Blanshard repeats, often in modern dress, old scandals and old wives' tales that one had assumed were forgotten, or else were confined, these days, to the spoken word alone.

> It would be idle to list the author's "facts" without appearing to
> set down the curious slanders beloved of the "Know-Nothings" of
> the Eighteen Fifites or of the Ku Klux Klan in the 1928 Presidential
> campaign.[218]

Like other members of the Intellectual Freedom movement, Fiske
dismissed complaints about Blanshard's publications as unwarranted
pressure by Catholic lay people and clerics. Apparently, members of
the Movement considered racial prejudice an evil, but not bigoted anti-
Catholicism. Blanshard's *American Freedom and Catholic Power*
consisted of an expansion of his articles published in the *Nation*. These
had resulted in the cancellation of subscriptions to that periodical by
New York City's high school libraries, an act vehemently criticized by
the leaders of the profession. In turn, Blanshard frequently commended
the American Library Association and its activists, as in his 1955
volume, *The Right to Read: The Battle against Censorship*. He
considered himself an opponent of Communism, but he believed that
the Vatican and the Kremlin posed equal dangers to America.[219]

Upon the completion of Fiske's work, the faculty of the School of
Librarianship at Berkeley—which had, in J. Periam Danton's words,
provided "the general supervision"[220] for the study—held a symposium
on the work and the social climate of library book selection. It was
decided that the value of the conference would be greater if the subject
was looked at "from broad rather than narrow vantage points."[221]
Thus, all the speakers but one were social scientists, not librarians.
The proceedings were published by the School the following year.
Danton, Dean at Berkeley from 1946 through 1961 and later a
premier figure in the field of international and comparative librarianship,[222] was delighted with Fiske's study, his School's role in
it, and the symposium papers. He declared in his introduction to
the published proceedings that the speakers' charge to view the subject from a "broad, and what might be called statesmanlike, view-
point, . . . was splendidly met."[223] He continued:

> Although it would be difficult to find a group of social scientists
> more diverse in interests, accomplishments, and backgrounds than
> our authors, many of the threads they have woven into their papers
> are remarkably similar. The reader will not, it is hoped, be

surprised to find in these fabrics the tough fiber of libertarianism—the championship of civil liberties—which, in one way or another, pervades almost every paper.[224]

Danton's pretentious pronouncements were hollow. Perhaps he misunderstood what libertarianism is: all of the contributors were left-wing statists and supporters of internationalist regulation. Equally erroneous was his characterization of the speakers as being "diverse in interests, accomplishments, and backgrounds." All nine were university teachers and only two had never received a degree, or taught, at the University of Chicago, Harvard, or Yale. (Danton received his doctorate in librarianship from Chicago.) Half of the contributions were shrill, partisan attacks on conservatives and anti-Communists.

Max Lerner declared in his presentation that contemporary America was nothing less than a battleground between the forces of light and darkness.[225] Harold Lasswell asserted that it was a period in which Americans' civil and political rights were not secure, and the country was dominated by fear, self-censorship, nativism, anti-intellectualism, and "anti-metropolitanism." He compared American anti-Communists to German Nazis.[226] Frederick Mosher, the token librarian among the presenters and a faculty member at the School of Librarianship who had been intimately involved with the Fiske study, raved about a "reign of terror" in America and "book burnings" by the USIA.[227] He assured his listeners that the coming years would be terrible: in the early 1950's, "Books and libraries had not yet become the object of attention of those who sought in California to protect America from the threat of Communist subversion, but there were signs that pointed toward libraries as an object of future attack."[228] Talcott Parsons expressed surprise that politics had been shown to have played such a small part in censorship attempts in California libraries.[229] Undaunted by these facts, he then blithely asserted that the political element was, nevertheless, the "precipitating factor"[230] in such efforts, working in combination with conservative religious and moral beliefs. Parsons shamelessly added that the supposedly neurotic emphasis on patriotism and loyalty among those most committed to laissez-faire government was caused "by well-known psychological mechanisms"[231] which he did not bother to specify in this piece. Fiske's contribution to the conference was a summary of her forthcoming book.[232]

Given the highly biased nature of both the Fiske study and *The Climate of Book Selection* symposium, it is ironic that Danton, the man overseeing both, became best remembered in the profession for his 1973 book, *The Dimensions of Comparative Librarianship*.[233] In it, he dismissed most work in international comparative librarianship as not being scientifically rigorous.

This symposium was not the first time Danton and his School had orchestrated what was essentially a political conference and published its proceedings. In 1951 he had initiated a meeting that was supposedly about the American public library. However, one of its three speakers, Librarian of Congress Luther Evans, devoted most of his presentation to the great services Unesco provided for libraries in other countries. He also managed to work in warnings about alleged attempts to pervert America's overseas libraries and the supposed dangers at home posed by censorial zealots.[234] In addition to their presentations, the speakers led two discussions, one of which was on "The Problem of Pressure Groups, the Incidence of Censorship, and the Obligation and Responsibilities of the Library and Librarian Concerning It." As with the Fiske symposium, Danton was delighted with the results. The speakers that had been most desired agreed to participate and, as Danton declared, "The gods smiled. . . ."[235]

The Fiske project was not only paid for by The Fund for the Republic, but The Fund had initiated the communication with the California Library Association that led to it.[236] This New York based organization financially supported other investigations of the role of "organized groups" in community controversies concerning library holdings.[237] One careful study of its work described yet another of its projects:

> Forty thousand dollars was allocated to produce a propaganda film, *Freedom to Read*, which was made available by the Fund to schools and organizations. The film was a distorted picture of the efforts of patriotic groups to keep subversive books out of public libraries. It had overtones of indignation against the attempt of Congressional committees to exclude books by Communist authors from United States Information Agency propaganda libraries abroad.[238]

The Fund had been established by the Ford Foundation in 1952 and came under the firm direction of Robert Hutchins two years later. (It should be noted that the Ford family has always maintained that by this time it had given up control of the foundation that bears its name.) Its major activity was financing academic studies that purported to prove that the threat of Communism from abroad, as well as from within America's borders, was negligible, and that there was widespread suppression of free speech and liberty in the United States due to anti-Communism. With millions of dollars at its disposal, its influence was widespread despite the fact that Hutchins, the researchers selected by The Fund, and the methodology and findings of their studies were repeatedly castigated by both liberals and conservatives in the anti-Communist movement, such as Sidney Hook, Dwight MacDonald, J. B. Matthews, and Arnold Beichman.[239]

Ellsworth and Harris' The American Right Wing

With the publication of *The American Right Wing*,[240] leading members of the library profession stepped entirely outside of their occupational roles in order to make a direct attack on the American anti-Communist movement. Subtitled *A Report to the Fund for the Republic*, it was written by Ralph E. Ellsworth and Sarah M. Harris and was based on the research and analysis they had begun in the late 1940's. As the director of the University of Iowa Library, Ellsworth had solicited publications for the "Right Wing" collection he had created there. It was said to be, for a time, the largest repository of its kind in the United States. Harris held the position of "Research Associate" at the library. Their study was issued in 1960, not long after Harris had passed away and Ellsworth had returned to his former position as head of the library at the University of Colorado. He was prominent in the profession for decades: in the 1950's, he was elected president of the Association of College and Research Libraries as well as the Colorado Library Association. His area of greatest expertise was library architecture.

It is significant that this purely political study with no direct bearing on librarianship was published by the University of Illinois Library School. It was the fifty-ninth issue in its Occasional Papers Series despite the fact that such Papers were formally required to "deal with some phase of librarianship."[241] It was not only an anomaly for the Series in terms of its subject but also its length. At fifty pages this was by far the longest of the Papers. Due to its size, a price of $1 was charged for it; all other Occasional Papers were given free to anyone interested. Harold Lancour, Assistant Director of the University of Illinois Library School, had served since 1952 as Chairman and Editor of the Publications Board which oversaw the series. Also on the seven-member Board was Robert B. Downs, Director of the Library and the Library School. No explanation was offered for the publication of this non-library work, but its outlook was clearly consistent with that of Downs. It may have been relevant that Lancour had directed the USIS libraries in France in 1952 and 1953 when the policies and practices of such libraries had been under attack by Senator McCarthy and others. (Lancour later resumed his involvement in international librarianship.) While the subtitle of the publication would indicate to the reader some sort of financial support by The Fund for the Republic, no description of its involvement was noted in the work.

Ellsworth declared that their research project had been undertaken because both he and Harris felt that what they termed the "Right Wing" was not truly understood by the scholars and others who wrote about it, such as Daniel Bell, Arnold Foster, Benjamin Epstein, and John Roy Carlson. They maintained that it was not only more dangerous than these supposed experts thought, but that it was becoming more menacing all the time.[242] The extraordinary fact here is that these investigators who were faulted were among the very strongest and most strident critics of the Right during this period.

Ellsworth and Harris demonized their so-called "Right Wing." According to them, it was comprised of ill-educated, racist, xenophobic paranoids who had adopted anti-Communism as their cause célèbre.[243] The authors included an uncommonly broad array of people under the rubric "Right Wing," so it not only took in those whom most conservatives at the time would have called "Far Right"—viz., Gerald L. K. Smith and members of various militia groups—but also William F. Buckley, Russell Kirk, J. Edgar Hoover, Richard Nixon, Barry Goldwater, the American Medical Association, and the American Bar Association. The authors asserted that despite the attacks of such self-styled "Conservatives" on those of the so-called "Ultra Right," they were not essentially different in outlook or philosophy.[244] Throughout Ellsworth and Harris' work, the terms *right wing* and *conservative* were used interchangeably.

The study concluded with a declaration that the Right-Wing was well-organized and "The result is a conservative government."[245] When the work was updated by Ellsworth and reissued by Public Affairs Press of Washington, D.C., in late 1961, his extreme views were even more pronounced. He complained that throughout most of the 1950's, the federal government had remained "stubbornly American."[246] He believed that the Right had recently increased in strength because many people in the United States thought that some of its major predictions had come true, such as the continued spread of Communism to Cuba and elsewhere.[247] Ellsworth declared that, in spite of the election of John F. Kennedy to the presidency, the extreme Right ultimately controlled the American government:

> Ten years ago, liberals, moderates, and uncommitted citizens could, and did, scoff at the Right Wing as a "fringe" group concerned in a crazy manner with unimportant issues. What they failed to understand, and what this report tries to clarify, is the fact that in terms of basic economic, political, social and governmental issues the Right Wing held the same beliefs as did the moderate conservatives of both major parties. They differed only in their concern with fringe issues, in their manner of speaking and in their sense of fair play.
>
> The significance of recent developments is simply that in a time of deep crisis, the moderates are more willing to go along with, and to be carried by, the extremists.[248]

Ellsworth and Harris' University of Illinois Occasional Paper received a positive, full-page review in *College and Research Libraries*, which declared it enlightening and useful despite its one-sidedness.[249] After its publication by Public Affairs Press, the study received more attention and was lambasted for its extremism by Howard Margolis in the prestigious journal *Science*. This careful analysis also condemned Robert Hutchins for refusing to dissociate his Fund for the Republic from the study which bore its ostensible endorsement. (Hutchins equivocated, declaring that since the title indicated it to be a report to—not from—the Fund, a disavowal was unnecessary.[250]) Even an evaluation in *Library Journal* by a member of the Intellectual Freedom movement agreed with the charges levelled by Margolis.[251] Russell Kirk, the conservative intellectual, declared in *National Review* that the Ellsworth and Harris work was an example of the quotidian attacks on conservatives by liberals in academia. Quoting Milton, he declared that while the latter claimed to merely want *liberty* for themselves and others, in actuality they sought *license*.[252]

NOTES

1. In response to an *American Libraries* article on international cultural relations by Charles A. Thomson, Chief of the Division of Cultural Relations of the State Department, Ludington wrote in 1944: "As a member of the United Nations, the United States has an obligation to make itself better known to other nations of the world. This should be done if for no better reason than to mitigate the evils of dollar diplomacy." (Flora B. Ludington, "Discussion" [following Charles A. Thomson's "The Emerging Program of Cultural Relations," *ALA Bulletin* 75 (Feb. 1944): 75-78], p. 78.) See also chapter five, note one.

2. Ludington, "Strengthening the Forces for Peace," 37-39.

3. Ibid., p. 37.

4. Ibid.

5. Ibid., citing Laves, "The United Nations and American Leadership in the World Crisis," *American Library Association Bulletin* 45 (March 1951): 79.

6. Laves, "The United Nations," 79-86. The quote is from p. 85. Laves' remarks appeared in different form in the *Saturday Review of Literature* (Feb. 24, 1951) and *Political Quarterly* (March-April 1951), a British journal.

Laves also commented on various domestic and international events. For example, he remarked: "More recently, as our own country has seemed to drift occasionally toward the equivalent of totalitarian witch hunting and persecution, courageous liberals have spoken out to renew our vigilance against such bigotry." (p. 86) He supported the United Nations armed response in Korea because he thought it represented the common will of humankind as expressed through the UN. (p. 79)

When Laves made his speech, he had recently accepted a teaching position at the University of Michigan at Ann Arbor.

7. Ludington, "Strengthening the Forces for Peace," p. 39.

8. Ibid., p. 37.

9. See Gary E. Kraske, *Missionaries of the Book*, pp. 233-34.

10. Flora B. Ludington, "The American Contribution to Foreign Library Establishment and Rehabilitation," in *International Aspects of Librarianship*, Papers Presented before the Eighteenth Annual Conference of the Graduate Library School of the University of Chicago, ed. by Leon Carnovsky (Chicago: University of Chicago Press, 1954), p. 112. The book also appeared (with different pagination) as *Library Quarterly* 24 (April 1954).

11. Ibid.

12. Ibid., p. 118.

13. Ibid., p. 124.

14. For a discussion showing how the domestic and international philosophies and activities were intertwined, see Louise S. Robbins, *Censorship and the American Library: The American Library Association's Response to Threats to Intellectual Freedom, 1939-1969* (Westport, CT, and London: Greenwood Press, 1996): pp. 75-78.

15. For brief professional biographies of Ludington and a list of her writings, see Anne C. Edmonds, "Flora Belle Ludington," in *Dictionary of American Library Biography*, pp. 322-24; and Margaret L. Johnson, "Flora Belle Ludington: A Biography and Bibliography," *College and Research Libraries* 25 (Sept. 1964): 375-79.

16. Robert B. Downs, "One Library World," *ALA Bulletin* (July-Aug. 1952): 215.

17. Ibid.

18. Lucile M. Morsch, "Promoting Library Interests throughout the World," *ALA Bulletin* 51 (Sept. 1957): 579-84.

19. President Dwight Eisenhower (June 1956), as quoted in Morsch, "Promoting Library Interests," p. 581.

20. Morsch, "Promoting Library Interests," p. 582.

21. Ibid., pp. 581-82.

22. Leon Carnovsky, "Introduction," in *International Aspects of Librarianship*, ed. by Carnovsky, p. v.

23. Ibid., p. vi.

24. Maurice B. Visscher, "The Interdependence of Knowledge and Information in the World Today," in *International Aspects of Librarianship*, ed. by Carnovsky, p. 11.

25. Ibid., p. 12.

26. Leon Carnovsky, "Patterns of Library Government and Coverage in European Nations," in *International Aspects of Librarianship*, ed. by Carnovsky, pp. 58-73. Carnovsky reported (p. 71) that most of his information about libraries in the USSR came from the master's thesis written by Arturs Baumanis at the Graduate Library School in 1952, "Principles and Practices of Soviet Librarianship."

27. Ibid., p. 71.

28. Ibid., p. 72.

29. Chase Dane, "Comparative Librarianship," *The Librarian and Book World* 43 (Aug. 1954): 141-44. In 1954, Dane began teaching a course on international comparative librarianship at the University of Chicago's Graduate Library School. A few years later, Dorothy Collings did the same at Columbia University's School of Library Service.

30. The different perspectives of these participants in the overseas efforts are described in Kraske, *Missionaries of the Book*, particularly pp. 16-17, 23-28, 32, 49-59, 85-86, and 138-46. Again, see above: chapter five, note one.

31. Ibid., pp. 231-32.

32. See Dan Lacy, "The Role of American Books Abroad," *Foreign Affairs* 34 (April 1956): 406.

33. Sidney Zion, *The Autobiography of Roy Cohn* (Secaucus, NJ: Lyle Stuart, 1988), p. 95. See pp. 11-12 on the voice in this book.

34. Kraske, *Missionaries of the Book*, pp. 232-34.

35. Ibid., p. 232.

36. Ibid., p. 233. See also Carl Milam, "Libraries, Scholars, and the War," *The Annals of the American Academy of Political and Social Science* 235 (Sept. 1944): 100-106.

37. See Lacy, "Overseas Book Program"; and Lacy, "Aid to National Policy," *Library Trends* 2 (July 1953): 146-70. James' primary pronouncement was "The Role of the Information Library in the United States International Information Program," *Library Quarterly* 23 (April 1953): 75-114.

38. Robbins, *Censorship and the American Library*, p. 77.

39. Robert B. Downs, "The ALA Today—A 1953 Stocktaking Report," *ALA Bulletin* 47 (Oct. 1953): 397.

40. Ibid., p. 398.

41. Ibid.

42. Robert B. Downs, *Perspectives on the Past: An Autobiography* (Metuchen, NJ, and London: Scarecrow Press, 1984), p. 159.

43. Cole, "Luther Evans," p. 26.

44. Robbins, *Censorship and the American Library*, p. 81.

45. American Library Association, "Overseas Library Statement," *ALA Bulletin* 47 (Nov. 1953): 487. The quotations from the Statement appearing in the following discussion are all from this page.

46. See J. [Jozip] Peters, *The Communist Party: A Manual on Organization* (New York: Workers Library Publishers, 1935), pp. 8-9, 16, 106, and elsewhere.

47. Dwight D. Eisenhower, "The President Speaks," (remarks at Dartmouth College, June 14, 1953,) *Library Journal* 78 (July 1953): 1206.

48. American Library Association, "Overseas Library Statement."

49. "Mr. Eisenhower then Defined His Ideas Further," *U.S. News and World Report* 34 (June 26, 1953): 45. See also p. 46. Similarly, Eisenhower's famous letter to the American Library Association concerned America's *domestic* libraries. (See Dwight D. Eisenhower, letter to Robert B. Downs, June 24, 1953, published as "President Eisenhower's Letter to ALA," *Library Journal* 78 [July 1953]: 1206.)

50. As quoted in Everett T. Moore, "Intellectual Freedom," in *Research Librarianship: Essays in Honor of Robert B. Downs*, ed. by Jerrold Orne (New York and London: R. R. Bowker, 1971), p. 16.

51. The text of the "Freedom to Read" statement can be found in American Library Association, Office for Intellectual Freedom, *Intellectual Freedom Manual*, 5th ed. (Chicago and London, 1996), pp. 135-40. The development of the document is described on pp. 133-35.

52. See Robbins, *Censorship and the American Library*, pp. 75-83.

53. For example, Arthur P. Young in his "Robert Bingham Downs," in *Leaders in American Academic Librarianship: 1925-1975*, ed. by Wiegand, pp. 86-87.

54. Robbins, *Censorship and the American Library*, p. 88.

55. Ibid., pp. 88-89.

56. Downs, *Perspectives on the Past: An Autobiography* (Metuchen, NJ, and London: Scarecrow Press, 1984): p. 159.

57. American Library Association, "Statement on Labeling," [July 13, 1951,] reprinted in American Library Association, *Intellectual Freedom Manual*, 5th ed. (1996), pp. 114-15.

58. American Library Association, *Intellectual Freedom Manual*, 5th ed., (1996), pp. 116-17.

59. Historians Peter Fritzche of the University of Illinois and Ian Kershaw of the University of Sheffield have attested to this. Both have written several books on Germany in this period.

60. "Mr. Dulles Told What was Done and Why," *U.S. News and World Report* 34 (June 26, 1953): 40.

61. Ibid.

62. Dulles' statement was reported in Robert J. Donovan, *Eisenhower: The Inside Story* (New York: Harper & Bros., 1956), p. 92.

63. See Eisenhower, "The President Speaks."

64. Eric F. Goldman, *The Crucial Decade and After: America, 1945-1960* (New York: Knopf, 1960), p. 253.

65. Utley, "Book Burners Burned," *The American Mercury* 77 (Dec. 1953): 35-39.

66. Couch, "Sainted Book Burners," *The Freeman* 5 (April 1955): 423-26.

67. Dan Lacy and Charles Kersten, "What Should Be the Function of Our Overseas Libraries?" Debate, moderated by Gunnar Back on *Town Meeting of the Air*, ABC Radio (New York: July 14, 1953), published in *Town Meeting*, vol. 19, no. 11 (1953), 15 pp. The debate could be heard on over three hundred ABC affiliates throughout the country. The listenership for *Town Meeting of the Air* was sometimes in the millions.

68. Lacy, "Overseas Book Program," p. 100.

69. Ibid., p. 105.

70. Ibid.

71. Ibid., pp. 101, 105.

72. Ibid., pp. 105-6.

73. Ibid., p. 106.

74. Ibid., pp. 110-11.

75. Ibid., pp. 99-100, 103-4.

76. Ibid., p. 102.

77. Ibid., pp. 101-102, 106-7.

78. Ibid., p. 111.

79. Ibid., p. 108.

80. The most accurate account of the overseas libraries scandal is in Roy Cohn's *McCarthy* (New York: New American Library, 1968; reprinted with additional preface and afterword as *McCarthy: The Answer to "Tail Gunner Joe"* [NBC/Universal, 1977], [New York: Manor Books, 1977]), pp. 75-92. Also valuable is the first-hand report on the overseas libraries by the former Communist Freda Utley, "The Book Burners Burned." She reported a lack of conservative books on America's domestic and international affairs. Utley was informed by the German *Amerika Haus* librarian in Hamburg that she had been instructed to not purchase her critique of the State Department's Asia policy, *China Story*, which she knew of through its German translation. Utley expressed contempt for the views on the overseas libraries expressed by the American Library Association. (She had lived in the USSR from 1927 to 1936 and become disillusioned with Communism. See her *Lost Illusion*, intro. by Bertrand Russell [Philadelphia: Fireside Press, 1948; London: Allen & Unwin.])

Rarely read by critics of McCarthy's overseas libraries investigation are the telling transcripts of his investigation: US Senate Committee on Government Operations, Permanent Subcommittee on Investigations, *State Department Information Program—Information Centers*; *Hearings*: Eight Parts: March 24, 1953-July 14, 1953; *Index*: Aug. 5, 1953; *Report*: Jan. 25, 1954 (Washington, DC: GPO, 1953-1954).

81. The information here about Stone is from Buckley and Bozell, *McCarthy and His Enemies*, pp. 195-97, 275-76, and 381-82. The information about the Institute of Pacific Relations and Frederick Vanderbilt Field is taken from Harvey Klehr and Ronald Radosh, *The* Amerasia *Spy Case: Prelude to*

McCarthyism (Chapel Hill and London: University of North Carolina Press, 1996), pp. 37-39. For a brief description of Silvermaster and the decoded Soviet transmittals which prove his guilt, see John E. Haynes, *Red Scare or Red Menace? American Communism and Anticommunism in the Cold War Era* (Chicago: Ivan R. Dee, 1996), pp. 96-98.

82. For a description of the documents found, see Ralph de Toledano, *Spies, Dupes, and Diplomats* (New Rochelle, NY: Arlington House, 1967), pp. 134-54.

83. Senator McCarthy's book, *McCarthyism and the Fight for America: Documented Answers to Quesions Asked by Friend and Foe*, was initially published in New York by Devin-Adair in 1952 and reprinted later that year as *The Fight for America* by Poor Richard's Book Shop in Hamilton, Montana. It included a positive foreword by William M. McGovern, professor of political science at Northwestern University. Devin-Adair was one of the primary conservative and libertarian book publishers in the 1950's, issuing works by John T. Flynn (the author and *Chicago Tribune* journalist), Frank Chodorov, and others.

84. Noted in Moore, "Intellectual Freedom," p. 7. When the *Post* inquired about McCarthy's book, the Boston Public Library responded that it was "on order."

85. This was well documented by Felix Wittmer in "The Leftwing Bias of the *Library Journal*," *National Republic* (Jan. 1955), as reprinted in his *Conquest of the American Mind: Comments on Collectivism in Education* (Boston: Meador Publishing, 1956), pp. 295-305; and analyses by well-known conservative writers like Ralph de Toledano in *The American Mercury* ("How Stalin's Disciples Review Books," 73 [Aug. 1951]: 14-20, and "The Book Reviewers Sell Out China," 73 [July 8, 1951]: 72-78); Irene Corbally Kuhn in *American Legion Magazine* ("Why You Buy Books that Sell Communism," [Jan. 1951]: 18-19, 53-55, 58-63); and George E. Sokolsky in his nationally syndicated newspaper column. Wittmer taught at New Jersey State Teachers College, later named Montclair State University. Despite his scholarship and prominence as a public speaker, his career in academia was a difficult and abbreviated one because of his anti-Communist views. De Toledano wrote numerous books on political subjects, was a nationally syndicated columnist, and held positions at *Plain Talk*, *National Review*, and, from 1948 to 1980, at *Newsweek*. He was still writing insightful articles in the new millenium.

86. See Felix Wittmer, *"Readers' Guide*, Undertaker of Conservative Articles," in his *Conquest of the American Mind*, pp. 306-22.

87. Fulton Lewis III, "A Guide to Red Reading," *American Mercury* 88 (June 1959): 53.

88. Harold H. Velde, in Committee hearings, 1953, as quoted ibid., p. 49. Both Lewis and Velde supported giving library users information about the Communist activities of authors.

89. Irene Corbally Kuhn, "Who Are the Censors?" *American Legion Magazine* (July 1954): 62.

90. Ibid., p. 14.

91. Ibid., p. 60.

92. Ibid., pp. 61-62.

93. Raymond Moley, Jr., *The American Legion Story*, with a foreword by J. Edgar Hoover (New York: Duell, Sloan, and Pearce, 1966), particularly pp. 356, 397. Richard Gid Powers attests to the American Legion's dedication to free speech and its opposition to extremists from the Left and Right in the 1950's. (See his *Not Without Honor: The History of American Anticommunism* [New York: The Free Press, 1995], pp. 262 and 306.) Powers is Professor of History at the College of Staten Island and the Graduate Center of the City University of New York. As reported earlier, he is also the author of a critical biography of J. Edgar Hoover: *Secrecy and Power: The Life of J. Edgar Hoover.*

94. Robbins, *Censorship and the American Library*, p. 50. See also p. 51. She noted the Sons of the American Revolution along with the American Legion.

95. See Laurence J. Kipp, "Report from Boston," *Library Journal* 77 (Nov. 1, 1952): 1843-46, 1887. Another version of this article was published as "Boston—The Library Did Not Burn," *The New Republic* 128 (June 29, 1953): 15-16. Philbrick, a native of Boston, had become well-known nationally for his testimony in court and before the House Un-American Activities Committee. He was also a frequent public speaker and wrote a newspaper column. His account of his infiltration of the Communist Party was published in 1952: *I Led 3 Lives: Citizen, "Communist," Counterspy* (New York: Grosset & Dunlap). In 1953 a television show based on his activities began a three-year run. He advocated the inclusion of Communist materials in public libraries. (See Philbrick's "Should Communist Books be Freely Available in Public Libraries?" *MLA* [Massachusetts Library Association] *Bulletin* 43 [Jan. 1953]: 1-3.)

96. *MLA* [Massachusetts Library Association] *Bulletin* 42 (Jan. 1952): 1-3.

97. Mrs. George Rodney Wallace, "It *Has* Happened in Massachusetts," *MLA* [Massachusetts Library Association] *Bulletin* 43 (Jan. 1953): 4-5.

98. Ibid., p. 4.

99. "It Happened in Pasadena," *California Librarian* 14 (Dec. 1952): 89-90.

100. J. E. Smith and E. B. Detchon, "It Happened in Burbank," *ALA Bulletin* 46 (March 1952): 85-87.

101. See Oliver Carlson, "What Really Happened in Pasadena?" *The Freeman* 1 (July 30, 1951): 681-84. *This Happened in Pasadena*, by David Hulburd, was published in New York by Macmillan in 1951.

102. This is expressed throughout his book, but see, in particular, Hulburd, *This Happened in Pasadena*, pp. 152-53. In a rare action, the publishing house made its own militant statements in the book concerning the events covered. (See Macmillan's "Introduction" and "Publishers Note," pp. vii-x, 165-66). MacMillan strongly supported Hulburd's theses.

103. Helen Haines, *Living with Books: The Art of Book Selection*, 2nd. ed. (New York: Columbia University Press, 1950). The first—and only other edition—had been published by Columbia in 1935. It had been reprinted every few years until the second edition appeared. All notes below refer to the second edition.

104. Haines, *Living with Books*, 2nd ed., p. 293.

105. Ibid., p. 404.

106. Ibid.

107. Ibid.

108. Ibid.

109. See Lottman, *The Left Bank*, pp. 274, 279-82, and *passim*. Bernard-Henri Lévy's account of French intellectuals' intense involvement in political argument shows Sartre to have been particularly accepting of the most barbarous violence by those he deemed "progressive." (Lévy, *Adventures on the Freedom Road, passim.*)

110. Haines, *Living with Books*, p. 404.

111. Ibid., p. 405.

112. Ibid., p. 403.

113. Ibid.

114. Ibid., pp. 515-16.

115. Ibid., p. 514.

116. See ibid., for example.

117. Ibid., p. 515.

118. Ibid., pp. 370-71. Referred to here are British works that were also published in the United States: E. H. Carr, *The Soviet Impact on the Western World* (London and New York: Macmillan, 1946); Harold Laski, *The American Democracy: A Commentary and an Interpretation* (London: Macmillan; New York: Viking, 1948); and Sidney and Beatrice Webb, *Soviet Communism: A New Civilization?* 2 vols. (London and New York: Longmans Green, 1935). Subsequent editions of the Webbs' work included new prefaces and appendices.

119. Haines, *Living with Books*, p. 406.

120. Ibid., pp. 405-6.

121. Helen Haines, "Balancing the Books: Reason Enthroned," *Library Journal* 73 (Feb. 1, 1948): 149-54.

122. Ibid., p. 150.
123. Ibid., p. 152.
124. Ibid.
125. Ibid., p. 153.
126. Ibid.
127. See, for example, Haines, *Living with Books*, p. xi; and Helen E. Haines, "Ethics of Librarianship," *Library Journal* 71 (June 15, 1946): 851.
128. Haines, "Ethics of Librarianship," p. 850.
129. Ibid.
130. Robert D. Harlan, "Helen Elizabeth Haines," in *Dictionary of American Library Biography*, pp. 223-26; and Ruth Warncke, "Helen Haines," in *World Encyclopedia of Library and Information Services*, 3rd ed., pp. 334-35, originally published in *ALA World Encyclopedia of Library and Information Services*, 1st ed., pp. 227-28.
131. Harlan, p. 225. He notes only Oliver Carlson's critique.
132. Warncke, "Helen Haines," p. 335.
133. Harlan, p. 225; Warncke, p. 335. Harlan mentioned that Haines had been disappointed for many years by what she had seen as librarians' lack of commitment to intellectual freedom.
134. Oliver Carlson, "A Slanted Guide to Book Selection," *The Freeman* 2 (Jan. 14, 1952): 239-42.
135. Elinor S. Earle, "Reply to Carlson," *ALA Bulletin* 55 (April 1952): 105.
136. Haines, *Living with Books*.
137. Haines, *Living with Books*, as quoted in Carlson, p. 239.
138. Ibid.
139. Ibid., p. 240.
140. Carlson, p. 242.
141. In 1982, this author, then unaware of Carlson's critique, wrote that in a 1938 article Haines' treatment of the social crises of the late 1930's sounded "like a parody of the radio or newsreel announcers of the time, [and that] Haines did not seem very sure or indeed very concerned with what the nature of the great social conflicts actually were." (Stephen Karetzky, *Reading Research and Librarianship: A History and Analysis* [New York and London: Greenwood Press, 1982], p. 68.)
142. Earle, "Reply to Carlson."
143. Everett T. Moore, "The Innocent Librarians," *ALA Bulletin* 55 (Nov. 1961): 861.
144. See George H. Nash, *The Conservative Intellectual Movement in America since 1945*, rev. ed. (Wilmington, DE: Intercollegiate Studies Institute, 1996), pp. 21-23; and "*The Freeman*," in *Dictionary of American Conservatism*, ed. by Louis Filler (New York: Philosophical Library, 1987), p. 130.

145. See: Harlan, p. 225; and Warncke, p. 335. Louise Robbins has declared that librarians were "shocked" by this attack on Haines but provides no evidence. (Robbins, *Censorship and the American Library*, p. 70.)

146. She wrote that ". . . it seems essential to analyze Carlson's accusations and in particular to study his quotations from *Living with Books* in their proper context." (Earle, p. 105.)

147. Haines, *Living with Books*, as quoted in Carlson, p. 239.

148. Haines, *Living with Books*, as quoted in Earle, pp. 105-6.

149. Earle, p. 106.

150. Carlson, p. 239.

151. Earle quoted (p. 106) the paragraphs below from Haines in an attempt to exonerate her of the charges levelled by Carlson. The material reproduced in Carlson's article were put in italics.

> Censorship concerned with sex extends far beyond legal control of pornography into the fields of creative and informational literature. Standard works by responsible authors on sex instruction and preparation for marriage and motherhood are too often eliminated from school use by organized attack, and similar outside pressures (with religion as chief motivating force) are directed at books on evolution and birth control. It should be remembered that Tennessee still maintains its law prohibiting the teaching of evolution and that campaigns for similar legislation in other states are frequently initiated.
>
> Political censorship, at times quiescent but never extinct, has drawn renewed strength (as was true after the First World War) from post-war reaction. Essentially nationalistic, focusing on so-called 'communistic doctrine,' 'Anti-Americanism,' and 'subversive literature,' strengthened by deepening hostility to Soviet Russia, and intensified by development of the U.S.-Soviet 'cold war,' it *rose in the late 1940's to a nation-wide hysteria. 'Treason' was read into acts, associations, and thoughts arbitrarily defined as 'disloyal'; books were suppressed or removed from libraries. Scholars accused of 'liberal thoughts' were dismissed from colleges and universities; 'loyalty tests' and 'loyalty boards' were set in operation for workers of every grade in the framework of federal, state, county, and municipal service. In spite of protest and resistant action by writers, publishers, teachers, scientists, librarians, many leaders in social and political thought, and a minority of newspapers, sanity and fair dealing seemed in eclipse.*
>
> In both political and moralistic aspects, censorship can become a dangerous and destructive influence, not only in publishing and

book selling but in library service, in education, and in intellectual and cultural life. On library book selection, problems are constantly encountered that arise directly from traditional acceptances of its prinicples [*sic*] and methods.

152. Carlson, p. 240, quoted by Earle, p. 108.

153. Haines, as cited in Earle, p. 108.

154. Earle, pp. 109-10; and Carlson.

155. Earle, pp. 109-10.

156. Carlson, pp. 241-42.

157. He considered Carlson's article typical of those that were criticizing librarians: "A rereading of both articles will repay anyone who wants to know more about the nature of such criticism of library policies." See Moore, "The Innocent Librarians," p. 861.

158. Harlan, p. 225.

159. Warncke, p. 335.

160. Robbins, *Censorship and the American Library*, p. 215n4.

161. Downs, *Perspectives on the Past*, pp. 157-60.

162. Ibid., p. 164.

163. See Couch, "The Sainted Book Burners," pp. 424-25.

164. Ibid., p. 165. The *Library Journal* debate of June 1, 1961 and August 1, 1961 is reprinted in full in Downs, *Perspectives on the Past*, pp. 165-73.

165. Downs, "Apologist for Censorship," as reprinted in his *Perspectives on the Past*, p. 165.

166. Kilpatrick, "Polemicist at Work," as reprinted in Downs, *Perspectives on the Past*, p. 169. Kilpatrick's views on censorship and civil rights were not akin to those of most of his fellow white Southerners. When Harper Lee's *To Kill a Mockingbird* (1960) was banned in one school district, Kilpatrick gave out free copies of the book to its students.

167. Robert B. Downs, "The Age of the Intellectual," University of Illinois Commencement Address, May 19, 1974, as reprinted in Downs, *Perspectives on the Past*, pp. 211-12. Downs was quoting Albert Guérard, the French-born historian and literary critic who immigrated to the United States at the age of twenty-six. Guérard held that America ". . . is not a territory and not a code, but a way of life." He considered himself a citizen of the world and was interested in the creation of a unitary world language. See his self-description in Stanley J. Kunitz and Howard Haycraft, eds., *Dictionary of Modern Literature* (New York: H. W. Wilson, 1942), pp. 583-84.

168. Robert B. Downs and Jane B. Downs, *Journalists of the United States: Biographical Sketches of Print and Broadcast News Shapers from the Late 17th Century to the Present* (Jefferson, NC, and London: McFarland,

1991), p. 3.

169. Ibid., p. 197.

170. Ibid., p. 209. Fans of *PM* still assert that critics of this New York daily, like James Wechsler, were merely "Red-baiters," although even they freely admit that it was openly radical, did not oppose the USSR, and included many known members of the Communist Party on its staff. For an example of such tortuous exculpations, see Dan Georgakas, "*PM*," in *Encyclopedia of the American Left*, pp. 579-81.

171. Downs and Downs, p. 323. Downs failed to identify the source of this criticism. It was *Time*, a magazine which for decades was best known for its pungent declarations and capricious views.

172. Sokolsky wrote several impressive books, among them a nine hundred page history of the world which tried to put the Asian past on an equal footing with that of the West (*An Outline of Universal History* [Shanghai: The Commercial Press, 1928]) and an analysis of twentieth century developments in China and Japan (*The Tinder Box of Asia*, rev. ed. [Garden City, NY: Doubleday, Doran, 1933]).

173. Downs and Downs, p. 125.

174. The most complete study of Duranty is S. J. Taylor, *Stalin's Apologist: Walter Duranty, The New York Times's Man in Moscow* (New York and Oxford: Oxford University Press, 1990). Malcolm Muggeridge, a correspondent in the USSR for the *Manchester Guardian*, had portrayed a recognizable Duranty and his mendacious journalism in his 1934 novel, *Winter in Moscow* (London: Eyre and Spottiswoode; Boston: Little, Brown, 1934; reprint: Grand Rapids, MI: William B. Eerdmans, 1987). An entirely open critique of Duranty appeared in 1940 in Muggeridge's *The Thirties in Great Britain* (Hamish Hamilton, 1940; reprint: London: Collins, 1967) and later in his *Chronicles of Wasted Time*, vol. 1: *The Green Stick* (London: Collins, 1972; reprinted in *Chronicles of Wasted Time: An Autobiography* ([1972-1973] New York: William Morrow; reprint: Washington, DC: Regnery, n.d.). Duranty was not a committed Communist but an amoral self-seeker.

175. "Everett T. Moore, 1909-1988," *Newsletter on Intellectual Freedom* 37 (March 1988): 37.

176. Everett T. Moore, "Intellectual Freedom," in *Research Librarianship: Essays in Honor of Robert B. Downs*, ed. by Jerrold Orne (New York and London: R. R. Bowker, 1971), p. 6.

177. Ibid., p. 5.

178. Ibid.

179. Ibid.

180. Ibid.

181. Ibid., p. 6.

182. Ibid., p. 7.

183. Ibid., p. 13.

184. Max Eastman, "An Open Letter to Rockwell Kent," [April 1950] in *Plain Talk: An Anthology from the Leading Anti-Communist Magazine of the 40's*, ed. by Isaac Don Levine (New Rochelle, NY: Arlington House, 1976), p. 393.

185. Peter Viereck, quoted in "Corliss Lamont," *Twentieth Century Authors: A Biographical Dictionary of Modern Literature*. First Supplement. Ed. by Stanley J. Kunitz and Vineta Colby. New York: H. W. Wilson, 1953. Pp. 844-45.

186. For example, see Lawrence J. Kipp, "How to Catch a Witch," *Library Journal* 78 (Dec. 1, 1953): 2071-75. Kipp, a librarian at Harvard College, had some interest in international librarianship. He had been involved in programs giving assistance to European libraries after World War II and efforts promoting the international exchange of library materials.

187. For example, see Robbins, *Censorship and the American Library*. Her second chapter is even titled, "Book Banning and Witch Hunts, 1948-52."

188. While 36 alleged witches were killed in New England—20 of them in only one town, Salem—approximately 50,000 were executed in Europe. Interestingly, witchcraft was not considered a heresy by the Russian Orthodox Church, and it did not persecute those considered to be witches. (See Richard M. Golden, "American Perspectives on the European Witch Hunts," *The History Teacher* 30 [Aug. 1997]: 411, 414.)

189. Thomas Hutchinson (1711-1780), one of the half-dozen most significant historians of early America in the eighteenth century, proudly pointed this out in his volume published in 1767, *The History of the Province of Massachusetts-Bay* (Boston: Thomas & John Fleet), which covered the period up to 1750. He was no obscure figure, being the last civilian to serve as the royal governor of Massachusetts. Moreover, his book was reprinted in England in 1795, and the last volume of his history was published in that country. The entire work, which included Hutchinson's collection of the most relevant primary sources, was reissued in 1936 by Harvard University Press.

It has been noted that "Hutchinson's devotion to objectivity and his reliance on original sources make his three-volume *History of Massachusetts-Bay* a solid work of scholarship." (Thomas J. Sehr, "Thomas Hutchinson," in *American Historians, 1607-1865*, ed. by Clyde N. Wilson [Detroit: Gale Research, 1984], p. 142.) Marc Mappen has indicated that "In regard to the writing of historians on Salem, perhaps the first genuine attempt to arrive at an objective view was . . . by Thomas Hutchinson, who had known some of the principal actors in the outbreak." (Mappen, "Suggestions for Further Readings," in *Witches and Historians: Interpretations of Salem* [Huntington, NY: Robert Krieger, 1980], p. 119.)

190. Everett T. Moore, "Why Do the Rightists Rage?" *ALA Bulletin* 56 (Jan. 1962): 26-31.

191. Ibid., p. 26.

192. Ibid.

193. Ibid., p. 29.

194. Ibid., pp. 29-30.

195. Ibid., p. 29.

196. Ibid., p. 30.

197. Ibid., p. 29.

198. Again, see: Felix Wittmer, "The Leftwing Bias of the *Library Journal*"; and Ralph de Toledano, "How Stalin's Disciples Review Books" and "The Book Reviewers Sell Out China." Irene Corbally Kuhn also provided convincing evidence of this phenomenon in "Why You Buy Books that Sell Communism," as did George E. Sokolsky in his Hearst/King Features column.

To buttress their charges, Moore and other anti-anti-Communist librarians frequently cited a two-page handout by Leon C. Hills, "How Are Books Selected for Purchase by Librarians?" (Remarks by Hills to the Mayflower Society of the District of Columbia, October 17, 1956. [Washington, DC: National Defense Committee of the National Society of the Daughter of the American Revolution; n.d.] One processed leaf, recto and verso.) However, it was atypical of the mainstream conservative attacks. The handout was not as well-written as the published critiques, and, unlike them, in two of its sentences it hinted of a possible conspiracy on the part of the political opposition. These two sentences focussed on the Melcher family, pointing out its involvement with *Library Journal, Publisher's Weekly*, and other influential publications.

199. Moore, "Why Do the Rightists Rage?" p. 27.

200. Ibid., p. 30, quoting Ellsworth and Harris.

201. Moore, "Why Do the Rightists Rage?" p. 30.

202. Marjorie Fiske, "Preface," *Book Selection and Censorship: A Study of School and Public Libraries in California* (Berkeley and Los Angeles: University of California Press, 1959), p. vii. Additional information on those involved in the study and its presentation to the professional community in California can be found in Fiske's Preface (pp. vii-ix) as well as her article, "Book Selection: Preliminary Plans," *California Librarian* 18, no. 1 (1957): 27-28, 57.

Throughout the book, Fiske stated that she believed in including all books in all types of libraries and that no objections based on supposed standards, a book's political or social statements, or alleged obscenity should be of any concern. The censorship of even one book would inevitably lead to more. (See Fiske, *Book Selection and Censorship*, pp. 65-68, 84, and elsewhere.)

203. The books were John H. Scharr, *Loyalty in America* (1957) and Harold M. Hyman, *To Try Men's Souls: Loyalty Tests in American History* (1960). The latter study was finanically supported, in part, by the Fund for the Republic.

204. See the large number of questions asked related to political and social questions: Fiske, *Book Selection and Censorship*, p. 138, IIIF5; p. 139, IVC and IVE; p. 141, F5; p. 142, E and F.

205. Ibid., pp. 45-47, 57, 80, 82, 132 table 26.

206. Ibid., p. 69.

207. For example, see ibid., pp. 58, 100.

208. Ibid., p. 112.

209. Ibid., p. 84.

210. Ibid., p. 110.

211. Ibid., pp. 46-47.

212. Ibid., p. 40.

213. Ibid., p. 49. This veteran social surveyor was apparently unable or unwilling to distinguish between correlation and causation.

214. See, for example, ibid., p. 51.

215. Ibid., pp. 10-11.

216. Ibid., p. 62.

217. For example, see the prize-winning article, William E. Benemann, "Tears and Ivory Towers: California Libraries during the McCarthy Era," *American Libraries* 8 (June 1977): 306.

218. John W. Chase, "Expanded Articles," review of *American Freedom and Catholic Power*, by Paul Blanshard (Boston: Beacon Press, 1949), *New York Times Book Review* (May 15, 1949): 15.

219. See Paul Blanshard's *American Freedom and Catholic Power*. Approximately 250,000 copies of the first edition were sold. It was expanded and reissued in 1958. See also: Blanshard, *The Right to Read: The Battle against Censorship* (Boston: Beacon Press, 1955); and Blanshard, *Communism, Democracy, and Catholic Power* (Boston: Beacon Press, 1951).

220. J. Periam Danton, "Introduction," in *The Climate of Book Selection: Social Influences on School and Public Libraries*, papers presented at a symposium held at the University of California, July 10-12, 1958, ed. by Danton (Berkeley: School of Librarianship, University of California, 1959), p. v.

221. Ibid.

222. His early interest in such matters was evidenced by his service as a delegate to the 1939 meeting in The Hague of the International Library Committee, the executive board of the International Federation of Library Associations. He wrote two books in the field of international comparative librarianship and served as a consultant in several countries.

223. Danton, "Introduction," in *The Climate of Book Selection*, ed. by Danton, p. vi.

224. Ibid.

225. Max Lerner, "Our Changing Society," in *The Climate of Book Selection*, ed. by Danton, p. 10.

226. Harold D. Lasswell, "The Atmosphere of Censorship," in *The Climate of Book Selection*, ed. by Danton, pp. 41-49.

227. Frederick Mosher, "Setting the Stage in California," in *The Climate of Book Selection*, ed. by Danton, pp. 54, 56.

228. Ibid., p. 54.

229. Talcott Parsons, "Implications of the Study," in *The Climate of Book Selection*, ed. by Danton, p. 80.

230. Ibid., p. 89. He also stated that librarians' major problem was their *anomie*.

231. Ibid., p. 88.

232. Marjorie Fiske, "Book Selection and Retention in California Public and School Libraries," in *The Climate of Book Selection*, ed. by Danton, pp. 66-76.

233. J. Periam Danton, *The Dimensions of Comparative Librarianship* (Chicago: American Library Association, 1973).

234. Luther Evans, "Free Libraries in a Free World," in *A Symposium in Public Librarianship: Three Addresses* (Berkeley: School of Librarianship, University of California, 1952), pp. 42-54.

235. J. Periam Danton, "Foreword," in *A Symposium in Public Librarianship*, p. v.

236. See Mosher, "Setting the Stage in California," in *The Climate of Book Selection*, ed. by Danton, p. 52.

237. See Fiske, *Book Selection and Censorship*, p. 38n.

238. Harold Lord Varney, "Fund for Whose Republic?" *American Republic* 89 (Aug. 1959): 6. As a young man, Varney had written novels that reflected his ideological support of the IWW. He later worked in public relations and wrote for several conservative journals.

239. For example, see Sidney Hook, *Heresy, Yes; Conspiracy, No* (New York: John Day, 1953), pp. 61-64; J. B. Matthews, "Hutchins to Investigate Communism?" *The American Mercury* 80 (June 1955): 71-81; Sidney Hook, "Six Fallacies of Robert Hutchins," *The New Leader* (March 19, 1956): 18-28; John A. Sessions, "A Misleading Guide to US Communism," *The New Leader* (Oct. 31, 1955): 25-27; Arnold Beichman, "Robert Hutchins Meets the Press," *The New Leader* (Nov. 21, 1955): 18-20. See also Thomas C. Reeves, *Freedom and the Foundation: The Fund for the Republic in the Era of McCarthyism* (New York: Knopf, 1969), pp. 157-58, 178-81. Reeves' book, based on his doctoral dissertation, is highly supportive of The Fund.

240. Ralph E. Ellsworth and Sarah M. Harris, *The American Right Wing: A Report to the Fund for the Republic*, University of Illinois Library School, Occasional Paper number 59 (Urbana, IL: University of Illinois Graduate School of Library Science, Nov. 1960) [50 p.]; updated ed. by Ellsworth (Washington, DC: Public Affairs Press, 1962) [63 p.]. The greater length of the revised version was largely a function of its typesetting. In actuality, Ellsworth added only a page at the beginning and three at the end.

241. Publications Board of the Occasional Papers series, untitled statement, in Ellsworth and Harris, *Right Wing* (Occasional Papers), back cover.

242. Ralph Ellsworth, "Preface," Ellsworth and Harris, *Right Wing* (Occasional Papers), p. 1; and Ellsworth and Harris, *Right Wing* (Occasional Papers), p. 33 notes 1-4.

243. See Ellsworth and Harris, *Right Wing* (Occasional Papers), pp. 22-23 on the adoption of anti-Communism. The other characteristics of the so-called Right-Wingers are noted throughout their work but are summarized on page 31.

244. Ibid., pp. 6-8, p. 33n3, and *passim*.

245. Ibid., p. 32.

246. Ellsworth, updated edition of Ellsworth and Harris, *The American Right Wing: A Report to the Fund for the Republic* (Washington, DC: Public Affairs Press, 1962), p. 1.

247. Ibid., pp. 43-46.

248. Ibid., p. 46.

249. Richard Zumwinkle, "Report on Conservatism," review of *The American Right Wing*, by Ellsworth and Harris, *College and Research Libraries* 22 (Sept. 1961): 401.

250. Howard Margolis, "Right Wingers Seem to Be Almost Everywhere," review of *The American Right Wing*, by Ellsworth and Harris, *Science* 134 (Dec. 22, 1961): 2025-27.

251. Donald V. Black, "Report on the Right," review of *The American Right Wing*, by Ellsworth and Harris, *Library Journal* 87 (Feb. 15, 1962): 745-46.

252. Russell Kirk, "License They Mean at Colorado," *National Review* 13 (Nov. 20, 1962): 393.

8

MAINSTREAM INTELLECTUALS AND ACADEMICS OPPOSE ANTI-COMMUNISM

The Mainstream Intellectuals' Assault on the Anti-Communists

Unfortunately, it has been the views of librarians like Robert B. Downs and Everett T. Moore that have dominated the profession for over fifty years. Thus, those Americans who sought to insure that Cold War era libraries—both domestic and overseas—included vital anti-Commuist works were dismissed as ignorant, intolerant, aggressive proto-fascists. Similarly prejudiced notions were commonly posited in the intellectual world of the 1950's and subsequent decades, a world which the leaders of the library profession were well acquainted with and were, to some extent, part of. The libel has continued to be declaimed by library historians.

A striking description of the alleged postwar absence of gray matter among conservatives and how this created a potential source of fascism was put forth by Lionel Trilling in December 1949 in the preface to his collection of essays, *The Liberal Imagination*. However, the last two sentences below are very rarely quoted or discussed.

> In the United States at this time liberalism is not only the dominant but even the sole intellectual tradition. For it is the plain fact that nowadays there are no conservative or reactionary ideas in general circulation. This does not mean, of course, that there is no impulse to conservatism or to reaction. Such impulses are certainly very strong, perhaps even stronger than most of us know. But the conservative impulse and the reactionary impulse do not, with some isolated and some ecclesiastical exceptions, express themselves in

ideas but only in action or in irritable mental gestures which seek to resemble ideas.

   This intellectual condition of conservatism and reaction will perhaps seem to some liberals a fortunate thing. When we say that a movement is "bankrupt of ideas" we are likely to suppose that it is at the end of its powers. But this is not so, and it is dangerous for us to suppose that it is so, as the experience of Europe in the last quarter-century suggests, for in the modern situation it is just when a movement despairs of having ideas that it turns to force, which it masks in ideology.[1]

Was Trilling unaware of the scholarship of Frank H. Knight, F. A. Hayek, Richard Weaver, and other academics? Why did he ignore the numerous writings of Walter Lippmann published in the previous fifteen years? How did he fail to publicly recognize the beliefs expressed by conservative literary figures, such as Herbert Agar, Robert Frost, Allen Tate, Robinson Jeffers, and Robert Penn Warren? (Some conservative intellectuals later did the same and have erroneously portrayed these years as a "Dark Age" of American conservative thought.)

How accurate were the charges of neofascism made against conservatives and anti-Communists that were generally accepted in liberal circles throughout the 1950's and afterwards? Instead of looking for those who some liberals would call "moderate" conservative anti-Communists, let us first recognize the existence of those conservative intellectuals and scholars who actively supported the bête noire of the leaders of the American Library Association—Senator Joseph McCarthy. They included, among others, William F. Buckley, James Burnham, John Chamberlain, Frank Chodorov, Eugene Lyons, L. Brent Bozell, Felix Wittmer, William Montgomery McGovern, and Suzanne La Follette. They were not usually accused of being fascists by serious political thinkers, but their avid readers were. Only Burnham and Lyons could have ever been considered anti-democratic—and then only in their youths when they were Communists—but members of the public who agreed with them about McCarthy were. It should be noted that even many conservative anti-Communists, like Peter Viereck, opposed the Senator, and that others, like Russell Kirk, were not enthusiastic about him. There were diverse views among those in the conservatives' anti-Communist movement:

there was no party line.

In 1952, then-liberal Irving Kristol, who considered McCarthy a demagogue, nevertheless indicted mainstream liberals of the day for their lack of concern about, and understanding of, Communism, Communists, and anti-Communism. He maintained that their views were disingenuous and intellectually untenable. Most, Kristol reported, considered Communists to be merely more outspoken in their supposed progressiveness than they were and therefore judged them by a different standard than they applied to those on the Right. In truth, he said, Communism was not a mere variant form of dissent but a movement whose aim was totalitarian: "a conspiracy to subvert every social and political order it does not dominate.[2] Unlike most liberals of the time, Kristol was not afraid to use explicit terms like "pro-Communist" or "front organization" when describing such realities. He went on to attack the "high moral posture" of those liberals who considered it "impossible to oppose Communism vigorously without walking into the arms of Black Reaction."[3] He made the highly significant observation that

> there is one thing that the American people know about Senator McCarthy: he, like them, is unequivocally anti-Communist. About the spokesmen for American liberalism, they feel they know no such thing. And with some justification.[4]

Kristol reported in 1995 that he had been widely attacked for this article in *Commentary*, the intellectual journal of the American Jewish Committee, and that it was the most controversial essay of his career.[5]

Sidney Hook, perhaps the leading liberal intellectual critic of Communism in this period, wrote in 1952:

> American intellectuals were more frightened of Franco in 1936 and of Hitler in 1933 than they are of Stalin today. . . . As country after country has come under Stalin's knife, concern in the colleges, in literary circles, even scientific quarters has *not* increased.[6]

That same year, James Burnham decried the neutralism of European intellectuals despite their access to information about Soviet regimentation, political prison camps, and so forth.[7]

As already reported, there was little concern about the USSR or

Communism expressed by prominent librarians in the 1940's, 1950's, or afterwards, and Americans who did express a fear of, or animosity towards, the Soviet Union were dismissed by them as unenlightened, paranoid neo-Nazis. This was the same view prevalent among social scientists, who avidly adopted the work of T. W. Adorno. He had left Germany when the Institute for Social Research ("The Frankfurt School") was closed upon Hitler's ascent to power in 1933. Adorno and his colleagues continued their previous study of the factors which lead to fascism and, in 1950, produced *The Authoritarian Personality*.[8] This one thousand page publication was sponsored by the American Jewish Committee as part of its multi-volume Studies in Prejudice Series. Utilizing circular reasoning and a variety of pseudo-scientific procedures, appropriating prewar German social structure as a universally applicable model, and completely ignoring the role of philosophy and ideology as well as actual political and social circumstances and events, Adorno and his team invented a pathology and a measure whereby conservative anti-Communists would, ipso facto, be labeled as having a psychological disorder: the so-called Authoritarian Personality. Those with this condition were deemed potential fascists, if not actualized ones. Moreover, the people Adorno and his colleagues adjudged *conservative* were said to be unlike the respectable, authentic ones of previous eras but were actually *pseudo-conservatives*, with traits bordering on the proto-fascist. At one point, they declared that conservatism of any kind was probably a mental disorder, not a true ideology, philosophy, or natural mode of being. Throughout this tome, the distinction between conservatism and fascism was consistently brought into question.[9] Tellingly, this massive study did not investigate the psychology of Communists.

These newly invented afflictions—the authoritarian/conservative/pseudo-conservative/proto-fascist personalities—immediately became popular weapons of liberal and left-wing intellectuals and professionals: they no longer had to *debate* their opponents, they merely had to *diagnose* them. This was far easier than refuting their evidence, ideas, and arguments. Even Margaret Mead, who was certainly no conservative,[10] criticized the wanton application of "the psychoanalytically oriented, German-modeled, authoritarian personality study, in which the character structure of lower-middle-class Americans is equated . . . with the character of lower-middle-class Germans as prone to victimize the weak."[11] (Given Adorno's flights of fancy, one

wonders how accurate his view of *Germans* was.)   Additional flaws
were pointed out by other social scientists.[12] Nevertheless, outside of
conservative circles, *The Authoritarian Personality* was generally
considered a landmark work: its thesis became widely accepted among
academics, intellectuals, and the cultured.   Interestingly, Leo Lowenthal, another transplanted member of the Frankfurt School who
wrote about the dangers of the Right in America, was married to
Marjorie Fiske when she conducted her study of alleged censorship in
California's libraries.

Leading scholars in the United States contrived a variety of
other supposed explanations for the desire among many Americans—particularly the mass of McCarthy's supporters—for a strong
stand against the USSR and its agents:

1. They were members of social groups experiencing
    downward mobility.
2. They were members of social groups experiencing upward
    mobility.
3. They were mindless followers.
4. They were mindful fascists.
5. They were old-fashioned American populists.
6. They were not old-fashioned American populists, but
    fascists.
7. They were European-style fascists.
8. They were American-style fascists.
9. They were isolationists.
10. They were international interventionists.[13]

Finding themselves confronted by a large percentage of the
population holding a contrary view of the world and its political and
military exigencies, the lumpen intellectuals were clearly in a state of
desperation.[14]

Among the influential and widely read scholars and intellectuals
who reacted most negatively to the wide popular support McCarthy
received were Richard Hofstadter, Daniel Bell, Nathan Glazer, Oscar
Handlin, Seymour Martin Lipset, Talcott Parsons, and David Riesman.
Their publications were filled with references to each other's works;
scholars have described how they influenced each other.[15]

In general, Hofstadter and the others viewed McCarthyism as

merely the most recent spasm of a deeply ingrained American populism that was authoritarian (à la Theodor Adorno), anti-intellectual, obscurantist, nativist, and paranoid. (It is significant that Hofstadter acknowledged more than once that he usually overstated his theses in his works, but argued that this was intellectually acceptable since his views had been neglected in the past. He was also not embarrassed to admit that his reasons for writing history, as well as his historical assessments, were directly induced by contemporary events.[16]) Some of the touchstone essays of these scholars were brought together in *The New American Right*, edited by Bell in 1955.[17] The theme and tone of the book is encapsulated in a statement in this collection: ". . . the American people are indifferent to the ordinary requirements of democracy."[18] The volume was enlarged and updated in 1963 as *The Radical Right*.[19] In some ways, its successor was *The Politics of Unreason* by S. M. Lipset and Earl Raab, issued in 1970.[20]

Throughout the 1960's, scare books about the alleged threat from conservative anti-Communists were written which appealed to a broader audience than just the intellectuals and the highly literate. Among these mud-slinging works were *The Far Right*, *Danger on the Right*, and *The Christian Fright Peddlers*, all issued by large, "mainstream" publishers: McGraw-Hill, Random House, and Doubleday.[21] Many of the studies in *The New American Right* had been supported financially by The Fund for the Republic. *The Politics of Unreason* and *Danger on the Right* were products of the Anti-Defamation League, which, like some other Jewish organizations, seemed afraid of another Holocaust.

Margaret Mead was one of the most incisive critics of the works of Adorno, Hofstadter, Glazer, Riesman, and the others of this school of social physicians, as well as of the popular articles that reflected similar ideas. As already shown, she condemned their fallacious application of psychoanalytical and cultural analyses of prewar Germany to the United States. Even worse, she held, was the neoisolationism these works displayed: all aspects of the conservative anti-Communist movement were attributed to Americans' psychological behavior or to social, economic, and political developments within the United States. (The overuse of psychological and social class concepts here was particularly egregious, in her view.) Mead deemed their castigation of American society irresponsible and unwarranted. She also noted that they paid no attention to international realities: a polarized world, a newly Communized China, nuclear weapons, Communist spies, Communist front organizations, and Communist manipulation through so-called "united fronts" with liberal groups. She observed that in their discussions of Joseph McCarthy ". . . there seems to be a persistent retreat from recognizing the [realities in the] rest of the world."[22]

Also important in exposing the methodological and substantive errors of Hofstadter, Bell, and the others was the social science research by Stanford University's Raymond Wolfinger and his protégée, Sheilah Rosenhack Koeppen. Her work confirmed Wolfinger's,[23] which had shown that the commonly accepted theories about the so-called Extreme Right anti-Communists were logically and empirically untenable. Koeppen's study of the Christian Anti-Communism Crusade demonstrated clearly that the members of this large, nationwide organization whom liberals consistently relegated to the Extreme Right were firmly committed to democratic principles and processes.[24] The Stanford research was definitely known to some of the influential anti-anti-Communists, but they were unwilling to let go of their baroque fabrications. Today, the assertions of Adorno, Hofstadter, et al are still being recycled while the research and analyses that refuted them are largely forgotten.

The Book World Opposes Anti-Communism

In the years following the war, and throughout the fifties and sixties, librarians were only one part of the so-called "mainstream" book world that rejected anti-Communism. The other participants were the publishers, book reviewers, and book sellers. The members of this subculture were similar in general outlook and political ideology.

In the two decades after the war, the number of conservative, libertarian, and anti-Communist books that appeared was artificially low because of the reluctance of the major publishers to issue them. Among those who had no alternative but to turn to one of the handful of small, conservative book publishers in the early years of this period were William F. Buckley, veteran journalist and author John T. Flynn, and—frequently—Friedrich A. Hayek. (To some extent, this paralleled the difficulty of even world-renowned conservative and libertarian academics in gaining positions at American colleges and universities.

Hayek's and Ludwig von Mises' appointments at the University of Chicago and New York University, respectively, were realized only through outside subvention.[25]) In the 1960's, books by Kevin Phillips, Senator Barry Goldwater, and Phyllis Schafley had to either be self-published or issued by conservative publishers, all of which had meager resources.[26] In part, the motivation of the "mainstream" publishers was ideological: they tended to have so-called "progressive" ideas. Indicators of their political orientation have already been mentioned, like their prominent role in writing the "Freedom to Read" Statement and their choice of Dan Lacy—the primary author of the American Library Association's declaration on the overseas libraries—to head the American Book Publishers' Council in 1953. However, there were also economic incentives and disincentives at work here. Publishers knew that books not considered "liberal" would probably not receive positive reviews and therefore would sell poorly to libraries and not be stocked by bookstores. There were only a half-dozen or so newspapers and magazines that provided the influential book reviews: *Library Journal*, *The New York Times*, *The New York Herald-Tribune*, *Saturday Review* (titled *Saturday Review of Literature* until 1952), and the *Chicago Tribune*. Only the Midwest newspaper took a strong anti-Communist stance in its reviews, and the impact of its critiques was largely regional.[27]

    A telling case where leftist ideological concerns overrode economic interests involved the decision of a major publisher in the 1940's to reject Hayek's *Road to Serfdom*, a sophisticated description by this libertarian of how free societies might gradually become totalitarian through the increasing power of government. The publisher's decision was made, in part, on the advice of an outside editorial advisor, William Miller, who insisted that the book was 'sensational' and 'unfit for publication by a reputable house.'[28] (As mentioned earlier, Miller was a friend of Richard Hofstadter, with whom he coauthored two textbooks on American history.) The first public report of this rejection appeared in a 1949 book Miller wrote on the publishing industry and its relationship to libraries[29] for the Public Library Inquiry, the landmark study initiated and overseen by the American Library Association. Miller's opinion remained unchanged in later years despite the publication of Hayek's volume by the University of Chicago and its subsequent extraordinary success.[30] Hayek reported that the book had been rejected by two other American publishers as well, despite the great interest it had already aroused when issued in England.[31]

In *The Book Industry: A Report of the Public Library Inquiry*, Miller displayed how different his views were from those of the conservative and libertarian anti-Communists. He stressed that the free market was injurious to high-quality publishing[32] but maintained that the publishers were nevertheless holding their own against the dark forces of economic, political, and social conformity:

> Despite these consequences [of open commerce] and those of the more obvious kind of censorship imposed by religious, political, and outside business groups, the book industry remains at least as open to ideas of all sorts and to the work of young and mature artists who for a time may set themselves against the main trend as any other big American opinion forum. . . . Comparatively, in an age of increasing deference to the market and particularly in a period of constricting and sometimes panicky fear for national security, the book industry has kept itself remarkably liberal and free.[33]

He then proceeded to demonstrate this supposed openness "to ideas of all sorts" and dedication to freedom by pointing to the publication of four books: one critical of Henry Ford, one critical of the Catholic Church, and one critical of the American Legion. The fourth, a collection of poetry by Robinson Jeffers, an opponent of Franklin Roosevelt's domestic and foreign policies, was faulted for its political views by its own publisher. Random House placed its critique on the book's jacket as well as in a special "Publishers Note" within the work itself.

In the early 1960's, there was a revealing instance of a politically moderate American publisher standing up to Communist pressure. The independent-minded William Jovanovich, President of Harcourt, Brace & World, was informed by Yugoslav agents that his friend, Milovan Djilas, would be harmed unless Jovanovich cancelled his plans to issue the dissentient's *Conversations with Stalin* in spring 1962. The publisher proceeded, as he believed his friend wanted him to. However, as he had greatly feared, the author was arrested and served four years in prison, half of them in solitary confinement with no heat in winter, no books for reading, and no paper for writing. It appeared that the only part of the American government willing to protest the treatment of Djilas and Jovanovich was the US Senate Committee on the Judiciary's Subcommittee to Investigate the Administration of the Internal Security Act.[34] Tellingly, neither the jailed activist nor the American-born publisher of Montenegran descent became a cause célèbre among the members of librarianship's Intellectual Freedom movement. Attempts to suppress critiques of Communism apparently lacked the power to motivate them.

A close look at the record makes it clear that the most prominent book review organs in the United States, as well as those geared specifically for librarians, tended overwhelmingly to undermine anti-Communist efforts. For example, Joseph McCarthy's 1952 book, *McCarthyism: The Fight for America*, was ignored by the major review media while *Ordeal by Slander*, by the apparently pro-Communist Owen Lattimore, was widely praised. The disparate treatment accorded these two books was protested in a statement to seven hundred newspapers signed by twenty-eight prominent anti-Communists, including John Chamberlain, Ralph de Toledano, William F. Buckley, Victor Lasky, Frank Chodorov, Morrie Ryskind, Suzanne La Follette, and Eugene Lyons. As McCarthy had done in his book, they refuted the charges frequently arrayed against him, like those concerning his methods.[35] William Buckley and L. Brent Bozell's well-documented and even-handed evaluation of McCarthy's charges (including those against Lattimore) and those of McCarthy's opponents was savaged by book reviewers when published in 1954. (Material released in the 1990's by the governments of the United States and Russia show how accurate the Senator's accusations generally were, as well as the assessment by Buckley and Bozell.)[36] Despite the intense British interest in McCarthy, as demonstrated, in part, by the publication there of several of the American books attacking him, Buckley was unable to find an English publisher willing to issue the objective work he had coauthored. Not surprisingly, the anti-McCarthy books received highly favorable reviews in Britain, as in the US.[37]

An interesting study by Felix Wittmer analyzed the book reviews in *Library Journal* over an eighteen month period in 1953 and 1954. Most were written by librarians. He found that three-fourths of all political books reviewed were left-of-center, only one-quarter were conservative. Moreover, almost all of the former received positive reviews and were highly recommended for libraries. This was the case, for example, with the works of Isaac Deutscher, like his admiring biography of Trotsky, *The Prophet Unarmed*. The same held true for *Saturday Review* editor Norman Cousins, who advocated world federalism in his *Who Speaks for Man?* In contrast, the anti-Communist or pro-capitalist books were consistently panned:

> James Burnham's *Containment or Liberation?*: 'exaggerations, insinuations, and unrealistic thinking.'

> Buckley and Bozell's *McCarthy and His Enemies*: 'a sustained and sometimes tasteless attack on those who do not agree with him [McCarthy].'

> Felix Wittmer's own *Yalta Betrayal*: 'While it is well-documented, it is repetitive and comes close to name-calling. . . . Cannot be recommended.'

> Friedrich A. Hayek's *Capitalism and the Historians*: 'many unreasonable attacks on noted scholars holding opposing views; . . . astounding prejudices.'[38]

Wittmer's sad fate in American academia is also relevant to this study. Born in Germany, he received his doctorate from the University of Munich in 1924. Because of his public opposition to the National Socialists, he was forced to flee Germany when Hitler came to power. A scholar of German and of history, he soon began teaching at New Jersey State Teachers College (later renamed Montclair State University), a position he held for seventeen years. However, he began expressing anti-Communist views in 1943. As a result, he became the unrelenting object of hostility and harassment by his colleagues. This forced him to resign—pensionless—in 1951.[39]

Ralph de Toledano, the author, journalist, jazz critic, and poet, provided damning evidence of pro-Communist distortion in his evaluation of book reviews in the *New York Herald-Tribune* and the *New York Times* in the 1940's and the 1950's.[40] Joseph Barnes dominated the review pages of both the daily *Herald-Tribune* and its weekly *Book Review*. In earlier years, Barnes had written for Communist-front publications issued by the Institute of Pacific

Relations and the American-Russian Institute. He was named as a Communist and a spy in sworn testimony by numerous former Communists and erstwhile agents: Whittaker Chambers, Louis Budenz, Alexander Barmine, Karl Wittfogel, and Hede Massing.[41] Not surprisingly, Barnes wrote positive reviews of Edgar Snow's untruthful *Pattern of Soviet Power* and Frederick L. Schuman's *Soviet Relations at Home and Abroad*. Snow was identified as a Communist agent by Budenz and wrote numerous books flattering to the Chinese Communists. Schuman, an academic whose works on the Soviet Union ranged from exculpatory to adulatory, had been described by a Senate committee as one of the most active members of Communist-front organizations in the United States. Barnes also wrote a favorable review of *USSR: The Story of Soviet Russia* by the ever mendacious Walter Duranty. When Barnes left his full-time position at the *Herald-Tribune* he became a senior editor at Simon and Schuster.

Most others in the *Tribune*'s stable wrote in a similar mode. Foster Rhea Dulles declared that Henry Wallace's *Soviet Asia Mission* was 'a heartening expression of faith in the Soviet Union.' Predictably, anti-Communist books by former Soviet officials Victor Kravchenko and Alexander Barmine were panned by Walter Kerr and Dulles respectively.

The New York Times praised its own Duranty for *Stalin & Co.*, as well as the Communist William Marx Mandel for his *Guide to the Soviet Union*. The latter book managed to contain nothing negative about the USSR in its five hundred pages. Like the *Herald-Tribune*, this newspaper also wrote approvingly of Schuman's aforementioned volume. As one might expect, a review by R. L. Duffus[42] questioned the veracity of Louis Budenz's *Men Without Faces: The Communist Conspiracy in the USA*. Budenz had been the managing editor of the *Daily Worker* for five years and had also worked in Communist covert operations within the United States. Granville Hicks was similarly dismissive of *The Whole of Their Lives*, Benjamin Gitlow's exposé of the Communist Party he had helped found and lead.

In a related study, de Toledano analyzed the book reviews on Communism in China that appeared in the *New York Times Book Review*, the *New York Herald-Tribune Book Section*, and the *Saturday Review of Literature*. He reported that the great majority—73—of the reviewers of 42 books were pro-Communist, 12 were what he called 'fence-straddlers,' and 7 were anti-Communist. Among those he identified as pro-Communist were Owen Lattimore, Edgar Snow, and Agnes Smedley. Smedley, involved in Communist activities world-wide for decades, left her entire estate to the head of the Communist Chinese army when she died in 1950 and requested that she be buried in the new Communist state. Not surprisingly, pro-Chinese Communist books were almost consistently praised in these influential newspapers and magazines. True to form, anti-Communist volumes, like Lin Yutang's *Vigil of a Nation*, were flayed by the pro-Mao journalist, Harrison Forman, as well as by Brooks Atkinson, remembered today mainly for his theater criticism rather than for his periodic political theatrics.[43]

It is relevant that when a few individuals with little money made an end run around the mainstream book world by forming the Conservative Book Club in 1961, it had thirty thousand members by the end of the next year and was selling 15-20,000 books per month by 1967. It distributed works by a variety of publishers and reprinted some conservative books itself. Its success encouraged its director, Neil McCaffrey, to found Arlington House in 1965, and it soon became the major conservative book publisher. Anti-Communist books were a staple of both the Conservative Book Club and Arlington House.[44]

NOTES

1. Lionel Trilling, "Preface," *The Liberal Imagination: Essays on Literature and Society* (New York: Charles Scribners' Sons, 1950; reprinted with new foreword, 1976), pp. ix-x. Ten years later, Daniel Bell also ignored reality when he declared that there was a liberal consensus among Western intellectuals. (Bell, *The End of Ideology: On the Extension of Political Ideas in the Fifties* [Glencoe, IL: The Free Press, 1960], p. 373.)

2. Irving Kristol, " 'Civil Liberties,' 1952—A Study in Confusion: Do We Protect Our Rights by Protecting Communists?" *Commentary* 13 (March 1952): 235.

3. Ibid., p. 232.

4. Ibid., p. 229.

5. Irving Kristol, "An Autobiographical Memoir," in *Neoconservatism: The Autobiography of an Idea*, by Kristol (New York: The Free Press, 1995), p. 19.

6. Sidney Hook, untitled essay, in *America and the Intellectuals* (New York: *Partisan Review*, 1953), p. 50; book originally printed as "Our Country and Our Culture" in *Partisan Review* (1952).

7. James Burnham, untitled essay, in *America and the Intellectuals*, p. 23.

8. T. W. Adorno and others, *The Authoritarian Personality* (New York: Harper & Bros., 1950).

9. See ibid., pp. 51-52, 181-82. The social scientists believed it "possible to investigate the relations of pseudoconservatism to 'genuine conservatism'— if, indeed, the distinction can be maintained. The question may be raised as to whether there is any deeply ingrained conservatism, within the individual, that does not derive its energy in large part from the personal need to curb one's own rebellious tendencies." (p. 51) In any case, even an authentic conservative "conceives of government as a tool of business." (pp. 162-63) Moreover, the modern economic system that conservatives support is dominated by large corporations: ergo, stated Adorno and his colleagues, they support corporate business, just as the fascists do. (p. 841)

10. For an analysis of her work and ideology, see Robert Cassidy, *Margaret Mead: A Voice for the Century* (New York: Universe Books, 1982).

11. Margaret Mead, "The New Isolationism," *The American Scholar* 24 (Summer 1955): 380.

12. Edward A. Shils believed that authoritarianism existed on the political Left as well as the Right and criticized Adorno and his co-workers for failing to address this. Robert H. Hyman and Paul B. Sheatsley declared, "Our major criticisms lead us inevitably to conclude that the authors' [Adorno et al.] theory has not been proved by the data they cite. . . ." Nevertheless, all three considered the study a major advance in social science which merely needed refinement. (See Shils, "Authoritarianism: 'Right' and 'Left,' " and Hyman and Sheatsley, *"The Authoritarian Personality*—A Methodological Critique," in *Studies in the Scope and Method of* The Authoritarian Personality, ed. by Richard Christie and Marie Jahoda [Glencoe, IL: The Free Press, 1954], pp. 24-49, 50-122. The quotation is from p. 119.)

It is significant that another popular book of the era, Erich Fromm's *Escape from Freedom* (New York: Rinehart, 1941), also dealt with "the authoritarian personality" and focused on fascism; any possible personality disorders of those on the Left were ignored. Not surprisingly, Fromm was also an immigrant from Germany where he, like Adorno, had been on the faculty of the Institute for Social Research.

13. These—and more—appear in Earl Latham, ed., *The Meaning of McCarthyism*, 2nd ed. (Lexington, MA: D. C. Heath, 1973; 1st ed. 1965.) The book is, in part, a sampler of the rich literature of this genre.

14. Samuel Stouffer, a liberal social scientist at Harvard University, remarked:

> To assume that most intolerant people among the rank and file are bad or sick would be to commit an error which, in the author's judgment, is all too common. This error is not unknown even among scholars, for a few of whom, incidentally, the "native fascist" may fulfill the same psychological need of a target upon which to project personal anxieties as may the "liberal" or the "intellectual" for a few other citizens. (Stouffer, *Communism, Conformity, and Civil Liberties: A Cross-section of the Nation Speaks Its Mind* [Garden City, NY: Doubleday, 1955; reprint: Gloucester, MA: Peter Smith, 1963], p. 223.)

These ideas were not stressed in Stouffer's book. His quantitative study, *Communism, Conformity, and Civil Liberties*, paid for by the Fund for the Republic, concluded that American anti-Communism was based on incorrect information reaching people who were not well educated. He believed that the issue of Communism was primarily one concocted by politicians engaged in partisan politics.

15. For example, see John Morton Blum, "Foreword" [1980], in *The Age of Reform: From Bryan to F.D.R*, by Richard Hofstadter (New York: Knopf, 1955; reprinted 1985), p. xiii. Blum noted that Hofstadter was influenced by Bell, Lipset, and Riesman, as well as C. Wright Mills and William Miller. Miller was Hofstadter's personal friend and collaborated with him on two American history textbooks.

16. See Peter Novick, *That Noble Dream: The "Objectivity Question" and the American Historical Profession* (New York: Cambridge University Press, 1988), pp. 337-41; and Michael Kraus and Davis D. Joyce, *The Writing of American History*, revised ed. (Norman, OK, and London: University of Oklahoma Press, 1985), pp. 313-21. Hofstadter's most relevant books for our discussion—those which bring together his essays and his views developed in the 1950's, were: *The Age of Reform* (1955); *Anti-Intellectualism in American Life* (New York: Knopf, 1963); and *The Paranoid Style in American Politics and Other Essays* (New York: Knopf, 1965). See page three in both *The Age of Reform* and *Anti-Intellectualism in American Life* for statements by Hofstadter declaring his presentist motivation and consciousness.

17. Daniel Bell, ed. *The New American Right* (New York: Criterion Books, 1955).

18. Nathan Glazer and Seymour Martin Lipset, "Polls on Communism and Conformity," in *The New American Right*, ed. by Bell, p. 149.

19. Daniel Bell, ed., *The Radical Right:* The New American Right *Expanded and Updated* (Garden City, NY: Doubleday, 1963).

20. Seymour Martin Lipset and Earl Raab, *The Politics of Unreason: Right-Wing Extremism in America, 1790-1970* (New York and London: Harper & Row, 1970).

21. Donald Janson and Bernard Eisman, *The Far Right* (New York: McGraw-Hill, 1963); Arnold Foster and Benjamin R. Epstein, *Danger on the Right* (New York: Random House, 1964); and Brooks R. Walker, *The Christian Fright Peddlers* (Garden City, NY: Doubleday, 1964).

22. Mead, "The New Isolationism," p. 381. Her other points were made on pp. 378-82. Mead was apparently not convinced that the intellectuals she wrote about were as "persecuted and repudiated" (p. 382) as they felt themselves to be.

23. Raymond E. Wolfinger and others, "America's Radical Right: Politics of Ideology," in *Ideology and Discontent*, ed. by David Apter (New York: The Free Press, 1964): 262-93.

24. Sheilah Rosenhack Koeppen, "Dissensus and Discontent: The Clientele of the Christian Anti-Communism Crusade," (Ph.D. dissertation, Stanford University, August 1967), particularly pp. 2-3, 20-24, 122-40. William F. Buckley, Jack Kemp, and President Ronald Reagan have been among the CACC's supporters. (See Fred Schwarz, *Beating the Unbeatable Foe: One Man's Victory over Communism, Leviathan, and the Last Enemy* [Washington, DC: Regnery, 1996].)

25. See Nash, *The Conservative Intellectual Movement in America since 1945*, pp. 346n57, 15, and 348n102.

26. William A. Rusher, *The Rise of the Right*, revised ed. (New York: National Review, 1993), pp. 171-72. Henry Regnery, the publisher of many of the most significant conservative and anti-Communist authors of the 1950's and 1960's—such as Stefan Possony, Louis Budenz, Freda Utley, and William F. Buckley—reported that he was unable to make a profit with the publishing house which bore his name so it went out of business. Regnery also published classic and modern philosophers. From 1949 until 1951, he published the seventy-two books used in the Great Books Program. However, the board of directors of the Great Books Foundation broke off this relationship before he could realize a profit from his investment: they were incensed by Buckley's *God and Man at Yale* and wanted nothing to do with the publisher of this new book. Despite the financial failure of Regnery's company, his involvement with publishing, as well as the Regnery imprint, were later renewed. (See Henry Regnery, *Memoirs of a Dissident Publisher* [New York and London: Harcourt, Brace, Jovanovich, 1979], pp. 248, 103-18, 170-73.)

27. Interesting facts about the relative difficulty of getting anti-Communist books published were noted in articles of the period: Kuhn, "Who Are the Censors?"; Kuhn, "Why You Buy Books that Sell Communism," pp. 54-55, 63; and Wittmer, *"Library Journal,"* p. 297.

28. See Miller's statements reprinted in Couch, "The Sainted Book Burners," p. 423.

29. William Miller, *The Book Industry: A Report of the Public Library Inquiry* (New York: Columbia University Press, 1949).

30. Again, see Miller's statements quoted in Couch, "The Sainted Book Burners," p. 423. On *The Road to Serfdom*'s success, see: George H. Nash, *The Conservative Intellectual Movement in America since 1945*, revised ed. (Wilmington, DE: Intercollegiate Studies Institute, 1996), pp. 3-6; Friedrich A. Hayek, "Preface to the 1956 Paperback Edition," *The Road to Serfdom*, with an introduction by Milton Friedman (Chicago: University of Chicago Press, 1994; originally published in 1944), pp. xxviii-xxxiii; and Milton Friedman, "Introduction," *Road to Serfdom*, pp. xvii-xx.

31. Hayek, "Preface, 1956," *Road to Serfdom*, p. xxix.

32. Miller, *The Book Industry*, pp. 27-64.

33. Ibid., p. 61. See also pp. 62-63.

34. See US Senate Committee on the Judiciary, Subcommittee to Investigate the Administration of the Internal Security Act and Other Internal Security Laws, *Yugoslav Interference with a U.S. Book Publisher: Testimony of William Jovanovich*, June 27, 1962 (Washington, DC: GPO, 1962).

35. See "McCarthy Critics Challenged by 28," *New York Times* (April 6, 1953): 7.

36. William F. Buckley, Jr., "Introduction to the New Edition," *McCarthy and His Enemies: The Record and Its Meaning*, by Buckley and L. Brent Bozell (New ed.: Washington, DC: Regnery, 1995; 1st ed., 1954) pp. vii-xiv. Arthur Schlesinger, Jr. called it 'a sick book' when first published. (Quoted on p. viii.) On Lattimore, see pp. 153-60. See also: M. Stanton Evans, "History's Vindication of Joe McCarthy," *Human Events*, Special Supplement (May 16, 1987): S1-S8; M. Stanton Evans, "McCarthyism: Waging the Cold War in America," *Human Events*, Special Supplement (May 30, 1997): S1-S8; and M. Stanton Evans, "Joe McCarthy and the Historians," *Human Events*, Special Supplement (Jan. 1, 1999): S1-S8.

37. See Buckley, "Introduction to the New Edition," in *McCarthy and His Enemies* (1995), pp. viii-xii.

38. See Felix Wittmer, *"Library Journal."*

39. See an account of his ordeal in E. Merrill Root, *Collectivism on the Campus: The Battle for the Mind in American Colleges* (New York: Devin-Adair, 1955), pp. 313-22.

40. Ralph de Toledano, "How Stalin's Disciples Review Books." The quotation and the information on the reviews in this and the following paragraph were obtained from his article.

41. The full story about Barnes will not be known until all relevant archives have been opened. A 1944 KGB communication recently made public indicates that Barnes was not one of *its* agents but was considered potentially useful. (See John Earl Haynes and Harvey Klehr, *Venona: Decoding Soviet Espionage in America* [New Haven and London: Yale University Press, 1999], p. 241.) The KGB was only one Communist organization running agents in the United States.

42. Duffus, the author of numerous non-fiction books, had a strong interest in reading and public libraries. He wrote *Books—Their Place in a Democracy* (Boston: Houghton, 1930) and *Our Starving Libraries: Studies in Ten American Communities during the Depression Years* (Boston: Houghton, 1933).

43. Ralph de Toledano, "The Book Reviewers Sell Out China," *The American Mercury* 73 (July 8, 1951): 72-78. Forman insisted in his own book, *Report from Red China* (New York: Holt, 1945), that the Chinese Communists were not interested in collectivizing China but in democratizing it. The scholar, Walter Kolarz, tersely noted when describing the book that Forman's "sympathies are pro-Communist." (Kolarz, *Books on Communism: A Bibliography*, 2nd ed. [London: Ampersand, 1963.]) Ampersand also published Robert Conquest's notable book on the USSR, *The Last Empire* (1962).

44. Ann Edwards, "The Story of the Conservative Book Club," *Human Events* (May 20, 1967), as reprinted in *The Best of Human Events: Fifty Years of Conservative Thought and Action*, ed. by James C. Roberts (Lafayette, LA: Huntington House Publishers, 1995), pp. 25-27.

9

AN OVERVIEW OF AMERICAN LIBRARIANSHIP AND THE SOVIET UNION, 1960-1985

From 1960 to 1985, the aims of Soviet librarianship remained essentially the same, both domestically and internationally. At home, it maintained its commitment to forcing Communist ideology on its own people. Despite its hostility to democratic ideas, it frequently developed links to the United States and other Western countries, largely to gain scientific and technical information in all fields, including librarianship. The latter took on added significance with the development of computers, reflected in the growing use of the term *library and information science* in the United States to denote the library profession. The basic tenets of Soviet librarianship had followed the USSR's troops into Eastern Europe, so library workers in countries like Hungary and the German Democratic Republic promulgated Communist ideology with only slight variations.

After 1960, American theories of library relations with the USSR again became part of the profession's general philosophy for dealing with the entire world, eclipsing the distaste and hostility that had begun to grow among a minority of the vocal librarians in the earlier years of the Cold War. To some extent, this reflected the general decline in anti-Communism among intellectuals and the highly educated. The new policy of international comparative librarianship was developed in tandem with British professionals. It was one of unbridled internationalism and political relativism.

The State of Communist Librarianship
and its International Relations

In its essentials, Soviet librarianship in the years 1960 through 1985 was the same as it had been since the Bolsheviks' coup. As in previous years, the primary purpose of libraries in the Soviet Union and the other Communist countries was to foster Communism. This was reiterated time and again.[1] "Reader guidance" was stressed, and librarians played a prominent role in determining the reading behavior of Soviet citizens.[2] Librarians who did not cooperate were still being imprisoned and tortured in the 1980's. While the facts about their mistreatment were now easier to obtain than in the past, the American library community was loath to get involved on their behalf, fearing that it would ruin the supposed "good relations" that existed between the librarians of East and West.[3]

Librarians in the USSR and the countries it occupied considered themselves part of a manichean world consisting solely of Communist and "bourgeois" forces. The former was considered scientific, progressive, effective—the wave of the future. The latter was dismissed as reactionary, "skeptical," unscientific—a dying remnant of a decaying order.[4]

As in the postwar years and the 1950's, Soviet librarians were bombastic.[5] They now *consistently* claimed to have the largest libraries, and the largest number of libraries, in the world. (As before, a *library* was conveniently defined as any collection in the USSR of fifty or more books, and a *book* was any paper item of more than a few pages.)[6] They even touted their public libraries as the most democratically run on earth.[7] The Soviet people were regularly celebrated as having the highest quality reading habits on the planet and being conversant with the best literature of all nations. Testimonials and data were piled atop each other to prove the superiority of the USSR to the Western countries, particularly the United States.[8]

The Soviets, with their dedication to fostering Communism, openly expressed contempt for American ideals concerning readers' freedom to read what they desired: it was alleged to be philosophically flawed, irresponsible, and devious. In the 1970's, one of their foremost librarians, O. S. Chubaryan, declared: "Only the lack of understanding (or unwillingness to understand) of how deep an imprint a book just read can make on a person's mind and how it can influence one's outlook and moral qualities explains the attempts to deny the importance of book propaganda and the guidance of reading and see in them a 'violation of personality.' "[9]   Moreover, he asserted, the American defense of 'free choice of books for reading' and 'non-interference of libraries in the field of people's reading' was an example of the ideological error of "formalism."[10]   (Formalism was a potentially fatal mistake in the USSR.)   Communist librarians also maintained that the belief in the right of an individual to choose his or her own reading matter was one of many "bourgeois" theories which were actually attempts to disguise the true social role of the library.[11]

There was no international debate on such issues because Americans rarely responded to these charges.   Their philosophy of international and comparative librarianship demanded comity at any cost; conflict was assiduously avoided.   The ideals of American democracy and liberty—and of American librarianship—were not defended against assaults from abroad.

In contrast, the Soviets reacted wildly to even muffled criticism, to perceived criticism, and to alleged criticism.   For example, in 1980 Boris Kanevskij, Director of International Book Exchange at the Lenin Library, attacked what he claimed were the

> bourgeois librarians who have taken up a hostile anti-communist stance. It is generally known that anti-communism is nowadays the basis of all forms of bourgeois ideology. In order to formulate spurious aims and slogans to attract the masses, the ideologues of the bourgeoisie are involved to a great extent in slandering the theory and practice of scientific communism.[12]

In the postwar era, the hostility expressed towards American librarianship varied in intensity, but it was even present during the years of so-called "détente."   No major change was apparent until 1988, three years after Gorbachev's rise to power.[13]

As discussed earlier, from its very inception Soviet international librarianship had stressed the importance of obtaining professional expertise from America and utilizing its library system as a conduit for Western scientific and technological knowledge. Lenin had realized the significance of obtaining scientific and technical information, and he established channels for doing so.[14] Krupskaya had clearly articulated the basic policy of the USSR regarding the use of American library expertise:

> We must use the experience of other countries, of capitalist countries, in every way we can; in technical services we must borrow all that we can. But we must build our own library—a library of a different kind, more in keeping with our socialist way of life.[15]

These essential ideas were maintained in the sixties, seventies, and most of the eighties.

The volume of Soviet relations with the West had varied in different periods. In the early 1950's, the Soviet Union had not only attempted to increase its efficiency in acquiring scientific information from abroad and distributing it throughout the country, but in disseminating it to the newly Communized nations.[16] According to Soviet officials, of special note here was

> the great political significance of this work in view of the fact that the distribution of books abroad, especially in the countries of the people's democracy, promotes the popularization of Soviet socialist culture, and fortifies the position of the camp of peace, democracy and socialism.[17]

After Stalin's death in 1953, the USSR had further intensified its efforts to obtain scientific and technical information from the West. Under Khrushchev's leadership, the number of libraries which were permitted to obtain books directly from overseas sources was increased. Until 1955, only two had been trusted with this privilege.

In 1957 the USSR had joined the primary international library organization, the International Federation of Library Associations and Institutions, which it had ignored since its founding in 1929. Soon, the Soviet Union began sending its librarians abroad on professional tours.[18] Efforts of this kind increased in the seventies, as the Communist librarians proclaimed that they were acting in accordance with the policy of détente.[19] Such activities facilitated the gathering of technical data from the West, the dissemination of Soviet propaganda, and the disarming of American librarians psychologically and philosophically.

Obtaining Western scientific and technical data was rarely difficult. VINITI, the All-Union Institute of Scientific and Technical Information, translated, abstracted, and photocopied enormous numbers of items annually.[20] Traditionally, it reproduced materials with no hesitation at all since the Soviet Union did not accept the concept of copyright until 1973. A large percentage of the abstracts VINITI made in the natural sciences were of items published in the United States, Britain, and other Western countries.[21] In 1970 alone, one million abstracts were made.[22]

The Anglo-American Ideology of International and Comparative Librarianship: Globaloney

By the early 1970's, American librarians and their articulate British colleagues had formulated an ideology of international and comparative librarianship that remained relatively stable through 1985. To a large extent, Soviet librarianship—like the rest of the Communist system—was now considered to be merely another variation among the world's institutions with which the West *had* to forge "good relations." This required accepting it on its own terms and accommodating to it. As already noted, conflict of any kind was to be avoided at all costs. The goal was an internationalized profession which, it was held, could play a vital role in the attainment of world peace, justice, and understanding. The ultimate aim was one global society and a global government.

There was a high degree of agreement on the major theses of the philosophy among those active in this area of the profession. Moreover, almost all of these adherents held positions of leadership within librarianship. Only a few outspoken librarians maintained a clear view of the USSR during this period, notably Paul L. Horecky, Eugene Slon, Robert Delaney, and the Englishman, George Chandler.[23] Not surprisingly, their work was not incorporated into the received body of knowledge of the profession. It is also significant that many of those with executive power in this area maintained a firm grip on the reigns of power. For example, Lester Asheim, head of the Office of International Relations of the American Library Association from 1961 through 1966, successfully fought off the efforts of ALA members for more input into, and accountability from, his Office.[24]

The Internationalist Imperative

Perhaps the most significant belief among leaders of this field of
international and comparative librarianship was that we now lived in a
"global village" in which the various nations had to cooperate and
unite. Many believed that library and information workers could be
instrumental in realizing the dream of One World because the field
itself was international, *in posse* if not *in esse*. Thus, John F. Harvey
commented on "the one world philosophy permeating this field,"[25] and
Lester Asheim wrote of "the hoped-for One World of Librarianship."[26]
To B. C. Vickery and A. G. Brown, international cooperation and "one
world of information" were inevitable: "As information science
continues to develop, so also will international cooperation, for . . .
information science, both in its theoretical base and its practical
applications, is essentially international in character."[27]

In the preface to their landmark *Encyclopedia of Library and
Information Science,* editors Allen Kent and Harold Lancour stated that
they were committed to building a new discipline—an integrated library
and information science—and that they were "equally committed to a
'one-world' concept of their science."[28]   Their stated goal was to
produce a work which was "non-national." Sylva Simsova maintained
that "internationalism is a natural outcome of life in a global village in
which neighbors of different cultures learn to live with one another."[29]
She held that "international understanding, which has often been given
as one of the objectives of comparative librarianship, will follow as
mutual understanding reduced any areas of friction."[30]   Others were
even more optimistic: Richard Krzys and Gaston Litton predicted that
extraterrestrial librarianship would someday supersede global librarianship.[31]

D. J. Foskett asserted that all humans would perish unless ignorance and mistrust gave way to knowledge and understanding. Since
librarians held key positions in the international communications
network, through cooperation and mutual assistance in librarianship
"we make a genuine contribution to the achievement of peace and
happiness for all men across the world."[32]   Louis Shores believed that
"our professional destiny is to lead this troubled world out of its
current dilemmas by teaching people everywhere to compare their
ideals and their societies."[33]   Libraries could become centers for fact-

based dialogues on issues of war, peace, trade, and education, and also help develop a world culture that focuses on the advancement of humankind. However, unlike many involved in international comparative librarianship, Shores held a positive view of the United States and other Western countries.

Closely connected with the concepts of One World and international cooperation was the idea of The Integration and Internationalization of Knowledge and Information. By supporting the "universality and integration of knowledge," Robert Vosper held that librarians would help heal the world's wounds, a world divided by ideological, linguistic, political and religious differences.[34] He declared: "Perhaps the universal language of the future will be MARC!"[35] (The acronym stands for Machine Readable Cataloging). Vosper reminded his colleagues that the dream of universal bibliographic control was an old one for librarians, citing Konrad von Gesner's sixteenth century attempt, *Biblioteca Universalis.*

Information scientists such as H. J. Abraham Goodman, Manfred Kochen, and Eugene Garfield were enthusiastic proponents of the international coordination and dissemination of the world's knowledge to solve the problems of mankind. Inspired by the utopian writings of H. G. Wells, they called their hoped-for product "The World Brain" or "The World Encyclopedia."[36] (Incidentally, while Wells had not been uncritical of the Soviet Union, he had tended to defend it decade after decade.[37])

The Equal Distribution of Information

A strong faith in the benevolent result of the integration and internationalization of knowledge led to the third major idea of those who were influential in Anglo-American international and comparative librarianship: the concept that information generated in the West—particularly information of economic value—should be made available throughout the world. E. J. Josey summed this up with his statement, "Equal distribution of data is certainly needed on the international level."[38] Like Josey, Joseph Z. Nitecki extrapolated from a concept that had sometimes been applied at the national level in the United States when he declared that the failure of libraries to cooperate internationally to give full information access to *all* of humankind was "discriminatory."[39]   Significantly, the free flow of information was frequently opposed when there was a belief that it might in some way promote American (or other Western) influence in the world. Thus, while the democratically elected governments of the United States and Great Britain consistently fought the efforts of Unesco, the Communist nations, and Third World countries to bring about a so-called "New World Information and Communication Order," it was supported by most of those Americans and Britains active in the field of international librarianship.[40]

Centralized Planning

The fourth generally accepted concept was the belief that centralized planning and government direction and assistance would be needed to attain the goals of international librarianship. (This coexisted with the contradictory notion that governments were incapable of bringing the people of the world together.) Krzys and Litton predicted that, during the lifetime of their readers, "Within each country certainly, or within a world government possibly, legislation will be enacted that will assure the realization of the constituent elements of a global librarianship."[41]

Vosper strongly supported central planning and government involvement, noting that the USSR had been the world's leader in this, with the West trailing, but improving.[42]   Foskett implied that the centralization in Eastern European countries had never actually stemmed from Communist political philosophy or exaction, but merely from a desire for efficiency![43]   In an article on international library education, Martha Boaz attributed the failure to centralize all of America's global pedagogical activities to the sad fact that the United States did not have a ministry of education.[44]   She quoted approvingly from *World Education: An Emerging Concept*: 'It will only be a matter of time until one world government is formed, unless separate national loyalties through gross miscalculation and chauvinistic aims destroy us first.'[45] Frederick Kilgour expressed the less commonly heard view that it was the United States, rather than the highly centralized countries, that was promoting the free and beneficial international exchange of information.[46]

Cultural Relativism

A major reason why many American and British leaders in this field were optimistic about the possibilities of international cooperation was that they saw strong underlying similarities among apparently disparate social and political systems, particularly between democratic and Communist societies. Thus in the 1960's, Foskett remarked that in Eastern Europe the Library was expected, among other things, to foster Communist propaganda. Some in the West would disagree, he declared,

> . . . but it is no different, in principle, from the patriotic fervour displayed by some American libraries in praising the American way of life. In fact it would be hard to find a really vital public library that was not, in one way or another, committed to the attainment of objectives that its society held to be worthwhile. We in this country [The United Kingdom], for example, cheerfully involve our public libraries in such things as productivity campaigns; do we ever pause to ask ourselves what is the aim of such campaigns?[47]

Similarly, in 1973 Harvey wrote:

> In a socialist country with a strong, central government, like Bulgaria, certain differences of organization and administration can be expected when comparison is made with Switzerland, having a different political and economic system. However, this paper assumes most of these to be differences in practice, not in policies, principles or goals. Perhaps, even USSR libraries can be examined by an American with standards modified only partially.
>
> The degree to which libraries in Bulgaria and Switzerland are comparable would decrease primarily as their goals differed. Of course, school library service philosophy, in socialist countries, for instance, is tied closely to the political, economic and social systems and attempts to reinforce them with many books explaining the socialist philosophy. However, political books in capitalist country school libraries are likely to explain the local political system, also.[48]

H. Allen Whatley managed to see many similarities between the philosophy and practice of book distribution in Communist countries and that in the West. For example, he equated Stalin's extensive purges of library bookshelves in the 1920's and 1930's with the practice found in democratic countries of relegating a few volumes to restricted-access collections.[49]

The playing down of distinctions among different societies was facilitated by the discouragement of value judgements, which were considered to be relative and therefore moot.[50] It was even stated that the successful international library worker was distinguished by his "lack of strong political and ethical ideas, his blandness. In fact, he finds strong feelings of any kind likely to be inhibiting and obsolete."[51] To some extent, this approach was engendered by a desire to create a science of comparative librarianship. However, another influential factor was indicated by a criticism expressed by one of those involved in the field, A. D. Burnett: the tendency for Westerners to omit the full truth from their reports on other countries because of their desire to promote international harmony.[52]

Criticism of the West

It was considered productive among those in international comparative librarianship to praise the countries of Eastern Europe and the developing world while criticizing the West. As already shown above, some of these judgements revolved around the centralization of library affairs and the international dissemination of information. At one conference on international librarianship, Patricia Schuman and E. J. Josey devoted large parts of their presentations to censuring the United States.[53]

According to veterans in this area of the profession, even the Western librarian who attempted to assist other countries was suspect:

> The International Man must be ever on guard against neo-colonialism. His ideal is service, but his obligation is also to counteract Western money and guns. Is he subtly peddling political or religious views along with his suggestions and advice?[54]

> We do not think of ourselves in political terms when we offer professional assistance to libraries, but the political implications are always in the minds of our hosts. Our protestation that we have no motivation other than pure altruism and professional commitment must contend with the incontrovertible fact that history, both ours and theirs, argues against so innocent an intention.[55]

Internationalization of the Professional Curriculum

It was held that library school courses in international and comparative librarianship should impart to students the internationalist philosophy. In addition, the idea that all courses in library and information science should be taught from an international perspective gained popularity.[56] J. Periam Danton, Martha Boaz, and Sylva Simsova stated that courses on the international and comparative aspects of library and information science should advance international cooperation and understanding.[57] Frances Carroll concluded an article on the subject with the view that "the many [international] library education activities should continue, and they will be nurtured by the forces of an international society."[58]

NOTES

1. See, for example: Sikorsky, "Library Planning," p. 38; Chubaryan, "Reading," pp. 52-53; and P. Molnar, "Bibliology," p. 6. This phenomenon is dealt with throughout George Chandler, *Libraries, Documentation, and Bibliography in the USSR, 1917-1971: Survey and Critical Analysis of Soviet Studies, 1967-1971* (London and New York: Seminar Press, 1972).

2. Chubaryan, "Reading," p. 58; and Gayle Durham Hollander, *Soviet Political Indoctrination: Domestic Mass Media and Propaganda since Stalin* (New York and London: Praeger, 1972), pp. 90, 97n60.

3. See: "The Agony of Reizia Palatnik," *Assistant Librarian* 64 (Oct. 1971): 146-49; Shirley Havens, "Harassment Soviet Style," *Library Journal* 97 (August 1972): 2531-34; Frode Bakken, "Matter of Conscience," [Letter,] *Assistant Librarian* 74 (Sept. 1981): 123; Jack Minsker, "Science, Shcharansky, and the Soviets," *Journal of the American Society for Information Science* 29 (Sept. 1972): 219-24; Alexander Lerner, "To Protest or Ignore? A Scientist's Alternatives in Reacting to the Persecution of his Colleagues," *Journal of the American Society for Information Science* 30 (Nov. 1973): 353-55; and Stephen Karetzky, "American Library Community Ignores Plight of Ukrainian Colleague," *Newsletter of the International Society of Jewish Librarians* 9 (Jan.-March 1985): 19, and the other items about Hanna Mikhaylenko in the same

newsletter, pp. 20-23. (The publication had formerly been titled, *The Jewish Librarians Caucus Newsletter*.) Palatnik, a librarian, and Shcharansky, an information scientist, were persecuted, in part, for Jewish and Zionist activities. Mikhaylenko, a school librarian in the Ukraine, drew the wrath of the authorities because she put books on Catholicism in her library.

4. See, for example, P. Molnar, "Bibliology," p. 6; Chubaryan, "Reading," p. 49.

5. See Chandler, *Libraries, Documentation, and Bibliography*, pp. 2, 4.

6. See Friedberg, *Russian Classics*, pp. x, 94n7, 180n. See also: Baumanis and Martin, *Soviet Book Statistics*; and Fenelonov, "Soviet Public Libraries," p. 46.

7. N. V. Gavrilov, in Chandler, *Libraries, Documentation, and Bibliography*, p. 27.

8. Osipova, "Popularity of Reading," pp. 94-96; Chubaryan, "Reading," pp. 55-57; and Serov, "Library Science," p. 179. A variety of myths and cults concerning reading in the Soviet Union and Russia are discussed in Stephen Lovell, *The Russian Reading Revolution: Print Culture in the Soviet and Post-Soviet Eras* (New York: St. Martin's Press; London: Macmillan, 2000).

9. Chubaryan, "Reading," p. 53.

10. Chubaryan, "Librarianship in the System of the Sciences," p. 337. For an explanation of the serious offense of "formalism," see R. N. Carew Hunt, *A Guide to Communist Jargon* (London: Geoffrey Bles, 1957), pp. 73-78.

11. See, for example, Serov, "Library Science," p. 177.

12. "Top Soviet Librarian Attacks Western International and Comparative Librarianship," *Focus on International and Comparative Librarianship*, vol. 11, no. 3 (1980): 29. For similar charges, see also Chubaryan, and others, *The Public Library: Its Role in Socio-Economic and Cultural Life of the Society (From Soviet Libraries' Experience)* (Moscow: V. I. Lenin State Library, 1974), p. 3.

13. Marianna Tax Choldin, "Access to Foreign Publications in Soviet Libraries," *Libraries and Culture* 26 (Winter 1991): 140-45.

14. Ibid., pp. 137-38.

15. Krupskaya, in "We Shall Fulfill Lenin's Instructions," 1936, in Simsova, ed., *Lenin, Krupskaya, and Libraries*, p. 46.

16. For example, see (1) Presidium of the Soviet Academy of Sciences, *The Work and the Position of the Staffs of the Library of the Academy of Sciences of the USSR and the Fundamental Library for the Social Sciences of the Academy of Sciences of the USSR*, (Lexington, KY: University of Kentucky Libraries, Margaret I. King Library, Occasional Contributions no. 19, Dec. 1950) [3 pp.] trans. by Peter Petcoff, from *Vestnik Akademii Nauk SSSR* (1950); and (2) Presidium of the Soviet Academy of Sciences, *The Work of the*

Libraries of the Academy of Sciences of the USSR in the International Book Exchange, (Lexington, KY: University of Kentucky Libraries, Margaret I. King Library, Occasional Contributions no. 25, March 1951) [2 pp.] trans. by Peter Petcoff, from *Vestnik Akademii Nauk SSSR* (1950). Petcoff worked at the Library of Congress.

17. Presidium of the Soviet Academy of Sciences, *International Book Exchange,* p. [1].

18. Chandler, *Libraries, Documentation, and Bibliography,* pp. 190, 38.

19. USSR Library Council, "Report on Activities September 1973-November 1974," *IFLA Annual,* 1975 (Munich: Verlag Dokumentation, 1975): 196-99. For other details on such involvements, see Choldin, "Access to Foreign Publications in Soviet Libraries."

20. Chandler, *Libraries, Documentation, and Bibliography,* p. 70.

21. Ibid., pp. 71, 134; Gregory Walker, *Soviet Book Publishing Policy* (Cambridge, England; and New York: Cambridge University Press, 1978), pp. 118-19.

22. Chandler, *Libraries, Documentation, and Bibliography,* p. 70.

23. See: Paul L. Horecky, ed., *Russia and the Soviet Union: A Bibliographic Guide to Western Publications* (Chicago and London: University of Chicago Press, 1965); Robert Finley Delaney, *The Literature of Communism in America: A Selected Reference Guide* (Washington, DC: Catholic University of America Press, 1962); Eugene Slon, *Open Access to Soviet Book Collections,* ed. by Donald C. Robbins (New York: Ukrainian Library Association of America; and Toronto: New Review Books, 1978); and Chandler. Chandler, director of the Liverpool Public Library and a historian of England from the seventeenth through twentieth centuries, also served as head of the National Library of Australia for several years.

Bohdan Wynar, who had been born in the Ukraine but eventually came to the United States, contributed a few short—but insightful—pieces on the Soviet Union and its librarianship, as well as on the failure of those in Western international and comparative librarianship to understand that Communist state. For example, see Wynar's reviews of *The Dimensions of Comparative Librarianship,* by J. Periam Danton; and *Libraries, Documentation, and Bibliography in the USSR,* by George Chandler; in *American Reference Books Annual* (Littleton, CO: Libraries Unlimited, 1974), pp. 78-79. Wynar correctly considered Chandler's 1972 book the best on the subject since Paul Horecky's 1959 *Libraries and Bibliographic Centers in the Soviet Union.*

24. See Stephen Karetzky, "The Asheim Assumption," (letter) *Library Journal* 122 (Nov. 1, 1997): 8.

25. John F. Harvey, "Toward a Definition of International and Comparative Library Science," *International Library Review* 5 (July 1973): 294. It should be noted that he claimed to reject the social/idealistic aspects of the

philosophy as inappropriate and impractical. He wanted comparative librarianship to become a field of scholarship justifiable in and of itself.

26. Lester Asheim, *Librarianship in the Developing Countries* (Urbana: University of Illinois Press, 1966), p. 2.

27. B. C. Vickery and A. G. Brown, "Information Science," in *Comparative and International Library Science,* ed. by John F. Harvey (Metuchen, NJ, and London: Scarecrow Press, 1977), p. 190.

28. Allen Kent and Harold Lancour, "Preface," in *Encyclopedia of Library and Information Science,* vol. 1, ed. by Kent and Lancour (New York: Marcel Dekker, 1968), p. xii.

29. Sylva Simsova, "Comparative Librarianship as an Academic Subject," *Journal of Librarianship* 6 (April 1974): 116.

30. Ibid., p. 117.

31. In *World Librarianship: A Comparative Study,* by Richard Krzys and Gaston Litton, with Ann Hewitt (New York and Basel: Marcel Dekker, 1983), pp. 201-3.

32. D. J. Foskett, "Comparative Librarianship," in *Progress in Library Science, 1965,* ed. by Robert L. Collison (London: Butterworths, 1965), p. 114.

33. Louis Shores, "Comparative Librarianship: A Theoretical Approach," in *Comparative and International Librarianship,* ed. by Miles M. Jackson (Westport, CT: Greenwood Press, 1970), p. 4. See also p. 23.

34. Robert Vosper, "National and International Library Planning," in *National and International Library Planning,* Key Papers Presented at the 40th Sesion of the IFLA General Council, Washington, DC, 1974 (Munich: Verlag Dokumentation, 1976), pp. 11-14.

35. Ibid., p. 11.

36. H. J. Abraham Goodman, "The 'World Brain/World Encyclopedia' Concept," *ASIS '87: Proceedings of the 50th Annual Conference of the ASIS* [American Society for Information Science] *Annual Meeting* (Medford, NJ: Learned Information, 1987), pp. 91-98, 256.

37. As reported earlier, Wells had refused to cooperate with an ACLU study that criticized the treatment of political prisoners in the USSR. His book about the new Communist state (*Russia in the Shadows* [New York: George H. Doran, 1921; reprinted: Westport, CT: Hyperion Press, 1973]) contained as much criticism of the Western democracies as of the Soviet Union. For a negative assessment of this book, see Henry Arthur Jones, *My Dear Wells* (London: Eveleigh Nash & Grayson, 1921; New York: E. P. Dutton). Jones had been a leading dramatist and proponent of intellectual freedom in Britain since the 1880's. Highly regarded in the United States, he was awarded an honorary degree by Harvard in 1907.

38. E. J. Josey, "Political Dimensions of International Librarianship," speech, conference sponsored by the Library Association of the City University of New York: "Shrinking World, Exploding Information: Developments in International Librarianship," New York, April 4, 1986. The presentation was later published in much altered form, but a videotape of the conference speeches was made.

39. Joseph Z. Nitecki, "National Network of Information in Poland," *Journal of the American Society for Information Science* 30 (Sept. 1979): 274-79.

40. See, for example: Thomas T. Surprenant, "Global Threats to Information," *Annual Review of Information Science and Technology,* vol. 20 (White Plains, NY: Knowledge Industry Publications, 1985), pp. 3-25; and R. C. Benge, *Confessions of a Lapsed Librarian* (Metuchen, NJ: Scarecrow Press, 1984), pp. 185-205. Brother Emmett Corry referred to "the phobic attempts of this country [The United States] to control the Third World's access to both technological information and communications channels," in *Unequal Access to Information Resources: Problems and Needs of the World's Information Poor* (Ann Arbor, MI: Pierian Press, 1988), p. v.

41. *World Librarianship,* p. 201.

42. Vosper, "National and International Library Planning," p. 10 and elsewhere.

43. Foskett, "Comparative Librarianship," in *Progress in Library Science,* p. 132.

44. Martha Boaz, "International Education: An Imperative Need," *Journal of Education for Library and Information Science* 26 (Winter 1986): 172.

45. M. R. Mitchell, S. S. Grin, and B. Sobel (Washington, DC: University Press of America, 1977), p. 65n3, as cited by Boaz, p. 173.

46. Frederick Kilgour, "Public Policy and National and International Networks," *Libraries and Information Science in the Electronic Age,* ed. by Hendrik Edelman, (Philadelphia, PA: ISI Press, 1986), pp. 1-10.

47. Foskett, "Comparative Librarianship," in *Progress in Library Science,* pp. 136-37.

48. Harvey, "Toward a Definition of International and Comparative Library Science," p. 314.

49. H. Allen Whatley, "European Librarianship," in *The Library in Society,* by A. Robert Rogers, Kathryn McChesney, and others (Littleton, CO: Libraries Unlimited, 1984), p. 132.

50. See, for example, Simsova, "Comparative Librarianship," pp. 117-20.

51. John Harvey, "An Anatomy of the International Man," *Wilson Library Bulletin* 47 (June 1973): 841.

52. A. D. Burnett, "Study in Comparative Librarianship, I," *Studies in Comparative Librarianship* (London: The Library Association, 1973), pp. 7-8.

53. Patricia Glass Schuman, "Recent Developments in U. S. Information Policy"; and E. J. Josey, "Political Dimensions of International Librarianship," at "Shrinking World, Exploding Information" conference.

54. Harvey, "Anatomy," p. 841.

55. Asheim, *Librarianship in the Developing Countries*, p. 67.

56. A rationale and detailed plan for internationalizing the curriculum was presented in *Internationalizing Library and Information Science Education: A Handbook of Policies and Procedures in Administration and Curriculum*, ed. by John F. Harvey and Frances Laverne Carroll (New York and London: Greenwood Press, 1987).

57. J. Periam Danton, *The Dimensions of Comparative Librarianship* (Chicago: American Library Association, 1973); Martha Boaz, "The Comparative and International Library Science Course in American Library Schools," in *Comparative and International Library Science*, ed. by Harvey, pp. 169-74; and Simsova, "Comparative Librarianship," p. 121.

58. Frances Laverne Carroll, "Library Education," in *Comparative and International Library Science*, ed. by Harvey, pp. 160-61.

10

THE BETRAYAL OF THE
PROFESSIONALS: WHY?

One might wonder why the leaders of a learned profession were so erroneous in their appraisal of Communist librarianship and the Soviet Union for over seven decades and were so willing to assist them. One could also wish to know why these same individuals frequently thought poorly of their own country and insisted on the necessity of creating a new social order, often fantastic in its character. These are particularly remarkable phenomena because the brutish ideals and activities of those who worked in Soviet libraries remained essentially unchanged for decades after they were promulgated by Lenin and Krupskaya. They were articulated and publicized in many languages. They were printed in Western journals and proclaimed at international conferences. Librarians from democratic countries visited the USSR for more than seventy years, speaking with its librarians and examining its institutions. Moreover, the despotic nature of revolutionary utopianism, particularly when promoted by intellectuals and mixed with socialist or statist ideas, had already been amply described between 1790 and 1860 by Burke, Tocqueville, Bastiat, and others.[1] Yet none of this resulted in a comprehension of the situation in the Soviet Union or of Communist attitudes towards the West. It is not possible to ascertain the reasons for this with certainty, but one can put forth some plausible explanations, some of which have been formulated by scholars in their analyses of similar phenomena among intellectuals. Of particular relevance here are the works of Paul Hollander, Thomas

Molnar, Karl Popper, Irving Kristol, Alexandr Solzhenitsyn, Andrei
Sakharov, James Burnham, Erich and Rael Jean Isaac, Jeane J.
Kirkpatrick, Lewis Feuer, Ludwig von Mises, Raymond Aron, M.
Stanton Evans, and Jean-François Revel.[2]

Pathologies: Psychological, Moral, and Cognitive

One or more of the following psychological, moral, and cognitive
pathologies may apply to the Americans (and the British) discussed in
this work:

1. Intellectual and/or emotional *infantilism.*
2. *Denial*: the unconscious blocking out of unpleasant—but
    sound—information and knowledge.
3. *Projection* of American, democratic, and benign assumptions
    concerning human goals, motives, and politics onto Com-
    munist leaders and librarians.   This dovetails with *faulty
    perception* and/or a *lack of imagination*: an inability to see that
    other people may truly be different from oneself.
4. *Utopianism*: immature, unrealistic hopes and fantasies con-
    cerning the attainable; wishful thinking.
5. *Alienation* from one's own society, sometimes combined with
    an irrational proclivity for another—real or fictive. These can
    be spurred on by *unwarranted guilt* or *masochism.* A neurotic
    need to be liked by, or to gain the affection of, strangers or
    foreigners may obtain.
6. *Thanatosis*: a death wish. Or, at the very least, a failure of
    the natural instinct for survival.
7. *Amorality, immorality, amoralism, immoralism, moral
    relativism* and/or *scientism,* particularly the unconscious or
    conscious suspension of value judgements and/or the inability
    or unwillingness to distinguish good from evil. These can be
    closely associated with a patronizing *cultural relativism* when
    dealing with foreign countries.

Conspiracism—the tendency to imagine plots where they do not
exist—must also be taken into account when analyzing the anti-anti-

Communists. (One is tempted to say that they saw anti-Communists under every bed.) Conspiracism has definitely not been confined to the Right, as many academics seem to believe. Daniel Pipes' peerless scholarship on the subject is highly relevant here.[3]

Liberal Versus Conservative Librarianship

A major reason why American librarianship was unable to reject Soviet librarianship, as well as the Soviet Union itself, was because for most of the period under consideration here the field lacked a conservative body of professional thought: the professional creed was entirely liberal. While some librarians were conservative in their private lives or their political ideology, their ethos of librarianship was still liberal.[4] The essential articles of twentieth century liberal thought and faith which made it possible for so many librarians to be willing to accept, admire, assist, or cooperate with Soviet librarianship and the Soviet Union were the following:

1. Internationalism: the belief that the United States should aid the rest of the globe and the conviction that Americans should become "citizens of the world."
2. Perfectionism: the conviction that people are infinitely malleable and that human societies can—and should—be made perfect.
3. The belief that the major obstacles to progress are ignorance or ill-functioning institutions. The former, it is asserted, can be remedied by education or information; the latter by better management.
4. The certainty that major societal changes are necessary.
5. A belief that social change usually results in progress.
6. An extreme faith in the efficacy of rationalism and centralized state planning and power.
7. A hostility towards capitalism.
8. A conviction that discussion and compromise can settle all disputes.
9. A belief that there are no moral absolutes.

Conversely, the absence of a vital conservative librarianship made impossible the objective critique of, and effective opposition to, the

USSR. Fundamental conservative elements include:

1. Nationalism: a primary concern for, identification with, and loyalty to, one's own country (and its citizens) rather than another country or countries.
2. The conviction that human beings and their societies are flawed and will always be so. The only thing that can be perfect is God.
3. The belief that many concepts, and alleged instances, of social progress in the past several centuries have frequently been illusory.
4. Surety that individuals are better able to know what is good for them than is government.
5. A strong commitment to the rights of individuals.
6. A recognition that government power must be stringently circumscribed.
7. Confidence that much knowledge and wisdom are embedded in a people's traditions and customs.
8. The understanding that social stability is necessary. Most political and social situations have evolved over a long period of time and exist because (1) they work and (2) they reflect the accumulated knowledge and wisdom of generations. They should not readily be tampered with. Healthy societies are organic entities and cannot be managed rationalistically, particularly along the lines prescribed by ideological principles. The latter course inevitably leads to tyranny.
9. A comprehension of the great economic and political virtues of capitalism.
10. A belief in the existence of good and evil, and an understanding of their inherent and eternal opposition.

These lists are not exhaustive but they suffice.[5]

The Flaws of Liberal Internationalism

Those librarians most involved with the Soviet Union and international library relations from 1917 to 1985 would be classified by most political scientists as *liberal internationalist* in mind-set. Marked among the characteristics of those espousing this philosophy are (1) an unrestrainable and uncompromising idealism or utopianism, (2) a rejection of policies based on realpolitik, (3) a disregard for American self-interest, and (4) a willingness to surrender American national sovereignty and military security to international regulation.

The foremost liberal internationalist of the twentieth century was Woodrow Wilson. Sigmund Freud, who coauthored a book about Wilson with William C. Bullitt, the lifelong diplomat who had worked beside the President, wrote this about him:

> Wilson . . . repeatedly declared that mere facts had no significance for him, that he esteemed highly nothing but human motives and opinions. As a result of this attitude it was natural for him in his thinking to ignore the facts of the real outer world, even to deny they existed if they conflicted with his hopes and wishes. He, therefore, lacked motive to reduce his ignorance by learning facts. Nothing mattered except noble intentions.[6]

He summarized Wilson's activities in foreign affairs as "a pretension to free the world from evil [which] ends only in a new proof of the danger of a fanatic to the commonweal."[7] Freud and Bullitt provided ample evidence of Wilson's extraordinary ignorance of the world outside of the United States and Britain, the world he tried so hard to refashion in accordance with his abstract visions.[8] Irving Kristol has noted that, under his presidency, the utopian notion of world citizenship became a *policy* of a major government for the very first time.[9]

It is ironic that so many of the self-righteous utopians in librarianship who preached about "international understanding" during the Cold War understood so little about both the domestic and international policies of the Communist states. Ignorance, naivete, fantasy, and arrogance were most evident in their assertions that the Communist and the democratic countries were essentially the same, and/or that it was the height of "professionalism" to unite us into "One World," one "Global Village." In reality, there was no "World Community" of nations with shared values and common aims. The essential struggle between tyranny and democracy was not comprehended, and the potential value of superficial "cooperation" (which was actually unilateral assistance) and of the international flow of information were grossly exaggerated. Jeane Kirkpatrick commented during the Cold War that the American conception of international harmony

> simply will not accommodate the predilection [of some other countries] for violence and a contempt for one another's right to survive. . . . [However,] we fall back again to imagining that profound conflicts in national goals are simply misunderstandings and that if only we understood each other better the apparent conflicts would in fact be dissolved. We think that others' goals only seem incompatible with ours. But our illusions do not contribute to the achievement of our goals.[10]

It should also be remembered that one of the aims of the post-World War II internationalists in American librarianship was the eventual demise of their country—after its power had been divvied up among all the other nations to create a more "equitable" world. This can certainly be considered, at the very least, an end result of alienation! In truth, the incapacity of American librarians to have an instinct for the preservation of their society bespoke a failure of their most basic natural elements. Alienation, paralysis of the survival instinct, and even a drive for self-extinction were as much in evidence among leading librarians of the twenties and thirties as those fifty years later.

Essential to this study of American librarians and the Soviet Union is the fact that Communism was, as Solzhenitsyn called it in 1976, "a concentration of evil . . . spreading throughout the world." He asserted:

> That which is against Communism is for humanity. Not to accept, but to reject, this inhuman Communist ideology is simply to be a human being. Such a rejection is more than a political act. It is a protest of our soul against those who would have us forget the concepts of good and evil.[11]

The leaders of the American library profession did not understand the moral, political, and military threat Communism posed.

After World War II, it became a popular idea among internationalists that the inhabitants of other countries are essentially "just people," fundamentally the same as us. Partially the consequence of projection, this cliché obscured important truths. True, we are the same in that we have two eyes, one nose, ten toes, and so forth. However, human beings have an extremely wide range of thought, emotion and behavior, and the cultures of the social groups they are part of also differ greatly. The acts of the Nazis, including the National Socialist librarians, during the 1930's and the 1940's should be frightening and instructive for the very reason that the Nazis *were* human beings, that is, "just people." Furthermore, individuals and social groups are organized into countries. It was relevant—and ignored by the internationalist librarians—that "the people" in Communist countries had no impact on their government decision-makers. Converting Communist librarians into Western-style demo-crats—an impossible task—would, in any case, have had no effect on the leaders of the Communist Party, and the librarians advocating freedom would have been quickly purged. To think otherwise was naive.

Librarians, the "New Class," and Intellectuals

A large number of the internationalist librarians and their sup-porters, particularly after 1970, appear to have been members of "The New Class" as it is defined by Irving Kristol, Norman Podhoretz, Peter Berger, and others.[12] To them, the term describes that increasingly large and powerful group in our so-called "post-industrial" society that produces or distributes knowledge and information; it includes university professors, journalists, teachers, and so forth. The ideology of this new social class they describe is internationalist, utopian, anti-capitalist, anti-middle class, and anti-religious. Its members have tended to identify with the left-wing of the Democratic Party. Those who comprise the New Class are described by those who study it as arrogant, self-righteous, frustrated, power-hungry, and enthusiastically supportive of far-reaching planning and social engineering. Their critics share Lionel Trilling's eventual dislike for, and fear of, the phenomenon he described and named—"The Adversary Culture"[13]—a creation of, by, and for the New Class. Rael Jean Isaac, Erich Isaac, and Peter Metzger have called them "Coercive Utopians" in their research on how they have attained positions of power in many American institutions and social movements.[14]

Relevant studies have been conducted on the international views of intellectuals, particularly their irrational attraction to Communism. (This, in part, inspired the aphorism of the great French sociologist Raymond Aron: "Marxism is the opium of the intellectuals."[15]) The research by Paul Hollander of the University of Massachusetts and Harvard's Russian Research Center are of particular significance and relevance. His extensive studies of "Political Pilgrims" have stressed the alienation of America's clerisy from its society and its expressed affinity for "progressive" alternatives, particularly those seen abroad.[16] While a portion of non-intellectuals have similarly succumbed, they have not done so to the great extent as intellectuals.[17] In the 1970's, some of the strongest attacks on Western cultural leaders came from dissident members of the Russian intelligentsia, like Andrei Sakharov and Alexandr Solzhenitsyn, who charged them with perverse anti-Americanism, deluded anti-anti-Communism, irresponsibility, faddishness, and cowardice.[18]

The radicalism of American and European intellectuals in the twentieth century was looked upon by the Soviets as being of great strategic value.[19] In the USSR and among some scholars in the United States, like Zbigniew Brzezinski, one popular term for the unwitting assistants of Communism was "Useful Idiots of the West." Its origin has often been attributed to Lenin himself.[20]

In a 1982 speech, Susan Sontag commented on the errors that she and many other Western intellectuals had made since the 1950's and on the liberal intellectual journals that had been dominant during this period:

> 'Imagine if you will, someone who read only the *Reader's Digest* between 1950 and 1970, and someone in the same period who read only *The Nation* or *The New Statesman*. Which reader would have been better informed about the realities of Communism? The answer, I think, should give us pause.'[21]

When the speech was reprinted, in part, in *The Nation*, this statement was omitted.

Sontag conceded that "The emigres from communism who we didn't listen to, who found it far easier to get published in the *Reader's Digest* than *The Nation* or *The New Statesman*, were telling the truth."[22] She admitted that many of the West's illuminati, including herself, had misunderstood Communism and had made their political judgements with double standards and fixed minds.[23] While they had loved justice, she said, they had not loved the truth.[24] Despite these admissions, Sontag felt compelled to begin her speech by criticizing the United States.

It must be remembered that others besides the literati and the leading librarians generally failed to comprehend and oppose the Communist threat. This situation began to grow worse in the 1960's with the increasing opposition to the Vietnam War and the growth of the so-called "counterculture." Some historians, like Richard Gid Powers, maintain that in the sixties anti-Communism almost died out in the United States. American journalists did a poor job of keeping their country's citizens apprised of developments in the Soviet Union. (They were equally incompetent in covering other areas of the world.)[25] American scientists also failed to provide their country with vital information. Richard Pipes asserts that the scientific community was largely responsible for the misguided, pre-Reagan nuclear strategy of the United States: its members did not perceive that the USSR thought it could one day win a nuclear war. This, he has written, "can charitably be described as an act of grave intellectual and political irresponsibility."[26] Presidents Nixon and Carter, as well as Secretary of State Kissinger, also accepted baseless notions about the intentions of the Soviet Union. As a result, they permitted it to reach military parity with the United States in the false belief this would make it a secure, contented, and peaceful state.[27]

NOTES

1. See: Edmund Burke, *Reflections on the Revolution in France* (London: J. Dodsley, 1790; as republished: with intro. by Russell Kirk [Chicago: Henry Regnery, 1955]); Alexis de Tocqueville, *L'Ancien Régime et la Révolution* (Paris: Michel Lévy Frères, 1856; as trans. and published: *The Old Regime and the French Revolution*, trans. by Stuart Gilbert [Garden City, NY: Doubleday, 1955], particularly pp. 137-41, 147-48, 156-57, and 205-6); and Frédéric

Bastiat, *La Loi* (Paris: Guillaumin, 1850: as trans. and published: *The Law*, trans. by Dean Russell [Irvington-on-Hudson, NY: Foundation for Economic Education, 1950.]) The first English translation of Tocqueville's 1856 book was published in London and New York the same year it came out in Paris. Bastiat's work was first issued in English three years after it was published in France. It is significant that all three men had been practicing politicians—elected legislators, no less—before writing these works and were thus well grounded in the realities of political affairs.

2. See: Paul Hollander, *Political Pilgrims: Western Intellectuals in Search of the Good Society*, 4th ed., with a new intro. by Hollander (New Brunswick, NJ, and London: Transaction, 1998) [previously subtitled *Travels of Western Intellectuals to the Soviet Union, China, and Cuba, 1928-1978*]; Thomas Molnar, *The Decline of the Intellectual* (New Brunswick, NJ, and London: Transaction, 1994); Molnar, *Utopia: The Perennial Heresy* (Lanham, MD, and London: University Press of America, with the Intercollegiate Studies Institute, 1990; first published: New York: Sheed and Ward, 1967); Molnar, *Authority and Its Enemies* (New Brunswick, NJ, and London: Transaction, 1995); Karl R. Popper, *The Open Society and its Enemies* (Princeton: Princeton University Press, 1950), Irving Kristol, *Neo-Conservatism: The Biography of an Idea* (New York: Free Press, 1995), Aleksandr I. Solzhenitsyn, *The Mortal Danger: How Misconceptions about Russia Imperil America*, 2nd ed., trans. by Michael Nicholson and Alexis Klimoff (New York: Harper & Row, 1981); Solzhenitsyn, *Warning to the West* (New York: Farrar, Strauss, and Giroux, 1976); Solzhenitsyn, "America: You Must Think about the World," and "Communism: A Legacy of Terror," reprinted in his *Détente* (New Brunswick, NJ: Transaction, 1976), pp. 7-38, 39-66; Andrei Sakharov, *My Country and the World*, trans. by Guy V. Daniels (New York: Knopf, 1975); James Burnham, *Suicide of the West: An Essay on the Meaning and Destiny of Liberalism* (Washington, DC: Regnery Gateway, 1985; first published: New York: John Day, 1974); Rael Jean Isaac and Erich Isaac, *The Coercive Utopians: Social Deception by America's Power Players* (Chicago: Regnery Gateway, 1983); Jeane J. Kirkpatrick, *Dictatorships and Double Standards: Rationalism and Reason in Politics* (New York: Simon and Schuster [and the American Enterprise Institute, Washington, DC], 1982; Kirkpatrick, *Legitimacy and Force*, 2 vols. (New Brunswick, NJ, and Oxford, England: Transaction Books, 1988); Lewis Feuer, *Ideology and the Ideologists* (New York: Harper & Row, 1975); Feuer, *Marx and the Intellectuals: A Set of Post-Ideological Essays* (Garden City, NY: Doubleday, 1969); Ludwig von Mises, *The Anti-Capitalistic Mentality* (Spring Mills, PA: Libertarian Press, 1972; first published: Princeton, NJ: Van Nostrand, 1956); Raymond Aron, *The Opium of the Intellectuals*, with new foreword by Aron, trans. by Terence Kilmartin (New York: W. W. Norton, 1962; first eds. in English: Garden City, NY: Doubleday, 1957, and London:

Secker & Warburg, 1957; originally published as *L'Opium des Intellectuels* [Paris: Calmann Lévy, 1955]); M. Stanton Evans, *The Politics of Surrender* (New York: Devin-Adair, 1966); Jean-François Revel, *The Totalitarian Temptation*, trans. by David Hapgood (Garden City, NY: Doubleday, 1977; originally published as *La Tentation Totalitaire* [Paris: Robert Laffont, 1976]); and Revel, *How Democracies Perish*, trans. by William Byron (Garden City, NY: Doubleday, 1984; originally published as *Comment les Démocraties Finissent* [Paris: Grasset & Fasquelle, 1983]). Some of Sigmund Freud's writings are relevant, including those on the death wish. (See his *Civilization and Its Discontents*, as translated and edited by James Strachey [New York: W. W. Norton, 1962]; first editions in English: trans. by Joan Riviere [New York: J. Cape and H. Smith, 1930; London: Virginia Woolf at the Hogarth Press, 1930]; originally published as *Das Unbehagen in der Kultur* [Vienna: Internationaler Psychoanalyticher Verlag, 1930]).

3. See Daniel Pipes, *Conspiracy: How the Paranoid Style Flourishes and Where It Comes From* (New York: Free Press, 1997), particularly pp. 20-25, 46-48, 147, 154-70, and 174.

4. Phyllis Dain has made this point well in regards to Harry M. Lydenberg. I am indebted to her for this and am suggesting that we broaden her clearly articulated insight. See her "Comments," *Newsletter of the Slavic and East European Section, Association of College and Research Libraries* 3 (1987): 47-49; "Harry M. Lydenberg and American Library Resources: A Study in Modern Library Leadership," *Library Quarterly* 47 (Oct. 1977): 451-69; and "Harry Miller Lydenberg," in *Dictionary of American Library Biography* (Littleton, CO: Libraries Unlimited, 1978), pp. 329-33.

5. The differences between liberal and conservative ideologies are described effectively in the writings of Russell Kirk and James Burnham. For example, see Kirk, *A Program for Conservatives* (Chicago: Regnery, 1954); and Burnham, *Suicide of the West: An Essay on the Meaning and Destiny of Liberalism* (Chicago: Regnery, 1985; originally published: New York: John Day, 1954). The influence of Edmund Burke is evident in the writings of both men.

6. Sigmund Freud, "Introduction," *Thomas Woodrow Wilson: A Psychological Study*, by Freud and William C. Bullitt (Boston: Houghton Mifflin, 1967), p. xii.

7. Ibid., p. xiii.

8. For example, see Freud and Bullitt, pp. 153-54. See also pp. 253-54 on Wilson's possibly fatal inattention to the Soviet Union during the treaty negotiations in early 1919.

9. Irving Kristol, "The Twisted Vocabulary of Superpower Symmetry," in *Scorpions in a Bottle: Dangerous Ideas about the United States and the Soviet Union*, ed. by Lisa Roche (Hillsdale, MI: Hillsdale College Press, 1986),

p. 15.

10.   Jeane J. Kirkpatrick, "The United States and the World: Setting Limits," speech, Dec. 1985, as reprinted in *Legitimacy and Force,* vol. 1: *Political and Moral Dimensions,* by Kirkpatrick, p. 377.

11.   Soltzhenitsyn, *Warning to the West,* p. 46.

12.   See their observations in B. Bruce-Briggs, ed., *The New Class?* (New Brunswick, NJ: Transaction Books, 1979). The term was first used in a quite different way in Milovan Djilas' critique of the Communist states. (See Djilas, *The New Class: An Analysis of the Communist System* [New York: Praeger, 1957].) Djilas, once a prominent member of the Yugoslavian Communist Party and a vice-president of the country under Tito, was jailed by his former comrade for a total of nine years due to his critiques of Communism.

13.   See Trilling, "Preface," *The Opposing Self: Nine Essays in Criticism* (New York: Viking Press, 1955), pp. ix-xiv; and Trilling, "Preface," *Beyond Culture: Essays on Literature and Learning* (New York: Viking Press, 1965), pp. ix-xviii.

14.   Rael Jean Isaac and Erich Isaac, *The Coercive Utopians.* The Isaacs have made a coherent and full description of these zealots. The term *coercive utopians* was coined by Metzger.

15.   See Aron, *The Opium of the Intellectuals.* The originator of this remark is sometimes said to be Clare Boothe Luce, but she never uttered it before the publication of Aron's volume.

16.   The term *pilgrimage* had occasionally been used in this political context before Hollander's landmark book. For example, see Sylvia R. Margulies' solid *Pilgrimage to Russia: The Soviet Union and the Treatment of Foreigners, 1924-1937* (Madison, WI, and London: University of Wisconsin Press, 1968).

17.   See Margulies, *Pilgrimage to Russia,* for an analysis of non-intellectual visitors to the USSR.

18.   See Sakharov, *My Country and the World* (1975); and Solzhenitsyn's *Détente* (1976); *Warning to the West* (1976); and *The Mortal Danger,* 2nd ed. (1981).

19.   Brzezinski, *Between Two Ages* (1976 ed.), p. 147.

20.   It is possible that Lenin did not formulate this particular term, but similar ones. See William Safire, "Useful Idiots of the West," *New York Times Magazine* (April 12, 1987): 8, 10.

21.   "Susan Sontag Provokes Debate on Communism," *New York Times* (Feb. 27, 1982): 27.

22.   Sontag, "The Hard Lessons of Poland's Military Coup," *Los Angeles Times* (Feb. 14, 1982): section 4, p. 2.

23.   "Susan Sontag Provokes."

24.   Sontag, "The Hard Lessons."

25. For example, see: Stephen Karetzky and Norman Frankel, eds., *The Media's Coverage of the Arab-Israeli Conflict*, intro. by Karetzky (New York: Shapolsky, 1989); R. Bruce McColm, *El Salvador: Peaceful Revolution or Armed Struggle?* (New York: Freedom House, 1982), pp. 7-9, 32-45; Peter Braestrup, *The Big Story: How the American Press and Television Reported and Interpreted the Crisis of Tet 1968 in Vietnam and Washington* (Garden City, NY: Anchor Press, 1978); and Herman H. Dinsmore, *All the News that Fits: A Critical Analysis of* The New York Times (New Rochelle, NY: Arlington House, 1969).

26. Richard Pipes, "Soviet Global Strategy," *Commentary* 69 (April 1980): 35-36, 38.

27. Zbigniew Brzezinski, speech at Columbia University (New York: April 1982.)

11

THE COMPLICITY OF
LIBRARY HISTORIANS

Introduction: Anti-Anti-Communism and Historical Revisionism

The unwillingness of the library profession to oppose the Soviet Union has been lauded by historians of librarianship. To some extent, this has been the result of factors already described, including those dealt with in the previous chapter. It has increasingly reflected the general decay in academia, particularly among historians.[1]

For the past several decades, the dominant literature of American librarianship dealing with the history of Soviet-American library relations, international librarianship, and related subjects—like intellectual freedom—have been interrelated. In many instances, they are clearly of one piece and essentially made out of whole cloth. The methodological and substantive flaws in such histories are enormous. Among the most blatant of these are the idealization of past anti-anti-Communist librarians and the uncritical acceptance of their extreme words and views as gospel. Similarly, the early tendentious histories have been adopted as scripture by later historians. Thus, histories of librarianship have traditionally relied on contemporary accounts of the fifties by those like Robert B. Downs and articles of the "It Happened in _____ " variety. Biased analyses, such as Marjorie Fiske's flawed 1959 study and the contributions in J. Periam Danton's *Climate of Book Selection*, have provided much shot for later histories of that period.

Ralph Ellsworth and Sarah Harris' hysterical 1960 report, *The American Right Wing*, has gained renewed currency in even the most academic-looking works of recent years. Conversely, the accounts by the most objective observers and scholars of the past have been ignored. Consequently, the genuine dangers posed by the Soviet Union and the international Communist movement it directed have been minimized, if not dismissed. According to these widely applauded studies of the past, the primary enemies of freedom and peace were those who were robust in their Americanism and anti-Communism.

In recent accounts of the history of librarianship, there is also a frequently sloppy utilization of evidence—or a failure to even look at the evidence. An easy use of banal phrases and epithets substitutes for analysis and insight. Moreover, one is consistently presented with the facile charge that the alleged evil doers of yore are the same as the supposed political demons of today: American conservatives and nationalists. This provides the foils for both the crusading librarians being written about and the historians of librarianship themselves.

Today's library historians based in universities' graduate schools of library and information studies not only accept at face value the specious testimony and flawed historical works that have emanated from within their profession, but they are further misguided by the products of the so-called "Revisionist" school of US history, which has come to dominate the discipline in American academia. In actuality, the antagonistic elements within this country's higher education have been with us far longer than most today assume. A 1920 work by George Santayana noted the attack upon the conservative principles of most Americans by revolutionary values advanced by the educational system.[2] As described earlier in *Not Seeing Red*, in the late twenties and early thirties, John Dewey and George S. Counts of Teachers College, Columbia University, were pointing to the Soviet Union as the society America should emulate. The facts also show that the academy of the late forties and the fifties, almost always misrepresented—then and now—as a stage for right-wing repression, was nothing of the kind.[3] It was far more hospitable to those on the Left than on the Right.[4] A systemic collapse was only years away.

The degraded state to which historians of the United States and its international relations had sunk in the decades after the late 1950's was made clear in a 1992 speech by John Lewis Gaddis.[5] The Ohio State University historian, who was soon to go on to a named professorship at Yale, admitted that since 1959 the revisionist version of US foreign policy first articulated by William Appleman Williams[6] had hardened into a new orthodoxy within colleges and universities and become the "conventional wisdom"[7] which now had to be reexamined. Williams had asserted that the Cold War was essentially caused by American aggressiveness. (Half of the dozen books he wrote dealt largely with Soviet-American relations. The USSR was usually presented as being more benign.) Despite his misgivings concerning Williams' views, Gaddis rationalized their widespread acceptance:

> When one considers the difficulties the United States created for itself in the world through its own hubris and arrogance during the 1960s and early 1970s, it is hardly surprising that Williams's tragic view of American diplomatic history seemed, to a great many people at the time, to make sense. To a great many people even today, it still does.[8]

Gaddis provided additional excuses for the failure of academia's historians to apprehend the truth about Soviet-American relations:

1. A scepticism about the actual influence of Communist philosophy *anywhere*. This came about, he said, because the professoriate had been "traumatized" by the excesses of McCarthyism.
2. A failure to believe that the USSR spied on the United States. According to Gaddis, this was a reaction to the exaggerated charges of Soviet espionage made by many.
3. A belief in the moral equivalence of the American and Soviet governments. Gaddis reported that historians had merely adopted this from international relations theory.
4. An inattention to the criticisms of Communism coming from those living under it. He offered no excuse or explanation for this.

The result, said Gaddis, was the failure of historians to realize the ruthlessness of Communist governments and the responsibility of the Soviet Union for the precipitation of the Cold War. These realities, he declared, were now clear to see due to the opening of archives in the former USSR and the public pronouncements of its erstwhile citizens.

However, this historian was unable to shake loose entirely from his intellectual roots. Thus, he asserted that both the rise and the fall of Communism were basically due to shifts in "underlying tectonic forces." These, as well as the other essential elements of twentieth century history, could best be understood by utilizing the most powerful and accurate concepts available: those of Karl Marx![9]

While Gaddis admitted that those who had lived under Communism seemed to agree with President Reagan's 1983 pronouncement that the USSR was an evil empire, he took little notice of those in the West who had understood Communism long before he himself had barely begun to. Moreover, he was unable to say anything positive about longtime anti-Communists like Richard Pipes and Jeane J. Kirkpatrick.

To be sure, the Revisionist school of William Appleman Williams did not hold complete sway over his academic discipline, but Williams *was* a professor of history at the University of Wisconsin at Madison and Oregon State University. Moreover, in 1980 he was elected president of the Organization of American Historians, the major association of historians of the United States. His colleagues had thus placed him at the very pinnacle of their field.

After Gaddis' call for a change in the orthodox revisionist approach—a challenge which has been strongly opposed by many historians—he continued to write on this subject in much the same way.[10] In 1996, Oxford University Press issued his book, *We Now Know: Rethinking Cold War History.*[11] As noted, Gaddis claims to base many of his recent insights on the opening of former Soviet archives. However, others—like Richard Pipes, Ronald Reagan, and the mass of the American people—saw things clearer *during* the Cold War than he and his fellow historians do now with the advantage of hindsight and the fuller access to Communist depositories. A more significant book than his *We Now Know* would be one titled *They Knew Then.* While the opening of the Soviet archives has added a depth to our knowledge of Communism, they have not altered the fundamental facts, which have long been known to those willing to see them.[12]

Gaddis' accounts of the historiography of this field have revealed more than he intended: he inadvertently complimented the veteran conservative anti-Communists. In 1992 he admitted that one reason he and his fellow academics had not accepted the idea that Communist ideology had played a role in the behavior of Communist states, or that there truly had been such things as "captive nations" and Soviet spies, was because he and his colleagues "worried that if we talked too explicitly about these kinds of things, we might wind up sounding too much like John Foster Dulles, or, for a more recent generation, Ronald Reagan."[13] Four years later, he said pretty much the same thing when he tried to explain why he and his fellow scholars studying the Cold War had avoided the fact that the Western countries were based on an ideology supportive of democracy and capitalism while the other side rested on Communist ideology:

> One reason for this neglect, I think, was the lingering legacy of McCarthyism within the American community. The excesses of the 1950s so traumatized us that, by the time I entered graduate school in the mid-1960s, *to talk about the ideological roots of Soviet foreign policy was to sound a little like a member of the John Birch Society, if not Tail-Gunner Joe himself.* Even in the field of Soviet studies, where ideology could hardly be dismissed, it [Communist ideology] tended to be explained as a rationalization for actions already decided upon rather than as a guide to action.[14] (Italics mine)

Gaddis reported in this 1996 article that on the question of the relative morality of the United States and the USSR during the Cold War, ". . . the people now most likely to sympathize with . . . [the] 'moral equivalency' position—or at least a watered-down version of it—are some of my colleagues within the academic community."[15]

The quick and widespread acceptance of the revisionist approach among American historians was extraordinary. In 1970, Charles S. Maier of Harvard University—no Cold Warrior, for sure—pointed out that "Few historical reappraisals have achieved such sudden popularity as the current revisionist critique of American foreign policy and the origins of the Cold War."[16] This occurred, he stated, despite the gross methodological, factual, and conceptual errors of its practitioners. He maintained that in their work ". . . the key issues hinge not upon facts or evidence but upon assessments as to how repressive or non-repressive contemporary liberal institutions are."[17] Opposition to the Vietnam War accelerated the acceptance of the new historical approach.[18] Maier's criticisms of the revisionists built, to some extent, on those made by Arthur Schlesinger, Jr. in 1967.[19]

Gary R. Hess' laudatory evaluation of the revisionist school and

its exponents admitted that even strong supporters of the foremost of
the inventive recensionists, William Appleman Williams, considered
his work "imprecise" and "misleading."[20] However, while his basic
methodological flaws and errors were conceded, his general conclusions
were nevertheless accepted: "Williams's apologists acknowledge but
tend to discount questions about the use of documentation, imprecise
terminology, and the relationship of specific events to the general
interpretation."[21]

Robert James Maddox, the author of a 1973 book critiquing the
New Left historians, sadly reported in 1996 that his condemnatory
volume had had no effect:

> The book changed nothing. The same and even more imaginative
> misrepresentations of the documents have continued to appear with
> dreary regularity in articles and monographs. They now adorn
> some of the most popular college texts.[22]

An interesting example of the many historians who were swept up
in the movement within the discipline is Frank Warren, who has
become more bold and left-wing since the sixties. Having written a
book "from a democratic left perspective" in 1966 which condemned
the inability of liberal intellectuals to view the Soviet Union critically
in the 1930's, he stated in the preface to the volume's 1993 reprint that
he was upset that he had been seen by some as supporting
"conservative or Cold War liberal anti-Communism."[23] He declared
that " . . . perhaps it was my fault for not resisting more the climate
of dispassionate 'objectivity' so prevalent [then] in the historical
profession and, instead, putting my full politics right out front."[24]
Moreover, he regretted that he had not been more understanding of,
and sympathetic to, the American Communists of the 1930's.[25]

The analysis and historiography of American anti-Communism,
overwhelmingly dominated by the Left since its very inception,
maintained some of the same basic theses as the Revisionists throughout
most of the twentieth century.[26] The field has proven itself to be
adaptable and highly imaginative. For example, some prominent
historians have asserted that from the late 1930's through the Cold
War, the American public, leading political figures, and even some
scholars *mistook* the Soviet Union for an aggressive, totalitarian country
because they naively confounded Communism with fascism.[27]

To a large extent, historians of librarianship imitate the worst in contemporary academic history. In universities, the field of history—like most of the social sciences and humanities—is now dominated by unreconstructed rebels of the 1960's who retain their romantic view of revolutionaries and anti-establishment movements of the past. The victory of the adversarial pathology has been convincingly described.[28] (Generally, the conditions are worse in secular institutions than in Christian ones.[29]) This is not a mere accusation by critics on the Right, but a triumph proclaimed by self-styled "progressives." The editors of the radical history reference work, *Encyclopedia of the American Left*, state in their introduction that

> . . . many scholars who had come of age within the 1960s political movements embarked upon academic careers or began working as film-makers, curators, archivists, or librarians. Many of these younger scholars selected radical movements of the past, including the controversial and many-sided history of the Communist Party, as their scholarly specialties.[30]

Paul Buhle also reports in this volume that by the late 1980's, "If radical history had once been rare in the authoritative *Journal of American History*, it now became commonplace."[31] And, as reported earlier, in 1992 Michael Kazin was pleased to declare that American historians are "overwhelmingly cosmopolitan in their cultural tastes and liberal or radical in their politics."[32]

Quantitative studies done over the past twenty years have supported the qualitative ones, clearly demonstrating that faculty members in academia—particularly in the social sciences and humanities—are usually liberal or left-wing. A 1989 Carnegie Commission survey found that 70% of the college instructors in both the social sciences and the humanities labeled themselves *liberal*, while only 15% and 18%, respectively, considered themselves *conservative*. A 1998 investigation uncovered that at the University of Colorado at Boulder, 184 of the 190 humanities and social science professors who were registered to vote were Democrats, 6 were Republicans. In May 2000, the American Council on Education and the American Association of University Professors released the results of a survey they had sponsored. When asked to describe their political leanings, faculty members in the social sciences, humanities, education, and business at

the nation's leading research universities responded as follows: 10%
"far left," 53% "liberal," 30% "moderate," and less than 1% "far
right."

The percentage of leftist professors is generally the highest at elite
institutions. For example, the history department at the University of
North Carolina at Chapel Hill has 49 registered Democrats on its
faculty but only 1 Republican. There are no Republicans in the history
departments of Cornell (29 Democrats) and Dartmouth (10 Democrats).
Reportedly, there are no conservatives among the 56 full-time faculty
members in history at Princeton University.[33]

The revisionist approach is a major element in the field of library
history. A full understanding of why prominent American librarians
did not adhere to the most significant values of their culture and their
profession could provide valuable insights into the problems
democracies will always face in maintaining their free societies. It is
not likely that such an understanding will come from the work of those
currently conducting research in relevent areas of library history. Most
fully sympathize with the librarians criticized in this book, and the
great majority of their studies fit comfortably within the adversarial
culture now entrenched in higher education—including the schools for
educating librarians. It is significant that over the past two decades
there have been numerous surveys by faculty members of these schools
of library and information studies to determine the race, gender, age,
academic background, and productivity of their colleagues nationwide.
However, unlike investigators in other fields, they have made no
attempts to determine their political orientation. The reason is clear
enough: the profession's much touted commitment to diversity does not
extend to this area.

Entire areas of library history related to the study of American
librarianship and the Soviet Union have been largely taken over by the
Left. One such subject is that of the Cold War's effect on American
librarianship. In 1998, the primary organization within the American
Library Association devoted to the history of the profession, the
Library History Round Table, invited Ellen Schrecker to speak at
ALA's annual conference. She is, according to then-Committee Chair
Louise Robbins, "a prominent historian of the McCarthy period."[34] In
truth, Schrecker's works are panned even by liberal historians for their
gross distortions. In his *New York Times* review of her most recent

book on the fifties, Thomas C. Reeves calls it the best example of commonplace "leftist tirades" and chides her for continuing "to cling to the absurd illusion of heroic Reds as the champions of the highest ideals of humanity."[35] Ronald Radosh has written a thorough analysis of this book's factual, conceptual, and methodological errors.[36] It is similar to her previous publications: Schrecker's 1986 book on Communists and alleged McCarthyite oppression was no less bizarre.[37] Her invitation to speak, when others could have provided a more balanced presentation, says a great deal about the Library History Round Table. So too does the fact that no one who would have challenged her theses was asked to serve as a respondent.

In a report on her presentation for the *Library History Round Table Newsletter*, Schrecker was described as "one of the leading scholars of the McCarthy period." It went on to say that "According to Schrecker, librarians were more courageous in fighting McCarthyist oppression than most professions," although she added that the relevant history of several disciplines remains to be studied. "Schrecker concluded that McCarthyism set back race relations, women's rights, cultural discourse and diversity, . . . and led to the Korean and Vietnam wars."[38] Such farfetched conclusions are common in her work, so it is alarming that at the time of this presentation Schrecker was a professor of history at Yeshiva University and had previously taught at Princeton and Harvard.

Schrecker has not been the only radical speaker invited to librarians' conferences to speak about intellectual freedom and censorship during the Cold War. For example, in 1997 Laura Nader, Professor of anthropology at the University of California at Berkeley, gave an address at the American Library Association annual conference. As with Schrecker's presentation, no one with a contrasting point of view was invited to debate the subject. A contemporaneous publication by Nader alleged that " . . . repressive and fear-generating events such as the cold war periodically appear in the history of American universities, thereby facilitating industrial and military regulation of academic affairs. . . ."[39] Published in a collection of essays issued by the New Press (located at the City University of New York), the contributors to *The Cold War and the University* included Noam Chomsky, Howard Zinn, and other conspiracy-minded members of academia's far Left.

Specific Examples

The important role of Everett T. Moore as an early creator and purveyor of the historical myths concerning librarianship's opposition to anti-Communism has already been described in the section on the Intellectual Freedom movement. However, it is interesting to note that even his wild claims were not sufficiently far-reaching for the library press. In 1971, *Library Journal* apparently attempted to add additional punch to an article by Moore which compared the threats to intellectual freedom in contemporary America with those in other times, primarily the years when McCarthy was a powerful Senator.[40] Moore's piece included a quotation which stated that acts like the authorization of wiretaps by US Attorney General John Mitchell at the behest of President Richard Nixon (in the government's investigation of a group charged with bombing the CIA headquarters in Madison, Wisconsin) may represent an assumption of executive power greater than anything since Oliver Cromwell declared himself the Lord Protector of England in 1653. *Library Journal* filled an entire page with a picture of Cromwell shortly before a battlefield victory and his subsequent arrogation of power above a photo of "Senator Joseph McCarthy at the Army-McCarthy hearings, in his role as 'protector of the United States,' "[41] as the caption read. One assumes that these visuals and explanatory text were the creation of *Library Journal*'s editors, who were apparently trying to best Moore in the journalistic-historical license department. Why did they use a picture of McCarthy rather than Nixon? This juxtaposition of a man coming to power via the sword with a legislator democratically elected to do what he was doing was a hubristic attempt to draw a parallel. (It may be relevant that *Library Journal*'s ever-interesting and socially pertinent editorials since the sixties sometimes seem to have replaced the "editorial we" with the "royal we.") At the time he wrote this, Moore was Assistant University Librarian and Lecturer in the School of Library Service at the University of California at Los Angeles.

A 1972 article about The Progressive Librarians' Council, which existed from 1939 until the mid-1940's—was, overall, very positive in its treatment of that organization. The author of this *Library Journal* piece,[42] Dr. Joe Kraus, a library historian as well as administrator, did note the group's sudden turnaround on America's involvement in World War II after the Soviet Union was attacked, its having the Stalinist

Rockwell Kent as a conference speaker, its vocal support of Communist labor leader Harry Bridges, and its newsletter's interview with the director of the American-Russian Institute. Nevertheless, the author never stated the obvious: that the PLC's first Chairman, librarian Phillip Keeney, was pro-Communist, and that, for those who controlled it, pro-Sovietism was the primary purpose of the association's existence. Instead, Kraus—like the former PLC members he quoted—focused on the apparently non-Communist elements of its agenda, thereby replicating a prototypical technique of such front groups.

He claimed that its newsletter "offered a freedom of expression that the *Library Journal*, *Wilson Library Bulletin*, and *ALA Bulletin* could not tolerate."[43] This is difficult to accept since the *P.L.C. Newsletter* clearly contained "freedom of expression" only for views it approved of. Kraus asked the rhetorical question, "Was it a left-wing organization?" and answers "Yes, of course, if one concedes that much that was *left* in 1939-44 has become *center* or *right-of-center* in 1972."[44] Thus, according to Kraus, the Progressive Librarians Council was merely ahead of its time. For this to be true, one would have to accept that agitation on behalf of the Soviet Union's agenda was acceptable by the early 1970's. Tellingly, the *C* word appeared nowhere in the article.[45]

This unwillingness—or inability—to utilize the word *Communism* was also evident in Robert Vosper's 1976 history of American international librarianship, "A Century Abroad."[46] In this *College and Research Libraries* overview, he mentioned that some American academic librarians who had met their Cuban counterparts in 1956 later assisted a few of them to relocate to the United States "when life became too complicated for them at home."[47] Too *complicated*? Such words and phraseology obscured the nefarious impact of Communism on librarianship and librarians. Vosper, who was the University Librarian at UCLA from 1961 to 1964, was deeply involved in international librarianship for much of his career.

An early historical work which is still relied upon by current researchers was William E. Benemann's 1977 "Tears and Ivory Towers: California Libraries during the McCarthy Era."[48] Benemann's *American Libraries* article was based largely on contemporary accounts like those of Everett T. Moore, "It Happened in Pasadena," The Fiske

Report, Danton's *Climate of Book Selection*, and other mainstays of the Intellectual Freedom movement. Some of his statements concerning the public's complaints about the texts in their schools and libraries were particularly caustic, and, as shown elsewhere in this book, have been quoted by recent library historians, who agree wholeheartedly with his views:

> Looking from the vantage point of the 1970s, it is difficult to imagine objections to the goals of the United Nations. But in 1952 the idea of a world federation was viewed with suspicion—or unalloyed hostility—by a number of Americans. They believed membership would require a lessened allegiance to the United States and would, more abhorrently, ask Americans to live in peaceful acceptance of their communist neighbors.
>
> These were the objections most frequently voiced, but some observers felt that opposition was motivated, at least in part, by other concerns. A closer look at UNESCO materials revealed proposals for lowering of barriers separating not only nations, but also races. Many felt that UNESCO sought an end to white supremacy in world affairs.[49]

Unlike most other chroniclers of this period, Benemann was very dissatisfied with the response of California librarians: he thought they had merely been "pelting storm troopers with popcorn."[50] As indicated above, the "storm troopers" he was referring to were those Americans who were wary of surrendering their country's sovereignty to some form of global federation, a traditional American stance still maintained by the majority of the population. As for Benemann's charge that such people were unwilling to live peacefully with the Communist countries of the world, no evidence of this was given anywhere in his work. The same was true for his assertion that white supremacism was actually at the core of some of their views on world affairs. As with his accusation of militarism, Benemann provided no facts to sustain this allegation of racism among Californians, and he never named the so-called "observers" who shared his views. His work was nothing more than a Brown smear, which accounts for its popularity among those who still cite it as a reliable historical account.

Anti-anti-Communism became further enshrined in American librarianship through the overwhelmingly positive biographical pieces published about its chief proponents. In his laudatory contribution about Robert B. Downs in *Leaders in American Academic Librarianship, 1925-1975*, published by the profession's national honor society, library administrator and historian Arthur P. Young uncritically accepted Downs' views concerning the alleged national hysteria in the 1950's and his conflation of the roles played by domestic public libraries and those of overseas federal libraries.[51]   In the same collection, Edward Johnson's treatment of Ralph E. Ellsworth's *American Right Wing* made it seem that this diatribe stemmed from Ellsworth's devotion to education and intellectual freedom.[52]

Wayne Wiegand's essay in *Leaders in American Academic Librarianship*, which he edited, focused on the professional life of Lawrence Clark Powell, who served as the director of libraries at UCLA from 1944 to 1961.[53]   He described him as a "successful defender of intellectual freedom who survived a brush with the McCarthy era's misdirected accusations against suspected Communist sympathizers. . . ."[54]   Central to this "brush" was Powell's appearance before the California State Senate Investigating Committee on Education in 1951.   Wiegand began his treatment of this by emphasizing Powell's "abhorrence of censorship."[55] He then declared that

> One of the most significant tests of intellectual freedom and, conversely, most concentrated efforts to censor during Powell's UCLA years centered in Wisconsin Senator Joseph McCarthy's self-appointed campaign against alleged Communist infiltration in American government and life.   Libraries did not escape the scrutiny of reactionaries in search of literature "sympathetic" to Communism.[56]

In truth, the Committee's activities were not part of any McCarthy effort or movement.   This Committee had been established in the 1940's, years before the Senator's anti-Communist work drew nationwide attention.   Moreover, similar activities in California had begun even before its creation: the California State Legislature's Fact-Finding Committee on Un-American Activities had been set up in January 1941 and was soon investigating the very real activities of pro-Communist and pro-Axis groups and individuals.

The work of the Committee on Education had already borne valuable fruit.   For example, as described later in this book, it had investigated the use in public schools of pro-Soviet texts written by well-known Stalinists, like *Land of the Soviets* by Marguerite and Maxwell Stewart. Its activities, including its investigation of Powell and his library, hardly seem to qualify as the "scrutiny of reactionaries in search of literature 'sympathetic' to Communism." Wiegand's placement of quotation marks around the word *sympathetic* makes it appear that he doubted either the existence of "literature 'sympathetic' to Communism" or the ability of the so-called "reactionaries" to discriminate between it and other material.

Wiegand's use of the cliché that McCarthy's activities were "self-appointed" is fallacious. He was democratically elected to the US Senate in 1946. His constituents supported his anti-Communist activism, so he was voted in again in 1952. Moreover, McCarthy did not appoint himself to his committee memberships or his positions therein.

It behooves anyone studying this period to understand why Lawrence Clark Powell—a man most remembered as a bibliophile—was brought in front of a State investigating committee. There were good reasons for the Legislature to carry out its legal responsibility of overseeing activities at the University of California at Los Angeles, as well as other educational institutions.[57] For example, Robert Gordon Sproul, the University's President, was also the Chairman of the Institute of Pacific Relations, a Communist-controlled organization. An examination of the Committee on Education's numerous reports shows that its members did not consider people like Sproul to be Communists, but naive anti-anti-Communists. However, some active members of the University's faculty and administration *were* in the Party. Moreover, UCLA had hosted a Communist-run conference that had received a warm welcoming speech from Sproul. It was also well known that in the 1940's the University of California Press had begun publishing a periodical in conjunction with the Hollywood Writers' Mobilization. At least three of the five editorial board members of *Hollywood Quarterly* were Communists: John Howard Lawson, Franklin Fearing, and Kenneth MacGowan. Despite protests from the California Legislature's Joint Fact-Finding Committee on Un-American Activities, the University's comptroller, and others, the defiant Press was still issuing it in the late forties.

It should also be pointed out that the Committee on Education declared publicly that Powell was not typical of those who usually testified before it: "His manner and conduct were in most striking contrast with that of witnesses heretofore set forth in this report."[58] According to the Committee, unlike most others he expressed no objections to the inquiry, answered all questions put to him, and was forthright. In actuality, he was less candid than he was given credit for.

Wiegand presented a distorted picture of Powell's appearance before the Committee. Almost nothing about the hearing was provided except the fact that Powell had confirmed that he had been a member of the Communist Party when he had been in college. This was actually a very minor element of the meeting: the Committeemen accepted his explanation that it had been a short-lived, youthful protest, and that he had never attended any Party meetings. Omitted was the fact that he was also asked about a statement in a Communist newspaper that he had been an active sponsor of a conference dominated by pro-Party writers. He denied this, so the Committee quickly dropped the subject. The great bulk of the questions asked of Powell centered on why his publicly-supported library appeared to be promoting anti-conservative and anti-anti-Communist publications on the subject of American education instead of presenting a balanced collection of views, as the Committee members thought it should.[59] They were, in effect, advocating education instead of propaganda, intellectual freedom rather than censorship.

Wiegand did note that the Committee's chairman—one of the alleged "reactionaries"—had been friendly towards, and supportive of, Powell during the hearing as well as afterwards.[60] He also stated that Powell received immediate backing from UCLA's president and the head of the University of California Board of Regents. In addition, Wiegand reported that

> Throughout the ordeal Powell continued to receive staunch support from California's conservative community, many of whom Powell had come to know through his book-collecting and publishing activities. Because of their defense, the entire incident quickly blew over.[61]

With this statement, Wiegand became one of the rare library historians dealing with this period to say anything positive about a group of conservatives while identifying them as conservatives.

Clearly, Powell emerged from the government hearing with support from powerful people across a broad political spectrum. Nevertheless, according to Wiegand ". . . the damage had already been done"[62] because a local newspaper report bearing a distorted, sensationalist headline about Powell quickly appeared on the newsstands. However, such headlines were then daily occurrences in most cities, as they still are in many places. Moreover, Powell promptly wrote up *his* account of his testimony, and it was carried in the same day's evening papers, on the radio, and in the next morning's newspapers.[63]

According to Wiegand, this "ordeal" left a "scar" on Powell, and after some years the scar became a source of pride for him. The historian also declared that it boosted Powell's standing among librarians as a "principled, symbolic leader"[64] at the time the profession was fighting "McCarthyism" by increasing its dedication to intellectual freedom. The views of both men are troubling. Anyone bothering to read the transcript of the hearing can see that there was nothing that should have been considered by anyone, including Powell, an ordeal. Similarly, nothing transpired there for any librarian to have been proud of. This had not been a drama about a heroic, freedom-loving librarian standing up to the forces of censorship and oppression. It had been the story of the propagandistic promotion of an anti-conservative and anti-anti-Communist political agenda in a tax-supported university library and the justifiable response by some members of the university community, and of elected public officials, that this was unacceptable.

Wiegand advised his readers to see Powell's autobiography if they wanted a more complete description of his encounter with the Committee.[65] However, Powell's inaccurate rendering was far less useful for understanding what actually transpired than the transcript of the hearing itself.[66] It is significant that nowhere in the body of Wiegand's essay or in its notes is there any indication that this historian read the proceedings. It appears that Wiegand's treatment of this event was based largely on Powell's self-serving autobiography and an interview with Powell: no other relevant sources were cited. Both Wiegand's account and Powell's autobiography used the term "ordeal"[67] to describe the call to testify and what transpired. Similarly, both works focused on the Committee's alleged great interest in Powell's past membership in the Party, even though this is not borne out by the hearing transcripts.

The accounts by the two men do not always coincide. While the librarian's memoirs reported that his own version of his testimony was quickly distributed through the media, this important fact was not mentioned in Wiegand's rendering. As noted, according to this library historian ". . . the damage had already been done"[68] because of the appearance of the first headline. He does not make it clear what this damage supposedly was.

Since Wiegand considered this entire affair an irrational search by McCarthyite reactionaries for Communist subversion, he failed to mention any of the actual reasons for this government hearing. A few of the background causes have already been cited, most of which indicated a great tolerance of, if not support for, pro-Communist activities at the University. Chief among the immediate grounds was a bulletin board display at the UCLA library. According to Powell, it had apparently angered one or more of the students or faculty members. A letter of complaint was mailed to the Committee, which then sent an investigator.

Powell dismissed the frequent allegations that UCLA was left-wing: "This was an old chestnut, often reroasted by the local newspapers, and was due to a small noisy minority of students and a few faculty."[69] He claimed that the campus was actually *conservative*, an assertion that, if true, makes the long, successful careers there of Powell and those he hired, like Everett T. Moore and Robert Vosper, truly remarkable.

Describing the origin of this investigation, the library director reported that ". . . a liberal junior member of Everett Moore's reference staff put up a bulletin board display of current periodical articles critical of legislative inquiries."[70] This characterization of the display was untrue. The transcript of the hearing shows that Powell had brought with him a list of the items in the display, and that some of the articles and pamphlets in it were discussed. Moreover, a photograph of the bulletin board had been taken and was reproduced in the Committee's published report. Thus, the actual items on exhibit were known to all involved and cannot be a subject of debate. Titled "Threats to the Schools," the display consisted of items indicating that the major danger to education came from anti-Communists; the Catholic Church; and citizens, like those in Pasadena, who opposed paying higher taxes to support a changeover to the so-called "progressive education" they disliked. It contained no items with opposing viewpoints, like articles about Pasadena from the *Freeman* or the report on the conflict there by the Senate Investigating Committee on Education.[71]

Thus, in Wiegand's piece, we have many of the major elements common in the historical treatment of this subject: an overreliance on the distorted and self-serving testimony of an anti-anti-Communist participant, a failure to look at the most revealing documentation, and an eagerness to condemn anti-Communists as repressive paranoids.

Robert D. Harlan, a professor at the University of California's School of Library and Information Studies at Berkeley, presented as *fact* the unsubstantiated view that Helen Haines' *Living with Books* was not partial to pro-Soviet works, and he did so in the profession's landmark *Dictionary of American Library Biography*, which appeared in 1978.[72] The same message appeared in the equally encomiastic biography of Haines in the 1980 *ALA World Encyclopedia of Library and Information Services*. It was written by Ruth Warncke, a former official of the American Library Association.[73] Warncke attributed the lack of widespread and open professional approval for *Living with Books* to librarians' timidity and their failure to support intellectual freedom.[74] Harlan apparently believed this too.[75]

The entries in the American Library Association's *World Encyclopedia* about librarianship in the Soviet Union and other Communist countries were written by librarians from those states and therefore followed the Party line. Similarly, predictable biographical sketches of people like Krupskaya, O. S. Chubaryan, and Lev Tropovsky were written by Soviet librarians. This selection of contributors accorded with the encyclopedia's general approach to foreign subjects, but it guaranteed the limited value of the work. Sad to say, the biographies of Soviet librarians that *were* written by those outside of Communist countries failed to describe the political nature of their subjects' work or the influence of Soviet politics on their lives. In this category must be included Ray Suput's entry on E. I. Shamurin and Herman Liebaers' contribution on Margarita Rudomino.[76] They resembled the works written about librarianship in the USSR by many of the contemporary internationalists and Soviet specialists in the United States, who have usually ignored or underplayed the horrific consequences of Communist rule.

In the 1990's, librarians with a background in Russian and Soviet Studies were showing clear signs that—unlike their scholarly predecessors in the late forties and fifties—they were not immune to absurd myths concerning Cold War America and Joseph McCarthy. Thus, in a 1995 history of the Soviet-American exchange of publications, Margaret Olsen[77] of the Slavic and East European Library at the University of Illinois declared that the mutual interest the Soviet Union and the United States had had in each other

> was undermined by distrust between the two governments. The Stalinist government was unwilling to exchange information freely with the West, and McCarthyism had a similarly depressive influence in the U.S. Three decades passed before the Soviet Union was truly open to the West, but the mid-1950's, when Stalin died and Senator Joseph McCarthy was discredited, were a major turning point that led to the proliferation of cultural exchanges in 1958.[78]

Olsen had sixteen pages in her *Library Resources and Technical Services* article to provide some evidence to substantiate her rough equation of Soviet obstructionism with that alleged to have originated in the United States, but she failed to do so. Moreover, earlier in the paragraph quoted above, she cited a classic scholarly article by Melville Ruggles on Soviet-American book exchanges. In that very piece, Ruggles had laid the blame for the lack of exchanges until the mid-fifties entirely on the USSR.[79]

In 1997 the Slavic Collections Curator at Yale University and the Library of Congress' Senior Exchange Specialist for Russia and the Baltic Countries[80] declared in a lengthy *Serials Librarian* article about large research collections like theirs that "Exchanges with the Soviet Union did not become truly effective and productive until the late 1950s. Stalin's death and the end of McCarthyism made this sudden growth possible."[81] There were thirty-five notes in the article helping to substantiate many of their statements, but none for this. The authors were apparently familiar with Olsen's article and trusted it, since four of their notes cited the work. It is possible that they merely accepted her word for the false parallel. Given the commonly accepted views among the highly educated today about McCarthy and Cold War America, such an untruth would be easy to imbibe and regurgitate.

The Internet has allowed contemporary librarianship to impart its distorted view of the history of Soviet-American relations to greater numbers of people than ever before. A prime example is the Web site established by Glenda Pearson, Head of the Microforms and Newspapers Collection at the University of Washington Libraries. "The Red Scare: A Filmography"[82] is a sneer at the long-held and commonly accepted American view that the Soviet Union and Communism were dangerous forces.

Donald G. Davis, a professor at the School of Library and Information Science at the University of Texas at Austin, is the longtime editor of *Libraries and Culture*, the premier American journal of library history. He has also coedited two valuable reference books in the field: a guide to American library history and the *Encyclopedia of Library History*.[83] Davis provided an overview of Soviet-American library relations during the Cold War in an article written for presentation at a 1998 international conference.[84] His work noted how the USSR prevented the free choice of reading material by its own citizens, crushed dissent in Eastern Europe, and hindered the free interchange of ideas at the 1970 IFLA conference in Moscow. Despite these brutal truths, his analysis was essentially flawed.

A fundamental distortion was its description of the primary conflict of the twentieth century as being between "capitalism and communism."[85] Freedom and/or democracy versus Communism would have been more accurate, although capitalism does seem a necessary component of free societies, where it serves as both an expression, and a progenitor, of liberty.[86]

Davis also maintained that

> . . . Cold War animosity and tension waned through the 1970s,
> . . . [and] the superpowers became less antagonistic, . . . [allowing]
> the Soviets and Americans slowly, warily, to progress slowly in
> their relations. . . . This all changed, however, with the dawning
> of the Reagan years. With Reagan's conservatism and comments
> on outlawing the "Evil Empire", the Cold War escalated once
> again. . . .[87]

The only individual Davis credited for helping to end Communism in Europe was Mikhail Gorbachev.[88]

These views do not accord with the facts, which show an aggressive Soviet Union growing militarily stronger throughout the seventies and confirm that the policy called *détente* was detrimental to America's security. Informed accounts of the Cold War also demonstrate the positive results of President Reagan's policies towards what truly was an evil empire.[89]

Davis also drew inaccurate and misleading parallels between the Soviet Union and the United States. For example, he declared them both subject to "the crippling paranoia of infiltration by the ideological other"[90] after World War II. He even *began* his piece with a passage describing an anti-Communist who was rending and burning some books merely because they contained the word *Communist*. This stereotypic portrayal was taken from a novel by Abraham Polonsky, identified by Davis as a "blacklisted Hollywood Ten writer."[91] Mentioning the fact that he was a longtime propagandist for Stalinism would have been more enlightening.

Davis strongly criticized Lucile Morsch's 1957 appeal to American librarians to help support their country's political and cultural foreign policy. To him, it had been a call aimed at "cold warriors" to promote "cultural imperialism."[92] Moreover, the implication was that this patriotic speech, described earlier, had been typical of its time. In truth, it had been unique among the orations by the American Library Association presidents, who had advocated a policy of appeasement.

Davis pressed his thesis of moral equivalence in, and bilateral culpability for, the Cold War: "As I. F. Stone said, '[E]very people has committed its sins.' "[93] (Stone should be best remembered for his perverse book claiming that the Korean War was not instigated by the Communists.[94]) Davis did not see a free world and a Communist world, but merely "feuding superpowers and their minion nations."[95] Similarly, he equated the tenets and actions of the Soviet and American librarians despite the fact that he also acknowledged that they reflected the governing philosophies of their countries. Thus, an American librarian at an international conference who declared that the central concerns of libraries in the United States were 'social responsibility, intellectual freedom and the freedom to read'[96] was guilty of "a none-too-stealthy example of American cultural imperialism" when he "offered to help other libraries around the world to achieve the same goals."[97] Can *offering* to assist people become educated and free seriously be regarded as oppressive?

Davis continued with these wrong-headed, cynical themes:

> Just as the nation-states of the Cold War era used the countries of
> the third or developing world to further their own game, so did the
> international cold warrior/librarians treat the libraries of the third
> world as backward and in need of a caretaker.[98]

> The United States, saturated with the doctrines of the Marshall Plan
> and fearing the threat of Communist infiltration, saw itself as the
> policeman and big brother to all the other peoples of the world.[99]

As a consequence, he wrote, at yet another international conference an
American described US libraries and "offered to help all the libraries
of the world 'follow suit.' " Yes, sniffed Davis, "a 'suit' tailor-made
after the pattern of America's own outfit."[100]

Pamela Spence Richards

Pamela Spence Richards was a leader in the fields of both library
history and international comparative librarianship when she passed
away in September 1999. Indicative of the status of this Professor at
Rutgers University's School of Communication, Information, and
Library Studies is the fact that she helped organize a 1996 joint
Russian-American conference that involved the American Library
Association, the Library of Congress' Center for the Book, the Rus-
sian Ministry of Culture, the Russian Library Association, and the
International Federation of Library Associations and Institutions
(IFLA). Afterwards, she edited the proceedings for *Libraries and
Culture*.[101] Richards also served as chair of IFLA's Round Table on
Library History from 1995 to 1997 and was then reelected for another
two-year term. She served on the editorial board of *Library Quarterly*,
widely considered the most prominent intellectual and scholarly journal
of the American library profession for the past seven decades. *Library
History*, the primary British periodical on the development of librarianship, included Richards as a member of its editorial board.

Her major publication on the history of Soviet-American library
relations, which appeared in *Library Quarterly* in 1998, is laden with
conceptual and factual errors. Titled "Soviet-American Library Re-

lations in the 1920s and 1930s: A Study in Mutual Fascination and Distrust," its primary thesis affirms the general moral and political equivalence of the two countries.[102] Thus, she declares that while the librarians of the United States and the USSR were greatly interested in learning about how their counterparts promoted readership, their relations were "distorted by politics"[103]: they were "constrained by the deep ideological reluctance of both the American and Soviet establishments to recognize any value in the other's library practices."[104] After the 1930's, she asserts, "geopolitics doomed them to mutual ignorance for most of the rest of the century."[105] This facile equation of the "establishments" of the countries is merely recycled New Left revisionist history. In truth, "geopolitics" were not to blame for any problems, but rather Soviet totalitarianism and aggression. Moreover, as we have seen, by the late 1940's many American librarians had a clear understanding of the USSR and its libraries. Unfortunately, the leaders of the field were not listening to them, and they continued to extend their hands in friendship until the Communist power succumbed.

Richards consistently refers to Soviet librarianship as a *profession* in her effort to draw false parallels between the countries. In truth, librarianship in the USSR was not a profession by any Western definition[106] of the term: librarians there had no philosophical or structural autonomy but were mere handmaidens of the state. She writes of the "important professional philosophical commonalities that have long gone unrecognized."[107] In actuality, the two groups were antithetical in their most essential values and goals.

False comparisons are also made between the open and politically diverse library collections in the United States and the tightly controlled ones in the Soviet Union. She states that before 1937 libraries in both countries had collections of works from—and about—the other in "research libraries with discrete clienteles,"[108] failing to note that most pro-Western books in Soviet research libraries were accessible only to those very few given this special privilege. Her undocumented assertion that public libraries in both countries were quite limited when it came to describing the others' "culture and accomplishments"[109] ignores the facts presented earlier showing the great amount of pro-Soviet materials in American public libraries before the Cold War. (One need only recall the popular books by Maurice Hindus and the encyclopedia articles of Walter Duranty, as well as Howard Winger's

1949 study showing the large proportion of pro-Soviet books in libraries.) Her explanation for this alleged mutual censorship resorts to sapless sociological theory: it is "typical of developed countries with rival ideologies."[110]

Richards alleges that the views of American librarians towards the USSR from the period after World War I through the 1930's generally reflected those of Americans in general, i.e., that the Communist country had nothing positive to contribute to civilization and should only be feared.[111] Alas, as I have shown, the librarians' views were not this close to the truth.

Not all of Richards' views are as novel as those reported so far. For example, she repeats the academic commonplace that there was "public hysteria"[112] in the post-Great War era. She also raises the typic bogey of J. Edgar Hoover.[113]

Richards is clearly in error when she writes of the "tentative, sometimes grudging, tone of American reports of Soviet progress in literacy and adult education before World War II."[114] As has been shown, their reports were almost consistently effusive. She claims that it was Stalin's purges begun in the second half of the 1930's that "put an end to the normal professional life in Russia."[115] As demonstrated early on in this book, normal professional librarianship ended with the Bolshevik coup in 1917. Stalin did not invent the purge, he merely perfected it.

Richards writes that "Among the isolated articles on library work in Soviet Russia in the American scholarly press in the mid-1930s, there are two positive accounts, the authors of both of which clearly anticipated criticism of their enthusiasm for Soviet practices."[116] She is referring to Margaret P. Coleman's moronic article in the *Wilson Bulletin for Librarians* and John Richmond Russell's piece in the *Journal of Adult Education* which insisted that propaganistic activities in Soviet libraries were insignificant.[117] (The reader is referred to the analyses of these articles earlier in this book.) One can easily establish that the *Wilson Bulletin for Librarians* and the *Journal of Adult Education* were not "scholarly." More importantly, Richards' statement above minimizes the very positive library press the Soviet institutions received *throughout* that decade and ignores the fact that not one major anti-Soviet article appeared in the United States. Additionally, her remark that both Coleman and Richmond anticipated criticism implies that people were reluctant, or even afraid, to voice such ideas. If anything, the opposite appears to have been true!

There are further problems with Richards' treatment. She considers Coleman's sophomoric questions about the essentials of American society and its librarianship to be "searching."[118] Coleman had asked—rhetorically—if American libraries were truly democratic and if American libraries and schools were not actually propagandists for capitalism just as those in the Soviet Union were for Communism? Common sense and a basic understanding of political affairs could have provided the answers. In short: *Yes*, American libraries were not only quite democratic but were more so than those in any other country. However, it is naive to expect any human institution to be perfect. *No*, general support for an economic system that had proven to satisfy humans' physical needs better than any other and was an apparent requisite for political democracy was not the same as complete support for an oppressive social/economic/political system.

Richards has a similarly high regard for Russell's unwillingness to condemn Soviet propaganda; her judgment should be distasteful to democratically minded librarians. She continues her tract: "But Coleman's and Russell's pleas to their American colleagues to judge Soviet librarianship separate from its overall political goals fell on deaf ears."[119] For some reason, she does not feel compelled to offer any evidence of this. Moving on to the next unsubstantiated assertion, she declares that within a year of the articles by Coleman and Russell ". . . the reports of Stalin's mass purges made all Soviet institutions suspect for generations of American librarians."[120] Unfortunately, this did *not* happen, as evidenced, for example, by the wartime affection evinced by the leaders of American librarianship.

Richards appears pleased that the Soviet librarians she discusses supported adopting American library techniques despite the fact that they were extremely critical of the goals of libraries in the United States and of the society in general.[121] They were not being broadminded or tolerant, as Richards implies, but merely cunning. And those Americans who helped such efforts were nothing less than accomplices. Why does sharpening the blade of the Communist intellectual guillotine merit praise?

In contrast, American librarians are criticized for not adopting Soviet innovations in "literacy training and adult outreach"[122] because of their association with propaganda activities. Again, no evidence is provided. Richards then declares that when the civil rights movement of the sixties moved American librarians to increase efforts to reach the underserved, techniques had to be independently developed that—she implies—could have been adopted from the Soviet model. [123] In truth, American librarians had plenty of domestic models from the twenties and thirties to choose from if they were looking for examples of outreach, such as those of Joseph Wheeler, director of Baltimore's public libraries. [124]

Richards' frequent insistence on equating the United States with the Soviet Union and the resulting distortion of the facts is flagrant when she writes about Frank A. Golder, the Stanford University historian and curator of the Russian collection at what was later named the Hoover Institution. [125] She declares that "Golder's plans for a collaborative Soviet-American institute at Stanford failed because of both the United States government's intransigence on the question of diplomatic recognition for the Soviet Union and Stalin's campaign for ideological purity, begun in 1928." [126] However, the very page in Golder's biography that Richards cites to back up her assertion about the American government refutes it! It is stated quite clearly that Golder was informed by a State Department official that it "had no objection [to the proposed institute] as long as an agency of the Soviet government, such as the Society for Cultural Relations, signed the agreement, rather than an official diplomatic representative." [127] The biographer goes on, citing Golder's own correspondence, to declare that while the Department could not *officially* promote such an interchange, it was not actually opposed to it. [128] Richards' second point is also incorrect. It is clear that although Golder's optimistic, idealistic project received its final rejection during Stalin's 1928 campaign for ideological purity, Soviet officials had been unwilling to agree to it the *previous* year too because the Soviet state had been refused permission to control the contents of the proposed institute's publications. [129] Moreover, Richards fails to mention Golder's problems as early as 1921—before Stalin's ascension—in getting Soviet approval to ship books and manuscripts he had collected back to California. [130] The editors of Golder's papers comment on his naiveté, specifically in regard to his plan for a Russian-American institute. His "illusion," [131] they say, was that he could avoid political subjects and focus merely on the social and economic: everything in the Soviet Union had become political.

Richards also distorts Golder's view of the Communists. She

quotes a remark of his showing his grief over the famine he witnessed in the USSR in 1921[132] while omitting more telling ones in the same book:

"The country is in ruins, and I wish I could see sunshine ahead. So much suffering, so much talking, so much arresting, so much stealing, so much demoralizing one finds nowhere else, and while Rome burns the [Soviet] leaders fiddle."[133]

Golder also wrote that he went about his job of collecting documents 'as if a sword hung over [him].'[134] He was followed everywhere by the secret police and was frequently accosted by them.

Richards quotes from a 1925 letter from Golder to Herbert Hoover published in a one-volume collection of the librarian's papers to buttress her assertions about Communist achievements and the American unwillingness to be instructed by them:

'We could . . . learn something from the Russian experiment. The Bolsheviks have not accomplished what they set out to do, but they have come a bit nearer to it than we thought possible. It will not do to be dogmatic on the question.'[135]

A statement he made two years later appearing only twenty-one pages after the one above was, overall, more telling:

While watching this [military] review I could not help but recall similar occasions. In 1914 I saw Nicholas II, in 1917 Kerenskii, and in 1923 Trotskii review the troops. How the mighty have fallen and how much blood has been wasted in these thirteen years! How little there is to show for it![136]

Had he not passed away in January 1929, Golder's view of the Communist state would almost certainly have been even more negative.

Despite its significant errors, Richards' study has been celebrated by her peers. In spring 1999, it was announced that it had earned her the American Library Association's annual award for Distinguished Published Research. Its supposed high-quality research methodology and significant findings were noted in the organization's pronouncements. The prize is bestowed by ALA's Library Research Round Table, the group within the Association that focuses on the area

denoted by its name.[137] The chair of the LRRT committee making the
selection was Lorna Peterson, whose valuations of works of library
history have been shown to be largely determined by her own
"progressive" ideology.[138]

Some of the defects in Richards' article appear in her other
publications as well. For example, when describing the East-West
tensions resulting from the USSR's political and military domination of
the countries to its west after World War II, she declares that the
proximate cause was "disagreement with the other Allies over the
future governance of Eastern Europe."[139] This avoids the essential fact
of brutal Communist imperialism.

Louise Robbins

Within librarianship, one of the most prominent of the contemporary attacks on American anti-Communism is Louise Robbins'
1996 *Censorship and the American Library: The American Library
Association's Response to Threats to Intellectual Freedom, 1939-
1969.*[140] Robbins, an Assistant Professor at the School of Library and
Information Studies at the University of Wisconsin at Madison, became
Associate Professor and Dean of the School soon after the book went
to press. Her position as Chair of the Library History Round Table
was mentioned earlier. She also headed the History Special Interest
Group of the Association for Library and Information Science Education in 1992.

Her book reprises all of the major phrases and clichés of anti-anti-
Communism put forth by the leaders of the Intellectual Freedom
movement in the 1950's. The misleading term *witch-hunt* is emphasized by its inclusion in the title of one of the work's five chapters,
"Book Banning and Witch Hunts, 1948-52." The propagandistic use
of this term has already been analyzed. Patriotic organizations like the
American Legion are called "right-wing, super-patriotic groups," and,
of course, are described as "self-appointed censors."[141] The term "self-
appointed" is an attractive pejorative to those on the Left. It is
frequently used to smear a voluntary group of citizens, most commonly
local in origin. (When there is *any* indication of communication or
cooperation among such groups, the specter of a far-flung conspiracy
is devised and promulgated.)   As previously noted, grass-roots

expressions of popular will are feared by "progressives," who consider them neofascist. Only pseudo-mass movements controlled and led by an elitist Left appear to suit them.

Anti-Communism is described by Robbins as consisting of censorial assaults by people on the Right resulting from their inability to adjust to social change, such as those epitomized by the civil rights, anti-war, and women's movements of the 1960's.[142] The widespread desire in the fifties for loyalty oaths for some government workers and educators was supposedly a symptom of "oath fever."[143] She believes in other contrived maladies, like the Authoritarian Personality.[144] J. Edgar Hoover, we are told, was an "obsessive" anti-Communist. (Even Emma Goldman, the radical he helped deport, declared that 'At least Hoover was fair.'[145] True obsessives are not capable of fairness. Moreover, if Hoover—and, by inference, the organization that carried out his directives—were irrationally preoccupied with opposing Communism, one cannot explain the FBI's failure to pursue some extremely important leads on subversion by Soviet agents.[146]) Robbins maintains that the Cold War "tapped a vein of intolerance"[147] in the country: domestic libraries were "under siege" in a right-wing attempt to label or remove books she terms *subversive*—in quotation marks.[148] The flaws in all of the aforementioned accusations are described throughout *Not Seeing Red*.

Throughout most of the book Robbins reiterates the views of the 1950's Intellectual Freedom movement leaders with no critical analysis or evaluation of the evidence. Their word is enough for her—quite frequently their very words. As mentioned before in the discussion of Helen Haines and her critic, Oliver Carlson, Robbins even parrots earlier Haines enthusiasts, erroneously asserting that Carlson's attack on Haines "was refuted point by point by Elinor S. Earle."[149] Almost all her assertions and allegations are based on those from within the Movement: their utterances are taken on faith. While apparently sufficient for Robbins, this should not be adequate for the inquisitive reader.

The failure to look at and evaluate factual evidence rather than merely rehash partisan testimony is physically reflected, to some degree, by the book's notes: they were not meant to be looked at by a reader seeking substantiation of some point. They are difficult to find at the back of the volume. Moreover, it is frequently arduous to discern the provenance of a statement because several citations are often thrown together in one endnote when several are actually needed. The task of matching an element in the narrative with the corresponding source is made even harder because the citations are often fashioned in a highly abbreviated form, and the book's bibliography—less than three pages long—contains only a small percentage of the referenced works. One must wonder why a publisher which was once known as a source of well-researched, academic books in librarianship did not insist on the basic building blocks of a scholarly work.[150]

What little historical context is provided in the book is based largely on revisionist studies by historians of the far Left, such as Athan Theoharis, David Caute, and Ellen Schrecker. They share her belief in the general intolerance of the American people and the egregious oppression of left-wing groups and Communists in the 1950's.[151]

Robbins' historical views can also be gauged, to some degree, by her brief analysis of more recent developments in intellectual freedom.[152] As she remarks in her introduction to this 1996 book, there is a contemporary political and social urgency to her subject:

> Today, as the United States appears to become even more conservative and to retreat from the values of pluralist democracy on which American librarianship's intellectual freedom ideology is grounded, the American library profession, which historically has embraced the dominant ideology, may be faced with more fundamental choices concerning its very identity than ever before.[153]

Clearly, Robbins has a penchant for seeing anti-democratic threats from the Right.

Not surprisingly, this volume has been extremely well received by the vocal members within librarianship because it reflects that group's general outlook and reaffirms their predecessors' allegedly heroic acts. Leaving nothing to chance, positive book reviews have been insured by the choice of reviewers. Thus, Zoia Horn, a lifelong activist in the Intellectual Freedom movement, gives it a rave evaluation in the *Journal of Education for Library and Information Science*,[154] the official journal of the Association for Library and Information Science Education. She even praises the obviously inadequate notes and bibliography, although not for the primary function these are supposed to serve: "The notes at the end form an abundant bibliographic record which can be invaluable in choosing and developing theses, or smaller papers."[155]

Prestigious *Library Quarterly* also provides a generous assessment of the book.[156] (Robbins, incidentally, is on the editorial board of the periodical.) One of the points this evaluation makes is that the volume "is well researched and the historical record is well documented."[157] The reviewer, Beverly Lynch, is best known in the field as an administrator and a former president of the American Library Association, an organization treated very favorably in the work. As with Zoia Horn, scholarly publication has been a marginal element of Lynch's career.

The book's short review in *Libraries and Culture* is open to more revealing interpretations. Carl Bowen Davis reports that "Robbins manages an exceptionally generous presentation of the actions of the many ALA movers and shakers from 1939 through 1969, allowing them to speak for themselves, to appear in their best light. . . ."[158] He remarks that there are "adequate notes."[159] Unfortunately, in the same issue of this journal an overview of the library history literature of 1995 and 1996 misjudges the book as "first-rate," "an outstanding piece of historical literature" containing "critical analysis." However, the usually generous author of this survey also refers to "that venerable institution, the American Library Association" in the same paragraph, indicating how one should measure his words about *Censorship and the American Library*.[160] He asserts that the book is an example of what he considers to be the recently increased sophistication of American library history.[161]

Other publications by Louise Robbins on the 1950's, like her 1994 "Anti-Communism, Racism, and Censorship in the McCarthy Era" in the *Journal of Education for Library and Information Science*, can serve as exemplars of this now-fashionable area for research. In this work, subtitled "The Case of Ruth W. Brown and the Bartlesville Public Library," she makes the startling assertion that a knowledge of the events in this small (population twenty thousand), segregated, company town in Oklahoma fifty years ago will not only reveal a great deal about Cold War anti-Communism in general, but also about America today.[162] She asserts that ". . . its major elements—anti-communism, racism, and suppression or censorship—were prominent themes of the McCarthy era, a time in which books or films that dealt

with race issues were often attacked as Communist propaganda."[163]
Her major source for the ideas in this quote is David Caute's *The Great
Fear: The Anti-Communist Purge under Truman and Eisenhower.*[164]
The absurd first sentence of the introduction to his diatribe reads: "The
great fear, like the threat of upheaval and expropriation that inspires it,
has been a recurrent phenomenon in the history of the bourgeoisie since
the French Revolution."[165] Caute's book does not improve as it goes
along.

Robbins continues: "A book-length exploration of the intersection
of these themes that played out in Bartlesville will shed light on the
motives of the censors of the 1950s and perhaps illuminate what lies
behind similarly ambiguous acts of censorship today."[166]   (The
promised book has recently been published and is discussed below.[167])
To this already inchoate mix which questions the authenticity of anti-
Communism she adds another element much favored today in library
historiography: ". . . it is clear that Ruth Brown needs to be viewed
from a feminist standpoint."[168]

The 1956 film *Storm Center* starred Bette Davis as a small-town
librarian almost single-handedly fighting the forces of darkness, viz.,
censorship and anti-Communism. If, as Robbins believes,[169] it was
based on the incidents in Bartlesville, the movie is even shallower than
its critics thought at the time. More recently, Leonard Maltin has said
of this film, which was made with the cooperation of the American
Library Association: "Not even Davis can uplift clichés."[170] Davis' foil
in the movie—the "typical American"—associates education, music,
book reading, and libraries with Communism. At the movie's end, the
library and its books burn, but the heroine literally vows to fight on to
the death.

A related article by Robbins about Bartlesville and the Bette Davis
film, "Fighting McCarthyism through Film: A Library Censorship Case
Becomes a *Storm Center*," was published in the *Journal of Education
for Library and Information Science* in 1998.[171] In it, she asserts that
the film itself, and the story of its actual production, mirrored the
essence of the events in Bartlesville and conditions in the country at
large: "the Technicolor reality of the Red Scare."[172]

Her purple prose results only in a black and white cartoon. On
one side of her caricature are the usual villains: "right wing anti-
Communists"[173] and "super-patriotic groups."[174]   The forces of

"virulent anti-Communism"[175] are embodied by individuals such as Richard E. Combs, Senator Joseph McCarthy, and "J. B. Matthews, professional anti-Communist."[176] (Given Professor Robbins' numerous publications attacking such individuals and their cause, would she be willing to call herself a professional anti-anti-Communist?[177]) Their agencies are the American Legion, the Knights of Columbus, the Catholic Legion of Decency, the House Committee on Un-American Activities, California's Tenney Committee, and so forth. Robbins charges that they all exacerbated the public's fears—which she believes was not difficult to do—by employing "Red scare tactics."[178] On the other hand, she also asserts that the passage of the McCarran Internal Security Act indicated that the Congress "was willing to sacrifice civil liberties for a sense of security,"[179] although she does not make it clear whose feelings of security she is referring to here. (Anti-anti-Communists have assiduously avoided mentioning the fact that the McCarran Act differed little in principle from many earlier state laws used to weaken the Ku Klux Klan and the German-American Bund.[180] This helps belie their claim that their concern has been for civil liberties, e.g., the right of free association.)

She maintains that politicians made allegations of Communist subversion solely for political gain, personal and otherwise.[181] Robbins is equally critical of "the power of a 'citizens' committee' like the American Legion"[182] and that of committed anti-Communist individuals. Interestingly, when describing anti-Communist efforts she frequently uses the word *crusade*.[183]

She also censures politicians for what she considers to be "assigning guilt by association."[184] (Elsewhere, she inaccurately claims that this was the essence of what she terms *McCarthyism*, which also included "witch-hunting.") It was allegedly used by those worried about a loss of political or economic power to induce fear and feelings of powerlessness in others.[185] Given the centrality of these indictments in numerous works, they warrant refutation. The accusations of witch-hunting and widespread fearmongering have been dealt with earlier.

Wanton charges against anti-Communists for "determining guilt by association" are as inaccurate as Robbins' assumption that the United States was Bartlesville writ large. The first of these allegations became common in some circles in postwar America, and is still repeated by many historians.[186] It is a fine example of assigning guilt by cliché.

Membership in the Communist Party, or in groups run by Party members, was usually only one piece of evidence that active opponents of Communism utilized in their investigations and analyses. It was certainly not a fact that should have been ignored. The right of association is a modern judicial construct derived, by some judges, from the First Amendment. Nonetheless, it has never been considered absolute by jurists and has been constrained by the understanding that a society has the right to preserve itself. Thus, it has been regulated in many areas, such as those involving: the public interest, national security, and criminal conspiracy; organizations with declared illegal purposes, including the violent overthrow of the government; and the act of associating with known criminals. As a result, statutes have been on the books regarding the personal associations of government employees, educators, police officers, criminals, and members of organized crime. Restrictions have even been upheld which prohibit the *appearance* of misconduct by some of these people. Thus, ignoring a person's associations to help determine whether he or she is in league with agents of a hostile foreign power would not only be absurd but would not accord with commonly accepted laws. The acceptance of using such regulations against Communists began declining in the 1960's, while it has increased for those in organized crime and terrorist groups: witness the 1970 Racketeer Influenced and Corrupt Organizations ("RICO") ordinance and the 1996 Anti-Terrorism and Effective Death Penalty Act.[187]

Membership in an organization, particularly active membership, is of obvious significance—but not to Robbins. She also dismisses as meaningless other genuine actions, such as signing an amicus curiae brief on behalf of the Hollywood Ten. This too is not an act, apparently, and to call it so is another example of "assigning guilt by association." One wonders what criteria—if any—would satisfy Robbins' demands to designate a deed as Communist or pro-Communist.[188] Illogically, she does not hesitate to declare people innocent or praiseworthy by association.[189]

Many of the highly educated in our society have been condescending in their attitude towards the vital anti-Communists. One can wonder whether this would have been different if the leaders of the American Legion or the House Committee on Un-American Activities had been the type to quote Cicero: "*Pares vetere proverbio cum paribus facillime congregantur.*"[190] Whether considered ancient wisdom or common sense, the understanding that "Birds of a feather flock together" lends additional credence to the arguments of the anti-Communist activists.

Being an extremist, Robbins insists several times that "virtually no one"[191] among the supposed anti-Communists truly believed that Communists or 'so-called subversives'[192] were any real threat to the United States. She is certain that their actual targets were the *liberals*.[193] In any case, Robbins seems to have no quarrel with Communists. To her, they were primarily Popular Front allies skilled in advancing liberal causes. Her sole professed political test for anyone is whether he or she supported "causes dear to liberals"[194]: racial integration, unionism, adherence to Constitutional rights, and opposition to fascism.[195] Those who pass include, among others, the Bartlesville librarian, the American Library Association and its Intellectual Freedom movement activists, Eleanor Roosevelt—and the Communist members of the Popular Front.

Robbins' beloved Front in the United States was actually a short-lived creation of the Communist Party undertaken on orders from the Moscow-based Comintern, the Communist International, in 1935. This alliance of Communists and non-Communists—heretofore forbidden by the USSR—was clearly to serve Soviet interests, not America's, and for this reason came to be vigorously opposed by some members of the Left, such as Norman Thomas, John Dewey, and George Counts. Some Communists and fellow travelers saw the light when the Soviet Union formed an alliance with Germany. Overnight, Communists in American Front groups ceased their diatribes against fascism. (The USSR proceeded to invade eastern Poland and Finland.) However, after the Soviet Union was attacked by Germany, Communists in the United States made another sudden about-face: they ceased their agitation against America's involvement in the war and demanded America's entry into the fray. Moreover, they immediately discarded their supposed devotion to progress in racial areas and unionism, declaring that all energy must be spent on defeating the Nazis. It was manifest that their overriding concern was the Communist motherland, much to the chagrin of many of their former allies in Front groups, like the black union organizer and civil rights leader, A. Philip Randolph.[196] This is all known by those with a basic knowledge of history. Thus, one wonders why Robbins views the Communist members of Popular Front groups so positively when they were obviously not truly committed to the causes she supposedly champions: racial integration, unionism, and anti-fascism. She should also be questioning the intelligence and the priorities of the non-Communist members of the Front groups.

Robbins' claims that anti-Communism was merely a ploy to combat the liberal causes supported by the Popular Front is supported by referring to an unconvincing book by Larry Ceplair and Steven Englund: *The Inquisition in Hollywood: Politics in the Film Community, 1930-1960.*[197] In fact, she cites this work several times to substantiate her views. Central to Ceplair and Englund's volume is their consideration of Communists primarily as effective members of American "progressivism,"[198] with the Popular Front coalition the most successful movement on the Left in American history.[199] This coalition's central objective was to oppose "international and domestic fascism."[200] Only such a Front could battle "the nativism which characterized the entire course of American history"[201] and protect the Left, which has "been periodically savaged by the forces of government and the Right since the days of Daniel Shays."[202] The authors mourn its absence in the fifties and sixties. Communists are necessary because—unlike liberals—they have backbone and political sagacity.[203]

In a review of *The Inquisition in Hollywood*, the liberal historian at the University of Wisconsin, Thomas C. Reeves, faulted the volume's "lack of objectivity, unevenness, and numerous flaws."[204] He believed many readers would be offended by "the young authors' left-wing bias,"[205] and pointed to their sympathetic portrayal of Communist screenwriters as idealistic artists, 'successful radicals,' 'progressives,' and 'seekers of justice.'[206] Even the Communist Party, he reported, was pictured "as an inspiring channel for social consciousness."[207]

David Culburt of Louisiana State University liked part of *The Inquisition in Hollywood*, but expressed concerns about the validity of the authors' research techniques.[208] This historian found unuseful their "conventional good guys/bad guys treatment of the Hollywood Ten, replete with moral indignation."[209] He also noted that their strong assertions about the dynamics of American politics and society went unsupported, like their declaration that the anti-Communist investigations of Hollywood were fueled primarily by the fear of unionism and hatred of socialism on the part of the country's 'corporate and political elites.'[210]

Walter Goodman, who had written a book[211] highly critical of the House Committee on Un-American Activities, also found their theses wanting. He was particularly disturbed by the authors' refusal to place the failure of the Communist Party of the United States where it belonged—on its slavish following of the dictates from Moscow.[212]

The handful of books which Robbins apparently relies on for her major ideas, and which she recommends to her readers, also includes *Scoundrel Time* by the notorious prevaricator and longtime (possibly lifelong) pro-Communist Lillian Hellman.[213] Reviews in journals across the non-Communist political spectrum—in *Dissent*, *Library Journal*, and *National Review*—have pointed out that it is based on factual errors, distortions, and fabrications.[214] Robbins also depends on Victor Navasky's deceptive *Naming Names*, which is comprised largely of misrepresentations and unwarranted assertions, as in his fierce condemnation of liberal anti-Communists, like Arthur Schlesinger, Jr.[215] Navasky has most recently distinguished himself by reasserting the now uncommon belief that Alger Hiss was not truly guilty of espionage.[216] Of course, David Caute's *The Great Fear* has a supporting role in this Robbins article too.

Another of Robbins' sources is a book about this period by journalist Stefan Kanfer, who compensates for his lack of scholarly research and compelling evidence with an attempt at a compelling title: *The Journal of the Plague Years*.[217] The absence of substantive data, objective scholarship, and credible theses in books of the anti-anti-Communist genre seems to have necessitated such titles alluding to frightening—albeit inapposite—events from distant centuries that still have the power to alarm. *The Inquisition in Hollywood*, *The Great Fear*, and *Journal of the Plague Years* are just a few of those that fit this pattern.[218]

The books Robbins relies on to support her theses in "Fighting McCarthyism through Film" have been discredited for many years. Much of the *reliable* information has now been summed up in the volume *Hollywood Party: How Communism Seduced the American Film Industry in the 1930s and 1940s*.[219] The very fact that a ludicrous anti-anti-Communist movie was made in 1955 with the backing of mainstream Columbia Pictures belies the myth of widespread fear and suppression in America. Nevertheless, works like Robbins' article still present the stock elements: "Red Scares"; deluded, retrograde, anti-Communists; "super-patriots"; neofascist citizens' committees; censorship; cruel and illegal investigating committees; and "The Blacklist." We have already been subjected to decades of fraudulent writings, feature films, and television documentaries with these caricatures. Some of the myths they have advanced are confronted in several parts of *Not Seeing Red*. The facts should be faced: the Communists had indeed been very active in Hollywood, as elsewhere, and that their goal was to attain Soviet objectives, not American ones.[220]

As for "The Blacklist," this usually refers to a particular anti-Communist effort in the film industry from the late forties through the fifties. It gravely affected relatively few people—most of whom were Communists or pro-Communist—and did so at a time when there was not only a Cold War, but a hot one in Korea which resulted in the battlefield deaths of more than 36,000 American soldiers and the wounding of an additional 100,000. Actors, writers, and others unable to find work in Hollywood on their own terms (it was easy to get removed from this blacklist) were still able to work at their crafts in New York with little trouble: there was no proscription of Communists in the scores of theaters there. In addition, television, which was also centered in New York, was a place where some Communists found employment by keeping their political views secret and getting hired by their comrades. Of course, there were many other jobs available because of the booming economy.

However, there was not just this one Blacklist one hears of all the time, but others as well. Most of the blacklisting in the entertainment world, particularly in Hollywood, was started by the Communists in the 1930's and continued in show business by those on the Left for several decades. It predated and outlasted the one aimed at Communists in the late forties and fifties, which provided relatively minor inconveniences for most of those affected by it. The evidence clearly shows that the Communists not only influenced the content of films for decades—despite the received knowledge that they did not—but also worked to destroy the Hollywood careers of patriotic Americans, such as John Charles Moffit, Fred Niblo, Jr., Jim McGuiness, and Morrie Ryskind (the Pulitzer Prize winning playwright who was later associated with the Marx Brothers' films). Unlike those martyrized in feature films, television documentaries, history books, and journals of librarianship, there was no way for *these* individuals to ever return to the lives they had led.[221]

What is the fate of a piece of writing like Louise Robbins'

"Fighting McCarthyism through Film"? The Library History Round Table of the American Library Association gave Robbins' work an award for being the 'best article written in English in the field of United States and Canadian Library History.'[222] Thus, the falsehoods that were brazenly generated largely by Communists, and readily appropriated by many leftists and liberals, are now ratified as scholarly truths.

The article was reprinted as a chapter in Robbins' *Dismissal of Miss Ruth Brown: Civil Rights, Censorship, and the American Library*, published by the University of Oklahoma Press in 2000. Most of the major theses of the book have already been discussed in treating her earlier publications, but some are made more explicit in this volume. Robbins apparently sees a connection of some sort between America's foreign policy and the postwar return ("encouraged—or mandated"[223]) of women to work within the home and family: "Containment was not just foreign policy applied to the US effort to keep communism corralled within a tightly defined Soviet sphere, it was domestic policy applied to society's efforts to keep women confined within the domestic sphere as well."[224] She asserts that "much, if not all"[225] of postwar anti-Communism developed merely because it suited the interests of conservative economic groups in battling liberal change, such as the advancement of unionism, "peace, consumer protection, social reform, advancement for women and minorities,"[226] and so forth. She affirms the necessity of using concepts of gender, race, and class to explain the story,[227] and again insists that events in the small, segregated, southern town of Bartlesville, Oklahoma, in 1950 have great relevance nationwide today. It is

> pertinent to our time, as cultural values are again perceived to be under siege, as fear of difference—race, gender, class, national origin, sexual orientation—once again is exploited, as discourse is again constrained and contested, and as conservative groups have again escalated their challenges to materials in library collections.[228]

The result of this, we are told, is as before: "censorship, intolerance, and suppression of the rights of others."[229] For those of the Left, such bogeys provide sustenance.

Cindy Mediavilla

Cindy Mediavilla's 1997 contribution to a University of Illinois'
Library Trends issue also typifies the contemporary historical studies
of librarianship, anti-Communism, and the Intellectual Freedom
movement. In "The War on Books and Ideas: The California Library
Association and Anti-Communist Censorship in the 1940s and
1950s,"[230] this Adjunct Associate Professor at San José State
University's School of Library and Information Science presents the
usual ingredients.

Helen Haines is the heroine, holding aloft the beacon of freedom
that inspired and guided the California Library Association's Committee on Intellectual Freedom. The Committee, in turn, garnered the
support of both the state association and the American Library Association.[231] Mediavilla's adulation of those in the Intellectual Freedom
movement is boundless. She reports that in 1941, future attacks on
books and ideas were predicted by the president of the California
Library Association in 1941 because of the 'worldwide'[232] rise of
fascism. That same year, she writes, Helen Haines warned that in the
United States there were already afoot 'repressive movements against
so-called "radical" literature which endanger free investigations.'[233]

As indicated in the title of the article, Mediavilla does not hesitate
to identify the evil enemy in this "War on Books and Ideas," and she
does so throughout the article: it is "Anti-Communist Censorship."[234]
The reader is presented with the standard culprits in works of this
genre: legislative investigating committees and their directors, like
California State Senator Jack Tenney and United States Senator Joseph
McCarthy; the US Chamber of Commerce; patriotic societies; and
concerned citizens. The anti-Communists also included "agitators like
Anne Smart,"[235] later referred to as "the infamous Anne Smart."[236]
Nothing positive is said of the anti-Communists, nothing negative about
those in the Intellectual Freedom movement.

Mediavilla accepts the basic fantasies of the Intellectual Freedom
movement. The only real danger to America, we are told, was fascism
and right-wing reaction. No threats were posed by Communists at
home or abroad; allegations to the contrary were mere ploys of the
forces of reaction.

Mediavilla cites the work of one researcher to explain the California State legislature's establishment of its Committee on Un-

American Activities. It was, she says, a response to "ten years of aggressive agitation by farm and dock labor unions," an attempt to "suppress 'radical' thoughts and actions."[237] While Mediavilla puts the word *radical* in quotation marks here, one should remember the destructive work by the powerful leader of the West Coast long-shoremen, Harry Bridges, an instigator of the 1934 General Strike in San Francisco. Consistently accused by conservatives of being a Communist, the opening of former Soviet archives has, not surprisingly, borne this out.[238] In true Intellectual Freedom movement tradition, Mediavilla never confronts the genuine threat posed by the USSR and its international agents. Moreover, she consistently ignores this state committee's investigations of pro-fascist, pro-Axis individuals and groups. It opposed National Socialism as well as Communism.

In addition to the stereotypical portraits of the major players in this drama, Mediavilla's article also exemplifies contemporary historiography in this subject area by its failure to provide hard evidence. The abstract of the work appearing at its beginning starts with the claim that it is based on "primary sources and related documents."[239] In truth, she frequently relies on secondary sources when obtaining the primary documents they discuss seems to be both required and easy. Moreover, these secondary sources are usually limited to a few short accounts written by members of the Intellectual Freedom movement. Here she is merely reiterating what we have heard many times before. When not ignored, primary documents are often misused. On a few occasions, she provides some social or political context for the events described, usually citing a single article or book. Frequently, she makes bold assertions without providing any evidence at all.

Examples of these methodological inadequacies are called for. Mediavilla claims that the years of Jack Tenney in California and Joseph McCarthy in Washington were times when ". . . belief in 'intellectual freedom' became equated with things 'subversive' and 'sinister.' "[240] This charge is not substantiated by anything in her piece. The adjectives "subversive" and "sinister" are taken from statements by California legislative committees specifically concerning the use in schools of the book *Land of the Soviets* and the textbook series *Building America*. The Joint Fact-Finding Committee on Un-American Activities found the former to consist of pro-Soviet, pro-

Communist propaganda—which it clearly was—and considered the use of this children's book in schools to have a "sinister objective."[241] As the Committee's twelve page report showed, those who wrote, edited, and distributed *Land of the Soviets*—Marguerite Ann Stewart, Maxwell S. Stewart, and the Institute of Pacific Relations—had been promoting Stalinism for years, as did the contents of this particular book.[242] Ignoring the copious evidence provided in its study, Mediavilla asserts that the Committee "quickly" condemned the volume *merely* because its editor was associated with Communists and fellow travellers.[243] As for the *Building America* series, the Committee issued an extensive, well-documented report describing its anti-Americanism. As will be shown later, Mediavilla dismisses this convincing, analytical study[244] without even examining it. The objective and thorough committee investigations revealing the brazen use of subversive and sinister propaganda in school classrooms confound Mediavilla's wanton charge that the committee was merely an opponent of intellectual freedom.

In discussing this period, Mediavilla is at the very least guilty of hyperbolism when she makes the extreme and naive claim that "For the first time, California's long-standing tradition of an educational system independent of politics was seriously threatened."[245] Few anywhere at any time would claim that public education is ever independent of politics. She cites one source for her accusation: a 1974 journal article about Jack Tenney.

Mediavilla writes of a five-year "censorship nightmare"[246] in Los Angeles, apparently based entirely on two short, intemperate, and misleading articles: "It Happened in Pasadena,"[247] from 1952, and William Benemann's 1977 "Tears and Ivory Towers: California Libraries during the McCarthy Era."[248] The latter, she says, quoting Benemann, showed the censors pitted against those supporting " 'world understanding,' as stated by the goals of the United Nations."[249] She continues to allow him to explain:

> In 1952 the idea of a world federation was viewed with suspicion . . . by a number of Americans. They believed membership [in the United Nations] would require a lessened allegiance to the United States and would, more abhorrently, ask Americans to live in peaceful acceptance of their communist neighbors."[250]

As already reported, the vicious claim that such Americans did not want peace was baseless. Moreover, Mediavilla should know that, close to half a century later, the majority of Americans are still wary of international government agencies and any plans for world federation.

Writing of the early fifties, Mediavilla insists that "The fear generated by the political climate of the period cannot be overstated."[251] Although the library profession had been seriously threatened, she reports that by the mid-1950's it "had weathered anti-Communism and appeared to be regaining its strength."[252] Still, there remained long-lasting traumas: "As Benemann poignantly relates, 'The daily tirade of [anti-Communist] headlines had infected the profession with a virulent and crippling strain of angst.' "[253] She also accepts the Fiske study's flawed estimation of the situation, namely, that efforts at censorship had traumatized most librarians into becoming self-censors.[254] She comments: "It is no wonder that Fiske found the ghost of McCarthyism present during many of her interviews, even though the outspoken senator had fallen into national disfavor long before."[255] Mediavilla then appears to strike out on her own with a novel theory apparently invented out of thin air: there had been a golden era in librarianship, but because of anti-Communism ". . . librarians once so committed to intellectual ideals and civil rights, began to doubt themselves and their professional affiliations."[256]

She reports that an article expressing concern about pro-Communist publications in libraries appeared in 'a strident anti-Communist newspaper.'[257] Neither these words nor the description of the article which follows are Mediavilla's but quotations from an article by John E. Smith. She has not bothered to read the item she condemns. Smith, a member of the American Library Association's Intellectual Freedom Committee from 1949 to 1952, was the coauthor of the 1952 scare article that appeared in the *ALA Bulletin*, "It Happened in Burbank."[258]

It should be noted that this southern California librarian, Smith, was clearly not afraid to express his opinions and showed no evidence of the fear and crippling angst allegedly widespread among librarians at the time. Others who were obviously not suffering from such afflictions were the librarians at the University of California at Los Angeles who set up, and allowed to stand, the one-sided display about

alleged right-wing threats to American education. As the chairman of
the California State Senate Investigating Committee on Education had
to remind the Intellectual Freedom movement librarians in his state,
they were supposed to present differing views on issues.[259]

Mediavilla admires the California Library Association and its
Intellectual Freedom Committee (IFC) for defending the use in schools
of the book, *Land of the Soviets*, and the textbook series, *Building
America*. As already reported, the former had been criticized by
California State investigating committees as pro-Soviet propaganda and
the latter for being extremely critical of the United States. Mediavilla
dismisses these charges. She implies that the definitive critique of the
work by a committee-appointed researcher, Richard E. Combs, and that
by the investigating committees themselves, was the state library
association's IFC pamphlet about the *Building America* series. It
"proved Combs's criticisms to be unfounded and exaggerated"[260] and
successfully "rebutted Combs's objections point by point."[261] Her latter
assertion has an unfortunate resemblance to the traditional Intellectual
Freedom movement mantra about Earle's invalid critique of Carson's
devastating attack on Haines' *Living with Books*. And in fact, as in the
apologias by those who defend Earle without scrutinizing the texts,
there is no evidence in this article that Mediavilla ever looked at *Land
of the Soviets*, any of the volumes of *Building America*, or Combs'
competent study.[262]

Apparently, fame and durability are the measures which Mediavilla
uses to judge authors and books. To her, it is ridiculous to think that
any famous author, or any text that has been in use for many years,
could seriously be considered radical, subversive, or pro-Communist.[263]
Is Mediavilla unfamiliar with the development of "progressive"
American textbooks in the thirties and forties under the influence of
Dewey, Counts, and their Teachers College colleague, Harold Ordway
Rugg? All three were profoundly dissatisfied with their country and
dedicated to rebuilding America along very different lines. The opposition to these texts by some academics and much of the general
public did not begin with the Cold War but had begun to gain force by
the second half of the thirties.[264] As for novelists, playwrights, and
other writers, the large number who were pro-Soviet, particularly
before the Cold War began, has already been recounted. This holds
true for the three she defends: Carey McWilliams, Langston Hughes,
and Sherwood Anderson.[265] McWilliams and Hughes distinguished

themselves by publicly supporting every Moscow-ordered campaign, like that supporting Stalin's show trials in the late 1930's. Anderson was a member of dozens of pro-Soviet and Communist front groups and worked for their causes until his death in 1941. In the 1950's, Hughes publicly repudiated his Party membership and pro-Communist writings, some of which were reprinted in a book Mediavilla uses as a source. Is she unaware of all this? Why is she shocked that government representatives believed that school textbooks which included writings by these people required examination for possible subversive themes? Would she approve of a text for children containing Hughes' "Worker's song," which advocates taking control of the country and changing its name to the USSA, the United Soviet States of America?[266]

While the three thousand words in the Intellectual Freedom Committee's pamphlet dealing with the textbook series do contain a few valid criticisms of Combs' findings and methods, most are not even an evaluation of his 126 page typed study or its published version but only of his points that were reported in a *Los Angeles Times* article on the controversy.[267] (Interestingly, the paper's headline for that day was "Czechoslovakia Seized by Reds.") The research team, headed by Helen Luce of the San Bernardino County Library, included librarians in that county's school district. Together, they read eleven volumes of the *Building America* series in their investigation—but did not bother to read the one report by Richard Combs they were supposedly evaluating.

Most of the shortcomings of *Building America* that Combs points out are very real. He was well qualified to undertake such an assessment. Having served as the counsel for several legislative committees investigating subversion, he understood both the sound estimation of evidence and the subject at hand. (An active anti-Communist on both the state and national levels for over three decades, he was also an avid book collector, helped promote the antiquarian book trade in California, and served in organizations like the Friends of the Bancroft Library of the University of California at Berkeley. He became a federal judge in 1970.)

As he charges, alleged negative aspects of American life receive much attention in the Series, but criticisms of the USSR and the Communist-controlled areas of China are infrequent. Helen Luce's research team tries to explain away all of his compelling points, but

usually fails to present any solid evidence that refutes his. For
example, Combs complains that all the photos of Soviet farm life show
well-fed people, give a general impression of prosperity, and were
obtained from official Soviet sources. The researchers admit that the
pictures portray Soviet society in a positive way but lamely plead,
"Perhaps no other kind [is] available than these from an official Soviet
agency."[268] Surely a disclaimer or explanation of some kind could have
been printed with the photos in the textbooks. Supporters of the series
claimed that its goal was to help students evaluate conflicting points of
view; such a caveat could have served this instructional purpose.

There are many other instances where Combs' critics are clearly
in the wrong. He points out the connections between the Soviet and the
Chinese Communist Parties; the evaluators reply that there is not
unanimity among experts on this subject. Combs objects to the fact
that only nine of sixty photographs on American community planning
present it positively. His critics retort that there are thirty positive
photos and thirty negative ones; apparently, they consider this a proper
balance. He declares that the contemporary American family is
unfairly judged a failure; the library team counters that he did not quote
fully enough, merely noting the first sentence of the following:

"But was the American family happier? No one can answer the
question positively. Far more homes were broken by divorce than
ever in history. By 1935, the rate was about 1 divorce to every 6
marriages."[269]

Clearly, the additional sentences only serve to bolster his charge.

Combs observes that left-wing groups in America are treated well
in the *Building of America* while conservative ones are not. For
example, there is a photo of a burning cross at the University of
Southern California but no explanation that this was not the work of
right-wing racists but of the Communist Party's youth organization. He
also decries the praise accorded the critics of the Sacco and Vanzetti
conviction. Ignoring these particulars, the researchers respond de-
fiantly that in these textbooks, "Groups are praised when they defend
civil liberties, criticized when they try to deny them."[270]

The California Library Association Intellectual Freedom Committee added a brief critique of its own to the small pamphlet it
published. After proclaiming its high regard for Luce's study, it

charges that Combs' report is biased, methodologically flawed, and full of distortions and misstatements.[271] Thus, the Committee claims that he unfairly attributes the Series to "so-called subversive authors and organizations, some of them having no connection with *Building America*."[272] This charge is false. Even one of the excerpts from the *Los Angeles Times* that appears in this pamphlet contains Combs' statement that the contents of the books are "*based* on the writings of some of the most notorious Communist sympathizers in the country."[273] (Italics mine) This criticism is not truly answered by the librarians. A list inserted by the California Library Association does show that Combs uses the term "Building America authors," which could have been honestly misinterpreted by one who did not read this lawyer's study. Those listed under this rubric were authors cited in the textbooks' notes and bibliographies, thus agreeing with that part of Combs' statement above about many of the works *Building America* was *based* on. (The Committee itself indicates this too, but still disdainfully and inaccurately charges, "It is evident that those who have attacked *Building America* do not understand the use of bibliographic citations."[274]) Not only are his terms fully spelled out in his complete report, but so is the fact that some of these "authors" were people who were praised in the body of the school books. In addition, he shows that some members of the Series' editorial board belonged to Communist-front organizations.[275] The writers of the textbooks are not identified in the works themselves, only the members of the editorial board.

Combs states that the authors he refers to were active in front groups—and so they were: Oliver LaFarge, Owen Lattimore, Carey McWilliams, Anna Louise Strong, Albert Rhys Williams, Louis Adamic, and others.[276] Some were no longer part of such organizations, but their works cited in this textbook series had been written while they had been. Others were still members, still sympathetic to the USSR, and extremely critical of the United States. Regarding the librarians' use of the dismissive phrase 'so-called subversive authors and organizations'—common among anti-anti-Communists of all periods—one wonders if they would have been willing to call anyone or anything *subversive*, aside from the anti-Communists and their efforts.

While this pamphlet that defended the *Building America* series was thin in both size and substance, it was considered by the education profession to be the best response to the textbooks' critics. Accordingly, an educationist at New York University who was a member of the *Building America* editorial board declared in a journal published by the National Education Association (which also owned the textbook series) that it was "the most complete refutation of the reports of the investigators working for the California State Senate."[277] He crowed that it successfully refuted the charges—"volume for volume."[278]

As reported, the other work Mediavilla defends is *Land of the Soviets*.[279] Its author was Marguerite Ann Stewart, Secretary of the Institute of Pacific Relations. Her husband, Maxwell S. Stewart, was the volume's editor. Marguerite Stewart wrote, or edited, several other books on political affairs, some geared for children. Her collaborators on these projects included Foster Rhea Dulles and Eleanor Lattimore, the wife of Institute mainstay Owen Lattimore. The publisher of these books was usually the Institute of Pacific Relations, working in cooperation with Webster Publishing of St. Louis, but she also wrote for the Foreign Policy Association. Maxwell Stewart was a member of scores of Communist front organizations, including the IPR. For about twenty years he was also editor of Public Affairs Pamphlets, which included among its specialties the widespread distribution of anti-anti-Communist literature, like Ralph E. Ellsworth and Sarah M. Harris' *The American Right Wing*. This outspoken defender of Stalin's purge trials and the murder and imprisonment of millions of innocent people in the second half of the thirties[280] also served as an editor of *The Nation* and of *Soviet Russia Today*. The latter was issued by the Communist-controlled Friends of the Soviet Union.

Only the title of the book, *Land of the Soviets*, is named in the text of Mediavilla's article. Omitted is any mention of the Stewarts or the involvement of the Institute of Pacific Relations in its publication. Mediavilla's bibliographic citation for the work not only omits Maxwell Stewart's name—which is printed directly under his wife's on the title page in equally large letters—but the fact that its publication was a joint venture with the IPR, whose name actually appears above that of Webster Publishing on the same page. Perhaps she is unaware of the prominent role of Maxwell Stewart and the Institute of Pacific Relations in the dissemination of sophisticated propaganda. One of the Institute's techniques was to issue such agitprop alongside sounder work.[281]

The book seems geared to the sixth-grade level. Its many photographs are almost entirely of ostensibly positive things about the Soviet Union: workers' rest homes, free dormitories for university students, a new apartment house, two smiling girls hugging Joseph Stalin, and so on. The work claims to present both the good and the bad in Soviet life, but there is actually little of the latter and Soviet flaws are generally excused. A young reader would learn that ". . . a great many of the basic rights outlined in the [Soviet] constitution have existed, to a large degree at least, ever since the establishment of the Soviet system."[282] In contrast to the United States, where ". . . all business is conducted primarily for the profit of the owner," in the Soviet Union ". . . the factories and other types of business are socially owned, that is, they belong to the population as a whole and are operated by the government, not for the profit of any one person or group of individuals, but for the benefit of all the people."[283] In the area of international affairs, throughout the 1930's it was the USSR that made the greatest effort of any country to prevent a war from breaking out in Europe. Its 1938 non-aggression pact with Germany was not only quite reasonable, but the Communist country was actually forced into it by the actions of England, France, and other countries. As for the fears of the American government that the USSR wants to precipitate revolutions throughout the world, they are unwarranted. Stalin changed this policy of Lenin in 1927 and exiled Trotsky, who opposed Stalin's peaceful intentions. The unnecessary lack of trust between the Soviet Union and the Western countries led directly to World War II, so political and social cooperation with the USSR should continue after the end of the war.[284]

As the California Legislature's Joint Fact-Finding Committee on Un-American Activities showed in its 1947 report,[285] and as I have demonstrated here, the California Library Association's Intellectual Freedom Committee was wrong to support the use of *Land of the Soviets* as a textbook for schoolchildren. Similarly, Mediavilla is wrong in ignoring the contents of this propagandistic work and the Fact-Finding Committee's report on the book. As she does throughout her study, she marshals unfounded assertions rather than facts to support the IFC and its anti-anti-Communist efforts. As with the works by Pamela Spence Richards and Louise Robbins discussed earlier, the essential thrust of Mediavilla's study was ratified in the major periodic review of library historiography.[286]

Jean Preer

One can see that the historical research on Cold War librarianship done in the 1990's provides no evidence that there was much concern among the leaders of the profession with the role American libraries could play in a nation whose civilization was clearly threatened from without by increasingly menacing Communist countries as well as by Communist subversion at home. Similarly, this is not a subject that interests the authors of these historical studies. They share the priorities of those they write about: the primary danger, they maintain, came from domestic anti-Communists.

Another example of this is "The American Heritage Project: Librarians and the Democratic Tradition in the Early Cold War" by Jean Preer of Catholic University's School of Library and Information Science. Her study of the American Heritage Project—in which public librarians nationwide led group discussions about the meaning of American democracy—refers to "the increasing suspicion and paranoia of the early Cold War."[287] She contrasts the Project favorably with those "organizations of all sorts [which] undertook to rekindle patriotic fervor and to define American values"[288] in these years. (By "all sorts" she appears to mean the anti-Communist groups.) The endeavor was paid for by the Fund for Adult Education, an organization created by the Ford Foundation. Its goals frequently paralleled those soon to be advanced by another Foundation offspring already described, The Fund for the Republic. Fighting anti-Communism was one of them.[289]

Preer declares that the Project had several purposes: to increase the public's appreciation of intellectual freedom, demonstrate that libraries are an essential agency sustaining free discourse, and broaden the library's appeal among both the general populace and politicians to increase the possibility that federal financial support for public libraries would be initiated. She maintains that the program was a success. However, one must question how successful it truly was since it largely avoided the most crucial threat to human freedom—and even human existence—the world had ever seen: sophisticated, aggressive, and militarily powerful Communist states led by the Soviet Union.

She reports that Margaret Monroe, a Project librarian and later a library historian, remembered the Project dialogs thusly: ". . . group members saw these discussions as a channel to release the pervasive tensions of the early McCarthy era and the library as the one place where people felt free to talk about such issues."[290] Preer presents this rather extreme and self-serving recollection against a background in which "campaigns against subversive literature had already led to attacks on libraries."[291] She quotes the former Director General of Unesco, Walter Laves, who expressed shock to American Library Association conferees about 'some self-appointed group of pseudo-patriots'[292] concerned about their library's holdings. Preer also notes the remarks at a conference on intellectual freedom where librarians were told by Julian Boyd, American historian and former library director at Princeton University, that 'our great and incomparable heritage of free inquiry is most in danger from friends within, not from enemies without.'[293] Thus, in true Intellectual Freedom movement tradition, Preer has the threat of Soviet aggression dismissed, the specter of domestic fascism raised, and the messianic mission of librarianship asserted.

Boyd's rabid speech deserves attention because of its lack of historical perspective and its distorted view of contemporary developments. He asserted that the current controversies concerning libraries comprised nothing less than a battle between 'tyranny' and 'liberty,'[294] and that "We need Committees of Safety perhaps even more than they were needed at the time of the American Revolution, for our liberties are in greater danger."[295] Organized in 1775, the various Committees of Safety served as de facto state governments for the Revolutionary populace, maintaining law and order, overseeing the militias, and so forth. As a historian of Colonial America, Boyd certainly knew this. Thus, what he was calling for at this conference was nothing less than an insurrection against the federal government. His blatant lunacy was either not seen by Preer or not found objectionable. This is merely another instance of extremism being accepted by those in the Intellectual Freedom movement and by its historians at the same time they rail against the supposed extremism of anti-Communists.

The war to stop Communist aggression in Korea is mentioned only in passing in Preer's article, despite the fact that it took place during the very years under discussion. It was of little significance to library leaders then, and is of little significance to library historians today.

Opposing Communism—even when endorsed by their beloved United Nations—is anathema to devotees of the Intellectual Freedom movement.

Preer exhibits a lack of accurate knowledge about the time period under consideration and a concomitant trust in unreliable, often radical, analysts. Thus, she repeats some of the usual canards about those years, e.g., that Senator Joseph McCarthy never did find any Communists in the State Department.[296] For information on academics, she recommends Ellen Schrecker's extremist *No Ivory Tower*,[297] whose exuberant embrace of American Communists even embarrasses many on the Left. Preer also declares that magazine articles of the day about attempts at censorship in public libraries "demonstrated the need for a strong and coherent position of principle and professional support."[298] The tendentious pieces she notes appeared in the *Nation* and the *New Republic*, two publications sometimes targeted in such attacks upon libraries.

The *Nation* article[299] she likes—a particularly good example of a bad source—was written by Matthew Josephson, the lifelong radical who had once written for the *Daily Worker*. Always loath to criticize the USSR, he ceaselessly maligned the United States. During the Cold War, Josephson denounced those liberals, like Arthur Schlesinger, Jr., Lionel Trilling, and Reinhold Niebuhr, who vocally opposed Communist totalitarianism.[300] His vicious, distorted article in the *Nation* drew strong criticism at the time from both conservative and liberal anti-Communists for its author's refusal to admit that known Communists were anything other than liberals and for his allegation that there was a reactionary, censorial conspiracy in the United States.[301] Josephson's article was part of a special issue of the *Nation* ostensibly devoted to "Civil Liberties." Other contributors included Carey McWilliams, Arthur Eggleston, and Kirtley Mather, who—like the magazine's editor, Freda Kirchway—always found it difficult to criticize Joseph Stalin's regime.[302] The *New Leader*, which was edited by William E. Bohn and Samuel Levitas and regularly included contributors like Arthur Koestler, Sidney Hook, and Bertrand Russell, criticized the orientation of this issue of the *Nation* in which Josephson's article fit so well:

> The most significant thing about the *Nation*'s special issue is what it leaves unstated. . . . In 64 pages dedicated to freedom the

Nation does not acknowledge that Communism exists, much less that it threatens the Bill of Rights. Surely this must demonstrate a lack of intelligence or honesty, or both. If it be argued that the *Nation* elected to deal only with the "domestic" threat, this reveals as provincial a view of the world as Colonel McCormick's. Would the same magazine, ten years ago, have devoted so much wordage to freedom without framing the issue against the overriding problem of the time, Nazism?

Editor Freda Kirchway goes even further than her contributors, for she sees the United States as "heading up the new counter-revolution" and leaves the impression that Russia is heading up the new revolution. . . . What it shows is that the *Nation*, not America, is gripped by fear—fear of reality, fear of truth, fear of struggle. . . . America, rejecting fear, whether McCarthy-induced or Kirchway-induced, has courageously and hopefully staked its future upon the victory of the only genuine revolutionary force in the world—democracy.[303]

While the American Heritage Project that Preer lauds did not *require* particular subjects or readings by its participants, the focus was clearly on the material in the book *Living Ideas in America*, edited by Henry Steele Commager and published by Harper in 1951. The well-known Columbia University history professor acknowledged in his preface that the concept for the volume came from the American Library Association.[304] He stated in his introduction, "I have tried to present opposing points of view, but it would be folly to pretend that I have been wholly objective in my choice of material or to attempt to conceal the fact that my own sympathies are those of a Jeffersonian liberal."[305]

The few selections and comments in *Living Ideas in America* that dealt with the Soviet Union made it clear that Commager did not think highly of that country and believed it should be opposed.[306] However, there was less than one would expect in his book about how to counter the USSR, an aggressive nuclear power (with the largest modern army in the world) that espoused a view of "the good society" that was antithetical to that of the United States. This would certainly seem to qualify as one of the "complex problems that confront our society today"[307] that he claimed the book would clarify. The editor's failure to deal adequately with Communism is indicated by the fact that although the war in Korea had begun at the end of June 1950 and this work was issued in 1951 (Commager's preface is dated August of that year), there is no mention of the conflict anywhere in the book.

Despite his claim to be a Jeffersonian, Commager frequently expressed opinions that did not reflect his mentor's belief in the wisdom of the general public or display this founding father's knowledge of, and respect for, those who held ideas different from his. For example, the historian caricatured all opponents of Roosevelt's New Deal as people who "associated reform with Socialism and, by a curious confusion, associated Socialism with Communism."[308] There were many selections with introductions by Commager inveighing against loyalty oaths and government investigations into subversive activities; no readings were provided in their defense. On the subject of requiring college faculty members to declare that they are not Communists, he remarked: "Here, as so often, those vocally most zealous for 'Americanism' and 'loyalty' were the first to violate the true principles of American democracy and to flout the Constitution."[309] In the same context he also referred to "superpatriotic alumni."[310] (It should be pointed out that many of these oaths not only placed Communism beyond the pale, but alluded to other doctrines that would have prevented a professor from freely seeking the truth and/or instructing his or her students to do the same.) Much of the volume dealt with the alleged dangers posed by anti-Communism.[311]

The other book which stemmed from the American Heritage Project was Gerald W. Johnson's *This American People*.[312] Johnson stated in his work that ". . . without the friendly interest of the American Library Association, represented by Dr. Ralph E. Ellsworth, Director of Libraries at the University of Iowa, this book would never have been undertaken. . . ."[313] Like Commager's work, it was supposed to relate current American crises to traditional American thought and values, and it too was published by Harper in 1951. However, unlike *Living Ideas in America*, it was nothing more than the entirely eccentric, dogmatic views of its author. His manifest goal was not to raise questions and encourage discussion, but to provide facile answers.

Johnson's previous books were popular works on American history, life, and politics. He was also a journalist and radio commentator. *This American People* was short in length and written mainly in a simple, informal style suitable for an eleven-year-old child. The ideas expressed were simplistic. For example, his description of anti-Communists was composed mainly of negative stereotypes:

> Unfortunately, though, belief in dictatorship in the form of thought
> control is not confined to Communists, nor to Fascists, nor to
> Czarists, nor to the Lamaists of Tibet. It is shared by some people
> who hate communism and who regard themselves as being as far
> from communism as the poles are apart. It is shared, or at least it
> is tolerated, by all those whose fear of the future is greater than
> their hope; and this is characteristic of many native-born Americans,
> some of them highly intelligent.[314]

The insubstantiality of the book is shocking. The following statement by Johnson on voting in America gives some indication of this:

> But the voter who votes by labels and catchwords and slogans
> instead of by thinking is not voting honestly. When we vote for a
> man because he is called a Democrat or a Republican, a Socialist or
> a Capitalist, a Red or a White, and not because we sincerely believe
> that he is the best man running for the job, then we are abandoning
> that honesty on which the Founding Fathers relied; and, of course,
> if we abandon their kind of honesty, then their kind of government
> cannot be expected to work for us.[315]

The concept that a politician may well be a member of a particular
political party for ideological reasons was apparently not considered
important by this author. Moreover, common sense would indicate that
a party directly controlled by a hostile foreign power and acting on its
behalf—as the Communist Party of the United States was—could
rationally be considered a fifth column rather than a legitimate,
indigenous political organization.[316]

Johnson made it clear that he detested the USSR.[317] However, he
declared that the Soviet Union was a threat to America only if
Americans were frightened by that country.[318] His assertions seemed
to indicate that the United States could be protected from the USSR
largely through the power of positive thinking!

He advocated a maximalist position on intellectual freedom. Thus,
he believed that while the Soviet Union had indeed erected an Iron
Curtain, the United States was doing so too, pointing to the fact that
American nuclear scientists had been prevented from communicating
with those in the USSR. While this would seem to have been a wise

precaution, to Johnson it indicated that America was already on the slippery slope downward. Once again, he declaimed his slogan that *fear* had outstripped *hope*.[319] He also made pronouncements that opposed any laws hindering the Communist Party in the United States, criticized those he claimed were against academic freedom, and ridiculed those who wanted young people to salute the flag in school.[320] Johnson also declared that Communism posed no threat within the United States because, at its contemporary rate of growth, the Communist Party would take forty thousand years for it to gain the majority of votes.[321] This was a red herring: anti-Communists did not believe that the danger posed by domestic Communists was their getting voted into power.

Fellow liberal Arthur M. Schlesinger, Jr., who liked the book's political orientation, pointed out some of its limitations:

> Unfortunately, Johnson confines himself in the main to restatements of the main themes of the American past without going much beyond affirmation in showing how they will help us ward off the concrete dangers of the present. . . . *This American People* gets vague and hortatory just when you want it to get down to business.[322]

Schlesinger also questioned Johnson's thesis that the domestic and international questions facing Americans could be answered merely by the wisdom of the past: new ideas and solutions might well be called for.

Both authors chosen to produce books for the American Heritage Project were known quantities. Commager and Johnson had written numerous works on contemporary political affairs, as well as American history, so their views on such things as active anti-Communism were already matters of public record.[323] The leaders of the library profession—particularly Ralph E. Ellsworth, chair of the American Library Association committee overseeing the selection of these books for the American Heritage Project—got what they wanted: two liberal works unsuitable for fostering a true interchange of ideas on contemporary American problems, particularly the threat posed by the Soviet Union and how to oppose it. And Jean Preer's celebratory history of this Project failed to analyze these two partisan books that were central to the endeavor.

Far-Left Models and Sources for
Contemporary Library Historians

An important element of the recent tendentious studies emanating from the schools of library and information studies are their full acceptance of fantastic New Left—and even Old Left—histories. These university-based historians of librarianship utilize these works by professional anti-anti-Communists to support their analogous theses, and they point their readers to them for further instruction. Some instances of this have already been given. Louise Robbins uses books by Ellen Schrecker, David Caute, Richard M. Freeland, and Athan Theoharis. Jean Preer finds works by Schrecker and Paul Boyer significant. A 1996 historical study by Christine Jenkins, an assistant professor at the University of Illinois' Graduate School of Library and Information Science, relies, in part, on a volume by Fred J. Cook. (Jenkins' research focuses on librarians of the 1950's battling "super-patriot pressure groups" and "Red-hunters" who did not want to send children's books overseas that were critical of the United States or were written by members, or former members, of "so-called 'subversive' organizations."[324] Note that the only word she puts in quotation marks here is *subversive*. Given some of the authors Jenkins names, this means that she believes that (1) even the Communist Party of the United States has never been subversive, and (2) prominent activity within Stalinist organizations was of no significance.)

Let us look at what some political moderates have written about the specific works relied on by historians of librarianship. One could counter their words by saying that there have been positive evaluations by other people, but the quality of such assessments would need to be considered. After all, when the scholarly journal of the primary organization of US historians selects the self-admitted theoretician of the Communist Party, Herbert Aptheker, to review a book by Ellen Schrecker, one would *expect* him to applaud her view that there was a widespread suppression of freedom throughout America in the 1950's, as well as in other periods.[325] And he does. The evaluations given below are from the dwindling number of those not on the far-Left who have been given the opportunity to appraise historical studies.

Like most moderates, Nathan Glazer has dismissed Schrecker's *No Ivory Tower: McCarthyism and the Universities*. In his review for *The New Republic*, he declared that he found little that was credible in her main point: that the domestic "Communist threat was nonexistent; the investigators were malign and self-interested; [and] their victims were well-intentioned men and women who acted out of the highest motives. . . ."326

Of Caute's *The Great Fear*, Arthur Schlesinger, Jr., wrote in the *New York Times Book Review*: "He gets too many facts wrong. . . . I really don't recognize the America of that period in Mr. Caute's feverish account. . . . The book's essential deficiencies, however, are analytical. Mr. Caute does not seem to have thought through what he is trying to say."327

The *Political Science Quarterly* review by John P. Roche of Tufts University stated that "Regrettably the major premise of *The Great Fear*—that under Presidents Truman and Eisenhower the United States suffered its greatest crisis in democratic values as anti-Communist posses terrorized the land—is merely ludicrous."328 *The New Yorker* dismissed the book because Caute was unable to perceive any of the legitimate concerns about Communism at the time. "Thus, most of his book becomes a dismal catalogue of American misdeeds on every level (federal, state, municipal) of every branch of government."329

Sidney Hook wrote a lengthy reaction to *The Great Fear* titled "David Caute's Fable of 'Fear and Terror': On 'Reverse McCarthyism.' "330 He attacked the author for his "fantasy picture of a nation swept by hysterias of fear synthetically contrived by its political leaders."331 He went on to say that even during the height of McCarthy's prominence, ". . . the leading newspapers of the country were criticising, indeed denouncing him. His methods, tactics and words were under impassioned attack in almost every large educational centre of the nation."332 Hook declared that Caute primarily—and erroneously—criticized the liberal anti-Communists rather than the actual wrongdoers, whom he identified as the Communists and their McCarthyite opponents.333 Giving numerous examples, he attributed the author's ideas to his "obsessions," "historical ignorance," "political ignorance," "naiveté," "political animus"334 and "anti-American animus."335 (Incidentally, Caute is English.) His methodological faults included "selective quotation" and "irresponsible exaggeration."336

The 1972 review of Richard M. Freeland's *The Truman Doctrine and the Origins of McCarthyism* in the *New York Times Book Review*337 was scathing. Freeland's thesis was that the basics of McCarthyist anti-

Communism were a natural outgrowth of Truman's policies. William Shannon, the reviewer, had covered Truman as a reporter and was now a member of the *Times'* editorial board. He observed that the author relied heavily on speculation rather than evidence and ignored facts and events which did not suit his interpretation, such as the ugly realities of domestic Communism and Communist expansion elsewhere in the world. Freeland also ignored the variegated and widely held anti-Communism found among the American people in the period under discussion. In essence, observed Shannon, Freeland had reprised the 1948 views of Henry A. Wallace and his Progressive Party. Such ideas, he said, could have found a commercial publisher (Knopf) only at a time when there was so much antagonism towards America's war in Vietnam. Freeland's book had originally been his doctoral dissertation.

Athan Theoharis' *Seeds of Repression: Harry S. Truman and the Origins of McCarthyism*[338] blamed the Cold War and what he called "McCarthyism" primarily on the Democratic President. One would have expected the Marquette University history professor to document his arguments carefully given their great departure from the views then typically held by academics and non-academics, but he did not: the volume had neither footnotes nor endnotes. Apparently, one was expected to accept all of the authors' statements on faith. The reviewer for the *Journal of Politics* declared the work "blatantly tendentious."[339] It received an equally negative assessment in *The American Historical Review*,[340] where it was pointed out that ". . . the Soviet Union was more than a 'bogie' manufactured by Truman and McCarthy . . . ," and that the book's theses were "simplistic," "poorly documented," and "unconvincing."[341] The *Annals of the American Academy of Political and Social Science* judged the volume unworthy of "engaging the attention of serious readers."[342]

Journalist Fred J. Cook had written nine books before producing *The Nightmare Decade: The Life and Times of Senator Joe McCarthy*[343] in 1971. One of these volumes was a defense of Alger Hiss, another a supposed exposé of the FBI. Thomas C. Reeves wrote in the *Journal of American History* of Cook's *Nightmare Decade*: "poorly researched, badly written, and aimed at the mass market, it demands no serious attention from scholars."[344] It presented a picture where Communist subversion was merely a right-wing fabrication. Its simplistic interpretations were based on inadequate source material. Reeves expressed the hope that his fellow historians would produce a comprehensive picture of the era: "Until we do gullible students will be citing Cook."[345] Reeves should have added gullible professors.

One does wonder how anyone could take a book seriously that has as its opening sentence: "It was a time of national paranoia in which the greatest power on earth expended its energies hunting for Communists under every bed; in which millions of average Americans looked fearfully over their shoulders, wondering whether *they* would be tapped next to explain themselves before the grand inquisitors."[346] In Cook's foreword and last chapter, he declared that another era of McCarthyism was beginning led by the likes of Spiro Agnew and George Wallace. Perhaps these alarmist sections provided a perverse appeal to some readers, thereby weakening their critical abilities.[347]

Paul S. Boyer's *By the Bomb's Early Light: American Thought and Culture at the Dawn of the Atomic Age* was the creation of a man obsessed by a fear of nuclear weaponry who believed that most other people were similarly fixated, or should have been.[348] "So fully does the nuclear reality pervade my consciousness that it is hard to imagine what existence would have been like without it,"[349] he told his readers at the beginning of this 1985 work. Atomic weapons, Boyer asserted, were "the supreme menace of our age."[350] A pacifist, a conscientious objector in the 1950's, and a longtime campaigner for disarmament, he was unable to do what most others could: control their fear and support political and military policies most likely to avert disaster. *By the Bomb's Early Light* minimized the genuine threat posed by the USSR during the Cold War and praised the judgments of revisionist historians like David Caute, Athan Theoharis, and Walter LaFeber.[351]

The fear of Communism, claimed Boyer, was foisted on the American people by the country's elites. It was a contrivance that redirected the fear of the atomic bomb. Boyer not only dismissed the threat posed by Communism, but he sometimes tried to deny Communism's very existence. For example, he was either unable or unwilling to clearly state that after World War II it was Communists who were attempting to seize control of Greece by force. Instead, he wrote of an American move in 1947 to provide "funds for military aid to aid a corrupt and repressive Greek regime in defeating its opponents in a bitter and murky civil war. . . ."[352] Either this alleged murk made it impossible for Boyer to see that those who had instigated this war were Communists, or he considered this fact of no importance.

It is interesting that Boyer has also written books about the Salem witch trials and about book censorship in the United States,[353] two other areas of great interest to anti-anti-Communist librarians. Both works, of course, purported to show the underside of American history. However, it is not surprising that this professor of history at the University of Wisconsin has still not forsaken his primary passion, and his longtime career, of writing about the USA's alleged evil involvement with nuclear weapons.[354]

McCarthyism *and the Library Historians*

Over the past half-century, charges of so-called "McCarthyism" have appeared so frequently in the aforementioned works by librarians and library historians that some discussion of this is necessary. In most cases, the use of this pejorative substitutes for the provision of facts and analysis. For fifty years, numberless accusations of McCarthyism have been irresponsibly—but effectively—used to cudgel or dismiss anti-Communists, often with no regard for their actual political views. Among the more highly educated, the fear of being labelled a McCarthyite has frequently made people reluctant to express anti-Communist sentiments, or to even utter the word *Communism*.[355] Historian Richard Gid Powers, a strong critic of McCarthy, has written that in the late fifties and the sixties discussions of Communism became rare because of the "hysteria over anticommunist 'extremism,' to a great extent manufactured and manipulated by self-styled 'moderates' to suit their own political purposes."[356] In 1980 Norman Podhoretz pointed out that ". . . a key term has quietly disappeared from the discussion of the Soviet-American conflict. It is the term 'Communism.' "[357] He stressed the impossibility of understanding the international situation without using this word and comprehending its meaning.[358]

As already reported, Louise Robbins offers a definition of *McCarthyism* that, unfortunately, is widely accepted. She charges that it consists primarily of "assigning guilt by association" and "witch-hunting" to instill fear in others.[359] Both derogatory clichés have already been critiqued in this volume, as has the fabrication that a "climate of fear" existed throughout the country due to overzealous anti-Communists. Since its inception in 1950 by *Washington Post* political cartoonist Herb Block ("Herblock"), and its widespread use by Owen Lattimore in the following months,[360] the meaning of *McCarthyism* has almost always been negative. Definitions offered by McCarthy and his supporters—that it was "Americanism with its sleeves rolled up," or "the refusal to accept totalitarianism of any kind"—did not prevail linguistically. However, this eponymic epithet does not even accurately describe the activities of Joseph McCarthy, let alone those of more temperate anti-Communists.

It is misfortunate that the image of the Senator held by most people today has largely been formed by a few negative lines in history textbooks and by highly inaccurate television documentaries and "docudramas." These portray him as an amoral opportunist, a ruthless—or even demented—troglodyte with no concern for the truth and no positive accomplishments.[361] The depiction is much the same in most works produced by academics.[362]

Many of his critics have always claimed that they opposed his methods, not his anti-Communist goals. This is belied by the fact that one rarely sees or reads comparable attacks on the equally combative approach used by many of his contemporary Congressional colleagues, including his foes. For example, Senator Ralph Flanders compared him to Hitler in a speech to the upper house. (Ironically, Flanders soon initiated the resolution to censure McCarthy for conduct unbecoming a Senator!) Historian Arthur Herman of George Mason University has written in his recent biography of the legislator from Wisconsin that "McCarthy's opponents could dish it out better than they could take it."[363] Fiery Congressional hearings like those McCarthy sometimes ran were not uncommon in the 1950's. McCarthy's pugnacity was certainly equalled by that of Senator Estes Kefauver, who so delighted liberals by his truculence in his public inquiries on crime early in the decade that he was later selected as Adlai Stevenson's running mate in the 1956 presidential election. (It should be noted that McCarthy's investigations, like Kefauver's, were entirely legal.) The hostility McCarthy elicited was thus not due as much to his manners or procedures as his aims. It is probable that a question raised earlier in this chapter would have to be answered in the negative when it comes to McCarthy. He would not have been viewed much more favorably among his detractors if he had been the type to elegantly declare: "It would be wise to recall Cicero's words, '*Pares vetere proverbio cum paribus facillime congregantur.' "*

The goal of many of his probes was to oust security risks in the federal government. He frequently did so using the guidelines of the various agencies themselves or even the specific recommendations of their own internal investigatory departments, which were being ignored. In these cases, the real reasons for the opposition to McCarthy included partisan party loyalty—as with Democratic politicians—and devotion to, or fear of, party leaders—as with those fellow Republicans who opposed him after Eisenhower became president.

A negative view of McCarthy has also been created by what today would be called *sound bites, pseudoevents,* or *media events.* For example, most historically aware people have seen, heard, or read the well-staged, rhetorical question to the Senator during the Army-McCarthy hearings by the crafty attorney, Joseph Welch, who quietly feigned a doleful judgment: "Have you no sense of decency, sir?" This sham, which drew applause from the journalists and opponents of McCarthy packed into the hearing room, immediately and irreparably harmed McCarthy's image since it was broadcast live on television and radio.[364]   In contrast, even today one does not hear any criticism of Welch's earlier remarks concerning "pixies" and "fairies," alluding to the belief held by many that McCarthy's assistants, Roy Cohn and David Schine, were not heterosexual.   Welch's tasteless, biased remarks elicited sustained laughter from the supportive audience. This too served to undermine the Senator and his investigating team. Welch, a cagey, self-possessed, New England trial lawyer, was treated like a hero by the mainstream news media throughout the hearings.[365]

The now widely held belief that journalists were afraid of McCarthy until the objective reporter, Edward R. Murrow, exposed him in early 1954 on his *See It Now* television program is false. Even two of McCarthy's most bitter critics broke ranks with their "progressive" colleagues and declared that Murrow's famous production was mere propaganda because he was so highly selective in his choice of film clips of the Senator.[366]   Moreover, McCarthy was justifiably angered by Murrow's carefully chosen remarks on this show that the Senator had 'given considerable comfort to our enemies,' indicating that in some way he had committed treason.   No one has paid much attention to the fact that Murrow soon afterwards declared on another of his CBS television news programs that McCarthy headed "a private Gestapo within the ranks of those employed by the federal government." The meaning of this remark was also clear: McCarthy was a dangerous Nazi.[367] Despite such egregious transgressions, the general academic consensus has been that McCarthy was an irresponsible assailant while Murrow was a perceptive, fair-minded journalist.

From the very beginning of McCarthy's high-profile anti-Communist efforts, he was opposed by the *New York Times*, the *Washington Post*, the *New York Herald-Tribune*, and other major newspapers.[368] Henry Luce, apparently deciding that McCarthy was déclassé, had *Time* magazine put the Senator on its front cover in October 1951, and had him savaged in the accompanying article for his alleged sartorial and political slovenliness.[369] (This received a factual rejoinder from Nora de Toledano in the *American Mercury*.[370]) The *Washington Post* was so eager to believe the worst about McCarthy, and so willing to do anything to prove it true, that in 1954 it helped pay a self-proclaimed spy on the Senator's staff. For most of the year, the leaders of the Democratic Party and the liberal Americans for Democratic Action were fooled and fleeced by this confidence man. The chief liasion with the bogus agent was ADA director Joseph Rauh, who four years earlier had criticized anti-Communists for their alleged 'confidential informants, dossiers, [and] political spies.'[371] None of the supposed sleuth's far-fetched stories were checked until shortly before a projected twelve-part series based on them was about to begin running in the *Washington Post*. All turned out to be fabrications, like the one about McCarthy's purported arms cache secreted in the Senate building which he and Roy Cohn intended to use to overthrow the government.[372] As one can see, the methods of these prominent anti-McCarthy forces were neither rational nor principled, but when made public they were not criticized by the major liberal newspapers of the day because their goal was considered laudable: to "get" McCarthy. Likewise, while this madcap story of the "spy" and his besotted "handlers" was well-known in the 1950's, it has rarely been mentioned by historians and by biographers of McCarthy because it does not fit the stereotypical picture they cleave to.

The snippets of McCarthy most often presented today usually show only McCarthy's blunt side, when he was most prone to seem heavy-handed or to hyperbolize. Does any book or documentary present anything from the 1952 televised interview with a subdued, genial McCarthy on the prestigious CBS news program *Chronoscope*? The answer, of course, is no, despite the fact that both a transcript and a videotape of the show are available.

Similarly, few people—and none of the historians of librarianship who frequently refer to the probes—bother to read the transcripts of the thorough, workmanlike hearings the Senator held to investigate the federal government's overseas libraries. These chronicles provide a compelling description of the libraries' failure to carry out their legally mandated objectives. For example, they did not provide as many anti-Communist books and periodicals as pro-Communist ones, and their shelves were filled with the works of William Z. Foster and other prominent Party members. In addition, the accounts show that McCarthy was actually courtly with witnesses who were honest with him, like Langston Hughes, whose Communist writings from earlier years were still being provided through these libraries. The person most abused at these hearings was McCarthy himself, who was consistently needled by hostile witnesses, like the Communist William Marx Mandell, whose books were carried by the libraries abroad. James Wechsler, the Editor of the *New York Post*, equated McCarthy with Stalin during his testimony.[373]

Not only did McCarthy uncover valuable information, but, more than anyone else, he alerted the American public to the government's laxness in opposing Communism abroad and at home. In some cases, he was responsible for the production of rigorous research. One example was the important report by his staff member, Robert Kennedy, which clearly showed how the ships of neutral countries and America's supposed allies were making war-related goods available to the Communists in China and Korea while young Americans were fighting and dying on the Korean peninsula.[374] And contrary to the received knowledge today, the senator from Wisconsin did make public a number of security risks, pro-Communists, and Soviet agents working in the federal government.[375] Significantly, he did so at a time when other political figures lacked the courage to do so. His unflagging bravery, like that demonstrated in World War II, is usually either disregarded or dismissed.[376]

Yes, McCarthy tended to overstate his case, but any misconceptions he may have had about the Soviet Union and Communism appear minor, and far less dangerous, when compared to those of most of his critics. Moreover, any slurs he made against others were—and continue to be—surpassed by those made against him. In the end, he doomed himself because his devotion to his cause surpassed his political acumen: he attacked flaccid anti-Communism among members of his own political party, just as he had done with Democrats.

While McCarthy did not have much of a following among academics and intellectuals, there were, and are, some who have closely studied his words and actions and have proceeded to clearly articulate and defend his contributions to the anti-Communist movement. The reader is referred to the writings of William F. Buckley, Willmoore Kendall, James Burnham, Frank S. Meyer, William Schlamm, Kenneth Colgrove, M. Stanton Evans, Arthur Herman and others. Many of them have also analyzed the widespread distortion of McCarthy's statements, methods, and goals, which has produced what Schlamm called the liberal/left "folklore of 'McCarthyism.' "[377]

Relevant discussions of McCarthy's supporters, antagonists, and the conflict concerning the overseas libraries have appeared earlier in this volume: in the material about Senator William Benton in chapter six, "The Overseas Libraries Dispute" in chapter seven, and in part of chapter eight.

The demonization of Joseph McCarthy by library historians; and their facile, uninformed, and total dismissal of his work; provide additional evidence of the quality of their scholarship. Their blithe and frequent use of the slanderous and propagandistic term *McCarthyism* has not revealed any truths, but obscured them.

NOTES

1. Descriptons and analyses of the triumph of the adversary culture in modern higher education are: Paul Hollander, "Higher Education: Reservoir of the Adversary Culture," in his *Anti-Americanism: Irrational and Rational*, with new intro. (New Brunswick, NJ: Transaction Publishers, 1995, pp. 146-214; originally published as *Anti-Americanism: Critiques at Home and Abroad, 1965-1990* [New York and Oxford: Oxford University Press, 1992]); Roger Kimball, *Tenured Radicals: How Politics has Corrupted Our Higher Education*, rev. ed. with new intro. (Chicago: Ivan R. Dee, 1998); "The Academy in the Age of

Political Correctness," section two of *Against the Grain: The New Criterion at the End of the Twentieth Century*, ed. by Hilton Kramer and Roger Kimball (Chicago: Ivan R. Dee, 1995), pp. 67-134; Dario Fernández-Morera, *American Academia and the Survival of Marxist Ideas* (Westport, CT, and London: Praeger, 1996); Edith Kurzweil and William Phillips, eds., *Our Country, Our Culture: The Politics of Political Correctness* (N.p.: Partisan Review Press, 1994); and the articles by David Bromwich, Margery Sabin, Denis Donoghue, Gertrude Himmelfarb, and Frank Kermode in *What's Happened to the Humanities?* ed. by Alvin Kernan (Princeton, NJ: Princeton University Press, 1997).

Since 1987, scores of articles on the decline and politicization of higher education have appeared in *Academic Questions*, the quarterly journal of the National Association of Scholars. It is essential reading for those studying this subject.

Other professional schools besides those in library and information studies have moved far to the Left in recent decades. See: Rita Kramer, *Ed School Follies: The Miseducation of America's Teachers* (New York: Free Press, 1991); Sally Satel, *PC, M. D.: How Political Correctness is Corrupting Medicine* (New York: Basic Books, 2000); Daniel A. Farber and Suzanna Sherry, *Beyond All Reason: The Radical Assault on Truth in American Law* (New York: Oxford University Press, 1997); and Aimee Howd, "Law Schools vs. Dissenting Views," *Insight* 15 (Dec. 20, 1999): 16-17, 39.

Books dealing primarily with the field of history are: Gertrude Himmelfarb, *On Looking Into the Abyss: Untimely Thoughts on Culture and Society* (New York: Knopf, 1994); and Keith Windschuttle, *The Killing of History: How Literary Critics and Social Theorists are Murdering Our Past* (New York: The Free Press, 1996). The lack of open debate within the history profession's usual channels of comunication are described in Tom Nichols, "H-Net and Beyond: A Real Academic Dialogue at Last," *Heterodoxy* 7 (March 1999): 1, 11-13. He believes that the Internet has begun to provide an outlet for scholars to express views not acceptable to the Leftist academic establishment, although submissions must sometimes be done anonymously to preserve people's careers. Liberal historian David Brinkley offers some insight into why academic historians seem incapable of writing fairly about conservatives in "The Problem of American Conservatism," *American Historical Review* 99 (April 1994): 409-29.

Even closer to the focus of this book are: John Earl Haynes, "The Cold War Debate Continues: A Traditionalist View of Historical Writing on Domestic Communism and Anti-Communism," *Journal of Cold War Studies* 2 (Winter 2000): 76-115; Haynes, "Historians Scramble for New Party Lines," *Heterodoxy* 4 (Sept. 1996): 8-9; Haynes, letter, *Reviews in American History* 25 (Sept. 1997): 528-30; Edward S. Shapiro, "Responsibility for the Cold War: A

Bibliographical Review," *Intercollegiate Review* (Winter 1976-1977), as reprinted in his *Clio from the Right: Essays of a Conservative Historian* (Washington, DC: University Press of America, 1983), pp. 255-62; Robert J. Maddox, *The New Left and the Origins of the Cold War* (Princeton, NJ: Princeton University Press, 1973); Lee Congdon, "Anti-Anti-Communism," *Academic Questions* 1 (Summer 1988): 42-54; Maddox, "A Visit to Cloudland: Cold War Revisionism in College Texts," *Continuity*, no. 20 (Spring 1996): 1-11. The reviews by Arthur Schlesinger, Jr., Nathan Glazer, and others described later in this work also show the lack of objectivity and the leftist tilt of books by prominent historians.

Nearly all of the aforementioned works show that the discipline of history is almost entirely populated by highly subjective "progressive" academics. It is not surprising, therefore, that the primary journals in the field—which are directly controlled by the two major associations, the American Historical Association and the Organization of American Historians, reflect these biases. So too do almost all the periodicals issued by other publishers. Not only do the "mainstream" journals distribute the new counter-culture historiography, but there are also academic journals catering solely to the most extreme on the Left. Thus, Cambridge University Press issues *Radical History Review*; Oxford University Press offers *History Workshop Journal*. In contrast to the numerous history journals on the Left, there is only one that is manifestly conservative: *Continuity*. Issued only twice per year by the Center for the American Idea, it has far fewer subscribers than either *Radical History Review* or *History Workshop Journal*.

The book publishers also know their audience and readily publish trendy, politically correct pseudo-scholarship in order to survive economically. (See William C. Dowling, "Saving Scholarly Publishing in the Age of Oprah: The Glastonbury Project," *Journal of Scholarly Publishing* 28 [April 1997]: 115-34.) In many cases, it is all too clear that publishers are *striving* to advance the anti-American cause. Thus, the City University of New York's New Press publishes books on the Cold War in which extremist authors of the far-Left, like Noam Chomsky and Howard Zinn, heap blame on the United States. (See Stephen Karetzky, "CIA Funds for Intellectuals," [letter], *The Chronicle of Higher Education* [May 12, 2000]: B13.)

Complementing the textbooks, journals, and monographs are the books issued in prestigious series and the reference works sold largely to libraries. There too one finds perverse "revisionist" views on the history of Soviet-American relations and the history of Communism.   Among these em-barrassments are: (1) the 1997 multivolume *Encyclopedia of U.S. Foreign Policy*, a product of the Council on Foreign Relations and Oxford University Press; (2) the volume in the *Cambridge History of American Foreign Relations* that covers the years 1945-1991, and (3) the *Columbia* [University] *History of the Twentieth Century.* Anyone looking for information on Julius and Ethel Rosenberg in the twenty-four volume *American National Biography*, a project overseen by the American Council of Learned Societies and recently issued by Oxford University Press, will learn that the couple may not only have been innocent of spying, but may not even have been Communists! (For a critique of these works, see Henry D. Fetter, "Victory into Defeat: The Cold War on the Reference Shelf," *Heterodoxy* 8 [June/July 2000]: 1, 8, 10-12.)

2. George Santayana, *Character and Opinion in the United States* (London: Constable, 1920; as reprinted: New York: George Braziller, 1955), pp. 28-29. Known for being critical of much that was—and remains—American, Santayana also recognized many positive aspects of the American national character. For example, in addition to the above mentioned conservative values, he noted the "fund of vigour, goodness, and hope such as no nation ever possessed before." (Ibid., p. 4) He also admired Americans' bravery, love of achievement, and absence of malice. Santayana maintained that the United States had expanded the admirable English notions of individual liberty, voluntary cooperation, and democracy. (Ibid., pp. 4, 109-10)

3. See the caricature drawn in Ellen Schrecker's *No Ivory Tower: McCarthyism and the Universities* (New York and Oxford: Oxford University Press, 1986). Some of the basic distortions of this work are pointed out in the book review by Nathan Glazer, "The Professors and the Party," *New Republic* (Oct. 6, 1986): 39-42. An early attempt by social scientists to *prove* the supposed chilling effect McCarthyism had on scholarly research does not withstand close scrutiny. The alleged findings were more closely related to the biases of the researchers and their subjects than to the data collected. (See Ernest van den Haag, "McCarthyism and the Professors," review of *The Academic Mind: Social Scientists in a Time of Crisis*, by Paul Lazarsfeld and Wagner Thielens, Jr. [Glencoe, IL: Free Press, 1958] *Commentary* 27 [Feb. 1959]: 179-82.) David Riesman helped carry out the Lazarsfeld-Thielens study.

Other critiques of the supposed oppression by the Right on campuses are: Sidney Hook, *Heresy,* Yes; *Conspiracy,* No (New York: John Day, 1953), pp. 61-64; Eugene Lyons, "Is Freedom of Expression Really Threatened? The Hysteria over Hysteria," *American Mercury* 76 (Oct. 1953): 22-33; Robert E. Fitch, "The Fears of the Intelligentsia: The Present Slough of Despond," *Commentary* 18 (Oct. 1954): 328-35; and John P. Roche, "Was Everyone Terrified? The Mythology of 'McCarthyism,' " *Quadrant* [Sydney] 33 (Sept. 1989): 31-39. Fitch, a theologian, was Dean and Professor at the Pacific School of Religion in Berkeley, California. Roche, a liberal in the fifties who became Chairman of Americans for Democratic Action, later became a political scientist at Brandeis and Tufts.

4. See: Francis G. Wilson, "Intellectuals and the American Tradition," *Education* [London] 63 (March 1943): 391-403; William F. Buckley, Jr., *God and Man at Yale: The Superstitions of "Academic Freedom,"* with new intro. by Buckley (Washington, DC: Regnery Gateway, 1986; originally published: Chicago: Henry Regnery, 1951); M. Stanton Evans, *Revolt on the Campus* (Chicago: Henry Regnery, 1961); Nancy Jane Fellers, "God and Woman at Vassar," *The Freeman* 3 (Nov. 3, 1952): 83-86; Patricia B. Bozell, "Liberal Education at Vassar," *The Freeman* (Jan. 12, 1953): 269-72; Robert Fitch, "The Fears of the Intelligentsia"; and E. Merrill Root, *Collectivism on the Campus: The Battle for the Mind in American Colleges* (New York: Devin-Adair, 1955). Russell Kirk covers the years 1953 through 1977 in *Decadence and Renewal in the Higher Learning: An Episodic History of American University and College since 1953* (South Bend, IN: Gateway Editions, 1978). Francis G. Wilson was a widely published political scientist at the University of Illinois. Root, a professor of English at Earlham College, wrote six books of poetry and several works of non-fiction. (An admirer, Robert Frost, puckishly called him "the second best poet in America.") Both Fellers and Bozell had attended Vassar. Bozell, the sister of William F. Buckley, Jr., wrote primarily about religion in the ensuing years.

5. John Lewis Gaddis, "The Tragedy of Cold War History," *Diplomatic History* 17 (Winter 1993): 1-16.

6. William Appleman Williams, *The Tragedy of American Diplomacy* (Cleveland: World, 1959). In 1962, a revised and enlarged edition was published by Dell of New York for widespread sale as a mass market paperback. Clearly, there was a large market for anti-American books of this type even before the Vietnam War began making such sentiments much more widespread.

7. See Gaddis, "The Tragedy of Cold War History," p. 7n30, and p. 15.

8. Ibid., p. 1.

9. Gaddis maintained that Marx and his philosophy were benevolent, but that the latter was distorted by Lenin and his followers. In truth, the facts about Marx's personality and his philosophy are quite ugly. (For succinct overviews, see Paul Johnson, "Karl Marx," in *Intellectuals*, by Johnson [New York: Harper & Row, 1988], pp. 52-81; Richard Wurmbrand, *Marx and Satan* [Westchester, IL: Crossway Books, 1986]; and Thomas Sowell, *Marxism: Philosophy and Economics* [New York: William Morrow, 1985].)

10. See, for example, John Lewis Gaddis, "On Moral Equivalency and Cold War History," *Ethics and International Affairs* 10 (1996): 131-48.

11. John Lewis Gaddis, *We Now Know: Rethinking Cold War History* (Oxford and New York: Oxford University Press, 1996). On the title page it is described as "A Council on Foreign Relations Book," implying some sort of subvention, but there is no explanation of this anywhere in the work.

12. Richard Pipes, "Introduction," *The Unknown Lenin*, p. 6; and Adam B. Ulam, "Preface, 1998: Lenin among the Bolsheviks," in *The Bolsheviks: The Intellectual and Political History of the Triumph of Communism in Russia*, by Ulam, with a new preface (Cambridge, MA, and London: Harvard University Press, 1998, p. 12; originally published 1965).

13. Gaddis, "The Tragedy of Cold War History," p. 8.

14. Gaddis, "On Moral Equivalency and Cold War History," p. 138. The reference to "Tail Gunner Joe" was a snide allusion to Senator Joseph McCarthy, who had used the sobriquet in his electioneering. This politician had earned the right to do so. (Gaddis, incidentally, never served in the military.) McCarthy, who had an automatic exemption from the draft because he was a judge, nevertheless enlisted in the Marines at the age of thirty-three and spent over two years in the Pacific during World War II. He frequently volunteered for combat duty and acquitted himself well in this capacity. (See Roy Cohn, *McCarthy: The Answer to "Tail Gunner Joe"*, [New York: Manor, 1977], pp. xii-xiii, 16, 274-75; and Thomas C. Reeves, *The Life and Times of Joe McCarthy: A Biography* [New York: Stein and Day, 1982], pp. 50-52.) Reeves, no supporter of McCarthy, admits that he participated in twelve aerial combat missions, encountered enemy fire, and did indeed utilize the tail gun.

15. Gaddis, "On Moral Equivalency and Cold War History," p. 132.

16. Charles S. Maier, "Revisionism and the Interpretation of Cold War Origins," *Perspectives in American History* 4 (1970): 313.

17. Ibid., p. 345.

18. Ibid., p. 313.

19. Arthur Schlesinger, Jr., "Origins of the Cold War," *Foreign Affairs* 46 (Oct. 1967): 22-52, particularly: 22-26, 24n3, and 52.

20. Gary R. Hess, "After the Tumult: The Wisconsin School's Tribute to William Appleman Williams," *Diplomatic History* 12 (Fall 1988): 485.

21. Ibid., pp. 496-97. Other noted Cold War historians who blamed the United States for the conflict were Denna F. Fleming, Gar Alperovitz, Lloyd Gardner, Athan Theoharis, Gabriel Kolko, and Edward Pessen.

22. Robert James Maddox, "A Visit to Cloudland: Cold War Revisionism in College Texts," p. 1. As noted above, his book was *The New Left and the Origins of the Cold War*.

23. Frank A. Warren, "Preface to Morningside Edition," *Liberals and Communism*, p. xvii.

24. Ibid., p. xxi. Another element here is that Warren had been raised in a radical family and was apparently returning to his roots.

25. Ibid.

26. This point is made well by Richard Gid Powers in his *Not Without Honor*, pp. 31-33, 43, and elsewhere.

27. For example, see Les K. Adler and Thomas G. Paterson, "Red Fascism: The Merger of Nazi Germany and Soviet Russia in the American Image of Totalitarianism, 1930's-1950's," *American Historical Review* 75 (April 1970): 1046-64.

28. See note one above.

29. See Stephen Karetzky, "The Vitality of American Catholic Higher Education," *Catholic Library World* 65 (Jan.-March 1995): especially pp. 21-22.

30. Marie Jo Buhle, Paul Buhle, and Dan Georgakas, "Introduction," *Encyclopedia of the American Left*, ed. by Buhle, Buhle, and Georgakas (Urbana and Chicago: University of Illinois Press, 1992; originally published: New York: Garland, 1990), p. xi.

31. Paul Buhle, "History, U.S." in *Encyclopedia of the American Left*, p. 323. The *Journal of American History* is the scholarly journal of the Organization of American Historians, the primary association of historians focusing on the United States.

32. Michael Kazin, "The Grass-Roots Right," p. 136. Kazin, Professor of History at American University, fully expounds his political philosophy in his book, *The Populist Persuasion*.

33. Paul Hollander, "Higher Education: Reservoir of the Adversary Culture," in his *Anti-Americanism: Irrational and Rational*, pp. 151-53; "Footnotes," *Chronicle of Higher Education* (May 1, 1998): A12; Daniel J. Flynn, "Off the Shelf," *Campus Report* (Oct. 1998): 6; and David Horowitz, *Hating Whitey*, p. 153. The ACE report is discussed in Peter Schmidt, "Survey Finds Widespread Faculty Support for Racial and Ethnic Diversity," *Chronicle of Higher Education: Today's News* (May 18, 2000): <chronicle.com/news>. The story in the weekly print version of the *Chronicle of Higher Education* was half the length of the daily online one. This information on the general political orientation of faculty members did not survive the cuts.

34. Robbins, "Message from the Chair," *Library History Round Table Newsletter*, n.s. 3 (Fall 1997): 1.

35. Thomas C. Reeves, "Are You Now . . . ," review of Schrecker's *Many are the Crimes: McCarthyism in America* (Boston and London: Little, Brown and Co., 1998,) *New York Times Book Review* (June 14, 1998): 22-23.

36. See Ronald Radosh, "The Two Evils: Communism, McCarthyism, and the Truth," review of *Many are the Crimes*, by Schrecker, and *The Soviet World of American Communism*, by Klehr, Haynes, and Anderson, *New Republic* (May 11, 1998): 38, 40-49.

37. See Nathan Glazer, "The Professors and the Party," review of Schrecker's *No Ivory Tower: McCarthyism and the Universities* (New York and London: Oxford University Press, 1986) *New Republic* (Oct. 6, 1986): 39-42.

38. Andrew B. Wertheimer, "Schrecker on McCarthyism," *Library History Round Table Newsletter*, n.s. 4 (Fall, 1998): 7. Wertheimer has made valuable contributions to library history and historiography.

39. Laura Nader, "The Phantom Factor: Impact of the Cold War on Anthropology," in *The Cold War and the University: Toward an Intellectual History of the Cold War* (New York: The New Press, 1997), p. 109.

40. Everett T. Moore, "Threats to Intellectual Freedom," *Library Journal* 96 (Nov. 1, 1971): 3563-67. One bright spot Moore found in the McCarthy era was Dean Acheson's steadfast support for Alger Hiss! (p. 3564)

41. In ibid., p. 3566.

42. Joe W. Kraus, "The Progressive Librarians' Council," *Library Journal* 97 (July 1972): 2351-54. Kraus was the director of libraries at Illinois State University at Normal. He had several articles on library history published, including contributions to the *Dictionary of American Library Biography*.

43. Kraus, "The Progressive Librarians' Council," p. 2354.

44. Ibid. This quotation was also placed under the title of the article by *Library Journal*'s editors to emphasize what they apparently considered the theme of Kraus' work.

45. One of the author's sources, former PLC member Edwin Castagna, told him that the political orientation of those in the organization ranged from 'luke-warm liberal to Marxist.' (Quoted on p. 2354.)

46. Robert Vosper, "A Century Abroad," *College and Research Libraries* 37 (Nov. 1976): 514-30.

47. Ibid., p. 523.

48. William E. Benemann, "Tears and Ivory Towers: California Libraries during the McCarthy Era," *American Libraries* 8 (June 1977): 305-9. At the time he wrote this, Benemann was a librarian at Golden Gate University Law Library in San Francisco.

49. Ibid., p. 306.

50. Ibid., p. 307.

51. Arthur P. Young, "Robert Bingham Downs," in *Leaders in American Librarianship: 1925-1975*, ed. by Wiegand, pp. 72-93. Young wrote *Books for Sammies: The American Library Association and World War I* (Pittsburgh: Beta Phi Mu, 1981).

52. Edward R. Johnson, "Ralph E. Ellsworth," in *Leaders in American Librarianship: 1925-1975*, ed. by Wiegand, pp. 115-16. Johnson was the director of libraries at the University of North Texas in Denton.

53. Wayne Wiegand, "Lawrence Clark Powell," in *Leaders in American Academic Librarianship: 1925-1975*, ed. by Wiegand, pp. 263-87.

By the time he wrote this, Wiegand had earned a master's degree in librarianship and a doctorate in history. He has taught in the schools of library and information studies at the University of Kentucky (1976-86) and the

378 *Not Seeing Red*

University of Wisconsin at Madison (1987 to the present). Wiegand has written and edited several books and articles on library history.

Powell headed UCLA's library until 1961 when he left to become the full-time director of the new library school at the University. He was elected President of the California Library Association in 1950, and of the Bibliographical Society of America, 1954-1956. Powell was accorded the American Library Association's most esteemed accolade in 1981: honorary membership.

54. Ibid., p. 284.

55. Ibid., p. 271.

56. Ibid.

57. The following material was taken from California Legislature, Joint Fact-Finding Committee on Un-American Activities, *Third Report: 1947: Un-American Activities in California* (Sacramento: The Senate, March 24, 1947), pp. 105-11, 321-22. Other Communist activities at UCLA and other educational institutions are described on pp. 95-144, 313-22, and elsewhere in this *Report*.

58. California State Investigating Committee on Education, *Tenth Report: The 1951 Hearings* (Sacramento: The Senate, Aug. 12, 1952), p. 61. See also p. 72.

59. Ibid., pp. 61-72.

60. Wiegand, "Lawrence Clark Powell," pp. 271-72. At the time, Chairman Nelson S. Dilworth was also a member of the California State Senate's Fact-Finding Committee on Un-American Activities. He was to serve on the Senate Finance Committee as well.

61. Ibid., p. 272.

62. Ibid.

63. Lawrence Clark Powell reported this in his *Fortune and Friendship: An Autobiography* (New York and London: Bowker, 1968), pp. 168-69.

64. Wiegand, "Lawrence Clark Powell," p. 272.

65. Ibid., p. 286n15.

66. California State Investigating Committee on Education, *Tenth Report: 1951*, pp. 61-72.

67. See Powell, *Fortune and Friendship*, p. 166.

68. Wiegand, "Lawrence Clark Powell," p. 272.

69. Powell, *Fortune and Friendship*, p. 166.

70. Ibid. Moore was then head of reference services at the library.

71. California State Investigating Committee on Education, *Tenth Report*, pp. 61-72.

72. See Robert D. Harlan, "Helen Haines," in *Dictionary of American Library Biography*, p. 225.

73. See Ruth Warncke, "Helen Haines," in *World Encyclopedia of Library and Information Services*, 3rd ed., pp. 334-35. As noted in the text, the entry originally appeared in the first edition of the work, the *ALA World Encyclopedia of Library and Information Services*, pp. 227-28. The only change made to the original 1980 entry was the addition of Harlan's sketch to its bibliography.

74. Ruth Warncke, "Helen Haines," in *World Encyclopedia of Library and Information Services*, 3rd ed., p. 335.

75. Robert D. Harlan, "Helen Haines," in *Dictionary of American Library Biography*, p. 225.

76. Ray R. Suput, "E. I. Shamurin," and Herman Liebaers, "Margarita Ivanova Rudomino," in *World Encyclopedia of Library and Information Services*, 3rd ed., pp. 770-71 and 726-27, respectively.

77. Margaret S. Olsen, "The More Things Change, the More They Stay the Same: East-West Exchanges, 1960-1993," *Library Resources and Technical Services* 39 (Jan. 1995): 5-21.

78. Ibid., p. 8.

79. Melville J. Ruggles, "Eastern European Publications in American Libraries," in *Iron Curtains and Scholarship*, ed. by Winger, p. 119.

80. Tatjana Lorkovic and Eric A. Johnson, "Serial and Book Exchanges with the Former Soviet Union," *The Serials Librarian* 31, no. 4 (1997): 59-85.

81. Ibid., p. 60.

82. Glenda Pearson, "The Red Scare: A Filmography," <http://www.lib.washington.edu/exhibits/AllPowers/film.html>, March 5, 1998.

83. Donald G. Davis, Jr., and John Mark Tucker, eds., *American Library History: A Comprehensive Guide to the Literature* (Santa Barbara, CA, and Oxford: ABC-CLIO, 1989; and Wayne A. Wiegand, and Donald G. Davis, Jr., eds., *Encyclopedia of Library History* (New York and London: Garland, 1994).

84. Donald G. Davis, "With Malice toward None: IFLA and the Cold War," *IFLA Journal*, vol. 26, no. 1 (2000): 13-20. *Libraries and Culture* is published by the University of Texas Press. Davis' work was written for presentation at a conference sponsored by the IFLA Round Table on History, "Books, Libraries, Reading and Publishing in the Cold War," Paris, June 11-12, 1998.

85. Davis, "With Malice toward None," p. 14. This is stated twice on this page.

86. The literature on these subjects is vast. Despite its hostility to many on the Right, a good starting point is Richard Gid Powers, *Not Without Honor: The History of American Anticommunism* (New York: Free Press, 1995). It shows how the concern for freedom was central to American anti-Communism. A prime example of the works stemming from this movement was Norman Podhoretz, *The Present Danger: "Do We Have the Will to Reverse the Decline*

of American Power?" (New York: Simon and Schuster, 1980). On the interrelationship of capitalism and freedom, see John Stuart Mill, *On Socialism* (Amherst, NY: Prometheus Books, 1987). Ironically, many librarians, particularly those in the Intellectual Freedom movement, frequently cite selected passages of Mill's *On Liberty* to buttress their ideology. They thereby distort the meaning of the book and his beliefs in general.

87. Davis, "With Malice toward None," p. 18.

88. Ibid., p. 19.

89. A few of the many studies that can be cited are: Podhoretz, *The Present Danger*; Richard Pipes, *Survival is Not Enough: Soviet Realities and America's Future* (New York: Simon and Schuster, 1984); Edward N. Luttwak, *On the Meaning of Victory: Essays on Strategy* (New York: Simon and Schuster, 1986); Jeane J. Kirkpatrick, *The Reagan Phenomenon and Other Speeches on Foreign Policy* (Washington, DC, and London: American Enterprise Institute, 1983), pp. 3-36; and Andrew E. Busch, "Ronald Reagan and the Defeat of the Soviet Empire," *Presidential Studies Quarterly* 27 (Summer 1997): 451-66. The evil nature of Communism was vividly described in the writings of Solzhenitsyn.

90. Davis, "With Malice toward None," p. 13.

91. Ibid.

92. Ibid., p. 16. The Morsch piece in question was her "Promoting Library Interests throughout the World," *ALA Bulletin* 51 (Sept. 1957): 579-84.

93. Davis, "With Malice toward None," p. 16, quoting a speech by I. F. Stone at the Ford Hall Forum on National Public Radio, April 12, 1983.

94. Irving F. Stone, *The Hidden History of the Korean War* (New York: Citadel Press, 1952).

95. Davis, "With Malice toward None," p. 14.

96. Ibid., p. 15, quoting a librarian in Michael P. Barnett, "IFLA in Liverpool: Return of the Native," *Wilson Library Bulletin* 46 (Jan. 1972): 469.

97. Davis, "With Malice toward None," p. 15.

98. Ibid.

99. Ibid., p. 16.

100. Ibid.

101. Pamela Spence Richards, ed., "The History of Reading and Libraries," Proceedings of an International Conference, June 19-21, 1996, Vologda, Russia, published as *Libraries and Culture: A Journal of Library History* 33 (Winter 1998).

102. Pamela Spence Richards, "Soviet-American Library Relations in the 1920s and 1930s: A Study in Mutual Fascination and Distrust," *Library Quarterly* 68 (Oct. 1998): 390-405.

103. Ibid., p. 390.

104. Ibid.

105. Ibid., p. 391.

106. See: Jean Key Gates, "Librarianship as a Profession," *Introduction to Librarianship*, 3rd ed. (New York and London: Neal-Schuman, 1990), pp. 79-82; and Jonathan A. Lindsey and Ann E. Prentice, *Professional Ethics and Librarians* (Phoenix: Oryx Press, 1985), pp. 1-4.

107. Richards, "Soviet-American Library Relations," p. 391.

108. Ibid., p. 403.

109. Ibid.

110. Ibid.

111. Ibid., pp. 397-98.

112. Ibid., p. 397.

113. Ibid., p. 398.

114. Ibid., p. 391.

115. Ibid., p. 399.

116. Ibid.

117. Margaret P. Coleman, "America, Russia, and Adult Education," *Wilson Bulletin for Librarians* 10 (Dec. 1935): 235-39; and John Richmond Russell, "Library Service in the USSR," *Journal of Adult Education* 8 (April 1936): 165-69.

118. Richards, "Soviet-American Library Relations," p. 400.

119. Ibid.

120. Ibid.

121. Ibid., p. 404.

122. Ibid.

123. Ibid.

124. See Wheeler's *The Library and the Community: Increased Book Service through Library Publicity Based on Community Studies* (Chicago: American Library Association, 1924). The difference between Wheeler's American approach and that of the Communists is evident in his book. He declares that the librarian's motive for wanting to bring library service to all is rightly based on "the strong belief that good books, widely read, will produce an intelligent people." (p. 9) Wheeler despises those with other motives. The American librarian, he says, "has the missionary spirit, but it is not that of the saver of souls, nor of the reformer, nor the pathological motive of the rectifier of social ills. It is only the desire to share with the whole population the contents of books which can prove of great help to them. . . ." (p. 10)

As an "outreach" librarian in Brooklyn in the 1960's, I can attest to the fact that there was no dearth of ideas or abilities among my colleagues.

125. Golder's work is best understood in the context of the development of the Hoover Institution Library. For the story of the Library and the scholar who directed it for twenty-four years, see Charles B. Burdick, *Ralph Lutz and*

the Hoover Institution (Stanford, CA: The Hoover Institution, 1974). On the changes in the Institution's name over the years, see Burdick, p. 35n.

126. Richards, "Soviet-American Library Relations," p. 394.

127. Alain Dubie, *Frank A. Golder: An Adventure of a Historian in Quest of Russian History* (Boulder, CO: East European Monographs, 1989; distributed by Columbia University Press), p. 181.

128. Ibid., pp. 181-82.

129. Ibid., pp. 182-89.

130. Ibid., p. 130.

131. Terrence Emmons and Bertrande M. Patenaude, "Introduction," in Emmons and Patenaude, eds., *War, Revolution, and Peace in Russia: The Passages of Frank Golder, 1914-1927* (Stanford, CA: Hoover Institution Press, 1992), p. xxiii.

132. Richards, "Soviet-American Library Relations," p. 394.

133. Golder, quoted in Dubie, p. 233n56. The word *Soviet* in brackets was inserted by Dubie.

134. Golder, quoted in Dubie, p. 130.

135. Richards ("Soviet-American Library Relations," p. 394) quoting a letter of Golder to Herbert Hoover, in Emmons and Patenaude, eds., *War, Revolution, and Peace in Russia*, p. 322. Richards noted page 318 as the source of the quote.

136. Golder, "A Trip to Russia," *A.R.A. Association Review* 3 (Jan. 1928), as reprinted in Emmons and Patenaude, eds., *War, Revolution, and Peace in Russia*, p. 343.

137. See American Library Association, "Recipients Named for Jesse H. Shera Award for Distinguished Published Research," <http://www.ala.org/news/v4n17/jessehshera.html> May 5, 1999, accessed Sept. 9, 1999. The award was shared with another article considered of equal value.

Richards' work was also positively received in the periodic review of the literature of library history. (See Edward A. Goedeken, "The Literature of American Library History, 1997-1998," *Libraries and Culture* 35 [Spring 2000]: 338.)

138. See Stephen Karetzky, letter, *Library Quarterly* 68 (Jan. 1998): 121-22.

139. Pamela Spence Richards, "Scientific Communication in the Cold War: Margarita Rudomino and the Library of Foreign Literatures during the Last Years of Stalin," *Libraries and Culture* 31 (Winter 1996): 239.

140. Louise S. Robbins, *Censorship and the American Library: The American Library Association's Response to Threats to Intellectual Freedom, 1939-1969* (Westport, CT, and London: Greenwood Press, 1996).

141. For example, see ibid., p. 50.

142. Ibid., p. 154.

143. Ibid., p. 43.

144. See p. 211n85.

145. Quoted in Ralph de Toledano, *J. Edgar Hoover: The Man in His Time* (New Rochelle, NY: Arlington House, 1973), p. 45. As an editor and correspondent for *Newsweek* and the *New Leader*, much of Toledano's work focused on the FBI; his biography of Hoover remains the best one. The *New Leader* was influential despite its small circulation. Its editors and contributors from 1940 through 1990 held a wide variety of political views, but all were anti-Communists. They included Daniel Bell, George Orwell, Willy Brandt, Bertrand Russell, Sidney Hook, John P. Roche, Milovan Djilas, and Alexandr Solzhenitsyn.

J. Edgar Hoover's *actual* views on Communism are contained in his informed—and moderate—popular books on the subject. (For example, see: *Masters of Deceit: The Story of Communism in America and How to Fight It* [New York: Henry Holt, 1958]; *A Study of Communism* [New York: Holt, Rinehart, and Winston, 1962]; and *On Communism* [New York: Random House, 1969].) Nevertheless, they are almost always dismissed because they are alleged to have been largely written by FBI staff members—a shabby treatment not accorded the writings and speeches of other public figures. Hoover was certainly a careful man: there is no reason to believe that the works bearing his name reflected his ideas any less than Theodore Sorensen's words reflected those which appeared under the name John F. Kennedy. Moreover, one can plainly see in Hoover's early public depositions on Communism in 1919 that this twenty-four year old law school graduate was well-schooled and an able writer. (See, for example, his early reports reprinted in his *On Communism*, pp. 76-79.)

Substantiating information regarding Hoover's authorship can be found in Richard Gid Powers, *Secrecy and Power: The Life of J. Edgar Hoover* (New York: The Free Press, 1987), pp. 66, 82, 343-44. However, Powers does not even mention two of Hoover's books in his six hundred page volume: *A Study of Communism* and *On Communism*. The book provides evidence of Hoover's diligent study of Communism and his dedication to knowing the truth about it. (See pp. 375-79) Nevertheless, this biography is essentially a strong indictment of the man.

For one account by a Congressman pertaining to the relationship between Emma Goldman and Hoover, see page 87 of Powers' book.

146. For example, the FBI failed to follow up on highly significant information provided to the government by Whittaker Chambers in the late 1930's and the 1940's. For some indication of the lapses in dealing with Chambers, see: D. M. Ladd, memo to J. Edgar Hoover, Dec. 29, 1948, reproduced in Robert Louis Benson and Michael Warner, eds., *Venona: Soviet Espionage and the American Response, 1939-1957* (Washington, DC: National

Security Agency and the Central Intelligence Agency, 1996), pp. 121-28. In his biography of Chambers, Sam Tanenhaus offers the explanation that in those years, ". . . the FBI, preoccupied with Nazi spies, was not interested in the Communist underground. . . ." (Tanenhaus, *Whittaker Chambers: A Biography* [New York: Random House, 1997], p. 170. See also pp. 203-4.) Tannenhaus' scholarly book has received accolades from Stephen Ambrose, John Kenneth Galbraith, and many others.

147. Robbins, *Censorship and the American Library*, p. 23.

148. Ibid., p. 77.

149. Ibid., p. 215n4.

150. Advocates of the abridged forms of notation now acceptable to some in academia are encouraged to read Gertrude Himmelfarb's "Beyond Method," in *What's Happened to the Humanities?*, ed. by Kernan, pp. 143-61; as well as Himmelfarb's "Where Have All the Footnotes Gone?" in her *On Looking into the Abyss*, pp. 122-30.

151. See ibid., pp. 22-23; 202, notes 49-51.

152. Robbins, *Censorship and the American Library*, pp. 157-63.

153. Ibid., pp. 7-8.

154. Zoia Horn, untitled review of *Censorship and the American Library*, by Robbins, *Journal of Education for Library and Information Science* 39 (Spring 1998): 236-39.

155. Ibid., p. 239.

156. Beverly P. Lynch, untitled review of *Censorship and the American Library*, by Robbins, *Library Quarterly* 68 (Jan. 1998): 92-94.

157. Ibid., p. 94.

158. Carl Bowen Davis, untitled review of *The Library Bill of Rights*, issue title of *Library Trends*, vol. 45, no. 1 (1996), ed. by Wayne Wiegand; and of *Censorship and the American Library*, by Robbins; *Libraries and Culture* 33 (Fall 1998): 454.

159. Ibid., p. 455.

160. Edward A. Goedeken, "The Literature of American Library History, 1995-1996," *Libraries and Culture* 33 (Fall 1998): 417.

161. Ibid., pp. 432-33.

162. Louise S. Robbins, "Anti-Communism, Racism, and Censorship in the McCarthy Era: The Case of Ruth W. Brown and the Bartlesville Public Library," *Journal of Education for Library and Information Science* 35 (Fall 1994): 331-36.

163. Ibid., p. 331.

164. David Caute, *The Great Fear: The Anti-Communist Purge under Truman and Eisenhower* (New York: Simon and Schuster, 1978). Caute devotes 1½ pages to librarians, including a paragraph on the case in Bartlesville. His other books deal with Communism and intellectuals, Frantz Fanon, Marx,

and political subjects of this type.

165. Ibid., p. 17.

166. Robbins, "Anti-Communism, Racism, and Censorship," p. 331.

167. Louise S. Robbins, *The Dismissal of Miss Ruth Brown: Civil Rights, Censorship, and the American Library* (Norman, OK: University of Oklahoma Press, 2000).

168. Robbins, "Anti-Communism, Racism, and Censorship," p. 333.

169. Ibid.

170. Leonard Maltin, *Leonard Maltin's Movie Video Guide, 1999.* (New York: Signet, 1998), p. 1307.

In contrast, Norma Sayre, former film critic for the *New York Times*, seems to like the movie, although she admits it is "simple-minded." Her major complaint appears to be that Davis is a mere civil libertarian: if she were a radical or a Communist, the movie would be making a more important point. (See Norma Sayre, *Running Time: Films of the Cold War* [New York: Dial Press, 1982]. The quotation is from p. 177. See also pp. 176, 181, 218.)

171. Louise Robbins, "Fighting McCarthyism through Film: A Library Censorship Case Becomes a *Storm Center*," *Journal of Library and Information Science Education* 39 (Fall 1998): 291-311.

172. Ibid., p. 307.

173. Ibid., p. 294.

174. Ibid., p. 305.

175. Ibid., p. 306.

176. Ibid., p. 304.

177. In addition to the items described here, see her "Racism and Censorship in Cold War Oklahoma: The Case of Ruth W. Brown and the Bartlesville Public Library," *Southwestern Historical Quarterly* 100 (July 1996): 19-48.

178. Robbins, "Fighting McCarthyism through Film," p. 306. See the other claims on the same page concerning the inducement of fear.

179. Ibid., p. 293. See also p. 307n7.

180. See John Earl Haynes, *Red Scare or Red Menace? American Communism and Anticommunism in the Cold War Era* (Chicago: Ivan R. Dee, 1996), pp. 167-69. The McCarran Act was passed in September 1950 when Congress overrode the veto of President Truman. It created a board to register all organizations deemed subversive and required them to provide information on their activities and membership. It also forbid the hiring of subversives in national defense work and barred entry to the United States by anyone who had ever been a member of a totalitarian organization. Never truly implemented—the Communist Party, for example, simply refused to register—its provisions were overturned by Supreme Court decisions in the mid-sixties which ruled that they violated the Fifth Amendment against self-incrimination.

181. Robbins, "Fighting McCarthyism through Film," pp. 296, 306. In the movie, a politician attacks the librarian "under the guise of patriotism for his own political advantage." (p. 296)

182. Ibid.

183. See ibid., pp. 293, 296, 301.

184. Ibid., p. 306.

185. Robbins, *Dismissal of Miss Ruth Brown*, pp. 154, 8.

186. William Safire, "On Language: 'First Things First,' " *New York Times Magazine* (Sept. 26, 1999): 39. Brief definitions of "guilt," "guilty," "association," and "association-in-fact enterprise" may be found in *Black's Law Dictionary*, 7th ed., ed. by Bryan A. Garner (St. Paul, MN: West Publishing, 1999).

187. See the decisions in the following court cases: *Adler v. Board of Education* (1952); *Scales v. United States* (1961); *Keyishian v. Board of Regents* (1967), dissenting arguments of Justices Clark, Harlan, Stewart, and White; *U.S. v. International Brotherhood of Teamsters* (1994); *U.S. v. Mason Tenders* (1995); and *Morisette v. Suffolk County Police* (New York, 1987).

188. See Robbins, *Dismissal of Miss Ruth Brown*, p. 150, for her remarks on J. B. Matthews' "tactics."

189. For example, she tries to link Ruth Brown with Helen Haines and Ernestine Rose, whom she *may* have met while attending summer classes at Columbia University's School of Library Service. Clearly an admirer of Haines and Rose, Robbins would like to believe that Brown learned about intellectual freedom from the former and library service to African-Americans from the latter. (See ibid., p. 34.)

190. This ancient wisdom pointing out that "Birds of a feather flock together" had earlier been stated by Homer.

191. Robbins, "Fighting McCarthyism through Film," p. 307n7.

192. Ibid., p. 294.

193. Ibid., pp. 293-94, 300, 306-7, 307n4.

194. Ibid., p. 294.

195. Ibid., pp. 307n4, 294.

196. Warren, *Liberals and Communism*, pp. 103-126. The twists and turns of the Popular Front as it served the interests of the USSR are described and rationalized by a historian Robbins cites in her research: Albert Fried, *Communism in America: A History in Documents* (New York: Columbia University Press, 1997), pp. 227-47.

A fascinating accusation made by Robbins is that "right-wing" anti-Communists cunningly changed the meaning of the word *front* to mean something negative, viz., a façade. (Robbins, "Fighting Communism through Film," p. 294.) Here, as elsewhere, she sees guile among conservative anti-Communists where it did not exist. The *Oxford English Dictionary* dates the earliest use of the word *front* to signify "A person, organization, etc., that serves as a cover for subversive or illegal actions" to 1905. (*OED* [Oxford: Oxford University Press, 1971].) There was no reason for Americans to reserve the use of that term to concepts later devised by Communist sloganeers. Moreover, the material she specifically cites as proof of this stratagem (e.g., Richard E. Combs, "How Communists Make Stooges out of Movie Stars," *American Legion Magazine* 47 [May 1949]: 14-15, 42-46) does not support her allegation that they say people joined Popular Front organizations to surreptitiously advance Communist causes. In the case of Combs' article, the point was made quite clear even in its title that many of those who joined Communist-controlled organizations had been fooled into doing so. Combs used the term *front* in only one way: as the *OED* defines it. The *f* was not capitalized in his article and he did not use the term *Popular Front*. And indeed, the organizations he wrote about *were* Communist front groups.

Robbins ignores the important fact that some of the professed causes of the Popular Front, like anti-fascism, were shared by conservative anti-Communists, such as those in the American Legion. The conservatives understood, however, that cooperation with Communists should be undertaken only as a very last resort and subjected to constant scrutiny. This stance was quite clear during the temporary cooperation between the US and the Soviet Union during World War II.

197. Larry Ceplair and Steven Englund, *The Inquisition in Hollywood: Politics in the Film Community, 1930-1960* (Garden City, NY: Anchor Press/Doubleday, 1980).

198. Ibid., p. xiv.

199. Ibid., pp. 98-99, 128, 152-53.

200. Ibid., p. 100.

201. Ibid., p. 162.

202. Ibid., p. 428.

203. Ibid., pp. 51-52, 152.

204. Thomas C. Reeves, review of *The Inquisition in Hollywood*, by Ceplair and Englund, *History* 9 (Feb. 1981): 92. Reeves is best known for his massive *Life and Times of Joe McCarthy*.

205. Reeves, review of *The Inquisition in Hollywood*, p. 91.

206. Ibid.

207. Ibid., p. 92.

208. David Culbert, review of *The Inquisition in Hollywood*, by Ceplair and Englund, *Journal of American History* 68 (June 1981): 186.

209. Ibid., p. 185.

210. Ibid.

211. Walter Goodman, *The Committee: The Extraordinary Career of the House Committee on Un-American Activities* (New York: Farrar, Straus and Giroux, 1968).

212. Walter Goodman, review of *The Inquisition in Hollywood*, by Ceplair and Englund, *New Republic* 182 (May 31, 1980): 32.

213. Lillian Hellman, *Scoundrel Time* (Boston: Little, Brown, 1976). On Hellman, see Norman Podhoretz, *Ex-Friends: Falling Out with Allen Ginsberg, Lionel and Diana Trilling, Lillian Hellman, Hannah Arendt, and Norman Mailer* (New York: The Free Press, 1999), pp. 103-38; and William Wright, *Lillian Hellman: The Image, the Woman* (New York: Simon and Schuster, 1986).

214. For example, see William F. Buckley, "And Who is the Ugliest of Them All?" Review of *Scoundrel Time*, by Hellman, *National Review* 29 (Jan. 21, 1977): 101-6; and John R. Marvin, review of *Scoundrel Time*, by Hellman, *Library Journal* 101 (May 11, 1976): 1110.

215. Victor S. Navasky, *Naming Names* (New York: Viking, 1980), pp. 52-55.

216. See his ludicrous explanation in Jacob Weisberg, "Cold War without End," *New York Times Magazine* (Nov. 28, 1999): 122-23.

217. Stefan Kanfer, *A Journal of the Plague Years* (New York: Atheneum, 1973). Diana Trilling dismissed the work as superficial. (Trilling, review of *A Journal of the Plague Years*, by Kanfer, *New York Times Book Review* [July 8, 1973]: 4-5.) The title was taken from books by Defoe and Camus.

218. There are numerous others, of course, such as: Stanley I. Kutler, *The American Inquisition: Justice and Injustice in the Cold War* (New York: Hill and Wang, 1982), which deals mainly with allegedly wronged pro-Communists; Griffin Fariello, *Red Scare: Memories of the American Inquisition* (New York: W. W. Norton, 1995); and Cedric Belfrage, *The American Inquisition* (New York: Bobbs-Merrill, 1973).

219. Kenneth Lloyd Billingsley, *Hollywood Party: How Communism Seduced the American Film Industry in the 1930s and 1940s* (Rocklin, CA: Forum, 1998). See also: Eric M. Breindel, "The Communists and the Committees," *Commentary* 71 (Jan. 1981): 46-52; and Ronald Radosh, "The Blacklist as History," *The New Criterion* 16 (Dec. 1997): 12-17.

220. See Billingsley, *Hollywood Party*.

221. See Hilton Kramer, "The Blacklist Revisited," in *The Twilight of the Intellectuals: Culture and Politics in the Era of the Cold War*, by Kramer (Chicago: Ivan R. Dee, 1999), pp. 70-80; Billingsley, *Hollywood Party*, pp. 47, 179, 263-73; Morrie Ryskind, with John H. M. Roberts, *I Shot an Elephant in My Pajamas* (Lafayette, LA: Huntington House Publishers, 1994), pp. 163-66; Joseph Farah, "The Real Blacklist," *National Review* 41 (Oct. 27, 1989): 42-43;

and "Hollywood Ignores Real 'Blacklist' Victims," *AIM Report*, vol. 26, no. 24 (Dec.—B, 1997): [1-2, 4-6]. See also Weinstein and Vassiliev, "Double Agent/Hollywood Hustler: The Case of Boris Morros," in their *Haunted Wood*, pp. 110-39.

Evidence of *leftist* blacklisting activity even appears in unlikely places like *The Fund for the Republic*'s condemnation of alleged right-wing blacklisting: John Cogley, *Report on Blacklisting*, vol. 1 (New York: The Fund for the Repulic, 1956), pp. 111-12. Sidney Hook noted "the record of activity and harassment by Communists against critics of Communism," but did not stress the active participation of liberals in this. (Again, see Cogley, vol. 1., pp. 111-12.) The ease with which Communists blacklisted in Hollywood could get work in New York's theater is shown in US House of Representatives Committee on Un-American Activities, *Communism in the New York Area (Entertainment): Hearings:* June 18 and 19, 1958; May 8, 1958; April 1, 1957 (Washington, DC: GPO, 1958).

Ryskind's early career was intertwined with that of George S. Kaufman and Ira and George Gershwin. He became a member of the editorial board of *The National Review* in the fifties. In his autobiography, he pointed out the hostility of the studio heads towards those they considered too anti-Communist. The business leaders believed that their charges against some in Hollywood would hurt the image of the industry, so they created yet another blacklist of conservatives who had worked in movies. (Ryskind, pp. 165-66, and elsewhere.)

222. Mark Tucker, "Report on Donald G. Davis Article Award," *Library History Round Table Newsletter* n.s. 4 (Spring 2000): 11. This was the first time that the award, named in honor of Donald G. Davis, Jr., was bestowed.

In the biennial review of library historiography, it was declared that "Louise Robbins displays her impressive scholarly skills. . ." in her article. "As usual, Robbins' work is well written and well documented and clearly reflects her skills as an historian." (Goedeken, "The Literature of American Library History, 1997-1998," *Libraries and Culture*, p. 318.)

223. Robbins, *Dismissal of Miss Ruth Brown*, p. 5.

224. Ibid. The narrowness of Robbins' social focus is reflected by the fact that she mentions the men returning from World War II only as a source of women's oppression or as a burden. Ignored is the fact that of the sixteen million men encouraged or mandated to join the armed forces, over 400,000 did *not* return and almost 800,000 did so wounded. Moreover, she does not even consider the possibility that most American women wanted to return to family life, or that more were grievously hurt by the loss of their husbands, sons, or brothers than the loss of their assembly line jobs. If such distortions are the result of her proclaimed feminist approach, the methodology is wanting.

225. Ibid., p. 6.

226. Ibid., p. 7. See also p. 6.
227. Ibid., p. 175 and elsewhere.
228. Ibid., p. 8.
229. Ibid., p. 9.
230. Cindy Mediavilla, "The War on Books and Ideas," *Library Trends* 46 (Fall 1997): 331-47.
231. Ibid., pp. 336, 343-44.
232. Ibid., p. 331.
233. Ibid.
234. See, for example, ibid., p. 342.
235. Ibid., p. 340.
236. Ibid., p. 342.
237. Ibid., p. 332.
238. See: Robert W. Cherny, "Harry Bridges," and Bruce Nelson, "San Francisco's General Strike," in *Encyclopedia of the American Left*, ed. by Buhle, Buhle, and Georgakas, pp. 106-7 and 672-74; Ed Shoemaker, "Harry Bridges," in *Biographical Dictionary of the American Left*, ed. by Johnpoll and Klehr, pp. 44-45; and Klehr, Haynes, and Firsov, *The Secret World of American Communism*, p. 104n24. Bridges was protected by leading members of the New Deal, among others. (See Eugene Lyons, *The Red Decade* [New Rochelle, NY: Arlington House, 1971; originally published by Bobbs-Merrill, 1941], pp. 231-34.) Supposedly reputable publishers still issue one-sided, romantic views of the General Strike that downplay Bridges' connection with Communism. For example, see David F. Selvin, *A Terrible Anger: The 1934 Waterfront and General Strikes in San Francisco* (Detroit: Wayne State University Press, 1996), pp. 57-59, 63-65. Selvin had been a journalist for West-Coast labor publications.
239. Mediavilla, "War on Books and Ideas," p. 331.
240. Ibid., p. 344.
241. Mediavilla cites "Summary of Findings of the California Joint Fact Finding Committee on Un-American Activities," in *Red Fascism: Boring from Within by the Subversive Forces of Communism*, comp. by State Sen. Jack B. Tenney (Los Angeles: Federal Printing Co., 1947), p. 643.
242. See "Land of the Soviets," in California Legislature, Joint Fact-Finding Committee on Un-American Activities, *Third Report: Un-American Activities in California* (Sacramento: The Senate, March 24, 1947), pp. 313-22.
For a brief description of the Institute and a description of how it spread propaganda through its publications, see Harvey Klehr and Ronald Radosh, *The Amerasia Spy Case: Prelude to McCarthyism* (Chapel Hill and London: University of North Carolina Press, 1996), pp. 37-39. As described elsewhere, the offices of *Amerasia*, one of its journals, was found to contain large quantities of top-secret American documents. This was merely some of the

evidence that the IPR was working on behalf of a foreign power.

243. Mediavilla, "War on Books and Ideas," p. 333.

244. Ibid., pp. 333-34.

245. Ibid., p. 344.

246. Ibid., p. 338.

247. "It Happened in Pasadena," *California Librarian* 14 (Dec. 1952): 89-90.

248. William E. Benemann, "Tears and Ivory Towers: California Libraries during the McCarthy Era," *American Libraries* 8 (June 1977): 305-9.

249. Mediavilla, "War on Books and Ideas," quoting Benemann, "Tears and Ivory Towers," p. 306.

250. Benemann, "Tears and Ivory Towers," p. 306, as quoted in Mediavilla, "War on Books and Ideas," p. 338.

251. Mediavilla, "War on Books and Ideas," p. 341.

252. Ibid., p. 340.

253. Benemann, "Tears and Ivory Towers," p. 308, as quoted in Mediavilla, "War on Books and Ideas," p. 342.

254. Mediavilla, "War on Books and Ideas," pp. 331, 341-43.

255. Ibid., p. 342.

256. Ibid., p. 344.

257. Ibid., p. 336. The newspaper was *Alert: A Weekly Confidential Report on Communism and How to Combat It*, published in Los Angeles by Jacoby and Gibbons and Associates.

258. John E. Smith and Evelyn Benagh Detchon, "It Happened in Burbank," *ALA Bulletin* 46 (March 1952): 85-87.

259. See California Senate Investigating Committee on Education, *Tenth Report: The 1951 Hearings* (Sacramento: The Senate, August 12, 1952), pp. 61-72. See pp. 62 and 69 for the committee chairman's statements on the responsibility of librarians to make opposing ideas available to library users.

260. Mediavilla, "War on Books and Ideas," p. 334.

261. Ibid.

262. See Richard E. Combs, "Critical Analysis of 'Building America' Series," in California, Senate Investigating Committee on Education, *Third Report: Textbooks* (Sacramento: The Senate, March 27, 1948), pp. 45-120.

263. Mediavilla, "War on Books and Ideas," p. 333.

264. Critiques of progressive education included: Michael Demiashkevich, *An Introduction to the Philosophy of Education* (New York: American Book Co., 1935); A. E. Bestor, *Educational Wastelands* (Urbana, IL: University of Illinois Press, 1953); Irene Corbally Kuhn, "Battle Over Books," *American Legion Magazine* (Oct. 1958): 20-21, 37-40; and Augustin G. Ruud, *Bending the Twig: The Revolution in Education and Its Effect on Our Children* (New York: Sons of the American Revolution, New York Chapter, 1957).

The experiences and views of a conservative textbook writer in the 1940's and 1950's are interesting and relevant: Donzella Cross Boyle, *American History was My Undoing: A Case Study of a Textbook* (Fullerton, CA: Education Information, 1961). The *Building America* series and Combs' critique are discussed on pp. 22-30 of Boyle's work. Education Information was a grassroots organization.

265. See Eugene Lyons, *The Red Decade*, with new preface (New Rochelle, NY: Arlington House, 1970; originally published: Bobbs-Merrill, 1941), pp. 129, 144, 250-54, 320-22, 346-51, 386-88. For the precise organizations they were members of, and the characteristics of these groups, see: US House of Representatives Special Committee on Un-American Activities, *Investigation of Un-American Activities in the United States: Appendix IX: Communist Front Organizations*, 3 vols. (Washington, DC: GPO, 1944); and the Committee's *Guide to Subversive Organizations and Publications*, rev. ed. (Washington, DC: GPO, Dec. 1961).

266. See Hughes' "Worker's Song," reprinted in Tenney, *Red Fascism*, p. 467. As indicated, Mediavilla uses those parts of Tenney's book that suit her purpose.

267. "Textbook Series Scored at Inquiry," *Los Angeles Times* (Feb. 25, 1948): 1, 7.

268. California Library [Association] Committee on Intellectual Freedom, *The Right to Know: An Analysis of the Criticisms of* Building America (N.p.: The Committee, June 1948, 18 pp.), p. 5.

269. Ibid., p. 9.

270. Ibid., p. 11.

271. Ibid., pp. 14-16.

272. Ibid., p. 15.

273. Ibid., p. 10.

274. Ibid., p. 14.

275. See Combs, "Critical Analysis of 'Building America' Series," in California Committee on Education, *Third Report*, pp. 48, 53-56, 66-69, and elsewhere.

276. Mediavilla, "War on Books and Ideas," p. 14. For a list of their memberships and the nature of the organizations, see US House of Representatives, *Investigation of Un-American Activities: Appendix IX: Communist Front Organizations*; and its *Guide to Subversive Organizations*.

277. Kimball Wiles, "*Building America*: A Case in Point," *Educational Leadership* 6 (Nov. 1948): 111. The division of the NEA that issued both this journal and the textbook series was its Association for Supervision and Curriculum Development, or ASCD.

278. Ibid., p. 112.

279. Marguerite Ann Stewart, *Land of the Soviets*, ed. by Maxwell S. Stewart (St. Louis: Webster Publishing Co. in cooperation with the Institute of Pacific Relations, 1942).

280. In 1938 Stewart wrote that on his recent visit to the Soviet Union he had seen no fear among the common people, as was being reported in the West. He declared that despite the admitted ruthlessness against "thousands," the purges were the result of "popular discontent" and showed that ". . . the material and political aspirations of the common people are beginning to be felt." (Maxwell S. Stewart, "Progress and Purges in Soviet Russia," *Nation* 147 [Sept. 17, 1938]: 265.)

281. See Lyons, *The Red Decade*, pp. 245, 259, 346, and elsewhere. For an interesting description of how Communists controlled the Institute and its sophisticated publications, such as *Pacific Affairs* and *Amerasia*, see Klehr and Radosh, *The* Amerasia *Spy Case*, pp. 38-39, 41-42, 168, 189-90. It is significant that the IPR served as a center for Communist espionage and propaganda despite the fact that many non-Communists were involved with it and the IPR received most of its financial support from the Rockefeller Foundation and the Carnegie Corporation. For a fairly complete list of Maxwell Stewart's formal Communist affiliations, see US House of Representatives, *Investigation of Un-American Activities: Appendix IX: Communist Front Organizations*. For information on Marguerite Ann Stewart's other frequent publisher, the Foreign Policy Association (which was similar in goals and methods to the Institute of Pacific Relations and the Public Affairs Institute), see Sheppard Marley, "Mrs. Dean's Foreign Policy Lobby," *Plain Talk* 1 (Nov. 1946): 16-20; and William Henry Chamberlin, "Anti-Anti-Communism: A Ford Investment," *National Review* 1 (April 11, 1956): 16-18.

282. M. Stewart, *Land of the Soviets*, p. 75.

283. Ibid., p. 6.

284. Ibid., pp. 84-94.

285. "*Land of the Soviets*," in California Joint Committee on Un-American Activities, *Third Report*, 1947, pp. 313-22.

286. See Goedeken, "The Literature of American Library History, 1997-1998," *Libraries and Culture*, p. 324.

287. Jean Preer, "The American Heritage Project: Libraries and the Democratic Tradition in the Early Cold War," *Libraries and Culture* 28 (Spring 1993): 167.

288. Ibid.

289. For example, it provided money to the Foreign Policy Association, a cousin of the Institute of Pacific Relations and the Public Affairs Institute. Again, for information on the FPA, see: Marley, "Mrs. Dean's Foreign Policy Lobby," and William Henry Chamberlin, "Anti-Anti-Communism."

290. Preer, "The American Heritage Project," p. 169.

291. Ibid., p. 171.

292. Ibid., pp. 172-73.

293. Julian Boyd, quoted ibid., p. 182. See note below.

294. Julian Boyd, "Free Communication—An American Heritage," in *Freedom of Communication: Proceedings of the First Conference on Intellectual Freedom, New York City, June 28-29, 1952*, ed. by William Dix and Paul Bixler (Chicago: American Library Association, 1954), pp. 10-11.

295. Ibid., p. 18.

296. To be precise, Preer referred to "Senator Joseph McCarthy's charge in February 1950 that Communists had infiltrated the State Department. Although a Senate committee found no basis for the allegation. . . ." (Ibid., p. 167) True, the committee of Democratic Senator Millard Tydings did reject all of McCarthy's charges, but it never undertook a real investigation: its only purpose was to protect the reputation of the Democratic Party by silencing McCarthy. However, the State Department itself then investigated McCarthy's charges, started proceedings against two-thirds of those he named, and dismissed most that did not resign. Those separated from the State Department included Soviet agents as well as obvious security risks. An excellent description of McCarthy's charges, the Tyding Committee, and the records of those accused, remains Buckley and Bozell's *McCarthy and His Enemies*, pp. 41-160, 360-63. See also M. Stanton Evans, "Joe McCarthy and the Historians," *Human Events*, Special Supplement (Jan. 1, 1999): S1-S8.

297. Preer, "The American Heritage Project," p. 167.

298. Ibid., p. 182.

299. Matthew Josephson, "The Battle of the Books," *Nation* 174 (June 28, 1952): 619-24.

300. See David E. Shei, *Matthew Josephson, Bourgeois Bohemian* (New Haven and London: Yale University Press, 1981), pp. 222-26, 250-51. When he died in 1978, he was writing a book defending Alger Hiss. (Shei, pp. 274-79)

301. See, for example, "Meet the *Nation* Experts on Civil Liberties," *New Leader* (July 14, 1952): 14, 22; and "The *Nation*'s Fear," *New Leader* (Jan. 1953): 22-23. See also, Eugene Lyons, "Is Freedom of Expression Really Threatened?" p. 29.

302. See Frank A. Warren's brief, but interesting, comments about Kirchway and her lack of concern for civil liberties in the Soviet Union in his *Liberals and Communism*, p. 190 and *passim*.

303. "The *Nation*'s Fear," *New Leader* (July 14, 1952): 22-23.

304. Henry Steele Commager, "Preface," in *Living Ideas in America*, ed. by Commager (New York: Harper, 1951), p. xviii.

305. Ibid.

306. Commager, *Living Ideas in America*, pp. 431, 652, 706-14, 721-22, 726-27.

307. Commager, "Preface," ibid., p. xviii.

308. Commager, *Living Ideas in America*, p. 479.

309. Ibid., p. 592.

310. Ibid.

311. See ibid., pp. 366-69, 394-424, 592-99.

312. Gerald W. Johnson, *This American People* (New York: Harper, 1951).

313. Ibid., p. 205.

314. Ibid., p. 98.

315. Ibid., p. 87.

316. This point was consistently made by foes of, and defectors from, the Party and its progenitors from the earliest years of Bolshevism. These charges have, of course, been entirely confirmed by the research in Russian archives since the demise of the Soviet Union, e.g., Klehr, Haynes, and Firsov, *The Secret World of American Communism*; Klehr, Haynes, and Anderson, *The Soviet World of American Communism*; Haynes and Klehr, *Venona*; and Allen Weinstein and Alexander Vassiliev, *The Haunted Wood: Soviet Espionage in America—the Stalin Era* (New York: Random House, 1999).

317. Johnson, *This American People*, pp. 97-98, 182-83.

318. Ibid., pp. 43-44.

319. Ibid., pp. 101-4, 109-10.

320. Ibid., pp. 108, 131, 55, 58.

321. Ibid., p. 98. While the situation of the United States was obviously different from that of Russia in 1917, it is important to remember that the Bolsheviks seized power there and ran the country although only a minuscule percentage of the country's population belonged to the Party and few even supported it.

322. Arthur M. Schlesinger, Jr., "Our Past—And Present," review of *This American People*, by Gerald W. Johnson, *New York Times Book Review* (Oct. 7, 1951): 6.

323. For example, see the following by Henry Steele Commager: "Washington Witch Hunt," *Nation* 164 (April 5, 1947): 385-88; "Who is Loyal to America?" *Harper's Magazine* 195 (Sept. 1947): 193-99; and "Red-Baiting in the Colleges," *New Republic* 121 (July 25, 1949): 10-13. Revealing, but published after *Living Ideas in America*, were Commager's "Was Yalta a Calamity?" *New York Times Magazine* (Aug. 3, 1952): 7, 48-49; and "Ten Guideposts for Our Foreign Policy," *New York Times Magazine* (Feb. 21, 1954): 7, 20, 22-23. These counseled against an energetic confrontation with Communism at home or abroad.

324. Christine Jenkins, "ALA Youth Services Librarians and the CARE-UNESCO Children's Book Fund: Selecting the 'Right Book' for Children in Cold War America,1950-1958," *Libraries and Culture* 31 (Winter 1996): 209-34.

325. That Aptheker was chosen as the book reviewer for this publication of the Organization of American Historians says much about the state of academic historiography. See Herbert Aptheker, review of *No Ivory Tower*, by Ellen Schrecker, *Journal of American History* 74 (Dec. 1987): 1093-95.

326. Nathan Glazer, "The Professors and the Party," review of *No Ivory Tower*, by Ellen Schrecker, *New Republic* 195 (Oct. 6, 1986): 40.

327. Arthur M. Schlesinger, Jr., "A Shameful Story," review of *The Great Fear*, by David Caute, *New York Times Book Review* (March 19, 1978): 44.

328. John P. Roche, review of *The Great Fear*, by David Caute, *Political Science Quarterly* 2 (Summer 1979): 361.

329. Untitled review of *The Great Fear*, by David Caute, *The New Yorker* (April 17, 1978): 138.

330. Sidney Hook, "David Caute's Fable of 'Fear and Terror': On 'Reverse McCarthyism,' " *Encounter* 52 (Jan. 1979): 56-64.

331. Ibid., p. 57.

332. Ibid., p. 63.

333. Ibid., p. 56.

334. Ibid., p. 57.

335. Ibid., p. 61.

336. Ibid., p. 63.

337. William Shannon, review of *The Truman Doctrine and the Origins of McCarthyism*, by Richard M. Freeland (New York: Knopf, 1972), *New York Times Book Review* (Jan. 16, 1972): 3-4.

338. Athan Theoharis, *Seeds of Repression: Harry S. Truman and the Origins of McCarthyism* (Chicago: Quadrangle Books, 1971).

339. Clarence Lasby, review of *Seeds of Repression*, by Theoharis, *Journal of Politics* 34 (Nov. 1972): 1328. Lasby taught history at the University of Texas at Austin, becoming chair of the history department in 1973. His publications were primarily on twentieth century America, particularly the Cold War era. The *Journal of Politics* was copublished by the University of Texas Press and the Southern Political Science Association.

340. Herbert Waltzer, review of *Seeds of Repression*, by Theoharis, *American Historical Review* 79 (Oct. 1974): 1291-92. Waltzer taught at Miami University.

341. Ibid., p. 1292. Waltzer also documented his criticism that "Theoharis neither understands nor likes politics," (p. 1292) preferring morality plays to reality.

342. Jeffrey M. Burnam, review of *Seeds of Repression*, by Theoharis, *Annals of the American Academy of Political and Social Science* 399 (Jan. 1972): 226. Burnam was Assistant Professor of Political Science at Northern Illinois University.

343. Fred J. Cook, *The Nightmare Decade: The Life and Times of Senator Joe McCarthy* (New York: Random House, 1971).

344. Thomas C. Reeves, review of *The Nightmare Decade*, by Fred J. Cook, *Journal of American History* 58 (March 1972): 1055.

345. Ibid., p. 1056.

346. Cook, *The Nightmare Decade*, p. 3.

347. Ibid., pp. ix-xi, 569-80.

348. Unimpressed by Boyer's book was David Seideman. See his "Hell and Hard Work," review of *By the Bomb's Early Light: American Thought and Culture at the Dawn of the Atomic Age*, by Paul [S.] Boyer (New York: Pantheon, 1985), *Times Literary Supplement* (March 14, 1986): 268.

349. Boyer, *By the Bomb's Early Light*, p. xviii.

350. Ibid., p. xx.

351. Ibid., pp. 101-4.

352. Ibid., p. 102.

353. Paul Boyer, *Purity in Print: The Vice Society Movement and Book Censorship in America* (New York: Scribner's, 1968); and Paul Boyer and Stephen Nissenbaum, *Salem Possessed: The Social Origins of Witchcraft* (Cambridge, MA: Harvard University Press, 1974).

354. Some of his recent works were reissued in a collection in 1998: Paul Boyer, *Fallout: A Historian Reflects on America's Half-Century Encounter with Nuclear Weapons* (Columbus: Ohio State University Press, 1998).

355. On the reluctance of individuals to call people Communists who *are* Communists, see Eric Breindel, "Calling a Comunist a Communist" (May 9, 1987), reprinted in *Passion for Truth*, by Breindel, pp. 17-19. See also pp. 19-21.

356. Powers, *Not Without Honor*, p. 274.

357. Podhoretz, *The Present Danger: "Do We Have the Will to Reverse the Decline of American Power?"* (New York: Simon and Schuster, 1980), p. 91. Podhoretz titled this chapter of the book "The Missing Term."

358. Ibid., pp. 90-95.

359. See Robbins, "Fighting McCarthyism through Film," p. 306; and Robbins, *Dismissal of Miss Ruth Brown*, pp. 154, 8.

360. Thomas C. Reeves is correct on the origin of the term *McCarthyism*. (See his *Life and Times of Joe McCarthy*, pp. 266-67.) On the popularization of the term by Owen Lattimore, see Arthur Herman, *Joseph McCarthy: Reexamining the Life and Legacy of America's Most Hated Senator* (New York: The Free Press, 2000), pp. 125-26.

361. A fraudulent television "docudrama" about McCarthy was *Tail Gunner Joe*, produced by NBC and Universal in 1977. Typical of the documentaries is *Senator Joseph McCarthy: An American Inquisitor*, produced for the popular A&E series *Biography* in 1995.

362. The most objective is Herman's recently published *Joseph McCarthy*. (His previous book was *The Idea of Decline in Western History* [New York: The Free Press, 1997].) Roy Cohn's more popular *McCarthy* catches the essence of the man and his work. A valuable biography is forthcoming from journalist and historian M. Stanton Evans.

363. Herman, *Joseph McCarthy*, p. 194.

364. Joseph Welch is described in the lengthy treatment of the Army-McCarthy hearings in Roy Cohn's *McCarthy*, pp. 124-219, particularly pp. 195-204. See also Herman, *Joseph McCarthy*, pp. 271-76.

365. For example, see "That Sly Counselor—Welch," *Newsweek* 43 (June 7, 1954): 27-28, 31.

366. Gilbert Seldes, "Murrow, McCarthy, and the Empty Formula," *Saturday Review* 37 (May 15, 1954): 25-26; and John Cogley, "The Murrow Show," *Commonweal* 59 (March 26, 1954): 618.

367. As quoted in A. M. Sperber, *Murrow: His Life and Time* (New York: Freundlich, distributed by Simon and Schuster, 1986), pp. 438, 469.

368. See Herman, *Joseph McCarthy*, pp. 230-32.

369. "Demagogue McCarthy: Does He Deserve Well of the Republic?" *Time* (Oct. 21, 1951): 21-24.

370. Nora de Toledano, "*Time* Marches on McCarthy," *American Mercury* 74 (Feb. 1952): 15-22. See also Joe McCarthy, "Statement on *Time* Magazine," in *Congressional Record* (Nov. 14, 1951), as reprinted in *Major Speeches and Debates of Senator Joe McCarthy Delivered in the United States Senate, 1950-1951*, by McCarthy (Washington, DC: GPO, n.d.), pp. 333-39.

371. Rauh in *The Progressive* (May 1950), as quoted in William F. Buckley, "The Testament of Paul H. Hughes," in *Up from Liberalism*, by Buckley, with a Reintroduction by Buckley, Foreword by John Dos Passos (Briarcliff Manor, NY: Stein and Day, 1984; originally published: New York: McDowell, Obolensky, 1959), p. 101.

372. See John Earl Haynes, "The 'Spy' on Joe McCarthy's Staff: The Forgotten Case of Paul H. Hughes," *Continuity: A Journal of History* 14 (Spring-Fall 1990): 21-61; and Buckley, "The Testament of Paul H. Hughes," in *Up from Liberalism*, by Buckley, pp. 101-16.

373. The widely referred to, but rarely examined, hearings on the federal government's overseas libraries are: US Senate, Committee on Government Operations, Permanent Subcommittee on Investigations, *State Department Information Programs—Information Centers; Hearings*: Eight Parts: March 24, 1953-July 14, 1953; *Index*: Aug. 5, 1953; *Report*: Jan. 25, 1954 (Washington,

DC: GPO, 1953-1954).

374. Robert F. Kennedy's scrupulous research for Senator McCarthy is an important element of the following publications by McCarthy's Committee on Government Operations, Permanent Subcommittee on Investigations: *Control of Trade with the Soviet Bloc* (Washington, DC: GPO, July 1953); and *Control of Trade with the Soviet Bloc: Hearings*, Part 1: March 30 and 31, 1953, Part 2: May 4 and 20, 1953 (Washington, DC: GPO, 1953). When McCarthy died in 1957, Kennedy grieved. He flew to Wisconsin to attend the burial.

375. See: James Burnham, *The Web of Subversion: Underground Networks in the U.S. Government*, with new preface (New York: John Day, 1959; originally published 1954), pp. 66-67, 175; Buckley and Bozell, *McCarthy and His Enemies*; and Joe [Joseph] McCarthy, *The Fight for America* (Hamilton, MT: Poor Richard's Book Shop, 1952, reprint of *McCarthyism and the Fight for America: Documented Answers to Questions Asked by Friend and Foe Alike* [New York: Devin-Adair, 1952]), pp. 27-30.

376. See note 14 above on his war record.

377. Buckley and Bozell, *McCarthy and His Enemies*; Willmoore Kendall, "McCarthyism: The *Pons Asinorum* of Contemporary Conservatism," in *The Conservative Affirmation*, by Kendall (Chicago: Regnery Gateway, 1985; originally published: Chicago: Regnery, 1963), pp. 50-76; Frank S. Meyer, "The Meaning of McCarthyism," *National Review* (June 14, 1958), as reprinted in *The Conservative Mainstream* (New York: Arlington House, 1962), pp. 187-93; James Burnham, "The Third World War," *National Review* 3 (June 1, 1957): 518; James Burnham, *Suicide of the West: An Essay on the Meaning and Destiny of Liberalism* (Chicago: Regnery Books, 1986; originally published: New York: John Day, 1964), pp. 219-20, 289-90; Kenneth Colgrove, "Senator McCarthy," as reprinted in the *Congressional Record* (June 24, 1952), inserted by Rep. Timothy P. Sheehan, and as reprinted in *Major Speeches and Debates of Senator Joe McCarthy*, by Joe McCarthy, pp. 1-3; and William S. Schlamm, "Prologue," in *McCarthy and His Enemies*, by Buckley and Bozell (1st ed., 1954), pp. vii-xv. (In recent years, Buckley has begun to criticize McCarthy, mainly for his actions after 1953.)

More recent are Arthur Herman's *Joseph McCarthy* and the following analyses by M. Stanton Evans: "History's Vindication of Joe McCarthy," *Human Events*, Special Supplement (May 19, 1987): S1-S8; "McCarthyism: Waging the Cold War in America," *Human Events*, Special Supplement (May 30, 1997): S1-S8; and "Joe McCarthy and the Historians," *Human Events*, Special Supplement (Jan. 1, 1999): S1-S8.

For a nuanced portarit of the various individuals and social groups that supported McCarthy, see Herman's *McCarthy*, pp. 158-82. Lionel Abel has described McCarthy's support among America's Trotskyites, who appreciated his attacks on the Stalinist Left. (See Abel's *Intellectual Follies: A Memoir of the Literary Venture in New York and Paris* [New York: W. W. Norton, 1984], pp. 74-77.)

CONCLUSION

The last decades of the Czarist regime saw the development of a liberal library profession in Russia eager and able to serve the rapidly growing number of literate people. World-famous library collections were created, guided in part by the philosophy that different points of view should be represented. The goal was to provide library services on the Western model to a country experiencing extraordinary economic and intellectual growth as well as social and political reform.

This progress ended with the Communist coup d'état which followed the 1917 Revolution. Its leader, Lenin, held that libraries were a highly significant tool for implementing his political program; he refashioned these institutions so that they could help reshape society. His ideas were embellished and implemented by his wife, Krupskaya, but it was Lenin whose name was consistently invoked in the decades that followed his death. The Communist government nationalized all libraries and purged their book collections of all religious items and other materials deemed politically counterproductive so that they would reflect the views of the Communist Party. Many librarians deemed uncooperative—rightly or wrongly—were imprisoned or killed, a practice that continued for almost seventy years.

Krupskaya stressed that all aspects of librarianship, from cataloging to reader guidance, had to be done from a Communist point of view. She and Lenin realized the importance of obtaining scientific and technical knowledge and data from the West, so they established library conduits to help accomplish this. Librarianship itself was one area where technics from the democratic countries were adapted to attain Soviet goals. This task was easy because American librarians were eager to help the new state. A few went there to live and to help create the "New Communist Man" and the "New Communist Society," while others served as temporary advisers on matters like library administration.

Some Americans assisted the Communists by producing adulatory accounts of libraries in the Soviet Union; such enthusiasts included leaders of the library profession. These visitors tended to ignore the accomplishments made before the Revolution, the destruction of books by the Bolsheviks, the widespread censorship, and the oppressive political and social goals of the Communists. They seemed unaware of, or uninterested in, the mass purges being carried out and the widespread, murderous Red Terror. Regulations which clearly indicated the tyrannical nature of the Soviet Union were explained away by these pilgrims; positive motives were imputed to most of what they saw. In contrast, the United States was derided. These tourists were harsh critics of American librarianship: as with democracy itself, it did not excite them, particularly when compared to the dynamism, certitude, and zeal they perceived in the USSR. They were impressed by the size of the Soviet library system and the active involvement of library workers in so-called "educational" projects. The essential differences between the nature of education in a democratic society and that of propaganda in a totalitarian country were clearly not understood. Almost no criticism of the Soviet library system emanated from any of the world's democracies. Analogous phenomena can be seen in librarianship's sister profession, education, where men like John Dewey and George S. Counts raved about the accomplishments of the Communists. While accurate critiques of the USSR had been made from its very inception by some perceptive journalists and political figures, librarians—like many cultural and intellectual leaders—chose to dismiss them.

After World War II, Lenin's library ideology followed Soviet troops into eastern Europe. Wherever it was inflicted, it carried its commitment to forcing Communist views on all people within its reach. After the death of Stalin, the Soviet Union forged even more efficient links with capitalist countries to increase the acquisition of scientific and technical information from abroad. The image of a non-threatening, cooperative country was projected when considered useful. The new, high profile of Soviet library and information scientists in the international arena was, in part, one aspect of the Soviet policy of "peaceful coexistence," and later, "détente."

Nevertheless, with the beginning of the Cold War, many American librarians finally began to view the USSR and its totalitarian form of librarianship accurately. To some extent, this paralleled the growing understanding of Communism throughout large parts of American society. It was also reinforced by objective scholarship about Soviet libraries, frequently by librarians who had fled from Communist countries or who were scholars in Slavic studies.

However, the leaders of the library profession remained unmoved. The primary threat they warned of was not that posed by the Soviet Union, but by the grass-roots American anti-Communists, whom they portrayed as ignorant neofascists. The crusade by these prominent librarians against anti-Communism that began in the late 1940's increased in the next decade, and their ethos gained general acceptance within the profession. Its paranoid, elitist outlook was frequently cloaked by the *professed* ideology of intellectual freedom, whose tenets were rarely used by its proponents to critique the USSR. The new-found fervor for a partisan version of this creed was in part fueled by the profession's piteous attempt to gain greater self-respect and social prestige.

Soviet librarians were bombastic, claiming to have the world's largest libraries, the best readers, and the soundest philosophy. They believed they were the harbingers of the future and that Western librarians, particularly those in the United States, were part of the decaying bourgeois order. The Soviets pilloried librarians in the democracies for clinging to allegedly irresponsible theories, like those supporting the individual's right to read what he or she wants. They also made the unfounded charge that Western professionals were antagonistic to them. This paralleled mainstream Soviet thought and action.

At the same time, American librarians, in concert with their British colleagues, were forging a theory of comparative librarianship and international library relations that remained stable from the early 1960's through the ascent of Gorbachev in 1985. Essentially, it was internationalist in nature and was at odds with mainstream political and public opinion during much of the Cold War which correctly viewed the USSR as a threat. It treated the Soviet Union as merely another country with which relations of all kinds should be close. After all, it was argued, the basic socio-political philosophy and system in that Communist entity was no better or worse than any other. The goal of these utopian, internationalist professionals was to create a unified, global profession in a unified, global society. Librarians, it was held, could do much to create a world based on peace and justice because the major requirement for this was the correct application of knowledge at the proper time and place. This necessitated central planning on a national and international level. It would also entail the worldwide distribution of American-produced information and technology. While American librarians professed political and cultural relativism, they found numerous opportunities to criticize the West. As with previous anti-anti-Communist movements, it was developed and embraced by the leaders of the profession. And as with the earlier movements, it has received no criticism from historians of the profession or those involved in international comparative librarianship.

As stated, the international philosophy and policy of American librarianship throughout the Soviet era developed with little relation to either the actual situation in the USSR or to public opinion in the United States. Numerous cognitive flaws and psychological, moral, and political pathologies were at fault here. (To an extent, these appear to be similar to those which thrived among some other highly educated groups, like intellectuals.) The lack of a vibrant conservative librarianship and the near-total ascendancy of an internationalist, liberal orientation both reflected, and accounted for, many of these defects.

Twentieth century American anti-Communism, which eventually won a great victory, stemmed primarily from a devotion to freedom. It developed within a variety of social, cultural, and religious venues in different time periods: labor unions, political movements and parties, patriotic organizations, the Catholic Church, and elsewhere. It had widespread support among the general population. It was even prominent among a portion of intellectuals, primarily those who considered themselves conservative or neoconservative.[1] However, anti-Communism never found fertile ground within the leadership of the library profession, which vigorously fought it from the end of World War II through the demise of the Soviet Union.

Those who have written the history of librarianship have validated the traditional anti-anti-Communism of the profession by parroting their predecessors. In recent years, such historians have usually been faculty members in graduate schools of library and information studies in large public universities. This has facilitated their increasing use of the methods and products of academia's adversarial historiography. The perverse results have been closely critiqued in this volume.

Scholars who seek a full understanding of why the leaders of American librarianship failed to comprehend and oppose Communism and support their country's democratic ideals could provide some valuable insights into the enduring problems free societies will always confront in one form or another. (Much courage will be needed since their findings will not be well received by their colleagues who are besotted by myths, misinformation, and chronic maladies.) The succumbing of the Soviet Union has not meant the disappearance of all dangerous countries, Communist and otherwise. Moreover, the compulsion of some individuals to transmogrify their own democratic societies is still strong, as are the related intellectual, moral, and psychosocial disorders described in this book.[2]

Given the unique status of the United States in terms of its citizens' freedoms, its power, and its longstanding role as the ultimate guardian of the globe's democratic countries, it is vital to *all* peoples that America retain its essential political and social character—including its national sovereignty—and play a preeminent role in the world.[3] The most important measure of the library profession will continue to be the extent to which it helps attain these goals.

NOTES

1. Overviews of these anti-Communist movements can be found in Richard Gid Powers, *Not Without Honor: The History of American Anticommunism* (New York: The Free Press, 1995); and John Earl Haynes, *Red Scare or Red Menace: American Communism and Anticommunism in the Cold War Era* (Chicago: Ivan R. Dee, 1996). Specific people, efforts, books, and articles on the subject are referenced in these two works and described in Haynes' *Communism and Anti-Communism in the United States: An Annotated Guide to Historical Writings* (New York and London: Garland, 1987). His *Annotated Guide* is updated by the publication he edits, *Newsletter of the Historians of American Communism.*

As described in chapter two, the essential nature of the Soviet Union and of Communists in the United States were widely understood by Americans in the years following the Bolshevik coup. A reading of the literature of this period should convince even the most sceptical on this point. One particularly striking source here are the numerous pamphlets of the time, such as that by the socialist David P. Barrows: *Are Berkeley Socialists Bolshevists?* (Berkeley, CA: n.p., July 31, 1919). The salvos from the Communists against American liberals and socialists leave little room for confusion about their goals. (For example, see *The White Terrorists Ask for Mercy* [Chicago: Daily Worker Publishing, for the Workers Party of America, February 1925].) A useful source for early declarations by revolutionary groups that is still used by historians of all political persuasions is the so called "Lusk Report," after New York State Assemblyman Clayton Lusk, head of the committee which carried out the study: New York [State] Legislature, Joint Committee Investigating Seditious Activities, *Revolutionary Radicalism*, 4 vols. (Albany, NY: J. B. Lyon, 1920). However, leftist historians usually explain away the exhortations to violence and the support expressed for worldwide revolution led from Moscow. They also criticize or dismiss that half of the Lusk Report which described the positive programs to Americanize immigrants—one type of educational work that many public libraries were then engaged in.

The mass of the American people opposed Communism for numerous reasons. Given their traditional belief in individual freedom, even socialism in its most benign form never held much attraction for them. (The most recent attempt at a comprehensive study of socialism's rejection in the US comes to this conclusion, albeit almost reluctantly. See Seymour Martin Lipset and Gary Marks, *It Didn't Happen Here: Why Socialism Failed in the United States* [New York: W. W. Norton, 2000].) Moreover, the bulk of the citizenry has liked the society much the way it has been, not merely what it might one day be transformed into. Not surprisingly, most Americans opposed any foreign country or outside force which threatened to radically alter the republic's social and political profile or diminish its national autonomy. In this regard, the commitment to the nation's democratic nature—which has always been a widespread and strong element of American patriotism—has been of special significance. (Powers' *Not Without Honor* is valuable on some of these points, as are many of the works of Irving Kristol over the past thirty years.)

Embracing change and progress, but not mesmerized by utopian ideologies, the great majority of the populace considered Communism an anathema. Generally, only a few social types were attracted by its revolutionary message. It is relevant that Winston Churchill denounced Communists and their sympathizers as 'a gang of ruthless and bloody-minded professors.' (Quoted and analyzed by Peter Viereck in his *Shame and Glory of the Intellectuals: Babbitt Jr. vs. the Rediscovery of Values* [Boston: The Beacon Press, 1953], p. 109.) William Buckley's concern about the hubris of academics led him to declare: "I am obliged to confess that I should sooner live in a society governed by the first two thousand names in the Boston telephone directory than in a society governed by the two thousand faculty members of Harvard University." (Buckley, "A Reply to Robert Hutchins: The Aimlessness of American Education," in *Rumbles Left and Right*, by Buckley, intro. by Russell Kirk [New York: Macfadden-Bartell, 1964; originally published: G. P. Putnam's, 1963], p. 103.)

Another important factor was that approximately twenty per cent of US citizens in the twentieth century were Roman Catholics: the Church was one of the major intellectual, cultural, and spiritual opponents of Communism since the inception of this political movement. Its vital network of neighborhood churches and schools, as well as its universities, were in active service against it. Catholic anti-Communism, which frequently included neopopulist elements, is best understood if one first reads the following encyclicals: Pope Leo XIII, *Rerum Novarum* (aka *The Condition of Labor*), May 15, 1891; Pope Pius XI, *Quadragesimo Anno* (aka *Reconstructing the Social Order*), May 15, 1931; and Pope Pius XI, *Divini Redemptoris* (aka *Atheistic Communism*), March 19, 1937.

Jewish anti-Communism has had a more complex history. The foremost Jewish magazine of its time, *The American Hebrew*, was an opponent of the Bolsheviks from the inception of their coup. (For example, see "The Week in Review," *The American Hebrew* 105 [July 11, 1919]: 202.) However, many Jewish emigrants from the Russian Empire initially assumed that any form of government and society must be better than those which fostered the pogroms they had fled. Nevertheless, the most widely read Yiddish daily, *The Forward*, became strongly anti-Communist after its socialist editor visited the Soviet Union in 1925. *The American Hebrew* and *The Forward* reflected the lack of widespread appeal for the new ism in the American Jewish community. Despite this, many Communist Party members in the United States were Jews.

Some of the Jewish anti-Communists, like labor leader David Dubinsky, maintained their opposition throughout their lives. However, many prominent Jewish opponents of the USSR, like Bertram Wolfe, Jay Lovestone, and Eugene Lyons, emerged as such only after becoming disaffected with the Party and/or the Soviet Union in the 1930's. Well known today is the significance of the Jewish anti-Communist neoconservatives—e.g., Norman Podhoretz and Irving Kristol—whose liberal political views (including their liberal anti-Communism) began to change in the late 1960's. Unfortunately, largely forgotten now except by a dwindling number of traditional conservatives, are Jews who were not men of the Left and who had worked early on with conservatives. Among these were Isaac Don Levine, Alfred Kohlberg, George Sokolsky, and Morrie Ryskind. A pioneering work about them is the recent study showing that the preeminent journal of conservative anti-Communism, *National Review*, which started in 1955, would probably not have been born or survived for long without the intellectual and financial support from a half-dozen of William Buckley's Jewish friends and colleagues. (See George H. Nash, "Forgotten

Godfathers: Premature Jewish Conservatives and the Rise of *National Review*,"
American Jewish History 87 [June/Sept. 1999]: 123-57.) Objective scholarship
is also lacking on others with strong ties to conservative anti-Communism, like
Rabbi Benjamin Schultz and his American Jewish League Against Communism. (See Powers, *Not Without Honor*, p. 229.) There is still no scholarly
biography of Roy Cohn.

Seedbeds of anti-Communism in the United States were the immigrant
communities from countries that were threatened, or already occupied, by
Communist forces. Additionally, workers in the American labor movement
frequently had firsthand experience with Communists who tried to take over
their unions: to know them was to not love them.

As noted elsewhere, it is frequently ignored that many Americans wisely
remained anti-Soviet during World War II despite the fact that many in the
Roosevelt administration mistook a temporary Soviet-American military alliance
against a common enemy for something greater. (A starting point on this
subject is George Sirgiovanni, *An Undercurrent of Suspicion: Anti-Communism
in America during World War II* [New Brunswick, NJ, and London: Transaction Publishers, 1990].) The eventual triumph of anti-Communism is described
in : Andrew E. Busch, "Ronald Reagan and the Defeat of the Soviet Empire,"
Presidential Studies Quarterly 27 (Summer 1997): 451-66; Jay Winik, *On the
Brink: The Dramatic, Behind-the-Scenes Saga of the Reagan Era and the Men
and Women Who Won the Cold War* (New York: Simon and Schuster, 1996);
and Peter Schweizer, ed., *The Fall of the Berlin Wall: Reassessing the Causes
and Consequences of the End of the Cold War* (Stanford, CA: Hoover
Institution Press, Stanford University; and Washington, DC: William J. Casey
Institute of the Center for Security Policy, 2000). Schweizer's book includes
contributions by Richard V. Allen, Frank J. Gaffney Jr., and Fred C. Iklé.

Many valuable anti-Communist organizations and efforts remain to be
studied objectively. For example, the American Bar Association had a variety
of useful committees on Communism in the 1950's and 1960's, such as (1) the
Special Committee on Communist Tactics, Strategy, and Objectives, and (2) the
Standing Committee on Education about Communism and Its Contrast with
Liberty under Law. (See the latter's well-done academic study *A Contrast
between the Legal Systems in the United States and in the Soviet Union* [N.p.:
American Bar Association, 1968]; as well as the Standing Committee on
Education against Communism's scholarly *Peace or Peaceful Coexistence?*, by
Richard V. Allen, foreword by Bertram D. Wolfe [Chicago: American Bar
Association, 1966].) The most ignored and/or unfairly maligned of these anti-
Communist groups have been the grass-roots organizations, like the Cardinal
Mindszenty Foundation, America's Future, and the Christian Anti-Communism
Crusade. Thus, while President Ronald Reagan, William Buckley, and Jack
Kemp have praised the Christian Anti-Communism Crusade and have

participated in its conferences, it has nevertheless rarely received serious or positive treatment by historians. In addition to distributing their own publications, such groups have also broadened the audience for books by James Burnham, William Henry Chamberlin, and others.

Similarly, there is a dearth of biographies of anti-Communists, and many of those that have been written have been produced by their strongest critics. An academic has recently dared to write a biography of Senator Joseph McCarthy that is far more objective than previous ones by professional historians. (Arthur Herman, *Joseph McCarthy: Reexamining the Life and Legacy of America's Most Hated Senator* [New York: The Free Press, 2000].) A significant book on McCarthy is forthcoming from M. Stanton Evans, the author of several authoritative works on American politics and history. He serves as the director of the National Journalism Center.

Much more research is also needed on the history of anti-anti-Communism and its many successes. Emerging soon after the Bolshevik coup in 1917, it developed its own culture and traditions. Studies would include descriptions and analyses of efforts to minimize the threat of Communism, demonize or otherwise undercut anti-Communists, pervert the American legal system, blacklist non-Communists in the film industry, and purge higher education of anti-Communists. Charges of alleged Red-baiting, harassment, blacklisting, "McCarthyism," and so forth, have traditionally been freely made by liberals and those on the Left who have opposed anti-Communism. In contrast, little attention has been paid to the very real calumnies, threats, job discrimination, professional contempt, and "Brown-baiting" (unfairly charging that someone is a Brownshirt [after the uniform of the Stormtroopers], i.e., a Nazi) that anti-Communists, including those in educational and cultural institutions, were routinely subjected to for most of the twentieth century and continue to endure today. Studies of the frequent "Brown Scares" by anti-anti-Communists could prove revealing. A few examples of material already done in this and closely related areas are: Daniel Hawthorne, *Judge Medina: A Biography* (New York: Wilfred Funk, 1952, pp. 217-92); Billingsley, *Hollywood Party*, pp. 47, 179; Ryskind, *I Shot an Elephant in My Pajamas*, pp. 163-66; Hook, *Heresy*, Yes; *Conspiracy*, No; Root, *Collectivism on the Campus*; Buckley, *God and Man at Yale*; Wittmer, *Conquest of the American Mind*; Kirk, *Decadence and Renewal in the Higher Learning*; Francis Spufford, "The Heretic" [Ronald Radosh], *New Republic* 214 (June 17, 1996): 41-42; Powers, *Not Without Honor*, pp. 163-67; Hollander, *Political Pilgrims*; and Kimball, *Tenured Radicals*.

With the record of Communist brutality and aggression becoming even fuller than it had been in the past, it should be obvious that the study of this movement and of those who did—or did not—oppose it (and why) is of great significance. Recent summaries of Communist atrocities and imperialism in the twentieth century include: Stéphane Courtois, and others, *The Black Book of*

Communism: Crimes, Terror, Repression, trans. by Jonathan Murphy and Mark Kramer (Cambridge, MA, and London: Harvard University Press, 1999; originally published as *Le Livre Noir du Communisme: Crimes, Terreur, Répression*, Paris: Robert Laffont, 1997); and Oleg Sarin, and Lev Dvoretzky, *Alien Wars: The Soviet Union's Aggressions against the World, 1919 to 1989* (Novato, CA: Presidio Press, 1996).

2. See the first sixteen pages of chapter ten and the scores of relevant studies cited in their notes. Some works which include analyses specifically of the political, social, and cultural developments of the past fifteen years are: Paul Hollander, "Modernity and Its Discontents," *Orbis* 43 (Fall 1999): 661-71; Hollander, "Introduction to the Transaction Edition: The Durable Significance of the Political Pilgrimage," *Political Pilgrims: Western Intellectuals in Search of the Good Society*, 4th ed., by Hollander (New Brunswick, NJ, and London: Transaction, 1998), pp. ix-lxii; Hollander, *Anti-Americanism: Critiques at Home and Abroad* (New York and Oxford: Oxford University Press, 1992); Hollander, *Decline and Discontent: Communism and the West Today* (New Brunswick, NJ, and London: Transaction, 1992); Hilton Kramer and Roger Kimball, eds., *The Betrayal of Liberalism: How the Disciples of Freedom and Equality Helped Foster the Illiberal Politics of Coercion and Control* (Chicago: Ivan R. Dee, 1999); Kramer and Kimball, eds., *Against the Grain:* The New Criterion *on Art and Intellect at the End of the Twentieth Century* (Chicago: Ivan R. Dee, 1995); Edith Kurzweil and William Phillips, eds., *Our Country, Our Culture: The Politics of Political Correctness* (Boston: Partisan Review Press, 1994); Georgie Ann Geyer, *Americans No More: The Death of Citizenship* (New York: Atlantic Monthly Press, 1996); Arthur M. Schlesinger, Jr., *The Disuniting of America: Reflections on a Multicultural Society*, revised and enlarged ed. (New York: W. W. Norton, 1998); and Thomas Sowell, *The Quest for Cosmic Justice* (New York: The Free Press, 1999). Some of these works affirm that the desire for radical change within the United States has become stronger because overseas models of utopia have disappeared. I think it is more likely that it reflects the coming to power of the sixties generation and the institutionalization of its adversarial stance to traditional culture.

The notion that the loss of American sovereignty is not only inevitable, but salutary, has gained a new respectability in the so-called "mainstream" media. For example, see Henry Grunwald, "A World Without a Country?" *Wall Street Journal* (Jan. 1, 2000): R44, R46. Grunwald is the former editor-in-chief of *Time, Inc.* and the former US ambassador to Austria. Two weeks after his piece appeared, the cover of *The New Republic* proclaimed in big letters: "America is Surrendering Its Sovereignty to a World Government. Hooray." (The article being touted was Robert Wright's "Continental Drift," *The New Republic* [Jan. 17, 2000]: 18, 20-23.) Some of the social, political, intellectual, and economic factors related to this are described in Christopher Lasch, *The Revolt of the*

Elites and the Betrayal of Democracy (New York: W. W. Norton, 1995), pp. 33-49, and elsewhere; and Patrick J. Buchanan, *The Great Betrayal: How American Sovereignty and Social Justice are Being Sacrificed to the Gods of the Global Economy* (Boston: Little, Brown, 1998), pp. 93-108, 261-92.

The military threat posed by China, and the lax American response, are best revealed in: US House of Representatives Select Committee on US National Security and Military/Commercial Concerns with the People's Republic of China, *Report*, 3 vols., submitted by Mr. [Christopher] Cox, Chairman (Washington, DC: GPO, May 25, 1999). See also: Aaron L. Friedberg, "Arming China against Ourselves," *Commentary* 108 (July/Aug. 1999): 27-33; Christopher Hitchens, "The Spies Who Fleeced Us," *The Nation* 269 (July 12, 1999): 8; James Lilley and Carl Ford, "China's Military: A Second Opinion," *The National Interest*, no. 57 (Fall 1999): 71-77; and Michael Pillsbury, *China Debates the Future Security Environment* (Washington, DC: National Defense University Press, 2000). On the dangers posed by the Democratic People's Republic of Korea, see Nicholas Eberstadt, *The End of North Korea* (Washington, DC: AEI Press, 1999).

As in the past, the American library profession usually courts Communist countries while savaging democratic and pro-Western ones. See the following by Stephen Karetzky: "American Library Community Ignores Plight of Ukrainian Colleague," *Newsletter of the International Society of Jewish Librarians* [aka *Jewish Librarians Caucus Newsletter*] 9 (Jan.-March 1985): 19; "The American Library Association Versus Israel," *Midstream* 31 (March 1985): 31-32; "Turkish Turbulence," (letter) *American Libraries* 29 (March 1998): 34; and "Cuba, Communism, Communication," (letter) *American Libraries* 29 (June/July 1998): 52.

3. The soundness of such a foreign policy, as well as its relationship to the battle waged during the Cold War, is made clear in Robert Kagan and William Kristol, "The Present Danger," *The National Interest*, no. 59 (Spring 2000): 57-69. Margaret Thatcher concurs in "Courage," speech, Washington, DC, Dec. 10, 1997, in *Leadership for America: The Principles of Conservatism*, ed. by Edwin J. Feulner, Jr. (Dallas: Spence Publishing, 2000), pp. 6-17; and her "Time for Leadership," *Hoover Digest: Research and Opinion on Public Policy* (Fall 2000): 8-21. See also: Elliot Abrams, "Why America Must Lead," *The National Interest*, no. 28 (Summer 1992): 56-62; Charles Krauthammer, "The Unipolar Moment," in *Rethinking America's Security: Beyond Cold War to New World Order*, ed. by Graham Allison and Gregory F. Treverton (New York and London: W. W. Norton, 1992), pp. 295-306; Coral Bell, "American Ascendancy and the Pretense of Concert," *The National Interest*, no. 57 (Fall 1999): 55-63; Ashley J. Tellis, "Smoke, Fire, and What to Do in Asia," *Policy Review*, no. 100 (April/May 2000): 15-34; Sen. Jesse Helms, "Respect the Sovereignty of the American People," speech to the UN Security Council, Jan. 20, 2000, *Vital*

Speeches 66 (Feb. 15, 2000): 268-72; and Cliff Kincaid, *The United Nations Today* (Owings, MD: America's Survival, 2000) [44 p.].

Many of the views on American foreign policy expressed in these works and those cited in note 2 can be found in Robert Kagan and William Kristol, eds., *Present Dangers: Crisis and Opportunity in American Foreign and Defense Policy* (San Francisco: Encounter Books, 2000).

BIBLIOGRAPHY

Aaron, Daniel. *Writers on the Left: Episodes in American Literary Communism.* New York: Harcourt, Brace & World, 1961. Reprinted: New York: Octagon Books, 1979.

Abel, Lionel. *The Intellectual Follies: A Memoir of the Literary Venture in New York and Paris.* New York: W. W. Norton, 1984.

Abrams, Elliot. "Why America Must Lead." *The National Interest,* no. 28 (Summer 1992): 56-62.

Adler, Les K., and Thomas G. Paterson. "Red Fascism: The Merger of Nazi Germany and Soviet Russia in the American Image of Totalitarianism, 1930's-1950's." *American Historical Review* 75 (April 1970): 1046-1064.

Adorno, T. W., and others. *The Authoritarian Personality.* New York: Harper & Bros., 1950.

"The Agony of Reizia Palatnik." *Assistant Librarian* 64 (Oct. 1971): 146-49.

ALA World Encyclopedia of Library and Information Services. Chicago: American Library Association, 1980.

ALA World Encyclopedia of Library and Information Services. 2nd ed. Chicago: American Library Association, 1986.

Allen, Richard V. *Peace or Peaceful Coexistence?* Foreword by Bertram D. Wolfe. Chicago: American Bar Association, 1966.

Alstedt, Valter. "Library Education in the Soviet Union." *College and Research Libraries* 19 (Nov. 1958): 467-70. Reprinted from *Biblioteksbladet* [Lund, Sweden] 9 (1957). Trans. by Thomas R. Buckman.

America and the Intellectuals: A Symposium. New York: Partisan Review, 1953. Originally published as "Our Country and Our Culture" in *Partisan Review* (1952).

American Bar Association, Standing Committee on Education about Communism and its Contrast with Liberty under Law. *A Contrast between the Legal Systems in the United States and in the Soviet Union.* N.p.: The American Bar Association, 1968.

American Library Association. "Message to Russia." *Bulletin of the American Library Association* 11 (June 1917): 328-29.

————. Overseas Library Statement." Adopted by ALA Council, June 25, 1953. *ALA Bulletin* 47 (Nov. 1953): 487.

————. "Recipients Named for Jessie H. Shera Award for Distinguished Published Research." < http://www.ala.org/news/v4n17/ jesseshera.html>. May 5, 1999. Accessed Sept. 9, 1999.

————. "Statement on Labeling." (July 31, 1951.) Reprinted in ALA, *Intellectual Freedom Manual.* 5th ed. 1996. Pp. 114-15.

American Library Association, Board on Resources of American Libraries and [the] International Relations Board. *Conference on International Cultural, Educational, and Scientific Exchanges.* Princeton University, Nov. 25-26, 1946. Chicago: American Library Association, 1947.

American Library Association, Office for Intellectual Freedom. *Intellectual Freedom Manual.* 5th ed. Chicago: American Library Association, 1996.

Amnesty International. "The Case of Hanna Mykhaylenko" and "Petition to USSR Minister of Health." *Newsletter of the International Society of Jewish Librarians* 9 (Jan.-March 1985): 20-21, 23.

Aptheker, Herbert. Review of *No Ivory Tower*, by Ellen Schrecker. *Journal of American History* 74 (Dec. 1987): 1093-95.

Arendt, Hannah. *The Origins of Totalitarianism.* New ed. New York: Harcourt Brace, 1975.

Armstrong, John A. *Ideology, Politics, and Government in the Soviet Union.* 3rd ed. New York: Praeger, 1974.

Arnot, R. Page. *The Impact of the Russian Revolution in Britain.* London: Lawrence and Wishart, 1967.

Aron, Raymond. *The Opium of the Intellectuals.* With new foreword by Aron. Trans. by Terence Kilmartin. New York: Norton, 1962. First editions in English: Garden City, NY: Doubleday, 1957; London: Secker & Warburg, 1957. Originally published as *L'Opium des Intellectuels.* Paris: Calmann Lévy, 1955.

Asheim, Lester. *Librarianship in the Developing Countries.* Urbana: University of Illinois Press, 1966.

"Avrahm Yarmolinsky—The List [of his Writings, 1909-1955]." *Bulletin of the New York Public Library* 59 (March 1955): 110-32.

Baaken, Frode. "Matter of Conscience." (Letter.) *Assistant Librarian* 74 (Sept. 1981): 123.

Backus, Oswald P., III. "Recent Experiences with Soviet Libraries and Archives: Uncommon Resources and Potential for Exchange." *College and Research Libraries* 20 (Nov. 1959): 469-73, 499.

Baldwin, Roger N. *Liberty under the Soviets.* New York: Vanguard Press, 1928.

Barasenkov, V. "The Saltykov-Scedrin State Public Library, Leningrad."

Unesco Bulletin for Libraries 11 (Feb.-March 1957): 32-35.

Barmine, Alexander. "The New Communist Conspiracy." *Reader's Digest* 45 (Oct. 1944): 27-33.

Barrows, David P. *Are Berkeley Socialists Bolshevists?* Berkeley, CA: n.p., July 31, 1919. (Pamphlet)

Bartlett, John, and others, eds. *Familiar Quotations.* 15th ed. Boston: Little, Brown, 1980.

Bassow, Whitman. *The Moscow Correspondents: Reporting on Russia from the Revolution to Glasnost.* Reprint: New York: Paragon House, 1989. Originally published: New York: William Morrow, 1988.

Bastiat, Frédéric. *La Loi.* Paris: Guillaumin, 1850. As translated and published: *The Law.* Trans. by Dean Russell. Irvington-on-Hudson, NY: Foundation for Economic Education, 1950. First English trans.: 1853.

Baumanis, Arturs, and Robert A. Martin. *Soviet Book Statistics: A Guide to Their Use and Interpretation.* Urbana, IL: University of Illinois Library School, Occasional Paper number 44, Dec. 1955.

————, and A. Robert Rogers. "Soviet Classification and Cataloging." *Library Quarterly* 28 (July 1958): 172-86.

Beatty, Bessie. *The Red Heart of Russia.* New York: The Century Co., 1918.

Beichman, Arnold. "Robert Hutchins Meets the Press." *The New Leader* (Nov. 21, 1955): 18-20.

Bell, Bernard Iddings. *Crowd Culture.* New York: Harper & Bros., 1952.

Bell, Coral. "American Ascendancy and the Pretense of Concert." *The National Interest*, no. 57 (Fall 1999): 55-63.

Bell, Daniel. *The End of Ideology: On the Exhaustion of Political Ideas in the Fifties.* Glencoe, IL: The Free Press, 1960.

————, ed. *The New American Right.* New York: Criterion Books, 1955.

————, ed. *The Radical Right:* The New American Right *Expanded and Updated.* Garden City, NY: Doubleday, 1963.

Benda, Julian. *The Treason of the Intellectuals (La Trahison des Clercs).* Trans. by Richard Aldington. New York: Norton, 1969. Previously published in New York: William Morrow, 1928; in London as *The Betrayal of the Intellectuals.* First French edition: *La Trahison des Clercs* (Paris: Bernard Grasset, 1927).

Benemann, William E. "Tears and Ivory Towers: California Libraries during the McCarthy Era." *American Libraries* 8 (June 1977): 305-9.

Benson, Robert Louis, and Michael Warner, eds. *Venona: Soviet Espionage and the American Response, 1939-1957.* Washington, DC: National Security Agency and the Central Intelligence Agency, 1996.

Benton, William. "Too Busy to Think?" *ALA Bulletin* 52 (June 1958): 441-43.

————. "William Benton Reports on Russian Libraries." *Library Journal* 81 (Nov. 15, 1956): 2650-51.

Berdyaev, Nicholas. *The Origin of Russian Communism.* Trans. by R. M. French. London: Geoffrey Bles, 1937, 1948. As reprinted: Ann Arbor: University of Michigan Press, 1960.

Bereday, George Z. F.; William W. Brickman; and Gerald H. Read; eds. *The Changing Soviet School: The Comparative Education Society Field Study in the U.S.S.R.* Boston: Houghton Mifflin, 1960.

Berkman, Alexander, ed. *Letters from Russian Prisons.* New York: Albert and Charles Boni, 1925.

Berkowitz, Bruce D. "Who Won the Cold War—and Why it Matters." Review essay. *Orbis: A Journal of World Affairs* 40 (Winter 1996): 164-71.

Berthold, Arthur B. "Dispensing Library Ammunition." *Wilson Bulletin for Librarians* 9 (Nov. 1934): 130-32, 135.

————. "Survey of Recent Russian Library Literature." *Library Quarterly* 17 (April 1947): 138-47.

————. "The Young Librarian." *Wilson Bulletin for Librarians* 8 (Jan. 1934): 296-97.

Besançon, Alain. "Forgotten Communism." *Commentary* 105 (Jan. 1998): 24-27.

Bestor, A. E. *Educational Wastelands.* Urbana, IL: University of Illinois Press, 1953.

Bethell, Tom. "But Can Juanito Really Read?" *National Review* 35 (Sept. 30, 1983): 1196-99.

Beyerly, Elizabeth. "A Russian Abstracting Service in the Field of Sciences: *Referativnyi zhurnal.*" *Aslib Proceedings* 8 (May 1956): 135-40.

Billingsley, Kenneth Lloyd. *Hollywood Party: How Communism Seduced the American Film Industry in the 1930's and 1940's.* Rocklin, CA: Forum/Prima, 1998.

Billington, James H. *Fire in the Minds of Men: Origins of the Revolutionary Faith.* New York: Basic Books, 1980.

————. *Russia Transformed: Breakthrough to Hope.* New York: The Free Press, 1992.

Biographical Dictionary of the Left. 4 vols. Ed. by Francis X. Gannon. Boston and Los Angeles: Western Islands Publishers, 1969-1973.

Black, Donald V. "Report on the Right." Review of *The American Right Wing,* by Ellsworth and Harris. *Library Journal* 87 (Feb. 15, 1962): 745-46.

Black's Law Dictionary. Ed. by Bryan A. Garner. 7th ed. St. Paul, MN: West Publishing, 1999.

Blanshard, Paul. *American Freedom and Catholic Power.* Boston: Beacon

Press, 1949. 2nd ed.: 1958.

————. *Communism, Democracy, and Catholic Power*. Boston: Beacon Press, 1951.

————. *The Right to Read: The Battle against Censorship*. Boston: Beacon Press, 1955.

Boaz, Martha. "The Comparative and International Library Science Course in American Library Schools." In *Comparative and International Library Science*. Ed. by Harvey. Pp. 167-80.

————. "International Education: An Imperative Need." *Journal of Education for Library and Information Science* 26 (Winter 1986): 165-73.

Bolubash, Anna. "The Great Ukrainian Famine of 1932-1933 as an Instrument of Russian Nationalities Policy, Part I." *The Ukrainian Review* 26 (Winter 1978): 11-23.

————. "The Great Ukrainian Famine of 1932-1933 as an Instrument of Russian Nationalities Policy, Part II." *The Ukrainian Review* 27 (Spring 1979): 31-59.

Booker, M. Keith. *Film and the American Left: A Research Guide*. Westport, CT, and London: Greenwood Press, 1999.

Bottomore, Tom, ed. *A Dictionary of Marxist Thought*. 2nd ed. Cambridge, MA; and Oxford, England: Basil Blackwell, 1991.

Bowen, Elizabeth. "Libraries in the USSR." *Ontario Library Review* 42 (May 1958): 114-16.

Bowker, R. R. "For Russia." *Library Journal* 42 (August 1917): 599-605.

————. "Help for Russian Librarians." *Library Journal* 47 (Sept. 15, 1922): 756.

————. "Relief for Russian Librarians." *Library Journal* 47 (June 1, 1922): 495.

————. Untitled editorials in *Library Journal*: 47 (April 15, 1922): 363; 48 (Feb. 15, 1923): 179; 48 (Nov. 15, 1923): 967; 49 (March 15, 1924): 287; 49 (Sept. 1, 1924): 741; 50 (Dec. 1, 1925): 1006.

————. "Who Will Help Russian Librarians?" *Library Journal* 47 (April 1, 1922): 310.

————. "Who Will Help Russian Librarians?" *Library Journal* 47 (April 15, 1922): 358.

————, and Zinovi Rechkoff. "Literature and Science in Russia." *Library Journal* 43 (March 1918): 164-66.

Boyer, Paul [S.]. *By the Bomb's Early Light: American Thought and Culture at the Dawn of the Atomic Era*. New York: Pantheon, 1985.

————. *Fallout: A Historian Reflects on America's Half-Century Encounter with Nuclear Weapons*. Columbus: Ohio State University Press, 1998.

Boyle, Donzella Cross. *American History was My Undoing: A Case Study of a Textbook*. Fullerton, CA: Education Information, 1961.

Bozell, Patricia B. "Liberal Education at Vassar." *The Freeman* (Jan. 12, 1953): 269-72.

Braestrup, Peter. *The Big Story: How the American Press and Television Reported and Interpreted the Crisis of Tet 1968 in Vietnam and Washington.* Garden City, NY: Anchor Press, 1978.

Breindel, Eric M. "The Communists and the Committees." *Commentary* 71 (Jan. 1981): 46-52.

Brinkley, David. "The Problem of American Conservatism." *American Historical Review* 99 (April 1994): 409-29.

Brooks, Jeffrey. *When Russia Learned to Read: Literacy and Popular Literature, 1861-1917.* Princeton, NJ: Princeton University Press, 1985.

Brown, Edward J. "Literature of the Humanities." In *Iron Curtains and Scholarship.* Ed. by Winger. Pp. 96-110.

Brown, William Adams, Jr. *The Groping Giant: Revolutionary Russia as Seen by an American Democrat.* New Haven: Yale University Press, 1920; London: Humphrey Milford and Oxford University Press.

Bruce-Briggs, B., ed. *The New Class?* New Brunswick, NJ: Transaction Books, 1979.

Bryant, Douglas W. "The American Scholar and Barriers to Knowledge." In *Iron Curtains and Scholarship.* Ed. by Winger. Pp. 13-27.

[Bryant, Louise.] "The First Woman of Russia: Nadezhda Krupskaya." In *Lenin's Impact on the United States.* Ed. by Daniel Mason, Jessica Smith, and David Laibman. New York: NWR Publications, 1970. Pp. 73-76.

Brzezinski, Zbigniew. *Between Two Ages: America's Role in the Technetronic Era.* Harmondsworth, England: Penguin, 1976. Originally published by Viking Press, 1970.

———. Speech. New York: Columbia University, April 1982.

Buchanan, Patrick J. *The Great Betrayal: How American Sovereignty and Social Justice are Being Sacrificed to the Gods of the Global Economy.* Boston: Little, Brown, 1998.

Buckley, William F., Jr. "And Who is the Ugliest of Them All?" Review of *Scoundrel Time,* by Hellman. *National Review* 29 (Jan. 21, 1977): 101-6.

———. *God and Man at Yale: The Superstitions of "Academic Freedom."* With new intro. by Buckley. Washington, DC: Regnery Gateway, 1986. Originally published: Chicago: Henry Regnery, 1951.

———. *Rumbles Left and Right.* Intro. by Russell Kirk. New York: Macfadden-Bartell, 1964. Originally published: G. P. Putnam's, 1963.

———. *Up from Liberalism.* With a reintroduction by Buckley. Foreword by John Dos Passos. Briarcliff Manor, NY: Stein and Day, 1984. Originally published: New York: McDowell, Obolensky, 1959.

————, and L. Brent Bozell. *McCarthy and His Enemies: The Record and its Meaning.* New ed. Washington, DC: Regnery, 1995. Originally published: Chicago: Henry Regnery, 1954.

————, and others. *The Committee and Its Critics: A Calm Review of the House Committee on Un-American Activities.* New York: G. P. Putnam's Sons, 1962.

Burbank, Jane. *Intelligentsia and Revolution: Russian Views of Bolshevism, 1917-1922.* New York and Oxford: Oxford University Press, 1986.

Burdick, Charles B. *Ralph Lutz and the Hoover Institution.* Stanford, CA: Hoover Institution Press, 1974.

Burke, Edmund. *Reflections on the Revolution in France.* London: J. Dodsley, 1790. As republished: Intro. by Russell Kirk. Chicago: Henry Regnery, 1955.

Burnam, Jeffrey M. Review of *Seeds of Repression,* by Athan Theoharis. *Annals of the American Academy of Political and Social Science* 399 (Jan. 1972): 224-26.

Burnham, James. *Suicide of the West: An Essay on the Meaning and Destiny of Liberalism.* Chicago: Regnery, 1985. Originally published: New York: John Day, 1964.

Busch, Andrew E. "Ronald Reagan and the Defeat of the Soviet Empire." *Presidential Studies Quarterly* 27 (Summer 1997): 451-66.

California. Senate Investigating Committee on Education. *Tenth Report: The 1951 Hearings.* Sacramento: The Senate, August 12, 1952.

————. *Third Report: Textbooks.* Sacramento: The Senate, March 27, 1948.

California. State Senate Fact-Finding Committee on Un-American Activities. *Fourth Report: 1948: Communist Front Organizations.* Sacramento: The Senate, March 25, 1948.

California Legislature. Joint Fact-Finding Committee on Un-American Activities. *Third Report: Un-American Activities in California.* Sacramento: The Senate, March 24, 1947.

California Library [Association] Committee on Intellectual Freedom. *The Right to Know: An Analysis of the Criticisms of* Building America. N.p.: The Committee, June 1948. (Pamphlet, 18 pp.)

Cannicci, Lynn [Amnesty International, USA]. Letter to Stephen Karetzky. March 3, 1985. Published in *Newsletter of the International Society of Jewish Librarians* [aka *Jewish Librarians Caucus Newsletter*] 9 (Jan.-March 1985): 22.

Carlson, Oliver. "A Slanted Guide to Library Selections." *The Freeman* 2 (Jan. 14, 1952): 239-42.

————. "What Really Happened in Pasadena?" *The Freeman* 1 (July 30, 1951): 681-84.

Carnovsky, Leon. "Libraries in Nazi Germany." *Library Journal* 59 (Nov. 1934): 893-94.

————. "Patterns of Library Government and Coverage in European Nations." In *International Aspects of Librarianship*. Ed. by Carnovsky. Pp. 58-73.

————, ed. *International Aspects of Librarianship*. Papers Presented before the Eighteenth Annual Conference of the Graduate Library School of the University of Chicago. Chicago: University of Chicago Press, 1954. Also published (with different pagination) as *Library Quarterly* 24 (April 1954).

Carroll, Frances Laverne. "Library Education." In *Comparative and International Library Science*. Ed. by John F. Harvey. Metuchen, NJ, and London: Scarecrow Press, 1977. Pp. 148-66.

Casey, Jane Barnes. *I, Krupskaya: My Life with Lenin—A Novel*. Boston: Houghton Mifflin, 1974.

Cashmore, H. M. "Libraries in Russia." *The Library Association Record* 39 (June 1937): 298-300.

————. "Russia." In *A Survey of Libraries*. Gen. ed. by L. McColvin. Pp. 308-44.

Cassidy, Robert. *Margaret Mead: A Voice for the Century*. New York: Universe Books, 1982.

Caute, David. *Communism and the French Intellectuals: 1914-1960*. New York: Macmillan, 1964.

————. *The Fellow-Travellers: A Postscript to the Enlightenment*. New York: Macmillan, 1973.

————. *The Great Fear: The Anti-Communist Purge under Truman and Eisenhower*. New York: Simon and Schuster, 1978.

Cebotarev, G. A. "The Library of the USSR Academy of Sciences." *Unesco Bulletin for Libraries* 10 (Oct. 1956): 225-26.

Ceplair, Larry, and Steven Englund. *The Inquisition in Hollywood: Politics in the Film Community, 1930-1960*. Garden City, NY: Anchor Press/Doubleday, 1980.

Chamberlin, William Henry. "Anti-Anti-Communism: A Ford Investment." *National Review* 1 (April 11, 1956): 16-18.

Chambers, Whittaker. *Witness*. With new preface by Robert Novak. Foreword by Milton Hindus. Washington, DC: Regnery, 1988. Originally published: New York: Random House, 1952.

Chandler, George. *Libraries, Documentation and Bibliography in the USSR, 1917-1971: Survey and Critical Analysis of Soviet Studies, 1967-1971*. London and New York: Seminar Press, 1972.

Chase, John W. "Expanded Articles." Review of *American Freedom and Catholic Power*, by Paul Blanshard. *New York Times Book Review* (May

15, 1949): 15.

Chesnut, Charlotte Forgey. *The Alabama Librarian* 2 (July 1960): 68-69.

The Chicago Manual of Style. 14th ed. Chicago and London: University of Chicago Press, 1993.

Childs, James B. "Russian Library Exhibit." (Letter.) *Library Journal* 68 (July 1943): 565, 566.

Choldin, Marianna Tax. "Access to Foreign Publications in Soviet Libraries." *Libraries & Culture* 26 (Winter 1991): 135-50.

―――. *"CA [Current Anthropology]* and Soviet Censorship: An Interrupted Conversation with My Father." *Current Anthropology Supplement* 37 (Feb. 1996): S129-30.

―――. "Censorship in the Slavic World: An Exhibition in the New York Public Library, June 1-October 15, 1984." New York: New York Public Library, 1984.

―――. "Censorship Under Gorbachev." *Solanus* 5 (1991): 130-42.

―――. *A Fence Around the Empire: Russian Censorship of Western Ideas under the Tsars.* Durham, NC: Duke University Press, 1985.

―――. "The New Censorship: Censorship by Translation in the Soviet Union." *Journal of Library History* 21 (Spring 1986): 334-49.

―――. "The Russian Bibliographical Society, 1889-1930." *Library Quarterly* 46 (Jan. 1976): 1-19.

―――. "Some Developments in Nineteenth Century Bibliography: Russia." *Libri* 27 (June 1977): 108-15.

―――, ed. *Access to Resources in the 80's.* Proceedings of the First International Conference of Slavic Librarians and Information Specialists. New York: Russica, 1982.

―――, ed. *Books, Libraries, and Information in Slavic and East European Studies.* Proceedings of the Second International Conference of Slavic Librarians and Information Specialists. New York: Russica, 1986.

―――, and Maurice Friedberg, eds. *The Red Pencil: Artists, Scholars, and Censors in the USSR.* With translations by Maurice Friedberg and Barbara Dash. Boston and London: Unwin Hyman, 1989.

Christie, Richard, and Marie Jahoda, eds. *Studies in the Scope and Method of* The Authoritarian Personality. Glencoe, IL: The Free Press, 1954.

Chubaryan, O. S. "Library Science in the System of Sciences." In *Reader in Comparative Librarianship.* Ed. by D. J. Foskett. Pp. 141-48.

―――. "Reading in Modern Society: Reading and Motivating Forces of Modern Society." In *Reading in a Changing World.* Ed. by Morhardt. Pp. 49-62.

―――, and others. *The Public Library: Its Role in Socio-Economic and Cultural Life of the Society (From Soviet Libraries' Experience).* Moscow: V. I. Lenin State Library, 1974.

————. "Librarianship in the System of the Sciences." *Libri*, vol. 21, no. 4 (1971): 336-49.

Church, Robert L., and Michael W. Sedlak. *Education in the United States: An Interpretive History.* New York: The Free Press, 1976. London: Collier Macmillan.

Churchill, Winston S. *Blood, Toil, Tears, and Sweat: The Speeches of Winston Churchill.* Ed. and intro. by David Cannadine. Boston: Houghton Mifflin, 1989.

————. *Churchill Speaks, 1897-1963: Collected Speeches in Peace and War.* Ed. by Robert Rhodes James. New York: Barnes & Noble, 1998. Originally published by Chelsea House, 1980.

————. *Winston S. Churchill's Maxims and Reflections.* Ed. by Colin Coote and Denzil Batchelor. Intro. by Coote. New York: Barnes & Noble, 1992.

Cipolla, Carlo M. *Literacy and Development in the West.* Harmondsworth, England, and Baltimore, MD: Penguin Books, 1969.

Clapp, Verner W. "About Russian Publications." (Letter.) *Library Journal* 71 (Aug. 1946): 1029.

Cogley, John. "The Murrow Show." *Commonweal* 59 (March 26, 1954): 618.

————. *Report on Blacklisting.* 2 vols. New York: The Fund for the Republic, 1956.

Cohen, Eliot A. "The Future of Force and American Strategy." *The National Interest* 48 (Fall 1990): 3-15.

Cohn, Roy. Letter to the author. Oct. 4, 1983.

————. *McCarthy.* New York: New American Library, 1968. Reprinted with additional preface and afterword as: *McCarthy: The Answer to "Tail Gunner Joe"* [NBC/Universal, 1977]. New York: Manor Books, 1977.

The Cold War and the University: Toward an Intellectual History of the Cold War. New York: The New Press, 1997.

Cole, John Y. "Archibald MacLeish." In *World Encyclopedia of Library and Information Services*, 3rd ed. Pp. 529-30.

————. "Luther Evans." In *Supplement to the Dictionary of American Library Biography.* Ed. by Wiegand. Pp. 22-26.

Cole, Toby. "A Library on the Soviet Union." *Library Journal* 70 (May 15, 1945): 476-79.

————. "A Special Libraries Conference on Russian Materials." *Library Journal* 71 (May 15, 1946): 730-33.

————. Untitled review of *A Guide to the Soviet Union* by William Mandel. *Library Journal* 71 (Aug. 1946): 1048.

Coleman, Margaret P. "America, Russia, and Adult Education." *Wilson Bulletin for Librarians* 10 (Dec. 1935): 235-39.

Coleman, Peter. "The Brief Life of Liberal Anti-Communism." *National Review* 41 (Sept. 15, 1989): 34-36.

―――. *The Liberal Conspiracy: The Congress for Cultural Freedom and the Struggle for the Mind of Postwar Europe.* New York: The Free Press, 1989; London: Collier Macmillan.

Collier, Peter, and David Horowitz. "McCarthyism: The Last Refuge of the Left." *Commentary* 85 (Jan. 1988): 36-41.

The Columbia Encyclopedia. 5th ed. New York: Columbia University Press, 1993.

Combs, Richard E. "Critical Analysis of 'Building America' Series." In California. Senate Investigating Committee on Education. *Third Report: Textbooks.* Sacramento: The Senate, March 27, 1948. Pp. 45-120.

―――. "How Communists Make Stooges out of Movie Stars." *American Legion Magazine* (May 1949): 14-15, 42-46.

Comfort, Nicholas. *Brewer's Politics: A Phrase and Fable Dictionary.* London: Cassell, 1993.

Commager, Henry Steele. "Ten Guideposts for Our Foreign Policy." *New York Times Magazine* (Feb. 21, 1954): 7, 20, 22-23.

―――. "Was Yalta a Calamity?" *New York Times Magazine* (Aug. 3, 1952): 7, 48-49.

―――. "Washington Witch Hunt." *Nation* 164 (April 5, 1947): 385-88.

―――. "Who is Loyal to America?" *Harper's Magazine* 195 (Sept. 1947): 193-99.

―――, ed. *Living Ideas in America.* New York: Harper, 1951.

Communism in Action: A Documented Study and Analysis of Communism in Operation in the Soviet Union Prepared at the Instance and under the Direction of Representative Everett M. Dirksen by the Legislative Reference Service of the Library of Congress, under the Direction of Ernest S. Griffith. Washington, DC: GPO, 1946.

Congdon, Lee. "Anti-Anti-Communism." *Academic Questions* 1 (Summer 1988): 42-54.

Conquest, Robert. *The Harvest of Sorrow: Soviet Collectivization and the Terror-Famine.* New York: Oxford University Press, 1986.

Cook, Fred J. *The Nightmare Decade: The Life and Times of Senator Joe McCarthy.* New York: Random House, 1971.

Cooney, Terry A. *The Rise of the New York Intellectuals: Partisan Review and its Circle, 1934-1945.* Madison, WI: University of Wisconsin Press, 1986.

Corry, John. "Hissteria: Why Do They Insist on Distorting History?" *American Spectator* 29 (May 1996): 46-47.

Couch, W. T. "The Sainted Book Burners." *The Freeman* 5 (April 1955): 423-26.

Counts, George S. "Dare Progressive Education Be Progressive?" *Progressive Education* 9 (April 1932): 257-63.
————. *Dare the School Build a New Social Order?* New York: John Day, 1932.
————. *The Prospects of American Democracy.* New York: John Day, 1938.
————. *The Soviet Challenge to America.* New York: John Day, 1931.
————, assisted by Nucia Lodge. *The Challenge of Soviet Education.* New York: McGraw-Hill, 1957.
————, and Nucia Lodge. *The Country of the Blind: The Soviet System of Mind Control.* Boston: Houghton Mifflin, 1949.
————, and others. *Bolshevism, Fascism, and Capitalism: An Account of the Three Economic Systems.* New Haven: Yale University Press for the Institute of Politics, Williams College, 1932.
Courtois, Stéphane, and others. *The Black Book of Communism: Crimes, Terror, Repression.* Trans. by Jonathan Murphy and Mark Kramer. Cambridge, MA, and London: Harvard University Press, 1999. Originally published as *Le Livre Noir de Communisme: Crimes, Terreur, Répression.* Paris: Robert Laffont, 1997.
Cox, Michael. Untitled review of *Still Seeing Red*, by White. *Political Studies* 46 (Sept. 1998): 841.
Cremin, Lawrence A. *The Transformation of the School: Progressivism in American Education, 1876-1957.* New York: Knopf, 1969.
Crossman, Richard, ed. *The God that Failed.* New York: Bantam, 1965. Originally published: London: Hamish Hamilton; New York: Harper, 1950.
Culbert, David. Review of *The Inquisition in Hollywood*, by Ceplair and Englund. *Journal of American History* 68 (June 1981): 184-86.
Curtis, Michael. *Totalitarianism.* New York and London: Transaction Books, 1979.
Dain, Phyllis. "Comments." *Newsletter of the Slavic and East European Section, Association of College and Research Libraries* 3 (1987): 44-49.
————. "Harry M. Lydenberg and American Library Resources: A Study in Modern Library Leadership." *Library Quarterly* 47 (Oct. 1977): 451-69.
————. "Harry Miller Lydenberg." In *Dictionary of American Library Biography.* Littleton, CO: Libraries Unlimited, 1978. Pp. 329-33.
Dallin, Alexander. "The Soviet Social Sciences after Stalin." In *Iron Curtains and Scholarship.* Ed. by Winger. Pp. 82-95.
Dane, Chase. "Comparative Librarianship." *The Librarian* 43 (Aug. 1954): 141-44.
Daniel, Hawthorne. *Judge Medina: A Biography.* New York: Wilfred Funk, 1952.

Daniels, Robert V. *Russia: The Roots of Confrontation.* Cambridge, MA, and London: Harvard University Press, 1985.

Danton, J. Periam. *The Dimensions of Comparative Librarianship.* Chicago: American Library Association, 1973.

————, ed. *The Climate of Book Selection: Social Influences on School and Public Libraries.* Papers presented at a symposium held at the University of California, July 10-12, 1958. Berkeley: School of Librarianship, University of California, 1959.

Davis, Carl Bowen. Untitled review of *The Library Bill of Rights,* issue title of *Library Trends,* vol. 45, no. 1 (1996), ed. by Wayne Wiegand; and of *Censorship and the American Library,* by Louise S. Robbins; *Libraries and Culture* 33 (Fall 1998): 453-55.

Davis, Donald G., Jr. "With Malice toward None: IFLA and the Cold War." *IFLA Journal,* vol. 26, no. 1 (2000): 13-20.

————, and John Mark Tucker, eds. *American Library History: A Comprehensive Guide to the Literature.* Santa Barbara, CA, and Oxford, England: ABC-CLIO, 1989.

DeKoster, Lester. *Vocabulary of Communism.* Grand Rapids, MI: William B. Eerdmans, 1964.

Delaney, Robert Finley. *The Literature of Communism in America: A Selected Reference Guide.* Washington, DC: Catholic University of America Press, 1962.

Delougaz, Nathalie. "Adaptions of the Decimal Classification for Soviet Libraries." *Library Quarterly* 17 (April 1947): 148-61.

————. "Some Problems of Soviet Librarianship as Reflected in Russian Library Periodicals." *Library Quarterly* 15 (July 1945): 213-23.

————. "Some Significant Trends in Soviet Book Production." *Library Quarterly* 19 (Oct. 1949): 250-62.

"Demagogue McCarthy: Does He Deserve Well of the Republic?" *Time* (Oct. 21, 1951): 21-24.

Demiashkevich, Michael. *An Introduction to the Philosophy of Education.* New York: American Book Co., 1935.

Dennis, Lawrence J., and William Edward Eaton. *George S. Counts: Educator for a New Age.* Carbondale and Edwardsville, IL: Southern Illinois University Press, 1980; London and Amsterdam: Feffer & Simons.

Derman, Henriette M. "Semen Afanasevich Vengerov, 1855-1920." *Library Journal* 46 (April 15, 1921): 349-50.

"The Development of Soviet Pedagogy." *Soviet Education* 25 (Nov. 1982): 34-101.

Dewey, John. *Impressions of Soviet Russia and the Revolutionary World— Mexico, China, Turkey.* New York: New Republic, 1929. Reprinted in *John Dewey's Impressions of Soviet Russia and the Revolutionary*

World—Mexico, China, Turkey. Intro. by William W. Brickman. New York: Teachers College, Columbia University, 1964.

————. "Why I Am Not a Communist." *The Modern Monthly* 8 (April 1934): 135-37.

Dictionary of American Library Biography. Ed. by Bohdan S. Wynar, George S. Bobinski, and Jesse Hauk Shera. Littleton, CO: Libraries Unlimited, 1978.

Dinsmore, Herman H. *All the News that Fits: A Critical Analysis of the News and Editorial Contents of* The New York Times. New Rochelle, NY: Arlington House, 1969.

Ditzion, Sidney. *Arsenals of a Democratic Culture: A Social History of the American Public Library Movement in New England and the Middle States from 1850 to 1890.* Foreword by Merle Curti. Chicago: American Library Association, 1947.

Dix, William, and Paul Bixler, eds. *Freedom of Communication: Proceedings of the First Conference on Intellectual Freedom, New York City, June 28-29, 1952.* Chicago: American Library Association, 1954.

Djilas, Milovan. *The New Class: An Anaylsis of the Communist System.* New York: Praeger, 1957.

Donovan, Robert J. *Eisenhower: The Inside Story.* New York: Harper & Bros., 1956.

Dovring, Folke. *Leninism: Political Economy as Pseudoscience.* Westport, CT, and London: Praeger, 1996.

Dowling, William C. "Saving Scholarly Publishing in the Age of Oprah: The Glastonbury Project." *Journal of Scholarly Publishing* 28 (April 1997): 115-34.

Downs, Robert B. "The ALA Today—A 1953 Stocktaking Report." *ALA Bulletin* 47 (Oct. 1953): 397-99.

————. "One Library World." *ALA Bulletin* 46 (July-Aug. 1952): 215-17.

————. *Perspectives on the Past: An Autobiography.* Metuchen, NJ, and London: Scarecrow Press, 1984.

————, and Jane B. Downs. *Journalists of the United States: Biographical Sketches of Print and Broadcast News Shapers from the Late 17th Century to the Present.* Jefferson, NC, and London: McFarland, 1991.

Dubie, Alain. *Frank A. Golder: An Adventure of a Historian in Quest of Russian History.* Boulder, CO: East European Monographs, 1989; distributed by Columbia University Press.

Dudley, Edward. "Libraries in the USSR." *Library Association Record* 61 (May 1959): 111-15.

Durant, Will. *The Lesson of Russia.* London: G. P. Putnam's Sons, 1933.

Dziak, John J. *Chekisty: A History of the KGB.* Foreword by Robert Conquest. Lexington, MA: Lexington Books/D. C. Heath, 1988.

Earle, Elinor S. "Reply to Carlson." *ALA Bulletin* 46 (April 1952): 105-10.

Eastman, Max. "An Open Letter to Rockwell Kent." *Plain Talk* (April 1950). As reprinted in *Plain Talk: An Anthology.* Ed. by Levine. Pp. 393-96.

———. "We Must Face the Facts about Russia." *Reader's Digest* 43 (July 1943): 1-14.

Eberstadt, Nicholas. *The End of North Korea.* Washington, DC: AEI Books, 1999.

Eddy, Harriet G. "Beginnings of United Library Service in the USSR." *Library Journal* 57 (Jan. 15, 1932): 61-67.

Edmonds, Anne C. "Flora Belle Ludington." In *Dictionary of American Library Biography.* Pp. 322-24.

Egbert, Donald Drew, and Stow Persons, eds. *Socialism and American Life.* 2 vols. T. D. Seymour Bassett, bibliographer. Princeton: Princeton University Press, 1952.

Egorov, Dmitri. "Russian Libraries since the Revolution." *Library Review* 2 (1929-30): 329-32.

Eisenhower, Dwight D. Letter to Robert B. Downs, June 24, 1953. Published as "President Eisenhower's Letter to ALA." *Library Journal* 78 (July 1953): 1206.

———. Remarks at Dartmouth College, June 14, 1953. Published as "The President Speaks." *Library Journal* 78 (July 1953): 1206.

Ellsworth, Ralph E., and Sarah M. Harris. *The American Right Wing: A Report to the Fund for the Republic.* University of Illinois Library School, Occasional Paper number 59. Urbana, IL: University of Illinois Graduate School of Library Science, Nov. 1960. [50 p.] Updated ed.: Washington, DC: Public Affairs Press, 1962. [63 p.]

Emmons, Terence, and Bertrand M. Patenaude, eds. *War, Revolution, and Peace in Russia: The Passages of Frank Golder, 1914-1927.* Stanford, CA: Hoover Institution Press, 1992.

Encyclopedia of the American Left. Ed. by Mari Jo Buhle, Paul Buhle, and George Georgakas. Urbana and Chicago: University of Illinois Press, 1992. Originally published: New York: Garland, 1990.

Evans, M. Stanton. "History's Vindication of Joe McCarthy." *Human Events,* Special Supplement (May 16, 1987): S1-S8.

———. "Joe McCarthy and the Historians." *Human Events,* Special Supplement (Jan. 1, 1999): S1-S8.

———. "McCarthyism: Waging the Cold War in America." *Human Events,* Special Supplement (May 30, 1997): S1-S8.

———. *The Politics of Surrender.* New York: Devin-Adair, 1966.

———. *Revolt on the Campus.* Chicago: Henry Regnery, 1961.

Evatt Foundation. *Seeing Red: The Communist Party Dissolution Act and Referendum 1951: Lessons for Constitutional Reform.* Sydney, Australia: The Evatt Foundation, 1992.

"Everett T. Moore, 1909-1988." *Newsletter on Intellectual Freedom* 37 (March 1988): 37.

Farah, Joseph. "The Real Blacklist." *National Review* 41 (Oct. 27, 1989): 42-43.

Farber, Daniel A., and Suzanna Sherry. *Beyond All Reason: The Radical Assault on Truth in American Law.* New York: Oxford University Press, 1997.

Fariello, Griffin. *Red Scare: Memories of the American Inquisition.* New York: W. W. Norton, 1995.

Fediai, Victor. "Expansion of Library Service in the USSR." *ALA Bulletin* 54 (May 1960): 379-81.

Fellers, Nancy Jane. "God and Woman at Vassar." *The Freeman* 3 (Nov. 3, 1952): 83-86.

Fenelonov, E. A. "Soviet Public Libraries." In *Libraries in the USSR.* Ed. by Francis. Pp. 39-50.

Fernández-Morera, Darío. *American Academia and the Survival of Marxist Ideas.* Westport, CT, and London: Praeger, 1996.

Fernow, B. "The Imperial Public Library of St. Petersburg." *Library Journal* 30 (Nov. 1905): 860-61.

Fetter, Henry D. "Victory into Defeat: The Cold War on the Reference Shelf." *Heterodoxy* 8 (June/July 2000): 1, 8, 10-12.

Feuer, Lewis S. "American Travelers to the Soviet Union, 1917-32: The Formation of a Component of New Deal Ideology." *American Quarterly* 14 (Summer 1962): 119-49.

———. *Ideology and the Ideologists.* New York: Harper & Row, 1975.

———. *Marx and the Intellectuals: A Set of Post-Ideological Essays.* Garden City, NY: Doubleday, 1969.

Feulner, Edwin J., Jr., ed. *Leadership for America: The Principles of Conservatism.* Dallas: Spence Publishing, 2000.

Filene, Peter G. *Americans and the Soviet Experiment, 1917-1933.* Cambridge, MA: Harvard University Press, 1967.

Filler, Louis, ed. *Dictionary of American Conservatism.* New York: Philosophical Library, 1987.

Fischer, Louis. *The Life of Lenin.* New York: Harper & Row, 1964.

Fiske, Marjorie. *Book Selection and Censorship: A Study of School and Public Libraries in California.* Berkeley and Los Angeles: University of California Press, 1959.

———. "Book Selection Study: Preliminary Plans." *California Librarian* vol. 18, no. 1 (1957): 27-28, 57.

Fitch, Robert E. "The Fears of the Intelligentsia: The Present Slough of Despond." *Commentary* 18 (Oct. 1954): 328-35.

Fleming, E. McClung. *R. R. Bowker: Militant Liberal.* Norman, OK: University of Oklahoma Press, 1952.

Flexner, Jennie M., and Sigrid A. Edge. *A Readers' Advisory Service.* New York: American Association for Adult Education, 1934.

Flynn, Daniel J. "Off the Shelf." *Campus Report* (Oct. 1998): 6.

Foner, Philip S., ed. *The Bolshevik Revolution: Its Impact on American Radicals, Liberals, and Labor.* New York: International Publishers, 1967.

Fonotov, Georgij. "Nadezhda Krupskaya." In *ALA World Encyclopedia of Library and Information Services.* 2nd ed. Pp. 424-25.

Foskett, D. J. "Comparative Librarianship." In *Progress in Library Science, 1965.* Ed. by Robert L. Collison. London: Butterworths, 1965. Pp. 125-46. Reprinted in *Reader in Comparative Librarianship.* Ed. by D. J. Foskett. Pp. 12-22.

———. "Comparative Librarianship as a Field of Study: Definitions and Dimensions." In *Reader in Comparative Librarianship.* Ed. by D. J. Foskett. Pp. 3-9.

———, ed. *Reader in Comparative Librarianship.* Englewood, CO: Information Handling Services, 1976.

Foster, Arnold, and Benjamin R. Epstein. *Danger on the Right.* New York: Random House, 1964.

Francis, Simon, ed. *Libraries in the USSR.* London: Clive Bingley, 1971.

Frankfurter, Felix. Letter to Franklin Delano Roosevelt. May 11, 1939. Published in "Judging Librarianship." *American Libraries* 26 (May 1995): 408, 411. Intro. by David Streeter.

Fraser, George. *Seeing Red: Undercover in 1950's New Zealand.* Palmerston North, New Zealand: The Dunsmore Press, 1995.

Fredricks, Jessica M. "A Glance at Russian Libraries." *Wilson Bulletin for Librarians* 10 (Dec. 1937): 233-37.

Freeland, Richard M. *The Truman Doctrine and the Origins of McCarthyism: Foreign Policy, Domestic Politics, and Internal Security, 1946-1948.* New York: Knopf, 1972.

Freud, Sigmund. *Civilization and its Discontents.* Trans. and ed. by James Strachey. New York: W. W. Norton, 1962. First editions in English: trans. by Joan Riviere; New York: J. Cape and H. Smith, 1930; London: Virginia Woolf at the Hogarth Press, 1930. Originally published as *Das Unbehagen in der Kultur.* Vienna: Internationaler Psychoanalytischer Verlag, 1930.

———, and William C. Bullitt. *Thomas Woodrow Wilson: A Psychological Study.* Boston: Houghton Mifflin, 1967.

Fried, Albert. *Communism in America: A History in Documents.* New York: Columbia University Press, 1997.

———. *Socialism in America: From the Shakers to the Third International.* Garden City, NY: Bantam Books, Doubleday, 1970.

Friedberg, Aaron L. "Arming China against Ourselves." *Commentary* 108 (July/Aug. 1999): 27-33.

Friedberg, Maurice. *Russian Classics in Soviet Jackets.* New York and London: Columbia University Press, 1962.

Fromm, Erich. *Escape from Freedom.* New York: Rinehart, 1941.

"The Fund for the Republic's Blacklisting Report Lacked a Few Fundamental Facts." *Saturday Evening Post* (Feb. 9, 1957): 10.

Futrell, Michael. "Banned Books in the Lenin Library." *Library Review* 130 (Autumn 1959): 184-86.

Gaddis, John Lewis. "On Moral Equivalency and Cold War History." *Ethics & International Affairs* 10 (1996): 131-48.

———. "The Tragedy of Cold War History." *Diplomatic History* 17 (Winter 1993): 1-16.

———. *We Now Know: Rethinking Cold War History.* Oxford and New York: Oxford University Press, 1997.

Garrison, Gretchen J. "Public Libraries and the World-Mind." *Wilson Bulletin for Librarians* 9 (Sept. 1934): 18-20, 31.

Gates, Jean Key. *Introduction to Librarianship.* 3rd ed. New York and London: Neal-Schuman, 1990.

Gay, Peter, and Gerald J. Cavanaugh. "Richard Hofstadter." In *Historians at Work.* Vol. 4. Ed. by Gay and Cavanaugh. New York: Harper & Row, 1975. Pp. 384-89.

Geller, Evelyn. *Forbidden Books in American Public Libraries, 1876-1939: A Study in Cultural Change.* Westport, CT, and London: Greenwood Press, 1984.

Geyer, Georgie Ann. *Americans No More: The Death of Citizenship.* New York: Atlantic Monthly Press, 1996.

Gide, André. *Return from the USSR.* Trans. by Dorothy Bussy. New York: Alfred A. Knopf, 1937. Originally published: *Retour de l'URSS.* Paris: Librairie Gallimard, 1936.

Gilbert, Sir Martin. *Winston S. Churchill.* Vol. 4: *The Stricken World: 1916-1922.* Boston: Houghton Mifflin, 1975.

———. *Winston S. Churchill.* Vol. 8: *"Never Despair": 1945-1965.* Boston: Houghton Mifflin, 1988.

Glazer, Nathan. "The Professors and the Party." Review of *No Ivory Tower*, by Ellen Schrecker. *New Republic* (Oct. 6, 1986): 39-42.

Gleason, Abbott. *Totalitarianism: The Inner History of the Cold War.* New York and Oxford: Oxford University Press, 1995.

Goedeken, Edward A. "The Literature of American Library History, 1993-1994." *Libraries and Culture* 31 (Summer-Fall 1996): 603-44.

―――. "The Literature of American Library History, 1995-1996." *Libraries and Culture* 33 (Fall 1998): 407-45.

―――. "The Literature of American Library History, 1997-1998." *Libraries and Culture* 35 (Spring 2000): 311-53.

Goldberg, Harold J., ed. *Documents of Soviet-American Relations, 1917-1933.* Vol. 1: *Intervention, Famine Relief, International Affairs.* Vol. 2: *Propaganda, Economic, Recognition.* Gulf Breeze, FL: Academic International Press, 1993, 1995.

Golden, Richard M. "American Perspectives on the European Witch Hunts." *The History Teacher* 30 (Aug. 1997): 409-26.

Goldman, Emma. *Living My Life.* New York: Knopf, 1931.

―――. *My Disillusionment in Russia.* [Includes *My Further Disillusionment in Russia.*] Intro. by Rebecca West. Biographical sketch by Frank Harris. As reprinted from an apparent 1925 unabridged edition: Gloucester, MA: Peter Smith, 1983.

Goldman, Eric. *The Crucial Decade and After: America, 1945-1960.* New York: Knopf, 1960.

Goodman, H. J. Abraham. "The 'World Brain/World Encyclopedia' Concept." In *ASIS '87: Proceedings of the 50th Annual Conference of the ASIS Annual Meeting.* Medford, NJ: Learned Information, 1987. Pp. 91-98, 256.

Goodman, Walter. *The Committee: The Extraordinary Career of the House Committee on Un-American Activities.* New York: Farrar, Straus and Giroux, 1968.

―――. Review of *The Inquisition in Hollywood*, by Ceplair and Englund. *New Republic* 182 (May 31, 1980): 31-32.

Gorokhoff, Boris I. "Soviet Views on International Book Exchange." *Library of Congress Information Bulletin* 11 (Sept. 8, 1952): 11-12.

Gottlieb, W. W. "Some Facts about Libraries in the USSR: Impressions from a Recent Visit." *Library Review* 130 (Summer 1959): 98-101.

Grayson, Benson L., ed. *The American Image of Russia, 1917-1977.* Intro. and comments by Grayson. New York: Frederick Ungar, 1978.

Great Soviet Encyclopedia: A Translation of the Third Edition (Moscow: Sovetskaia Entsiklopedia Publishing House, 1970). New York: Macmillan, 1973.

Gregory, Agnes. Letters to the author. May 8, 1997; May 13, 1997.

Gregory, H. A. "Libraries in Soviet Russia." In *Australian Institute of Librarians Meeting and Conference Proceedings.* Vol. 2. Melbourne: Brown, Prior, and Anderson; Dec. 1940. Pp. 118-24.

―――. "Why I Enlisted: Some Talks with the Man in the Street in Central

Europe." Talk over Radio Station 3XY. Melbourne, Feb. 8, 1939.

Grierson, Philip. *Books on Soviet Russia, 1917-1942: A Bibliography and a Guide to Reading*. London: Methuen, 1943. Reprint: Twickenham: Anthony C. Hall, 1969.

Grunwald, Henry. "A World Without a Country?" *Wall Street Journal* (Jan. 1, 2000): R44, R46.

Gvosdev, Yuri. "Publishing and Book Distribution in the USSR." In *Iron Curtains and Scholarship*. Ed. by Winger. Pp. 43-50.

Haag, Ernest van den. "McCarthyism and the Professors." Review of *The Academic Mind*, by Lazarsfeld and Thielens, Jr. *Commentary* 27 (Feb. 1959): 179-82.

Hackett, Alice Payne. *Seventy Years of Best Sellers, 1895-1965*. New York and London: R. R. Bowker, 1967.

Haffkin Hamburger, L. [L. B. Khavkina]. "The Institute for Library Science at Moscow." *Library Journal* 50 (Dec. 1, 1925): 991-93.

———. "Libraries in the Soviet Union." *ALA Bulletin* 20 (Oct. 1926): 260-64. Reprinted in: *Libraries* [Chicago] 31 (Dec. 1926): 502-6; and *The Librarian and Book World* [London] 16 (Dec. 1926): 134-39.

———. "Russian Librarians Send Thanks." (Letter.) *Library Journal* 48 (Feb. 1, 1923): 128.

———. "Russian Libraries." *Library Journal* 40 (March 1915): 168-73.

———. "State Institute for Library Science in Russia." *Library Journal* 48 (Feb. 15, 1923): 171-72.

Haimson, Leopold H. "Three Generations of the Soviet Intelligentsia." In *Iron Curtains and Scholarship*. Ed. by Winger. Pp. 28-42.

Haines, Helen E. "Balancing the Books: Reason Enthroned." *Library Journal* 73 (Feb. 1, 1948): 149-54.

———. "Committee on Intellectual Freedom to Safeguard the Rights of Library Users to Freedom of Inquiry." *California Librarian* 3 (Dec. 1941): 138-39.

———. "Ethics of Librarianship." *Library Journal* 71 (June 15, 1946): 848-51.

———. *Living With Books: The Art of Book Selection*. New York: Columbia University Press, 1935.

———. *Living With Books: The Art of Book Selection*. 2nd ed. New York: Columbia University Press, 1950.

Handlin, Oscar. *The Distortion of America*. 2nd ed. New Brunswick, NJ, and London: Transaction, 1996. First edition: Little, Brown, 1981.

Harding, Stan. *The Underworld of State*. Intro. by Bertrand Russell. London: George Allen & Unwin, 1925.

Harlan, Robert D. "Helen Haines." In *Dictionary of American Library Biography*. Pp. 223-26.

Harries, Owen, and Robert Tucker. "A Note on *The National Interest.*" *The National Interest* 1 (Fall 1985): 3-4.

"Harrison Salisbury Says 'Library of Russia [is] Like the Circles of Hell.' " *American Libraries* 14 (Dec. 1983): 699.

Harvey, John F. "An Anatomy of the International Man." *Wilson Library Bulletin* 47 (June 1973): 837-41.

————. "Toward a Definition of International and Comparative Library Science." *International Library Review* 5 (July 1973): 289-319. Reprinted in *Reader in Comparative Librarianship*. Ed. by D. J. Foskett. Pp. 33-49.

————, ed. *Comparative and International Library Science.* Metuchen, NJ, and London: Scarecrow Press, 1977.

————, and Frances Laverne Carroll, eds. *Internationalizing Library and Information Science Education: A Handbook of Policies and Procedures in Administration and Curriculum.* New York and London: Greenwood Press, 1987.

Havens, Shirley. "Harassment Soviet Style." *Library Journal* 97 (August 1972): 2531-34.

Hayek, F. A. [Friedrich A. von Hayek] *The Road to Serfdom.* With new intro. by Milton Friedman. Chicago: University of Chicago Press, 1994; originally published in 1944; reprinted with new preface by Hayek in 1956.

Haygood, William Converse. "Libraries in the Union of Socialist Soviet [*sic*] Republics." *Library Journal* 61 (June 1, 1936): 435-39.

Haynes, John Earl. "The Cold War Debate Continues: A Traditionalist View of Historical Writing on Domestic Communism and Anti-Communism." *Journal of Cold War Studies* 2 (Winter 2000): 76-115.

————. *Communism and Anti-Communism in the United States: An Annotated Guide to Historical Writings.* New York and London: Garland, 1987.

————. "Historians Scramble for New Party Lines." *Heterodoxy* 4 (Sept. 1996): 8-9.

————. Letter. *Reviews in American History* 25 (Sept. 1997): 528-30.

————. Letter to the author. Oct. 30, 1998.

————. *Red Scare or Red Menace? American Communism and Anticommunism in the Cold War Era.* Chicago: Ivan R. Dee, 1996.

————. "The 'Spy' on Joe McCarthy's Staff: The Forgotten Case of Paul H. Hughes." *Continuity: A Journal of History* 14 (Spring-Fall 1990): 21-61.

————, and Harvey Klehr. *Venona: Decoding Soviet Espionage in America.* New Haven, CT, and London: Yale University Press, 1999.

Heilbut, Anthony. *Exiled in Paradise: German Refugee Artists and Intellectuals in America from the 1930's to the Present.* New York: Viking

Press, 1983.

Heller, Scott. "Academic Politics Color Reactions to 'Annals of Communism.' " *Chronicle of Higher Education* (Feb. 28, 1997): A18.

————. "Yale Editor Brings Hidden Records of Soviet Communism to Light." *Chronicle of Higher Education* (Feb. 28, 1997): A15.

Hellman, Lillian. *Scoundrel Time.* Boston: Little, Brown, 1976.

Helms, Sen. Jesse. "Respect the Sovereignty of the American People." Speech to the UN Security Council, Jan. 20, 2000. *Vital Speeches* 66 (Feb. 15, 2000): 268-72.

Herman, Arthur. *Joseph McCarthy: Reexamining the Life and Legacy of America's Most Hated Senator.* New York: Free Press, 2000.

Hess, Gary R. "After the Tumult: The Wisconsin School's Tribute to William Appleman Williams." *Diplomatic History* 12 (Fall 1988): 483-99.

Hills, Leon C. "How Are Books Selected for Purchase by Librarians?" Remarks to the Mayflower Society of the District of Columbia, Oct. 17, 1956. Washington, DC: National Defense Committee of the National Society of the Daughters of the American Revolution, n.d. One processed leaf, recto and verso.

Himmelfarb, Gertrude. "Beyond Methodology." In *What's Happened to the Humanities?* Ed. by Alvin Kernan. Princeton, NJ: Princeton University Press, 1997. Pp. 143-61.

————. "Where Have All the Footnotes Gone?" In *On Looking into the Abyss: Untimely Thoughts on Culture and Society.* By Himmelfarb. New York: Knopf, 1994. Pp. 122-30.

Hodgkinson, Harry. *The Language of Communism.* New York: Pitman, 1955. Published in London by Allen & Unwin as *Doubletalk: The Language of Communism.*

Hoffer, Eric. *The True Believer: Thoughts on the Nature of Mass Movements.* Intro. by Sidney Hook. New York: Time, 1963.

Hofstadter, Richard. *The Age of Reform: From Bryan to F.D.R.* New York: Knopf, 1955; reprinted 1985 with 1980 foreword by John Morton Blum.

————. *Anti-Intellectualism in American Life.* New York: Knopf, 1963.

————. *The Paranoid Style in American Politics and Other Essays.* New York: Knopf, 1965.

Holland, Kenneth. "Prospects for a Freer Exchange of Knowledge." In *Iron Curtains and Scholarship.* Ed. by Winger. Pp. 124-29.

Hollander, Gayle Durham. *Soviet Political Indoctrination: Domestic Mass Media and Propaganda since Stalin.* New York and London: Praeger, 1972.

Hollander, Paul. *Anti-Americanism: Irrational and Rational.* With new intro. New Brunswick, NJ: Transaction Publishers, 1995. Originally published as *Anti-Americanism: Critiques at Home and Abroad, 1965-1990.* New York and Oxford: Oxford University Press, 1992.

―――. "Modernity and Its Discontents." *Orbis* 43 (Fall 1999): 661-71.

―――. *Political Pilgrims: Travels of Western Intellectuals to the Soviet Union, China, and Cuba.* With new preface. Lanham, MD, and London: University Press of America, 1990. Originally published: New York and Oxford: Oxford University Press, 1981.

―――. *Political Pilgrims: Western Intellectuals in Search of the Good Society.* 4th ed. With new intro. by Hollander. New Brunswick, NJ, and London: Transaction, 1998.

―――. "Reassessing the Adversary Culture." *Academic Questions* 9 (Spring 1996): 37-48.

"Hollywood Ignores Real 'Blacklist' Victims." *AIM Report,* vol. 26, no. 24 (Dec.—B, 1997): [1-2, 4-6].

Hook, Sidney. "David Caute's Fable of 'Fear and Terror': On 'Reverse McCarthyism.' " *Encounter* 52 (Jan. 1979): 56-64.

―――. *Heresy, Yes; Conspiracy, No.* New York: John Day, 1953.

―――. "Six Fallacies of Robert Hutchins." *The New Leader* (March 19, 1956): 18-28.

Hoover, J. Edgar. *Masters of Deceit: The Story of Communism in America and How to Fight It.* New York: Henry Holt, 1958.

―――. *On Communism.* New York: Random House, 1969.

―――. *A Study of Communism.* New York: Holt, Rinehart, and Winston, 1962.

Horecky, Paul L. *Libraries and Bibliographic Centers in the Soviet Union.* Bloomington, IN: Indiana University, 1959.

―――, ed. *Russia and the Soviet Union: A Bibliographic Guide to Western Publications.* Chicago and London: University of Chicago Press, 1965.

Horn, Zoia. Review of *Censorship and the American Library,* by Louise S. Robbins. *Journal of Education for Library and Information Science* 39 (Spring 1998): 236-39.

Horne, Herman Harrell. *The Democratic Philosophy of Education: Companion to Dewey's Democracy and Education.* New York: Macmillan, 1932.

Horowitz, David. *Hating Whitey: And Other Progressive Causes.* Dallas: Spence, 1999.

Horowitz, Irving Louis. "The Conscience of Castrologists: Thirty-Three Years of Solitude." In his *Conscience of Worms and the Cowardice of Lions: Cuban Politics and Culture in an American Context.* New Brunswick, NJ, and London: Transaction, 1993. Pp. 15-36.

Hovde, David. "LHRT Executive Committee Meeting." *Library History Round Table Newsletter.* N.s. 3 (Spring 1998): 2-4.

Howd, Aimee. "Law School vs. Dissenting Views." *Insight* 15 (Dec. 20, 1999): 16-17, 39.
Hulburd, David. *This Happened in Pasadena*. New York: Macmillan, 1951.
Hunt, R. N. Carew. *A Guide to Communist Jargon*. London: Geoffrey Bles, 1957; New York: Macmillan.
Hyman, Harold M. *To Try Men's Souls: Loyalty Tests in American History*. Berkeley and Los Angeles: University of California Press, 1960.
Ilin, M. *New Russia's Primer: The Story of the Five-Year Plan*. Trans. by George S. Counts and Nucia P. Lodge. Boston and New York: Houghton Mifflin, 1931.
"The 'Index' of the Soviet Inquisition." *The Slavonic Review* 4 (March 1926): 725-32.
Isaac, Rael Jean, and Erich Isaac. *The Coercive Utopians: Social Deception by America's Power Players*. Chicago: Regnery Gateway, 1983.
"It Happened in Pasadena." *California Librarian* 14 (Dec. 1952): 89-90.
James, Henry, Jr. "The Role of the Information Library in the United States International Information Program." *Library Quarterly* 23 (April 1953): 75-114.
Janson, Donald, and Bernard Eisman. *The Far Right*. New York: McGraw-Hill, 1963.
Jenkins, Christine. "ALA Youth Services Librarians and the CARE-UNESCO Children's Book Fund: Selecting the 'Right Book' for Children in Cold War America, 1950-1958." *Libraries and Culture* 31 (Winter 1996): 209-34.
Johnson, Edward R. "Ralph E. Ellsworth." In *Leaders in American Academic Librarianship: 1925-1975*. Ed. by Wiegand. Pp. 95-123.
Johnson, Gerald W. *This American People*. New York: Harper and Brothers, 1951.
Johnson, Margaret L. "Flora Belle Ludington: A Biography and Bibliography." *College and Research Libraries* 25 (Sept. 1964): 375-79.
Johnson, Paul. *Intellectuals*. New York: Harper and Row, 1988.
———. *Modern Times: The World from the Twenties to the Eighties*. New York: Harper and Row, 1983.
———. *Modern Times: The World from the Twenties to the Nineties*. Rev. ed. New York: Harper Collins, 1991.
Jones, Henry Arthur. *My Dear Wells*. London: Eveleigh Nash & Grayson, 1921; New York: E. P. Dutton.
Josephson, Matthew. "The Battle of the Books." *Nation* 174 (June 28, 1952): 619-24.
Josey, E. J. "Political Dimensions of International Librarianship." Conference speech at "Shrinking World, Exploding Information." April 4,

1986.

Kagan, Robert, and William Kristol. "The Present Danger." *The National Interest*, no. 59 (Spring 2000): 57-69.

————, eds. *Present Dangers: Crisis and Opportunity in American Foreign and Defense Policy*. San Francisco: Encounter Books, 2000.

Kahan, Stuart. *The Wolf of the Kremlin*. NY: Morrow, 1987.

Kandel, I. L. *Comparative Education*. Boston: Houghton Mifflin, 1933.

————. "Comparative Education." In *Educating for Democracy*. Ed. by John I. Cohn and Robert M. W. Travers. London: Macmillan, 1939. Reprinted: Freeport, NY: Books for Libraries, 1970. Pp. 422-42.

Kanfer, Steven. *A Journal of the Plague Years*. New York: Atheneum, 1973.

Kardos, Bela Talbot. "Bookshelves behind the Iron Curtain." *Idaho Librarian* 5 (Oct. 1953): 25-27. Reprinted from the *Christian Science Monitor*.

Karetzky, Joanne L. *The Mustering of Support for World War I by* The Ladies' Home Journal. Lewiston, NY, and Lampeter, Wales, UK: Edwin Mellen Press, 1997.

Karetzky, Stephen. "The American Library Association Versus Israel." *Midstream* 31 (March 1985): 31-32.

————. "American Library Community Ignores Plight of Ukrainian Colleague." *Newsletter of the International Society of Jewish Librarians* [aka *Jewish Librarians Caucus Newsletter*] 9 (Jan.-March 1985): 19.

————. "The Asheim Assumption." (Letter) *Library Journal* 122 (Nov. 1, 1997): 8.

————. "CIA Funds for Intellectuals." (Letter) *The Chronicle of Higher Education* (May 12, 2000): B13.

————. "Cuba, Communism, Communication." (Letter) *American Libraries* 29 (June/July 1998): 52.

————. Letter. *Library Quarterly* 68 (Jan. 1998): 121-22.

————. *Reading Research and Librarianship: A History and Analysis*. Westport, CT, and London: Greenwood Press, 1982.

————. "Turkish Turbulence." (Letter) *American Libraries* 29 (March 1998): 34.

————. "The Vitality of American Catholic Higher Education Today." *Catholic Library World* 65 (Jan.-March 1995): 21-29.

————, and Norman Frankel, eds. *The Media's Coverage of the Arab-Israeli Conflict*. Intro. by Karetzky. New York: Shapolsky, 1989.

Karintsev, N. "Moscow Libraries." *Information Bulletin*. Washington, DC: Embassy of the USSR, June 8, 1941. As reprinted in *Library Journal* 68 (July 1943): 565-66.

Karlowich, Robert A. "Harry Miller Lydenberg and Soviet Libraries in 1923." *Newsletter of the Slavic and East European Section, Association of College and Research Libraries* 3 (1987): 35-44.

————. "Libraries, Bibliographies, and Books in Russia in 1917-1935: A Preliminary Bibliography of Books and Serials on the Period Published in the Soviet Union, 1946-1985." In *Books, Libraries, and Information in Slavic and East European Studies*. Ed. by Choldin. Pp. 129-43.

————. "Stranger in a Far Land: Report of a Bookbuying Trip by Harry Miller Lydenberg in Eastern Europe and Russia in 1923-24." *Bulletin of Research in the Humanities* 87, nos. 2-3 (1986-87): 182-224.

Kartashov, N. S. "The Unified Library System in the USSR." In *International Librarianship Today and Tomorrow*. Comp. by Price and Price. Pp. 81-94.

Kasinec, Edward. "Iurii O. Ivaniv-Mezhenko (1892-1969) as a Bibliographer during His Years in Kiev, 1919-1933." *Journal of Library History* 14 (Winter 1979): 1-20.

————. "L. B. Khavkina (1871-1949): American Library Ideas in Russia and the Development of Soviet Librarianship." *Libri* 37 (March 1987): 59-71.

————. " 'Old Cadres' in Practical Service of the 'Book and Revolution': The Case of A. Iu. Malein (1869-1938)." *Libri* 35, no. 3 (1985): 250-59.

————. "P. N. Berkov and the Beginnings of Soviet Russian Book Studies (1923-1935)." *Libri* 31, no. 3 (1981): 258-70.

Kazin, Michael. "The Grass-Roots Right: New Histories of U.S. Conservatism in the Twentieth Century." *American Historical Review* 97 (Feb. 1992): 136-55.

————. *The Populist Persuasion: An American History*. New York: Basic Books, 1995.

Kent, Allen, and Harold Lancour. "Preface." In *Encyclopedia of Library and Information Science*. Vol. 1. Ed. by Allen Kent, Harold Lancour, and William Z. Nasri. New York: Marcel Dekker, 1968. Pp. xi-xii.

Kent, Charles Deane. "Book Selection in the USSR." *Ontario Library Review* 43 (Nov. 1959): 284-86.

————. "The Leningrad State Library." *Canadian Library Journal* 16 (Sept. 1959): 67-70.

————. "Leningrad State Library Institute." *Library Journal* 84 (Nov. 15, 1959): 3528-30.

————. "The Library of the Hermitage in Leningrad." *Library Review* 17 (Spring 1960): 320-21.

Kernan, Alvin, ed. *What's Happened to the Humanities?* Princeton, NJ: Princeton University Press, 1997.

Khmelnitsky, Eugenia. "Research in the Bureau of Labor, Kharkov, Ukraine." *Special Libraries* 19 (July-August 1928): 183-85.

Khrushchev on the Shifting Balance of World Forces: A Selection of Statements and an Interpretive Analysis: A Special Study Presented by Sen. Hubert H. Humphrey: Prepared by the Legislative Service of the Library of Congress. Washington, DC: GPO, Sept. 1959.

Kilgour, Frederick. "Public Policy and National and International Networks." In *Libraries and Information Science in the Electronic Age.* Ed. by Hendrik Edelman. Philadelphia, PA: ISI Press, 1986. Pp. 1-10.

Kimball, Roger. *Tenured Radicals: How Politics Has Corrupted Our Higher Education.* Rev. ed. with new intro. Chicago: Ivan R. Dee, 1998.

Kimmage, Dennis, ed. *Russian Libraries in Transition: An Anthology of Glasnost Literature.* Jefferson, NC, and London: McFarland, 1992.

Kincaid, Cliff. *The United Nations Today.* Owings, MD: America's Survival, 2000. [44 p.]

Kipp, Laurence J. "Boston—The Library Did Not Burn." *The New Republic* 128 (June 29, 1953): 15-16.

———. "How to Catch a Witch." *Library Journal* 78 (Dec. 1, 1953): 2071-75.

———. "Report from Boston." *Library Journal* 77 (Nov. 1, 1952): 1843-46, 1887.

Kirk, Russell. *Decadence and Renewal in the Higher Learning: An Episodic History of American University and College since 1953.* South Bend, IN: Gateway Editions, 1978.

———. "License They Mean at Colorado." *National Review* 13 (Nov. 20, 1962): 393.

———. *A Program for Conservatives.* Chicago: Regnery, 1954.

Kirkpatrick, Jeane J. *Dictatorships and Double Standards: Rationalism and Reason in Politics.* New York: Simon and Schuster (and the American Enterprise Institute, Washington, DC), 1982.

———. *Legitimacy and Force.* 2 vols. New Brunswick, NJ, and Oxford, England: Transaction Books, 1988.

———. *The Reagan Phenomenon and Other Speeches on Foreign Policy.* Washington, DC, and London: American Enterprise Institute, 1983.

Klehr, Harvey; Haynes, John Earl; and Anderson, Kyril M. *The Soviet World of American Communism.* New Haven, CT, and London: Yale University Press, 1998.

———; Haynes, John Earl; and Firsov, Fridrikh Igorevich. *The Secret World of American Communism.* New Haven, CT, and London: Yale University Press, 1995.

———, and Ronald Radosh. *The* Amerasia *Spy Case: Prelude to McCarthyism.* Chapel Hill and London: University of North Carolina Press, 1996.

Knightly, Phillip. *The First Casualty: From the Crimea to Vietnam: The War Correspondent as Hero, Propagandist and Myth Maker.* New York and London: Harcourt, Brace, Jovanovich, 1975.

Koch, Stephen. *Double Lives: Spies and Writers in the Secret Soviet War of Ideas against the West*. New York: Free Press, 1994.

Koch, Theodore W. "The Imperial Public Library, St. Petersburg, Second Paper: The Story of a Hundred Years." *Library Journal* 40 (Feb. 1915): 93-108.

Koeppen, Sheilah Rosenhack. "Dissensus and Discontent: The Clientele of the Christian Anti-Communism Crusade." Ph.D. dissertation, Stanford University, August 1967.

Kohn, Hans. *Basic History of Modern Russia*. Princeton, NJ: Van Nostrand, 1957.

Kolarz, Walter. *Books on Communism: A Bibliography*. 2nd ed. London: Ampersand, 1963.

Konecny, Peter. "Conflict and Community in Soviet Institutes of Higher Education, 1921-1928." In *History of Higher Education Annual, 1992*. University Park, PA: Pennsylvania State University, 1992. Pp. 69-84.

Kornweibel, Jr., Theodore. *"Seeing Red": Federal Campaigns against Black Militancy, 1919-1925*. Bloomington and Indianapolis, IN: Indiana University Press, 1998.

Korsch, Boris. *The Brezhnev Personality Cult—Continuity: The Librarian's Point of View*. Jerusalem: Marjorie Mayrock Center for Soviet and East European Research, Hebrew University of Jerusalem, 1987.

―――――. *The Permanent Purge of Soviet Libraries*. Jerusalem: Soviet and East European Research Centre, Hebrew University of Jerusalem, 1983.

―――――. "The Role of Readers' Cards in Soviet Libraries." *Journal of Library History* 13 (Summer 1978): 282-97. Originally published in Hebrew in *Yad Lakoré* 15 (April 1976): 135-45.

Kramer, Hilton. "The Blacklist as History." *The New Criterion* 16 (Dec. 1997): 12-17.

―――――. "Protecting the Rosenberg Myth: *N. Y. Times* Trying to Minimize Rosenbergs' Role as Soviet Spies." *Human Events* 53 (May 16, 1997): 14.

―――――. "The 'Red Baiters' were Right—But *N. Y. Times* Ignores Spy Story." *Human Events* 52 (March 22, 1996): 5.

―――――. *The Twilight of the Intellectuals: Culture and Politics in the Era of the Cold War*. Chicago: Ivan R. Dee, 1999.

Kramer, Hilton, and Roger Kimball, eds. *Against the Grain:* The New Criterion *on Art and Intellect at the End of the Twentieth Century*. Chicago: Ivan R. Dee, 1995.

―――――, eds. *The Betrayal of Liberalism: How the Disciples of Freedom and Equality Helped Foster the Illiberal Politics of Coercion and Control*. Chicago: Ivan R. Dee, 1999.

Kramer, Rita. *Ed School Follies: The Miseducation of America's Teachers.*
New York: Free Press, 1991.

Kraske, Gary E. *Missionaries of the Book: The American Library Profession
and the Origins of United States Cultural Diplomacy.* Westport, CT, and
London: Greenwood Press, 1985.

Kraus, Joe W. "The Progressive Librarians' Council." *Library Journal* 97
(July 1972): 2351-54.

Krauss, Michael, and Davis D. Joyce. *The Writing of American History.*
Rev. ed. Norman, OK, and London: University of Oklahoma Press,
1985.

Krauthammer, Charles. "The Unipolar Moment." In *Rethinking America's
Security: Beyond Cold War to New World Order.* Ed. by Graham Allison
and Gregory F. Treverton. New York and London: W. W. Norton,
1992. Pp. 295-306.

Kristol, Irving. " 'Civil Liberties,' 1952—A Study in Confusion: Do We
Protect Our Rights By Protecting Communists?" *Commentary* 13 (March
1952): 228-36.

―――. *Neoconservatism: The Autobiography of an Idea.* New York: The
Free Press, 1995.

Krupskaya, N. K. ["Nadezhda Krupskaia"]. "A Bolshevist *Index Expurgatorius.*" *Living Age* 322 (July 5, 1924): 26-28. Reprinted from *Pravda*
(April 9, 1924).

―――. *On Education: Selected Articles and Speeches.* Trans. by G. P.
Ivanov-Mumjiev. Moscow: Foreign Languages Publishing House, 1957.

―――. *Reminiscences of Lenin.* Trans. by Bernard Isaacs. New York:
International Publishers, 1975.

Krzys, Richard, and Gaston Litton; with Ann Hewitt. *World Librarianship:
A Comparative Study.* New York and Basel: Marcel Dekker, 1983.

Kuhn, Irene Corbally. "Battle Over Books." *American Legion Magazine*
(Oct. 1958): 20-21, 37-40.

―――. "Who Are the Censors?" *American Legion Magazine* (July 1954):
14-15, 59-62.

―――. "Why You Buy Books that Sell Communism." *American Legion
Magazine* (Jan. 1951): 18-19, 53-55, 58-63.

Kunitz, Stanley J. "The Roving Eye." [Editorials.] *Wilson Bulletin for
Librarians* 9 (Nov. 1934): 137-38, 166; 10 (Nov. 1935): 194-95; and 10
(March 1936): 469-70.

―――, and Howard Haycraft, eds. *Dictionary of Modern Literature.*
New York: H. W. Wilson, 1942.

Kurzweil, Edith, and William Phillips, eds. *Our Country, Our Culture: The
Politics of Political Correctness.* Boston: Partisan Review Press, 1994.

Kutler, Stanley I. *The American Inquisition: Justice and Injustice in the*

Cold War. New York: Hill and Wang, 1982.

Kuzin, N. P., and R. B. Bendrovskaia. "Basic Directions in the Development of Soviet Pedagogical Science during the Prewar Years." Trans. by Arlo Schultz. *Soviet Education* 25 (Dec. 1982): 74-84.

L., N. "Russia." *Library Journal* 49 (April 1, 1924): 336, 338.

————. Untitled editorial. *Library Journal* 49 (April 1, 1924): 342.

Lacy, Dan. "Aid to National Policy." *Library Trends* 2 (July 1953): 146-70.

————. "The Overseas Book Program of the United States Government." In *International Aspects of Librarianship*. Ed. by Carnovsky. Pp. 98-111.

————. "The Role of American Books Abroad." *Foreign Affairs* 34 (April 1956): 405-17.

————, and Charles Kersten. "What Should Be the Function of Our Overseas Libraries?" Debate. Moderated by Gunnar Back. *Town Meeting of the Air*. ABC Radio. New York: July 14, 1953. Published in *Town Meeting* vol. 19, no. 11 (1953). 15 pp.

Lasby, Clarence. Review of *Seeds of Repression*, by Athan Theoharis. *Journal of Politics* 34 (Nov. 1972): 1328.

Lasch, Christopher. *The American Liberals and the Russian Revolution*. New York: McGraw-Hill, 1972. Originally published: New York: Columbia University Press, 1962.

————. *The Revolt of the Elites and the Betrayal of Democracy*. New York: W. W. Norton, 1995.

Laves, Walter H. C. "The United Nations and American Leadership in the World Crisis." *ALA Bulletin* 45 (March 1951): 79-86.

Lazarsfeld, Paul, and Wagner Thielens, Jr. *The Academic Mind: Social Scientists in a Time of Crisis*. Glencoe, IL: Free Press, 1958.

Leich, Harold M. "The Society for Librarianship and Russian Librarianship in the Early Twentieth Century." *Journal of Library History* 22, no. 1 (1987): 42-57.

Lenin, Vladimir Ilich. *Lenin and Books*. Comp. by A. Z. Okorokov. Moscow: Progress Publishers, 1971.

————. *Lenin and Library Organization*. Comp. by K. I. Abramov. Moscow: Progress Publishers, 1983.

————. *V. I. Lenin: Selected Works*. 3 vols. Moscow: Progress Publishers, 1970-1971; reprinted from Lenin's *Collected Works*.

Lerner, Alexander. "To Protest or Ignore? A Scientist's Alternatives in Reacting to the Persecution of His Colleagues." *Journal of the American Society for Information Science* 30 (Nov. 1973): 353-55.

Letters. *ALA Bulletin* 34 (Sept. 1940): 478-80.

Levine, Isaac Don. *Eyewitness to History: Memoirs and Reflections of a*

Foreign Correspondent for Half a Century. New York: Hawthorn Books, 1973.

—————. *The Man Lenin.* New York: Thomas Seltzer, 1924.

—————, ed. *Plain Talk: An Anthology from the Leading Anti-Communist Magazine of the 40's.* New Rochelle, NY: Arlington House, 1976.

Lévy, Bernard-Henri. *Adventures on the Freedom Road: The French Intellectuals in the Twentieth Century.* Trans. and ed. by Richard Veasey. London: Harvill Press, 1995. Originally published as *Les Aventures de la Liberté.* Paris: Bernard Grasset, 1991.

Lewis, Fulton, III. "A Guide to Red Reading." *American Mercury* 88 (June 1959): 48-53.

"Libraries in Soviet Russia." *Literary Digest* 93 (April 9, 1927): 28.

"Library Activities in Russia." *Library Journal* 49 (March 15, 1924): 292.

Library of Congress, Congressional Research Service. *World Communism, 1964-69: A Selected Bibliography.* Vol. 2. Washington, DC: GPO, 1971.

Library of Congress, Legislative Reference Service. *World Communism: A Selected Annotated Bibliography.* Washington, DC: GPO, 1964.

Library of Congress, Legislative Reference Service. *World Communism: A Selected Annotated Bibliography.* (Addendum.) Washington, DC: GPO, 1964.

"Library of Kazan Students." In *Great Soviet Encyclopedia: A Translation of the Third Edition.* Vol. 3. P. 716.

"Library Progress in Russia." *Libraries* 35 (Dec. 1930): 454-55.

"Library Reorganization in Russia." *Libraries* 36 (April 1931): 158.

Liebaers, Herman. "Margarita Ivanovna Rudomino." In *World Encyclopedia of Library and Information Services.* 3rd ed. Pp. 726-27.

Lilley, James, and Carl Ford. "China's Military: A Second Opinion." *The National Interest*, no. 57 (Fall 1999): 71-77.

Lincove, David A. "Propaganda and the American Public Library from the 1930's to the Eve of World War II." *RQ* 33 (Summer 1994): 510-23.

Linderman, Eric G. "A. Robert Rogers: The Influence of His Canadianism on His Work as a Library Educator." *Libraries and Culture* 35 (Fall 2000): 499-513.

Lindsey, Jonathan A., and Ann E. Prentice. *Professional Ethics and Librarians.* Phoenix: Oryx Press, 1985.

Lippmann, Walter, and Charles Merz. "More News from the *Times.*" *New Republic* 23 (Aug. 11, 1920): 299-301.

—————. "A Test of the News." *New Republic Supplement* (Aug. 4, 1920): 1-42.

Lipset, Seymour Martin, and Gary Marks. *It Didn't Happen Here: Why Socialism Failed in the United States.* New York: W. W. Norton, 2000.

Lipset, Seymour Martin, and Earl Raab. *The Politics of Unreason: Right-Wing Extremism in America, 1790-1970*. New York and London: Harper & Row, 1970.

Lorkovic, Tatjana, and Eric A. Johnson. "Serial and Book Exchanges with the Former Soviet Union." *The Serials Librarian* 31, no. 4 (1997): 59-85.

Lovell, Stephen. *The Russian Reading Revolution: Print Culture in the Soviet and Post-Soviet Eras*. New York: St. Martin's Press; London: Macmillan, 2000.

Lowenthal, Leo, and Norbert Guterman. *Prophets of Deceit: A Study of the Techniques of the American Agitator*. 2nd ed. Foreword by Herbert Marcuse. Intro. by Max Horkheimer. Palo Alto, CA: Pacific Books, 1970. First edition lacks Foreword: Harper & Bros., 1949.

Ludington, Flora B. "The American Contribution to Foreign Library Establishment and Rehabilitation." In *International Aspects of Librarianship*. Ed. by Carnovsky. Pp. 112-24.

———. "Strengthening the Forces for Peace." *MLA* [Massachusetts Library Association] *Bulletin* 41 (July 1951): 37-39.

Luttwak, Edward N. *On the Meaning of Victory: Essays on Strategy*. New York: Simon and Schuster, 1986.

Lydenberg, Harry Miller. "Avrahm Yarmolinsky: Introduction." *Bulletin of the New York Public Library* 59 (March 1955): 107-9.

———. "Books for Europe." *Bulletin of the American Library Association* 18 (Aug. 1924): 222.

———. "Books for Foreign Countries." *Bulletin of the American Library Association* 20 (Oct. 1926): 368-69.

———. *History of the New York Public Library: Astor, Lenox, and Tilden Foundations*. New York: New York Public Library, 1923. Reprinted: Boston: Gregg Press, 1972.

———. "An International Board? Why? What for? What Does It Do?" *ALA Bulletin* 38 (Nov. 1944): 457-63.

———. "What Some Friends in Europe Say about Us." *Library Journal* 53 (May 15, 1928): 437.

Lynch, Beverly P. Untitled review of *Censorship and the American Library*, by Louise S. Robbins. *Library Quarterly* 68 (Jan. 1998): 90-92.

Lyons, Eugene. *Assignment in Utopia*. New York: Harcourt, Brace, 1937.

———. "Is Freedom of Expression Really Threatened? The Hysteria over Hysteria." *American Mercury* 76 (Jan. 1953): 22-33.

———. *The Red Decade*. With new preface. New Rochelle, NY: Arlington House, 1970. Originally published: Bobbs-Merrill, 1941.

———. *Workers' Paradise Lost: Fifty Years of Soviet Communism*. New York: Funk & Wagnalls, 1967.

MacLeish, Archibald. "Libraries in the Contemporary Crisis." *Library Journal* 64 (Nov. 15, 1939): 879-82.

Maddox, Robert James. *The New Left and the Origins of the Cold War.* Princeton, NJ: Princeton University Press, 1973.

———. "A Visit to Cloudland: Cold War Revisionism in College Texts." *Continuity*, no. 20 (Spring 1996): 1-11.

Maichel, Karol. "Czechoslovak National Bibliography: A Historical Sketch." *College and Research Libraries* 18 (July 1957): 269-74.

———. "Russian Current Bibliographies, 1772-1917." *Library Quarterly* 28 (Jan. 1958): 38-44.

———. "The Russian Exchange Program at Columbia University." *Library Resources and Technical Services* 2 (Fall 1958): 254-58.

———. "Russian Retrospective Bibliographies." *Library Quarterly* 28 (April 1958): 122-31.

Maier, Charles S. "Revisionism and the Interpretation of Cold War Origins." *Perspectives in American History* 4 (1970): 313-47.

Main, Stephen J. "The Creation and Development of the Library System in the Red Army during the Russian Civil War (1918-1920): A Historical Introduction." *Library Quarterly* 65 (July 1995): 319-32.

Mäkinen, Ilkka. "Libraries in Hell: Cultural Activities in Soviet Prisons and Labor Camps from the 1930s to the 1950s." *Libraries and Culture* 28 (Spring 1993): 117-42.

Malia, Martin E. "Report on the Principal Results of Martin E. Malia's Acquisitions Trip to the USSR." Appendix to the *Library of Congress Information Bulletin* 15 (July 16, 1956): 389-92.

Maltin, Leonard. *Leonard Maltin's Movie and Video Guide, 1999.* New York: Signet, 1998.

Manuel, Frank E. *A Requiem for Karl Marx.* Cambridge, MA: Harvard University Press, 1995.

Mappen, Marc, ed. *Witches and Historians: Interpretations of Salem.* Huntington, NY: Robert Krieger, 1980.

Margolis, Howard. "Right Wingers Seem to Be Almost Everywhere." Review of *The American Right Wing*, by Ellsworth and Harris. *Science* 134 (Dec. 22, 1961): 2025-27.

Margulies, Sylvia R. *The Pilgrimage to Russia: The Soviet Union and the Treatment of Foreigners, 1924-1937.* Madison, WI, and London: University of Wisconsin Press, 1968.

Marinelli, Anne V. "Librarianship from an International Point of View." *College and Research Libraries* 10 (Oct. 1949): 319-20.

Marley, Sheppard. "Mrs. Dean's Foreign Policy Lobby." *Plain Talk* 1 (Nov. 1946): 16-20.

Marvin, John R. Review of *Scoundrel Time*, by Hellman. *Library Journal*

101 (May 1, 1976): 1110.

Marx, Karl. "The Civil War in France." [1871] Reprinted, in part, from the Foreign Languages Publishing House [Moscow] edition, in *Basic Writings on Politics and Philosophy: Karl Marx and Friedrich Engels*. Ed. by Lewis Feuer. Garden City, NY: Doubleday, 1959. Pp. 363-90.

———, and Frederick Engels. *Selected Works*. Moscow: Progress Publishers, 1975.

———, and Friedrich Engels. "Manifesto of the Communist Party." [1848.] English edition of 1888. Reprinted in *Basic Writings on Politics and Philosophy: Marx and Engels*. Ed. by Feuer. Pp. 1-41.

Matthews, J. B. "Hutchins to Investigate Communism?" *American Mercury* 80 (June 1955): 71-81.

"McCarthy Critics Challenged by 28." *New York Times* (April 6, 1953): 7.

McCarthy, Joseph. *The Fight for America*. Hamilton, MT: Poor Richard's Book Shop, 1952. Reprint of *McCarthyism and the Fight for America: Documented Answers to Questions Asked by Friend and Foe*. New York: Devin-Adair, 1952.

———. *Major Speeches and Debates of Senator Joe McCarthy Delivered in the United States Senate, 1950-1951*. Reprinted from *The Congressional Record*. Washington, DC: GPO, n.d.

McColm, R. Bruce. *El Salvador: Peaceful Revolution or Armed Struggle?* New York: Freedom House, 1982.

McColvin, Lionel R., general ed. *A Survey of Libraries: Reports on a Survey Made by the Library Association during 1936-1937*. London: The Library Association, 1938.

McCormick, Charles H. *Seeing Reds: Federal Surveillance of Radicals in the Pittsburgh Mill District, 1917-1921*. Pittsburgh: University of Pittsburgh Press, 1997.

McFadden, Charles J., O.S.A. *The Philosophy of Communism*. New York: Benziger Brothers, 1939.

McKay, George L. "A Bibliography of the Published Writings of Harry Miller Lydenberg." In *Bookmen's Holiday: Notes and Studies Written and Gathered in Tribute to Harry Miller Lydenberg*. Ed. by Deoch Fulton. New York: New York Public Library, 1943. Pp. 5-26.

McNeal, Robert H. *Bride of the Revolution: Krupskaya and Lenin*. Ann Arbor: University of Michigan Press, 1972.

McWilliams, John C. *The Protectors: Harry J. Anslinger and the Federal Bureau of Narcotics, 1930-1962*. Newark, DE: University of Delaware Press, 1990.

Mead, Margaret. "The New Isolationism." *The American Scholar* 24 (Summer 1955): 378-82.

Mediavilla, Cindy. "The War on Books and Ideas: The California Library

Association and Anti-Communist Censorship in the 1940s and 1950s," *Library Trends* 46 (Fall 1997): 331-47.

Medina, Harold R. *The Anatomy of Freedom.* New York: Henry Holt, 1959.

Medved, Michael. "As Bad as it Gets." *American Legion Magazine* 145 (Aug. 1998): 18-22.

"Meet the *Nation* Experts on Civil Liberties." *New Leader* (July 14, 1952): 14, 22.

Melgounov, Sergey Petrovich. *The Red Terror in Russia.* London and Toronto: J. M. Dent, 1925. From German trans. of Russian version: Berlin: Vataga, 1924.

Mendel, Arthur P. "The Formation and Appeal of 'Scientific Socialism.' " In *Essential Works of Marxism.* Ed. by Mendel. New York: Bantam, 1965.

Meyer, Frank S. "Principles and Heresies: The Meaning of McCarthy." *National Review* 5 (June 14, 1953): 565-66.

Milam, Carl H. "Help for Russian Librarians." *Library Journal* 47 (Oct. 15, 1922): 870.

————. "Libraries, Scholars, and the War." *The Annals of the American Academy of Political and Social Science* 235 (Sept. 1944): 100-106.

Miliukov, Paul. *Bolshevism: An International Danger: Its Doctrines and Its Practice through War and Revolution.* London: Allen & Unwin, 1920. Reprint: Westport, CT: Hyperion, 1981.

Mill, John Stuart. *On Socialism.* Amherst, NY: Prometheus Books, 1987.

Miller, William. *The Book Industry: A Report of the Public Library Inquiry.* New York: Columbia University Press, 1949.

Milum, Betty L. "Luther Evans." In *World Encyclopedia of Library and Information Services.* 3rd ed. Pp. 289-90.

Minsker, Jack. "Science, Shcharansky, and the Soviets." *Journal of the American Society for Information Science* 29 (Sept. 1972): 219-24.

Mises, Ludwig von. *The Anti-Capitalistic Mentality.* Spring Mills, PA: Libertarian Press, 1972. Originally published: Princeton, NJ: Van Nostrand, 1956.

"Mr. Dulles Told What Was Done and Why." *U.S. News & World Report* 34 (June 26, 1953): 40, 42, 45.

"Mr. Eisenhower then Defined His Ideas Further." *U.S. News & World Report* 34 (June 26, 1953): 45-46.

Mohrhardt, Foster E. "Verner Warren Clapp." *Dictionary of American Library Biography.* Pp. 77-81.

————, ed. *Reading in a Changing World.* Papers Presented at the 38th Session of the IFLA General Council, Budapest, 1972. Munich: Verlag Dokumentation, 1976.

Moley, Raymond, Jr. *The American Legion Story.* With a foreword by J. Edgar Hoover. New York: Duell, Sloan, and Pearce, 1966.

Molnar, Pal. "The Conception and Interrelation of Bibliology and Library Science Formulated in Recent Debates in Socialist Countries." *Libri* 18, no. 1 (1968): 1-34.

Molnar, Thomas. *Authority and Its Enemies.* New Brunswick, NJ, and London: Transaction, 1995.

———. *The Decline of the Intellectual.* New Brunswick, NJ, and London: Transaction, 1994.

———. *Utopia: The Perennial Heresy.* Lanham, MD, and London: University Press of America, with the Intercollegiate Studies Institute, 1990. First published: New York: Sheed and Ward, 1967.

Moore, Everett T. "The Innocent Librarians." *ALA Bulletin* 55 (Nov. 1961): 861-62.

———. "Intellectual Freedom." In *Research Librarianship: Essays in Honor of Robert B. Downs.* Ed. by Jerrold Orne. New York and London: R. R. Bowker, 1971. Pp. 1-17.

———. "Threats to Intellectual Freedom." *Library Journal* 96 (Nov. 1, 1971): 3563-67.

———. "Why Do the Rightists Rage?" *ALA Bulletin* 56 (Jan. 1962): 26-31.

Moore, Harry Thornton. "Witch Hunters at Work." *The New Republic* 19 (June 19, 1935): 158-61.

Morsch, Lucile M. "Promoting Library Interests throughout the World." *ALA Bulletin* 51 (Sept. 1957): 579-84.

Moshensky, O. "Soviet Libraries." *Library Review* 91 (Aug. 1949): 157-58.

Mostecky, Vaclav. "The Library under Communism: Czechoslovak Libraries from 1948 to 1954." *Library Quarterly* 26 (April 1956): 105-17.

Mott, Frank Luther. *Golden Multitudes: The Story of Best Sellers in the United States.* New York: Macmillan, 1947.

Muggeridge, Malcolm. *Chronicles of Wasted Time: An Autobiography.* Washington, DC: Regnery, n.d. Previously published: New York: William Morrow, 1973-1974. Originally published in two volumes: Chronicle I: *The Green Stick*; Chronicle II: *The Infernal Grove.*

———. *The Thirties in Great Britain.* London: Collins, 1967. Originally published: London: Hamish Hamilton, 1940.

———. *Winter in Moscow.* London: Eyre and Spottiswoode; Boston: Little, Brown, 1934. Reprint: Grand Rapids, MI: William B. Eerdmans, 1987.

"Murrow's TV Program Exposes Book Banning." *Library Journal* 80 (May 15, 1955): 1245-46.

Nash, George H. *The Conservative Intellectual Movement in America since 1945*. Rev. ed. Wilmington, DE: Intercollegiate Studies Institute, 1996.
————. "Forgotten Godfathers: Premature Jewish Conservatives and the Rise of *National Review*." *American Jewish History* 87 (June/Sept. 1999): 123-57.
Navasky, Victor S. *Naming Names*. New York: Viking Press, 1980.
Nazmutdinov, Ildar K. "Union of Soviet Socialist Republics." Trans. by Thomas L. Mann. In *ALA World Encyclopedia of Library and Information Services*. 2nd ed. Pp. 818-22.
Nelles, Walter. *Seeing Red: Civil Liberty and Law in the Period following the War*. New York: American Civil Liberties Union, Aug. 1920. [12 pp.]
New York [State] Legislature. Joint Committee Investigating Seditious Activities. *Revolutionary Radicalism*. [aka the "Lusk Report."] 4 vols. Albany: J. B. Lyon, 1920.
Nichols, Thomas M. "Mules, Missiles, and McCarthy: CNN's *Cold War*." *International Journal* 54 (Summer 1999): 418-25.
Nichols, Tom. "H-Net and Beyond: A Real Academic Dialogue at Last." *Heterodoxy* 7 (March 1999): 1, 11-13.
Nitecki, Joseph Z. "National Network of Information in Poland." *Journal of the American Society for Information Science* 30 (Sept. 1979): 274-79.
Novick, Peter. *That Noble Dream: The "Objectivity Question" and the American Historical Profession*. New York: Cambridge University Press, 1988.
Nyholm, Jens. "Russia Wants to Know Us." (Letter.) *Library Journal* 63 (Oct. 1, 1943): 777.
O'Brien, C. Bickford. "Russian Libraries—The Door Swings Open." *College and Research Libraries* 18 (May 1957): 217-21.
O'Neill, William L. *A Better World: The Great Schism: Stalinism and the American Intellectuals*. New York: Simon and Schuster, 1982.
Olsen, Margaret S. "The More Things Change, the More They Stay the Same: East-West Exchanges, 1960-1993." *Library Resources and Technical Services* 39 (Jan. 1995): 5-21.
Olson, Everett C. "Russian Literature in the Natural Sciences." In *Iron Curtains and Scholarship*. Ed. by Winger. Pp. 69-81.
Osipova, I. P. "Popularity of Reading in the USSR." In *Reading in a Changing World*. Ed. by Mohrhardt. Pp. 91-100.
The Oxford Dictionary of Quotations. 4th ed. New York: Oxford University Press, 1992.
Oxford English Dictionary. Oxford: Oxford University Press, 1971.
Parrish, Thomas. *The Cold War Encyclopedia*. New York: Henry Holt, 1996.

Payne, Robert. *The Life and Death of Lenin.* New York: Simon and Schuster, 1964.

Pearson, Glenda. "The Red Scare: A Filmography." <http://www.lib.-washington.edu/exhibits/AllPowers/film.html>. March 5, 1998.

Pelling, Henry. *America and the British Left: From Bright to Bevan.* New York: New York University Press, 1957. Originally published: London: A. and C. Black, 1956.

Peters, J. [Jozip] *The Communist Party: A Manual on Organization.* New York: Workers Library Publishers, 1935.

Philbrick, Herbert A. "Should Communist Books Be Freely Available in Public Libraries?" *MLA* [Massachusetts Library Association] *Bulletin* 43 (Jan. 1953): 1-3.

Pillsbury, Michael. *China Debates the Future Security Environment.* Washington, DC: National Defense University Press, 2000.

Pipes, Daniel. *Conspiracy: How the Paranoid Style Flourishes and Where It Comes From.* New York: Free Press, 1997.

Pipes, Richard. *Communism: The Vanished Specter.* Oslo and Boston: Scandinavian University Press, 1994.

———. *Russia under the Bolshevik Regime.* New York: Knopf, 1993.

———. *The Russian Revolution.* New York: Vintage, 1991.

———. "Soviet Global Strategy." *Commentary* 69 (April 1980): 31-39.

———. *Survival is Not Enough: Soviet Realities and America's Future.* New York: Simon and Schuster, 1984.

———, ed. *The Unknown Lenin: From the Secret Archives.* New Haven, CT, and London: Yale University Press, 1996.

Podhoretz, Norman. *Ex-Friends: Falling Out with Allen Ginsberg, Lionel and Diana Trilling, Lillian Hellman, Hannah Arendt, and Norman Mailer.* New York: Free Press, 1999.

———. *The Present Danger: "Do We Have the Will to Reverse the Decline of American Power?"* New York: Simon and Schuster, 1980.

Pope Leo XIII. *Rerum Novarum* (aka *The Condition of Labor*). Encyclical. May 15, 1891.

Pope Pius XI. *Divini Redemptoris* (aka *Atheistic Communism*). Encyclical. March 19, 1937.

———. *Quadragesimo Anno* (aka *Reconstructing the Social Order*). Encyclical. May 15, 1931.

Popper, Karl R. *The Open Society and Its Enemies.* Princeton, NJ: Princeton University Press, 1950.

Possony, Stefan T. *Lenin: The Compulsive Revolutionary.* Chicago: Henry Regnery, 1964.

———. *Waking Up the Giant: The Strategy for American Victory and World Freedom.* New Rochelle, NY: Arlington House, 1974.

————, ed. *Lenin Reader*. Chicago: Henry Regnery, 1966; with the Hoover Institution, Stanford University.

Powers, Richard Gid. *Not Without Honor: The History of American Anticommunism*. New York: The Free Press, 1995.

————. *Secrecy and Power: The Life of J. Edgar Hoover*. New York: The Free Press, 1987.

Preer, Jean. "The American Heritage Project: Librarians and the Democratic Traditions in the Early Cold War." *Libraries and Culture* 28 (Spring 1993): 165-88.

Presidium of the Soviet Academy of Sciences. *The Work and the Position of the Staffs of the Library of the Academy of Sciences of the USSR and the Fundamental Library for the Social Sciences of the USSR*. Lexington, KY: University of Kentucky Libraries, Margaret I. King Library, Occasional Contributions no. 19, Dec. 1950. Trans. by Peter Petcoff. [3 pp.] From *Vestnik Akademii Nauk SSSR* (1950).

————. *The Work of the Libraries of the Academy of Sciences of the USSR in the International Book Exchange*. Lexington, KY: University of Kentucky Libraries, Margaret I. King Library, Occasional Contributions no. 25, March 1951. Trans. by Peter Petcoff. [2 pp.] From *Vestnik Akademii Nauk SSSR* (1950).

Price, Joseph W., and Mary S. Price, comps. *International Librarianship Today and Tomorrow*. New York and Munich: K. G. Saur, 1985.

Rader, Inge Antonie. "Krupskaya: Pioneer Soviet Educator of the Masses." Ph.D. dissertation, Southern Illinois University, 1974.

Radosh, Ronald. "The Blacklist as History." *The New Criterion* 16 (Dec. 1997): 12-17.

————. "The Two Evils: Communism, McCarthyism, and the Truth." Review of *Many Are the Crimes*, by Schrecker; and *The Soviet World of American Communism*, by Klehr, Haynes, and Anderson. *New Republic* (May 11, 1998): 38, 40-49.

Rakov, Lev. "The Leningrad Public Library." *The Library World* 51 (May 1949): 221-22.

Ravkin, Z. I. "The Development of Pedagogical Science." *Soviet Education* 25 (Dec. 1982): 7-73.

Raymond, Boris. *Krupskaia and Soviet Russian Librarianship, 1917-1939*. Metuchen, NJ, and London: Scarecrow Press, 1979.

Reagan, Ronald. "Remarks at the Annual Convention of the National Association of Evangelicals in Orlando, Florida." March 8, 1983. In *Public Papers of the Presidents of the United States, Ronald Reagan, 1983*. Washington, DC: GPO, 1984. Pp. 359-64.

Reed, John. *Ten Days that Shook the World*. Foreword by V. I. Lenin. Preface by N. K. Krupskaya. New intro. by John Howard Lawson. New

York: International Publishers, 1967. Also published with intro. and
notes by Bertram D. Wolfe, New York: Vintage, 1960. Originally
published in U.S. and England: 1919.

Reeves, Thomas C. "Are You Now . . . ." Review of *Many are the
Crimes*, by Ellen Schrecker. *New York Times Book Review* (June 14,
1998): 22-23.

————. *The Life and Times of Joe McCarthy*. New York: Stein & Day,
1982.

————. Review of *The Inquisition in Hollywood*, by Ceplair and Englund.
History 9 (Feb. 1981): 91-92.

————. Review of *The Nightmare Decade*, by Fred J. Cook. *Journal of
American History* 58 (March 1972): 1055-56.

Regnery, Henry. *Memoirs of a Dissident Publisher*. New York and London:
Harcourt, Brace, Jovanovich, 1979.

"Reiza Palatnik—A. L. Asked to Take Action." *Assistant Librarian* 64
(Dec. 1971): 188.

"Reizia Palatnik." (Editorial.) *Assistant Librarian* 64 (Oct. 1971): 145.

Remnek, Miranda Beaven, ed. *Books in Russia and the Soviet Union: Past
and Present*. Wiesbaden: Otto Harrassowitz, 1991.

"Report on Russian Libraries." *Library Journal* 84 (Jan. 15, 1959): 161.

Revel, Jean-François. *How Democracies Perish*. Trans. by William Byron.
Garden City, NY: Doubleday, 1984. Originally published as *Comment
les Démocraties Finissent*. Paris: Grasset & Fasquelle, 1983.

————. *The Totalitarian Temptation*. Trans. by David Hapgood. Garden
City, NY: Doubleday, 1977. Originally published as *La Tentation
Totalitaire*. Paris: Robert Laffont, 1976.

Ribuffo, Leo P. *The Old Christian Right: The Protestant Far Right from the
Great Depression to the Cold War*. Philadelphia: Temple University
Press, 1983.

Richards, Pamela Spence. "Scientific Communication in the Cold War:
Margarita Rudomino and the Library of Foreign Literatures during the
Last Years of Stalin." *Libraries and Culture* 31 (Winter 1996): 235-46.

————. "Soviet-American Library Relations in the 1920s and 1930s: A
Study in Mutual Fascination and Distrust." *Library Quarterly* 68 (Oct.
1998): 390-405.

————, ed. *The History of Reading and Libraries in the United States and
Russia*. Proceedings of an International Conference, June 19-21, 1996,
Vologda, Russia. Published as *Libraries and Culture* 33 (Winter 1998).

Richardson, John V., Jr. "The Origin of Soviet Education for Librarian-
ship: The Role of Nadezhda Konstantinovna Krupskaya, Lyubov'
Borisovna Khavkina-Hamburger, and Genrietta K. Abele-Derman."
Journal of Education for Library and Information Science 41 (Spring

2000): 106-28.

Robbins, Louise S. "Anti-Communism, Racism, and Censorship in the McCarthy Era: The Case of Ruth W. Brown and the Bartlesville Public Library." *Journal of Education for Library and Information Science* 35 (Fall 1994): 331-36.

———. *Censorship and the American Library: The American Library Association's Response to Threats to Intellectual Freedom, 1939-1969.* Westport, CT, and London: Greenwood Press, 1996.

———. *The Dismissal of Miss Ruth Brown: Civil Rights, Censorship, and the American Library.* Norman, OK: University of Oklahoma Press, 2000.

———. "Fighting McCarthyism through Film: A Library Censorship Case Becomes a *Storm Center.*" *Journal of Education for Library and Information Science* 39 (Fall 1998): 291-311.

———. "Message from the Chair." *Library History Round Table Newsletter.* N.s. 3 (Fall 1997): 1-2.

———. "Racism and Censorship in Cold War Oklahoma: The Case of Ruth W. Brown and the Bartlesville Public Library." *Southwestern Historical Quarterly* 100 (July 1996): 19-48.

Roberts, James C., ed. *The Best of* Human Events: *Fifty Years of Conservative Thought and Action.* Lafayette, LA: Huntington House Publishers, 1995.

Roche, John P. Review of *The Great Fear*, by David Caute. *Political Science Quarterly* 2 (Summer 1979): 361-62.

———. "Was Everyone Terrified? The Mythology of 'McCarthyism.' " *Quadrant* [Sydney] 33 (Sept. 1989): 31-39.

Roche, Lisa, ed. *Scorpions in a Bottle: Dangerous Ideas about the United States and the Soviet Union.* Hillsdale, MI: Hillsdale College Press, 1986.

Rogers, A. Robert. "Censorship and Libraries in the Soviet Union." *Journal of Library History, Philosophy, and Comparative Librarianship* 8 (Jan. 1973): 22-29.

———. "Some Impressions of Three Russian Libraries." *Ohio Library Association Bulletin* 43 (July 1973): 4-10.

———, Kathryn McChesney; and others. *The Library in Society.* Littleton, CO: Libraries Unlimited, 1984.

Romerstein, Herbert, and Eric Breindel. *The Venona Secrets: Exposing Soviet Espionage and America's Traitors.* Washington, DC: Regnery, 2000.

Roosevelt, Franklin Delano. Memo to Felix Frankfurter. May 3, 1939. Published in "Judging Librarianship," *American Libraries* 26 (May 1995): 408, 411. Intro. by David Streeter.

Root, E. Merrill. *Collectivism on the Campus: The Battle for the Mind in*

American Colleges. New York: Devin-Adair, 1955.

Rosenfield, Leonora Cohen. *Portrait of a Philosopher: Morris R. Cohen in Life and Letters*. New York: Harcourt, Brace, & World, 1962.

Rostow, W. W. *The Stages of Economic Growth: A Non-Communist Manifesto*. Cambridge: Cambridge University Press, 1961.

———. *The Stages of Economic Growth: A Non-Communist Manifesto*. 2nd ed. Cambridge: Cambridge University Press, 1971.

———, with Alfred Levin. *The Dynamics of Soviet Society*. New York: W. W. Norton, 1953.

Rudd, Augustin G. *Bending the Twig: The Revolution in Education and Its Effect on Our Children*. New York: Sons of the American Revolution, New York Chapter, 1957.

Rudomino, Margarita Ivanova. "The All-Union Library of Foreign Literature." *Unesco Bulletin for Libraries* 10 (Oct. 1956): 226-28.

———. Untitled letter. Dec. 10, 1942. Trans. by Gerda Beherns. Published in *Library Journal* 68 (Oct. 1, 1943): 777.

Ruggles, Melville J. "Eastern European Publications in American Libraries." In *Iron Curtains and Scholarship*. Ed. by Winger. Pp. 111-23.

Rusher, William A. *The Rise of the Right*. Rev. ed. New York: National Review Press, 1993.

———. *Special Counsel*. New Rochelle, NY: Arlington House, 1968.

Russell, Bertrand. *The Practice and Theory of Bolshevism*. 2nd ed. New York: Simon and Schuster, 1964. Originally published: London: Allen & Unwin, 1920.

Russell, John Richmond. "Library Service in the USSR." *Journal of Adult Education* 8 (April 1936): 165-69.

"Russian Libraries Today." *Library Journal* 49 (Sept. 1, 1924): 727-29.

"Russians Free Librarian Raiza Palatnik from Prison." *Library Journal* 98 (March 1, 1973): 679.

Ruud, Charles A. "The Printing Press as an Agent of Political Change in Early Twentieth-Century Russia." *The Russian Review* 40 (Oct. 1981): 378-95.

Ryskind, Morrie, with John H. M. Roberts. *I Shot an Elephant in My Pajamas*. Lafayette, LA: Huntington House Publishers, 1994.

Safire, William. "First Things First." *New York Times Magazine* (Sept. 26, 1999): 36, 39.

———. *Safire's New Political Dictionary*. New York: Random House, 1993.

———. "Useful Idiots of the West." *New York Times Magazine* (April 12, 1987): 8, 10.

Sakharov, Andrei. *My Country and the World*. Trans. by Guy V. Daniels. New York: Knopf, 1975.

Santayana, George. *Character and Opinion in the United States*. London: Constable, 1920. As reprinted: New York: George Braziller, 1955.

Sarin, Oleg, and Lev Dvoretsky. *Alien Wars: The Soviet Union's Aggressions against the World, 1919 to 1989*. Novato, CA: Presidio Press, 1996.

Sarolea, Charles. *Impressions of Soviet Russia*. 2nd ed. London: Eveleigh Nash & Grayson, 1924.

Satel, Sally. *PC, M. D.: How Political Correctness is Corrupting Medicine*. New York: Basic Books, 2000.

Sayre, Norma. *Running Time: Films of the Cold War*. New York: Dial Press, 1982.

Schaar, John H. *Loyalty in America*. Berkeley and Los Angeles: University of California Press, 1957.

Schlesinger, Arthur M., Jr. *The Disuniting of America: Reflections on a Multicultural Society*. Revised and enlarged ed. New York: W. W. Norton, 1998.

———. "Origins of the Cold War." *Foreign Affairs* 46 (Oct. 1967): 22-52.

———. "Our Past—And Present." Review of *The American People*, by Gerald W. Johnson. *New York Times Book Review* (Oct. 7, 1951): 6.

———. "A Shameful Story." Review of *The Great Fear*, by Caute. *New York Times Book Review* (March 19, 1978): 1, 44-45.

———. *The Vital Center: The Politics of Freedom*. With new intro. by Schlesinger. Boston: Houghton Mifflin, 1962. Originally published 1949.

Schmidt, Peter. "Survey Finds Widespread Faculty Support for Racial and Ethnic Diversity." *Chronicle of Higher Education: Today's News* (May 18, 2000), <chronicle.com/news>.

Schoenfeld, Gabriel. "Twenty-Four Lies about the Cold War." *Commentary* 107 (March 1999): 28-35.

Schrecker, Ellen. *Many Are the Crimes: McCarthyism in America*. Boston and London: Little, Brown, and Co., 1998.

———. *No Ivory Tower: McCarthyism and the Universities*. New York and Oxford: Oxford University Press, 1986.

Schuman, Patricia Glass. "Recent Developments in U.S. Information Policy." Conference speech at "Shrinking World, Exploding Information." April 4, 1986.

Schwarz, Fred. *Beating the Unbeatable Foe: One Man's Victory over Communism, Leviathan, and the Last Enemy*. Washington, DC: Regnery, 1996.

Schweizer, Peter, ed. *The Fall of the Berlin Wall: Reassessing the Causes and Consequences of the End of the Cold War*. Stanford, CA: Hoover Institution Press, Stanford University; and Washington, DC: William J.

Casey Institute of the Center for Security Policy, 2000.

Sehr, Thomas J. "Thomas Hutchinson." In *American Historians, 1607-1865*. Ed. by Clyde N. Wilson. Detroit: Gale Research, 1984. Pp. 141-46.

Seideman, David. "Hell and Hard Work." Review of *By the Dawn's Early Light*, by Boyer. *Times Literary Supplement* (March 14, 1986): 268.

Seldes, Gilbert. "Murrow, McCarthy, and the Empty Formula." *Saturday Review* 37 (May 15, 1954): 25-26.

Selvin, David F. *A Terrible Anger: The 1934 Waterfront and General Strikes in San Francisco*. Detroit: Wayne State University Press, 1996.

Semenev, V. "A Russian View of the Lenin Library." *Wilson Bulletin for Librarians* 9 (Nov. 1934): 237-38.

Serov, V. V. "Library Science and Some Problems of Library Education in the USSR." *Libri* 19, no. 3 (1969): 175-90.

———. "Union of Soviet Socialist Republics." In *ALA World Encyclopedia of Library and Information Services*. 2nd ed. Pp. 567-71.

Sessions, John A. "A Misleading Guide to U.S. Communism." *The New Leader* (Oct. 31, 1955): 25-27.

Shannon, William. Review of *The Truman Doctrine and the Origins of McCarthyism*, by Freeland. *New York Times Book Review* (Jan. 16, 1972): 3-4.

Shapiro, Edward S. *Clio from the Right: Essays of a Conservative Historian*. Washington, DC: University Press of America, 1983.

———. "Liberalism and the College History Textbook." *Continuity: A Journal of History*, no. 16 (Fall 1992): 27-45.

Shavit, David. *United States Relations with Russia and the Soviet Union: A Historical Dictionary*. Westport, CT, and London: Greenwood Press, 1993.

Shaw, Ralph R. "About Russian Publications." (Letter.) *Library Journal* 71 (Aug. 1946): 1029.

———. "International Activities of the American Library Association." *American Library Association Bulletin* 41 (June 1947): 199-232.

———. "Wars Begin in the Minds of Men." *American Library Association Bulletin* 40 (Nov. 1946): 419-20.

Shei, David E. *Matthew Josephson: Bourgeois Bohemian*. New Haven and London: Yale University Press, 1981.

Shores, Louis. "Comparative Librarianship: A Theoretical Approach." In *Comparative and International Librarianship*. Ed. by Miles M. Jackson. Westport, CT: Greenwood Press, 1970. Pp. 3-24.

"Shrinking World, Exploding Information: Developments in International Librarianship." Conference sponsored by the Library Association of the City University of New York. New York: April 4, 1986.

Shteppa, Konstantin F. *Russian Historians and the Soviet State*. New Brunswick, NJ: Rutgers University Press, 1962.

Sikorsky, N. M. "Library Planning in the Soviet Union." In *National and International Library Planning*. Ed. by Vosper and Newkirk. Pp. 35-42.

Simsova, Sylva. "Comparative Librarianship as an Academic Subject." *Journal of Librarianship* 6 (April 1974): 115-25. Reprinted in *Reader in Comparative Librarianship*. Ed. by D. J. Foskett. Pp. 50-65.

———, ed. *Lenin, Krupskaia, and Libraries*. Trans. by G. Peacock and Lucy Prescott. London: Clive Bingley; Hamden, CT: Archon Books, 1968.

———, ed. *Nicholas Rubakin and Bibliopsychology*. Trans. by M. Mackee and G. Peacock. London: Clive Bingley; Hamden, CT: Archon Books, 1968.

Sirgiovanni, George. *An Undercurrent of Suspicion: Anti-Communism in America during World War II*. New Brunswick, NJ, and London: Transaction Publishers, 1990.

Skrypnev, N. "The 'Krupskaja' State Library Institute, Leningrad." *Unesco Bulletin for Libraries* 13 (April 1959): 84-86.

Sleeper, Raymond S., ed. *A Lexicon of Marxist-Leninist Semantics*. Alexandria, VA: Western Goals, 1983.

Slon, Eugene. *Open Access to Soviet Book Collections*. Ed. by Donald C. Robbins. New York: Ukrainian Library Association of America; and Toronto: New Review Books, 1978.

Smith, John E., and Evelyn Benagh Detchon. "It Happened in Burbank." *ALA Bulletin* 46 (March 1952): 85-87.

Smits, Rudolph. "Bibliographic Control in the Soviet Union." *College and Research Libraries* 17 (July 1956): 350-52.

Sniegoski, Stephen. "Joseph R. McCarthy and the Historians." *Modern Age* 29 (Spring 1985): 132-42.

Snowden, Mrs. Philip. [Ethel Snowden.] *Through Bolshevik Russia*. London and New York: Cassell, 1920.

Sokolsky, George E. *An Outline of Universal History*. Shanghai: The Commercial Press, 1928.

———. *The Tinder Box of Asia*. Rev. ed. Garden City, NY: Doubleday, Doran, 1933.

Solzhenitsyn, Aleksandr I. *Cancer Ward*. London: Bodley Head, 1962.

———. *Détente*. New Brunswick, NJ: Transaction, 1976.

———. *The Mortal Danger: How Misconceptions about Russia Imperil America*. 2nd ed. Trans. by Michael Nicholson and Alexis Klimoff. New York: Harper & Row, 1981.

———. *Warning to the West*. New York: Farrar, Straus, and Giroux, 1976.

Sontag, Susan. "The Hard Lessons of Poland's Military Coup." *Los Angeles Times* (Feb. 14, 1982): Section 4, p. 2.

"Soviet Research Libraries." *CU News* [University of California General Library] (May 29, 1957), as reprinted in *Library Journal* 82 (Nov. 15, 1957): 2892.

"The Soviet Teacher: The Training of Pedagogical Cadres." *Soviet Education* 25 (Nov. 1982): 7-33. Trans. by Arlo Schultz. From *Studies in the History of the School and the Pedagogical Thought of the Peoples of the USSR, 1914-1941*, ed. by N. P. Kuzin, M. N. Kolmakova, and Z. I. Ravkin (Moscow: Pedagogika Publishers, 1980).

"The Soviets Take Stock of Russia's Schools, Libraries and Movie Houses." *Library Journal* 44 (March 1919): 184-85.

Sowell, Thomas. *Marxism: Philosophy and Economics*. New York: William Morrow, 1985.

———. *The Quest for Cosmic Justice*. New York: Free Press, 1999.

Spargo, John. *"The Greatest Failure in All History": A Critical Examination of the Actual Workings of Bolshevism in Russia*. New York and London: Harper & Bros., 1920.

———. *The Psychology of Bolshevism*. New York and London: Harper & Bros., 1919.

Sperber, A. M. *Murrow: His Life and Times*. New York: Freundlich, distributed by Simon and Schuster, 1986.

Spufford, Francis. "The Heretic." *New Republic* 214 (June 17, 1996): 41-42.

Sroka, Marek. " 'Soldiers of the Cultural Revolution': The Stalinization of Libraries and Librarianship in Poland, 1945-1953." *Library History* 16 (Nov. 2000): 105-25.

Stam, David H. "A Bibliography of the Published Writings of Harry Miller Lydenberg, 1942-1960." *Bulletin of the New York Public Library* 64 (June 1960): 298-302.

"Statistics on Stilts." *Bookmark* [University of Idaho Library] 12 (Dec. 1959): 48.

Stelmakh, Valeria D., ed. *The Image of the Library: Studies and Views from Several Countries*. Haifa, Israel: University of Haifa Library, 1994.

Stevens, Norman D. "Ralph Robert Shaw." In *Dictionary of American Library Biography*. Pp. 476-81.

Stewart, George R. *American Place-Names: A Concise and Selective Dictionary for the Continental United States of America*. New York: Oxford University Press, 1970.

Stewart, Marguerite Ann. *Land of the Soviets*. Ed. by Maxwell S. Stewart. St. Louis: Webster Publishing, in cooperation with the Institute of Pacific Relations, 1942.

Stewart, Maxwell S. "Progress and Purges in Soviet Russia." *Nation* 147 (Sept. 17, 1938): 265-67.

Stieg, Margaret F. *Public Libraries in Nazi Germany*. Tuscaloosa and London: University of Alabama Press, 1992.

Stone, Irving F. *The Hidden History of the Korean War*. New York: Citadel Press, 1952.

Stouffer, Samuel. *Communism, Conformity, and Civil Liberties: A Cross-section of the Nation Speaks Its Mind*. Garden City, NY: Doubleday, 1955. Reprint: Gloucester, MA: Peter Smith, 1963.

Streeter, David, ed. "Judging Librarianship: Are Library Leaders Trained— Or Born?" *American Libraries* 26 (May 1995): 408, 411.

Stuart, Mary. " 'A Potent Lever for Social Progress': The Imperial Public Library in the Era of the Great Reforms." *Library Quarterly* 59 (July 1989): 199-222.

————. *Artistocrat-Librarian in Service to the Tsar: Aleksei Nikolaevich Olenin and the Imperial Public Library*. Boulder, CO: East European Monographs, 1986; distributed by Columbia University Press, New York.

————. "Creating a National Library for the Workers' State: The Public Library in Petrograd and the Rumiantsev Library under Bolshevik Rule." *Slavonic and East European Review* 72 (April 1994): 233-58.

————. "The Evolution of Librarianship in Russia: The Librarians of the Imperial Public Library, 1808-1868." *Library Quarterly* 64 (Jan. 1994): 1-29.

————. "Vladimir Stasov and the Professionalization of Librarianship in Russia." *Solanus*, n.s. 7 (1993): 17-34.

Supplement to the Dictionary of American Library Biography. Ed. by Wayne Wiegand. Englewood, CO: Libraries Unlimited, 1990.

Suput, Ray Radoslav. "The Contribution of E. I. Shamurin to Soviet Librarianship." Ph.D. dissertation, Case Western Reserve University, 1972.

————. "E. I. Shamurin." In *World Encyclopedia of Library and Information Services*. 3rd ed. Pp. 770-71.

Surprenant, Thomas T. "Global Threats to Information." In *Annual Review of Information Science and Technology*. Vol. 20. White Plains, NY: Knowledge Industry Publications, 1985. Pp. 3-25.

"Susan Sontag Provokes Debate on Communism." *New York Times* (Feb. 27, 1982): 27.

"Susan Sontag's God that Failed." *Soho News* (March 2, 1982): 10-13, 42+.

Sutton, Antony C. *Western Technology and Soviet Economic Development*. 3 vols. Stanford, CA: Hoover Institution on War, Revolution, and Peace, Stanford University, 1968-1973.

A Symposium in Public Librarianship: Three Addresses. Berkeley: School of Librarianship, University of California, 1952.

Szebenyi-Sigmond, Judith. "Libraries and Information Services behind the Iron Curtain." *American Documentation* 10 (April 1959): 108-15.

Szekely, Beatrice Beach. "Introduction." *Soviet Education* 25 (Dec. 1982): 3-6.

Takce, Ethel M. "Soviet Libraries in the War." *Library Journal* 69 (May 1, 1944): 384-88.

Talese, Gay. *The Kingdom and the Power.* New York and Cleveland: New American Library, 1969.

Tanenhaus, Sam. *Whittaker Chambers: A Biography.* New York: Random House, 1997.

Taylor, S. J. *Stalin's Apologist: Walter Duranty, The New York Times's Man in Moscow.* New York and Oxford: Oxford University Press, 1990.

Tebbell, John. *Between Covers: The Rise and Transformation of Book Publishing in America.* New York and Oxford: Oxford University Press, 1987.

————, and Mary Ellen Zuckerman. *The Magazine in America, 1741-1990.* New York and Oxford: Oxford University Press, 1991.

Tellis, Ashley J. "Smoke, Fire, and What to Do in Asia." *Policy Review,* no. 100 (April/May 2000): 15-34.

"Textbook Series Scored at Inquiry." *Los Angeles Times* (Feb. 25, 1948): 1, 7.

"That Sly Counselor—Welch." *Newsweek* 43 (June 7, 1954): 27-28, 31.

Thatcher, Margaret. "Courage." Speech. Washington, DC, Dec. 10, 1997. In *Leadership for America.* Ed. by Feulner. Pp. 6-17.

————. "A Time for Leadership." *Hoover Digest: Research and Opinion in Public Policy* (Fall 2000): 8-21.

Theoharis, Athan. *Seeds of Repression: Harry S. Truman and the Origins of McCarthyism.* Chicago: Quadrangle Books, 1971.

Thomas, Lately. [Steele, Robert V. P.] *When Even Angels Wept: The Senator Joseph McCarthy Affair—A Story without a Hero.* New York: William Morrow, 1973.

Thomson, Charles A. "The Emerging Program of Cultural Relations." *ALA Bulletin* 75 (Feb. 1944): 75-78. "Discussion" by Flora B. Ludington, Charles H. Brown, Mary Gould Davis, and Ralph Munn, pp. 78-81.

Thorp, Willard. "American Writers on the Left." In *Socialism and American Life.* Vol 1. Ed. by Egbert and Persons. Pp. 599-620.

Tocqueville, Alexis de. *L'Ancien Régime et la Révolution.* Paris: Michel Levy Frères. 1856. As trans. and published: *The Old Regime and the French Revolution.* Trans. by Stuart Gilbert. Garden City, NY:

Doubleday, 1955. First English translation: 1856.

Toledano, Nora de. *"Time* Marches on McCarthy." *American Mercury* 74 (Feb. 1952): 15-22.

Toledano, Ralph de. "The Book Reviewers Sell Out China." *The American Mercury* 73 (July 8, 1951): 72-78.

————. "How Stalin's Disciples Review Books." *The American Mercury* 73 (Aug. 1951): 14-20.

————. *J. Edgar Hoover: The Man in His Time.* New Rochelle, NY: Arlington House, 1973.

————. *Spies, Dupes, and Diplomats.* New Rochelle, NY: Arlington House, 1967.

"Top Soviet Librarian Attacks Western International and Comparative [Librarianship]." *Focus on International and Comparative Librarianship,* vol. 11, no. 3 (1980): 29.

Trilling, Diana. Review of *A Journal of the Plague Years,* by Kanfer. *New York Times Book Review* (July 8, 1973): 4-5.

Trilling, Lionel. *Beyond Culture: Essays on Literature and Learning.* New York: Viking Press, 1965.

————. *The Liberal Imagination: Essays on Literature and Society.* New York: Charles Scribner's Sons, 1950. Reprinted with new foreword, 1976.

————. *The Opposing Self: Nine Essays in Criticism.* New York: Viking Press, 1955.

Trotsky, Leon. "Leninism and Library Work." First published in *Pravda,* July 10, 1924. Trans. by Tom Scott. In *Problems of Everyday Life and Other Writings on Culture and Science.* By Trotsky. New York: Monad Books, 1973, distributed by Pathfinder Press. Pp. 143-61.

Tucker, Mark. "Report on Donald G. Davis Article Award." *Library History Round Table Newsletter.* N.s. 4 (Spring 2000): 10-11.

Turner, I. Bruce. "Ralph Shaw." In *Leaders in American Academic Librarianship, 1925-1975.* Ed. by Wiegand. Pp. 288-319.

Twentieth Century Authors: A Biographical Dictionary of Modern Literature. First Supplement. Ed. by Stanley J. Kunitz and Vinetta Colby. New York: H. W. Wilson, 1953.

Ulam, Adam. *The Bolsheviks: The Intellectual and Political History of the Triumph of Communism in Russia.* With new preface. Cambridge, MA, and London: Harvard University Press, 1998. First published 1965.

Untitled editorial. *Library Journal* 57 (Jan. 15, 1932): 74.

Untitled review of *The Great Fear,* by Caute. *The New Yorker* (April 17, 1978): 138.

U.S. House of Representatives Committee on Un-American Activities. *Communism in the New York Area (Entertainment): Hearings:* June 18 and 19,

1958; May 8, 1958; April 1, 1957. Washington, DC: GPO, 1958.

U.S. House of Representatives Select Committee on U.S. National Security and Military/Commercial Concerns with the People's Republic of China. *Report*. 3 vols. Submitted by Mr. [Christopher] Cox, Chairman. Washington, DC: GPO, May 25, 1999. [aka *The Cox Report*]

U.S. House of Representatives Special Committee on Un-American Activities. *Guide to Subversive Organizations and Publications*. Rev. ed. Washington, DC: GPO, Dec. 1961.

————. *Investigation of Un-American Propaganda Activities in the United States: Appendix, Part IX: Communist Front Organizations*. 3 vols. Washington, DC: GPO, 1944.

U.S. Senate Committee on Government Operations, Permanent Subcommittee on Investigations. *Control of Trade with the Soviet Bloc*. Washington, DC: GPO, July 1953.

————. *Control of Trade with the Soviet Bloc: Hearings*. Part 1: March 30 and 31, 1953; and Part 2: May 4 and 20, 1953. Washington, DC: GPO, 1953.

————. *State Department Information Program—Information Centers*. *Hearings*: Eight Parts: March 24, 1953-July 14, 1953; *Index*: Aug. 5, 1953; *Report*: Jan. 25, 1954. Washington, DC: GPO, 1953-1954.

U.S. Senate Committee on the Judiciary, Subcommittee to Investigate the Administration of the Internal Security Laws. *Yugoslav Interference with a U.S. Book Publisher: Testimony of William Jovanovich*. June 27, 1962. Washington, DC: GPO, 1962.

USSR Library Council. "Report on Activities, September 1973-November 1974." *IFLA Annual, 1975*. Munich: Verlag Dokumentation, 1975. Pp. 196-99.

Utley, Freda. "The Book Burners Burned." *The American Mercury* 77 (Dec. 1953): 35-39.

Varney, Harold Lord. "Fund for Whose Republic?" *American Mercury* 89 (Aug. 1959): 3-10.

Varvarina, E., comp. *Russian Librarianship during the Time of* Perestroika *(1987-1991): Digest*. Trans. by E. Azarova and O. Azarova. Moscow: Rudomino All-Russian State Library for Foreign Literature, 1993.

Vickery, B. C., and A. G. Brown. "Information Science." In *Comparative and International Library Science*. Ed. by Harvey. Pp. 181-200.

Viereck, Peter. *Shame and Glory of the Intellectuals: Babbitt Jr. vs. the Rediscovery of Values*. Boston: Beacon Press, 1953.

Visscher, Maurice B. "The Interdependence of Knowledge and Information in the World Today." In *International Aspects of Librarianship*. Ed. by Carnovsky. Pp. 1-11.

Vladimirov, Lev. Speech. Columbia University, School of Library Service.

New York: March 16, 1968.

Volkogonov, Dmitri. *Lenin: A New Biography*. Trans. and ed. by Harold Shukman. New York: The Free Press, 1994.

—————. *Stalin: Triumph and Tragedy*. Ed. and trans. by Harold Shukman. New York: Grove Weidenfeld, 1991.

Volodin, Boris F. "History of Librarianship, Library History, or Information History: A View from Russia." *Library Quarterly* 70 (Oct. 2000): 446-467.

Vosper, Robert. "A Century Abroad." *College and Research Libraries* 37 (Nov. 1976): 514-30.

—————. "National and International Library Planning." In *National and International Library Planning*. Ed. by Vosper and Newkirk. Pp. 9-14.

—————, and Leone I. Newkirk, eds. *National and International Library Planning*. Key Papers Presented at the 40th Session of the IFLA General Council, Washington, DC, 1974. Munich: Verlag Dokumentation, 1976.

Vronskaya, Jeanne, and Vladimir Vronskaya. *The Biographical Dictionary of the Former Soviet Union*. London: Bowker-Saur, 1992.

Walker, Brooks R. *The Christian Fright Peddlers*. Garden City, NY: Doubleday, 1964.

Walker, Gregory. *Soviet Book Publishing Policy*. Cambridge and New York: Cambridge University Press, 1978.

Wallace, Mrs. George Rodney. "It *Has* Happened in Massachusetts." *MLA* [Massachusetts Library Association] *Bulletin* 43 (Jan. 1953): 4-5.

Walling, William English. *Sovietism: The ABC of Russian Bolshevism—According to the Bolshevists*. New York: E. P. Dutton, 1920.

Waltzer, Herbert. Review of *Seeds of Repression*, by Theoharis. *American Historical Review* 79 (Oct. 1974): 1291-92.

Waples, Douglas. "Guiding Readers in Soviet Russia." *Bulletin of the American Library Association* 26 (Oct. 1932): 762-67.

Warncke, Ruth. "Helen Haines." In *World Encyclopedia of Library and Information Services*. 3rd ed. Pp. 334-35. Originally published in *ALA World Encyclopedia of Library and Information Services*. 1st ed. Pp. 227-228.

Warren, Frank A. *Liberals and Communism: The "Red Decade" Revisited*. With new preface. New York: Columbia University, 1993. Originally published: Bloomington: Indiana University Press, 1966.

Washburne, Carleton. *Remakers of Mankind*. New York: John Day, 1932.

Webster's New Universal Unabridged Dictionary. [Based on the *Random House Dictionary of the English Language*, 2nd unabridged ed., 1993]. New York: Barnes & Noble, 1996.

Webster's Third New International Dictionary of the English Language. Ed. by Philip Babcock Gove and others. Springfield, MA: G. & C. Merriam

Company, 1981.

"The Week in Review." *The American Hebrew* 105 (July 11, 1919): 201-2.

Weinstein, Allen, and Alexander Vassiliev. *The Haunted Wood: Soviet Espionage in America—the Stalin Era*. New York: Random House, 1999.

Weisberg, Jacob. "Cold War without End." *New York Times Magazine* (Nov. 28, 1999): 116-23, 155-58.

Wells, H. G. *Russia in the Shadows*. New York: George H. Doran, 1921. Reprinted: Westport, CT: Hyperion Press, 1973.

Wendt, Lloyd. *Chicago Tribune: The Rise of a Great American Newspaper*. New York and Chicago: Rand McNally, 1979.

Wertheimer, Andrew B. "Schrecker on McCarthyism." *Library History Round Table Newsletter*, n.s. 4 (Fall 1998): 7.

Whatley, H. Allan. "European Librarianship." In *The Library in Society*. By Rogers, McChesney, and others. Pp. 113-38.

Wheeler, Joseph L. *The Library and the Community: Increased Book Services through Library Publicity Based on Community Studies*. Chicago: American Library Association, 1924.

Whitby, Thomas Joseph. "Account of a Library Visit to the USSR, May-June 1957: A Report Submitted to the Graduate School of Library Service, Rutgers University." Washington, DC: n.p., Oct. 1957. 103 pp. Mimeographed.

———. "Development of the System of Legal Deposit in the USSR." *College and Research Libraries* 15 (Oct. 1954): 398-406.

———. "Evolution and Evaluation of a Soviet Classification." *Library Quarterly* 26 (April 1956): 118-27.

———. "Impressions from a Library Tour of the Soviet Union." *D.C. Libraries* 29 (Oct. 1958): 65-69.

———. "Libraries and Bibliographic Projects in the Communist Bloc." In *Iron Curtains and Scholarship*. Ed. by Winger. Pp. 51-68.

———. "National Bibliography in the USSR." *Library Quarterly* 23 (Jan. 1953): 16-22.

———. "Soviet Libraries Today." *ALA Bulletin* 53 (June 1959): 485-89.

White, John Kenneth. *Still Seeing Red: How the Cold War Shapes the New American Politics*. Boulder, CO: Westview Press, 1997.

White, Stephen. *Britain and the Bolshevik Revolution: A Study in the Politics of Diplomacy, 1920-1924*. New York: Holmes & Meier, 1979.

The White Terrorists Ask for Mercy. Chicago: Daily Worker Publishing for the Workers Party of America, February 1925. (Pamphlet)

Whitehead, Don. *The FBI Story*. Foreword by J. Edgar Hoover. New York: Random House, 1956.

Who Was Who in the USSR. Comp. by the Institute for the Study of the USSR (Munich). Ed. by Heinrich Schulz, Paul Urban, and Andrew

Lebed. Metuchen, NJ: Scarecrow Press, 1972.

Who's Who in American Education, 1957-58. 18th ed. Ed. by Robert C. Cook. Nashville: Who's Who in American Education, 1957.

"Whose Liberties?" *New Leader* (Jan. 1953): 31.

Wiegand, Wayne. "Lawrence Clark Powell." In *Leaders in American Academic Librarianship: 1925-1975.* Ed. by Wiegand. Pp. 263-87.

————, ed. *Leaders in American Academic Librarianship: 1925-1975.* Pittsburgh, PA: Beta Phi Mu, 1983; distributed by the American Library Association.

————, and Donald G. Davis, Jr., eds. *Encyclopedia of Library History.* New York and London: Garland, 1994.

Wilcox, E. H. *Russia's Ruin.* New York: Scribner's Sons, 1919.

Wiles, Kimball. "*Building America*: A Case in Point." *Educational Leadership* 6 (Nov. 1948): 108-15.

Wilson, Francis G. "Intellectuals and the American Tradition." *Education* [London] 63 (March 1943): 391-403.

Wilson, Lucy L. W. *The New Schools of New Russia.* New York: Vanguard Press, 1928.

Wilton, Robert. *Russia's Agony.* London: Edward Arnold, 1918.

Windschuttle, Keith. *The Killing of History: How Literary Critics and Social Theorists are Murdering Our Past.* New York: Free Press, 1996.

Winger, Howard W. "The Exchange of Ideas in the Advancement of Knowledge." In *Iron Curtains and Scholarship.* Ed. by Winger. Pp. 3-12.

————. "Introduction." In *Iron Curtains and Scholarship.* Ed. by Winger. Pp. 1-2.

————. "Public Library Holdings of Biased Books About Russia." Occasional Paper number 1. Urbana, IL: University of Illinois Library School, July 1949, 12 pp.

————, ed. *Iron Curtains and Scholarship: The Exchange of Knowledge in a Divided World.* Papers Presented before the Twenty-Third Annual Conference of the Graduate Library School of the University of Chicago, July 7-9, 1958. Chicago: Graduate Library School, University of Chicago, 1958. Also published (with different pagination) as *Library Quarterly* 28 (Oct. 1958).

Winik, Jay. *On the Brink: The Dramatic, Behind-the-Scenes Saga of the Reagan Era and the Men and Women Who Won the Cold War.* New York: Simon and Schuster, 1996.

Wittmer, Felix. *Conquest of the American Mind: Comments on Collectivism in Education.* Boston: Meador Publishing, 1956.

Wolfe, Bertram D. *An Ideology in Power: Reflections on the Russian Revolution.* Intro. by Leonard Schapiro. New York: Stein and Day, with the Hoover Institution, Stanford University, 1969.

————. "Krupskaya Purges the People's Libraries." *Survey*, no. 72 (Summer 1969): 141-55.

————. *A Life in Two Centuries: An Autobiography*. New York: Stein and Day, 1981.

————. *Three Who Made a Revolution: A Biographical History*. New York: Stein and Day, 1984. First ed.: Dial Press, 1948.

Wolfinger, Raymond E., and others. "America's Radical Right: Politics and Ideology." In *Ideology and Discontent*. Ed. by David Apter. New York: The Free Press, 1964. Pp. 262-93.

Wood, Neal. *Communism and British Intellectuals*. New York: Columbia University Press, 1959.

Woody, Thomas. "International Versus Nationalistic Education." *Educational Outlook* 6 (March 1932): 149-52.

————. *New Minds: New Men? The Emergence of the Soviet Citizen*. New York: Macmillan, 1932.

————. "Political Education in Russia." *School and Society* 28 (Dec. 1, 1928): 665-73.

————. "Ten Years Passed." [Parts I and II.] *Educational Outlook* 3 (Jan. 1929): 86-106.

————. "Ten Years Passed." [Part III.] *Educational Outlook* 3 (March 1929): 161-78.

World Encyclopedia of Library and Information Services. 3rd ed. Chicago: American Library Association, 1993.

Wright, Robert. "Continental Drift." *New Republic* (Jan. 17, 2000): 18, 20-23.

Wright, William. *Lillian Hellman: The Image, the Woman*. New York: Simon and Schuster, 1986.

Wynar, Bohdan. Review of *The Dimensions of Comparative Librarianship*, by Danton. In *American Reference Books Annual*. Littleton, CO: Libraries Unlimited, 1974. Pp. 78-79.

————. Review of *Libraries, Documentation and Bibliography in the USSR*, by Chandler. In *American Reference Books Annual*. Littleton, CO: Libraries Unlimited, 1974. P. 78.

Wurmbrand, Richard. *Marx and Satan*. Westchester, IL: Crossway Books, 1986.

Yarmolinsky, Avrahm. "Censorship in Russia." *The Russian Review* 3 (July 1917): 93-103.

————("Yarmolinsky, Avraham"). "The Duumvirate." Review of *Lenin*, by Leon Trotzky [New York: Minton Balch] and *Leon Trotzky: The Portrait of a Youth*, by Max Eastman [New York: Greenberg]. *New York Herald-Tribune Books* (June 28, 1925): 8.

———— ("Yarmolinsky, Abraham"). "Exploring Russia." *The Bookman* 46 (Dec. 1917): 481-86.

———— ("Yarmolinsky, Abraham"). "The Internal Policy of the Bolsheviki." *Current History* 8 (April 1918): 68-72.

———— ("Yarmolinsky, Avrahm"). *The Jews and Other National Minorities under the Soviets.* New York: Vanguard Press, 1928.

———— ("Yarmolinsky, Abraham"). "The Kennan Collection." New York: New York Public Library, 1921; reprinted from the *Bulletin of the New York Public Library* (Feb. 1921).

————. *Literature under Communism: The Literary Policy of the Communist Party of the Soviet Union from the End of World War II to the Death of Stalin.* Bloomington, IN: Russian and East European Institute, Indiana University, 1960.

———— ("Yarmolinsky, Abraham"). "More Bolshevist Legislation." *Current History* 8 (June 1918): 455-58.

————. "New Ideas and Ideals in Soviet Russia." *Current History* 22 (June 1925): 402-7.

————. *Road to Revolution: A Century of Russian Radicalism.* New York: Macmillan, 1959.

———— ("Yarmolinsky, Avraham"). "The Russian Public Library." *Library Journal* 47 (April 15, 1922): 352-53.

————. "The Slavonic Division—Recent Growth." *Bulletin of the New York Public Library* 30 (Feb. 1926): 71-79.

————. "Soviet Libraries." *College and Research Libraries* 5 (Sept. 1944): 351-56.

Yarros, Victor. "The Library and the Book in Russia's Revolutionary Movement." *Library Journal* 43 (March 1918): 147-51.

Ybarra, Michael J. "Blacklist Whitewash." *New Republic* (Jan. 5 and 12, 1998): 20-23.

Young, Arthur P. "Robert Bingham Downs." In *Leaders in American Academic Librarianship: 1925-1975.* Ed. by Wiegand. Pp. 72-93.

"Young Dewey." [Review of John Dewey's *Impressions of Soviet Russia.*] *New York Herald-Tribune Books* (March 31, 1929): 10.

Zion, Sidney. *The Autobiography of Roy Cohn.* Secaucus, NJ: Lyle Stuart, 1988.

Zumwinkle, Richard. "Report on Conservatism." Review of *The American Right Wing*, by Ellsworth and Harris. *Library Journal* 87 (Feb. 15, 1962): 745-46.

INDEX

Caute, David, 334, 361, 364,
384-85n164
*The Great Fear: The Anti-
Communist Purge under
Truman and Eisenhower*,
336, 341, 362
Censorship:
in California, study of, 231-34
Downs and, 224
Fiske's views, 252n202
Haines and, 248-49n151
Josephson and, 356
Khmelnitsky and, 80
Kilpatrick and, 249n166
Krupskaya and, 17-18
Kunitz's view, 86
Mediavilla and, 344, 346-47
in overseas libraries, 226, 243n80
revisionist histories and, 317
Robbins' views, 336
Soviet, 19, 20, 172
Counts and, 121
Gregory's view, 83
and international exchange of
books, 165
Kent's view, 167-68
Library Journal and, 62-63
library press and, 85
Lydenberg and, 67
proscribed books, 18
Waples and, 73
U.S., librarians and, 203-4
of conservative material, 210-14
*Censorship and the American
Library: The American Library
Association's Response to Threats
to Intellectual Freedom, 1939-
1969*, Robbins, 332-35
Central Committee, Communist
Party, 16, 20
Centralization, liberalism and, 293
Centralized book selection, Soviet,
159
Centralized planning, ideas of, 282

"A Century Abroad," Vosper, 315
Ceplair, Larry, *The Inquisition in
Hollywood: Politics in the Film
Community, 1930-1960*, 340-41
Chamber of Commerce, U.S., 103,
344
Chamberlain, John, 106, 218, 258,
266
Chamberlin, William Henry, 409n1
Chambers, Whittaker, 383-84n146
Chandler, George, 25, 279, 287n23
Change, radical, desire for, 410n2
Chernyshevskii, N. G., 15
Chesnut, Charlotte Forgey, 166
Chicago Tribune, 126, 137n140, 264
Chief Committee for Political
Education, 58
Childe, V. Gordon, 128
Children's libraries, Krupskaya and,
30-31
China, military threat from, 411n2
Chinese Communists, Forman and,
274n43
Chodorov, Frank, 218, 258, 266
Choldin, Marianna Tax, 10n10,
35n29
Chomsky, Noam, 313, 372n1
Christian Anti-Communism
Crusade, 229, 263, 408-9n1
Chronoscope (TV program), 368-69
Chubaryan, O. S., 22, 276, 322
Churchill, Winston, 11n15, 44,
187n67, 406n1
Citizens' committees, 337
City University of New York, New
Press, 372n1
Civilization, American, Counts'
views, 122
Civil rights movement, Richards'
views, 329-30
Civil Service Loyalty Review Board,
209
Clapp, Verner W., 145, 183n10
Class distinctions, MacLeish and, 88

Sproul, Robert Gordon, 318
Stalin, Joseph, 19, 20, 21, 22, 135n88
New York Times and, 127
Stalin, Souvarine, 129
Stalin & Co., Duranty, 268
Stalinism:
  Krupskaya and, 27-28
  textbook promotion of, 346
Stalinist organizations,
      Jenkins' views, 361
Stalinization, of libraries, 16
State Department, U.S. , 209
  and ALA International Relations
      Board, 155n31
  Information Centers, 192
  and McCarthy, 394n296
  overseas libraries, 148, 197-210
State Scientific Library, Soviet, 59
"Statement on Labeling," ALA, 203-4
"Statistics on Stilts," 162
Status, professional, librarians and,
      203
Steffens, Lincoln, 46
Stevenson, Adlai, 230
Stewart, Marguerite Ann, 346, 352
  Land of the Soviets, 318
Stewart, Maxwell S., 346, 352,
      393n280
  Land of the Soviets, 318
Stone, I. F., 325
Stone, William T., 170-71, 209-10
Storm Center (film), 336
The Story of Philosophy, Durant, 50,
      54-55n39
Stouffer, Samuel, 271n14
Strachey, John, 128
"Strengthening the Forces for
      Peace," Ludington, 191, 260-61
Strong, Anna Louise, 208, 351
Subversive materials, labeling of,
      ALA and, 203-4
Studies in Prejudice series,
      American Jewish Committee,
      260-61

Sulzberger, Arthur Hays, 137n141
Suput, Ray, 322
Sutton, Antony C., 89n5
Szebenyi-Sigmond, Judith,
      "Libraries and Information
      Services behind the Iron
      Curtain," 163-64
T
"Tail Gunner Joe," 375n14
Tail Gunner Joe (TV program), 9n7,
      398n361
Takce, Ethel M., "Soviet Libraries in
      the War," 143
Talmon, J. L., 161
Tanenhaus, Sam, 384n146
Tate, Allen, 258
Teachers:
  Russian, and Communism, 17
  Soviet, Dewey's view, 113
Teachers College, *Comparative
      Education Studies* series,
      115
"Tears and Ivory Towers: California
      Libraries during the McCarthy
      Era," Benemann, 315-16, 346
Technical information: foreign
      sources, 59-60
  Western, Soviets and, 277-79, 401,
      402
Technical librarianship, Soviet,
      163-64
Technical materials:
  American, supplied to Soviets, 164
  exchange with Soviets, 166
Television:
  and anti-Communism, 8-9n7
  Communists and, 342
  and McCarthy, 367-69, 398n361
  See also media
Ten Days that Shook the World,
      Reed, 127, 137n143
Tenney, Jack, 344
  Mediavilla and, 345, 346
Tenney Committee, California, 337

ABOUT THE AUTHOR

Stephen Karetzky holds a doctoral degree from Columbia University as well as master's degrees from both Columbia and the California State University. He has written and edited several books, including *Reading Research and Librarianship: A History and Analysis* (which won an award from the American Society for Information Science) and *The Media's Coverage of the Arab-Israeli Conflict*. He has taught in the schools of information and library studies at the State University of New York at Buffalo, Haifa University (Israel), and San José State University. Dr. Karetzky is the Library Director and an Associate Professor at Felician College in New Jersey.

Additional information is available in *Who's Who in America* and *Who's Who in the World*, both published by Marquis.